Reactions to participating in sessions with Moita

"She looks right into your soul, and there's nothing that's not there for that look. I've never seen anybody look at somebody with such total love. But at the same time there's this Puckish attitude, like she's having fun with us. Like she knows something really good about us, some really good surprise that's in store for us, and she's kind of smiling and keeping it to herself."
— *Frank*

"That is truly a mind-blowing experience. There were a few moments there where I could just feel my consciousness being totally drawn in. 'What's going on here?!' *Neat*. I really didn't expect it to be as intense. It felt like somebody who's been helping you all your life behind your back, and you don't know it, all of a sudden stands in front of you and says, 'Here I am.'"
— *Lisa*

Reactions to the Moita material

"The information conveyed in these conversations with Moita is comparable to the more famous Seth material. Comparing Moita with Seth, I find her much less bombastic in tone, which one would expect of a feminine being. Much other channeling like Edgar Cayce and *A Course in Miracles* is couched in formal language. In print, Moita comes off as having great charm because of her gentleness, humor, and articulate use of colloquial English. I was very moved by the moment one person tried to embrace this spirit, and her response."
— *Elihu Edelson, Both Sides Now*

"I would be most happy if Moita would give me a message as to the opinion of the unobstructed world about the choices we have taken. There are so many hours I would like to sit with you; listen; ask questions; receive answers. I will dream up a place and a time when we can connect. Until then, a big, big hug for all the messages, the love and the support, from your old medicine woman."
— *Dr. Elisabeth Kübler-Ross (1981)*

Reactions to

<u>*Mind Leap: Intimate Changes and Communication Between Worlds (2010)*</u>

"Reading *Mind Leap* was one of the most delightful experiences of my summer. First, I found it an absolutely intriguing story of personal challenge and human relationships, exceedingly well told. But second, and most important, I found it highly inspiring. There are many times in my own spiritual journey that I wonder whether it is all worth the effort – whether there really is a greater reality. This book is a powerful incentive to keep going, an inspiration and a source of hope!"

— *Joyce E. Ansell, literary editor*

"*Mind Leap* is a sincere record of paranormal experiences, highly symbolic dreams [and] encounters with wise entities from the spiritual realm, such as a gentle soul named Moita channeled by Siofra Bradigan.

"Letts presents a fascinating journal of his darkest and brightest moments... packed full of astonishing descriptions and mysterious details from the disturbing to the uplifting. For those who enjoy the pursuit of different realities, Letts will not disappoint. His work educates and entertains, focusing on the extraordinary capabilities of the human spirit."

— *ForeWord Clarion review*

"I would highly recommend *Mind Leap* to all who would be open to the changes we are experiencing as the turning point to a New Age approaches. The messages and learnings that came through David Letts and his associates are prophetic and relevant for this time, and those of us who are less sensitive can learn much from reading this material."

— *Elihu Edelson,* <u>*Both Sides Now*</u>

"David Letts made a huge contribution by helping the presences known as Loria and Moita come into the lives of many of us. He has a marvellous facility for comprehending the channeled messages in the context of surrounding events and has a gift for describing their deeper import for those fortunate to be there at the time or who read about it now. As well, I am astounded at the depth and profundity of David's dreams and the fine uses to which he has put them. Many seem to tap a source similar to channeling and remind me of Carl Jung's powerful dream-life. This material is deep and takes concentration; but for those who are ready, it is a very rich reading experience."

— *Dr. William H. Wynn, Emeritus Professor of Psychology, University of Regina*

Also in the Mind Leap series:

<u>*The World Conspires: Weaving Our Energies to Renew the Earth (2011)*</u>

Mind Leap series

EARTH DREAM AWAKENING

To Help Found a New World

DAVID W. LETTS

with SIOFRA BRADIGAN *and* MOITA

Title page image:
Design of "Swallows" crop circle appearing
at Adam's Grave, Wiltshire, U.K., on August 4, 2003.
Courtesy of Bert Janssen.[1]

Order this book online at www.trafford.com
or email orders@trafford.com

Most Trafford titles are also available at major online book retailers.

Printed in the United States of America.

ISBN: 978-1-4669-4948-5 (sc)
ISBN: 978-1-4669-4947-8 (e)

Trafford rev. 08/06/2012

 www.trafford.com

North America & international
toll-free: 1 888 232 4444 (USA & Canada)
phone: 250 383 6864 • fax: 812 355 4082

Contents

Of Names and Notes

Names and identifying details have been changed or removed in order to preserve confidentiality for many of the people and certain places in this story.

Superscript numbers in the text correspond to Endnotes referring to sections of *Mind Leap* or of *The World Conspires* or to other sources by author, date and any page references, linked to the Bibliography. A superscript number followed by the letter "N" indicates that the endnote includes an author comment – for example, this one about ellipses and transcription procedure generally[2N]. Such comments, like a few footnotes at the bottom of pages, provide additional information or clarify the author's perspective on the subject being discussed.

All that has happened in the past, all of Earth's history, man has created in his dream. And the end of time will come when man wakes up and realizes he has been dreaming.

– Earth Goddess (October 4, 1981)

For us, this is a labour of love. Instead of man creating only on his own, as an individual self set apart from the rest of the universe, this time he is involved in a co-creation – and we are the co-creators. Those who are here have arrived to help found a new world.

– Moita (June 24, 1979)

David's Introduction

So we begin a little early, trying to stack the deck.
– Earth Goddess

June Solstice 2012

On one level, this is the story of a young family wresting themselves from modern life in a North American city to find a very different, rustic existence close to nature and a circle of new friends in remote mountain valleys of the British Columbia interior.

But immediately the questions: Why this university psychology teacher and this legal secretary, a mother with two young children, suddenly heading off into the northern wilds? With what resources? After what planning? Toward what goal? With whom as a guide? And there is the rub, since answers are hardly obvious on the surface – especially the guide. Our travellers, you see, are a *mystic* and a *psychic*, who have come together as partners in a quite out-of-the-ordinary quest.

So it is through a dramatic inner as well as challenging outer landscape that this family will be journeying. Will they find the people, consciously unknown to them, whom they seek? Will they reach the unexpected place where their outer and inner searches converge? More surprisingly, given that the year is 1979, how will their quest connect with a planetary evolution in consciousness that is to culminate many years in their future – with what may be called the great change, the dimensional shift, the awakening of 2012 and beyond?

Readers will indeed be following the twists and turns of this family's difficult migration from city to "bush", and the adventures that follow. But there are more levels to this story that will unfold simultaneously, tied to the *"experiment in communication between worlds"* that these people – Kelly and myself – began together during the personally tumultuous year that led up to our move.[3N]

Kelly* and I first met – outwardly speaking – through an Expansion of Consciousness workshop I was co-leading on the Canadian prairies (Regina, Saskatchewan) in the spring of 1978. Inwardly, though, I'm sure we had already "met" in the dream-state six months earlier. In my dream, a then-unknown woman appeared beside me, pointing upward to a snowy mountain peak consisting of a high natural bridge over a tiny alpine valley. She excitedly whispered: *"No one lives up there. It must be an incredible experience to go there!"* To a degree outwardly, and certainly inwardly, this is just what Kelly and I would end up doing together.

Many strong connections came quickly to the fore as Kelly and I interacted in and out of our workshop. Then, near the end of a past-life regression in which I was guiding her, a calm, gentle, wise voice – quite different from Kelly's usual breezy personality – began to speak through her. This clear presence referred to approaching choices that would create our future together. From my past

---

* Before this book is over, Kelly will choose a new name to express her personal/spiritual changes. Siofra Bradigan is a Celtic name, meaning "spirited elf".

experience with other channelings (more than from my decade of psychology training), I recognized a higher energy source communicating, with genuine, measured intent. So I asked, "Who is speaking now?" The reply came: "She has her own name for me. She calls me Moita."

Moita (pronounced *Moy*-tuh) would explain that she is Kelly's origin, spiritually speaking – Kelly's "oversoul" or "entity" – as well as being linked to me and many others we either already knew or were yet to meet. Moita would also say she was coming to serve as a guide, as a doorway and as a mirror – roles that would continue to expand in meaning as our communication evolved. (Further insight regarding what fitted Kelly and me for our parts in this story, *because of* being "two such different souls", will be given in the Intermission between Parts One and Two.)

But why make this contact when Moita did? This is an age, Moita would emphasize, in which we and many other open-hearted explorers were needed . . . to awaken and make real a better dream of Earth . . . "to help found a new world". Our ongoing contact with Moita – this unconventional, ever-stimulating friend and teacher – and her higher-dimensional colleagues would be the key to our move away from the urban mainstream into relative solitude in the northern woods, where we could nurture seeds for the future.

(Readers new to this literature can get a sense for how true channeling feels, what it requires of its participants, its implications and potentials, pitfalls and rewards, through "A Letter from Kelly" and "Art of Communication" that follow this Introduction, as well as from the Preface to the *Mind Leap* series included near the end of this book. But the limitation, of course, that cannot be overstated is that channeling is first and foremost a *direct experience* for all involved – a crucible of feelings, energies and subtle perceptions at which transcribed words can only hint. We address this by including experiential descriptions and participants' conversation wherever possible, but readers are invited to connect the dots with their own intuitions and explorations.)

There is a specific reason that this experiential quest from 30-some years ago is highly relevant to us in 2012. People today may be surprised by this. Whatever their feeling for the transformations now under way, they may not realize the degree to which present changes were being prepared and prefigured in the heady 1970s to early 1980s period. But a quick look back to the few years around 1980 should bring a shock of recognition. Striking parallels suggest how much we today might learn from insights and discoveries that were well ahead of their time then.

After a decade or two of burgeoning movements concerned with human rights, war and violence, political/economic corruption, the environment, holistic health, women's, men's, gay/lesbian and children's issues, personal growth, consciousness expansion, and upsurging spiritualities (new and ancient, orthodox and esoteric), there was a sense of changes accelerating on many levels.

The very Earth was erupting in many volcanoes, huge earthquakes and tsunamis, some suggestively synchronized with emotional human events. Severe storms churned through an atmosphere lurching from one temperature extreme to another. Fires and pollution from fossil fuels and other chemicals choked the air, as holes developed in the atmosphere's protective layer. Still, society went on resolving environmental conflicts in favour of ever more development rather than ecological integrity, while species at risk paid the price of lost habitat. The Sun too was erupting with record levels of sunspots and flares, while planetary alignments and a returning comet were seen as further threatening Earth's geological and polar stability.

The nuclear arms race hung like a sword of Damocles over the world, as a superpower invaded Afghanistan. Closer to the strategic Middle East, Iraq and Iran went to war and, after its anti-modern, religious revolution, Iran held hostage the U.S. embassy – leading to an oil shortage and skyrocketing energy prices. Economic recession and the neo-conservative agenda gripped the West as predictions spread of economic collapse. Meanwhile allegations circulated of yet deeper conspiracies among shadowy groups to control world events for their own benefit.

Finally, the election of a right-wing U.S. president (backed by the gun lobby, fundamentalist church groups and the corporate elite), who aimed to confront an array of "evils" both foreign and domestic, lent weight to prophecies about End-Times – the Rapture, Armageddon and Second Coming, thought due by the Millennium if not sooner.

Simultaneously, though, a wave of open-minded, holistic explorations by individuals and groups was leading to a counter-prophecy of transformation and planetary rebirth, through cooperation with higher energy levels.[4N] For example, it was during the 1970s that one of the clearest demonstrations of an emergent "New Age" became widely known around the world – the vibrant community and miraculous garden at Findhorn, Scotland. This beacon of light would not have been born or continued evolving without the spiritual channelings and faithful application of its founders.[5]

Findhorn became famous because it demonstrated the potential for partnering with invisible realms of nature and spirit in order to make whole again a civilization whose abuses of power threatened to destroy itself, even all life on the planet. That Kelly and I had each faced up to power abuses earlier in our own lives – as in her struggles against a violent, alcoholic father, or my student activism and resistance to the Vietnam War – was one of many reasons we were drawn to spiritually oriented communities like Findhorn as learning and healing centres for the "New Age".

We were also drawn to a vision of community by information of a subtler kind, revealing our reincarnational history in a beautiful and what would now be considered "magical" city in far ancient times called Musili. More background will be given soon[6], but the relevant point is this: In that long-ago city, a group of us with Moita as our guiding spirit vowed to return together in body, bringing light and joy to a world that was (relatively speaking) dark and empty – meaning today. Intuitive links to some of those returning friends and to potential places to create community would add to the "invisible guidance" Kelly and I would follow, eventually pointing toward the British Columbia interior. In this country of high peaks, clear streams and deep forests, a variety of creative, independent people had already come to live by the "lamplight glow", and we would join them.

This book is a tapestry woven from three interrelated, not easily separable threads: **Journey**, **Perspective** and **Tales of Power**.

Journey: Chapter 1, "A Step in the Right Direction", describes our move from prairie city to mountain wildness. Then chapters 3, 6 to 8, 9 (part) and 11 to 14 continue this adventure as it unfolds over the next two years. I've included a Photo Album (pp. 401-405) to convey a feeling for the places involved, as noted in the text at appropriate points. Readers will meet many newly made friends, who bring their own openness and searching questions to our sessions, lending reality to our vision of community – though often in ways, and on levels, we are not expecting. This quest, guided by Moita and her own higher level, Amar, will culminate in channeled appearances of the Earth Mother (or "Goddess"), as laconically quoted at the beginning of this Introduction.

Perspective: Complementing these more people-oriented sections are chapters devoted to key subject areas. In chapters 2, 4, 5, 9 (most) and 10, Moita and Amar give their perspective on the evolution of the cosmos and life on Earth, civilizations ancient and modern, how technology, politics, religion and war play into humanity's cultural divide, and the process of planetary transformation. At several points, channelings through Thespian Michaels, Jane Roberts, David Spangler and Ray Stanford will be drawn upon to supplement and/or compare to our own material.

Tales of Power: Lastly, shorter, interspersed segments share our experiences dealing with darker forces on the subtle and not-so-subtle planes. Here Kelly's psychic sensitivity provides witness in five linked "tales", partly involving other incarnations of ourselves and friends as well as those of a world-famous healer and her threatening nemesis.

Varied as these components are, readers will find that they very much interrelate in spirit and content via the channelings at their core. What can be learned from these communications and events of three decades ago? What light do they shed on the upheavals through which our world has been passing and the wholer future we are called to co-create? Each reader will glean her/his own unique insights from these experiences, touching as they do upon many issues of personal and social transformation. But some wider lessons for today that are specific to this volume of the Mind Leap series fall under three headings – *power*, *probabilities* and *prophecy*.

Power, Moita explains, is energy used for control under conditions of alienation. For want of wholeness, of care consciously exercised, power creates destructive scenarios. The modern world is replete with the predictable results of power, from myriad modern frustrations to human tragedies to widespread catastrophes. Prophecy underscores the lessons of these probabilities (whether physically realized or not, and for whom) while aspiring to the alternative – the path with heart, the way of transformation, harmonizing Earth and Spirit. To assist the sinking in of these lessons, Appendix A provides a sampling of this book's channelings on these three themes.

From the Prologue on, quite a different understanding of recent world history emerges: a drama of contending timelines – of evolving probabilities, ranging between ultimate destruction and optimal growth – to which all of us have been contributing our energies and choices, positive or negative, consciously or unconsciously. Coming to realize the level of threat through which humankind has so far passed with the indispensable aid of our invisible allies, we may approach Earth's imminent awakening with a heightened sense of responsibility, humility . . . and blessed joy.

A LETTER FROM KELLY
(SIOFRA BRADIGAN)

Circa 1982

Dear Reader,

I've decided that the best approach is to pretend you have just heard about our work with Moita, and have written me a letter asking me about it. You're curious about how I discovered I had this "gift" and what it's like to be a channel for an energy-presence such as Moita seems to be.

Perhaps you're a little skeptical and somewhat uneasy about asking such questions. After all, you have heard about various strange cults and the dramatic and sometimes deadly effects they have on their members. But that's okay – because skepticism doesn't bother me in the slightest. As a matter of fact, I'm skeptical myself, and *I'm* at the centre of this phenomenon!

Oh, not skeptical that it isn't real – at least, not at the time it's happening. But it's hard to know exactly what to call it, how to phrase it. It refuses to be quantified or pegged nicely. And sometimes, as I don't go into trance at all, I am skeptical about the "truth" of what comes through. Actually, Moita herself has explained that it is a cooperative effort between her world and ours, and that whatever comes through is changed by the nature of the channel – in this case, me, my thoughts, my hidden needs and desires, my perceptions of reality.

So, now that I know you are a real person, just like me, with your own wisdom and life experiences to draw on, I can talk to you as I do to all my friends – straight (*my* kind of straight!). You're free to disbelieve absolutely everything I say – I can't force you to believe me. But, for my own sense of personal integrity (after all, I *do* have to live with myself forever, you know), I'm going to say to you that everything I put down on paper or that comes from my mouth is *truth as I perceive it*. I cannot make any absolute claims. I only know what I see and feel is real for me. What *you* see and feel is real for *you*.

I've always been what is commonly known as a "psychic" – but I don't like the word. I've spent my whole life thus far trying to accept me for me, without definitions that tend to limit me. I'm just a person who is willing to admit to her intuitions and perceptions, and who is trying to understand how the universe *really* works – aside from what I've been told in school, by the newspaper and radio and TV, by friends and relations. I want to be me – and that means I have to let go of preconceived notions of the way things are in order to find out what works.

Yes, I've had many strange things happen to me – only, for me they're not strange, they're normal.[7] I've had experiences of telepathy (such as with my father while growing up), premonitions and prophetic dreams, unusual "coincidences", and a healing energy that comes through my hands. I haven't as yet seen a ghost, but I *have* seen Moita.

Moita has a talent for the absurd. It helps to dissolve the mythos of a spiritual teacher. She is not interested in followers. (I imagine she's already much too busy and too fulfilled to have time or room for them.) So, talented as she is, one of the first times she chose to show herself to me was while I was up on a hydraulic lift at three o'clock in the morning in a big city downtown service station – actually *I* was in a car, and the *car* was on the lift!

It's hard to describe what that was like, but I wasn't afraid. She was obviously a beautiful being to me. There was an exchange of thoughts, but the encounter was brief because I didn't know what to say. I can't remember it ending as such. I guess I just floated out of the space where she was visible.

But I've never forgotten it, either. Seeing her filled me with a desire to see her again – to be *with* her. It was like being an orphan and then finding your real mother – and all the fears you had about why you'd been deserted, what was wrong with you, were dissolved. I knew she loved me, and that knowledge filled me and helped me through some very rough times over the next seven years: life experiences that prepared and strengthened me so that I would finally be ready to let her speak through me to others.

When it began, when she first actually spoke through me, I wasn't even consciously aware that it was happening. I was in the midst of a personal crisis, a painful breakup in a relationship. The words that I spoke gave a larger perspective – certainly not how I would have usually been able to speak of it. (How many of us could talk about our own pain calmly, as if it belonged to someone else?) David recognized a presence and asked who was speaking now. There was a sudden rush of energy to my mind, and she repeated the name that came to me in that earlier experience: Moita.[8]

It was as natural as breathing after that initial breakthrough. She came spontaneously, sporadically, for short periods of time. Those first few months were exciting as well as confusing. We had to be ready to change our state of mind at the drop of a hat, never knowing when she would come to speak. She came only when she was needed, and said only as much as we could hear and understand at that time.

She has never told us what choices we should make: these, she has said, are our own – and if she made them for us, we would not become strong. That impressed me. She has said that it is important to make mistakes so that we can learn. That is how she got to be where she is, and her level gives ours the same freedom so that one day we can join them. That impressed me, too.

I was upset and worried from time to time about whether it was real. But over the last four years she has proven to *my* satisfaction that she is not a secondary personality I created to fulfill some need within me, and she isn't a demon from hell bent on possessing me for her own evil ends. I was there, and I speak from my experience. Except for the rarest of exceptions, there was never any coercion involved.[9] I was always willing to let her in, and she was always willing to leave when she was done.

I did realize after a while that, if she so chose, she was powerful enough to "possess" me in a negative sense. But having the power to do something to someone, and *not* using that power, says volumes about her purpose and her sense of integrity and what level she comes from – at least, to me.

There will always be those that see something sinister and frightening in this. That's okay, because they will never *be* a channel – not in this life. But I *am*, and I feel honoured to be able to help in this way, even though I recognize that a lot of hard work on my part went into preparing me for the role I have chosen.

My experience of her inside me is hard to put into words. It's like reality shifts a little. My mind buzzes with energy; the air comes alive; the walls of the house dissolve into insignificance. It's not that they disappear, but that we no longer attach any importance *to* them, so they cease to exist in our reality. What does matter is her presence: the sense that you are really being looked at and listened to completely, maybe for the very first time in your life. I'm carried upward on a wave of energy and "eternal nowness". Time passes, and yet it passes more slowly, or more *richly*.

Each question that is asked becomes the most important question that has ever been asked, no matter how trivial it may sound to others. She shows by her intentness that she believes in *your* reality as well as her own. Though oftentimes the answers are hard to understand for a while, or not what you expected, it's obvious that she cares enough, loves enough, to make the attempt at opening the lines of communication between the levels. She *shares* her perspective – her broader insight into why the question was asked in the first place – but she does not *impose*: "Do not stop questioning or testing the truth of what you receive. In the end analysis, you are the only one who can decide what you perceive of all this and what applies to you directly."

As you read the excerpts from the many sessions we have held since this began, you will note that the quality of the exchange between others and Moita has grown and evolved, and I have become more comfortable with the idea as I have grown to know and accept myself. I do not foresee any *end* to this process of growth. There is always one more step, one more barrier to dissolve, one more discovery to make or remember about the nature of reality and the universe.

Her purpose in coming is simple, really: to make us aware that we are not alone and that we have within us tremendous potential for real love and compassion – for giving back to the universe joyfully and freely the gifts we have received, for learning how to become the co-creators of our world; to let us know we can remake our lives into works of beauty – if we will but take the reins in our hands, be responsible for our own action, and learn from our mistakes.

These words came from me, and yet I can make no claim to them. I am the channel, the vessel, through which they came – but they are more than I know of myself. We are *all* channels, and we are all mysterious, beautiful and worthwhile. If she never gives me another thing, knowing that we all matter is gift enough.

Love,
Kelly

THE ART OF COMMUNICATION

Channelings 1980/2012

"Prophetic and relevant for this time", said Elihu Edelson when *Mind Leap*, the first volume in this series, appeared in 2010. Why would the editor of *Both Sides Now* – one of the longest-running underground papers in North America, integrating politically left/antiwar and New Age spiritual perspectives – "highly recommend" a story of channelings from some 30 years ago "to all who would be open to the changes...as the turning point to a New Age approaches"?[10N]

One of Moita's prime purposes in the 200-plus sessions she held with us was exploring the *art of communication* between levels – and as a master, teaching it to both the human participants and to numerous entities who were in attendance non-physically. No doubt partly as a consequence, Moita's prediction that many more channels for such communication would be opening in the future has certainly proven true during the intervening years.

Today numerous channeling sources may be found, on the internet and in print, speaking about the changes of 2012 and beyond. Probably the best-known clearing-house website, and most useful to myself, is www.the2012scenario.com. Besides relevant news, the site features channelings attributed to "ascended masters", "galactics" (higher-dimensional ETs) and "celestials" (angelic realms). But as explained in the next section and by the 2012 Scenario site itself, individual discernment is needed to assess which among the variety of available sources are most credible, trustworthy and wise. To date, I personally have felt close to and trusting of the messages from Archangel Michael through Linda Dillon and the Federation of Light through Blossom Goodchild. My sense is that sources like these are continuing in the spirit of the channelings from Moita, Amar and the Goddess that fill this book with consistent love and light.*

So, how to answer my opening question? I believe the core vision, heart-knowing, insight into multidimensional reality, and ways of opening to higher energies communicated by Moita et al. are the most important keys for any of us to understand today's changes and to "ascend" with our transforming Earth. As well, their predictions of possible events furnish a history of probabilities – the dire ones having been mostly averted with their help, if current channelings be correct – and an outlook on what likely still lies ahead. While this sketching of futures has always been secondary, it is included to tell our story in the context of the time and to provide a perspective of decades on current prophecies that can so rivet the attention of people around the world today.

Finally, our story of working with higher energies toward community offers lessons for those seeking guidance on the threshold before us now. It illustrates an analogy given by Goodchild's source[11] – that prophecy is a chess game, where the *human reaction* to messages and events affects our higher levels' next moves, changing the predicted future. Confusion and frustration might be reduced if learnings from channeling relationships in previous decades became better known.

---

* Appendix B indexes all channelings mentioned, while Appendix C indexes dreams and regressions.

Clarity about Communications

One recurring theme should be highlighted from the start. A common assumption would prove quite misleading if applied to this and other experiential quests. But by keeping this "clarity" well in mind, there can be fuller awareness – a more accurate context – as events unfold.[12N]

Assumption: We can immediately judge experiences as being valuable psychic/spiritual messages with obvious meaning OR as being merely subjective with no real value at all.

Few readers would seriously think one can judge experiences at first glance. But we do tend to react instantly to things based on the information ready to hand and our past experiences and biases. In a book of mysteries that unfold over time, this tendency may create a lot of misunderstanding.

This assumption is dual in nature: two outlooks that are mirror images, and both incorrect. These attitudes are like two people – a true believer and a dyed-in-the-wool skeptic – who could argue endlessly about experiences like dreams, visions, channelings, psychic impressions, and so on, because the two of them have so much in common beneath their opposition. The believer approaches any experience like this as a direct and usually literal revelation of truth – pure and simple. The skeptic dismisses all such experiences as invalid, subjective imaginings – on principle. The reality, however, lies in between – and far beyond.

It is well-known that dreams, for example, come in many flavours. Some seem exceedingly random and crazy, or charming in their silliness. Others seem to reflect actual and perhaps serious situations or feelings in one's life. Still others are not realistic but make a powerful impression, as if speaking with intent of deeper things. Clearly, to make any headway with dreams, to understand the different types and apply the right approach to each, requires interest, awareness and dedication. Sometimes even the "superficial" ones will turn out to contain a nugget of real value. Sometimes the first view of a complex dream will give way over time to another, and then to another, and another.

What can be said about dreams applies to many types of non-ordinary awareness. There is a learning and growth curve to discovering where their truth lies. The more experience one has, the better one can become at teasing out clues, connecting threads, and recognizing or finding a deeper level of truth than first meets the eye. Rationality and objective evidence play a role here, so "merely subjective" this process is *not*. But intuitive flashes and heartfelt insights also prove essential, pointing to solutions where reason is stuck up a blind alley.

Inner communications can seem mysterious and ambiguous to us because they evoke a different type of reality than usual. How, then, can we be sure what level of contact is being made and how much significance to give it? The source that is communicating can also *change*, in midstream. For example, an entity who is apparently speaking through a channel may slide, without saying so, into an entity on a lower or higher level. Will the human participants even notice?

Thankfully, there *are* "pointers" to use in deciding what is or isn't a good-quality communication. After going through the interpretive process mentioned above, then stepping back to see the experience in perspective, one can ask:

- ➢ how insightful and balanced is the viewpoint conveyed?
- ➢ how accurate are any statements or signs of a factual truth?
- ➢ how wise, ethically and psychologically, is the manner of relating?
- ➢ how coherent, yet sensitive and creative, are the images and words?
- ➢ how deep and harmonious is the energy that infuses them?
- ➢ how intimately does the message relate to the individual(s) present?
- ➢ how consistent and unified is the entire body of communications?

Moreover, we are not at the mercy of which levels may make contact. We are in far more control than the beginner realizes. The secret, which we discover through trial and error, is that our own state of mind, the clarity of our own energy, determines the quality that will be able to be expressed.

Inner communications, in whatever form, are thus a *participatory, co-creative and evolving partnership* between levels. This, on top of everything else, means their reality is far more subtle and complex than either of the opposing assumptions with which we started would suggest. This subtlety and complexity demands that those on a spiritual path develop "discretion". We must become able consciously to discriminate among levels of apparent contact. We must also learn to choose from among a variety of messages which apparent truths actually relate to ourselves.

These lessons of spiritual development also apply, doubly, to compiling and writing this book. So, the dreams and visions, the psychic impressions and communications, that appear here have *not* been included because their validity and meaning are assumed to be obvious at face value. Those experiences that *have* been included are here because – at the time they were received, and during the days, weeks, months and anywhere up to *30 years* since that time – they were found to contribute an important thread of insight into the characters and/or understanding of this multidimensional reality. Again as an example, some dreams are immediately grasped. Others become clear in light of further dreams or after the events the dreams may have foreshadowed. Still others require long-term re-evaluation in the context of changing life experience, yielding a new outlook on the past.

Ultimately, the reader gets to participate in this co-creative partnership. The final key to the validity and meaning of inner experience is its dependence on you and me. The truth that is true for all is embedded in everyone's perception somewhere, *along with* what is individual. Thus, in the end, and very practically speaking, the truth of an experience is many-fold, depending on perceivers and the experiential universes in which we live. Allowing for this, we hope there is enough common ground within our various realities to make this sharing worthwhile for you too.

Clarity: We must carefully assess the sources and meanings of spiritual communications by employing rational/intuitive pointers. As communications reflect the states of their human co-creators, the characters, authors and readers all need to practise spiritual discrimination.

℘   ℘   ℘

PART ONE

Prologue

HOW *NOT* TO USE POWER

Experiences of heightened energy are often signs of breakthrough, of growing openness and understanding. But since energy brings power, a harmonious context is critical – a sense of balance and natural limits, of care and self-knowledge, of intimate relatedness to Earth and Spirit. As ample demonstration, we begin with an extreme case, perhaps the archetypal example of energy in *disharmony* with nature and cosmic reality.

When Kelly and I plan our trip from the Canadian prairies to the U.S. mid-Atlantic states for late March-April 1979, we little realize we are manoeuvring ourselves into nearly front-row seats for the most frightening of the year's lessons about power and its misuse: the Three Mile Island nuclear "accident" near Harrisburg, Pennsylvania.

Starting on March 28th, design, mechanical and operator failures combine to cause a major loss of coolant to the Three Mile Island reactor. The unprecedented result: a partial core meltdown with significant radioactive contamination of air and water. But not only "mistakes" are to blame. Behind this "accident" lies a history of political expediency and corporate greed. Why else rush the reactor into service, despite major problems, shortly before the end of 1978, in time to reap a huge tax break? And even as the crisis unfolds in late March, authorities take a few days to acknowledge its seriousness. Then they warn that hundreds of thousands of people may need to be evacuated.

This first well-publicized proof that even "peaceful" nuclear energy threatens life on Earth is one of many parallels between the time of our story and today. In the decades following Three Mile Island, the world will see two Level 7 nuclear "incidents", the most destructive category possible: at Chernobyl in 1986, and in the wake of Japan's massive earthquake and tsunami in 2011.

But nuclear energy is just one of many areas of modern technological power where stark lessons are escalating. Together, they force the question: *How can humanity awaken to transform Earth's dream . . . before it becomes an utter nightmare?*

It is on the evening of the second day of the crisis at Three Mile Island that Kelly and I meet with an Edgar Cayce study group in suburban Washington, D.C. As TV weather reporters pay close attention to wind directions over Pennsylvania and Maryland, 80 miles has come to feel very close. Our peace of mind has not been helped, either, by seeing the newly released film *The China Syndrome* this very afternoon – synchronistically, about a near-meltdown at a nuclear power station.

Moita session #81 (Kelly, David, Cayce study group / March 29, 1979)
(Replying to the obvious question from a participant tonight, Moita stresses the greater context of this particular crisis – including not just nuclear power but human consciousness, the nature of

time and probability, and the fate of the Earth itself.)

Jane: I am wondering whether nuclear accidents are going to be a continuing danger. Power company people are saying there's no danger, and scientists are saying there *is*. I'm wondering who's right and what we can do about it.

MOITA: In many ways, nuclear energy is like electricity. They use it, but they know not what it is or where it comes from. From *here*, many things that come to your world as energy are but extensions from another reality into this one, like worlds rubbing together. Out of its element, when it crosses the realities, it sets up a vibration that is counter to the one in which you live. That is what they see as radiation. It is not that the energy in itself is counter; but the pressing together of it, the forcing it in a small space where it does not belong, creates that kind of a change.

        It is like: If you lived inside the Earth...and happened to live beneath the ocean [but knew not what an ocean was], and [if you] discovered that by driving a hole in your ceiling you could cause water to rush through and [could] channel it and use the energy for your own purposes, you would not be aware of the immensity of the energy that you tapped, not ever having seen it.

Jane: So do you think we are going to have more and more of these things, because we tap such a great energy?

MOITA: It is not an energy that can be controlled for long...

(Later Moita returns to this subject, revealing a surprising connection to an event many would wish to forget.)

MOITA: I said once before that you have all experienced the end of the world – though you do not know it. These things are so related. People are very upset about this "accident" that may or may not be an accident. They remember with some part of themselves what the world looked like when all that energy was released and the devastation that it can cause.

Jane: Are you talking about the destruction of Atlantis?

MOITA: I was talking about just a few years ago . . .

Jane: Oh, just a few years ago. *(showing her confusion)* Hmm.

MOITA: . . . on another line of probability.

Jane: I guess I'd better sit back and let you explain it, since I don't know what you're talking about!

MOITA: As each one of you grows separately, you have many possibilities. You can choose different futures. There are many points in your life when you can make such a choice, to change the energy of your existence completely. As each individual has this happen to them, the world has it happen as a whole as well in its development towards unity.

        There was a time not far distant where a choice was made by the world-consciousness *not* to manifest a world destruction. That destruction was avoided on a physical level. But the reality of that possibility still existed in its own right – as when you dream and you go to a different realm, your dreams have reality too. They travel on from you after you are finished dreaming, and have an existence of their own as well.

This probability was experienced by many people, and the probability was presented for a reason: to make you all more aware of what could happen to your world if you chose to let it. We hope this lesson will help prevent the same kind of thing happening in your future.

Jane: I hope so too.

MOITA: But it is an effort of *all* of you to help prevent it. In this last century, many lessons have been given showing how power can destroy if it is not used properly, and the different types of power that are available. If you would come into your heritage and know yourself, you must also know how *not* to use power.

ം   ം   ം

The "once before" that Moita discussed "the end of the world" as a real probability was in a session three weeks earlier, from which excerpts will be given shortly. But Kelly's understanding of Moita's meaning is confirmed by this exchange a year later: referring to 13 notorious days in October 1962 that were anything but peaceful.

Moita session #135A (Kelly, David, workshop group / February 25, 1980)

Jim: I read a book where people travelled between different time-lines. There was one reality where the Russians had reached Cuba with their missiles and so forth. People in our reality, in the world that we think of as ours, were somehow affected by the knowledge that at any time that they made a decision, millions of reflections of themselves were doing things just about the same or opposite...

(Moita's response accepts that we do in fact experience these different probability lines on other levels of our being.)

MOITA: It is true...that on another time-line, during the Cuban missile crisis, the world was destroyed effectively. And that is one reason why so *many* people are against nuclear energy now, because they have tuned into that reality and learned the consequences of misusing energy.

ം   ം   ം

Before starting our spring 1979 trip to the East coast, however, rumours reached us of far more extensive crises to come: "disasters" being fully and deliberately planned by elite elements in the world, involving many of the forms of power our civilization has misused.[13N] Some of these conspiracy prophecies are being channeled and/or circulated by apparently "New Age" sources, but the irony is that only slightly different versions are being pushed by right-wing, fundamentalist groups. In 1979, just as 30-plus years into the future, these stories reference a web of more or less behind-the-scenes organizations frequented by servants of a world power elite, called the Illuminati or the Cabal – with links, as some tell it, to dark forces beyond the Earth and physical plane.

These predictions raise many questions – as much about the receivers and circulators of such "revelations" as about the credibility of their content and the advisability of dwelling on them. They certainly underscore the importance of discernment and each of us listening to our own inner voice, while being willing to take a stand on issues of good and evil manifest in the world around us.

More of Moita's views on this will be given in Chapter 9. But the relevant point for now is contained in the following excerpts, including her reference back to October 1962.

Moita session #77 (Kelly and David / March 9, 1979)

David: Are there conspiracies at work in the world, for example, to create a depression as a means to greater power and wealth for a few?

MOITA: There are many levels of conspiracy at work here! *(laughing, as she includes herself)*

There are those who would control the world's economy for their own ends. There are times when others' ends may appear to be ugly, but can serve good purposes too. It all works together. It will take a great many shocks to wake up many people. You have received some already, on the political scene. But still many people will not believe that there is that possibility, and that the world is made up of people and not governments.

It would be nice to have a *whole* world instead of one separated into small pieces. They say a house divided against itself cannot stand. That is what your world has become. And the houses themselves – the individual houses – are also divided. You are all in pieces, and you seem to have lost your direction, your sense of inwardness that expresses itself creatively in an outward form. This is what you are seeking, and this is what you need in order to help rebuild the world as it should be...

Some of these things are like possible other lines, as in what we would speak of reincarnationally, on a world level. People tune into different wavelengths, or different universes, and there are some where this conspiracy is more devastating than it may be here. None of these things are totally inaccurate. Much depends on the line you are standing on. Those who see other levels also act as a warning to show where the possibilities may lie, and how they can be prevented from happening. If a man can see his own destruction before the possibility of his own destruction arises, he can prevent it by being aware of it.

David: When you speak of some possibility happening or not, do you only mean happening to a specific set of individuals who experience the universe that way? Is there any sense in which one line happens more "factually" than another, for everyone?

MOITA: On another level, you all experience each possible future line of your development and your world's development. You are all aware of the lesson that you are learning from that other set of possibilities or circumstances. It's just that some of you are more close to that line and can see it more clearly than the others. You are all involved in it together. It is a matter of degree of perception, not a matter of truth or reality.

You have experienced the end of the world and what it would be like to have the entire face of the planet destroyed by your own energy. But you are not in that world now. You are in this one, and hopefully the lesson of that one will keep this one safer. It is like a *huge* dream, where anything can and does happen.

ɬ   ɬ   ɬ

One week into the Three Mile Island crisis, technicians are surprised to discover that the radioactive hydrogen "bubble" that was growing inside the stricken reactor has now nearly vanished, reducing the likelihood of a catastrophic explosion. And so, the world begins to catch its breath. But as we collectively seem to wake from this latest self-created nightmare, will we grasp the lesson?

Moita session #83 (Kelly, David, Marlene, Frank / April 5, 1979)

MOITA: I am very relieved that your bubble is lower.
David: This whole episode seems to have been choreographed perfectly as a teaching.
MOITA: Unfortunately, there are so many that we choreograph [that] no one notices. It is only a matter of time.
David: Before people will *have* to recognize it?
MOITA: There are so many patterns that are so plain for us to see, and many put them off as circumstance or coincidence. There has been a great deal of interest in this spot. Much energy has poured from many corners of the world, much concern for those who live near. It would seem unfitting if all that concern did naught. But then again, sometimes stupidity can overrule concern. We must work with the minds we are given.
Marlene: We really don't have anything else to work with!
MOITA: I mean *me*, not you!

ɬ   ɬ   ɬ

You are all in pieces, and you seem to have lost your direction, your sense of inwardness that expresses itself creatively in an outward form. This is what you are seeking, and this is what you need in order to help rebuild the world as it should be.
– Moita (March 9, 1979)

This book traces a radically new direction for planetary culture – based not on power over others and the Earth, exercised externally, in isolation and ignorance of larger realities, but on self-knowledge, partnership and community on *all* the levels of human being. That essence is what's important, not details of lifestyle. But Kelly and I are given a taste of this new direction early in our trip east, as we visit a small, spiritually-based community formed by people very like ourselves.

On a windy night in spring, Kelly and I sit with four members of the Associations of the Light Morning community in a lantern-lit cabin in the hills of western Virginia.[14] We pass among us the

Sioux peace pipe I have brought with me from the Great Plains, placing within its crucible the personal histories, feelings and dreams that we would mingle, merge and then release upwards, even as the rising smoke.

Moita session #80 (Kelly, David, A.L.M. group / March 24, 1979)

(As the wind is heard roaring outside:)

David: The spirit moves on many levels tonight...

(And my hand, holding Kelly's, suddenly reacts as if to a gust of energy.)

MOITA: You like the wind?.

David: It seems I felt its rush through my hand!...

MOITA: *(to Terry:)* What does your heart tell you? It is the only true voice that you have.

Terry: My heart tells me that we're orphans.

MOITA: Trapped on an island?

Terry: I was thinking of the heritage of the Indians as we passed the pipe, the generations it nourished. We're like cultural orphans.

MOITA: There are many such cultures that have seemingly been lost. *(pause)* You are trying to find a way back, but you are orphaned for a reason. Rituals and culture sometimes do prevent growth as well, and when they are lost they are lost for a reason. Their essence is not gone. *(pause)* You *can* make new rituals, enriching them with your new experience and keeping them more alive...

Nora: I'm thinking about this place – we who live here, you who pass through . . . What's it for?

MOITA: Large changes start in small places. Everything affects everything else. When you live in a reality without coincidence, small seemingly unimportant things carry great weight. Your thoughts fly from here and they touch others. You as yourself do not see what changes may be wrought in those flying thoughts. You are helping to weave a network of light.

Nora: Why?

MOITA: Perhaps the world has lived in darkness too long. It is a time of awakening, of returning; a time of many lessons. You all have lived without joy too long. *(pause)* Perhaps you can look on this as the true coming of spring in man's development. He has spent the winter sleeping. Now it is time for him to wake up.

Nora: What's our spring for in man's development?...

MOITA: You are here to learn love and what that means; and in the learning of that lesson, finding your joy and your beauty of self. You are putting behind self-punishment and regret.

Each one of you is great enough to contain the whole universe... Being is its own justification; it does not need a reason. Life is energy and it takes many forms, and each one is just as beautiful as each other...

Fern: As one of the blind men touching the elephant, how do you, from your perspective, view the group of us here at A.L.M.?

MOITA: You need to see this more as a whole. And in order to do that, you must spend less time trying to take things apart and looking at the pieces. Much more is at work here than what appears. To have faith in that "more" is a way of seeing, of removing the blindfolds.

I too have to take some things on faith. Powers greater than I channel their energy through me, just as they are seeking to do through you. That is one reason you are here.

Fern: How do you see the service you perform toward us? I ask because it may help me understand what our proper service might be for each other.

MOITA: I answer only what is asked. I give only what can be received.

Terry: How do you understand the Christ-consciousness?

MOITA: How do you understand love? Love is an energy in and of itself. It flows freely and does not bind itself to anything, for everything it touches is also love.

Terry: Why is this love not as visible in the world of today as it once was?

MOITA: Nothing about the world has changed since the time man began. The love has always been here, and it always will. The only thing that has changed is man's awareness. Man has cut himself off from that.

Terry: And why did we do that?

MOITA: In order to learn . . . *not* to.

ॐ   ॐ   ॐ

———————

Chapter 1

STEP IN THE RIGHT DIRECTION

Much energy has been put into planning this life, and you had – will have – an unusual amount of cooperation from others in carrying it through. All roads lead to the same, highly probable route you have chosen.
– Moita (January 16, 1979)

"If you would give your life to the spirit," Moita has told us, "there is a time to *start*." What forms of action would express an awareness of the coming New Age? New openings to other levels of ourselves, new depths of communication with spirit, may lead naturally to new forms of sharing in community with others. Perhaps this is also how we find our balance to flow with higher energies and arrive at a vision for manifesting them: awakening to a new dream that will not destroy but express and enhance the whole potentialities of Earth.

Our "highly probable" future, Kelly and I have come to believe, is to help to create an intentional community in which people may heal, learn and grow in greater harmony with nature and spirit. Travelling this road, there will be more apparent delays, more turnings, and more "travel at your own risk" signs than we ever would have anticipated. But there will also be rewards, as when we experience the results of that planning and cooperation, discovering ourselves at the meeting-point of positive energies on many levels. These energies are what draw us forward along the unknown route to our goal – or should I say, the unknown route that *is* our goal.

New Age community – during the late 1970s, best exemplified by the Findhorn Community in Scotland – is mentioned as early as Moita's second written communication through Kelly. This comes at a time when our personal destiny together, within a loose-knit group of young adults who are drawn to meditation and psychic exploration, is still unclear. Also unclear to all of us at this point is Moita's behind-the-scenes role as a group entity uniquely suited to guide the formation of such a community.

<u>Moita written channeling #4 (Kelly / July 6, 1978)</u>
MOITA: It is not permitted just yet to say exactly what [this communication] has to do with David, except that it concerns you both – and has connections with the community...

In order for the community to work, it must be based on love – in all its manifestations. On the ability to allow others their own freedom of expression in many ways.

Higher consciousness is fine providing it does not cut one off from the rest of humanity. The whole idea of man is to be able to become one with others in a very real sense without the fear of losing one's own oneness.

By mid-fall 1978, Kelly and I have come together as a couple and co-workers, centred around our evolving adventure with Moita. As far as down-to-earth progress toward the goal of a larger community, though, we feel increasingly bewildered by questions of *how*, and *who*, and *when*, and *where*. Moita's role is to fend off our impatience, suggest the state of mind and heart in which intuitions will come, and remind us of the priority of *why*.

Moita session #40 (Kelly and David / November 11, 1978)

David: Dream images continue to occur about places for a community to be built. Is there anything you can say about the way such a place should be found? How much of an ordinary, practical searching out of places is in the plan . . . if there is a plan? I assume nothing much can happen till after the winter – I could be wrong!

MOITA: The way time has a tendency to congeal itself into small units?!
           It is rather difficult to start a community in the winter. Spring is a much better time!... Providing you *continue* to put all of your energy into your "now", things will fall into place. If there is a plan, that is the only one. The universe is willing to give you anything you want, providing you *allow* it to.

David: Then trying to plan and search would probably just get in the way.

MOITA: You do not have much to plan *on*, at the moment! Your community will be made up of people, so people are the first place you should put your energy. It does no good to have a place without the people...

David: Taking the example of Findhorn, it started with very few people but had the place.

MOITA: True. They also were pushed to where they went, without a plan apparent.

No answers are forthcoming, either, even three months later – beyond an assurance "the universe" is active behind the scenes.

Moita session #70 (Kelly, David, 5 others / February 17, 1979)

David: I get the feeling that living in the city, in the old ways, should come to an end soon. "Giving our life to the spirit" seems to involve a radical break at some point. Can any time-frame for this be given?

MOITA: You will find this to be a rewarding spring – perhaps not in exactly the way you would envision it, however. Things are moving very well.

In March and April, then, Kelly and I visit our families on the East coast and the Associations of the Light Morning community in Copper Hill, Virginia, where we hold the session that ended the Prologue. We go to A.L.M. wondering whether it may be the people and place we have been seeking. Being there, we are warmed by the energy of community, the sharings of its members and their gentle, organic way of life. But we come away feeling we may have a slightly different note to sound in the emerging melody of New Age centres. We also realize that we wish to be involved in the very beginnings of the community that will be ours.

So we return home determined to send out feelers in enough new directions to hit upon that road "we" have already laid out. Soon after our arrival, Moita passes on essential wisdom for our present and future.

Moita session #84 (Kelly and David / April 14, 1979)

David: For me, the hope of community in a more permanent sense is tied to moving to the country, and we have many questions about when, where, how and who. I wonder if the answer to these must still be "focus on the present", or that we must have the attitude of almost "Thy will be done". It's not something we're to do, to plan, to desire in a specific way – that the most important thing is to try to become vessels or channels for other levels to work through us. Is that how you see it?

MOITA: *(long pause)* You have said it very well. *(pause)*

There certainly are practical aspects that must be worked out when the time comes, and it would be better for you to live in the country – *easier* on you. There are many things for you to learn in the city that are not easy. If you were done with your learning, you would not be here. *(pause)*

Your way is still filled with people. You are a stepping-stone for others. You help them light their own candles. I sense you still feel much alone and isolated.

David   There aren't that many people, that we consciously know of, that we are helping in that way you speak of.

MOITA: The smallest stone can start an avalanche, and the stone may not think it's great nor be aware of the avalanche it caused. It is not easy to measure. These kinds of things are very often those remembered longer. And in days to come, as the world develops, some of what you have said will be looked upon again. Once a light has been lit, it can shine on in darker corners before its owner is aware that it has a light within it.

But you must keep yours burning too. You can hold your ideal of community without restricting the form it may choose to take or the manner of its coming. Your community exists within you and in your attitude towards others, in how open you are willing to be, how much you are able to share, and how little you are willing to judge the paths they are following. *(long pause)*

If you take your joy in the moment and live your life to its fullest, even if it came to pass that your dreams were turned to dust, you would not have had a wasteful or unhappy life. Those who dream too far ahead spend their life trying to arrive. And when their dream turns out to be different than what they had hoped, they have wasted so much time striving for nothing...

(Kelly says later that as I ask my questions about community, Moita is saying to her "Love leads the heart, and faith the mind. Faith is a better driver [than the mind].")

MOITA: Now that you are back, perhaps we can do this more often.

David: That will be good...

MOITA: We are building a strong foundation, with much care and love. *(pause)* Have a joyous heart!

ço   ço   ço

As so often happens, by absorbing such messages, we unknowingly release movement in the direction of our dreams. Just three weeks later, a letter is written initiating a major step forward on our path. That letter has a history behind it: feelers long ago sent out that are only now returning to us.

Back in early 1978, a friend first mentioned the Associations of the Light Morning community to me and Ruth, my then-partner in the Loria channelings and Sunseed workshops[15N]. Sensing our affinity, we sent the A.L.M. people copies of our journal *Rays from Starflower*. The *A.L.M. Journal* subsequently quoted our Regina group's statement of purpose from an article on networking. That brief mention was read by Christopher and Becky of remote Sunrise Farm in the British Columbia interior, who then wrote Ruth and me this letter.

July 22, 1978

Dear Starflower,

We just read about your group in an *A.L.M. Journal,* and felt like connecting with you. The quote we read seemed like a good way to describe what we'd like to do here, too. To build a "loving community" that would "explore what it means to live in harmony with other people, with nature and with spirit, during an era of planetary transformation." There's sure a need for such places, and we hope to help one happen on our 160 acre farm in a mountain wilderness of northern B.C.

If any of you are in the area, or just feel like getting out in some beautiful "bush", we'd be happy to have you visit us...

Love,
Sunrise Farm

Chris and Becky subscribed to *Rays* and ordered the booklets of Loria communications. Another letter was written in the fall – unwittingly, *one day after* the Moita session excerpted above about where and with whom our community will develop.

November 12, 1978

Dear Starflower,

We'd like to mention that we are looking for others to form a community with on our land... We have long hoped to see a new and conscious sort of community here, and maybe a school of some kind. It's hard to know how much to push for such a thing, as we want it to happen naturally and in its right time. But we also want to let people know who seem to share a similar vision, as your group certainly does.

For the most part there are just the two of us here as permanent residents. We look forward to sharing this land and our life with more people...

Love to all of you,
Christopher

Enclosed was a photo of "Dawn at Sunrise Farm", showing a meadow, trees, and 7,000 foot mountain.

The spirit behind the words, and the beauty of the scene, certainly drew me – as they did Ruth, though by this point we had separated. Ruth's interest in the possibility of helping to build a community at Sunrise Farm led me not to respond to the letter myself. I felt that her need to make a connection with new people in a new place at this point might be greater than mine, as I was just beginning to live with Kelly and her children. Having wanted Ruth's and my child to be able to grow up in the country and in community, I did not wish to compete for an invitation to join Sunrise Farm, and so tried to put aside my desire to go there.

Ruth did initiate an exchange of letters with Chris and Becky, provoking more tantalizing photographs and plans for a visit the following summer. Later, though, Ruth put off the idea of rural living in order to continue at university. Learning of this, Kelly and I still hesitated to contact the Sunrise Farm people again, figuring they had been given Ruth's side of the painful events leading to our separation and probably would not be interested in us anymore. This paranoia reflected our sense of isolation in Regina at the time.

We were interested, however, that Becky and Chris did subscribe to our new format of *Rays* devoted to the Moita channelings, once we resumed publishing in March 1979. Thoughts in that same general direction were expressed in this dream of mine during the second week of April.

"Yukon Creek Community" dream
David / April 14 (?), 1979

I come upon an old trading post and other old log buildings arranged in a circle. A number of people our age are living here. I ask what community this is and am told Yukon Creek Community. "Do you realize how far that is?" I reply, thinking of the distance from Regina. I am nevertheless deeply impressed by talk of "many healings being done, and to be done, here".

One month later comes a similar dream.

"New Dimension Co-op" dream
David / May 7-10, 1979

There is a phone call concerning conferences on healing to be held soon in Regina and one other New Age centre. Then I find myself outside a set of buildings with a sign reading "New Dimension Co-op" (or "Community"). I see there is a bookstore and other facilities to be used both by residents and the general public.

Driving around, I arrive at a spot where a group is gathered and find that I recognize these people! It feels like returning for a visit to the A.L.M. Community, but much more joyous in that I see old friends of mine. We greet each other warmly, and I kiss and hug one lady friend. She, however, speaks of a need to restrain herself amid my open joy at seeing her. But I point out that we can return here every year for the rest of our lives to renew the closeness. We need not wall ourselves off in fear of having to part. Behind the buildings I glimpse the foothills of a Western mountain range.

ભ ભ ભ

I'm not sure if we ever notice it, but it is during these same few days in early May that the fateful letter is written, described earlier as "a major step forward on our path". It gives such a sense of surprised excitement and happy intimations of the future when it arrives, because it shows the Sunrise Farm folks have not prejudged our path – seeing no barrier in my now living and working with Kelly and Moita.

May 8, 1979

Dear David,

We are enjoying the latest copies of *Rays* – it's good to feel that contact in our lives – though we miss Ruth and Loria and wonder what has become of them [since she has] abruptly stopped writing.

After an especially solitary and contemplative sort of winter, also a heavy and changeful one, we're really wanting some people to share this place and our vision. Just this morning I was saying I think we're a bit like a fish out of water, trying to do this thing here by ourselves – get this farm happening and living such an isolated life. I know it's been a necessary stage for us, but we keep feeling it's time for something more, that we are meant to be doing this as a community. Though basically we do trust it will happen as and when it should – and try not to be overly impatient. (I wonder if Moita would have any feelings or ideas about us . . .)

Happy springtime to you...

Love,
Becky (& Chris)

Needless to say, Kelly and I write them back immediately, telling of our strong wish to connect with people to whom we would feel close enough to build community. Very aware of what a leap into the unknown this is, but unable to shake the sense that our destiny has come riding to us on Becky's letter, we ask if we may visit them this summer.

By the end of the month we are anxiously awaiting Chris's and Becky's reply. Then, on one of the few days before June 4th, I receive this dream.

"Mandala from Sunrise Farm" dream
David / June 1-3, 1979

We receive the awaited response from Sunrise Farm. It is written in the form of a mandala, with spokes radiating from a central hub. Chris and Becky say they were very excited to receive our letter and are looking forward to our visit. They say to bring all the copies of Rays *that we have, so they can put them in the outhouse.*

(Waking, I hope they mean for reading purposes!)

When we finally do receive Becky's reply, we discover that it was written on June 4th – and that perhaps the preceding *dream* letter I received was "written" because they could not at the time write a physical one.

June 4, 1979

Dear David,

...It felt *so* good to get your letter – just to be in touch with some people, as you say, "seriously involved in new age consciousness". (In the few days since we got your letter we've had company and no time or space to sit down and write you.) With the changes coming so fast these days, it can feel pretty lonely to not be sharing them with anyone – on deeper levels than we have been... On top of the collective changes, it's a very intense time.

July or August would be fine for visiting... We really look forward to meeting you!...

Much love,
Becky

Becky's longer letter, written three days later, is moving in its honest expression of sadness about Ruth and me, combined with a clear (and all too rare, in our experience) refusal to be judgmental. At the same time, she is very open about her own growing and changes.

ço   ço   ço

Spring – which this year doesn't come to Saskatchewan till mid-May and June – does indeed prove "rewarding". We have not yet received these last two letters from Sunrise Farm when we hold the following session with Moita, so we are still unsure which direction we are being led. But for a number of reasons we do feel a corner has been turned – to be confirmed by meetings both expected and unexpected.

Moita session #93 (Kelly and David / June 6, 1979)

David: For a while it seemed we were cut off from other members of the group here that we know have shared previous lives together. And now: several old/new friends deeply involved in New Age consciousness have joined our new workshop; some of the group are finally requesting *Rays* again; plus we've had other new/old contacts by mail and phone. Maybe people are coming together a bit more again.

MOITA: People never stop changing.

David: I imagine there still might be others in the group going back to Musili that we haven't met yet, or don't know we've met? *(pause)*

MOITA: It would seem rather wasteful, if there were no others, to have me here.

David: Wasteful? Because you're helping to bring some of those others together?

MOITA: One does not require a group entity without a group.

David: A group that is going to stay together? I mean, there *have* been enough people that we have known, though not many of them working together on *this* level.

MOITA: True. I am here to pave the way.

ప్ర   ప్ర   ప్ర

That the possibility of community is not only still with us, but more real and alive than ever, relieves us no end. And our excitement multiplies on receiving Becky's letters – as if confirming Moita's "paving the way".

Moita session #95 (Kelly and David / June 14, 1979)

MOITA: There are some who wonder why it might be necessary to have something like me around in a community. *(pause)*

David: Go on . . . !

MOITA: I was waiting! I heard that coming. Kelly was curious to see if I was right!
          This kind of communication serves as a reminder, and it helps to clear those who are involved in working through their own spaces. It brings them up above their confusion for a while. It is also a way to keep your goal from losing its vitality, making it more than just an idea – more of a living presence. That is why doorways are made: so they can be used...

          (After a long silence, as both of us also feel Loria's energy:)

MOITA: You are becoming reunited with many old friends – or at least, reacquainted. *(smiling)*

David: That's good to hear. *(feeling she must be including the Sunrise Farm people)*

MOITA: Perhaps the time for solitude is ending.

As more and more signs accumulate that our path is about to take a definite and exciting turn toward the country and toward community, we still seek a few Regina friends who share our vision enough to join our search. During our spring Sunseed workshop, we've felt much commonality with Owen and Hazel, a couple who have been quietly pursuing spiritual studies for some time. We invite them over one evening to explore why we should have come together at this point in our lives. Our talk of radical changes, both personally and in the world, brings Moita. So we invite her to speak with us.

Though Moita makes an unusual number of suggestive and indeed prophetic statements in this session, we all eventually recognize that our roads are leading in different directions. A further difficulty in communication proves to be Hazel's perception of Moita as part of an extraterrestrial civilization bent on taking over planet Earth, for our own good!

Moita session #96 (Kelly, David, Owen, Hazel / June 24, 1979)

MOITA: There has been much talk of change.

Hazel: More and more people are seeing the need for change. People are optimistic about being able to change. *(with a sigh)* The middle class is uptight, though. Do you experience all these human concerns very much, Moita?

MOITA: I experience them a great deal. That is why I am here. The few can do what the many cannot... *(pause)* Cities are becoming an unsafe place to be.

Hazel: I say, may God have mercy upon them.

MOITA: It is not mercy they need.

Hazel: They will receive judgment.

MOITA: They are receiving their own judgment. They have set it up themselves. And the Earth is going through its own cleansing process – and so are you...

Owen: Your view is that people should be leaving the cities (?).

MOITA: Not everyone *can*. But some must prepare, so that when things are finished there will be something for others to go to. *(pause)* That is why I have come: to help prepare for those who will be left behind.

Hazel: *(sighs)* I used to be afraid of it, you know. I used to have dreams, and I've become less afraid as time has gone by. I've seen all the suffering that goes on every day, and know all the various irritations and wearinesses that exist, and I'm not afraid so much now. I see it and, well, a good lesson could be an interesting thing to observe, you know. It could be a chance to show a lot of compassion and a lot of love for a lot of people.

MOITA: Your compassion would be better served if you had a stronger foundation from which to work – if there were something substantial, something concrete, something to offer to those who are lost. Words of comfort are fine and have their place. But in a world that is filled with change and confusion . . .

Hazel: Now, what are you talking about – this "concrete"? Do you see something?

MOITA: Those who are here have arrived to help found a new world.

Hazel: Are you talking about yourself and your particular group, your disembodied companions, or . . . ?

MOITA: Not just mine. There are others.

Hazel: Do you think you're going to do something in this situation more direct than you've done in the past? What kind of a thing have you got in mind?

MOITA: For us, this is a labour of love. Instead of man creating only on his own, as an individual self set apart from the rest of the universe, this time he is involved in a co-creation – and we are the co-creators.

(In what follows, Hazel seems to misunderstand. Moita means that her level is to co-create with our human level.)

Hazel: Huh! You're going to try and contact people in a more direct way, then, and more directly communicate your ideas about human life and change. Huh!

MOITA: I am here in part as a guide . . .

Hazel: *(interrupting)* Yeah, but do you think . . . ?

MOITA: . . . in part as a door, and in part as a mirror.

Hazel: Whew! I don't know if humans are going to be willing to . . . I don't know! I myself, I like being . . . Man *might* accept extraterrestrial *advice*. I don't know if he will accept extraterrestrial *government!* – unless he's *forced* to it.

MOITA: We use no force from here. And we are not speaking of government. We are speaking of discovery and of creation.

Hazel: Well, man doesn't even like to be governed by . . . *(laughing)* Hmm. But if he's in an absolutely crummy state after all these changes, I guess he'll have to get help where he can.

MOITA: Our hope is that *some* can get help before, and be ready.

Owen: I suppose it's a question what the appropriate preparation is.

MOITA: Those who are unprepared are unprepared for a reason – to learn by it. Those who are ready, and prepared to meet the changes before they happen, are also there for a reason – to help the others. And they both learn and benefit from the experience.

You are not living alone in the universe. The Earth is very much a part of this plan. It is, in a sense, its own defence against destruction. It has a body, and its organs are being misused and becoming diseased and blocked in many ways. It either must cleanse itself dramatically, or die. Hazel should understand the process better than any of you, since she has already lived through what the Earth is coming to.

(Moita refers to Hazel's near-death experience due to illness several years ago – an experience that opened her to a new perspective on life.)

Hazel: *(laughing)* That's correct, I have. Yes, I've dreamed it too.

MOITA: I am speaking more of your own personal experience with a body, and what happens when it is blocked. You still have many toxins that must be released.

Hazel: Mm-hmm. Well, I don't know. I think it's going to hurt man's pride.

MOITA: I hope so!

Owen: For sure! That's one good thing we can count on!... *(laughter)*

MOITA: It is time for doers. Creation does not happen by staying still. Creation in any form requires energy, requires interest and input. You can take what has been given to you and use it to good advantage... Inner searchings must eventually be able to turn outward again and be given back.

If a New Age is to come, what will it be built for...if not for those who come after? Those who are builders build not for themselves so much as they build for their children and all the children that come later.

The New Age is yours to experience in its beginnings, but not in its flower – not in this life. But the flower must be nourished, and the seed must be sown. Even if the seed is sown on barren soil, one day, when the Earth changes and the soil becomes more rich, the seed will find root and it will grow, for nothing is ever wasted.

We are here to bring to you a practical way to use love, a way to find out what love really is, and to let it flow out into the world again where it has been so sorely missed and has been misunderstood in its entirety...

David: We've seen the negative side of man can go very far. To see the balance, we need to know how far the positive can go. I'm wondering if you can say more about "a practical way to use love".

MOITA: Perhaps I should have said the physical manifestation of the energy in form. There is no one particular way to manifest it. Each will find a different road to that. But it is the energy itself, the opening of doors between people as well as worlds, that is of the prime importance. You all need love. It nourishes your soul. It is to you the food as the Sun is to the plant. So there is need for man to open the door and let not just *our* energy – but his own – flow out.

We think that now is the time when you should be preparing on a physical level, because it will take some time – not just for you – before you will know, or be able to know, how you can best serve the energy that comes to you. It is not easy to open yourself up sufficiently when you are in the midst of these turmoils.

And if the world [of all life-forms] is to have a say in its own destiny, it also must be a partner in your endeavours to create channels. That is why there has been talk of "the country" – although it is inadequate to describe what it means to be in a place where the world can touch you. You cannot but be changed by the experience.

Hazel: So you're saying that these two are going to go to the country and start working there soon?

MOITA: I said that it would be wise. It would bear more fruit, in time for it to be needed.

Owen: I have felt that Hazel and I are right where we ought to be right now. I have certainly not been feeling any real prompting to get out of the city at the moment or to leave Regina...

MOITA: The prairies are a good place to learn many things.

So ends one of the fullest Moita sessions as far as intimations toward the New Age are concerned, for which preparation is needful on many levels. Though we now realize Owen and Hazel will not be joining our westward venture, Moita has made the most of our shared energy this night, speaking with profound directness for these emergent times. "Those who are here" – meaning, I think, on both her level and ours – "have arrived to help found a new world." Together, "we are the co-creators" of what will become a new reality shaping humanity's future.

ക   ക   ക

We also discussed the energy of the prairies in the session ten days earlier, after receiving the most recent letters from Sunrise Farm.

Moita session #95 (Kelly and David / June 14, 1979)

David: Loria once spoke of the energy on the prairies here as being a very good quality for laying the foundations of what we're doing now. Could you say anything about the quality of energy there would be in a place like Sunrise Farm? *If* we were to go there, what sort of different energy-space would that involve? What kind of work would be appropriate there?

MOITA: For one, you would not just be living in [British Columbia] – you would be living in isolation from [large numbers of] people. *(pause)*

(with a laugh) You would in some ways be closer to our realm, for you would be higher up, where the atmosphere is thinner. Sometimes the atmosphere acts as a buffer between our world and yours. For us, it looks somewhat like a fog – the thicker it is, the more difficult it is to see through. It would be a clearer place. You would be able to dispose of more toxins in your body, and your mind perhaps.

I think you are grounded enough not to let the mountains take you away. Living in the prairies makes you part of them even after you leave.

David: I thought of that. If we were going somewhere else, obviously we'd be bringing the part of ourselves that developed here.

MOITA: It would have been difficult to develop anywhere else, for you would be carried away on a wind, and nothing to keep you on the ground. It is difficult to get carried away in Saskatchewan.

David: *(laughing)* It *is* windy!

MOITA: But enthusiasm is slow to start. People here are generally closer to themselves; and so, they find it difficult to be close to others or to take them into their hearts. One remains an outsider a long time on the prairies. They do not change easily... *(long pause)*

David: I'm wondering if living in as much isolation as Sunrise Farm would involve, at the beginning at least, would be a good, even necessary, way to begin. It depends on what we're after.

MOITA: There is no need for you to be cut off from people – even living in isolation.

David: Uh-huh. That's what I thought you meant.

MOITA: It is a very different feel.

David: Which do you mean: living out of the city or . . . ?

MOITA: Living among your brothers and sisters [in nature] who have different forms than you.

ॐ   ॐ   ॐ

We are surprised in both these June sessions to hear Moita speaking so positively about a move to the mountains. Previously, it took me a little time to accept and appreciate Saskatchewan as a potential place for starting a community. Then, as told in *Mind Leap*, after I became enthused about possibilities in the vicinity of an aboriginal medicine wheel site, my hopes were dashed as communication broke down both within our group and with local residents. As a result, we have grown more wary of jumping to conclusions and rapidly projecting ourselves into the future.

Now Moita is turning the tables and clearly urging this next leap into the unknown – though she would say it is our own higher selves that seek it. The chance to be in much closer contact with nature is definitely crucial here, though we don't yet realize how far that may lead or its implications.

The prospect of moving to B.C. is inviting, however, and recalls a crucial dream of mine from the previous fall, which can be taken both symbolically and literally. The dream contrasted drought-stricken prairie with a land of clear streams and evergreen forest. Within the dream, I considered the forest area too much to hope for – though, if feasible, clearly a better place to buy land. Now, as we hold this next session, we are in the midst of preparing for what seems our momentous trip west.

Moita session #98 (Kelly and David / July 3, 1979)

David: Do you have any comments on our upcoming meeting with Becky and Chris of Sunrise Farm? We've been thinking a fair amount about that. What will we need to be aware of in that meeting?

For example, I imagine we may represent some complementary aspects, so there may well be differences to be open to. Previously we've had a tendency to seize on one or another person as a potential co-worker, and then become aware of the different paths we are on. Those are just some of my thoughts.

MOITA: Some of the experiences that you have been going through are to help teach you to be open to differences in others. Being aware of that and being accepting of differences will be necessary for you in a community.

The most important thing that you can bring to this meeting, besides your own awareness of yourself, is the willingness to share your own fears and misgivings as well as your anticipation. For, if something is built here, it must be built openly. Everyone must have their eyes open and seeing, so they know what they are doing and why they are doing it. It cannot be strong if it is built upon uncertainty and deceit – not that I would think *(smiling)* you are deceitful. It is a comparison between different kinds of communities and how they are formed,...and why they may or may not survive their beginnings. It takes work and a great deal of dedication to make this kind of thing your life. *(long pause)*

(One of the thoughts Kelly picks up during the above is that in conversation with others we must be able to speak from deeper within ourselves, from our true motives, rather than just superficially or intellectually.)

MOITA: If things feel right, and [if] you all decide that you would be willing to explore what it would be to be together, there is much that can be done from this level and much that can be learned in an interaction with us.

        (smiling) I am inviting myself.

David: *(laughing)* You're quite welcome to.

MOITA: It is so difficult for people who have never experienced this. You are quite comfortable with the idea. You have gone through many changes, many openings in your own awareness. Your flow is more fluid than it was. But for those who are first starting, there are many things they must go through to achieve the familiarity and the openness that is needed in order to gain the most benefit from this type of experience...

(Long silence, as we both are experiencing very vividly what Moita calls "changing the reality of the room". Light patterns "swoosh" about – Kelly's word – engulfing the walls and each other's faces, with a hum in the air.)

David: Soon perhaps we can talk out of the city.

MOITA: Mmm. Outdoors, and without vehicles making their noisy rounds. If you still wish to record, you will have to have batteries! There are some conveniences to your modern world!

David: *(laughing)* It is good to have you as our travelling companion.

MOITA: *(wry smile)* Fortunately I do not need to ride. We shall say goodnight now.

ଡ଼   ଡ଼   ଡ଼

We wonder later if Moita's last comment presages all the car troubles we, with Kelly's two young children, will experience on our long, difficult journey. (And the major thunderstorm hitting Regina the day before our departure may be another omen.) This nearly 3,000 mile trek is also to include a swing through southern B.C.'s Okanagan Valley, where we have been developing further contacts.

Some distance out of Regina, I realize that Christopher's carefully drawn map is still lying on our desk at home! Thus, five days, 1,200 miles, and a couple hundred dollars later, as we start up the Sunrise Valley road in early afternoon, we have only a topographical map and our rather hazy recollection of directions to go on. Our lack of a map, our unreliable car, and the challenge of the road that awaits us, seem exquisite symbols of the uncertainties and naïveté we need to work through in order to be open, grounded and clear enough for the meeting with Chris and Becky. Through the ordeal, we will certainly arrive in a different mental space than when we first set out.

We're not sure whether we're making a mistake as I turn off the gravel logging road for an ever bumpier dirt track winding up the northern side of Sunrise Valley. With luggage on top covered by a canvas tent, our brown 1969 VW station wagon – practical enough (when functioning) for the city – is soon bouncing and scraping its way over ruts, rocks and logs, as we minutely plot our course to avoid the worst of the boulders and mud holes. At one point the car comes to a grinding halt, stalled on a log-reinforced beaver dam precariously perched, with a slight downward tilt, overlooking a cascading stream! Kelly and the children walk ahead, leaving me to get myself out of this. Thankfully, I am able to start up and drive off on the first attempt, without skidding any further towards the edge. Soon after, we decide we can't risk riding in the car any further.

Parking off the "road", we stuff essential clothing, food and supplies into packs and set off on nearly blind faith that Sunrise Farm – or at least some form of shelter – lies not too many miles further, and that 7-year-old Donovan and 4-year-old Arista can manage to hike as far as we have to go. As the hot afternoon wears on through a haze of mosquitoes, we pass some anonymous shacks and a gate across our path. Later, a fork in the road forces another dubious decision.

Kelly's energy is giving out, what with the weight of her pack and her hypoglycemia, when we stumble upon an old Jeep truck with a fractured windshield parked in the grass. By this time functioning on sheer will power, she tells me later, Kelly is for pushing ahead, without our supplies, what she hopes will be the short distance remaining. I reluctantly agree, substituting for my pack a tired 4-year-old.

Finally, we are overjoyed to spy a hand-painted red and green sign, bearing a horizontal figure 8 enclosing a double yin/yang, nailed to a tree at yet another fork in the road. Then, further still than we expect, a second yin/yang infinity sign labelled "Sunrise Farm" marks the entrance to a hayfield. Across the field, past some trees, and by a gate, we are walking hand-in-hand through a meadow overhung with beautiful tall trees, leading to the large, framed house that we are relieved to see has smoke rising from its chimney! Climbing the steep outdoor stairs to the main floor, we are greeted with smiling faces and open arms by Becky and Chris . . . who seem so comfortably familiar.

We have never met before in this life, of course. It nevertheless amazes us no end, after coming so far, to learn moments later that strong, pony-tailed Chris used to live in an area in Washington, D.C. that Kelly often passed when she lived there . . . and that shorter, dark-haired Becky attended high school in the town right next to mine in the New Jersey suburbs of New York City – across an entire continent from the isolated mountain meadow of our meeting.

Becky's small figure belies the long work days she has put in for years, maintaining her spartan farmhouse, a dozen goats, brood of chickens, several dogs, 10 to 20 cats and large vegetable garden, ever since she and her husband (who now lives elsewhere) bought this remote homestead. She has chosen this life in touch with nature and simple things, away from mainstream society. But it is a solitary one that has at times depressed her, despite her current relationship with Chris. There is also occasional contact with neighbours Greg and Dawn – who live further up the valley in a more artistically hippie home – and other visiting friends and correspondents, for whom Becky does astrology charts.

Kelly and I are impressed by Becky's and Chris's welcoming openness. And we are refreshed as well as stretched during a stay that includes milking goats (at which Donovan too becomes adept), hauling water from the creek, grinding grain, picking veggies for dinner, cooking and heating with wood, rebuilding a hay wagon, riding horse, visiting the crescent-mooned outhouse, being butted by a temperamental goat and a black sheep with a penchant for females, gathering medicinal red clover, singing and playing guitar, talking for hours, hiking and mountain-viewing, and skinny-dipping in a nearby chilly stream. *[Photo Album #1 to #4]*

Subsistence farming here is extremely challenging – full of hard work in the absence of most modern conveniences. For example, without electricity or much money, there are no power tools, lighting is by lamp oil and there's only a trapdoor root cellar for cooling food. But though it represents a huge change from our recent urban lives involving day jobs at university and a legal office, Kelly and I are moved by the very real, down-to-earth integrity of Sunrise Farm. Then one day, the longing of the four of us to connect in some ongoing way, despite many reasons against our simply moving immediately to the farm, is resolved. We accept Chris's suggestion to move instead to the nearest large town, as soon as we are able.

Balancing the outward emphasis of our days at Sunrise, one evening Chris, Becky and Greg observe my guiding Kelly in a hypersentience (past life recall) session. It is not the easiest experience for Kelly physically, due to the summer heat and several insects' taking advantage of her still body (despite my best efforts to find them!). But the session is definitely worthwhile for unexpectedly revealing a life shared with Becky that parallels some emotions familiar to her today. It also reveals the full context of a dramatic scene Kelly saw a couple years earlier on first using her crystal ball. As this ancient life relates to misused power and attendant disaster, as discussed in the Prologue and Tales of Power segments, we will return to Kelly's experience in Chapter 4.

As for Christopher, both Kelly and I have quickly felt a strong bond with him, and a further dimension to this will emerge surprisingly over a year later. I will experience an ecstatic flying dream that ends with a letter from Chris, including the supposed Bible quotation, "The prince is free." When I ask Moita whether the quote has only some general significance about Chris, she stuns me by saying, "It connects to your Raven dream." As Kelly then sees images from this first remembered archetypal dream in my life, received over a decade earlier, popping out of my head, I laugh: "Wow! The two princes!"[16]

In my "Raven Transformation" dream (circa 1970), a fellow prince and I have vowed to leave our familial castle to ride off into the woods seeking adventure. But I lose sight of him at the same moment that a daimonic Raven appears outside the castle windows – staring, screeching and even pecking in my direction. Eventually realizing that this Raven is my brother transformed, I climb to the sill of a large, arched window . . . and step out. Together then, two ecstatic ravens soar into freedom, into our open future.

So I will ask Moita, "When I first had the dream, was it about Chris and me?" She will reply,

"Let us say, as with your dreams of Kelly before you met, you will grow to identify certain dreams with those you become close with." And I will say, "Well, I certainly can identify Chris with that brotherly kind of feeling, and I can't think of many others that would fit it that closely."

It seems so very appropriate, then, that Chris and I should have met in a forested land of ravens, enriched by the Indian culture in which Raven is a powerful mythic being. Just which reincarnational ties underlie our bond, however, will remain an open question.

ى   ى   ى

Finally, on the last night of our all-too-short, first visit at Sunrise Farm, tall, blond Greg, his long-dark-haired, recently pregnant wife Dawn and their newborn baby Kari join Chris and Becky and us in a lantern-lit circle to invite Moita's presence. This very full session touches on many issues ranging from universal concerns that will remain critical through 2012 and beyond – threats to life on Earth, the conflicted state of humanity, and the challenge of achieving a dimensional shift in consciousness – to our own attitudes and purposes, individually and together, at this great time of change. We are also happy to learn that Moita feels as positively about our decision as we do.

Moita session #100 (Kelly, David, Chris, Becky, Greg, Dawn, Kari / July 16, 1979)

Chris: Do you have any feelings about this place and what purposes there might be here? I'd be interested to know...

MOITA: What do *you* see as far as your purposes?

(As Chris begins to speak again, the energy level rises and Moita becomes more and more present. Kelly begins to feel very spacey.)

Chris: That there *is* one. Just the sort of place it is – a way of life, of being. Something that people can partake of when they come – not so much sending out ideas of certain ways, or talking about them; it's too conceptual. It's a way of life that speaks more strongly. *(pause)* All the little things too – day in, day out.

MOITA: The act of letting your meditation become a way of life?

Chris: That says it. *(pause)* I felt good about Kelly and David going to [nearby town]. I find myself seeing them there a lot in my imagining.

MOITA: Helping to manifest it.

Chris: I feel I want to . . . I don't know how clear it needs to be, how much needs to be said. I want there to be a lot of space about how soon or what happens between us in this place. But that step right there feels good.

MOITA: It is a step in the right direction, and it is good to take one step at a time.

Chris: That's been one of my problems – taking too many at once, not going anywhere.

MOITA: Something that is built slowly, in the right kind of slowness, is usually something that can last.

Chris: Mm-hmm.

MOITA: There are those who go so slow, they never take a step... *(laughter; pause)* It is very
            important for this time of man for him to learn to open his heart and let energy flow
            outward, without fear.

Greg: Can that be as well accomplished in a secluded environment as in the midst of the
            hubbub and the chaos?

MOITA: Some depends upon purposes. There are individuals who can do it in the midst of a
            hubbub, and that is well for them. Those who are there can have a glimpse of what it can
            feel like, what they may be missing in their own lives. It is easier to do it when they are not
            under daily pressures as much, the fast kind of life – although there are pressures out in the
            wilderness as well . . .

Chris: Yeah.

MOITA: . . . and deadlines. But they are of a different nature.

Chris: You make them yourself a lot.

MOITA: They *do* have more life to them. Many have forgotten how to enjoy simple things – or
            rather, things that *seem* simple to them now.

Chris: Lost their depth.

MOITA: Yes. But the depth is still there.

Chris: That explains a lot of the purpose I'd like to see here. There are a lot of ways to do the
            same things – it can be very different.

            (We are interrupted by sounds of Morgan, the head goat, trying to climb the stairs to the house!)

Chris: Morgan is excited.

MOITA: Sounds like he's trying to get in!

Dawn: How come we're so cut off?

MOITA: From other people?

Dawn: From everything outside this planet, or this little island we're on. I don't know if I can
            explain it with words. I was hoping you'd just catch it.

            *(The feeling behind this question seems to match Terry's comment about our being "orphans" –
            during another lantern-lit session, the one at the A.L.M. Community, from the Prologue. There was
            also much discussion then about purpose.)*

MOITA: There are many reasons. *(pause)* It was necessary: in order to develop a sense of
            selfhood, separateness, the individuality of man; in order to develop his . . . logic. But the
            time is coming to reunite the other parts that have been left behind and to become more in
            touch with the world and the things in it. It has been a different growing period.

            You could, in a sense, relate this time in history to the end of the child in the womb,
            who thinks of himself only as an individual and has nothing else around him, not
            recognizing the beat of the world. And when he is born, there is much distress, some pain
            and fear, thrusting into a new world that he has no experience of. Senses are opened that he
            has not used, so there is a period of confusion. But he travels from being a thought *(Kari
            cries)* to being.

Dawn: The time you speak of – is it for everybody? Is it a major turning point?

MOITA: Everyone will be affected by it.

Dawn: Has it happened before . . .

MOITA: The turning point?

Dawn: . . . on this planet, with these people?

MOITA: There have been many endings and many beginnings. Each one fulfills a different purpose, but each one is hard to go through at the time. Something that fails to grow, dies; and life is here to be lived, enjoyed.

Greg: Is just trying to enjoy life a good enough path?

MOITA: If you define "enjoy life" as being part of it, exchanging energy with it, rather than just doing things that others define as pleasurable..., then, yes, that is path enough. It helps to open up your own centre of creativity – connects you with your source and lets things flow out. So the path naturally follows.

Greg: Is creativity a good path to follow?

MOITA: Creation is an act of love, love manifested in form. The form does not matter. It is the love that goes into making it that decides if it is worthwhile or not.

Greg: The form does not matter?

MOITA: That's what I said.

Greg: How about the guys that are logging and other such activities? Are they also pursuing a good enough path?

MOITA: You mean chopping down trees?

Greg: Yeah.

MOITA: They are not living with life unless they are doing it with a great deal of consciousness, [unless they] know what they are doing and how to redeem the energy loss as much as possible. The world would not refuse man shelter if it were reasonable. Do you know many loggers who love trees?

Greg: Yeah, I do.

Dawn: But maybe not as deep as we do.

MOITA: It should be difficult to kill a friend. Then you know you would only do it if it was very necessary.

David: You spoke before *(on June 24th)* of building a new way of life, and that the other parts of the world should be able to participate in creating that. Could you say more about what that could mean?

Chris: What did you mean by "other parts of the world"?

David: Other life-forms. *(i.e. nature's creatures and nature spirits)*

MOITA: The Earth and the air. After all, it is the Earth's body that you are sharing. That is one thing that has been forgotten.

Chris: Mm-hmm. It should be a grateful sharing.

MOITA: It is not a wise child who destroys his own mother and then has no nourishment.

Chris: That's what's happening. It's funny how close we are to destroying it at the same time that so many people are seeing so much better, too.

MOITA: Not very coincidental.

Chris: I suppose not. Nip and tuck.

David: Even if the great majority of people were to reach the point of wanting to live very differently, there are still many poisonous situations that have already been created – some of them not readily cured by physical means even, that we know of. Are there other ways that the planet can be cleansed?

MOITA: Do you mean other than . . .

David: . . . physical means.

MOITA: Since the entire Earth has been in a sense created by man – his reality, his poisons – they can also be uncreated. It takes a great deal of energy. There must be a balance. If there were enough people making an effort to absorb bad energy, many of these things would take care of themselves in a much shorter time than man would think. But the thing is: in order to do so, all of the things that are creating the poisonous situations must cease.

Greg: Say there was a majority who wished for these to cease, but there was a powerful minority that did not wish to cease, could the thoughts or efforts of those who are in the majority stop, change, the actions and the intent of the others? I guess what my question boils down to is: How much can your own reality-making make other people's reality?

MOITA: What could happen would be that you would force the minority group into a different universe altogether.

Greg: Whew! By thought? By sheer mental power alone – non-physical?

MOITA: If you have two universes that are existing on the same plane that are totally contradictory to each other, the situation could not be sustained for long. Either pressure would make the physical manifestation of the minority's ideas totally unfeasible or they would gradually dissipate – their energy would be useless without backing; or something would break, something would explode, there would be a disaster – which is the possibility that you are all heading towards, not just between each other but between yourselves and the world as well.

Anything is possible if you can conceive of it in your mind and put enough energy into it. The kind of energy we are talking about is active energy rather than passive...

(During these last sentences, we hear many goat calls. Becky goes out to discover a goat has been trying to get in through the fence and has gotten its head stuck.)

MOITA: The man who sits on the lonely mountain and meditates by himself, and decides what he thinks the world should be, does accomplish nothing.

Greg: Except, earlier you said that in seclusion you can open your heart better.

MOITA: Yes, but then one must also learn to use the energy that's available to you. It is to be shared.

Greg: So, in that case, you should be in the chaos and the hubbub . . .

MOITA: Not necessarily.

Greg: . . . in order to share it, being with the most number of people.

MOITA: There are different ways of sharing. It is not the numbers you share with. It is the quality of your sharing that matters most. If you have a very high quality, you can change other people from within, and they in turn will change others.

Chris: A little of that goes a long way.

(Becky returns from freeing the goat.)

MOITA: You see, I have a concept of reality that is not the same as your experience of it. But I am not content to stay in my reality and watch yours. We are here to help your reality be changed by yourselves, and with us, and with the world. We are not isolated from you. We are *very* active. And we share our energy as much as possible, and never feel the lack...

This is a particularly delicate operation, because the worlds are not totally together enough to let through a complete representation. This is a filter, and sometimes filters can get clogged or other things can go wrong.

Chris: *(with a laugh)* How is the filter flowing tonight?

MOITA: It depends. Each time I speak, it is different. Some depends upon the energy that is put into what is asked. The deeper the questions go, the more energy there is, and in the wake of that energy my presence can flow in.

Chris: That's good to know.

MOITA: That is where we touch you closest – from deep within...

Chris: I had a dream last night that I went to a town where there were a lot of nice people, and they were talking about Moita. I don't remember very much literally, but it was a dream I've been feeling all day. Nice dream . . . nice people.

MOITA: That is another place where we are close – in your dreams – and you can learn a great deal in them. The feelings are usually the things that are remembered easiest. Details come later and sometimes are not as important.

Becky: Do you stay close to Kelly during the day? Do you try to make contact at other times?

MOITA: In a sense, I am always close. It depends upon what she is doing, or thinking, or feeling, as to how close I can be felt by her. It is true of all of you. When you are calmest or most still, we are nearest. Mostly the responsibility for contact is on your end. We can only go as far as you let us.

(Kari has begun crying, so Greg takes her out of the room with him.)

MOITA: If we were here to impose our will upon you, things would not be the same. Then there would be no barriers that could keep us out. But since we are here not to impose but to impart and share of ourselves, even if we see you making mistakes or doing things that are not in tune with the world and you, we would not dream of stopping you, for then we would be doing you a great disservice.

Becky: But I feel often the desire to be in touch, but not able to.

MOITA: It is something felt by many.

Becky: It seems to be such an elusive contact – slips away so easily.

MOITA: When you lose your worry about being in touch, you will find that being in touch is easier. The difficulty with reaching us is that it is too simple.

Becky: Mm-hmm.

MOITA: It is something that is as easy as living, or as easy as thought. And sometimes, even if you do not feel us, if you think of us our presence is there. Being relaxed is important. *(pause)*

           I think I should leave... *(to Chris:)* I am glad I have met you.

Chris: I am glad too.

MOITA: *(to the others:)* And you. Perhaps we shall all meet again! Good night.

Others: Good night.

           (From conversation afterwards:)

Chris: It was really nice having that dream last night. It made me feel much more wanting to connect. It really was an intricate dream, with a lot of different sorts of people. I was travelling; and as I got to this town, I went in this store looking for somebody. The lady in the store said something about Moita, that they were connected with her.

David: Last night I dreamed of a newsletter put together and stapled just like *Rays*. On a strip across the front there were really brightly coloured countryside scenes – trees and hills.

Kelly: *(to Chris:)* I must say, when you asked your first question – about purposes – she really came in a lot, and I was dizzy.

Chris: I felt like that sometimes too. It seemed like it came in waves through the whole thing...

Kelly: I saw you sweating. *(with beads on his forehead, all agree)* You really looked like you were getting a lot of rushes, I must say.

Chris: It was kind of neat. I remembered some places, all right *(with a laugh)* – remembered what it's all about.

ಀ   ಀ   ಀ

Two other dreams of mine – from our first night at Sunrise Farm and the night of the session – show Chris and Becky and Kelly and me first knocking down mortared brick walls in order to build a new foundation with more space inside; and secondly, being woven together in an ever-changing pattern through the action of a large screw, as in a vise, while travelling a curving path through woods.

Returning to Regina from our trip, we have an overall feeling of relief and joy at how well this adventure of ours has begun, despite our awareness of huge challenges and unknowns ahead. Then, during our first session at home, Moita provides this further reality check.

Moita session #103 (Kelly and David / July 28, 1979)

David: I'm interested in your view of how the visit with Chris and Becky went, and where we are in the process I guess we all hope is going to unfold.

MOITA: Are you sure you know what you are asking?

David: It's pretty general. *(pause)*

MOITA: There is not as much unity as there should be. None of you have gotten down to the business of exploring doubt and fear.

David: Mm-hmm.

MOITA: As long as it remains unexplored, it will seem larger than it need be. But then, you will be spending the season of within *(i.e. winter)* – hopefully – exploring many things.

Finally, a dream of mine from the same week combines scenes and thoughts about the Associations of the Light Morning people with those of Chris and Becky and life at Sunrise Farm. It is a dream that does not romanticize away the difficulties ahead. I am not able to remember specifics to record in my journal, but the essence of the dream – and of the time of transition we are all entering – finds its way onto paper[17N] nearly as follows:

"When we meet other travellers along the way, is it an occasion for subtle combat, for competing, pulling back and defending, asserting one's view over the other's? Or is it an occasion for opening, for mutually surrendering to allow a mingling, some new being to be born from the substance of both?

"Remember what Moita said about fears and misgivings as well as anticipation – for there are problems in any meeting of different streams. We have chosen these problems as ways of growing. They are not things to regret or be embarrassed about. We are choosing to join with others from different streams in order to make a new way of life possible. In that joining we disappear for a time; we give ourselves up. What we identify as ourselves, as our own, seems lost to sight. But eventually we will bob to the surface and find a larger identification with the new being we have created. We will have truly 'reincarnated' with a broader foundation that is able to endure the changes to come."

Chapter 2

A NEW HEAVEN AND A NEW EARTH

"How did the universe begin?"
(#1 of the "10 Biggest Unanswered Questions in the Universe"*)

For decades, astronomers and physicists have been labouring via hugely expensive technology (space telescopes, particle accelerators, etc.) to come ever closer to what they conceive as the origin of the universe. The "big bang" theory accounts for their observations of an expanding cosmos and recordings of high-energy, subatomic events believed to match the state of the universe only a second after it began. But they remain stumped by the concept of a primal explosion, from an infinitesimal point of infinite energy at time = zero, that apparently created all the matter of our known universe as if "out of nothing".

This being "the biggest unanswered question", how we think about the beginning of the universe can reshape our entire outlook on reality and existence. But by continually trying to reach the infinite only by physical, external methods and concepts, how will mainstream scientists ever find the answer that lies precisely beyond those? Ironically, it makes perfect sense that that answer can only be encountered in a different manner.

As it is not Moita's way to expound at length on philosophical issues, here I turn first to another source. The following channeling, received through Thespian Michaels's waking vision, seems to me one of the best descriptions of the primal essence of things – explaining how the universe could not only "begin" but be *continually* created:

> Clear Light is the primal essence in its pristine state. It permeates all Creation. It is the very nature of the Creator and that which the Creator uses to bring everything into existence... It is unlimited potential awaiting birth and exists, eternally unchanging, holding all possibilities and outcomes in perfect balance. It remains dormant and without definition until acted on by focused consciousness. When a thought, word or action is directed by any intelligent life, such a stimulus instantly activates the Clear Light and causes it to take the form of whatever is projected.[18]

This is the dimension missing from physical scientists' hunt for the beginning of the universe – the "source field" (Wilcock 2011) that provides for so much else as well that science excludes from

---

* Chosen by physicists around the world for CBC Radio's *Quirks and Quarks* program (January 2, 2010).

reality, including the very nature of human being and consciousness.

It is time that the Mysteries of Clear Light be given back to humanity. These teachings have been both lost and suppressed for thousands of years and you vitally need them now. Although you are not yet aware of it, you have always had the ability to create whatever you needed out of Clear Light. Your Self, your I AM consciousness, is the director of this unlimited energy. This I AM consciousness is in everything that exists, from the smallest particle to beings vast beyond imagining, since each in turn is part of the Creator. God is always aware of Itself, therefore we...are also self aware.[19]

It will become obvious this is Moita's starting point as well, though usually expressed in more personal and familiar terms. Witness her saying goodbye to our first-ever workshop group:

If there is anything I wish to say to all of you before I go, it is that...we just are another form of this existence, the same as you; and that we hope all of you find your own centre of joy and let that flow out, because life is here to be loved, not to be destroyed. And we are in everything that you see. You can never be alone, none of you, because the force of love that has created this world lives in it still and flows out to anyone who will receive it, and it brings with it health and joy. Life is not just your body. It is an existence, a way of thinking – and it goes beyond just the here and now.[20]

This unbounded, conscious energy, "the force of love", is the point of departure for any story that can be told, indeed anything that can be said, about life and the world around us. And this will be evident as we now explore the macrocosm: not simply outer space as known to astronomers but, as described by Moita, "a universe of presences".

The Heavens as Macrocosm

This chapter delves into a subject of great interest to participants in the Moita sessions that we hold after our move to the British Columbia interior in 1979. While distant in so many ways from mainstream scientific institutions, this remote country setting is an excellent place to *experience* nature – and particularly to view, feel close to, and wonder about, all that shines in the day and night skies. Then, after being moved by the heavens above, it is a special treat to turn to inner space for answers to our questions. A query from a first-time participant is a good place to begin our exploring.

Moita session #164 (Kelly, David, Jim, Peter / November 30, 1980)
Jim: Do you have a different idea of how the solar system was formed?
MOITA: Different from what?
Jim: What I was taught in school.

MOITA: Mm-hmm.

Jim: Could you explain?

MOITA: It parallels some physical-level theories to an extent. The Universe was energy, [in] one form. In the beginning there were no separate beings; there were no planets. It was like that for a long time. It is difficult to explain how things changed, what caused them to alter. But the energy that was the Universe began to diversify, to coalesce, to attract and repel, until it formed separate pockets of energy that related to each other. Earth was not the first such pocket that began to descend through layers of energy to become matter. But the pattern is the same, though the timing is different for each.

ೊ   ೊ   ೊ

We have referred to this primal energy, the original and everlasting "stuff" of the Universe – a wholeness prior to differences, opposites, separate things and beings – as the Clear Light, or the energy of love. What, then, does it mean that the matter of our bodies and physical world comprises just one "layer" of this reality, having "descended" – in other words, having been *created* – from the primal energy? And beyond that, where is it all going – is there a direction inherent in the universe?

Whenever Moita responds to our astronomical questions, we must be prepared for her to take them further afield, dropping hints of something beyond. Here is one case, prompted by my question about some recently reported, intriguing phenomena, including the return of Halley's comet in 1985.

Moita session #86 (Kelly and David / April 29, 1979)

MOITA: Perhaps before we start talking about signs that may appear in the future, we should consider some of the beginnings. Kelly is very interested in all of these things. *(smiling)* She has talked of nothing else since I came!...

Taking you back to when it started, this time: ...the Universe was one Being and not many, and it spread itself out across the emptiness of its own Mind – which may be a spiritual interpretation of the "big bang" theory... The pieces of energy all started in the same place and spread out. And when they reached the farthest point away from their centre, they stopped and began going back. It is a giant flux.

ೊ   ೊ   ೊ

In the above, did you catch "its own Mind", and her reference to "when it started, this time"?

Moita session #164 (Kelly, David, Jim, Peter / November 30, 1980)

Jim: The universe seems to have been expanding, physically at least, and there is a debate whether it will slow and come back or not. Is the plan for the future of the universe open, or is it going to keep expanding?

MOITA: On the spiritual level, the object of the game is to get back together and to become more than what it was before it separated. So, yes, it would tend to rejoin and begin another cycle. This is not the first universe.

ം   ം   ം

Thus Moita assures us the primal energy of the Universe is alive with qualities of Mind – of awareness and thought on a cosmic scale – and intimates that, at one or many levels, it has always been this way. Throughout her communications, Moita refers to the protean capacities of this energy. She says it is the essence of the higher worlds, invisible to most of us, in which she and other entities exist. By focused intent, they direct and transform this creative energy from subtle to more dense, more material levels of reality, assisting embodied beings in our evolution.

Moita session #81 (Kelly, David, Cayce study group / March 29, 1979)
Doris: Where are you coming from – is it the spirit world?
MOITA: [Our world] co-exists with yours in the same space..., but it is separated by vibrations of energy. Your world is in the process of raising its energy level upwards, if you will, and we are reaching down to touch it, so that our worlds will come closer together. It is closing a gap. It is *all* of us who exist in this universe being able to touch each other and work together towards creating a more whole humanity... By coming here, I give you a taste of what it will be like for our world to touch yours, because here in this world at this moment our worlds are touching.

ം   ം   ം

I think of Michelangelo's ceiling fresco in the Sistine Chapel as Moita speaks of our reaching out to touch, bringing our worlds together. This is possible because we *are* of the same nature. It is the ancient idea of man as microcosm, carrying within us the essence of the macrocosm, in which the heavens are alive and aware. We experience this not only by thinking deeply but as we give credence to our feelings, allow ourselves to sense the wholeness of life, and open intuitively to meanings known to earlier cultures, even as we reinterpret them for today.

Moita session #86 (Kelly and David / April 29, 1979)
MOITA: I know you are aware that stars are more outward manifestations of other beings than they are actual physical balls of gas and energy. That is merely how they appear here, on your level, and how you view them...
         In your own solar system you have many forms of life, not all of them visible to your eye, and each set of energy has its own reason for being here. Some of the energy formed earth, and some formed plant, some animal and some man. And there were others (*i.e. other*

life forms of a less physically visible nature). That is why you are so connected to the Earth, and why it is so much a part of you, and you it. But the pieces develop with different speeds, finding their way back to the centre of things, and there are many outward expressions of that discovery... There is nothing that happens within the universe that does not affect all of its parts. Those who were taught the ancient astrology were given that in a clear form, some of which has been lost through time.

৯৯ ৯৯ ৯৯

These wider understandings from an earlier, more intuitive age can add to, rather than deny, the purely physical scientific knowledge of which our civilization is rightly proud. However, our pride should not rest on presuming ourselves the first astronomically advanced culture. Chapter 4's close look at major civilizations of the past will correct this widespread error . . . but Moita can't help pointing out Jim's slip of the tongue right here.

Moita session #165 (Kelly, David, Jim / December 21, 1980)

Jim: It seems the Egyptians and Dogon tribe of Nigeria knew that Sirius is a double star – a dark star revolving around a bright one – and they knew that long before they had telescopes. *(at this, Moita coughing deliberately and laughing)* Well . . .

MOITA: Long before *this current civilization* had telescopes. Astronomy is a subject that has been looked into by other civilizations. Many of the apparent amazing data astronomically that [have] been brought to light through archaeology [were] passed down from Atlantis.

৯৯ ৯৯ ৯৯

Moreover, there are many purposes, and insights, and energies, for which telescopes are quite unnecessary. Now we encounter Jim again – a lone individual sitting in silence on a mountain forestry lookout in the British Columbia interior, surveying the expanse of life above and below him for signs of fire – outer *and* inner.

Moita session #150 (Kelly, David, Jim, 2 others / July 17, 1980)

MOITA: I have seen you many times.

Jim: Hmm. I've been doing the best meditating in my life.

MOITA: When you meditate as well as you have been, you become clearer to us.

Jim: *(laughs)* And to myself?

MOITA: Hopefully.

Jim: Yeah, it's been really beautiful. I've been getting a strong sense of the Earth and the forest as living entities. That's been very strong on my mind.

MOITA: And what does it have to say to you?

Jim: Mainly reassurance in the midst of some pain and problems. We are all part of the single entity of the Earth. And that is still very healthy – more than I would have thought.

MOITA: It has a resilience that few would suspect.

Jim: Hmm. I'm just beginning to realize that.

MOITA: Life in such abundance must find expression... It is good that you do not feel lost in the vastness of life...

Jim: I've thought a lot about the Sun as spirit, the god of our solar system.

MOITA: The focus, the life-giver... The Sun is a very patient being – or *beings*, since it is not comprised of just one. It is *many*. On our level, it is not the same physical manifestation. It appears altered – its purposes more subtle, but also more vibrant. It is only on the physical that the Sun is a star, a ball of fire. Here, it is the eye of spirit opening from one level to another, giving of the Creative Forces to all within its realm, without stint or measure. You could say it is partly our source of life and energy.

Jim: But it is more than one, as well, you say – a conglomerate?

MOITA: Spirits who reach a certain level and have the desire to give continuously are attracted or drawn to this centre of energy. And so, they partake of its . . . (hmm) . . . position, job, joy. *(laughter)* There is not a word to describe its purpose adequately. It is somewhat like a magnet in drawing things into itself and at the same time giving back whatever it draws, as well as a doorway.

(Kelly will later describe seeing "the Sun as a glowing heart in the middle of a huge mist. The glowing centre flows through the mist outward in all directions, particle by particle. The mist is flowing in different densities around its central focus, encompassing the entire solar system.")

ဢ   ဢ   ဢ

Jim is our most frequent asker of astronomical questions, as shown again here.

Moita session #164 (Kelly, David, Jim, Peter / November 30, 1980)

Jim: Suddenly I think of Saturn.

(Kelly and I laugh, as we were definitely planning to ask about Saturn tonight, after publication of recent Saturn photos from the Voyager space probe.)

Jim: Why are two of its rings braided? Is there any special metaphysical meaning for that?

MOITA: There is – besides your telepathy. Both Jupiter and Saturn are very much like the Earth was, in that they are non-solid. The essence of their energy is different, so the physical matter they manifest is different. Saturn's consciousness is very . . . (several words, neither fit) . . . elaborate, diversified, joyful and colourful, bursting (?).

            The rings, for us, are like your northern lights. They are more of an other-level phenomenon than they are physical. Particles of such minute size are not difficult to manipulate from this level. So, many of the beings – spiritual beings – that are part of

Saturn's consciousness inhabit the rings. The outer rings, which are braided, are a symbol: the intertwining of polarities. It does not need to follow known physical laws, because the principles behind the experience are as yet outside man's understanding of law...

Peter: Does this mean Jupiter and Saturn are younger in time?

MOITA: No – that they were chosen not to become as physical. They are the centres of some of the higher spiritual beings of the solar system.

ം   ം   ം

One way to connect with the energies of the spheres is participating in their yearly, monthly and other cycles. The night of the spring equinox finds a group of people outdoors, gazing through a small telescope at a conjunction of planets and other celestial lights, while mindful as well of their astrological meanings. Later, they gather in a circle indoors.

Moita session #179 (Kelly, David, Jim, 2 others / March 20, 1981)

MOITA: How are you this evening?

Jim: Very good. Celebrating all the auspicious stellar events tonight.

MOITA: The heavens are filled with signs.

Jim: I was wondering how you might see the significance of the coming together of so many energies: of the Moon with its unconscious currents, and Saturn and Jupiter which seem to be two ends of a polarity scale – all three of them aligned tonight on the equinox. What kind of energy do you see descending upon us from such a dance?

MOITA: One that brings a great deal of change with it, and more awakenings from deeper levels; a drawing up of the race unconscious; more old patterns being played out – slightly different players.

Jim: But with a chance to make a better result, I would hope.

MOITA: So would I... This event paves the way for others to follow.

Jim: There seems to be quite a balance to it all: Jupiter representing the very positive, mellow, expansive aspects of consciousness, where Saturn has always been the more restrictive, dues-paying, difficult energy; and they're both together with the unconscious of the Moon. It almost includes the whole expanse of experience from sorrow to joy, being magnified at once. Perhaps this is a time we can put into perspective the many positive and negative things that have happened to us, see them in relation to each other. *(very long pause, as they gaze at each other)*

MOITA: Saturn is undergoing a transformation. Soon it will no longer be associated with "restrictive".

Jim: Is that part of the energy change of the beginning of the New Age?

MOITA: Yes. Many bonds will be let loose, because they will be understood. Man can only restrict himself when he does not understand himself. So, when he comes into his new awareness, he will no longer be bound.

Jim:　　　Well, Saturn's restrictions have always been there in order to teach. So I suppose, if the lesson is learned . . .

MOITA:　　Just as when the student learns all the teacher has to offer and the teacher leaves, so too do the restrictions once the lesson is learned. *(pause)* Man has chained himself to this Earth, and he is rattling the chains trying to attract attention. So the rest of the universe is becoming attracted to man's plight.

Jim:　　　More so than in the past?

MOITA:　　More so than since the beginning. He has the whole history of Earth behind his plea now.

Jim:　　　The extra energy seems to be needed, the way events seem to be going in the wrong direction rather than the New Age direction – on a *political* stage. Which may have nothing to do with what's really going on. *(laughs)*

MOITA:　　Help will come unlooked-for, and for a while unnoticed...
　　　　　　You always ask astronomy questions. *(laughs)* Not always. *Lately.*

Jim:　　　...That's one of my main passions in life, the stars – always has been.

MOITA:　　And how the destiny of the Earth is weaved among them.

Jim:　　　And more and more the concept that each star is a sentient being rings true to me.

MOITA:　　Yes, we have a very active universe. You know that Jupiter has the higher beings of the solar system, besides the Sun.

Jim:　　　I know it's the closest thing to being its *own* sun...

MOITA:　　The sunspots are also collected groups of beings. So there is a great deal of activity, at the moment, between other beings in the solar system, and the Earth is being bombarded by energy. *(pause)* There is a whole other level to astrology. Not many connect with it well, but there are a few... In one sense, you are all just parts of a single Mind... Someday perhaps *you'll* be a great mind with a universe inside! *(laughter)*
　　　　　　Mike would appreciate that one. *(referring to our friend, now away)* He is always trying to get me to do some "cosmic humour". *(laughter)*

೧　೧　೧

Turning back through the seasons, we come to rest near another major node in Earth's yearly cycle as experienced from the northern hemisphere: the winter solstice or "Festival of Sun-Return".

Moita session #44 (Kelly and David / November 24, 1978)

David:　　We would like to hear what you would say on the meaning of Christmas.

MOITA:　　Each of us here have their own ideas on the meaning of Christmas, mostly depending on what areas of humanity we have been involved in. I have experienced many forms of Christmas, before Christmas was named, when it was a time of year to celebrate the coming of the Sun, the returning of the life-giving energy and the warmth and the light. It is still for me the return of that energy more than it is the celebration of a single entity's manifestation.

Those of you who experience this time of year as one of giving and one of joy help also to bring us closer together. And we do enjoy the warmth. And it would be well if that kind of consciousness could be carried through for more of the year.

୨ଵ   ୨ଵ   ୨ଵ

From Earth's relations with brother Sun, we turn to sister Moon.

Moita session #42A (Kelly and David / November 14, 1978)

David: Can you talk some about the cycles of the Moon, including the Full Moon tonight?

MOITA: There are many things I could say. Spiritually speaking? Or from my perspective what the Moon does to people in your reality?

David: Mm-hmm.

MOITA: Since each planet has a soul of its own, it also follows that the Moon has one too. And as it travels its way around your planet and its face turns away, the influence of its psychic energy turns away also and faces the Sun, and they merge. When it comes around the other side and faces the Sun with the Earth between and they merge again, the Earth is in the centre. Therefore, it is part of the merging between these other two beings. And whenever you are at the centre of a merging, everyone is affected, depending on how much of the merging they're willing to accept, where they are at at the time, what their perceptions are of it. Some cannot accept it – they react violently – just like some cannot accept love and react violently towards it...

So, there is a great opportunity for good or ill when the merging is available. There is energy to be tapped or experienced in joy – one reason why lovers like a Full Moon, because when they are in love they intuitively know what that energy is and they get the most benefit from it. *(pause, while Moita and I silently look into each other's eyes)*

David: But then there's the quality of the New Moon, the dark of the Moon. From what you've said, it would seem that it was simply the absence of the merging, and I gather that there's a definite quality to that as well?

(Another pause follows, this time because Kelly's thoughts – not knowing how Moita will answer this, feeling that perhaps Moita has gotten trapped by her own words – have begun to interfere. Moita looks away in order to refocus and then returns to David as she begins speaking.)

MOITA: When you are bathed in the light and are facing it, you cannot see for the brightness. But when the light stands behind you, it illuminates. *(pause)*

David: You've just said a great deal.

MOITA: It has been said before.

ᔇ ᔇ ᔇ

The ancient All Hallows' Eve was a moveable feast day at the Dark of the Moon closest to the midpoint between fall equinox and winter solstice. During our gathering to celebrate this night traditionally set aside for opening the door between the worlds, we are given more about the New Moon – and are reassured (with a new twist) about an old controversy.

<u>Moita session #161 (Kelly, David, Jim, Margaret, 2 others / November 7, 1980)</u>

Jim: Besides being a time of beginning that can set the tone for the rest of the month, what quality of energy does the New Moon itself generate?

MOITA: As with all things, as seen from Earth, there is a polarity to the energy in people's reaction to it, or their interpretation of it. *(pause)*

      The New Moon is always a time of reflection rather than a time of activity. Some people think the Dark of the Moon is a good time for doing things they wish to be hidden; and so, they have made of it a time of hiding – not because of any quality of the New Moon but because of their associations with it. From my level, and to levels that are higher than mine, it is a time when hidden thoughts are illuminated; and so, you see, they are quite mistaken in what they use the energy for.

Jim: Is there a special quality to the New Moon this time of year in respect to the All Hallows' Eve celebration?

MOITA: With the energy changes that have been brought to the Earth, this time of year becomes a gateway. It is the beginning in the change of energy from one season to another, from the outer to the inner. *(pause)* As often happens when you open a door for the first time, the energy can seem overwhelming because it is unfamiliar and has been so long shut out – by some of us. *(pause)* You like these answers?

Jim: *(laughs)* Yeah, I heard that one... *(very long silence follows, as they continue to look to each other)*

MOITA: *(to Margaret)* You had another question you were asked to ask.

Margaret: *(pause)* Oh! *(laughter)* Oh, I can't stand it. Is the world round or flat? *(laughter)*
   (Margaret's son sent along this question after a discussion of it in school.)

MOITA: Perhaps rather than giving just a direct what-it-is, he would find it interesting to know *why* it is.

      When energy is attracted together in one place, it always forms a sphere, for then the energy can travel around from one point to another and evenly distribute itself. When an entity reaches a certain stage of development where he no longer requires the trappings of a body, he too becomes a sphere . . . of thought... So it is that the Earth is round.

Margaret: Well, I'm very pleased to know that. *(laughs)* I'm kind of relieved! *(laughter)*

MOITA: At least, then you do not have to worry about falling off. *(laughter)* There are enough things to plummet from already. *(laughter)*

ഔ   ഔ   ഔ

Now Mike puts in an appearance, shortly after another Full Moon.

<u>Moita session #135B (Kelly, David, Mike, 6 others / March 2, 1980)</u>
Mike: Were you outside last night?
MOITA: In the Full Moon?
Mike: I was wondering how you would have perceived the beauty of the night from your
            plane.
MOITA: When the Sun and the Moon join together over the Earth, it is a very bright and
            colourful union – an experience that clouds do not interfere with.
Mike: Do you see the Moon and stars as we see them? Or I guess you'd see the spirit behind
            them. Does it look a lot different?
MOITA: Yes, it does look much different. The only thing in your experience that would be
            comparable is the one you had...not long ago. That would give you some idea of the
            intensity of the light, the awareness.
(She refers to Mike's re-experiencing his soul's creation, during meditation a week earlier.[21])
Mike: The intensity of the Moon?
MOITA: And the Sun and the stars. You know it is not an easy thing to describe in mere words.

ഔ   ഔ   ഔ

We humans have often sensed a great omen in the rare alignment of Sun, Moon and Earth that
creates a solar eclipse. As one such eclipse approaches, Moita suggests a way of perceiving it
appropriate to this time of transition.

<u>Moita session #72 (Kelly, David, 5 others / February 24, 1979)</u>
David: There is to be an eclipse of the Sun the day after tomorrow. I'm wondering what that
            involves on other levels as far as the energy goes.
(The last total solar eclipse visible in North America in the 20th century is due the morning of
February 26th.)
MOITA: [We] spoke of illumination at the...New Moon, when that energy lighted things up and
            showed the way. So here you have an unusual event where there is an even merge, and the
            path of illumination – in the form of darkness – crosses the face of your world.
(By "even merge", Moita refers to the Sun and Moon appearing of equal size during a total
eclipse. With "darkness", she adds the blotting out of the Sun's light during an eclipse to the
simultaneous Dark of the Moon when, she says, what is hidden or missed may be revealed.)
MOITA: It can be seen symbolically as the Angel of Light and Truth wielding his sword and

slicing through those things that are not looked at. There is no doubt his presence causes waves – certainly more than dropping a pebble in a pool. And one part of the world cannot be affected without affecting other parts.

ᥱ   ᥱ   ᥱ

Throughout these sessions, the heavens have been presented as the ancients knew them to be: a mirror of the depths of the human mind and soul. Thus humanity is the microcosm in whom the heavens are reflected.

This final, unexpectedly touching exchange occurred in a romantic setting. Our small group sits in the lantern-lit loft of a cabin overlooking the hayfield we have all helped to harvest and bale till sundown. Above this field we will later view an especially brilliant meteor shower.

Moita session #152 (Kelly, David, 2 others / August 11, 1980)

David: How does the energy appear from your perspective on this night when the Earth is passing through the tail of a former comet?

MOITA: There are many small mergings between the Earth and the Outer Earth.

David: "Outer Earth"?

MOITA: You could also say "invisible". Just as the body has an aura that extends beyond the physical form, so too does the Earth. Particles passing through this auric field and towards the Earth's outer shell create small openings through which energy passes. And as you each have a larger self of which you are a part, the Earth also has a greater spirit of which it is one expression. It is for the Earth very much like [our] two worlds joining here at this moment. *(long silence)*

David: In the last couple of days, Kelly and I seem to have been doing much melting into each other – and this seems like just one more form of that.

MOITA: So it has been for you too. *(or "two")*

(Conscious of our "Earth" and "Sun" polarity as souls, tracing back to our first incarnations together – as described in the Intermission – Kelly and I feel Moita may be speaking about much more than our present personalities during the last few days . . . as our silent gaze continues.)

The Vital Earth

Our descent brings us now to the vital ground of Earth . . . which may not be as solid as we think. That the Earth itself is a powerful entity, encompassing many lesser levels of energetic beings, is something that we in this age are to learn well, according to prophecy. Arrayed across the Earth's body are lines and nodes where heightened energy may be felt and measured, reflected in the positioning of neolithic monuments, ancient temples, medieval cathedrals, indigenous sacred sites and contemporary crop circles. Plant and animal life channels and mirrors these local energy fields and energetic spirits of the Earth – as human cultures once understood and experienced.

From many cultural angles, this awareness is now returning as part of a participatory world-view, which Moita expands into further dimensions of time and perspective. Consider her experience of a tree.

Moita session #185 (Kelly, David, Jim, Margaret / May 30, 1981)

Margaret: From where you are, can you see many thousands of versions of one thing?

MOITA: Yes. I can see a thing as it passes through all time, and I can see a thing as it is seen from others', as well as it is seen through all of my, development. And I see a thing not just in one plane alone.

From where you are, you see physical things: tree, leaves, branches, bark, insects. From here, I see the roots – the energy – seeking the centre, the Earth. I see the light coming up out of the ground, surging through the branches, pouring out its essence, lighting the sky around it, touching the birds, attracting. And I see how it relates to me as a spirit, as a doorway to love, to the soul of the Earth. Those are some of the things I see in a tree.

৯   ৯   ৯

We, too, can open to such experience.

Moita session #135B (Kelly, David, Jake, Chris, Helen, 4 others / March 2, 1980)

MOITA: There are many spirits around here that are beginning to awaken in the woods. *(i.e. now that winter thaw approaches)*

Jake: I wanted to ask you about a place where there's a pine tree on a ridge, that seems to be a spot that is a unit, a whole of some sort. What is different about this place?

MOITA: There are many currents of energy running through the Earth. And there are certain trees that are chosen by the energy [of the nature spirit or *deva*] that is responsible for its area to reach down farther into the Earth and tap that energy and bring it up into the air where it can be utilized more readily by others. Some would call these mini power points. I would call them *power wells*, a reservoir that can be tapped in times of need.

Jake: I feel I have tapped this one spot to gain strength, to be balanced. I get a sense for the different feelings of areas. And I don't know how much of that is subjective or if I should continue to trust my intuition – that what I feel is in fact related to what is happening there.

MOITA: Points such as this do not just contain the energy of the moment, but also the memory of other times.

Jake: Other times in my life, or in previous lives?

MOITA: It can be . . . other times in your lives that would resonate with other times of this part of the Earth...

(From conversation after:)

Kelly: I saw a picture of the Earth like an atom, with all these lines going around it and connecting at the core, at the centre.

Chris: I really liked the description of a well for going deep in the Earth.

Helen: That place is really neat, up on top of a hill under a big old pine tree. Deer sleep there – you can tell – and a moose sleeps there. It's just like a different land, like a neat house!

℞ ℞ ℞

Limiting beliefs can blind us to what lies beyond ourselves. The poetry of this session near the winter solstice illustrates the playful wonder that is so often missed.

Moita session #125 (Kelly, David, workshop group / December 17, 1979)

Glen: Do nature spirits really exist? I mean, I've read stories about them; I really believe in them. Does that mean it's true – I've created my own reality at that point?

MOITA: Let us say that the Earth has a reality of its own as well.

Glen: So there are different beings, not just . . . okay. I kind of believe sometimes that if I believe in something, it's going to be there. But even if I don't, they still exist?

MOITA: In their reality, they exist. You can take yourself out of the reality so that they do not exist for you. They still are themselves, and they still are real. They still interact in their universe and follow the rules they have set out for themselves and their own development. It is only each individual's focus of perception on them or away from them that decides for the individual if they are real or not...

David: Moita, two years ago, when I was standing in the woods with some snow falling, I heard a tinkling noise like bells which I didn't know to be within me or outside. And the only thing that felt right was finally to decide it was something like the snow fairies.

           So I'd like to ask, could you share what goes on, from your perspective, as the nature spirits bring about such an event as snow falling into a forest? How is that a work of art?

MOITA: *(closing eyes)* Well, there are air spirits involved in it to a great extent, for they gather the crystals together to make clouds. They have an energy about them that says "fluffy and soft", and there is a great dance in the wind, bringing all these things together in one place. How can you describe a fairy dancing in the air?

           And when things are just right, they think they are coaxing snowflakes out of clouds, and each one is a work of art. They are very much into how each snowflake must look, and some of them get into where each snowflake should fall. And this energy, in the form of beauty, descends from the heavens into the trees.

           Then the tree spirits begin to decorate. They very much like the effect of snowflakes on green branches and...train their trees to grow their branches at the right angle to catch the snowflakes. And throughout it all, there is always a dance – a very earthy joy, a very simple joy, and unassuming. That is at least one kind of snowstorm. *(pause)*

Fairies are very simple and peaceful beings who only wish to make the Earth beautiful and fruitful. They have no desires beyond that.

Mike: Do they change? Do they go through cycles like we do?

MOITA: Some.

Mike: Do they evolve?

MOITA: Again, some. They grow in different ways. They can grow in complexity. They usually have no desire to do so. They are very much children and have that simplicity and wonder.

Mike: How are they created? Where do they come from?

MOITA: They come from the universe. They *are*, and they exist. They *be*, and have no fear of identity.

Glen: Moita, did you ever visit the Findhorn garden in Scotland? Or have you ever heard about it? You must have seen it.

MOITA: I have heard of it.

Glen: I've read some books about it. They believe that everything comes from above, and there's God beyond everything. Beyond the nature spirits there is one entity, there is one energy. Is that true?

MOITA: All life comes from one source.

Glen: Is that the source that man calls God?

MOITA: He does call it that.

Glen: It's all within us, true?

MOITA: It is within – within each.

Glen: There's another thing I'm really curious about. One of the people associated with Findhorn said he met some elves at a couple of different places. Are they nature spirits manifesting themselves in a different way, or are they a life form like we are? I mean, I don't know what *we* are, anyway . . . *(laughter)* . . . I'm not going to ask you! *(laughter)*

MOITA: There are many different types of nature spirits, and you have given each type a certain name. They each have different functions.

Glen: And he also said he encountered Pan, that was the god of the forest. Does he oversee the functions of all the nature spirits?

MOITA: You could say that. He is in a sense their teacher. He is the overall pattern that they gain their energy from. He guides. He is in a very real sense the personification of the Spirit of the Earth – one personification.

Glen: I forgot what I was going to ask. It doesn't matter.

(The reason may be the unexpectedly deep energy that Kelly and others of us feel as Moita speaks of Pan – as any who have heard or read the writings of R. Ogilvie Crombie or ROC, the man Glen referred to, can well imagine.[22] Moita chooses to end the session at this point.)

ॐ   ॐ   ॐ

The Lord of the Earth – as an energy to be experienced, who does not "lord" it over us – will come up twice more in connection with a beautiful forested, glacial canyon complete with waterfalls.

Moita session #188 (Kelly, David, Carl, 3 others / July 6, 1981)

Carl: Have you ever been to the canyon?

MOITA: Yes.

Carl: Are there a lot of entities there? Because you can *feel* them. Do you know any of them?

MOITA: I will tell you a secret: it is one of Pan's favourite places.

Carl: *(whisper)* Best spot in the world!

ço   ço   ço

The "secret" is passed on to 10-year-old Ben, whose visit with us this summer will soon be capped by a hike up to the glacier with young Donovan and me. Ben's acceptance reflects his being raised by psychically open parents.

Moita session #189 (Kelly, David, Ben, Donovan / July 19, 1981)

Ben: Will we see Pan on our hike?

MOITA: Do you know who Pan is?

Ben: Kelly just told me he's a spirit that likes the canyon.

MOITA: He is one manifestation of the Earth Spirit, the soul of the planet, the soul of the planet's nature. He is somewhat like me in that he oversees a large group of spirits.

Ben: How will we know we're around him? *(pause)*

MOITA: You can be standing quiet in a glade and all of a sudden the world will look different. When you see the world with a different set of eyes, when you see it as beauty, then you are becoming close to Pan, feeling his presence.

Ben: Will all of us feel his presence or . . . ?

MOITA: That is up to each of you, and to your ability to be still within and sense more subtle vibrations or thoughts, feelings. When you can see the air, then you can see Pan.

ço   ço   ço

More mysteriously yet, Kelly once came across a report of another (unidentified) spot in British Columbia where a woman passed through a non-physical "doorway" into a land of legend . . . and managed to return.

Moita session #43 (Kelly and David / November 21, 1978)

David: Could you tell us anything about unicorns, with reference to this woman's experience of visiting them?...

MOITA: And what do you want to know of unicorns – if they are real?

David: The kind of reality they may have.

MOITA: Her experience was real. There are many things that happen in this world, and there are other worlds besides this one.

David: Could one enter that world through many places in this one?

MOITA: Not many. There are some connections. There are places where the worlds rub close together or in a sense occupy the same space, and those are the doorways that can be used by people from one to the other – sometimes only in one direction. They are not always both ways – which, of course, is the danger in finding one, because you may be able to leave and not return, and no one will know of your experience except for yourself...

There are two kinds of unicorns – maybe more, but at least two. One is as a symbol of purity and freedom, and that one is not exactly a *deva* but a spirit of a kind that people use for different purposes and has a reality of its own in that. And then there are the unicorns that used to be here and left us then for a time. They would be hard to see now because they are not as dense as man has become. So their disappearance along with the disappearance of many legends – particularly nymphs and wood spirits – is quite similar. Man has evolved to the point where he has lost part of his sight... Some of these legends will come back to life.

ဢ   ဢ   ဢ

It may seem odd to devote so much attention to the now normally invisible dimensions of life on Earth, with less mention of the visible. It is the non-physical levels, however, that are the *origin* of those material forms with which most of us are much more familiar.

The elementals, fairies, elves, devas and angels of the natural world, and the soul of Earth itself: these are the great omission in all the debates between Biblical creationism, intelligent design and Darwinian evolution. Yet as some scientists now acknowledge their failure to find critical "missing links" between species, and recognize how relatively sudden, simultaneous, internally consistent mutations enable fringe populations to survive extinction, they have moved beyond belief in random, soul-less mechanisms as explanations for the evolving order of nature. It should not be long before the quantum physicists' nods to consciousness and freedom – as inherent in the nature of reality and all life – will alter biology's conception of the origin of natural forms.

Moita session #209 (Kelly, David, 2 others / December 1, 1981)

David: All the forms of nature, the plants and the animals, have they come out of each other over time the way the evolutionists say?

MOITA: That is a large-scope question. *(laughter)*

David: Mm-hmm, well, you're a large-scope person to ask. *(laughter)*

(When readers come to the rest of this session in Chapter 13, they will understand how "large"

I really mean – i.e. that the speaker here exists not "only" as Moita.)

MOITA: How do you explain that to one who is in a form? It begins in the non-physical planes. Nothing begins *here*. This is where it finds expression. And all things interconnect. In a sense, all things grow out of each other. Things become a more perfect expression of a form of energy. All of them are trying to become more of what they know they can be. So, on this plane there are changes in form that relate to their ability to manifest more completely, more surely.

Man sees evolution from the other end of things. He sees it as a natural order, which it is; but he sees it as a haphazard order, which it isn't. Why would an insect look like a stick unless it chose to? It makes no sense! Where did he get the blueprint to form that kind of a body, if not from the tree first, and then created a body to look like a tree?!

David: Man thinks it was pure chance.

MOITA: So many coincidences?

David: All the others died. *(with a laugh)*

MOITA: Because they did not look like sticks?! *(laughter)* Perhaps they died because they were not perfect, in a sense; because they saw the stick and realized it was a much better form! It made much better sense, so they all opted to become sticks too! *(soft laughter; pause)*

If it were true that only the strongest survived, man wouldn't be here. He is not the strongest of...creatures. He is different, and that makes him special. But that does not make him stronger; it just makes him different... The plants did come first, before the insects and before the mammals. Of course, the Earth was first, before them all.

David: And man was last, but his body did not come out of changes in the apes directly, I gather.

MOITA: They were experiments in form, to see what kind of form was best. And when the form was decided upon, then the experiments were no longer needed. Sort of like the difference between an actual stick and an insect's stick. It became the prototype, generally speaking.

David: So then the human spirit began densifying from the more spiritual level where it was?

MOITA: Where it awakened from, yes. It was not conscious for a long time. It was just a pool of energy. And then it became separated into smaller components, and it started on the process of becoming self-aware and separate. It became attracted to the Earth, to experimentation, and created form to continue that experiment and then became one with it...

I told you before why man was special...: because he could choose consciously, for all the others just naturally belong. They have no questions about who they are or if they should be here. They know; they are a part.

ം   ം   ം

Now, to summarize Creation in seven . . . sentences.

Moita session #164 (Kelly, David, 2 others / November 30, 1980)

MOITA: All of the races of the Earth were created not from what is known as evolution on a physical level, but were formed from the spirit. Evolution happened from the top down, not from the bottom up. Spirit is cause; matter is effect. Scientists look from the physical only. They have not yet identified the unifying principle that is in all matter, but they also do not recognize the power of creation. They will never find a "missing link". There *is* none.

ço   ço   ço

As all living species seek to perfect their expression in form, so do each of their members. We arrive now at more of the popular questions in our sessions: What is the consciousness of various animals, and how are animal and human souls related?

Moita session #135A (Kelly, David, workshop group / February 25, 1980)

Louanne: I've been realizing my emotional involvement with the animals in my life. I was wondering: What happens to animals when they die? Do they have the energy in their minds to reach your level of reality?

MOITA: Their spiritual development is somewhat different, in that all animals are part of the same soul. Each species has its own oversoul, an energy reservoir from which they come. It is like humans only on the surface, in that a part of that soul breaks off to become an animal. But the contact between the beings – the one who is in a physical body and the one who is in another reality – is something that is never broken. There is always an interaction going on between the two realities, and each animal is striving towards its own concept of perfection, trying to emulate that greater energy of which it is a part. And so, when an animal dies, it goes back and becomes part of that greater whole again.

Louanne: Very similar to what we do as people.

MOITA: Yes, except that as people that individual soul can change levels and go on to something else. In the animal kingdom, unless the spirit of an animal gains the desire to become human, it remains in that pool of energy from which it originally sprang.

ço   ço   ço

Moita session #113 (Kelly, David, Becky, Chris, Dawn, Greg, Rick / September 29, 1979)

(Russell, the family dog, lies in the centre of our circle of energy.)

Greg: What kind of entity do animals have, like Russell? (pause)

MOITA: They have sort of an oversee-er, a prototype of energy – the perfect Russell. (laughter, as Russell seems at times decidedly imperfect in his nervousness)
           Each dog manifests a different facet of that energy, just as each person manifests a different facet of a soul in each life. But they're not the same kinds of entities. It is almost

like having a living blueprint. The entity may not look like Russell exactly, but it would be what Russell would be striving *towards* – not necessarily just right now...

New life is usually created on our level first – moulded and shaped. And then the processes that you call mutation or evolution work towards becoming that model that has been created on a non-physical level...

Rick: Does Russell – and all of what we consider lower animals – feel actual conscious thought the way we do? Or do they just feel on a much more basic level and react? And then, within that, would Russell be striving consciously to develop himself, or would he just be being led by his entity?

MOITA: *(laughing)* Hmm! We are covering some very unusual subjects tonight! *(laughter; pause)* Russell, as Russell, ... would not be conscious of striving towards perfection the same way you would be, because you would have your own idea of what perfection was and Russell would have a model – a *visible* model.

Several: Hmm!

MOITA: Animals are more aware in many ways of what is really going on in the world. But they do not have that uniqueness that the human spirit can bring – the ability to interpret and, by interpreting, making changes. Russell could not of himself decide that his model is not what he wished to be.

Rick: Are we unique on this planet in having such a spirit, or do other species share that sentience?

MOITA: Not in that way. Other species share an intelligence, an awareness and a consciousness, but it is of a slightly different form. They do not go on to evolve beyond what they are, although it would be within the realm of possibility if they acquire the desire to go beyond. They are not limited except by their essence.

ക   ക   ക

Moita session #105 (Kelly and David / August 8, 1979)

David: What is the consciousness of whales and dolphins like, and how does it compare with man's?

MOITA: Whales are *very* . . . *delicate*. In some ways they are more complex than man. They are very benign and gentle creatures. They live in a world of sound and thoughts. They are able to extend themselves through the water and be in direct contact with their world. They have little difficulty in seeing *us*.

At the moment they are somewhat confused. They have been persecuted for a long time, yet they will still at times extend their friendship and help to man. The many instances of whales and dolphins guiding ships are no accident. They are very conscious acts – their attempt to bridge the gap between two completely different life-forms. The sea is full of life – much life.

David: I was a bit surprised to hear you speak of whales as more complex. Man often seems extremely complex, because of his confusion, his being out of touch. In a sense, whales would seem more simple in comparison.

MOITA: Some would consider *my* consciousness more complex than man's, yet I do not lose touch. I don't use "complex" to mean the inability to keep one's thoughts in order. Whales are very in touch with their environment. Not needing hands, they do not make things which distract them from it.

                 ❧   ❧   ❧

Moita session #117 (Kelly, David, workshop group / November 5, 1979)

Erica: Can animals be reincarnated as people ever? And if we wish, can *we* sometimes come back as an animal?

MOITA: You can experience what it is like to be an animal. Depending on where you are in your own development, it can be wise or unwise. For if you are not complete enough, you may choose to *remain* an animal – at least for a while, longer than intended. Any experience is open to any soul, and it is not always necessary to become something, in a reincarnational sense, to experience it...[23]

         (turning to C.) And I should also say to you that sometimes an animal *can* gain a desire to become a human. *(short pause)*

C.:   *(starting to laugh)* Yeah . . . ?!

    (C. has already mentioned feeling she was an otter in some previous existence.)

MOITA: And it is not that often that it happens. *(pause, as they gaze at each other)*

C.:   What would be likely to precipitate something like that happening?

MOITA: Most likely it would be contact. It could be a dramatic incident – for instance *(Moita smiles)*, being freed from a trap. *(pause)*

C.:   Wow. *(laughing)*

Beings from Space

Returning seemingly to the heavens, another phenomenon has proved an equally popular subject for questioners: UFOs and extraterrestrials, beings not of this Earth – or at least, not physically so. Here, once more, the form of manifestation may disguise the spiritual reality, and the truth or intent behind some channeled communications may have been "lost in translation".

Moita session #139 (Kelly, David, workshop group / April 7, 1980)

Kim: Did man evolve from the sea as scientists say, or did the space people colonize Earth?

MOITA: The legend of beings coming from other realms to populate the planet is based on manifesting spirits, those non-physical beings who collected near the Earth and then were drawn into it and its influence and became physical. On one hand, you could say they were beings from outer space, since they were not born of woman, not then – but not in the sense the question was meant.

Kim: About 10 years ago, I had the opportunity to speak with a group that claimed to be in contact with space people. I asked them where my race came from *(Kim is Japanese)*, and they told me we were from a planet about 30 light-years away. Is that so?

MOITA: The different races were formed when those beings manifested on Earth and chose what they felt was the proper combination of physical and spiritual attributes. None of the races originated anywhere except within man's mind – on the Earth, and [as] part of it.[24N]

Those are meant more as metaphors – man's need to explain his presence in other ways. It is still easier for him to explain what he sees as anomalies by introducing outside forces when he has not realized that he himself is a very versatile creator and needs look no farther than his own backyard for many explanations. I am not saying that these things are, on one level, untrue. I am saying, from my perceptions, that they are meant...more as a parable, perhaps – like a dream, and those [as] symbols.

ço   ço   ço

Moita session #74 (Kelly and David / March 1, 1979)

(Amar's appearance this evening is prompted by a question about those non-physical beings, called Speakers in the Seth material, attendant on man's early evolution. That response will be given in Chapter 4. As part of his longest conversation to date, Amar also answers this final question.)

David: Recently we were told of a book in which the author describes the different life-forms on other planets. According to this writer, all the other planets in our solar system have a more advanced consciousness than there is on Earth at this point.

AMAR: Earth is known for its underdog attitude. *(laughter)* That's its biggest problem! The question is: What is "advanced"? And what is not? And also, which universe it is you are looking in. There are an infinite number of possibilities. Almost any theory a man can imagine will have basis in reality in one universe or another. [The author] is misinterpreting some of his insights, giving them more physical reality than they deserve.

It is not always easy to tell the difference between what you are involved in as physical and what we are involved in as non-physical – since they are both just as real. But you cannot get to ours in a ship. So there is no contradiction, either. It is just a matter of here. *(i.e. a confusion resulting from our limited, physical perspective)*

ço   ço   ço

Moita session #130 (Kelly, David, workshop group / February 4, 1980)

Alice: Moita, you've heard talk here, or maybe from where you are, about people from outer space. Is this true? Are there actually people on other planets?

MOITA: There *are* beings on other planets. There is life on *all* planets. Some is physical and some is not. But most of the "beings from outer space" are from *inner* space, like *me*. *(pause)* Our perception can appear very alien [to you], and some [entities] are not as used to communicating in different levels.

ৡ   ৡ   ৡ

Moita session #94 (Kelly, David, workshop group / June 11, 1979)

(One of our funniest exchanges with Moita begins when she suddenly turns to Tim and says:)

MOITA: You had a question for me?

Tim: How do you know?

MOITA: I spy... *(pause, followed by Tim's asking a question about ghosts)*

Tim: Is that the question you knew I had in mind?

MOITA: No, I was thinking of another. But we will deal with "What are ghosts?" first...

(Moita's answer has appeared elsewhere.[25] Later in the session, Moita again turns to Tim:)

MOITA: Have you remembered your other question?

Tim: I wanted to ask . . . uhh . . . what are UFOs? And is it a problem today in our world?

MOITA: UFOs? You still are not at the question! *(laughing)* Hmm.

I would not say that UFOs are a problem. See yourself in a house that is long and straight and has many rooms, each one taking up a small space. The house is...one room wide, many rooms thick. You are standing in one of these rooms. In the room you are in, you know where everything is and how everything behaves. In the rooms next to you on either side, there are others who know what is in *their* rooms.

If you were standing in your room and someone from the room next to you put their arm through your wall, and their arm was shaped perhaps . . . *(laughter)* . . . [to] not look like an arm and that was all you saw . . . *(laughter)* . . . (do you like this?) . . . you would not know what was in the room next to you. You would only know what came into yours. *(laughing)*

I have made this very simple – or tried to! *(laughter, coughing)* Do you know the point I am getting at?

Tim: Yeah... There's no threat, then.

MOITA: If you went up and punched the arm . . . *(laughing)* . . . what do you think it would do?

Tim: If I what?

MOITA: If you went up and punched the arm . . . *(laughter)*

It's also a matter of what you think is dangerous. An earthquake is dangerous to those who are in it. But it has its own reasons for being. And those who die in an earthquake are really not dead, either. This is not . . . *(laughing hysterically)* . . . prime real estate, as far as the galaxy is concerned! *(laughter)*

Owen: "Be it ever so humble, there is no place like home." *(laughter)*

Hazel: You mean that UFOs are not entities attempting in some way or other to take over the space here.

MOITA: Perhaps they're accidentally crashing through the wall.

Hazel: They have a space of their own, and for some reason it's easy now to crash through the wall? Why are we seeing more of them?

MOITA: There are more *of* you to see them.

Tim: Could it be they're challenging us?

(Moita shakes her head.)

Tim: No? Because our planet's vibration level is stepping up?

MOITA: There are many universes that surround your Earth, not just the physical one. When [beings go] from one reality to another, they cannot pass through the door without changing. They are never exactly what they appear to be. My energy goes through a change when it comes here. I open a door between two realities, but the door itself is neither one nor the other. It is not truly either here or there.

            If you can understand that you shape the world around you – you have all entered into an agreement as to what composes the reality of the world – then you would also agree, for the most part, what something coming from another reality would look like. Your expectations would colour the lens that you view the world through. If you expect another energy presence to have the form of a flying saucer, it will assume that form for you. If you expect that it will have the form of an ancient god that you have read of, then it may assume that form as well. What you see through this reality's lens is not what you would see if you existed in the reality that the energy comes from. Disappointed?

Tim: Mm-hmm.

Hazel: Everybody loves a conspiracy.

MOITA: Oh, there *are* conspiracies.

Hazel: There are. *(in mock deadpan shock, followed by more laughter and coughing)*

    And what conspiracies does Moita have in mind? How does this lead to Tim's "real" question? Tune into future chapters . . .

    ৎ   ৎ   ৎ

    All of Moita's answers are highly attuned to the way our questions are worded, and the assumptions and motives behind our asking them. Thus, to Kim's question "Did the space people colonize Earth?" (April 7, 1980 session), she replies, "Not in the sense the question was meant", i.e. assuming a physical civilization physically travelling here. She then refers to "non-physical beings who collected near the Earth", as if coming from elsewhere on non-physical planes, "and then were drawn into...its influence and became physical." Her answers are further tied to the probabilities as perceived when questions are asked – as when referring to "this time", i.e. circa 1980 – which may or may not have applied in the same way earlier and may or may not apply later.[26N]

I believe this accounts in the next excerpts for what can *appear* a blunt denial of extraterrestrials now visiting Earth. Where questions like the ones below seem to assume literal travel by physical beings between planets, Moita emphasizes a more basic point: what we would consider visiting "space beings" today are primarily from *inner* space – originating, and even materializing their bodies and craft from non-physical dimensions.[27N] Moita and Amar make it clear that they themselves are inherently spiritual beings, integrally linked to humanity's evolution on Earth. Moita also indicates that she cannot yet reveal all the specifics of what is or may be going on.

Moita session #115 (Kelly, David, workshop group / October 15, 1979)

Mike: Are there people travelling here from other planets?

MOITA: Not at this time.

Mike: What's the worldwide phenomenon that people call UFOs?

MOITA: If you were standing outside and you were looking at the stars, wondering if there were other beings with whom you could communicate – others who had a more evolved awareness or a more advanced civilization; and in this wondering, became open to yourself, to a deeper level within, and a door from your world into mine opened and someone from another reality stepped through that door; depending on the space you were in at the time, you could see a flying saucer and occupants and even communicate with them, or you could see an angel descending from the stars or a spirit or even a shooting star.

Much depends on what symbol you place in your heart when you are searching for contact. And there are places on your Earth where you could say the distance between realities is thinner, and these phenomena are more frequent in those places than in others.

᪣   ᪣   ᪣

Moita session #191 (Kelly, David, workshop group / July 29, 1981)

Phyllis: Could you tell us something about the UFOs that are appearing around us? Are they trying to teach us something here on Earth?

MOITA: My universe and yours are drawing together. This energy has been separated from man for a long time. As we draw closer, as our presence becomes more obvious, you will see us in many forms. There is no true perception of the spirit. Each time I am seen, I am seen as something different. Some have seen me in the past as a presence from another planet, even though I am from here.

There are also beings on *all* of your planets, though they have different forms from you, forms that you are not able to perceive physically. Some of them are also bending their thoughts and presence in this direction. The Earth is their sister. They are concerned for her health. How these images are interpreted will depend on your own awareness of the energy.

There are no beings from any planets outside of this solar system on Earth at this time.

There are times in Earth's history when such beings have visited in different forms. There will come a time, when this crisis is passed, when such beings may come again.

ও   ও   ও

Moita session #180 (Kelly, David, Dawn, 17 others / March 28, 1981)

Dawn: Are we the only planet that has our kind of people? Like, are there more of us elsewhere?

MOITA: Do you mean a physical form similar to this?

Dawn: Mm-hmm.

MOITA: There are other planets in the universe that have chosen a form like yours.

Dawn: Will we be ever able to reach them?

MOITA: It is within the realm of possibility, far in the future. There is much to go through first, between here and there.

ও   ও   ও

Moita session #42B (Kelly, David, Spencer / November 17, 1978)

Spencer: There have been reports of UFO phenomena in South America, of beings emerging and saying they have come to try and help the Earth raise its consciousness at this time. What have you to say of those?

MOITA: *Some* of those are *us*.

Spencer: People clothing the phenomenon in terms they can understand?

MOITA: Yes, in terms that are more readily *acceptable* than the actuality. *(pause)* There is no doubt there are other beings and spirits. However, if *I* were one of *them*, I would not be coming to Earth at this time in its history. I would be *watching*, waiting to see what happened next before I ventured too near.

Spencer: If you don't put your fingers in the fire, you won't get burned?

MOITA: You must understand that I cannot be more specific.

Spencer: Not if it's something we have to work out on our own? But you are willing to make yourself available. You're able to go at least that far.

MOITA: Yes, we are. We also have our responsibilities in this.

Spencer: You're responsible in how you use your energy.

MOITA: Yes. The consciousness of man must be raised if you are to be able to continue in your evolution and to prevent the destruction of your world.

Spencer: Is that why you're here – to help raise the consciousness of man?

MOITA: To bring our worlds more closely together. It is hoped that you will in the future be able to see us and work with us on this...

(Later, Spencer picks up on the implications of the above statement.)

Spencer: Could you materialize?

MOITA: That requires a great amount of energy.

Spencer: But you can *do* it, can't you.

MOITA: Yes. *(pause)* If all those on my level materialized on yours, how do you think it would affect those who are here? Would they look on it as a gift, or would it cause fear and perhaps a feeling of awe in them? Would they look on us as gods? We are not here to be gods.

(Spencer sits looking at Moita in silence for a while.)

Spencer: You know something? Your universe makes a helluva lot of sense!

(As Moita then begins to leave, Spencer suddenly grabs her arms and gives her a big kiss. She looks at him in surprise and says:)

MOITA: I'm not used to such an overt show of affection!

Tales of Power #1

SPIRIT JOURNEY INTO THE DARK

The first hint of the life that will connect the first and last of these "Tales of Power", and set the tone for all of them, comes in Kelly's dream during our first winter together.

"Vision of Glowing Feather" dream
Kelly (February 13, 1979)

I am reading a book by Buffy St. Marie on the Plains Indians of Saskatchewan. Buffy tells of an encounter between a white male physician and an old Indian woman healer. At one point, the two compare their diagnoses of a patient. The doctor's opinion is medically based, while the Indian elder diagnoses psychically.

The patient is another Indian woman with very strange "symptoms". One night she is sitting on a power point and sees a white eagle feather glowing brightly before her. Every time she approaches, the feather moves away to the north, so she can only follow it, never touch it. Though she wishes to give the feather to someone else, she realizes she cannot pass it on because she can never get close enough.

In another part of Buffy's book, she describes her feelings while being among her Indian people: "Sometimes when my people are in council, they appear to be very much together, very kind and understanding. When they are in council, this is true. But when council is broken and they go their separate ways, some of them can be cruel and vindictive."

Then I am looking on a map of Saskatchewan to locate this place. There is a town name and an area marked in red, which seems not too far away. I remember Loria's words that there are a number of power points in North America, and any of them would be suitable for a community.

This dream first draws our attention by seeming to indicate a potential Saskatchewan location to build our community. But a few weeks later, Kelly uncovers a past life sharing these common elements: the challenge of maintaining harmony within an Indian tribe, psychic healing, power points, the direction (north) around the Medicine Wheel symbolizing wisdom, and bright magic animating an eagle feather. As well, a talented, energetic, inspiring "St. Marie" is no accident wherever Moita is present.[28N] It is time to introduce the medicine woman.

ও ও ও

Carla comes to us on March 2, 1979 in Regina, wishing to recover her memories of a possible past life as an American Indian. As she arrives, Kelly and I have no idea that a tale of black magical power awaits us, involving key lives of our future group in British Columbia . . . and of a world-famous friend, and of her nemesis.

But as we are introducing our method of past-life regression – Marcia Moore's "hypersentience", a less controlling approach than formal hypnosis[29] – Kelly becomes aware of Moita's presence. Very insistently, she receives the picture of both Carla and herself being subjects in the regression, because they were *together* in the life that Carla is seeking! The prospect sounds intriguing, of course. But never before have I guided a specific, detailed regression for two – likely quite a rare procedure because of its various pitfalls.

Kelly feels quite hyper about all this . . . until I bring out my Lakota peace pipe. As Kelly takes the pipe in her hands, she calms right down. She almost feels that Indian ancestors are standing behind her, saying all will be well. We then spread two mats on the floor for the women, with space between for Carla's moccasins, the peace pipe and me. Generally, we agree that at each stage I will ask Carla to describe her experience before Kelly does the same. After all, Carla has initiated this, her first regression. Then I begin the deep relaxation induction and some visualization exercises.*

When you can get the main characters together in an effort to relive or recreate or experience [a past life], there is nothing that cannot be done. Some depends on how many are involved in the particular instance. When there are only a few, this kind of interaction with the past is more easily accomplished, because you have with you the raw material that created it, or is creating it.
– Moita (March 9, 1979)

Asked to visit "an ideal place of retreat", Carla first avoids an Indian setting but Kelly finds herself sitting by a large, deeply blue lake, seeing low green hills and snow-covered mountains beyond. Behind her is an expanse of prairie grasses flowing in the breeze. "I feel the air is alive. I know the animals, and each has its place, and so do I." Kelly says no more at the time, but will exclaim afterward: "Did I ever feel like an Indian woman!" She sees herself in Indian clothing and knows she is waiting for something.

I next suggest they allow an image to come of "the best possible teacher for you". Here, without knowing it, Carla starts tuning into the life she seeks: "I get the feeling that somebody is standing with a long, black cape blowing around them. He has a really lined and weathered face. He has a lot of wisdom, but there's something weighing him down a lot – heavy knowledge that maybe isn't very happy. I feel that he doesn't want to let me know any of the bad, just the good."

In turn, Kelly says she hears chanting, which will continue, rising and falling in volume,

---

* For simpler, clearer reading, I will often summarize and otherwise abridge or rearrange the ensuing trialogue among Carla, Kelly and myself as guide, including some later conversation.

accompanied by a lot of energy: "Sometimes so low it's painful or feels threatening; and then so high, out beyond my hearing. I know if you listen, the words will take you somewhere – somewhere within. There's power in the voice. [The singer] shows many sides of himself, many faces. His form changes with his song."

Then I guide my subjects through the "star-gate", a tunnel of light that will issue upon a life they're living together as Indians. The women later describe spinning or potential out-of-body sensations as they move through the tunnel's swirling colours.

Then: "I feel as though I'm on the prairie," Carla says, "and the wind is just whipping around me." The wind is almost pushing her back, blowing her dress and hair, taking her breath. She sees a prairie sky, with clouds of different colours prior to sunset, above slightly rolling terrain of endless grass. It is pleasant, but she doesn't understand why she is there.

I return to Kelly, still sitting by her lake. She reports: "I am here to seek a message. There seems to be trouble – much illness among the very young and the very old. So I have come to an ancient place to wait for an answer."

Asked to move ahead till a message comes, Kelly describes being drawn to a special, very deep pool of water. "I see reasons. We have killed too much. We have forgotten our balance, forgotten our ancestors." It is a painful, harsh revelation as the tribe's excuses are ripped away, exposing truth. Kelly is shocked and afraid as she senses what must be done, then grows resigned and accepting. As she will explain later, there is a feeling of a "sacrifice" being necessary – though the thought of someone actually being murdered, as if to placate the gods, revolts and terrifies her.

"I know what I must do," Kelly reports. But for Carla's sake, she does not explain: "It is not time to speak." So I ask Carla what is happening with her. Enigmatically, she replies: "I can see myself in the middle of a big prairie, but I can't find myself in it. I don't know if it's me on that prairie or not." Soon the scene clarifies enough to say, "I feel someone just walking aimlessly. It feels like it's someone I'm following. They're dressed in flowing black robes" – thus, appearing to refer back to the "teacher" image she received earlier.

I have Carla move ahead till she and the robed figure arrive somewhere. After a pause, she says: "There's a place [with] a lot more plants, different plants that have mysterious medicinal qualities. This man seems to have a really close kinship with these plants." "Why," I ask Carla, "has he brought you here?" Another long pause. "He seems to want to have me learn about them."

"And how do you feel about that?" I inquire. Carla replies thoughtfully, "This man, he's someone I'd have mixed feelings about. There are some things that aren't good or not at all pure. I don't trust him, although I want to trust some of the things he's saying. There's almost a dark energy coming from him that you can almost see," she adds with a little laugh.

"What do you fear he might want to do? Or how would it affect you?" I ask.

"I don't know," says Carla. "I can never tell that in people. It seems that he is giving me something. But he's [also] trying really hard to get something *from* me, and I don't know what. I feel like he wants me to take some plants – take them away and go with him. A part of me wants to, but part of me feels strong that there is something in him that's not good. I still doubt my feelings a lot.

It's like there's two sides, and they balance each other out."

(Carla will later say, "I carried a lot of my traits into being that person. Even in this life, I can never make up my mind because I have to weigh out all sides.")

At this point, part of me thinks I should go back to Kelly, but I'm afraid to disrupt Carla's continuity. Also, I'm not yet sure the women's experiences are even connected. So I start to ask Carla to move ahead again . . . when Kelly, agitated, whispers, "No, wait!" . . . So I tell Carla I'll be back, and ask, "Where are you, Kelly?"

Kelly spills it out: "I am trying to reach her on her journey! – make her remember who she is. That is not a man she follows! She must be wary. The vision in the water told me: The only way to get what we needed was to send one of our girls into the prairie to follow who came, and that she could pick only one plant. And she must not forget that who she followed was not one of our light brothers, but a darker one. Because of what we did, we gave up our right to get the answer in the right way, and there would be many attempts to change or trick. So all our thoughts are bent in your [Carla's] direction."

(After the session, Kelly will elaborate – underscoring the ways this was a hypersentience session like no other. "I was getting all these danger signals. I was starting to breathe really hard with this huge panic inside. It was not like a thing we were remembering, [but] a thing I was experiencing at the time.")

(Continuing the conversation afterward, I will say that when Kelly whispered "No, wait!", it suddenly "made everything real for me in the present, as if the whole thing was at stake right now!" Kelly will agree: "Well, that's how it felt! As far as I was concerned, it was happening at that instant. If she'd gone ahead too soon, without my being able to tell her what was going on, I didn't know what was going to happen! There was great urgency. It had been building up for quite a while. And when you said that about moving ahead, I thought, "No! No! You can't do it!")

(Kelly will continue, speaking afterward to Carla: "When you were talking about whether to trust [the dark one] or not, I was shouting out, 'Don't trust him! Don't trust him!' It seemed that the evil part of him had to do with what the tribe had done." And then, reflecting what Kelly would only discover herself well into the session: "Something about leaving your body *wiped some memories away – like of where you came from. And that was the biggest danger of going in there.")*

(That Carla, unknown to us all during the regression to this point, has been describing an out-of-body experience in that life accounts for the vagueness and confusion of her descriptions – and her struggle to perceive and respond to Kelly's input. This will become clear in later conversation:

Carla: *I heard what you said, and I was trying really hard to focus my mind on it, but it was kind of floating by me. I could pick up little bits and pieces.*

Kelly: *That's exactly how it would have happened in reality!*

Carla: *Yeah, I couldn't focus on it at all, and that's why I was so really unsure.*

Kelly: *I was trying to get that message through to you somehow, so some part of you would know, so you wouldn't forget and wander aimlessly forever following this guy and looking at plants. That was why I had to be there; otherwise you'd have no anchor to come back to.*

Boy, I was anxious to get you back. I was worried.

Carla: *I was too! I was worried that I was going to do something that was going to be totally destructive to so many people.)*

During the session, when Kelly's warning ends, I ask Carla what she is experiencing. "Do Kelly's words call up anything?" She replies, "I can see where my confusion comes from easier. But I can't see into this person any differently."

I ask if Kelly has anything more now, and she answers, "I know her name." Rather than have Kelly reveal it, I ask Carla to be open to her name as I count to 5, but "No name comes to me."

Finally, addressing Kelly, I ask, "Shall we move on to see how this resolves itself? Where are you now and what's happening?"

Kelly answers: "In a lodge. She lies before me on a mat." Not understanding, I ask, "How has she gotten here?" Kelly explains, "This is where she journeyed *from*." Having just realized it herself, Kelly finally makes clear to me that the girl has been travelling out-of-body. "So her body has been here," I confirm, "which explains why she couldn't see herself." Kelly repeats: "I am watching over her and protecting her." Aware of what the girl is experiencing, all Kelly can do is "contact her by her name – Kenawachee (Kee-nah-*wah*-chay) – and help her remember where she is and why."

Now there's an interesting turn. With Kelly focused in the other life, following Kenawachee's travelling spirit while their bodies sit or lie in the lodge, Carla reflects on the situation from the viewpoint of her current life:

Carla: Kelly said she was protecting me, and I don't know why I'm always being protected by people. I don't know if I need it, or if they need to feel that I do, but I'm always having that.

Kelly: Only a fool goes into a battle with only one sword. I would have made this journey myself, if I had been allowed to.

David: Why were you not allowed to make it yourself?

Kelly: It is part of our punishment to put our youngest in peril, and to show her bravery. The protection I can give is scant. I can only keep her connected to her body, and make her remember her name. She is there alone; I am but a shadow. She does not know I am there. All are looked after when they journey in this way. And one *(herself in this case)* always goes as a shadow, so if there is no return there is knowledge of it.

(Afterward, Kelly will tell Carla: "You were doing it for the tribe. It was a ceremonial thing. I felt responsible because you were the one who had to go out and do it, where I would have done it myself because I had more experience in that. You had never gone there yourself. It had to be someone who'd never gone – that was what we were told.")

When I check with Carla again, she answers from within the journey: "I'm still trying to make a choice whether to trust this person and take what he wants me to take, or to not trust him and take nothing. There's a big conflict within myself as to what's the best thing to do."

"Okay," I say, "we're going to move ahead to a scene that will show how you decide, what the result is. Try to just be open to what comes, as I count . . ."

After a pause, Carla responds: "I'm leaving with nothing. And I feel really light about it. I can feel myself running, but not a frightened kind of running – light. I think that I maybe did a thing that wasn't bad – except that [man] feels there's negative feelings. I seem to be back on the prairie I was on before. It feels good to be back, but it seems as though I have some destination in mind – I don't know where."

I ask Carla to "move to when you reach that destination". Soon she reports: "I'm in a place where there's more green – a forest. I can feel there's a home for me in that forest." I ask her to move till she arrives "home".

"I can see a very small building almost like a goat hut," Carla says, "but not exactly. I'm looking on the outside, but I see a loft inside with a ladder." Meanwhile, Kelly sees the goat hut Carla describes superimposed over the lodge where she's aware of herself and Kenawachee's body being – the lodge's high roof and smoke hole somewhat fitting the loft image.

(So is Carla close to seeing – by returning to – the lodge where Kelly says her body lies? Later, Carla will offer that she wanted to be an Indian and in the scene Kelly saw her in, but she was *fighting against it* because she felt it might just be her wish. Thus the little goat hut rather than the lodge. It's not what regression skeptics would expect, but such self-doubting is a common block to smoother remembering of past lives.[30N])

"Is there anyone else around here?" I ask Carla. Interestingly, she says, "I can't see anybody, but it almost feels as though it's quite full of people." At my questioning, she allows that "When it seems there's a lot of people, [the place] doesn't seem that small." I ask, "This feels like your destination, like home?" Carla says promisingly, "It feels comfortable. It feels like I'm really used to it."

It's again time for me to switch. "Okay, let's see what Kelly has been experiencing." But there's no response . . . So intent on the experience, Kelly thinks to herself: "Kelly. Who is Kelly?" She literally doesn't know who "Kelly" is anymore! "Now wait a minute," she continues, "I should know who Kelly is." I edge closer to her on the mat, saying, "Are you . . . ? What's happening with you?"

Feeling thoughts in her direction, coupled with impatience at the dead silence, Kelly decides, "He must mean me." So she speaks: "I was feeling very proud that she did not take anything. She was not there to take – only to find what it was he would show her. There was *one* plant that was the cure for the disease, which Kenawachee needed to locate and then be able to lead the tribe to. If she'd touched anything, however, she would have been 'rooted' in his world. That had to be her choice, so she could not be told. She has passed a greater test than any of us." (Carla will later comment that whenever she sees something she likes, she's always reaching out . . . but then afraid to touch, even now.)

"Who is the man?" I ask. "I cannot speak his name," says Kelly. "He is a dark spirit, one who preys upon innocent minds." (And Carla will later add: "The spirit appeared to me as a medicine man. Except he reminded me of a worm – kind of a sneaky-type person.")

Kelly then points out that we're not done: "She must return. She must remember her people and come home to the fire in the lodge. She cannot see us. She is still in the other world."

So, picking up on her earlier reference to a place "full of people", I propose to Carla:

David: I'd like you to try something. See yourself in what you call 'home'. See it with the feeling there are people there. Let those people appear; let your body appear for you. Describe any experience that comes as you try that... *(pause)*

Carla: I can see quite a lot of women sitting and talking to each other in a language that I don't understand. There's an Indian woman – North American Indian.

David: One woman stands out?

Carla: The group are old women, nattering at each other. And there feels to be one woman who's younger. But I feel a lot younger than all of them, like about 12.

David: Where are you?

Carla: Watching. My skin feels brown. It feels a lot more in tune with the Earth.

David: Can you describe more of this scene, the place you're in?

Carla: The place has gotten a lot bigger. It seems pretty full with those women. I can only watch them. It seems as though we're not even together. I'm standing quite far away, looking on at them, and they don't even notice me. I don't understand the language they're speaking. But the younger woman who is there, she doesn't say anything.

Kelly: You're not yet seeing what is there in physical form. You're still seeing both worlds. I am the only one in the lodge besides yourself. Those others are past *(i.e. the ancestors)*. That's why they cannot see you. But you are closer.

(I decide to use Carla's current situation as a clue so that, through Carla, Kenawachee also can return fully to her body. This takes us to the end of the session:)

David: Just as an experiment, I'd like you to imagine that you're lying on a mat in [this lodge]. Try to feel yourself lying there beside this woman you've seen. *(pause)*

Carla: I can just vaguely put myself into that situation. I can feel it mildly. But I feel really strongly that Kelly was a person whose duty . . . that did have to try and protect me, that did have to try and give me some sort of a shield.

David: Can you describe her?

Carla: She's young, and she seems really dark *(she's dark-skinned, or aware of dark energy?)* except there's this really radiant type of light just coming from her. It seems as though she's really light at the same time. She seems to have really a lot of wisdom. Even though she's young, she seems really, really old – in her knowledge.

David: What is she wearing?

Carla: Some sort of robes, really loose clothing.

David: How is her hair?

Carla: It's long, straight.

David: How does your body feel?

Carla: I don't really feel very much a part of that body. Maybe I feel so disconnected from it because in Kelly's presence, which is very overwhelming.

David: Okay, can you imagine moving around, touching your body with your hands, stretching, getting into the feel as you move?

Carla: Yeah, I can. It feels like I would feel now.

David: *(to Kelly)* Do you have any more to say at this point?

Kelly: I am content. I feared she would not return.

David: Do you feel finished?

Kelly: Mm-hmm.

(So I invite the two women to come back to their bodies, on the mats here in the living room -- to return alert and refreshed and able to remember their experience. Later, as our post-session conversation begins to wind down, these comments:)

Carla: *(to Kelly)* You don't really have an Indian person's features, but you really look like an Indian woman to me for some reason.

Kelly: Maybe there *is* a reason – what we just went through!

David: It was pretty neat, I think. Especially the different levels of it: the being out-of-body within that life, and being sort of out-of-body here and now as we do this; the blending of this life's experience with that one and with the spirit world. I really sensed a transparency with experiences at different times flowing together. I'm almost tempted to say we've made history tonight.

Carla: *(to Kelly)* I felt there was a big difference in how you related to it, as [happening in] the present. You were completely absorbed in the other life, and it seemed as though I was looking at the other life from the viewpoint of me in this one... I'm quite glad that I did it with you at the same time. It seems a lot more interesting.

Kelly: Well, I'm glad that Moita's idea worked out. It must have been her idea; that's where it came from.

Carla: Yes, I'm glad it all worked out.

Kelly: Thank God the universe is safe! Everything's back in its proper order... Whew! But the more we do these, the more I'm beginning to think that we, right now, are actually affecting what we were doing then.

In a session on March 9th, Moita reveals one more, unsuspected reason that our actions and awareness now – particularly *Kelly*'s actions and awareness – can affect that other life. "You see," Moita says, "for her, that life comes *after*." Though that life lies in our historical past, Kelly, as a soul, is yet to become that medicine woman.

Chapter 3

SWIFT WINGS OF CHANGE

The tempo of upheavals in and around the Earth is clearly accelerating as the 1970s reach their finale. Amid worldwide climatic abnormalities, earthquakes, tidal waves and volcanic eruptions, bellwether California experiences a series of major tremors, culminating on August 6, 1979 in the strongest quake along the San Andreas fault since 1911, shaking the centre of the state including San Francisco.

Do other, more devastating possibilities await within the next few years, bringing massive disruptions not only to North America but shaking the planet as a whole? In these years surrounding 1980, Moita will be raising such disasters as probabilities for which people like us should be prepared, in order to be useful to those who are not.

Two days later in Regina, the intimate connection between these natural upheavals and changing states of human consciousness is especially brought home to Kelly and me. On the early evening of August 8th, a violent wind and rain storm, including two tornadoes, rips a broad swath through the city. For us, it is only hours after the end of the legal battle over my separation from Ruth. The animosity generated in court seems to find expression in the menacing reddish-grey clouds that Kelly first notices boiling through the sky. She senses a non-physical dimension to those clouds as well: human thought-forms contributing to the destruction soon to be wreaked on many roofs, windows, signs and vehicles.

The storm seems one more signal – if indeed our Regina learnings are now over – that we should soon be leaving this prairie city for the rural, remote British Columbia interior. Its heavy drama recalls the ominous thunderstorm that day back in early July, as we were making last-minute preparations for our first trip to Sunrise Farm – and of other hasty departures, in other times and places, as well.

Moita clearly wants us to view our world's present state, and probable cataclysms that may or not be physically realized in the near future, in the context of previous critical transitions – such as the crisis that led to the founding of ancient Musili. Before delving into our session this August 8th evening, here is further background on Musili and what preceded its founding, based on *The World Conspires*:

> Musili was a very ancient and beautiful city of light. Its present location, though the Earth has changed considerably in the meantime, could roughly be northern Spain. Cities like Musili, though quite real in their own time, have come down to us through the ages as myth and fairytale. Musili and its crystal towers and walls were erected and maintained with a highly advanced art/science of sound. Life was very happy and harmonious and healing,

for all things were done with awareness of their place within the whole.

Musili was founded by part of a larger group that had previously lived in Asia Minor. This larger group left the ancient Asia Minor city of Kyrionis (Keer-ee-*oh*-nis), splitting in two directions: one moving west to found Musili, and the other moving east to the area that became the Himalayas. Many members of the group then lived later incarnations in the two resulting civilizations as they matured. The groups split to develop two complementary approaches to reality – the creative/intellectual ("outward and light") and the earthy/intuitive ("slow and inward") – and are only now, in this transitional period, joining themselves and their polar tendencies together once more.[31]

Moita session #105 (Kelly and David /August 8, 1979)

David: A lot of psychic energy was released tonight.

MOITA: Kelly was watching. *(pause)* There seem to be parallels between San Francisco and Kyrionis.

(The inhabitants of Kyrionis in ancient Asia Minor did not heed warnings of their city's imminent destruction until after a first devastating earthquake. Kelly re-experienced this dramatic shared life, which preceded the life of our group's predecessors in Musili, during a regression the previous winter.[32])

MOITA: Some people say earthquakes rarely strike populated areas, because there are fewer of them. *(i.e. compared to the whole surface of the Earth)*

David: On the assumption quakes aren't connected with people.

MOITA: Precisely. And that the Earth doesn't know where the people are...

It may be that the whole California coast is vulnerable... California is a good example of a place that has lost its natural balance. It produces much more than it needs, and uses artificial means to increase its production. There is much that is artificial there. Each state has its own consciousness. The consciousness of Washington state, for example, is much different than California's.

ৡ   ৡ   ৡ

Three nights later, we hold our last group session in Regina, having invited four close friends to hear of our July trip to British Columbia. It is a significant gathering, as the others are about to embark on new ventures as well: Eileen and Gerald moving for a year to be close to Louis, the psychic and spiritual teacher on Orcas Island, Washington; and Neale – with the help of Eileen, Gerald and Steven (also Roy, who is not present) – preparing to launch a New Age bookstore in Regina.

It is certainly fitting that over one and a half years since first making his presence known to Eileen and others, Amar chooses this occasion to finally speak directly through Kelly to these members of our Regina group. The conversation with Amar has already been presented in *The World*

Conspires[33], but some of the exchange with Moita is given below.

<u>Moita session #106 (Kelly, David, Eileen, Gerald, Neale, Steven / August 11, 1979)</u>
MOITA: *(to Gerald)* You're bursting! *(laughter)*

(Kelly is suddenly seeing Gerald lit up like the Sun – more as pure energy than a person sitting next to her. Gerald, for his part, has just been gazing at his hand and experiencing all the blood and energy it contains, as if ready to spurt out at the slightest prick to the skin!)

Gerald: Yeah, I *feel* that way... I feel that someone has just cranked up the energy, or increased the vibrational rate; that things are just being accelerated – *meant* to move faster; that the move toward spiritualization is just being *pushed*.

MOITA: Yes.

Gerald: ...I think there are some who are going to feel the new energy as . . . It's going to drive them mad; they're not going to be able to cope with the energy. There are others – like us in this group, I *think* – who are meant to tune to that energy and figure out how to help the others. Am I anywhere near right in that?

MOITA: Well, the acceleration began with the first energy change a few years ago *(the one publicly predicted as "the end of the world as we know it", on June 13, 1976).* And then last fall the second and third change which we initiated have brought our worlds closer together.[34] In a sense, we are more like rubbing each other than having a space apart. This energy, we knew, would affect people in many ways: frighten many people; some would definitely lose their grounding. But it was their choice not to be ready enough when it happened, a lesson for some to take to another time to understand what steps are needed in order to be ready.

But the happenings that the world has planned for Earth are closer than many would think – not just the physical ones, but the political and social and economic changes as well. It would not do for us to wait too long, because then things would have started...their downward movement.

What needs to be done with the world is building a network of understanding and love between those who *are* aware of things, *do* know what's happening – a putting aside of thinking that *their* place in the wheel of life is more true or more important than another's. There are so many views that can be held concerning reality, and even those that are at opposite sides are not in contradiction. It is a time to learn acceptance of others; and in order to do that, you must learn acceptance of your own view, yourself...

As you become more cleansed, as your own vibration rate rises, you will find many things that you were not previously aware of will affect you a great deal. The more your body leaves heavier things behind – toxins and poisons – the more the lighter, subtle worlds can reach you.

ॐ   ॐ   ॐ

On August 28th, the day before our scheduled departure for B.C., as I am loading up the VW and our newly acquired, mid-60s-era pickup, Kelly's friend Jerry drops over to see her. It is surely an ironic touch to our last day in Regina that Kelly's last Moita session there should be with this person who first brought the two of us together – but who, as it turns out, treats "Moita" as one big joke.[35]

Despite our Volkswagen's collapsing in Alberta, forcing kids, cats, plants and us to pile into our heavily laden truck with an added trailer behind, we (but sadly, not the Dieffenbacchia) arrive safe and sound at our alpine town destination on the Labour Day weekend. There Paula, another friend to whom the Sunrise Farm folks introduced us in July, has said we can pitch tents in her backyard. During the following week of chilly, rainy weather, we also arrange a makeshift kitchen, dressing room and even transcript office in her woodworking shop. Despite the awkward, disorienting circumstances, camping out by our new friend's moist vegetable garden is an image of the rebirth under way in our lives. We've certainly come far from the dry prairies.

With the exception of a yoga teaching job for Kelly, we seem to be meeting nothing but dead ends in our search for a house and employment until that next weekend. Then – in the space of three days – I snag a hotel cooking job (no experience necessary), the local community college invites us to give a talk and workshop in the nearby Kindle Valley (a more accessible and more populated area than where Sunrise Farm is located) and we are interviewed by the local newspaper. Best of all, we are invited to hold a first Moita session in Paula's home with a group of her friends.

One of the participants is Joe, a medical doctor, who enters quite remarkably, ceremoniously offering the hostess a just-picked puffball mushroom approaching a foot in diameter! But at the end of the evening, Joe does something even more remarkable. He invites Kelly, me and the children, at very reasonable rent, to move into the main part of his charming, three-storey farmhouse situated on a hill overlooking a wide river valley and surrounding mountains! Joe will continue to live in the sunny, modern addition, but we will share meals and household tasks with us. Joe's acreage includes a tall evergreen forest and fair-sized lake – and it harbours, Joe understands, an Earth power point.

This wonderful solution falling into our laps through the "medium" of offering a Moita session leaves no doubt that long-prepared manoeuvring has suddenly surfaced in our lives. Dr. Joe Townsend is a socially and spiritually minded physician in his early 40s, who also owns land in the Gulf Islands near Victoria. Separated from his wife a while ago, the new challenge in his life is a cancer diagnosis, for which he is exploring both medical and alternative healing solutions. As he needs to travel, our staying in his farmhouse and being able to welcome him home serves several purposes for all concerned. And given his generosity, we will not be too surprised to learn, through further high-energy sessions, that Joe is a returning friend from the life of our group in Musili.[36]

୨ଚ   ୨ଚ   ୨ଚ

The next week, I return alone by truck to Regina to pick up the rest of our stored belongings. Mid-trip, I happen to notice headlines in an Alberta newspaper which call to mind Edgar Cayce's predictions about major earth changes to come. On a single day, September 12th, a massive earthquake hit the South Pacific (8.0, centred in Indonesia), Italy's Mt. Etna had its most violent eruption in 20 years, and Frederick – the most destructive hurricane in a century – slammed into the U.S. Gulf Coast. Needless to say, I feel even more urgency to complete my circuit back to B.C.

After my return trip to the prairies, September 24th is set for Kelly and me to whet interest in our community college workshop. We are to speak to residents of the Kindle Valley at the lodge serving as a community meeting-place – a rustic, rambling building looking out on one of the best fishing rivers in B.C.

On the night in question, we're not sure how long our drive north up to and into the valley should take. So, unfamiliar with the Kindle's unlit, mostly unpaved, winding roads, we arrive about a half-hour late. Apparently to the 20 or more patient attendees, though, this only puts us on "Kindle Valley time". Our audience happily includes Chris and Becky, who just "happen" to have come to town because of a runaway horse and heard of the event.

Speaking first, I describe some of the inspirations in my life, including my "Raven Transformation" dream, the Seth material and Findhorn Community. With little Arista sitting on her lap, Kelly then speaks from the heart of our personal changes and spiritual openings. After she is done, there are enthusiastic responses from a number in the audience. One expresses that we have managed to arrive at the right time to act as catalysts for many to share their openings and work toward the "New Age" – this from Jim, not the only ex-Californian living in the valley who is soon to join our workshop.

Two suggestive experiences follow. My dream three nights later carries a premonition of old/new friendships to unfold from our Kindle Valley talk. I dream I hear a woman's voice inside my head clearly saying, "*Now is the time for a meeting.*" Then I'm amazed to meet up with close friends from my peace activism days. After joyful hugs, we talk of living together as a group, *if* we see a shared purpose and *if* we're free of other commitments. These "ifs" hint of challenges that may temper the joy of renewing past connections.

As well, shortly after our Kindle Valley talk, a friend phones Kelly from the Okanagan Valley in south-central British Columbia. She tells about many people suddenly turning up there whose personal guidance has led them to the area for purposes of "New Age" work. Two in particular, Joan and Arthur, have been very excited to hear about our communications with Moita, as they themselves hope to create a healing and growth centre in southern B.C. In addition, our friend has discovered a number of locals are independently storing away food, some having been guided to do so in order that it last through the disruptions expected from coming Earth changes.

In the wake of this, we are eager to invite Moita's presence. But her message this time is unexpectedly sobering, as she speaks of another worst-case probability line involving the Vancouver area . . . which mercifully will *not* be realized.

Moita session #112 (Kelly and David / September 26, 1979)
David: How do you see all of these seemingly very rapid and exciting comings-together,

happening both here and in the Okanagan?

MOITA: I would see them as a sign that things need to be gotten ready. *(pause)* Not everyone will see this sign – only those that are becoming ready.

David: Is there anything you can say about why this is happening in the Okanagan? Or is that simply the area that we're more connected to at the moment?

MOITA: It is no accident that Ogopogo is in the area. There is depth there, a sense of the Earth reaching down into itself – deep roots.

(The supposedly mythical sea monster, named Ogopogo since pre-European settlement times, is believed this very year to have reared its head – on film – from the deep waters of Lake Okanagan.)

MOITA: There are reasons why many people are coming to these areas, particularly to the [Okanagan]. With the probable devastation of the Vancouver area, there will be many who will flee inland. It would not be wise to concentrate those who are needed most too far from an area that will supply a great many needful people.

David: Can you say more about that probable devastation and the source of it? Manmade or Earth changes? I know the two are connected, but will it be Earth changes there producing the devastation?

MOITA: There are a number of possibilities yet. One could be strictly physical disaster... A fault line does run up the West Coast and into Alaska. There is also the possibility of an Earth tremor or quake triggering a disaster in a nuclear power plant, if it happens that the building of the plant goes through.

David: Where may that plant be built?

MOITA: This is one that is in the States, [relatively close] to Vancouver.

David: Hmm. Can you give any time-frame for that?

MOITA: Right now, we would say between '82 and '85 would be the most likely time period. There is also another side to why people are gathering in these areas. If enough energy can be accumulated and put into positive endeavours – if enough people become aware of changing within themselves – having the energy that much closer to a place that is probably going to experience much physical change can help to alleviate some of it. It still could all be avoided.

David: Do you think we might have some work appropriate to us in a setting like Vancouver on a temporary basis? Should we explore the possibility of trips there?

MOITA: There are many people in Vancouver who will be ready to leave at the right time, and there are those that you could connect with before. It is an area of great disruption already. Many things are happening on many levels. There is not a sense of clearness to the city or many of the people. They gather together information along very unusual paths, and much of what they do is not well connected...

(During the above, Kelly sees pictures of a huge tidal wave smashing the Pacific coast from the west. When Moita speaks of the nuclear power plant, she sees not an explosion but a seeping out of radiation like insidious fingers. The earthquake alone is better – nice and clean – though it cripples

the city, felling power lines and skyscrapers.)

(It is then a relief to focus on our own location farther north:)

David: I want to ask about the energy of this land we live on now, since Joe has mentioned that it lies on a power point.

MOITA: Are you asking me if it is?

David: Yes, but to elaborate on what kind of energy might be here. *(pause)*

MOITA: Perhaps a better understanding of ley lines would be helpful. With a ley line of energy that runs from one point to another on the surface of the planet, not every point on that line is a power point, but every point is a *potential* power source that can connect with the overall energy pattern in the line itself. And there are new points being created all the time. As the Earth changes, so does its expression of energy.

There is an energy centre here, but there are some far older ones in the area with much more energy fairly close at hand. This place did not become a place of energy until in this century. So it is young and new, not as potent as others. When a new point opens, those who experience it in a sense help it to grow, and they nourish its energy and help to dictate what feel it will have, what characteristics it will bring out in others. In some ways, a new point is easier to cope with than an old one – more malleable. Older ones can be far more dangerous to the inexperienced. *(long pause)*

The energy here is connected very strongly to the air rather than the earth.

(That this place is a hilltop, subject to many winds, would seem to fit.)

David: My guess would be that some of the older ones you mention would have been known to the Indians. I wonder if some of them would still be places identified with Indians in this region.

MOITA: Definitely. You can be fairly certain that any place the Indians have built their totems and their lodges has been a place of power, and probably still is.

David: Recently a friend made a curious statement to me – that the Indian culture around here did not have a spiritual side to it...

MOITA: My perspective of this is that for the Indians in this area their spirituality was something that was lived more than it was spoken of. It was an inner knowledge – something which they found difficult to put into words,...something they would not speak of to others very often. *(pause)*

It is difficult enough to use your language. English is a language more suitable for describing objects than feelings or intuitions. The Indian language is more suitable for these matters, since it speaks more clearly of the Earth and the things that are of it. And they use an innate understanding of the workings of the spirit in life. It is not abstract.

ৎ   ৎ   ৎ

A few days after this September 26th Moita session, our sketchy knowledge of nuclear plans for northern Washington state is filled out by reading of a proposed power plant on the Skagit River. Many groups, some in Canada and some in the U.S. – notably the First Nations residents of the area – have been protesting the proposal for reasons that include the danger of an earthquake.

We have nowhere seen information regarding the possibility of quakes in that specific area, but a week or two later we find an article in the *Vancouver Sun* about a 1971 geological study indicating possible deep faults in the Skagit region. After being tipped off to the existence of the study, the Nuclear Regulatory Commission has to pressure the Puget Sound Power & Light Company to make the study public. Then, because the study has been released, the U.S. Geological Survey rescinds its earlier ruling that the plant design is adequate to withstand anticipated earthquakes. NRC hearings on the proposed plant, under way at the time, are immediately adjourned to assess the "new" information.

(In subsequent years, huge cost overruns will result in the scrapping of most nuclear power plans for Washington state. Based on the consortium's acronym, this public financing disaster becomes lovingly known as WHOOPS!).

ও   ও   ও

Sharing Joe's property is certainly a comfortable introduction to community and rural life in northern B.C. There's a trail uphill into tall woods and an old barn to explore. *[Photo Album #5]* The farmhouse has natural wood, stained glass, and most modern conveniences. (Only when the pipes freeze in winter will I get to chop holes through river ice to haul back our drinking water.)

During the fall, we and the kids enjoy canoeing on Joe's lake surrounded by gold- or red-turning trees amid the evergreens. Then one afternoon it occurs to me that our cat Silkie would like to join our paddling adventure. But as we five head out together, he is not so sure. Soon Silkie is walking the gunwales, nervously eyeing the water below, then standing atop the prow, looking ashore and meowing loudly as only a Siamese can. So we decide to return our reluctant passenger to land. But with 50 feet still remaining, our intrepid feline decides he can't trust us and must make it on his own! He leaps in, swimming instinctively toward the closest bit of solid matter he sees, finally scrambling up some tree branches trailing into the lake. After I manage to disengage him, I bring the little "drowned rat" ashore, wrapping him in a towel and assuring him his canoeing days are over.

Then our first experience of the magical depth of nature known for millennia by the Indians of the area comes on an autumn night of northern lights. This rural hilltop is perfect for watching the aurora colours swirl through the heavens – and, surprisingly to us, for *hearing* them as well. As the lights intensify, so too does an electric energy, like faintly heard static. But then a louder, wonderfully eerie sound greets our ears: from the folds of the hills around us, coyotes repeatedly raise their yips and howls in response to the surges of light in the night sky. This becomes one of many experiences of wild nature we are glad to be able to share with our young children through our move to British Columbia.

At the end of September, we pay a return visit to Sunrise Farm – an easier expedition now that we know where we're going! During our short stay, we hold a session in which Becky and Chris, neighbours Dawn and Greg, and Greg's brother Rick all participate. Moita's words and energy this night truly bring home how closely our inner and outer worlds intertwine – giving hope and direction for change.

Moita session #113 (Kelly, David, Becky, Chris, Dawn, Greg, Rick / September 29, 1979)

Dawn: In the last session we had *(July 16, 1979)*, you were talking about the bad, foul energy that's on this Earth because of man. Did you say that the Earth can be cleansed if this energy is absorbed, transformed?

MOITA: Transformed or transmutated.

Dawn: So I've been thinking quite a bit about that, and I want to understand more about absorbing and if it's something that all people can try.

MOITA: It's something that all can do, and all *should* do. You transform energy that is here in an unacceptable form by changing yourself from within, by accepting your place in the world, your responsibility for how the world is now, and going about in a creative and positive manner to express this change of view of yourself. Everything starts from one and works [outward].

  You cannot change another so that their energy is better. By trying to change another, you are creating more "bad" energy, because then you are neglecting the prime responsibility for changing yourself and giving others the freedom to do their own learning.

  This is how the world will change, in one time or another. This is how each can help to alleviate all those possible futures, so that perhaps the easier one can be chosen, the one with the least amount of pain. If you all love life and enjoy it, life will be good to you.

Dawn: Mmm. I hope so. *(pause)*

Rick: Does the creation of machineries cause bad energy?

MOITA: It is the way machinery is used that will determine if it causes bad energy or not. It would be *better* if man could create his machines with more knowledge or more awareness of energy and the way it works.

Chris: It's nice to know about changing yourself... There's that thing to work with right there, at least. It's a handle to everything else.

MOITA: Mmm. It helps to take away that feeling of helplessness, and seeing the immensity of the task before you, if you would change the entire world.

Chris: Mm-hmm. It would keep the changes and the magic from happening, certainly.

Dawn: I was also wondering if medicine men, chief Indians and shamans are able to absorb a whole lot more because of their understanding, and if that's part of their purpose amongst the tribes: to absorb the kinds of energy man creates just by being man. Is that one of their major duties?

MOITA: It would be difficult for them to heal if they were not able to touch another's energy and take away things that were not useful. So, yes, they are some of those who can help to change energy because of their awareness. But it is only a small part. The energy we are dealing with here that needs to be changed is energy that has accumulated over many thousands of years – what man has done to man, the thoughts that man has had and put into effect by thinking them. Many things need to be cleansed.

ぺ   ぺ   ぺ

Two weeks later, we begin our seven-week "Psychic Frontiers" workshop in a friendly home setting in the Kindle Valley. Aged from late 20s to early 40s, group members agree we should begin with a Moita session. So 16 of us (the largest group to date) join our energies in a circle. With the following question from Jim, a good-looking, sandy-blond-haired man of medium build, the conversation seems to pick up where our Sunrise Farm session left off.

Moita session #115 (Kelly, David, workshop group / October 15, 1979)

Jim: The concept of time I've read coming from you is the hardest concept for me to grapple with. The future, I would strongly believe, is totally undetermined – we can change it. And yet, I don't believe in time as moving in a line from past to future, either. So I'm confused.

MOITA: You are not alone. *(Jim laughs; pause)* It is hard to believe that all times are occurring at once, but that is what is happening – not just all times and all of your lives occurring at the same moment, but also all of your *possible* lives are also occurring in that same moment... Depending upon where you place your focus, you will bring one or another of those possible futures into your reality and experience.

Jim: I can believe in the existence of many possible futures, but is there one that is somehow more important or more generally focused? Or is it a random, infinite number of possibilities to choose from?

MOITA: When you speak of the evolution of a world, there are many possible futures. But depending upon how many individual focuses go in one direction, it will tip the...scales into one line or another. The future is changeable when you believe that you have created the entire Earth and your life and your part in it. But so long as you do not believe in your own energy, you will see the world travelling in a haphazard and unpredictable manner.

Jim: So is it possible, then, for a very small number of individuals to have a major impact on the evolution of an entire world?

MOITA: When their energy is more focused, more directed, more aware and more conscious, it does not take that many individuals to change a world. You can build upon a base of awareness, and awareness itself will become contagious. You all speak to each other on other levels; you are all linked together. You cannot help but affect those who are near you.

In this, it is like playing dominoes – providing you have all the pieces lined up.

Jim: That's a very hopeful message in a time where the vast majority of beings appear to be refusing to wake up. And it's very easy to get very cynical if you believe that it's going to take a majority waking up in a very short time. But perhaps if it did not require a majority to wake up in order to salvage the planet . . .

MOITA: You see, a little of belief can be a dangerous thing, for then you desire to see quick results. And when you do not see them on the surface where you hope to see them, you soon lose what small belief you had, and so you also lose what gain you have made.

To believe that you can change the world by being yourself instead of having to change others – in this belief, you can become strong, and you can grow and not lose your only centre, for then the centre of the universe is within and does not hinge upon other people's reactions. Theirs [are] not as important, and they will not thrust your own growth aside. And in staying in that place – in that centre, in your world – then you will see change happening from within others who are around you, and that change will be a lasting one, not one on the surface. It will be one that will carry through the rest of man's evolution – one he will not forget...

Myrna: How do you explain the polarized energy that has come to be, [both] in this particular area and throughout the world?

MOITA: By "polarized", do you mean one camp against the other?

Myrna: *(with a laugh)* So to speak.

(Many have been surprised during recent months to see the population of this valley split badly over the issue of herbicide spraying. Moita addresses the deeper problem by describing a context of changing consciousness.)

MOITA: When people begin to open up, a great part of it is fear of the unknown, of things that mankind cannot touch or see. They cannot be measured, therefore they cannot be anticipated. And man feels helpless and in many ways threatened or trapped if he cannot see what is before him and measure its worth or its danger. As more people open to this kind of energy, this reality begins to change. As the distance between your world and mine becomes less, more and more people will become frightened.

They do not know what they will find. They are afraid of themselves more than anything. Some of them have come here so they cannot remember what it is they wish to forget... Here is their only sanctuary, and their sanctuary is rapidly crumbling around them. They may try and hurt, on a physical level, others who represent to them this threatened security. But they do it because they do not understand that there is nothing to fear, and that if they accepted themselves, others would accept them too.

They are sometimes hard to live with, but they need to be loved – if not directly, at least indirectly, through understanding of their plight. And they will not understand that either, and it too will increase their fright. But some of them – not all – will recognize the door that is being opened, and they too shall walk through and join you.

Myrna: I hope so. *(pause)*

MOITA: Each will need to choose for himself. All eventually will learn, regardless of how long it seems to take or how rough the world they choose. Someday they grow and accept themselves. So do not despair for those who seem to lag behind. You are only seeing them in this life, and your acceptance now may help them later. *(long silence)*

Jeff: Kelly was saying earlier that you'd told them moving to this area was "a step in the right direction". What pulled them here?

MOITA: Let us say, it is a place where there are options, and an optimum future line converges here. *(pause)* That is as much as you shall get. *(laughter)*

Chris: That's pretty good. Sounds positive, anyway.

Jim: What kind of line was that, again?

MOITA: An optimum future line. This is how those from my reality help you shape your future: by influencing you and those who are open, and helping you to choose the best places for growth – be they positive or negative in your eyes.

ᔑ   ᔑ   ᔑ

We learn the very next morning (October 16th) that another major earthquake has struck California, this time near the Mexican border, causing widespread injuries and damage. On the same day, massive undersea land shifts are blamed for unprecedented tidal waves that flood the French Riviera. November will bring the largest evacuation in North American history as over 200,000 people are forced to leave Mississauga, Ontario, because of a train derailment and fire threatening to loose deadly chlorine gas. Simultaneously, thousands more are evacuated in Florida as a propane car catches fire.

Beginning in November as well, international relations are suddenly revealed as much more precarious than they previously appeared through Iran's seizure of the U.S. Embassy and its employees. This event will touch every person on the planet, not merely in terms of oil supplies but by adding fuel to a potential Great Power struggle over the Middle East, perhaps linked to prophecies of another world war.

Worried as many are about these dangers, special care needs to be given so as not to lose touch at times with our own centre, and thus also with our ability to play a positive role with those around us. This message is given repeatedly during our early months in B.C. – as when Moita answers the two next, quite different questions.

Moita session #114 (Kelly, David, Evelyn / October 12, 1979)

Evelyn: What of my family who live elsewhere in Canada? Do you see anything in our future?

MOITA: Canada is entering a rather difficult period, economically and politically. There are many changes of concepts that will be occurring, and *are* occurring, in this country – not, of course, only here but all around the world. The most important thing to understand in these times is that you are here to become more yourself, and to let go of your own fears and worries about what other people are going to have happen to them. When you try to take on another person's woe, you do not help them and you cripple yourself... If you take one step, accept yourself and love yourself, and let yourself flow outwards into your life. You will see that your life shall change in ways you may not be able to anticipate.

℘ ℘ ℘

Moita session #116 (Kelly and David / October 27, 1979)

David: Your talk of the need to prepare for those who will flee places devastated by Earth changes and other disruptions made me think our work may involve mobilizing resources just to sustain life. Am I right that in order to meet that kind of need, we're not talking about a small, comfortable community evolving spontaneously up in the woods somewhere but more large-scale organizing? It's a problem not knowing what numbers we're talking about.

MOITA: You must also remember there will be many such places set up.

David: Mmm. That's good.

MOITA: There is no doubt that it will not be very easy at first if many come to you for help. But the period of adjustment will not last that long, and of those who come most will find what they need at the time and then branch out to organize their own centre.

Do not worry. Those things that will be needed will be there. If something must be done, you will feel it. The most important thing for you to do is to be comfortable with yourself and your environment, to feel that you have what *you* need.

David: Mm-hmm. It's probably my best time to know what others need too.

MOITA: When you try to anticipate others' needs, you may neglect your own and, by so neglecting your own, not know what they will need either.

℘ ℘ ℘

This coming together, this tuning into oneself that enables our being in deeper touch with others, becomes very real when we gather several weeks later for a second Moita session in the Kindle Valley. As our sense of closeness and trust grows, something like a catalyst *does* seem to be at work, just as Jim anticipated – setting dominoes falling, both during these workshop gatherings and at other times. (And regarding Jim in particular, this is the first time a Kindle Valley friend confirms a link to the group of our reincarnational ancestors that migrated from ancient Kyrionis.)

Moita session #117 (Kelly, David, workshop group / November 5, 1979)

Jim: Three weeks ago, Kelly noticed my face going through some changes in talking to you – changes involving some sort of silver mask on my face as well as a Tibetan kind of scene. I've been curious ever since whether that could possibly relate to the descendants of those from Kyrionis who went east, to the Himalayan region, in order to delve within spiritually – like the Hermit card of the Tarot, which we were talking about. Did my past life have some connection to that? *(but after a pause, doubting Moita will answer)* I know you often don't answer reincarnational questions . . . *(laughter)* . . . of that nature.

MOITA: That is not the reason for my silence. One must . . . communicate with other levels first. But there are two different lives that are involved here, not just one.

The first, with the silver mask, is connected to an ancient warrior race, part of a ceremonial dance before going to war. There is a tribe in Africa that are spiritual descendants of this time period, and they have heightened abilities. They communicate, without drums, directly with each other.

Jim: Could that be the Masai? That just happens to be the tribe in an area of Africa I've studied and always been fascinated with. They were a warrior tribe until the white man came, but have gone downhill ever since. Eventually I wanted to ask you about Africa . . . *(laughter)*

Chris: Beat you to it.

MOITA: There are *reasons* for those interests. Interesting, is it not?

Jim: Mm-hmm! That you should bring up Africa – that's really very interesting.

(After the session, Jim will add: "When she said Africa, I just about hit the roof. It's one of the strongest passions of my intellectual life since I was a kid, and I never understood why.")

MOITA: Now to number two. *(pause)* You did not come from Kyrionis to Tibet in the original . . . voyage (?). You arrived at a later time to that settlement, or . . . form of learning. You were attracted to it, the energy it was putting out, and had made a choice to seek another path than the one you had been on previously. [You] felt that since you had not much background, it would be best to start slowly. So you chose a place that was distant, where you could work through many of your own blocks without the distraction of intense relationships.

Jim: It feels like this life might be somewhat of a balance to that one for me – that I'm strongly attracted to drawing myself into intense relationships.

MOITA: You could say that it is in a way a weaving together of those two lives: the warrior, who was very aggressive and outward; and the monk, who was very inward and thoughtful. That is why both were seen together, for they are both connected to this one, even though at first glance they are very different. So you take strength and wisdom and put it into action.

Jim: So in this life I've got to bring what I've learned from both of them together...
            Is the change-over to the New Age occurring among all the entities as well?

MOITA: It affects the entire realm of creation.

Jim: So there are similar tensions and inertias to overcome on the higher levels as there are here? Is the struggle there too as well as here?

MOITA: Not how you would define struggle. We are ecstatic that it is happening. We look forward to the changes it would bring. We are not opposed. If there are those who are opposed, they are no longer here, for we need not stay in one place. We are not bound to the Earth except by choice. And so, we are willing partners in this endeavour. *(pause)* Are *you* opposed to the partnership?

Jim: Oh, not at all. We need all the help we can get. But there's so much opposing the New Age here, and I wonder if that's a reflection of higher levels – the old gods hanging on somehow... *(pause)*

MOITA: Each one being different in their approach to developing wholeness, there are many problems in communication that arise. These entities are not opposed on this level, but they are working through old, unresolved conflicts from a physical plane. Those who die do not always become reunited with their whole self. There are many who still have not recognized that they have a greater part. And these are the ones who fight most a change in consciousness such as this. It is, in effect, forcing them in a corner.

Since you perceive in our world what you bring to it, dying is not always a freeing experience. And some are caught up in punishment and in retribution, and have not yet seen the futility of this circle of energy they have created. And until they reach a certain point, until they begin to break through their barriers, we cannot assist in their development, for they are free to choose how they will live and exist.

This age is one of their important stepping-stones, for there will be many who are near breaking through. And forcing them to face themselves with the energy that is changing will bring many to our realm of influence, so that they can be guided when they wish to be and know they are accepted and understood. Fear keeps many here. Does that clarify?

Jim: Quite a bit, yes.

Chris: It appears to me that if you're afraid, you're not even really here to what you can enjoy by being here.

MOITA: You are trapped in your own world. And it is true you cannot enjoy the one that is here for all. *(pause)*

Jake: I'm glad to hear that you're willing partners with us. I would like to have a direct awareness of the love of the Earth, and I'm heartened to hear that it's all coming, when it's ready to come. *(pause)*

MOITA: *(slowly)* Many here say "thank you", for we feel the depth to your words.

(Kelly will say afterward that all of a sudden, during the above, she can see entities all over the room. Moita's answer is like a consensus of opinion. One participant will later remark that tall, strong, full-bearded Jake seems to be expressing the feelings of our whole group as well. Many will sense that several layers of conversation are occurring at once between Jake and Moita, as Jake's obvious sincerity deepens the energy level for all.)

Jake: I'd certainly like all the guidance I could get. But I suppose I have to work my own way through most of it.

MOITA: Sometimes the most we can guide is by being a light for others to experience and see. Then they can come to it in their own unique way.

Jake: I want to see the light.

MOITA: The light has been all around you. There is much light here. Open your heart, and then you will feel it and see it more clearly. For it is not with your eyes that you see – it is with your heart.

Your heart is the door that opens onto the world and lets the light of love flow out. And when you have an open heart, you will also meet others who also have a light shining within them. And you see light in the sky and in the Earth, and it shines through you when you touch your feelings of oneness with creation. You have much guidance by staying still and allowing yourself the freedom to flow, for it is within yourself that we reach you, not without...

(Afterwards, Jake describes his experience in this period to Kelly: "Partly I'm trying to see with my eyes, I guess, and she tells me that isn't how you see. At times it seems that I see expressions of pain or sadness. I see expressions that aren't light. I don't know how things feel from your end.")

(Kelly replies: "There's one point where all of a sudden I feel: what's happening here? I can see a fog in front of my face (wherever it is I am). And I can see it flashing, and I know that Moita is presenting images, pictures, different faces to you. I'm not clear why, or what the pictures are. She'll sometimes act as a mirror. I'm feeling a lot of warmth and compassion. At one point I feel almost like tears.")

(Later in the session, Moita turns to not-quite-kempt, long-haired Mike – who, though he had much to ask at the first workshop session, has been silent so far tonight.)

MOITA: And the master of questions has nothing to say? *(laughter)*

Mike: Uh, well, now that you mention it . . . *(laughter)*

A couple of nights ago, I sat down to read one of your pamphlets on dreams.[37] There was a Full Moon beaming in the window right onto my head, and I started thinking about you and my higher self or whatever – just the feeling of it – and something really deep happened. I had to close my eyes and meditate. It was the only way I could deal with it. It made me cry. It's been years since I've felt it that deep in myself. I meditate fairly regularly, and this wasn't a normal trip. I went on an intense journey for an hour or so. I just wondered if you knew about that.

And I should mention: today there was a strong breeze that blew my hair – with all the doors closed – and a grey mist hanging around my head for a couple of seconds. I just thought I'd ask you, since you're more in tune with those things than I am. *(laughter)*

MOITA: Do you remember where you went?

Mike: Uh, no, not really. It's almost like a dream now – going through the universe, but not in orderly sequences. I seem to remember seeing things come out of my own brain, maybe thought-forms out of my third eye – many stars, lights.

MOITA: Exactly what are you asking?

Mike: Well, such an unusual experience – they don't happen that strongly with me very often. And the cue was with this dream workshop pamphlet. I *was* thinking of you; I have strong feelings about you. And we all have entities, right? Seeing as how we're all in this group thing, I was wondering if there was any relationship. I know of other people who have been having dreams, and there's been energy spilling out into the surrounding community. People's minds are moving. I don't know besides that.

MOITA: Well, you all chose to open to each other, to the energy of being together, and to yourselves. My energy can serve as a doorway for many. And in thinking of me, or my presence as you know it, you reactivated your experience of me within you. For while we are here, I am within each, so that you all have that key to your own doors. And that energy triggered your opening more to yourself.

Mike: My higher self?

MOITA: You could say that this was more in the way of a gift from your higher self to you, to this part that is you. There are times when each individual opens enough to experience things of this nature. It is not always something that can be repeated or something that can be done at will. This is why some people say that it is only by the grace of God that things like this are received. But it is more your openness, and your not consciously trying to form an experience, that these kinds of experiences can come.

(This is the first of those markedly altered states that Mike will experience as stimulated by our sessions, some of which have been shared previously.[38] *Now, more after-session comments:)*

Kelly: That experience that you were talking about, Mike? I had one like that this afternoon. It was really strong, like floating out of my body. I could hear Moita talking. It all had to do with love. It all just flowed from one thing to another and lasted about a half-hour. It was amazing. I just kept getting bathed with this fantastic energy, and it kept getting impressed on me the reality of love, what love really is – the energy of *creation*. That's what we're supposedly trying to connect with, and that's one of the purposes of this kind of communication: to let that out so we can connect with that again...

C.: It seemed that whenever Moita would talk to a person, that person's energy would be amplified, and the room would just ring with that person's energy.

Jake: That's the nice thing about holding hands – it sort of spreads itself around, too.

C.: Sometimes it felt the whole group was rising up into the air.

Erica: My hands were going up. My [physical] hand wasn't moving, but I felt it.

(After the tape ends, Jim expresses his feelings about this session, which began with Moita's reincarnational information about him. He says that tonight has been a leap forward in that his last lingering doubts about Moita have been removed. He says he feels cleansed, almost reborn, and very positive about where things are moving.)

ও   ও   ও

Our way is not to prove quite so smooth, nor these feelings quite so unanimous, however. It is Becky of Sunrise Farm, at one of the next two workshop meetings, who brings a visitor named Ike.[39]

I wonder if I should ask Ike to leave, since usual workshop practice is not to let any newcomer detract from the cohesiveness that a group has created over time. But as Ike is known to several group members, who seem accepting of his presence, and since Becky is the one bringing him, I decide to go along. Strictly speaking, it is not a wise decision for the workshop – though perhaps some larger purposes may eventually be served.

If not from genuine interest, we don't know why Ike should want to be here, since he volunteers very little about himself. But I am very much bothered when he does not participate with everyone else in a group fantasy journey I guide – instead, sitting in a chair, merely observing. Possibly this gap in group energy contributes to one participant's fearfully blocking out a likely reincarnational episode and not returning to the workshop thereafter.

When the group shares their experiences, Kelly describes the sequence of vivid dragon symbols she was getting, leading to a sense of integrating the natural/spiritual energy they represent for her. (It is interesting that this ancient image for the higher fairy realms – no, the dragon need not symbolize bondage to the unconscious – was condemned by new Christian converts as a heathen idol when King Arthur bore it into battle on his family banner in that age of transition to Christianity in Britain.)

Making the all-too-common mistake of interpreting another person's experience according to one's own symbolism, Ike's fundamentalist fervor then seizes upon Kelly's dragons as evidence of devil worship! He goes on to accuse me of hypnotically controlling people's minds, and the rest of the group of allowing themselves to be mesmerized. Later he moves on to Moita – whom he, of course, has never experienced – as a further example of sorcery and manipulation. (Only later will we learn that while nearly starving to death up north, Ike experienced a vision of himself as the reincarnation of a certain Old Testament prophet who made similar charges in his own day.)

The group reacts by attempting to explain and reason with Ike – attempts that lead nowhere. Then some members express hurt feelings and anger that he should barge in and lay this trip on us without any firsthand experience of what he's talking about. And this does seem the critical point: only someone who is on the outside looking in could think of applying such out-of-the-way concepts to our group's experiences together. All in all, it is an "interesting" experience, not without its humorous side, to have such opposite perspectives interact face-to-face – especially since Ike will not be the last in the valley to put forth such views.

We will soon learn that Becky has invited Ike to join her at Sunrise Farm, out of their growing friendship and because he is the kind of hardworking, outwardly oriented organizer she feels the farm needs. Actually, it was during the previous "heavy, changeful winter" that Becky's relationship with Chris began coming apart. Now in a few more months – *sadly*, for Kelly and me – Chris will be leaving the farm and B.C., heading first to India and later the U.S.

As for Becky, again to our regret, we will largely lose contact with her as well for most of the next three years, while she and Ike work to get Sunrise Farm into better physical shape. Meanwhile Ike will moderate his view of us, begin to read some *Rays*, and even dream positively about Moita.[40]

Thus both Chris and Becky virtually disappear from our view by the spring of 1980. But as they pursue their separate paths, we are fortunate in the other new friends we are making, particularly in the Kindle Valley. A rather similar trend will nevertheless hold true for our contacts with many of these individuals and couples over the next few years: couples (whom we'd rather perceive as solidly together) coming apart, and individuals withdrawing or leaving the area, for purposes of their own.

But this is jumping too far into the future, when our fall workshop has not yet been allowed its culmination. And though November 26th is the last scheduled meeting, we as a group already know it is but a beginning. The "dominoes" have been set tumbling for many of us during these weekly gatherings – ensuring that they will continue, though less frequently, through the months to come.

A number among the group have also discovered Moita to be a rich touchstone in their meditations between the weekly workshop gatherings. Even more intriguingly, many have found themselves dreaming of great birds – ravens, hawks, eagles – that in some cases have transformed into human or spirit beings.

One of my own such experiences was a virtual repeat of my "Eagles Are Coming!" dream-vision during the same week of early November one year before, as the 1978 energy changes approached.[41N] In this new dream, I unroll a poster to reveal a huge, colourful, shining eagle, which I know is related to our Kindle Valley friends. Later I see people wearing smaller, translucent eagles on their heads, as if mounted on circular hats.

Most spectacularly, Mike awakens from one dream in which Moita, as a column of energy, has been introducing him to his own entity, as another column of energy. Then, before his open eyes, he perceives a huge, three-dimensional eagle, wings outspread, fly upward toward and vanish into his head! We begin with some of Moita's answer to Mike's question about this experience.

Moita/Amar session #122 (Kelly, David, workshop group / November 26, 1979)

MOITA: Well, it is difficult to do this with words. The eagle has for many ages been a symbol of far-seeing, clear seeing, removed from the Earth. And you were in an altered state of consciousness, were you not?, and in that sense far from this Earth...

There are *always* many levels to symbols, and they represent all facets of the symbol. It is symbolic of the rising energy of the Earth toward our level, yet still able to return. It also is symbolic of your desire to touch something that is higher than what you are.

Mike: Did I make that vision? Did I produce that eagle in my mind?

MOITA: Much depends on which "I" you speak of. This "I" that you speak from now is a very small part of you, the larger "I". It is the part that is focused in this time, focused in this particular moment, in this life. But you have an "I" that sees through many other "I's" similar to this one. You call that your soul, but it has an identity as well as you. And when you, as a focus, open yourself to other levels of reality, you create doorways between yourself and your soul-self. Each doorway reacts in a different manner. But each time that door is opened, something goes through from one self to the other.

For some it is not as dramatic as yours. There are those who only get thoughts or insights into who they are and what they are, who connect with that energy and then seek to channel it into their life and help it express itself. Each one of you is unique in how you will react to an opening such as that, and also unique in what you will experience. *(pause)*

David: It seems surprising to me how many of us have, nevertheless, dreamed of a very similar kind of bird. It made me wonder – in addition to all the things you've said, the levels you've spoken of – if there is a higher level coming *down*, as it were, using that kind of symbol as a medium to contact us, to interact with us (?).

(The energy has been rising during the asking of the question. But now, as Moita closes Kelly's eyes, she feels her heart chakra opening and starting to pound. Soon she experiences something like a thick pillar of energy pouring down through her. Her eyes open, but a minute or two elapses till the energy is right to speak. Meanwhile I am feeling the same pounding of my heart, rushes through my body, and sweating, as I wait for Amar – Moita's own higher level – to answer.)

AMAR: Only those that are open will see this sign.

David: How do *you* see its meanings? *(pause)*

AMAR: It is a very powerful presence.

David: Coming to many around the planet now?

AMAR: Only to those who are open. *(pause)* This is not the question that brought me here.

David: Was that question about the prophecies we were discussing earlier?

AMAR: That is in my line.

(Earlier in the evening, Kelly and I summarized for the group the channelings presented in the book Fatima Prophecy: Days of Darkness, Promise of Light*. They are deeply impressive transmissions through Ray Stanford, of the Association for the Understanding of Man, concerning prophecies first communicated during the 1917 visions at Fatima, Portugal. Attributed to the Virgin Mary, their source was actually, as the book clarifies, the Angel of the Mother of Jesus.)*

(These prophecies were later set down in a letter that was to be released in 1960 by the Roman Catholic Church, but was not. They warned of the danger of world war, other social upheavals and Earth changes, as well as the incredible days – said to be near the end of the 20th century – when a "cosmic-solar event" would occur, the poles of the Earth would shift, and the human body would mutate, opening the way for a New Age. These are further examples of probability lines, first seen in the early 20th century and still considered relevant future possibilities as of these 1970s.)

David: What can you share with us at this time about that? *(long pause)*

AMAR: Be bending as the willow, for those who can't bend will be broken. *(pause)* When change comes, it has swift wings; it waits for no man. And if you would be ready, you will prepare yourself. *(pause)*

It is no easy task that we undertake, to turn about the destiny of the world when it is running headlong into disaster. If it was something we could accomplish alone, it would have been done eons ago. *(pause)*

Myrna: Have you read the letter from Our Lady at Fatima? Do you know what She said?

AMAR: She said many things that have come to light in other ways since that passage was blocked. We do not put all of our energy into one place. There are many in the world who have received the same information.

(to Mike:) Do you think I am as fearsome as that?

(Amar is now referring to a subsequent dream Mike experienced, which seemed to involve both Moita and Amar along with futuristic cars.)

Mike: You mean at the garage? Imposing, maybe. You didn't scare me. Very distinguished. *(laughter)* Um, then that was you in my dream?

AMAR: You knew me at the time.

Mike: Yeah, well, I always doubt myself a little bit.

AMAR: You have more truth in you asleep.

Mike: Hmm. I may not have understood the ending of what I was being shown, unless it meant violence in the world.

AMAR: There will be violence... Just as the Earth is erupting in physical disaster, so is man erupting in anger and fear.

Mike: And the best thing we can do is to be as open and as loving as possible, just keep putting good vibes into the Earth? Is there any more positive, strong direction we can take? I guess there's nothing stronger than love. I guess there are probably no shortcuts either, but I just feel like there's . . . I know I have a long way to go myself. How do we turn into power-generating stations to be a good influence on all things?

AMAR: The key is within. You hold it in your hand. I cannot turn the lock. As I said, if this could be done alone, it would already be accomplished.

Jim: When we gather together in a group such as this, are we assisting in this great work of turning the world around?

AMAR: By assisting and helping yourself and in turn helping others to find themselves, you are helping to prepare a road into the future so others may follow after you. There is great purpose here.

Jim: And each of us may have an important role to play in creating that road?

AMAR: Each of you who decides to set his foot upon it will be important to it. And in your heart, you know it is true.

Jim: It sounds like what I'm here for.

AMAR: We hope many are here for the same reason. If you know this is what you are here for, you have already opened the door. Now it is up to you to make your opening not just an idea but a reality. Reality is conceived first in thought and then energy manifested in form. *(pause)*

There are still many universes to choose from. Will you make a world of light or one of darkness? You are at a crossroads, and time is short. Make love your reality – and then we can all be together, and One.

(These last sentences are uttered as Amar looks from one to another of our group, so that each person experiences one of his phrases directed to him or her individually, and yet also to everyone as a whole. This culminates the truly incredible energy ever since I asked my first question – a period when many have found themselves unable to focus on Amar-through-Kelly's face, as it shifts,

becomes transparent, even invisible to some. Mike will say later that not only does he see the pillar of energy surrounding Kelly's body, but everyone in the circle is luminescent to his gaze.)

(After his final speech, Amar closes Kelly's eyes. In a few moments, Moita returns with a quiet laugh. Mike shifts in his chair.)

MOITA: You are squirming?

Mike: Just making a few adjustments. *(laughter)*

MOITA: He has a flair!... *(laughter)*

Helen: How can we help to prepare our children for the changes? Do you think it's good to talk to them about them or to let them be a surprise?

MOITA: Would *you* like that kind of a surprise?

Helen: I think I'd like to know a *little* about it ahead of time.

MOITA: That is why we are here to speak of these matters – so that they won't come as a surprise. It is time for hiding to cease. Each one of you has the right to make choices, and it need not be as frightening as some would make it. Your understanding what will happen, and the reasons why it is happening and the good that can come out of it, would help a great deal to lessen the shock. *(pause)*

Jake: The beauty of your presence overflows my heart.

MOITA: And your acceptance lights mine. *(pause)* And so, now each of you has *seen* love as a force. I know you are all reluctant to let me go. *(laughter)*

Mike: Can you tell us a cosmic joke first? *(laughter)*

MOITA: They must come spontaneously.

Mike: Right. *(pause)*

MOITA: One reason why there have been many experiences here of my presence at other times is [that] in this setting each of you has taken a part of my essence within yourself, so that it may be brought out later.

(said very intently:) I *have* come as a door, and this is how I may be opened. So, I need not say goodnight, for I never truly leave.

(Moita closes her eyes and Kelly returns. But we all by silent agreement continue to hold each other's hands, feeling our energy as a group and Moita's presence within us – which may be one and the same.)

(When we finally collect our minds again, we all have much to say on Amar's first appearance in the Kindle Valley. A few excerpts:)

Jim: From the first time, I've seen Moita change – her face going indistinct and the features changing – and each time it's been more intense. But with *Amar*, it went off the end of the scale! *(laughter)*

(to Kelly) I couldn't focus on your face. There was just a light reflecting off your eyes – that's all I could see for a while.

Kelly: *(to me)* You really looked to me like you were on the spot when you were talking to Amar. You're sitting in this little circle, with all this light blasting down on your head, and you can't get away – like, "Oh gee, I didn't really want to ask that question!"

David: I didn't feel *that* way, but very locked in. I could hardly move or break the gaze. The sense I got of what he was implying about the sign of the eagle was that it was like the Christ-consciousness – "a very powerful presence".

Kelly: A very powerful, *active* thing.

Jim: He sounded almost evasive, repeating "Only those who are open will see this sign." I don't think he *was* evasive – just my own lack of understanding.

Kelly: It seems like when Amar talks, he's speaking to almost a whole different level of person. He talks in universals, and he expects you to make the leap to try and grasp what he means.

Mike: What the *hell* did he mean about "it would have been done eons ago"? That really threw me! It's hard to comprehend the gravity of what seems to be ahead.

Jake: It's been a grave situation for thousands of years.

C.:   Maybe it's a little *more* desperate.

Kelly: This seems to be a little more than the average desperateness. This is like "The End of the World as You Know It"!

Jim: I found it a little bit disturbing in that *he* sounded worried. Somehow I expected this reassurance: "Everything's going to be all right."

David: It depends on us . . .

Mike: We've got to figure out what we're doing! Moita said small groups can have an effect. We've got to do *something* – but what?

Jim: I feel like we're all Frodo . . . and we've all been given the Ring!

৯   ৯   ৯

_____

Chapter 4

CYCLE OF CIVILIZATIONS AND CONSCIOUSNESS

It is no easy task that we undertake, to turn about the destiny of the world when it is running headlong into disaster. If it was something we could accomplish alone, it would have been done eons ago.
— *Amar (November 26, 1979)*

Amar's message to us during his first appearance in the Kindle Valley betrays a perspective not just of millennia but of eons, over which human consciousness first emerged and untold civilizations have arisen and fallen. A deeper understanding of the evolutionary process at work within ourselves today depends on greater insight into these previous ages of Earth.

The Seth channelings through Jane Roberts spoke of higher beings called Speakers,[42] responsible for initiating major advances in the evolution of human consciousness on Earth. It should be expected, then, that a question about the Speakers might open a chapter such as this. But when I asked the following question, I did not expect one of *them* actually to "speak"!

<u>Moita/Amar session #74 (Kelly and David / March 1, 1979)</u>

David: Could you tell us how you understand the concept of the Speakers?

MOITA: *(pause)* Maybe not. *(pause, closes eyes; then slowly:)*

The Speakers are those that grasp the ideas of other realities and form them into something that is more easily related to physical existence. They give these gifts and then others build on them. There are Speakers now who have come, because a new world is being created, to give their ideas. They are also doorway openers. They show others the door, but it is for them to walk through. Some of these types [of beings] work on other levels even more than they do on this one, trying to create the doorways from the top down rather than from the bottom up. *(pause)*

David: Is it possible to speak about the "original" group of Speakers as far as this Earth's evolution is concerned – a group that incarnated, in some sense, on this planet?

(A long silence, her eyes remaining closed. Then they open, beaming toward me a forceful, even fierce, energy that is unmistakeable. There is a huskiness to the voice, as our new visitor begins:)

AMAR: So you wish to know of Speakers, now, do you?! *(pause)* What would you know?

David: From what I've heard, my impression is there was a quantum leap forward or upward in the consciousness of early man when the Speakers came. The Speakers have also been said to have brought the first language to Earth – that called Sumari in the Seth material.[43]

I was asking about the original coming of the Speakers, if it happened at a certain time (?). *(pause)* Could you tell us how you view that?

AMAR: Carefully picking your words, I see! *(I laugh)*

When we first arrived . . . *(pausing, as his use of first person sinks in)* . . . things were much different! There was no such thing as thought. There was much Earth activity during that time, but there were some small areas of apparent quietude where man had developed – as a spirit only, not as a body as yet – but as a spirit with no thought, more like a cloud, something carried on currents with no will of its own.

(Meanwhile, Kelly is receiving images of early times on Earth, as she will describe later: "I get a picture of the world covered with volcanoes, with smoke everywhere, all kinds of activity. There is a lot more land and less water. I can't see anything I recognize as far as continents. It seems there is a little bit of water, and in the middle of that there is a clear space of quiet – almost like a Garden of Eden. I see some coloured fogs moving around – drifting clouds, formless blobs of energy with different colours, almost like amoebas." Note how this fits the idea in Chapter 2 of Clear Light energy beginning to coalesce and divide, eventually materializing in the various life forms, including man.)

AMAR: So we came to give it form, since the time had come – and man was changed and knew thought. In a sense, we awakened latent abilities, small germs of consciousness that were already there – that was our job – so they would develop and become more than blobs.

(Kelly will say afterward that being awakened was "a total shock – like getting hit in the head with a bolt of lightning: all of a sudden finding out you've had amnesia for the last 3,000 years.")

David: Of what manner was your coming?

AMAR: Not with trumpets. *(with a laugh)*

David: In visible form?

AMAR: Not really, no. Not at that time.

David: *As* physical as man was?

AMAR: *(quiet laugh)* That would be hard, to be *as* physical as man was...

David: Even though your consciousness was much different, were you like man in other ways?

AMAR: They did not know what to think of us. We were rather frightening when we woke them up. It is even more difficult than awakening someone in a dream to realize where they are. It was before language was invented – *physical* language. We have not come only once, but you asked of the first.

David: Would you speak of other times, too?

AMAR: Man had much growing to do first, in getting acquainted with this new position he found himself in, before language could be introduced – or the *idea* of language. It grew gradually: transforming thought-forms from one to another, becoming physical and non-physical, sort of flowing back and forth from one state to another. *(pause)*

In a sense, the language was an awakening itself. It was that kind of a language, one that *taught* and *showed* relationships between them and their environment *and us*. We also were physical and were not. It was somewhat like projecting an image well enough to have it seen.

(There is a period of silence while we gaze at each other. Kelly will describe her experience this way: "My eyes begin to change. I have a hard time keeping up with the constant changes in the shape of your face. I see you as an old man again, in this life, with even more character this time than before. There is this really together, inner certainness of self, with no doubting – a lot of strength.")

(A series of faces are then seen. "It seems like I know all these people. It is like seeing reincarnational faces coming up in a line and then going back to the end of the line to wait their turn again." At the same time, "the muscles in the back of my neck are all tightened with Amar's energy. I feel solid, like I have huge, square shoulders and am at least eight feet tall!")

AMAR: Now what do you see?

David: I see a face I've seen before – I describe it as Indian. *(another long pause, as I see the image that has come in the midst of Amar's energy)* It seems timeless – ancient, but not old.

ৎ৵   ৎ৵   ৎ৵

Once before this, in order to explain her own creation by a human group, Moita described the state of humanity in this early period: a fluid, diffuse consciousness which the philosopher Owen Barfield has called "original participation" with the Creative Forces of the universe. She implied then that this cycle is a *spiral* of development, leading to a more conscious, individualized form of creation – at least relatively speaking, what Barfield has termed "final participation."[44]

As the human spirit has transformed, so has the Earth. Consciousness did not evolve *from* matter. The human mind and its world have developed as mirror images, changing together from amorphous subtlety toward greater ego/object distinctiveness . . . and now, as the spiral turns, toward a new level of integration.

Moita session #34 (Kelly, David, Alex / October 18, 1978)

MOITA: In the early times, when man first became near-body, he wasn't body yet. He was in the process of becoming associated with the idea of taking on physical form, although he could still change his form at will. He could also change the forms of those things that were around him, although he did not understand how it was accomplished. It was an instinct. It was not a conscious creation either, in that sense, except it was done with the whole being and there was not a separation from the other levels as there has been at this time.

     Man has the capability to do this [type of creating] now as well as then. He had to go through those steps in between first *(i.e. becoming separated from other levels of spirit)* before he could realize his own responsibility in being able to create other life-forms, becoming as a god – or as he sees what a god is. It is not something that should be done lightly, because the creation is tied to its creator, just as we are all tied to ours.

ৎ৵   ৎ৵   ৎ৵

Mu (Lemuria)

As when humanity was first awakened to thought, this evolution is not always smooth and steady; it has its periods of rapid, culminating transformation. One reason for looking back to past periods of great change is that we are involved in another such time today. Those beings and those parts of ourselves that have participated in earlier transitions can help us now, as we open to them. In these next sessions, some first-time participants begin to learn of Moita's own past.

Moita session #153 (Kelly, David, Jim, Lorna, Cindy / August 16, 1980)

MOITA: I bring change. Change is fearful. But I, by myself, am not bringing it. It is here already. I am but one symptom.

Lorna: But change is always here! I mean, nothing ever does stay the same. So people always have to deal with that.

MOITA: But there are always those who *cannot*. You see it in recent history and in ancient. Many times things have changed and most of the people have fought it.

Lorna: Yeah. What change do you mean? Do you mean a *drastic* change, a change that we can't anticipate, and soon? I feel that you're talking about pretty soon. *(laughter)*

MOITA: Yes.

Lorna: And drastic. Something that hasn't really happened before.

MOITA: Something that *has* happened before, but that man has forgotten.

Lorna: That we don't know about, right. Happened when? *Long* time ago.

MOITA: Very long ago, when I was last here on Earth. Little more than 50,000 of your years.

Lorna: What were you?

MOITA: That will be difficult to say. I did have a body of sorts, and I was female – if you can call that kind of a body one or the other. But the world was definitely not like this. It does not fit this physical description at all!

Lorna: Was it the same mass?

MOITA: It was the same, but it had not solidified to this extent. It has been a process of becoming more dense throughout time. It started off very expanded. So your bodies have become more dense than mine was, as well as your Earth. And the consciousness of man has changed in a like manner.

ৎ ৎ ৎ

Moita session #130 (Kelly, David, workshop group / February 4, 1980)

Louanne: The civilization that Kelly told us you came from 50,000 years ago – she mentioned the name "Mu". Is that correct?

MOITA: That is what it has been called. *(i.e. Mu – or Lemuria, as in the Edgar Cayce readings – located in what is now the South Pacific region)*

Louanne: Okay. In that civilization, did they teach you the same way you're trying to teach us right now – how to develop the flow, to follow our feelings? Did they teach you that, or were you just one of those people within your civilization who had that insight? Like, how did you develop as the presence you are now? *(laughter)* That's loaded, I know.

MOITA: I am the sum of all of my experiences.

Louanne: Did you just have gifted experiences, then, to bring you where you are? I would like to think of myself as you in 50,000 years, you know? That would be great!

MOITA: There is no reason why you cannot be.

Louanne: Yeah, okay, now that I know that I want to stay more open to myself and to light the light within and follow that, I want to know: How did you know to do that 50,000 years ago? Was there someone there to say, "Sit down, I want to tell you a few things"? *(laughter)* Or did you just develop naturally? I don't think *I* would have just developed.

MOITA: When I existed in Mu, there was not this gap between the worlds. Our teachers, or our higher selves, were there for us almost in body to speak with and to experience. But thought was different as well. We did not have the sense of identity that you do. That was not part of man in that time. He was naturally all flow. He had no memory; he had no names for himself or others. He existed only to exist. And when something happened, that was all there was – what was happening in that moment. And when it passed away, the memory of that experience passed with it. It was only in the end of the civilization that we changed.

Louanne: Why did you change? Did you think it was necessary?

MOITA: The seed was sown long before, and language was born. And when language was born, memory came after. When things could be named, they achieved identity. And when we recognized their identity, we could remember them when we named them.

Herb: Our downfall, then, was just another part of this development?

MOITA: Yes. Descending into forgetfulness, so that identity could be born – individuality. *(pause)* And now you are coming out of that, so the two worlds – the two types of consciousness – can be reunited.

Herb: Would you say that's as things swing? Rhythm?

MOITA: I would call it "balance." But "harmony" fits well.

ৡ   ৡ   ৡ

Moita session #156 (Kelly and David / September 16, 1980)

David: I have been wondering what it was like in the previous times of transition on Earth. Could you help to fill out our understanding of previous cultures and give a sense for the overall pattern of development? I know it's a vast area to cover.

MOITA: The entire history of humanity?!

David: I know... Can Mu be considered the first major civilization on Earth? It depends upon how we define that, I guess.

MOITA: For the purposes of your time, Mu is the essential beginning...

David: You said before that the face of the Earth was much different – less dense and more malleable than now?

MOITA: *(pause; closes eyes)* There were some solid parts, and in those places there was life similar in that it had form and substance. It is somewhat like what happens to a gas as it becomes more solid. It descends through layers of awareness, becomes more attached to the physical. When our bodies were in their less physical state, we could flow and mingle with other life-forms and thoughts and elements that were still in that refined state. There were clouds of colour, waves and currents, that were followed. And each experience was the only experience. There was no memory. The end of Mu came when language was born, and memory with it.

David: Did the destruction of the land of Mu occur as the result of destructiveness in the civilization on a par with that of present-day culture?

MOITA: It was not that we became destructive. But once we gave names, once we defined boundaries of existence, the world began to coalesce, to become what we defined. We created sameness where before each moment was unique. With memory, there came comparisons. Things were jumbled together, lost their distinction. Each spirit began to choose what body they would use. The end of an age does not always come from violence. Changing your view of reality changes your world for all time. Memory was the beginning of Atlantis, and the death of Mu...

          This is one place where the female aspect of humanity was blamed for the change, or you could say "the fall from grace".

David: Why the female?

MOITA: We created language. There was a difference between what you would see as the male and female in Mu. I speak better for my part than for the other. The men did not have the seed for creating anything. So when I say "we", I mean literally the females created language and then taught it to men. *(said with characteristic dry humour:)* The apple again.

David: What, then, was the role of men in Mu?...

MOITA: What I said before of the nature of the spirit is what men did, and women too until the change. How can one define a non-role?...

          We did not at the time see what was happening as our decline. We gave Earth to a new race of man, and were left behind... *(tears forming in Moita's eyes)*

          (Some of this feeling for the last days of Mu can be glimpsed in this memory that surfaced in Kelly soon after we met: "the vivid reliving of being a wise-woman in the Mu era. I am standing in a grove of trees – the Singing Grove –with many women sitting on the ground in a circle around it. There is a sense of newness and wonder in my song. It is a time before there are words, but the sounds themselves are an explanation of how the world works. It is the beginning of language, of naming. A great outpouring of love and life is very evident throughout." I think this is probably Moita's own memory, before Kelly became a soul separate from her.)

David: Were there survivors of the civilization that carried parts of the culture to other lands?

MOITA: This was a very gradual process. It did not happen instantaneously. Those who chose their form before the Earth had condensed enough were destroyed by their eagerness. But those who held back, who waited, settled lands that were more stable. *(pause)* Japan and the Philippines were once part of Mu. Some of the other islands are remnants...

(On January 9, 1979, Moita mentioned that "Mu was mostly destroyed before Atlantis started," but also "their destructions overlapped each other in some ways." By the second age of Atlantis, she said, "What was left of Mu...was mostly remnants, or small pockets, isolated islands, mostly tribal cultures.")

David: Did some of the surviving wisdom of Mu feed into Atlantean culture?

MOITA: Those who were newly created and did not understand having no memory effectively cut themselves off from their own beginnings. We [the elders] were scorned because we did not use the power of memory... Buddhism and many other so-called Eastern religions were based on what came before – I would say, the memory of no-memory. Their description of the universe as a void is the closest man could then come to describing no-thought. They wished to return to this different state. Their ancestors saw the potential danger of language, but they failed to see the greater danger of trying to recreate the past; and so, they failed to live in the present.

David: It is a paradox still experienced by many trying to enter into Eastern religions. There is much striving after non-striving, or whichever of the many forms the paradox may take.

MOITA: There was no need for us to strive for non-striving, since it was our nature. They chose to try to change their own natures, instead of accepting themselves as they were.

৯০   ৯০   ৯০

Thus the origin of traditional Far Eastern culture's distinctive emphasis lies in ancient Mu. And the Western fascination with the East over the last several centuries represents the "rising" of Lemuria into modern consciousness, where it may contribute to the new, larger unity man now seeks.

Moita session #164 (Kelly, David, Jim, Peter / November 30, 1980)

Peter: Where did the Native people come from that populate this area? *(i.e. British Columbia)*

MOITA: ...There have been many civilizations on this Earth – some physical, some not – that have been lost in time and upheavals of the Earth. Many of the people that are native to this land are descendants in one way or another of the civilization that existed in what is now the Pacific, one of the first physical civilizations of Earth.

৯০   ৯০   ৯০

Moita session #159 (Kelly, David, Jim / October 19, 1980)

David: I had a dream last night in which a person involved in New Age activities sent us a map of interior B.C. – not very geographically accurate, I don't think. But the Kindle Valley appeared on it with some reference to an ancient civilization. I wonder if that is just symbolic of feelings I have about the energy here. But I wonder too if there may be more than that...

MOITA: Mu was not far from here. This area served as a colony for the continent. Just as Atlantis had its colonies, so we had ours. The Eskimo *(i.e. Inuit)* culture is a remnant of the Mu culture.

David: Was this part of the continent shaped pretty much then the way it is now?

MOITA: In Mu's latter days, this part was fairly solid, although it was still somewhat eruptive.

David: So would I have been involved in a life here at that time – being a colonizer, perhaps?
           (pause)

MOITA: We'll see if you get another dream!...

Jim: It's thought by geologists now that everything west of the Rocky Mountains was previously not a part of North America, and that the mountains were created by this piece of land crashing into the rest of the continent. I was wondering if that land movement could have had something to do with the sinking of Mu and have happened about that time. If so, this piece of land we're on could have been in the middle of the Pacific then. Can you shed any light on that?

MOITA: When Mu sank, there was a great undulation of the Earth's crust. There was much movement, although it was essentially a slower wave. Mu did not sink as quickly as Atlantis... *(pause)* It is not always easy to piece together what parts of the Earth were where when.

Jim: They all seem to have moved around quite a bit.

MOITA: *(laughing)* Most definitely. But I would say that your conjecture is probably accurate, at least as far as the time-frame is concerned.

Jim: So what is now the Kindle Valley could literally have been almost anywhere to the west of here in earlier periods of history.

MOITA: It most certainly was closer to the water.

৯   ৯   ৯

Atlantis

The history of Atlantis spans several ages between the time of Mu and roughly 12,000 years ago.[45] The further back we go in Atlantean civilization, just as in Mu, we find that human consciousness and the Earth itself are more fluid and subtle, more in touch with other levels of spirit, than their apparently more separate and dense states in recent centuries.

One member of the first dream workshop we led together found her fantasy journey, hypersentience session and dreams during the weekend all drawing her back to that energy – and most particularly to fish, even one floating in air!

Moita session #48 (Kelly, David, workshop group / December 3, 1978)

Bonnie: I had a symbol today, Moita. Do you think you could give me some information?

MOITA: Your fish.

Bonnie: Yes, my fish. And my fishes in the pool yesterday when I was in the cavern, and going fishing last night in my dream.

MOITA: Your fish for you is an ancient symbol, one that you have had near you many times. Seeing it suspended in the air is reminiscent of some of the energy and the power that has been associated through you with that particular symbol.

Being a symbol of water, it was also sometimes used as a symbol of Atlantis in some of the cults that sprouted up around the edge of the continent. And you were involved in the sharing of some of that kind of energy that you received from the sea and from those creatures.

There were different types of individuals on the continent. Some were in tune with the elemental energies: fire, water, air and earth. You were more of a specialist in that rather than concentrating solely on the elemental of water, you went more into the life-force and energy of the creatures in the ocean. And in that time, with the Earth being different, water was lighter. And so, a fish from then, if it were placed in the oceans now, would undoubtedly fly . . .

Bonnie: Oh, neat!

MOITA: . . . because it would be so light. And also, the air was heavier, and it would be able to be suspended; it would hold it up.

That is some of the energy that is coming close here – some of the changes that the Earth has gone through and backed off from, that kind of awareness and that kind of closeness to the life that's around. One of the things that we are breaking through, and one of the things that you are rising up to, is a different awareness of the same kind of energy – a more subtle awareness, but still it is essentially the same. Man has learned to be more responsible in some ways for his actions, and hopefully will take that with him – his independence, or his view of self – and use that different view to gain some more insights into what is actually happening around him...

Whenever these ancient symbols come up, it is a very positive sign that you are touching closer to your own roots, and drawing on that energy that you had once and bringing it forward into this life.

৵   ৵   ৵

But the most remembered and, perhaps for now, most relevant juncture in Atlantean history is its dramatic destruction. For the cause of its collapse, we return to the account begun earlier.

Moita session #156 (Kelly and David / September 16, 1980)

David: Can we move now to Atlantis?

MOITA: By leaps and bounds?!

David: I gather it had a very long history. Can you convey to us a sense for the overall pattern of phases it went through? *(pause)*

MOITA: *(eyes closed)* After the birth of memory and things were defined, the birth of will was not far behind: the desire to not only know what was around your environment but to be able to control to a certain extent that environment. Memory became something admired, sought after; and those who had the greatest memories were considered the greatest beings. And soon, once the environment became more orderly, those who had the greatest memory and had developed a greater will began to use it on others like themselves. *(pause)*

So there were seeds from the beginnings – seeds that craved dominion over others, and greed. *(smiles ruefully)* Such small beginnings, and such devastating results. The first small descent, and man plummets! In the age of Atlantis, will ruled man. He did not learn control or the understanding of power, of what its use could do or undo. Atlantis was very much like this culture is now in an outward form. They developed tools to help them control their environment.

David: Were those tools quite similar to the ones developed today?

MOITA: All tools that are concerned with control take on similar forms.

The prophecies that are so quoted from the Bible and other sources [as being about the end-times of this current era] are in some cases the history of Atlantis, a description of its end and a foretelling that this civilization, which was then in its infancy, would follow a similar path.

      ৎ   ৎ   ৎ

Not quite in the same category of tool, but relevant to this point, is the famous Crystal Skull – the real one, notwithstanding cinema fiction – rediscovered in 1927 beneath an altar-stone at Lubaantun, then British Honduras, by Professor Mitchell-Hedges. Formed without melting or grinding, in perfect symmetry, from a single, huge, flawless crystal unique to the area, experts have concluded that known indigenous techniques could not have created it, nor can present-day technology reproduce it.

The jawbone, discovered nearby, is suspected of having once been attached to the female skull with balanced weights, enabling it to move freely as if in speech. Moreover, a light placed beneath the skull was found to focus itself in but one place – behind the eye sockets, causing the eyes to glow. The skull is thought to have been used as an oracle, convincingly if not virtually alive.

As told in Richard Garvin's book *The Crystal Skull*,[46] when a researcher forgot to lock the skull in a safe upon finishing work one day, objects were found to fly around the room and strange noises were heard in its vicinity. Once the investigator, himself a skeptic, was shocked to turn and find a bright white aura surrounding the skull to a distance of nine inches.

In the midst of these occurrences, Mitchell-Hedges's daughter, on a sudden intuition, removed the skull to a Canadian bank vault where no one could any longer touch it. She had grown certain the skull could prove very dangerous to the world if it fell into the wrong hands. As beautiful as it is strange, the skull continues to excite curiosity, including our own.

Moita session #154 (Kelly and David / August 28, 1980)

David: Kelly suggested I ask about the Crystal Skull: where it comes from, by whom it was made and how, the possibilities surrounding it.

(Moita looks down and away from my eyes in order to concentrate better, undoubtedly because of Kelly's interest.)

MOITA: It was manufactured during the earlier periods of Atlantis, and it was used as a communication device between realities. Man is now discovering more about the invisible bands of energy. He has made many leaps since radio. The energy waves that we utilize in order to speak are similar. They are less easily detected, less dense, slower. Each mineral has certain frequencies which it resonates with, and the shape of the stone helps to channel certain energy.

It was made prior to the period of regression that man went through, before we lost contact with this physical reality. It was foreseen that a time would come when communication would be cut off, essentially. So it was thought by some with whom I am acquainted that such an intermediary, that did not depend upon the life-force of a body or a personality of a body, would be more useful in times to come – more dependable.

We could still use it, except it is not together. Unfortunately, it was not foreseen that, as all things can be used for good or ill in the world of man, so also could this. And it was not uninfluenced by those levels that surrounded it. As when you open to any on this plane, the thoughts of those who utilized it influenced what would come through – even more than someone's personality. In a way it has no buffer or filter, so it became a thing of power and a thing of fear for part of its history.

ৡ   ৡ   ৡ

Now we arrive at the sequel to last chapter's exchange in search of Tim's "real" question. Having just deflated the view that extraterrestrials are engaged in physical space travel to Earth these days, Moita keeps the game alive by remarking, "Oh, there *are* conspiracies . . ."

Moita session #94 (Kelly, David, workshop group / June 11, 1979)

Owen: Well, a more evasive answer than that would have indicated you are unwilling to divulge anything about these conspiracies. However, the tone . . . *(laughter)* . . . indicates that you would volunteer some information on one or two of them! *(laughter)*

MOITA: I am a stoolie! *(laughing)* Which one would you like?...

Hazel: Well, would anyone be interested in hearing any explanation about the Bermuda Triangle?

Tim: *(half-whisper)* Yeah!

MOITA: Now we come to the question! *(laughter)* Rather roundabout, I might say...

Now we're getting into alternate realities again. This seems to be the topic for this evening. Simply put, the Bermuda Triangle is a time-flux area, a place where the division between past, present and future is very thin, and sometimes non-existent.

Tim: What about the sinking of Atlantis? Does that have anything to do with it?

MOITA: You are talking of the crystal.

Tim: Yeah.

MOITA: That has a great deal to do with why time is thin there.

(Moita refers now not to the Crystal Skull, but to the giant crystal used by Atlanteans for power generation and much else, according to Edgar Cayce.[47])

Steven: Are people developing crystals again for focusing energy today?

MOITA: They have already, with the laser. And they have used the crystal to store information, as a miniature computer... It *is* a focuser of energy.

Tim: From what source?

MOITA: The air. "Cosmic radiation" is what some people call it. There is energy all around you all the time in many forms. Different crystals have the property of being able to absorb particular types of this energy...

The Atlanteans were, near the end, experimenting with the idea of time travel. They had reached a point where they felt they could in a sense colonize the planet not just at their present time but in their future times as well.

Hazel: How would they get around the problem of the decomposition of matter to its primal state when it reaches the speed of light?

MOITA: When you step through the veil of time, you do not travel at a speed. You travel through a veil, through an imaginary partition that you yourself have created. If you were open, any spot you sat in on the entire planet could be travelled backwards and forwards in time, and you could see what happened to everything around you.

Hazel: And can you do that in your mind now, without sending your body there?

MOITA: People do it with their minds a lot. That's why you have seers, clairvoyants, prophets, from one age to another.

Hazel: And the Atlanteans were trying to find a way to send people there, you say?

MOITA: They wanted to go beyond the spirit. You could say it was the ultimate in conquering the world, to think one could conquer it through time.

Owen: Are you implying the crystal had something to do with this, and the thinness of time in the Bermuda Triangle is a function of those experiments in some way?

MOITA: That is the area that they concentrated their most energy in, and where they conducted their more dramatic experiments. That is one of the things that contributed to the destruction that followed. In trying to warp time, the Earth answered. And this period in history is one of the times they were aiming for, in particular.

Owen: I was wondering about that when you first said something about it.

MOITA: So we get to conspiracies too! *(laughter)*

David: And some of those who are here in their bodies are part of that?

MOITA: Some of those who were lost [in the Bermuda Triangle] were those who were trying to get here in other ways. You cannot have the same entity occupying the same space from two different times without some kind of unusual reaction – something like an explosion, but not an explosion either. Many of the people that disappear in that area are those entities that are, in that time, trying to come forward. They meet somewhere in the middle and self-destruct in a way – not permanently; nothing is permanent. But of course, they're not the only ones.

It is not always easy to say who was in Atlantis, and doing what, from looking at them in this life and what they do now. Many changes go on in-between, and, depending on which aspect of their souls they are showing . . . (I have a dangling sentence I cannot finish.) The one from Atlantis would have already experienced the explosion [that destroyed the continent] in his time and then gone on to develop as an entity. Many of those would be very careful people in a lot of ways, especially as far as this kind of energy is concerned. They would be reluctant to get back into it because of that memory...

Hazel: You mean that these experiments that were failures would leave a deep impression on these entities of the harmfulness of them, and they would take a dim view of experiments with time travel?

MOITA: Mm-hmm, or other types of energy. Some people who have come back here from Atlantis now are those that are most into the anti-nuclear movement, because it was an energy that was similar to that that destroyed Atlantis. And also, many of the young people who were in the war – either World War I or World War II – were born very quickly afterwards in the baby boom. Many of those were ones who were most against war in this last decade, because they remembered very freshly what it was like to be in battle.

ॐ   ॐ   ॐ

As members of that same generation and active in anti-war and anti-nuclear causes, it would make sense that Kelly and I were among those present at the destruction of Atlantis.

A few months before we met in this life, Kelly had this experience:

I didn't start using [my crystal] ball regularly...till after a man I'd never seen before visited our house. Without my being aware of it, he happened to touch my chair, and this weird electric shock ran all through my head and body. Wanting to know more, I held the crystal ball with my eyes closed. I saw this man and me standing on a hill, raising our arms to the sky, and lightning coming down in answer. I didn't know what it meant at the time, but the contact with this man seemed to awaken something in me. [48]

It is during the hypersentience session we held at Sunrise Farm in July 1979 that Kelly relived the incarnation ending with this lightning scene. She learned that she was among those who, having been forewarned of the danger, left the doomed continent in time, carrying to Egypt what could be preserved of Atlantean knowledge and wisdom. The man whose presence triggered the original memory was her twin brother, lover and soul-mate in that life (her "other half"). After teaching the local inhabitants for a time, the two of them grew homesick and returned by boat to the scene of devastation. Finding that only the mountains remained above the waves of the Atlantic, they became entrapped in mud and debris. They called the lightning down so they could consciously die there together.

Again, the session in which Moita gives her overview of world history is an opportunity for me to ask a number of questions related to Kelly's hypersentience experience. Moita's succinct answers shed important light on the mystery linking Egyptian, Mayan, Incan and even Judeo-Christian civilization, and related Earth changes. She confirms what many researchers have suspected: that these cultures drew upon a previous civilization not recognized by our conventional history. And if the Mayan calendar that ends a cycle in 2012 traces back to Atlantean knowledge, it may explain why Atlanteans focused on this time period now for their time-travel experiments.

Moita session #156 (Kelly and David / September 16, 1980)

David: Did I know Kelly in that life? Did we leave Atlantis around the same time?

MOITA: You left Atlantis around the same time, but you went north and she south. You travelled south later, but she had gone. And so, in some ways you were together, in others apart.

David: Was the shape of Africa different then, such that we went to Egypt rather than someplace further west [in Africa]?

MOITA: Egypt was almost entirely on the [western] coast. The sinking of the Atlantean continent started a rise in the land off the then continental shelf. The "Great Rift" is one remnant of what once was the coastline.

(The Great Rift is a huge scar across the face of northeastern Africa today. So, according to this, all the land to the west of it would have risen since Atlantis's sinking.)

David: Was there a shift in the Earth's poles around that time?

MOITA: There was. Egypt was one place that was less affected than many other places...

David: Were there other survivors, or earlier colonizers, who carried aspects of Atlantean culture elsewhere?

MOITA: There was one [such carry-over] in Peru, and the Mayans were also descended from Atlanteans.

What started off as a carefully kept record of events [of Atlantis's history and destruction] quickly became, when understanding of its technology was lost, a story of things that were little understood – [regarded by later cultures as] legend, and then prophecy. For how could it relate to themselves when they could see nothing that even seemed similar to that which was described? *(pause)* By believing in this as prophecy, man set himself upon the road to rediscover those things which were mentioned but whose knowledge had been lost.

(Long pause, as Moita gazes very pointedly into my eyes.)

David: There seems to be a great intentness in your look, as if you're saying I was involved.

MOITA: As I was one who helped to create language, so you were one who sought to preserve the records and brought them to Egypt.

(Moita's point, in part, then, is that I have some responsibility for the eventual effect of those records, once their true understanding became lost. And here I am again, keeping records! The above is the second time Moita speaks of my own life then. The first appears below.)

৯ ৯ ৯

Moita session #56 (Kelly and David / January 9, 1979)

David: Are portions of Atlantis going to be rising within our lifetimes?

MOITA: I *hope* so, but it may be some time before one recognizes them as portions. There is still that temple in Egypt to be uncovered... You were involved in putting in the records...

(Edgar Cayce predicted that two temples from Atlantean times would be discovered, one having sunk beneath the ocean with the destruction of the continent and the other – a pyramid located between the Sphinx and the Nile River at Gizeh – buried under sand. Both temples were said to contain all the records from Atlantean civilization.[49])

MOITA: There was a reason why so many records of Atlantis were destroyed or buried. There was so much arrogance in the people, it was better that way, so your world had a chance to start off more fresh. But the arrogance is still there, and the rediscovery of Atlantis will take some of that from you.

৯ ৯ ৯

Egypt

Nourished in its beginnings by the gifts of a dying civilization, Egypt carried through its long history into the origins of European culture a tradition of ancient wisdom. More than anything else, the pyramids have symbolized that hidden and, to some extent, lost awareness.

Moita session #96 (Kelly, David, Owen, Hazel / June 24, 1979)

MOITA: The pyramid has long been used as an instrument to gather energy, physically and mentally... You could say that that symbol describes the type of energy base from which we work... It is a base of power, of energy, of creativity; and the more people there are at the base of a pyramid, the more energy there is coming through the top.

ço   ço   ço

Moita session #139 (Kelly, David, workshop group / April 7, 1980)

Don: Is it beneficial to meditate under a manmade pyramid?

MOITA: The form of the pyramid can help to focus a great deal of energy. That is why it was built in that particular shape. It will all depend upon the individual person who is inside. For some, the amount of energy that can be generated will be too much and they will not benefit from the experience. They will become less grounded; their awareness will dissipate into air. For others, it may be what they need. They may be ready to accept it, do something with it. And then there are some who would not notice it at all. They would not be aware of any change in energy...

Isabel: Does the Great Pyramid contain the answers to our past and our future? Will they be found in this century?

MOITA: The Great Pyramid...contains many predictions of the past, but its predictions do not go past the end of this age... Some have already been brought to light. Much of the importance of the pyramid is being lost, for it has served its purpose in having been built as a symbol, as a focus point, in ages before this one.

Isabel: Was that its only purpose, as a symbol?

MOITA: A symbol serves its purpose to raise the awareness of man. And when man's awareness is raised to a certain level, he understands the symbol and therefore has no need of it anymore. That is how a symbol serves its purpose. That is how knowledge serves its purpose, in bringing you to the point where you can go beyond it.

Isabel: Has the world reached that point, then?

MOITA: What happens to man after the age of the pyramid's predictions will be an open-ended proposition, [and the more so] the fewer symbols he brings with him. For, just as a symbol can help to raise man's awareness, at a certain point it will also contain it and keep it from going beyond the symbol itself.

ço   ço   ço

What is potentially true of the pyramid applies equally to the symbolism of any religions or secular ideologies today. Once a symbol becomes an idol, dogma and intolerance are not far behind.

Gwen: Religions are there to help people, I guess. But it's complicated for everybody because each of them, it seems, figures it is the one best way...

MOITA: It seems to be a matter of becoming too wound up in the part of the truth you have seen, and believing it is the whole picture instead of just one part – not just with religion, but with any view of the world as it is. Each person seeing the universe from [their] own perspective, if they fail to see there is more than one universe, they will naturally assume what they have seen is all there is.

      Religion is, relatively speaking, rather new. It is an attempt to regain a lost unity with the soul and the spirit. At one time, this level and your level were not separated; they were one, freely interacting. When the separation began, there was an attempt to put into symbols the awareness that was being lost. But once the awareness was lost completely, the understanding of the symbols was gone as well. And so, we are now entering an age when the symbols will become alive and fall away – because the understanding will once more be gained, and then symbols are no longer necessary.

ൟ   ൟ   ൟ

In regaining that understanding, one of the first steps is righting imbalances, for the depth beyond the symbol is reached through our own centre. The masculine emphasis of the pyramids had a feminine counterpart. Present-day technocracy requires a similar corrective.

Moita session #96 (Kelly, David, Owen, Hazel / June 24, 1979)

Hazel: You remind me, Moita, of my grandmother and my aunts while I was growing up in the American South. Your personality and some of the feelings and vibrations I get from you remind me of that very, very peaceful serenity. And that reminds me in some ways of Isis, the Egyptian "Great Mother" goddess. Man has gone away from that strongly feminine aspect. I think it once might have been more a part of his consciousness.

      You're a female? Well, I mean, if you people have those sorts of ideas?

MOITA: Let us say that this particular aspect of me is feminine in nature, and man was once very closely connected with this level...

Hazel: *(interrupting)* Well, it just isn't as predominant. Man is more polarized towards control.

MOITA: He is more isolated from his environment. He controls nothing.

Hazel: Mmm. He controls himself.

MOITA: Ah, does he now?! He may be control-oriented, but he still does not control anything.

Hazel: *(laughing with the rest of us)* True.

ൟ   ൟ   ൟ

Comments by Owen and Hazel are a springboard for quite a dissertation by Moita during a subsequent private session. It beautifully weaves together many themes in this chapter.

Moita session #98 (Kelly and David / July 3, 1979)

David: Both Owen and Hazel have said they feel a strong link to Isis in you. Also, Hazel has brought up the idea that many of the souls present on Earth now trace their histories back through a different planet – this, from a book they have read. Do you have any remarks on either or both of these?

MOITA: As far as different souls coming to Earth from other planets, there are some things I can say on that. I perceive it is more a problem with definition than it is with the concept itself. As the Earth has evolved, it has had other forms. It has not always looked as it does now, nor has it always been composed of the same elements. It has gone through many stages of development. The Earth I knew was nothing like this Earth and could very well be considered another planet.

(At this point, both Kelly and I think of Rudolf Steiner's referring to different stages in the evolution of Earth and human consciousness by using the names of other planets, or other classical gods as if they were the names of planets.[50] That Earth itself may in previous ages have appeared a different planet, just as man's form has changed through time, may shed further light on contacts now with apparent extraterrestrials.)

MOITA: There are different backgrounds to souls who have experienced the other forms of Earth. Some who have left in the earlier period of history and have had little contact in between would find it difficult to manifest on this plane without a great deal of disorienting information coming through. They would have a sketchy background to the realities that others are aware of here and now. There would be a very concrete gap in communication.

You know that words are not necessarily the easiest part of the communication, and that the vehicle through which we speak dictates much what can be said in what manner. If one with this lack of background would choose to communicate with others, the concepts that they consider normal would...feel very alien to the vehicle they were using, and the terms they would choose would have the colour of that alien feeling to them. This is in reference to where Hazel and Owen received this information – the books that were written on these souls. The information has to have come from somewhere!

It is true that some entities from other spheres of influence travel to Earth from time to time in order to broaden their own perception, to let go of some of their concepts of reality, expand their view. Mostly, those who are here are those who began here. It is not in the way of the universe to confuse or muddle a kind of spirit's development with many foreign influences. You do not take a polar bear and put it in the desert. *(laughter)* It would not survive long, and it would not benefit either...

Owen and Hazel have many strong memories of the time of Egypt. To them it is more of an ancient civilization than a new one, as it is for me. *(She notices my quizzical look.)* Not trying to be confusing there!

David: You mean "new" from the viewpoint of your own incarnation?

MOITA: *(nodding assent)* Many of the people involved in Atlantis reincarnated in Egypt because of some of its parallels in development and its connection to the Atlantean continent before the continent fell. The atmosphere was more open in Egypt's early history to many of the psychic creative forces that were made aware in Atlantis.

The Atlanteans – some of them – looked on Mu as the mother culture. If one were to look at the two civilizations in the philosophy of the East, Mu would be the mother element and Atlantis would be the father element, or one would be the intuitive and the other the intellect. Even though the creative forces were utilized in the Atlantean culture, the type of manifesting was different, or perhaps the reason for it was different. And Egypt was very much into the two polarities. I, as a representative in feel for the Mu culture, would bring up many memories of the feminine elements in Egypt for Owen and Hazel. For them those memories are fresher.

Everyone connects things and people with experiences of their own that have a similar feel, even though they may not be at all connected. It is something...important to be aware of: that you make judgments, without even knowing it, by connecting things to others or other unrelated instances...

One reason why there are so many apparently confused beings on the planet now is because of the different lines of development that are coming together in this end of an age. You have those who were at the end of Mu, and who continued on Earth, that are here mostly to try to avoid destruction from their own pasts; and those from Atlantis who are here to remake choices that were once made. Unfortunately, not all will remake this choice, but they have the opportunity to do so at this time.

And there are many civilizations that have decayed and fallen through the use of power – like Egypt and Greece – who are also coming together now to either fight old battles that have not been forgotten or remake the history of their own past and change the future. In a period of time such as this when the world is in flux, it is difficult to separate the many influences and strands of development that are together, and it can appear to be very confusing.

But the Earth's problems have been caused by man's own mistakes, and he cannot conveniently put the blame on other entities that are flooding the world. Too often he has used things such as that as scapegoats to escape his own responsibility. We would not have that happen, if it can be avoided. This is what the New Age is for: to wake man up and make him realize that the world is his, and its problems are also.

I have made a speech!

ॐ   ॐ   ॐ

Chapter 5

FROM GENESIS TO END-TIMES

That portion of humanity's current "cycle of consciousness" represented by the Judeo-Christian tradition claims but a few thousand years out of the many millennia stretching back through Egypt, Atlantis and Mu. For this chapter, focusing within that one tradition alone, we see that a veil was drawn across the understandings and failings of previous civilizations. Learning was to begin anew, with an increasingly rational, literal, moral emphasis suited to a further stage in the development of ego-consciousness.

Today, however, when some form of Christianity has been carried into all nations, a majority of the world's peoples continue to inhabit non-Christian spiritual environments – to the extent their lives are meaningfully defined at all in non-secular terms. Keeping this broader perspective in mind should help in understanding Moita's attempts to uncover the *essential* truths hidden within our questions on Biblical topics.

Being the religious tradition with which we in the West are most familiar, the gaps in this brief survey will be obvious – and what *is* said more controversial. The point is that these excerpts communicate certain *perspectives*, more or less whole, channeled through human beings, with the goal that we look at some of the founding experiences of our civilization with a fresher eye, a more open mind.

Moita session #130 (Kelly, David, workshop group / February 4, 1980)

Barb: What role does the Bible play in civilization as *we* know it? What is the purpose of the Bible? Because that's the closest thing that I can relate to what *you* are, what the Bible teaches about life hereafter. Do you know who wrote the Bible and why we have it?

MOITA: In any writing from one level to another, you must consider that it is filtered through human beings, through the personality that they have at the time, just as this communication – although it is a very direct one – is still filtered and it is not totally true from my level. So it is the same with everything that comes through to the Earth. That is the reason why Jesus came to the Earth in person: so that the words would have meaning, so that there would be a living Presence that was *not* filtered by a man or a woman who had their own . . . inequities within themselves, impurities or dense vibrations.

Any inspirational writing can serve to heighten your own intuition. The result of looking within yourself – of finding the God within you – will make the writings unnecessary. Until man can see that the love of the universe is an energy that can flow from him and have a *real* effect upon his reality, he will continue to lean on the inspiration of others.

These experiences are very individual, and everyone interprets them all differently. The

Bible is no different. Many battles have been waged over interpretations of someone else's experience whom no one has ever met. And no one has been able to ask the question of them, how did they view it? And words can get lost and changed throughout time.

For some, it serves as an important doorway; for others, it serves as a block. It is all dependent upon who you are and how you view your purpose, how whole you have become within yourself, how alone you can stand within the universe – knowing you are *not* alone, but not having to lean upon a tree for support, one that you have experienced in its growth to some extent, but one that is not you.

⋙ ⋙ ⋙

Old Testament

The questions that have been asked of Moita concerning Old Testament events are very few, but we can say that in the following questions we have at least begun at the beginning. Moita's answers here to questions about the biblical creation story can be compared to her fuller treatments of the origin of the universe in Chapter 2.

Moita session #113 (Kelly, David, Becky, Chris, Dawn, Greg, Rick / September 29, 1979)

Dawn: This question may seem sort of silly, but I was given a book about the creation of the world according to the Bible by [a certain denomination]. They really believe in a literal seven-day creation. I guess that's a big question to ask *(laughs)* – about the creation, to ask how it occurred.

MOITA: Well, perhaps a more accurate interpretation would be seven stages, although one could look at it in many lights. If you exist in a place where time has no meaning, how can you judge if it is what you call a day? For some, a day may mean a thousand years here.

(Interestingly, this echoes the verse in 2 Peter 3:8: "But, beloved, be not ignorant of this one thing, that one day is with the Lord as a thousand years, and a thousand years as one day." [51])

Dawn: Yeah, I knew the question was sort of clumsy. *(laughs)* I knew that answer could not be clear yes or no.

Greg: But were there seven stages?

MOITA: If you need to divide it up...

Dawn: Can you describe – hmm, here's another huge, vague question – the Creator, God?

MOITA: *No. (laughter)* That is something that cannot be described.

Dawn: Yeah. Maybe that's the wrong word, then.

MOITA: It is a difficult idea that you are trying to get across, so it is hard to choose the right words for it. It is a vague feeling, a reaching out for understanding. "God" is a word, but a word that means something different for each. If God is All, He is everything you can conceive of Him, and then He is more.

Greg: You refer to God as "He". Would you say it would be equally She, or it is equally neither?

MOITA: I would say that the view that most people hold of God is of the more masculine, but I would not say He is one or the other. It is just a matter of convenience to speak of it that way. What else would I use?

Greg: "It"?

MOITA: "It" . . . does not sound right either.

℅   ℅   ℅

Moita session #115 (Kelly, David, workshop group / October 15, 1979)

Mike: How did we come into being? *(pause)*

MOITA: Creation is an act of focus and a sharing of energy. And for me, a sharing of energy is also an act of love. How would *you* describe it?

Mike: Creation? Uh, well, love is the highest thing I can think of. So, whatever life is, if it was created, must have been created through some kind of love. But . . . I just don't understand how it came about. I can't comprehend God and the universe and all these things. So, I mean, I'm ignorant at the moment.

MOITA: There are many images that would suffice to explain, in part. Many have been used already. Taking a filled cup of water and turning it upside down and letting its contents spill – sharing, growing, each droplet being an individual essence. There is one image. The idea of the seed on the flower, or the many seeds, being picked up by the wind and flown over the Earth, each one part of the original plant, each one separate. You give your love to someone else. They take it and change it until you may not recognize it. And yet you have, in part, created a new person by giving of yourself, and they have helped you by changing. *(pause)* You see? Creation happens all around you.

℅   ℅   ℅

In the following two excerpts, Moita shows how two phenomena from the Old Testament era – one that seems a curiosity, while bearing a mystery; the other traditionally regarded as the Holiest of Holies, Indiana Jones notwithstanding – can be better understood within the wider context of humanity's evolution of consciousness.

Moita session #155 (Kelly, David, Judi / August 30, 1980)

Judi: This has been bugging me for a long time: the Methuselah question. Why is the oldest man in recorded history passed over in the Bible without any exclamation point or explanation? It strikes me as an indication that there was a time when people knew that physical existence was able to go on and on and on, much longer than we allow ourselves to stay in our bodies now. That's the only way my logical mind can make sense of it.

MOITA: You are *close. (Judi laughs)* Man's body was different then. It was not as dense as it is now; and so, it did not decay as quickly. Your energy is tighter, more bound up in a closer sphere. Bodies were looser. They flowed more easily back and forth between worlds. The spirit was more aware of renewing the physical. Now that awareness has grown very dim.

It is still true that man renews his physical, but he grows weary of the task very soon; and not being aware of the process, it becomes difficult to do, on an unconscious level, after a certain period of time. It is somewhat more complicated or complex with a denser form than it is with the less dense body man had before.

And the Bible is not the only place you will find references to men who have gone beyond what you would deem a reasonable length of time on Earth. In Egypt you will find more than one who is recorded – some with, and some without, exclamation points. *(laughter)*

୨ଚ   ୨ଚ   ୨ଚ

Moita session #135B (Kelly, David, Mike, 6 others / March 2, 1980)

Mike: The Ark of the Covenant in the Old Testament – people thought the voice that came out of it was the voice of God. Was that a symbolic thing? Was that something related to the Speakers?

MOITA: There was more than one Ark. The one that you speak of was one of many. And it was, in a sense, an actual machine... You could say it was similar to what is happening now – a communication between levels of being, an aid in focusing on this plane from another, instead of using a human channel. It was built at a time when the worlds had already separated a fair bit but had not retreated *this* far. If it were built, it would still generate a great deal of energy, but it would be difficult for us to utilize it in the same manner as before.

Mike: Who was speaking through it? Well, I guess it could be anybody.

MOITA: Or any number. It would not have to be just one voice, or rather I should say one thought-focus. We can combine.

୨ଚ   ୨ଚ   ୨ଚ

So too do traditional concepts like heaven and hell shed their opaque stereotypes when viewed as stages in an evolution of consciousness that can be recognized and grown through or toward. The questioner below refers to a book we have referenced in our workshops, already cited in Chapter 3.

Moita session #137 (Kelly, David, workshop group / March 17, 1980)

Louanne: In *Fatima Prophecy*, they speak of eight levels, heaven being at the top and hell being at the bottom.[52N] They put it in good terms for us everyday people so we can understand it. Are we in all of those levels at once?

MOITA: Those are levels of awareness, and the hell they speak of is the physical – being the densest or the lowest in vibration. You *are* in all of them at once, but when you are in this one you are not aware of the others. As you progress through each, you become aware of those you have passed through and know that there are those that you are going to. But it is not until you have reached the highest you can attain that you can remember all at once and *be* all at once. It is not something that you could connect with in this immediate time/place, but something that you will gradually grow to remember as your awareness expands itself, as you can encompass more memory and more experience.

Louanne: Are all of us capable of reaching that highest level . . .

MOITA: Yes.

Louanne: . . . in one of our lives?

MOITA: It is not so much that you reach it in a life. There are few that reach that level from a physical plane alone. Most develop basic talents in a physical, and go on to develop them further in a spiritual one and continue their growth on other planes – so that man here does not see the fruits of his own labour, except in those moments in man's history when one from a very high level comes in a physical form to show that it is possible to be both.

Louanne: For instance, Jesus? Mother Mary? Are these kinds of levels what you're referring to? Yourself?

MOITA: What you have spoken of first. I have not taken on a physical in a very long time, nor do I have plans for so doing. But there have been Masters that have walked the Earth, and their purpose has been to show man, as an example, the presence, the energy, the love, that is available in the universe if man will open himself up and let it touch him...

Right now, there is little love available to see with the eyes, but there has always been love available to feel with the heart, if one would open. And many have found that path, and many who have found it have left [the earth-plane]. And so, you see about you those who have not learned, as well as some of those who *are learning*. So you judge mankind from this angle and do not see all of those who have attained their awareness – who are *still* here but cannot be seen, only felt. You are climbing a great mountain.

๛   ๛   ๛

New Testament

With this mention of a high Being walking the Earth, we make our transition to the New Testament. Our first excerpts combine to suggest how far a religion can stray from the outlook of its original prophet and exemplar – in this case, how great can be the disparity between Jesus's own reality and the Jesus that people have been willing to accept. Or at the very least, if this presumes too much, these readings illustrate some very different perceptions of what that reality was. Below Moita gives her perspective on Christ's first coming, and only a hint beyond it.

Moita session #113 (Kelly, David, Becky, Chris, Dawn, Greg, Rick /September 29, 1979)

Rick: I want to ask about the individual, if indeed there was one, whom we call Jesus.

MOITA: Do you want to know if Jesus was a real person? If he was aware where he came from? What Jesus thought?

Rick: I'm wondering how he interacted with the people around him.

MOITA: He accepted them as they were and loved them. And he felt pain for them, but he knew he could not take their pain from them – that they had to do it themselves. You will find references in the Bible to Jesus's ability to see thought-forms, and that he said if each of you could see what he could see, the world would weep. *(tears coming to her eyes, matching the feeling in her voice; pause)*

     I will say yes, he was a real man, and he was from . . . a different level than I.

Rick: You say he accepted people. That sounds somehow passive, whereas he's generally thought of as having a very active role.

MOITA: Do you think it is easy to accept others?

Rick: No. *(laughter)* But when you talked about his being able to visualize thought-forms, I remember him seeing a "demon" in a person and telling it to leave. Somehow that sounds like more than just accepting the person. He's taking an active role, trying to dictate what goes on with the other person.

(Previously in this session, Moita said people are usually unaware of what their thoughts do to other people. She mentioned how the effects of people's unacknowledged negative thoughts were interpreted in Jesus's time as the work of "demons". See Chapter 9 for the full discussion.)

MOITA: Ah, but you see, we are looking at only one level. You do not know for sure the kind of interactions that went on between Christ and the person's entity. You do not know why the person was born in that time. And perhaps he was born only to be there at that moment so that Christ could show what could be done with the energy that he brought – since nothing is an accident, and everything is planned out ahead of time, especially in a life of a Great Teacher.

Greg: Are there comparable Great Teachers, or one, among us on Earth today? *(voice fading out, as if feeling he shouldn't be asking)*

MOITA: Today?

Greg: Yes.

MOITA: There is . . . but he is as yet unknown.

(Moita looks toward me in silence, perhaps expecting a question – but my mind is blank.)

In a future chapter, Amar himself will be more forthcoming about this as yet unknown Teacher. But on the day after Christmas 1979, when I ask about the mission of such a Being, Moita answers,

"The only thing I can say at this moment is to expect the unexpected. We must walk a fine line." Meanwhile Kelly gets flashing images she cannot understand – though one seems to be of Christ saying to a crowd, "Come unto Me." The meaning she gets from "walk a fine line" is that such an incarnation is planned so carefully, a wrong word in the wrong place and time would be like unravelling many preparations already under way.

ॐ ॐ ॐ

Moita session #124 (Kelly, David, Duggan, Caroline, 4 others / December 16, 1979)

Duggan: I'm having a lot of confusion and wondering about Christianity. That's what we grew up with in this country, and I don't know whether I can accept it. I don't know whether what the church is teaching is a distortion of what Christianity was or was intended to be. Could you enlighten me at all?...

MOITA: In any question like this, there are so many aspects to it. There are many angles, possible avenues, to explore.

Duggan: Why did Christianity leave out reincarnation? Was it ever a part of its teachings?...

MOITA: Yes, it was. There are still some veiled references to it they have not managed to eradicate. There was a desire on the part of the people who became powerful in the beginning of the church to seem more different than anything else that had been offered before. Christ came not just for those who considered themselves "chosen" – he came for *all* men – and they were jealous of this.

     For you see, there were so many prophecies that heralded his arrival for them and them alone, that when he did make himself manifest and they found he was not what they expected, and that he was here to open up all men to themselves and to each other, they did not want to lose this feeling of being special. It gave them a sense of importance and power over others. You could say their egos were hurt, when they had been raised to believe this so strongly, to find the reality was different.

     If they left in reincarnation, there would be many difficult questions that would arise. For instance, if one could incarnate in a different religion, how would you know who were the chosen ones? Was it just a body that would happen to be there at the time? Would your best friend perhaps have been in India or in China and worshipped Buddha or even known him, and yet now he is your neighbour and married to your daughter? It could be very ticklish, in many ways. That is only one.

     It is not the first time that something has been given to the church and then not released to the people. And so, Christ tried to get his message across in words they would not be able to lose, saying such simple things as "doing unto others", which includes your enemies as well as your friends. It is not that hard to see that his teachings were universal and were not merely directed at those who expected him and then did not want him. You could also say, on another level, that this is a lesson in expectations.

ళ ళ ళ

Moita session #122 (Kelly, David, workshop group / November 26, 1979)

Gary: I'm not too curious about past lives ever, because I know we've got to learn right now at the present time. But two of the most powerful experiences of my life have been when I've seen a vision of the Christ. I'm just wondering if you could tell me if I lived at the time when he was on Earth [and] if I may have seen him.

MOITA: It is not uncommon for those who have seen Christ once to wish to be near him a second time. There are many New Age people who have been here before – if not with Christ, with other Masters. *(pause)*

    There are many reasons why you are adamant against churches. One who has walked the same road will know when there are things being done that were not intended.

Gary: Um, I don't follow that last part.

MOITA: I think others do. *(smiling)* Perhaps you are too close to it. Let us say, if you came in a life and developed a method of meditation that would help others to know themselves, and then returned a number of years down the road into another life where this form of meditation had become a school of thought which was being utilized to control others rather than teaching them to free themselves, you would . . .

(This sentence is interrupted by the need to change tapes. Moita's thought is obviously that Christianity has, to some extent, followed the same pattern.)

MOITA: I think you understand my drift.

Gary: Yeah, it just came to me.

MOITA: You would not be happy with changes that have been brought about.

Gary: So I *have* seen him before (?). *(pause)* It's like pulling teeth – I feel like a dentist! *(laughter)*

MOITA: Do you really *need* an answer?

Gary: No, you're right, I really don't – because he's near anyway, so it really doesn't matter. But you've helped me understand my feelings about organized religion. Maybe I can lose that anger now a little bit...

MOITA: It will not help you.

Gary: Right. It gets in the way of the love you're supposed to feel – even for your enemies.

ళ ళ ళ

Christ brought a presence and message of love, an acceptance of diversity rather than narrow-minded bigotry or zealotry. It is also true that Christ's mission involved him more directly with the clash of opposing forces, as finally in his own arrest and crucifixion – making way, in Christian belief, for the resurrection, which can symbolize reconciliation in a higher consciousness.

Rightly understood, then, Christianity is one of many modern paths no longer looking back to the nirvana of no-memory in Mu but working toward the recovery of wholeness, a new level of integration. Symbolically, the crucifixion may be seen as a turning-point in this evolution, which makes it also a point of controversy when different views of the universe meet.

The question asked below is one specific part of a more general question about the differences between the Edgar Cayce and Seth communications. Moita's response to the larger question is that Cayce spoke for the whole of human awareness while Seth offered his own individual outlook on reality.[53]

Moita session #137 (Kelly, David, workshop group / March 17, 1980)

Mike: Seth's account of the crucifixion doesn't ring true to me. Is that something that he just believes happened because he projected himself along a possible line of experience? How did he come up with that?

(In Seth Speaks,[54N] *Seth describes a moment during an incarnation of his in the Holy Land at the time of Jesus's death. He had not even heard of Jesus, in that incarnation, when another man, drunken at the time, told him Jesus had been taken away by the Essenes while some other drugged individual took his place on the cross. Seth later describes these as the true facts in the course of saying that Christians have misunderstood self-sacrifice to be a positive spiritual act, rather than an unnecessary negation of the joy of life which a high Being like Christ would never have committed. There is a parallel to some Gnostic attitudes in this, as discussed later.)*

MOITA: There are many levels to the experience of the Christ-consciousness. And it would be difficult to go through them all and the things that came to affect individual awareness of that event. It is something like the Medicine Wheel, in that each brings his own perception to the experience. Sometimes, though, it is necessary to be able to take all of those views together and even raise your awareness a level higher in order to see that kind of reality – the true significance of an event in the history of man and his spiritual development.

(Actually, Seth himself states that various levels of reality must be recognized here. He maintains that the crucifixion was a psychic event, like a mass dream that interacted with the human psyche in a profound manner, contributing an idea *that was more important to history than the physical events.[55] Moita's response to Mike focuses on Seth's literal account of the crucifixion and seems to reflect her different assessment of the many relative values and perceptions involved. She speaks of Jesus accepting his death in an excerpt appearing later in this chapter.)*

MOITA: Seth was looking at this experience not so much from the angle of the impact that the advent of Christ had upon man. He was seeking to explain from a more physical level some of the things that happened – from a drier outlook, from a less whole view (?). It is like the six blind men and the elephant. *(laughter)* And Seth is one of the blind men who is holding the trunk...

Mike: He has no access, in his state of development, to the Akashic Records?... *(i.e. the reservoir of knowledge of all events in all times, or their energy imprints, that can be tapped by those reaching high enough on non-physical planes)*

MOITA: Those records are also prone to individual perception. Where you are in your development will determine what you see. What kind of outlook you bring *to* it will determine what you take *from* it.

Mike: Well, he probably would sway a lot of people. I know he has some people *I* know, because he presents himself as knowing a lot of things, having more access to that kind of reality. I just find it hard to understand how he would so miss the whole thing, if *I* got the right perception of what happened myself.

MOITA: I have tried very hard to explain to you how that happens.

Nora: I find that a very interesting question because I've read both Cayce and Seth too. But I really appreciated what Seth was saying because it did give me a different point of view, a different input. I don't think I've reached any final conclusion about it, but I found it very interesting – something to really think about.

MOITA: It helps you stretch your mind.

Mike: Yeah, well it did that for me too . . . until the end.

ॐ   ॐ   ॐ

Gnostic Approaches

Whether or not the Essenes kidnapped Jesus, as Seth relates, before the culminating act of his mission, they and other mystic groups did play a major but largely unpublicized role in the beginnings of Christianity, including the recognition of Mary as the intended "vessel" for the coming of the Messiah within the Essene community at Mt. Carmel, according to the Edgar Cayce readings.[56] Circa 200 A.D., however, those identifying themselves as Gnostics – from the Greek *gnosis*, knowing through experience rather than intellectually or through mediators – were expelled from the church as heretics.

Texts discovered in Egypt in 1945 delineate many of the early Gnostic views in their sharp divergence from orthodox tradition. Elaine Pagels's *The Gnostic Gospels*[57] contrasts orthodox emphases on male church authority, the gulf between God or Christ and individual humans, and the literal, physical aspect of Christ's life and teaching, with the Gnostic stress on Jesus's words and mission in their inner, symbolic significance for an individual's path to self-knowledge, wholeness and spiritual maturity – recognizing the God within. Like Seth, the Gnostics stressed the eternal, living Christ over the crucifixion, and opposed what seemed the orthodox love of martyrdom for its own sake.

The best of the Gnostic gospels, however, are not in Moita's view an accurate basis for evaluating Gnosticism as a historical movement. Similar comments might equally apply to other movements which define themselves in opposition more than in wholeness.

Moita session #144 (Kelly and David / May 27, 1980)

David: I've been excited by reading *The Gnostic Gospels* because of the great similarity between many Gnostic points of view and approaches to reality that have been coming through communications like this in recent years. It almost seems like the New Age might be defined as that time when Gnostic Christianity comes into its own after the spread of the orthodox variety. What can you tell us, from your perspective, about who the Gnostics were, and how similar their view of the world was to what you have been giving us?

MOITA: It would be difficult to generalize, since each was a very individual experience. You could say that the break between the Gnostics and the orthodox was very much symbolic of the differences between the intellect and the intuition; and in that case, the intellect, rational side, won over a greater proportion of the people because it was a time of unrest, and because they could not cope with standing on the edge of reality, willing to take a plunge into the unknown.

But neither, on the whole, was a very balanced view. Each made the same mistakes, although they clothed them in different terminology. Both felt they were right and they were the only way and all others were ignorant and incapable of understanding. Although the Gnostics professed equality, and in many ways were equal among their [members], they did not extend this concept farther than the individuals who were close to them. They still saw the universe through a lens of their own making, and they coloured the world around them until it became harsh and unyielding. And so, they created for themselves a battlefield in order to fight for their new intuition and for their right to follow their own path.

And because of this, the orthodox [attitude] was the same: that the Gnostics were irresponsible, impractical and just as power-hungry and egotistical as they were – although then they had someone else to pin the rap on since they needed not to look to themselves for egotism. They could point to another and create a cloud over those who were between these viewpoints. They fogged the issues to make things unclear, because each was afraid that their own inadequacies would be brought to light.

This is in a way what is happening now, except on a slightly different level. Hopefully there is much more balance and less looking to prove [one's] path is better. As the age began, so shall it end. And you have seen the beginning of that ending in the dissatisfaction that people have expressed with organized religion and power structures. That the naming of a man to a position automatically gives him contact with God and with the Creative Forces is a foolishness that goes beyond understanding, and there are many who are waking up to this reality. You are all part of the same humanity, and you are all different expressions of the same whole. One does not lead any, but everyone should lead himself.

There is always a danger when doors are open between the worlds. Each time a Teacher has stepped through the door and made himself touchable, people have taken only that which they can understand or can use, and thrown away the rest – both sides missing the whole.

The Gnostics, then, were close to New Age thinking in important ways, but were not free of egotism or dualism. Despite Gnosticism's suppression, an underground tradition of esoteric Christianity has continued through the centuries, surfacing to prominence in various ways as it has been rediscovered by individuals and groups. One of the earliest flowerings of this tradition (a later one would be philosophical alchemy), seeded by the encounter of Christianity and the indigenous Druidic religion in early Britain, has been remembered ever since for its vivid projection of a spiritual ideal.

Moita session #153 (Kelly, David, Jim, Lorna, Cindy / August 16, 1980)

Jim: In my meditation work, I've been dwelling a lot with the myth cycle involving Merlin, King Arthur and the Round Table: those stories that have been handed down and seem to have a lot of spiritual significance to a lot of people. I wonder if you could tell me anything about Merlin and where the stories originated.

(Silence, as Moita closes Kelly's eyes. Meanwhile, Kelly hears a discussion between the entities present as to how much and which parts of a large story can be told on this occasion, with the suggestion that perhaps more can be made available later. Then Moita opens Kelly's eyes.)

MOITA: It is difficult to separate the fact from the fantasy, and yet the fantasy has more reality to it as far as a spiritual path and spiritual development are concerned. The idea of Merlin being born old and living backwards is significant. It symbolizes that when you enter into a life you have already gained the knowledge that life holds for you. And you bring into it also what understanding you have learned from your other existences – other lives and in-between. He was one who was aware, who had not lost this knowingness. And so, it was as if he went backwards, since he knew the deed before it happened.

The time he lived in was one more fluid in some ways. It was less structured. There was more belief in the unexplainable. And so, manifestations were easier. It is to be noted that...around that time there are recorded many visions, miracles, whatever name you wish to call them. And many have wondered why there seem to be fewer in...your time.

Many of the people involved [with the Round Table] represented parts of a single soul manifested, playing themselves out against themselves – desires and needs and angers and guilts – to see what would arise from such an encounter.

The Grail was real in its way. It is an ideal that can be attained by some. There are many roads and many paths. Each one leads to a different doorway. The Grail is only found behind one; and so, it is an exacting path – as are many others. It is the *union* with the Christ-consciousness, or the soul-self. It is a quick and hard road when compared to others.

(Kelly is seeing a cup with bright, flashing lights coming out from it like rays of a sun. Jim is also seeing many visual changes during the talk of the Grail. Jim will mention later that the idea of those involved being part of a single soul is intriguing, since in his meditations he has been

visualizing himself seated in each of the 12 positions around the Round Table. These 12 seats can be coordinated with the zodiac, of course.)

෧ ෧ ෧

Moita session #171 (Kelly, David, Jim / January 17, 1981)
Jim: Can you tell me how old the symbol of the Round Table is, where it originated?
MOITA: The idea of joining in a circle to increase energy, to create a vortex, a place of attraction to higher realities, is so ancient there is really no time that can be put upon it. The idea of a table became more material after astrology had been given to the Atlanteans in their second age. Astrology was given from other levels because of the broadening distance between [our worlds]. In many ways it is a translation of spiritual concepts, of being one with the universe, of all things affecting each part. It was meant to be used as a tool for man to understand the nature of reality when he could no longer consciously connect.
Jim: When he could no longer connect *directly*, so a symbol was used, to point the way . . .
MOITA: . . . to him learning how to connect again. *(long pause, gazing)*

෧ ෧ ෧

"Second Coming" and New Age

"As the age began, so shall it end." Many are recognizing the beginning of that ending in the unrest that rises within each of us and fills our world. We are again living in a time of prophecy, and of applying those prophecies contained in the Bible to current events.

Moita session #115 (Kelly, David, workshop group / October 15, 1979)
Mike: Many are saying the "Second Coming" talked about in the Bible will happen soon. How exactly do you see that – as a consciousness change? There's going to be lots happening. Our backs are going to be up against the wall. Are we going to change and evolve at a crisis point? *(pause)*
MOITA: There are so many things. *(pause)* When the Christ-consciousness manifests itself on Earth . . . *(pause)* . . . it is, in a sense, the completeness of all of man expressing itself in a single form. It is all of your wisdom and all of your love and all of your acceptance and understanding brought together in one place at one time. And this kind of physical manifestation only occurs at key points in man's evolution – places where he has opened a door into himself. Man chooses when this will occur.

෧ ෧ ෧

A "Second Coming" would manifest the completeness of man, but individuals have different conceptions of what that means and how it may all come about. In the next excerpts, Moita alludes to the startling New Age prophecy of a separation of worlds, which in my experience first appeared among earlier channelings through David Spangler.[58] Though the separation of worlds seems to bear a tragic aspect, it respects the choices of souls and may offer the best hope for Earth's future.

Moita session #124 (Kelly, David, Duggan, Caroline, 4 others / December 16, 1979)

Duggan: I've had difficulty understanding what the "Second Coming" of Christ means. Does it mean a new consciousness within society? Like, the millennium is ending and there's prophecies of big changes soon. I know that church-going Christians sort of believe that someone's going to come down out of the sky and wave a magic wand and take all the good people up to heaven and burn all the bad people. I *think* that's what they mean.

MOITA: Basically, that *is* what they think. *(i.e. at least the more literal-minded believers)*

Duggan: Uh, like I can't accept that. But what I think is going to happen is that there is going to be a new search for the spirituality in man, or a new awakening of consciousness. Is that what is meant by the "Second Coming" of Christ?

MOITA: There is a chance that it could happen *both* ways, in that there are many souls who have created a reality where this is possible, this [fundamentalist] kind of "Second Coming". It will not be to their benefit as they think. You could say that they are leaving this Earth and starting another one, somewhere else.

But there are many things that are happening and will happen. And the new awareness of man will seem to be a very sudden thing, although it has been building slowly over many thousands of years. And there will be many physical changes. Much will depend upon *how* aware man becomes. They speak of this as a New Age because the Earth is being reborn. And the changes the Earth is going through are its cleansing of itself, so that it will be ready to receive man as a partner.

Remember that churches are composed of individuals, and the universe is composed of love, and not all individuals are open enough to receive that energy. The Christ-consciousness came to show what happens when someone *is* open to love and the law of the universe. This is what man is striving for, and in that lies control of your own destiny. He accepted his death because he knew it would serve himself and all those around him and would be but a passing thing. So he made his choices with his eyes open.

Caroline: Will this new Christ-consciousness affect everybody during the "Second Coming" of Christ, only in different ways according to their reality? Like, some people might think of being up in heaven with God, and others who don't even *know* Christ or God exists, or even think about it, may create their own reality differently. How are we all going to become Christ-conscious if we all have such different realities of it? How can we all be One?

MOITA: But you all are One already, only you are not aware of it. You see, these are so many . . .

Caroline: *(interrupting)* Will people be *aware* of it?

MOITA: So many of the things that are happening and will happen are all part of the same . . .

Caroline: What did you mean by saying that during the "Second Coming" some Christians will in a sense be taken from this Earth?

MOITA: They are choosing not to stay and try to work through [man's problems on Earth]. This is their "out" they are using. They are using this as...their escape hatch. They are fearful and afraid and not ready to enter a New Age. It has a great deal to do with their expectations from the *first* coming, and those that have chosen to veil the reality.

You are all One in one place. But for now things go in different directions, or so they seem, each to find his way back to home and self. They are making it easier for those who will be left behind, for they are taking their influence away. They are freeing the Earth, in a sense, for they have kept it locked in this particular reality because of their belief and the strength of it and the strength of their fear. By giving themselves this doorway, and leaving *this* Earth behind, going on to that other one that they are expecting, those of you who have chosen to be here through this time and afterward to help remake man's awareness and to heal the Earth will be freer to do so.

ॐ   ॐ   ॐ

Moita session #120 (Kelly and David / November 18, 1979)

David: In the Book of the Revelation, the "Second Coming" of Christ is tied to the climactic battle of Armageddon to be fought over the Holy Land. Many channelings, including *Fatima Prophecy*, associate this with a world war over the Middle East. I can handle the idea of Earth changes much better than I can accept that scale of warfare in the nuclear age. Can you tell us, from here, what the likelihood of that kind of thing happening is?

MOITA: *(words accompanied by a feel of very heavy energy)* Unless your leaders become more loving and in touch with the spirit within, there is a very good possibility that man will express his fear in this form. It is not something to be spoken of lightly, nor should you be comfortable with the idea. War is like an alien pestilence that is visited upon the Earth and all of its spheres of influence. That is why it is harder to accept, for it is not of the Earth; it does not have the same cleansing effect.

At least, it is a passing thing. *(pause)* There is something that has been noted here, and it is that man *is* in effect living one of Christ's commandments – doing unto others as he would do unto himself. But he has forgotten the greatest and the first. He must love himself first before he can do unto others in the right way.

(Note how this differs from Jesus's two greatest commandments as reported in Matthew 22:37-39: "Jesus said unto him, Thou shalt love the Lord thy God with all thy heart, and with all thy soul, and with all thy mind. This is the first and great commandment. And the second is like unto it, Thou shalt love thy neighbour as thyself."[59] What has been presented as loving a heavenly God can now be understood as loving the God within each.)

ଔ ଔ ଔ

Moita session #140 (Kelly, David, workshop group / April 9, 1980)

Harriet: Moita, I was wondering, if this holocaust happens to the world *(referring to great upheavals and/or war before the dawning of a New Age)*, what happens to the ones who don't survive? What happens to their souls?

MOITA: It will depend upon their awareness when they die or shortly after. Some will not be able to accept newness and change because they have been unable to do so in their own development for a long time. They will be given an opportunity to develop in another place, on another earth, and start the new cycle again.

       Those who can accept will continue to interact with the Earth. When new bodies are formed, there will be souls to fill them. And as the Earth moves into its new awareness, the spirit realms will also become more visible, and the distance between your world and mine will be less. There will be more direct communication, more conscious cooperation with man's own evolution and development.

       No one will ever truly die. Once a soul is born, the spark is never extinguished. They may move away from your awareness in many ways, but that spark is still there developing. This is all a passing thing.

Harriet: So the soul will always come back in a physical form?

MOITA: Not all souls. The idea is eventually to leave behind the need to come into a physical body. But the idea here is that even those who leave the Earth, because they cannot accept it, will not expire. They will just be removed.

ଔ ଔ ଔ

According to Biblical prophecy, the end-times will see the final confrontation between Christ and his opposite, battling for the hearts of men. But for a New Age to dawn, the coming years must also bring man's saving realization that he has created this battleground out of his own self-fear, and that the way of love lies not in victory but acceptance.

Moita session #130 (Kelly, David, workshop group / February 4, 1980)

Marcia: Can you look forward and see what's happening to mankind in the future – the next 50,000 years *(laughing)*, or even 100? What's it going to be like?

MOITA: That will depend upon the choices you make now. This time period is a nexus, a whirlpool, a crossroads. There are paths before you that lead into the future – some of them not pleasant, some of them extremely promising. That is why we are here: to help you choose the road that leads not to destruction but that leads to life, and to this change of man and his awareness, to the reuniting of [our] worlds, and the type of spirit that was before and that has grown in-between.

The Earth is going through a birthing, and it is going through a death first before it can be reborn. And so, you are going to experience many changes in many ways – physical and spiritual. It is important for each individual to take it upon himself to see the world change for better. To do that, he must see himself change towards wholeness. And that is the message we are here to bring: that you can change the world, and you can do it by starting from yourself. And if enough of you do it, indeed things will have changed and the face of the world will be different.

Marcia: Do you see an Antichrist coming – like extreme trouble, for everybody, not just for a few?

MOITA: I see many troubles. Man as a whole has a spirit. As with the individual, when he dies and faces all of his fears, or when he grows before his death and his ego and his fears begin to fight for their existence; so it is with the Earth and the consciousness of man. As man begins to evolve, and begins to pass through these fears that he has built up over so many centuries, those fears will begin to form to make their last stand, to fight for their reality, for their existence, for they cannot live without man and his belief. They die when belief in them dies. And so, that energy, that conglomeration of fears from all of man, will make itself known, and many will call it the Antichrist, for it is in many senses anti-life. I am not sure if that confuses or enlightens.

Marcia: A little of both...

(Moita is beginning to withdraw her energy, as the session has been a long one . . . but Shelley feels impelled to speak up.)

Shelley: You were just saying we could change the world by starting within ourselves. Well, I'll tell you, it gets really frustrating, you know. I am really afraid about what's happening. I feel that we have no control, you know? And, oh sure, it's all very nice to think if I change and somebody else changes and so on . . . But I can just try my hardest and it just doesn't seem to happen. I feel really helpless, and angry, and sad, when I watch the news and hear about the stupid things that are going on and the cruelty we're capable of. It makes me think perhaps there's something more to it. Surely we're not capable of being that ugly. Surely there must be something . . . *(sighs)*

MOITA: You are looking for an outside influence?

Shelley: Well, I'm looking for two things. One, I'm really questioning whether or not we can make a difference. I mean, it takes a whole lot of people, and then you have to get through the idiots who are in the decision-making process and that seems to be pretty hopeless. And the other thing that I'm confused about is that I wonder how people are capable of doing very savage and cruel things like torturing people. I'm wondering if that really is coming from us, or maybe some people are being used by other things up there.

(Moita's energy returns in full force to respond to these important questions, making sure her answers get through despite Kelly's fatigue. The following is delivered with determined intensity.)

MOITA: I will say to that last that, in some cases, yes, it is true, because there *are* other energies.

But these energies have been created by man himself, and have been given reality by man, just as the Antichrist of Marcia's question is a real phenomenon. It is the individual being involved that opens himself up *to* that energy that causes it to happen. It is the individual's prime responsibility to stop that from happening, by seeing himself and seeing what he is doing. Many cruelties happen through ignorance, and evil that is committed with a lack of understanding is not as evil as one that is committed when it is known exactly the effect the act will have upon the other and upon the life-force of the planet in general.

I am not saying that this path I see for man in the future is going to be one that will be easy to obtain. There is much work involved, and it will take everyone who has it within himself to open in order to do this work. The Earth has been created by you – all of you. Each one of you has added your energy to make this reality more real than any other, and it can be *changed* by you in how you view it. It does not mean that you ignore the ugliness that is there. It means that you focus yourself upon the beauty and, by so focusing, the ugliness itself will begin to disappear. It is not something that is done overnight. It is something that takes time. But it cannot be done except from each person.

There *is* hope. That is why *I* am here, why all of us send our love to all of you. We know there are trying times ahead. We are there to add our energy, our compassion and our understanding to all of the pain and all of the fear you will have to go through in order to see the end of this darkness and the beginning of the light.

Do not think that you are in this alone. You have many allies. And we are not at all ashamed to ally ourselves with you, for we see your beauty and we see your light, and we are here to help you let it shine. It is a choice you must make within yourself: to add your light to the light that is growing, or to turn your back and face the darkness and feed it. You cannot change the darkness by being within it.

And I really *must* leave for now, at least from this level. *(to Shelley:)* Thank you very much...and *all* of you *(looking around circle)* for adding your energy and your thoughts. Good night.

Tales of Power #2

MIND CONTROL IN ATLANTIS

I got that [J.B.] was in Atlantis and he was "on the dark side of the Force". He was an impetus behind Atlantis's sinking, by taking that energy and bringing it in and consciously focusing it, misusing it.
— Kelly, after Moita session (April 16, 1981)

Two days after Kelly receives the above information about a person currently controversial in channeling circles, I guide her in a past-life regression. Our goal is to uncover how her counterpart may have interacted with J.B.'s counterpart near the end of Atlantean civilization. (J.B. will be identified, and will serve as a focal point, in all three remaining Tales of Power after this one.)

Kelly's responses to my questions in this session very clearly reflect her identity in the other life as a young, virginal temple priestess, naive until now about the power structures of the society in which her Order has been operating. And her immersion in the past life seems to extend even to not knowing who is asking her the questions!

Hypersentience session #182 (Kelly, with David guiding / April 18, 1981)

Kelly: *(sigh)* I seem to be in some place very dark, some place I don't like. *(deep sigh)* I'm in a cave, and there isn't any way out. *(deep sigh)*

David: What blocks the way?

Kelly: Stones – many stones. Boulders.

David: Do you know how they have ended up blocking the way?

Kelly: Yes. They were put there by someone else – many someones. Women. They put me in the cave and then they blocked it up.

David: How did they feel about you? Why were they doing that?

Kelly: I don't believe them. *(vehemently)* I think they're liars. They don't understand the Laws. They're doing things wrong – very wrong. And the people: they don't know; people don't understand what they're doing.

David: What do they lie about?

Kelly: Everything! *(gasp)* I go back in my mind and see the Temple where I came from. The people bring us food, gold, questions. They pay for their questions.

There's this leader who comes. He brings much gold for answers. But they do not tell him the answer to his questions. They make one up that is not true.

David: Why do they do this? *(long pause)* What are you experiencing?

Kelly: Some kind of change, but I feel I am somewhere else – in a room. Walls – I can see them; they're cool to the fingertip. Cool stone – marble, white, cream. Then I hear voices down the hall. Some people are coming. I feel suddenly like I'm not supposed to be in here.

I see myself in some kind of robe – white, floor-length, long sleeves. Woman – long, dark hair. A silver band around my head – wire. No, not silver – platinum. There's a reason why it's here – something to do with communication. It's a receiver (?). It brings me words, understanding. It is a sacred object.

I am here in this room looking for some answer. A question has been asked.

(She means the question I asked above: "Why do they do this?" I don't realize it yet, but my question has taken her back in time in this other life.)

Kelly:	I see a row of books, but someone is coming and I look for a place to hide. *(pause)*
David:	Can you find a place?
Kelly:	Yes. Cupboard. Inside a cupboard – small, cramped, dark.
David:	And it works? Or are you discovered?
Kelly:	It works. *(whisper:)* I almost hear them. I see someone in the crack. *(whisper, as if afraid she'll be heard:)* He's the one.
David:	Which?
Kelly:	He is just different. He's the leader. *(gasp)*
David:	Now what?
Kelly:	They're coming over here – he and *her* – closer to where I'm hiding. He says, "Is this the Book?" She says, "Yes, it is the one we spoke of before." He says, "Does it have the information I'm after? Show me where it is. I must see it. I must see it now!" She says, "It is not permitted for someone not of the Order to touch the Book." He's mad. He calls her a fool popin . . . jay (?).
David:	Who is this "she" here?
Kelly:	She is the leader of the Order.
David:	Uh-huh, and he is the leader . . .
Kelly:	. . . of a large part of the country. It seems there is a machine in this Book – directions for making a machine, one that shoots light. It would be those who were before who understood these things. Someone must have written the Book. *(large sigh)* Does this answer the question?
David:	Okay, I'm getting there. The priestesses don't tell him the truth for fear of what he would do?
Kelly:	This is a private conversation – only he and she. I am an interloper. I'm not supposed to hear this, and I am in danger because of it. I don't think anyone else is in on this. She, at the last minute, is reluctant to let him have the Book. It's a sacred Book. Her and I . . . are not friends. *(pause)* He seems to be telling her that even if it is a *risk* for him to take the Book, in the end she will benefit.
David:	Do you know how he means that?
Kelly:	He doesn't know how to interpret the writing. It's useless to him without an interpreter.

He will use her. He promised her things – power. She is crazy for power anyway! I think she sees to use him. She seems very sophisticated, sure of herself.

I . . . they're not making any sound. *(Kelly makes a clucking sound.)* And I think they're doing something. *(i.e. having sex)* I'm glad I cannot look!

Ah. In the end she talks him out of taking it. And he agrees to come to study it with her and arrange to bring others who may have better understanding how it could be manufactured. They walk out of the room.

I know I ought to get out of here. But I have to look at the Book . . . see picture: some long barrel (?), curled, twisted; flare at the end; handle; crystal; some apparatus.

David: And do you understand what they were used for?

Kelly: I touch my hand to that thing on my head. See pictures of bright red light starting forest fires, killing (?). It's a weapon! A ruby gun.[60N]

Must be some war coming. Why would they need a weapon? It's good I do not live in the city.

David: Where are you now?

Kelly: I'm leaving the room, *(makes clucking sound again)* and I just realized I did a silly thing. *(snorting)* I closed the Book! – and they left it opened. I hope they don't . . . hmm. *(pause)* Ah. My name is Talia.

David: What's happening now?

Kelly: Someone just ran up to me and said, "Talia, my sister, where have you been? I have been so worried about you!" I went for a walk in the hills to do some thinking. Something is going on and I don't like it, and I'm not supposed to leave the Temple grounds. She's been trying to cover up for me. She doesn't think I should go out. She's afraid. *(pause)*

I tell her that we've got to get out of here before they find out that I know. I've been under false impressions. That man is no leader *at all* but someone who desires to *kill* the leader, and he *(the leader)* must be warned.

She's going to stay behind, but then she realizes if she stays behind, she'll be worse off than if she comes with me.

David: What is her name?

Kelly: *(pause)* Leana.

David: So where do you go?

Kelly: I see us creeping through tall grass in the dark. Woods coming up – safety in the woods. We're going on a long journey, if we must go to the City, several hundred miles to the west of us. *(pause; long sigh)*

David: What now?

Kelly: I've learned a lot since I left the Temple. Life is very hard for my people. They are all poor.

David: What makes it hard for them? Why are they so poor?

Kelly: All this land seems to be under some curse. The soil does not nourish; nothing flourishes – desolation. There's been some ancient disease visited . . . upon these . . . souls. I have never gone this way. I came from another part. But they're sickly, thin, oppressed. Wonder what I'll find when I get to the City.

David: Okay, can we move ahead to when you get there – or if anything unexpected happens as you're getting there, before you get there?

Kelly: I'm leaving my sister at a cottage, saying goodbye, telling her to wait for me here where she'll be safe and have strength, know I'll be back to get [her].

I've got different clothes now. I managed to get some more suitable clothing so I won't be noticed as I enter the City. It's a walled city. There a gate – not a wooden gate; a metal gate. Very ornate carving around its edges: snakes and dragons and boars; and some man standing with a rod in his hand that shoots lightning.

David: This is a weapon?

Kelly: After what I saw in the Book, it could be. Before I would have said it was a picture of a god, one of our gods. Now I wonder. But the gate is only open for certain hours.

David: Can you get in now?

Kelly: Yes. There is a travelling caravan of merchants. I slip in with them. *(pause)*

David: As you move through the City, can we come to your next major encounter or your destination?

Kelly: I tell this fool of a guard I have to see his Lord. I step on his foot. He's impudent! I cannot tell him I'm a priestess.

David: What does he do?

Kelly: He doesn't have a chance to do much. The object of my journey has walked by and spotted me, wants to know what the commotion was all about.

David: Can you describe him?

Kelly: He's *fat*, or should I say overly *stout*. It's not polite to call people "fat". Somewhat bald, though he seems to have a fair bit of hair. Wears big robes, lots of trinkets.

David: Do you get a chance to speak to him?

Kelly: Now something has definitely gone wrong. I talk to him and then he calls in someone else – another man, who I don't like and I don't trust. There's something about him – *sneaky*. He looks nice enough, much nicer than his Lord: much slimmer; he's tall; white hair; very strange, angular face; extremely long nose; long face – narrow, almost pointed; strange eyes – yellow . . . He has yellow eyes. *(voice sounding more trancelike)*

David: And how does he react to what he learns?

Kelly: Very smooth, but there's something odd. I feel . . . Yes, he's trying to speak to me through this band, which I have managed to hide with a head covering. Makes me uneasy. It seems that he must be involved with that other, and I am found out or at least suspected. *(pause)* Pressure is building. I have to *leave*, get out of his presence.

There. The farther I go, the less burdensome it becomes. It must have something to do with distance – maybe electromagnetic currents? He is the one you are looking for. *(i.e.*

another incarnation of J.B.) The other is just as much a tool as the leader of our Order. But I wonder where he comes from. His face is so odd. I keep seeing it.

I can't see what I *alone* can do. Somehow I must convince others. There are so many people here, someone must believe me. *(pause)*

David: Do you find anyone else?

Kelly: Through some women. I uncover a band of men who are involved in some kind of resistance. Rogues, mostly, looking for loot. I have to show them some of my powers to convince them I am who I say I am. They are as obnoxious as the guard. *(pause)*

David: Do they believe you then?

Kelly: They name me the Bright Lady.[61N]

David: What powers did you show them?

Kelly: The band I wear, it can create an aura of light around my body that is visible to any. It is electromagnetic; things do not go through it easily. And I can also lift small objects at a distance and create fire. Small things. But they have seen nothing, so it is not small. *(pause)*

David: What do they do, now that they're convinced?

Kelly: They want to kill everybody *(laughs)* – figure that will solve it. What to do with these idiots?! I want to talk to the masses, tell them that the priestesses can no longer communicate with the forefathers as they say they can, and that they are trying to manipulate men into creating distress – controlling. I dislike this intensely. I am no less a manipulator.

David: How do you manipulate?

Kelly: *(pause)* I permit an aura of mystery to surround me – sometimes a display of knowingness that I do not feel.

I do not seek to replace him. I see there is little hope of accomplishing anything in this manner. And his face still dominates my thoughts. I begin to feel drawn towards him.

David: Is there something you recognize in him?

Kelly: *(pause)* The display of the force that is out of the past. I see he controls a great many people through his thoughts. I feel that I have become one of them.

David: How do you feel controlled?

Kelly: Blinding headaches. They come through my band. They disrupt my pattern of thought. *(pause)*

I seem to have broken free. Somehow I removed the band and put it aside.

David: Was it an act of will to be able to remove it, do you know?

Kelly: Yes. It was difficult.

David: Is there anything in particular you did to develop that will?

Kelly: *(pause)* There's a very strange scene. I wander through the palace into a room, and there is a skull on an altar. *(i.e. a crystal skull)* It . . . it . . . *(pause)* I think the band activates it somehow.

David: And what happens to it then?

Kelly: It's a woman's voice speaking. *(definitely Moita, Kelly later confirms)* She says, "You will be free. Remove the band." I think I have been here merely to observe. I did not know I was here under compulsion. That is how he works. He makes you think you are there for a reason you are not – one that sounds sensible, plausible, acceptable.

David: What is this place in the palace?

Kelly: It is a small temple within, a room he uses. Often I have seen him come here. I have wondered what was inside. I wonder what he does.

David: So now you've removed the band.

Kelly: Yes, and I see that the only thing to do is to leave before I am captured. *(pause, huge sigh)*

David: So what is happening now?

Kelly: I make a quick trip to my rogues. I tell them that I think the key would be to steal the skull, that it is being used somehow to control people. But I cannot lead them. I have to get out of the City entirely. I don't know if they quite believe me. They are afraid. *(pause)*

I get my sister. I didn't leave soon enough. I see flying ships! They run us down.

David: What do they do to you?

Kelly: Take us back to the Temple. We have broken the Law. *(pause)*

David: And then what?

Kelly: I am where I was – waiting, to die.

David: And where is your sister?

Kelly: In a place like mine, alone.

David: What do you experience as you wait?

Kelly: *(pause)* Sorrow, grief, but peace too. I've heard reports that at least they succeeded in their last task. *(referring to the rogues)*

David: Do you know anything of the effect that might have had?

Kelly: *(pause)* At first they were stunned – then questions.

David: What kind of questions?

Kelly: About his origin.

David: Do you know what that was?

Kelly: I think he is some sort of composite. *(i.e. a hybrid or android?)* Maybe a throwback. He wasn't born. He came from someplace else.

David: Another physical place?

Kelly: I think so. I don't know where. He doesn't seem to belong here. There are vague legends about his arrival – something about a light falling from the sky.

David: How is he referred to? What is his name?

Kelly: The word I get I am not certain of.

(Kelly is dubious, as it is a word she has read in comics.)

Kelly: It is *N'garai. (pronouncing Ne-ga-ree) (pause)* It means "demon". *(pause)*

David: Okay. Before you die, are there any other experiences that draw you? Or move to the experience of your death. *(long pause)* Can you describe what happens?

Kelly: It feels good to be out and back into the sun and the air.

David: As you look back over your life, what do you feel are the things you learned or didn't learn? How does it look from this perspective?

Kelly: I am fairly pleased in my part, although I do not like the idea that I fell prey so easily to his influence.

David: What in you enabled him to do that? Do you see that?

Kelly: My desire to take an active part in preventing his plans. I may have been able to affect him more from a distance. *(pause)*

David: How could you have done that?

Kelly: I would have learned more about the other planes [of reality] and influenced him.

David: Okay, I'd like to go through some of the people in this life we've just done, and let yourself say who, if any, Kelly knows that are the same. Okay. N'garai?

Kelly: That one I have not yet met, but he is J.B. *(see Tales of Power #3)*

David: Okay. How about the leader of your Order? *(long pause)*

Kelly: I know there is someone in this life, but it seems to have been a brief meeting.

David: Any sense of when or where?

Kelly: Wait. There it is: [name].

(Kelly names the woman whom she healed of a collapsed aura a few years ago, as told in Mind Leap*. The woman then met her in the dream-state, asking Kelly's help with her confused identity. Kelly was shown her "book of lives", revealing the woman's recent life as a Nazi concentration camp guard who enjoyed her work. Murdered after the war by a camp survivor, she immediately returned in this life motivated by revenge – the guard's personality warring with her new identity.)[62]*

David: Okay, now try the same thing with the man who wanted to see the Book. *(long pause)*

Kelly: Leroy.

(The last we heard, Leroy continued to trance-channel without knowing who will speak or recalling what occurs. We learned of him through our friend Rena, who knew him personally. Rena's interactions with him came up several times in The World Conspires*.[63N] Indeed, there are striking parallels between Leroy's and J.B.'s irresponsible approaches to channeling in this life, as will be seen in Tales of Power #3. Some related comments from Moita will appear in Chapter 9.)*

David: All right. Now try the same thing with the Lord in the City. *(long pause)*

Kelly: The only face is Otto. *(i.e. Kelly's long-time acquaintance, also physically very large, who is very adept at going out of his body and who turned up by that means during a Moita session in* The World Conspires*.[64])*

David: All right. Do the same thing with your sister.

Kelly: Rena. *(see note about Leroy above)*

David: And finally picture the rogues and see if anyone Kelly knows comes to mind.

Kelly: *(laughs) (long pause)* I see four: you, Roy, Jim and Gerald.[65N]

David: Anything distinguishing the different ones or their part in what happened?

Kelly: You were rather sour, moody, angry.

David: At everything?

Kelly: There was much to be angry about. Gerald was the leader. He had a hard exterior, but was very soft inside – a big heart. Jim never took anything seriously. He was always laughing, and he thought it was all great fun, since he didn't want to be ruled. Roy was big, strong, not very smart, carried a big axe, knew how to use it.

David: Okay. Can we try one more thing going in the opposite direction? Do you find any person in that life who is known to Kelly as Eileen? *(wife of Gerald)*

Kelly: One of the priestesses in the Temple: a very small, slight woman; mousy, daunted, sort of like a trapped animal. She was young . . . a child...

David: Okay, one more person going in the opposite direction. Do you see anyone in that life whom Kelly knows as Ted? *(Kelly's first husband, as mentioned in Tales of Power #4)*

Kelly: Yes. He was a clerk in the palace.

(Kelly will say later that the skull was the Crystal Skull found by Prof. Mitchell-Hedges. She comments that the scenes were quite vivid and real for her, even though her conscious mind thought there were many things that struck her as anachronistic. It seems evident that this life occurred during a time of Atlantean history after the first destruction and before its final collapse.)

(Once the identity of J.B. is revealed in Tales of Power #3, one last identification won't be surprising. Kelly feels fairly certain that Elisabeth Kübler-Ross was someone in the palace, possibly the Leader's wife: a rather uncertain, dominated woman.)

Chapter 6

UNLOCKING OUR HEARTS

As fall 1979 comes to an end, Kelly and I can feel that the faith on which we moved from the prairies to British Columbia was well-placed. Besides the Kindle Valley friendships we have now made, we will make more friends through a winter workshop in the town closest to our hilltop home, and through an early spring workshop will renew our connections in the Okanagan Valley.

Still, we might *seem* to be marking time in terms of the greater goal of forming a community in which the New Age could become living, everyday experience. How is that goal to be realized, though – by trying to impose some preconceived program, or by being open to change and the truth beneath appearances, where we all have life challenges to work through? The latter was our path back in Regina, and it is the experience we will meet in this new part of the country as well. Rather than leaving behind our own past, we will allow it to sensitize us to similar situations that others around us are now facing.

Members of our Kindle Valley workshop will frequently recall Amar's message from the final session (at the end of Chapter 3): "Now it is up to you to make your opening not just an idea but a reality." The words signify painful, vulnerable, bewildering times of change and insecurity to be undergone by many of the group in the months following. After that last workshop session, Mike urged, "We've got to do *something* – but what?" For a number of our friends, life will answer that question more quickly and directly than they may have wished.

The truth is that in the year Kelly and I arrived, a cycle of upheaval in personal relationships was just beginning among some of those we come to know best. Consequently, the extended winter of 1979-1980 is a time of many realizations and subsequent movements out of old relationships into new couplings or phases of aloneness, and the old/new selves that go with them. Changes set in motion during this period run so deep that people may still be coping with their effects through the next spring, summer and fall.

Thus the focus of many of our sessions following our first Kindle Valley workshop is not grand designs for the future but very immediate, heartfelt sharings with individuals experiencing turmoil in their lives. Here some of our closest friends bring the feelings and concerns stirred by their changes to Moita, sensing a need for the information she may provide, her more balanced perspective, and perhaps the energy of her caring most of all.

Because of the personal nature of these changes, and their many commonalities, I will be giving these excerpts anonymously and without regard to chronology. In this way, I hope their universality will be recognized: as steps, however dimly understood at first, toward opening us and "making love our reality". How else can we help to found a new world than by becoming new ourselves?

(These are conversations occurring between January and November 1980 involving close to a dozen people living in or near the valley and connected in various ways. Participants will simply be identified by alphabetical letters, in order of appearance here – except C., already taken by one friend in all transcripts – regardless of repeated participation or chronology.)

ை   ை   ை

In most mind-expanding experiences, artificial boundaries are let down to reveal the natural flow of life, so that both individuality and love shine forth more clearly in their paradoxical unity. It is easier to speak than to do, of course, and there are periods when perspective on our confusion is not possible unless we are open enough to accept some deeper journeying first. Below is Moita's response to one friend's quandary, and the excerpts following elaborate the theme.

A.:   I've been having a lot of thoughts and I'm not sure where they come from. My mind keeps going to things that I don't seem to have any control over. It sometimes seems to be kind of a prison. Is the mind really like that?

MOITA: Your mind will *seem* a prison until you find the key to unlock your heart. The mind is a finite thing, and it only has limited experience in one existence. In order to connect with your greater self, with your wider understanding of the nature of life, you must pass through your heart first, and then your mind will become a tool. You will be able to use it as a focus instead of as a confusion of thoughts that seem to have no meaning or place. The heart is that centre which goes into confusion and chaos and comes out as order and balance and meaning. Your feelings will speak more clearly to you than your thoughts.

ை   ை   ை

B.:   Do you have anything to say about what is meant by "God's will", and giving yourself over, letting life just flow? Is it an attitude to have about your life?

MOITA: From my perspective, it means to let go of the single-focus identity of this one form; to know that there are other parts of yourself, of which you are only this one expression, that know what you are here for and are aware of the laws that govern the functioning of your universe. To give yourself over to the will of God is to let yourself be guided by that higher awareness which is part of you, not worrying where your path may lead, but having faith and knowing it is leading where you need to go.

When you stop projecting yourself into an uncertain future, you can give yourself over to the moment; and this is where the future is *made*. Even if the future is filled with difficulties or pain, accepting them as a part of your own growing experiences, knowing they are things you need to learn, will make them less painful. And in some cases they may not then be necessary, for you may have learned the lesson you need.

This is the lesson...in the story where the Lord asks [Abraham] to kill his son [Isaac] for

God; and he agrees, although he wishes his son to live for he is his only son. But by admitting to himself that he may not be aware of all of the meanings in this, he has learned that which he is meant to learn, and therefore the murder is stopped. It is very much a symbolic story. When you are willing to give sacrifices, sacrifices are no longer needed.

B.:   That's true.

MOITA: Of course, then they would not be looked upon as sacrifices, either.

૭   ૭   ૭

Whether we feel we have sought it ourselves, or that it has been thrust upon us from outside, the period of breaking through an impasse can seem to increase the confusion, as the opposing feelings become so much more focused on the immediate. The differing positions and perspectives in an interpersonal situation on this physical plane make it difficult to feel any wholeness and balance within it, whichever part is ours to play.

Below, D. comes to Moita while facing a difficult choice about relationships, and E. attends with him out of concern for D. and the others involved.

D.:   It's good to be with you again. I've thought of you. You have been aware of some changes going on in my life, and I've wanted to talk with you about them.

MOITA: *(smiling)* You look nervous.

D.:   I'm not sure how to approach all this. I have a feeling you might have a better idea.

MOITA: There are many things for people to discover about themselves, their natures. The Earth is in turmoil and the people are in turmoil with it. Your own values on life are being questioned by yourself. Situations help to broaden your perspective. You are not just a being who has been created now in this one life. You have a past and a future that goes beyond your own awareness of the moment. If a life was placid and easy and straight, would you look for answers in a deeper place? Strife serves as a means to reach within, to force you to face yourself. *(pause)*

D.:   It seems like, in the questioning of values, I don't know if I have much choice even left – if I'm already in the current more than I realize. It seems there's a choice between continuing with [my partner of recent years] or leaving and drawing near to [name]. I wonder if I see my choices very clearly.

MOITA: I told you . . .

D.:   I know! *(laughing) (thinking she's saying he has to discover it himself)*

MOITA: . . . you're learning to follow your heart. Your heart is the leader of your soul, not your mind. There are always alternatives. Following your heart, you will find the right road to become a whole spirit; and becoming whole, you will then be able to give of yourself to others – not just to one in particular. It is a greater goal than just a change in lifestyle...

         Do you desire to become an instrument of light . . .

D.:　　　　Yes...

MOITA:　　. . . bringing light into the world through your heart and your joy?

People have a tendency to see all relationships from just this one perspective, that this is the only one and there are no others. Broaden your view and help others to broaden theirs. Life is a delicate tapestry of connections and energy and purpose; and when each can find the movings of their own thread, they make the whole more beautiful and easier to see. Find your thread and show your own beauty to those around you. Do not be afraid for them to see your fumblings and your joy, or your uncertainty when you are uncertain.

D.:　　　　I *am* uncertain, and I see more fumblings than clear paths. I don't know which is the clear path.

MOITA:　　Then it would be wise for you to see clearer before you move along your path. If you would become a channel for your own life-force, you should let unclearness fall away from you, [in order] to walk a path that you can see with all of your heart. To see a path clearly does not mean to see one without pain. It means to accept all that taking that path entails, and embracing the sorrow as well as the joy. *(long pause, looking into each other's eyes)*

At least you will know we are all near...

(Tears come to D.'s eyes, as they do Kelly's occasionally during these exchanges.)

MOITA:　　Although sorrow is difficult to go through and experience, it helps a person to know themselves. Sorrow is a doorway to the inner workings of one's spirit. It is a cleansing fire that clears away the unimportant things in its wake, but only if a person can accept it enough and know it for what it is. It is a gradual process. Many individuals will go through many different kinds of lives or situations before they recognize pain as a friend and a teacher. And when they have done this, they have opened a door to joy and freedom...

Just as pain and sorrow [are] a tool for the individual to find himself, so is strife and difficulty for man as a whole. Things are being pushed. It will either be man recognizes himself in unity, or he destroys himself and his world – or at least this chance for unity will be passed. Nothing is ever truly destroyed.

E.:　　　　I don't know why it bothers me so much to think of the human conflict going on and on and on. I guess I just wish that somehow people could quit hating . . .

MOITA:　　It is their fear that makes them think they hate. Man is afraid to know himself. He is afraid of what he thinks he'll find.

E.:　　　　Where does that fear come from, though?

MOITA:　　It is difficult to believe he is afraid of love. *(long pause)* To man's mind, when he dwells here on your Earth, he sees love as a force that will take away his individuality, destroy his uniqueness.

E.:　　　　Fear of being hurt.

MOITA:　　And of losing his freedom of choice... *(pause)*

(smiling toward D.) You know you must make your own choice... *(long pause)* Each time you meet someone you have known from before – someone with whom you have a

strong connection – it is then your choice as a conscious being here and now to decide if that connection will be renewed or strengthened. You must look within and see what kind of future you wish for yourself. Each must make this choice alone. And although you are responsible for your own connections with others, you cannot make their choices for them nor take the burden of their life upon your shoulders, for they each have also chosen to be here...

E.:   I am confused.

MOITA: Do you know why?

E.:   Conflict. Trying to understand a system, kind of feeling that there isn't one.

MOITA: You are seeking a higher guidance or a knowing that there is that kind of guidance for man and his world, and that the things that you see are not just haphazard.

E.:   Yeah, that ties in, because to me part of the confusion and the turmoil is caused by us not being able to . . . When we go through life, we make decisions, and somehow we have to follow through. You can't always be seeking through someone else a deeper understanding of yourself.

MOITA: Each one of you seeks this understanding in different ways. When you get to the point where you know yourself first and do not need another to feed back your own understanding, what you would call mistakes or misguided directions or unwise choices would not be made in the first place. Until man learns the functioning of his own energy, he will continue to make mistakes. That is how he learns. *(pause)*

I have an easier time accepting what happens to you and others in a life, since I am no longer bound by these rules... *(pause; then D. resumes:)*

D.:   There were times when I asked for your guidance but was afraid what your guidance would be.

MOITA: It is not uncommon to have such fears. You may find that, when you give up your desires or your fear of losing them, they shall come forth in a clearer guise for you. We do not demand that you give up anything you are not willing to. You as the greater self may have different desires than you as your everyday self, but very often more than one purpose can be served with the same desire... *(long pause)*

And what are you seeing?

D.:   I'm feeling more open from my heart... I feel love.

MOITA: I have seen so many go through change. *(pause)* Although each thinks his case is unique. *(D. laughs)*

(Kelly will say afterward that she can sense Moita's 50,000 years of watching people having these fears in the process of growing. She has acceptance and love for them even when they are making what seem disastrous mistakes. "What patience! Sometimes it's like watching a kid learning how to walk – or crawl.")

D.:   I've had this little worry that, in my life so far, I have, one might say, bounced from one person to another. While I feel like there's been some change and openings, I hope this isn't my path for the rest of my life.

MOITA: Have you ever wondered about *our* relationships – those of us who are not in bodies, and how we handle these intricacies?

D.:   How?

MOITA: Of course, we do not have the forgetting and then the need to open to know ourselves. We remember our pasts and the differences in relationships. But there is only one rule, if you can call it that here, and that is to give of yourself when you are with one who will accept what you have to give.

I have very few souls that I have a continuous connection with through all of my development – although there are a few. It does not mean that I give any less to those that I have a shorter connection with. It is just that they have gone along a different path than I. When you meet on your path and embrace instead of throwing stones, your partings will not be wrenching. Of course, it does not translate as well in words as it does in feelings. *(pause)* Also, I can split myself if there is more than one that requires my attention. I need not be in just one place and one time. That solves many problems. *(pause)*

I can see you have missed us.

D.:   *(smiling)* You used a word with two meanings.

MOITA: I use many words with more than one meaning and level...

(looking at me) Do you have a question?

David: Through what D. has been saying, I've been reliving Kelly's and my experiences two years ago, separating from former partners. There are similar patterns, including the fear that following your guidance might mean having to abandon my desires.

(Kelly then receives the thought from Moita, "Am I such a terrible taskmaster?!")

David: It's amazing how whole the system of the universe is.

MOITA: At least, the part I play in.

ક   ક   ક

The transforming third, the sacrifice, pain as friend and teacher, sorrow as the spirit's cleansing fire – all working toward making of us an instrument of light . . . As we begin to see through Moita's eyes, literal, melodramatic physical life becomes a pageant of spiritual advance or retreat, with universal significance – a view that nonetheless proves extremely practical in keeping our balance amid events which would otherwise overwhelm us in a nightmare of guilt, confusion or grief.

Waking life is indeed but another kind of dream – a message spelled out in symbolic scenes, a reflection of self – that can terrify and enrage, or teach and fulfill, depending how we choose to view it. When all aspects of the dream can be recognized as oneself, then judgments – whether moral or psychological – on the parts played by different persons in our life lose their relevance, leaving us to accept our path as a chosen way of liberation.

F.:   I have the weirdest dreams. Either they're all a real fantasy world that could never happen to me, or they're nightmares. And the fantasies are usually nice dreams and I won't dream them again, but the nightmares I will. Does that mean something?

MOITA: Nightmares very often are the more important ones. They return until you understand them, until you come to a point where you can see their message. Their messages are usually not as frightening as are the dreams [themselves]. The world of dreams is dramatic because it speaks in pictures to make a simple point. Sometimes the picture must be very elaborate, or so it would seem.

It is a universal language, the language of symbols, but each person has a different meaning for each symbol. All of the things that you see in your sleep are different parts of yourself and how they feel about your life, what they see happening to you. You can befriend yourself or you can fight yourself. And when you are fighting or rejecting your different personalities or projections, you will have turbulent dreams.

The path to spiritual development is through acceptance of *all* – what appears negative and what you feel is positive – that lies within yourself. You do not destroy an impulse by fighting it but by accepting it as it is, growing *through* it. It is not easy to say precisely what I intend when I say this. Some will think I am propounding an immoral outlook on life; but then one must understand true morality before such a judgment can be made. A clear heart, a true heart, is one with no dark corners or hidden shadows. Shadows do not disappear when you turn your back on them. They disappear when they themselves are turned into light.

ప   ప   ప

(As Moita becomes present, both Kelly and G. are aware of a "really strong tenderness" from Moita all centred around G. After a silent exchange:)

MOITA: It is never easy, is it.

G.:   No. I've been feeling so intensely involved in what seems like karma or lessons about love that it's hard to see clearly. It feels like a real opening, but it isn't easy. Can you give me any insights into the past that might help? Or maybe that isn't important right now.

MOITA: It is the past you are learning to *let go of*. The things that you are feeling fall away are your attachments to those happenings of yesterday.

G.:   Yeah.

MOITA: Many yesterdays. And it is frightening not knowing where your tomorrows are leading you, or if you will have the strength to meet whatever challenges may come. *(G. nods)* You do have help.

G.:   I do. In other people, you mean? And in you?

MOITA: In all of those who have love for you. The New Age will be one where love is redefined, where it becomes a freedom rather than a bondage. You would not have someone bound to you through guilt.

G.: No. No. But love seems to form bonds, doesn't it?

MOITA: It brings with it its own sense of touching, a continued connection. But in order for it to be that kind of true bond, it must not be unhealthy, unwhole.

G.: Yeah.

MOITA: I love many, in many ways. Yet the love I hold for each of you does not make any of my other loves less . . .

G.: That's true, that's true.

MOITA: . . . because my love comes from a clear heart. I do not need another's assurance, for I know myself and I have seen my own beauty.

G.: That's a nice strong place.

MOITA: It is a place that is reached through difficulty and pain. When you can let go of what you see as your own desired ending, you will free not only yourself but others to make an ending that may be more right, although it may end up to be the same. It is not *what* happens; it is *how* it happens.

G.: Yes, I can see that. That's true.

MOITA: It is easier to see at the moment than it will be tomorrow.

G.: I know. I've been feeling the need to be stronger, and it's hard to know sometimes how to do that. I don't want to be weak, but I guess time will build the strength, probably.

MOITA: It is important for you to share how you feel with others. You have too often in the past concealed your thoughts, your fears. You have drawn a veil between how you feel and its cause, and you are now finding the veil is being torn. Strength is not being invulnerable. Strength is accepting the pain as well as the joy, and sharing it with others. Through sharing you learn to stand alone, but you need not be lonely. You all stand alone anyway.

G.: That's true.

MOITA: This is the yearning for completion that you feel when you are in a body... Bodies are barriers in a way. They stop your thoughts – so it seems to people – from reaching another. The desire to be free and able to flow into another's soul is what you experience in your closest moments – [beyond] the fear of always being contained within oneself, unable to ever truly know another...

Some people come into bodies because they are afraid of that joining, afraid of being unable to conceal their thoughts, their intentions, their fears and inadequacies. And so, sometimes it happens...when a moment of union occurs – those rare moments when one can join with another, even if it is briefly – that the one that has fear will cut themselves off from the experience of merging.

(smiling, looking toward G.) In your case, it is – or was – your fear of being unfaithful to another's memory. You understand?

G.: I feel like that fear is passed now, though.

MOITA: It has led you to here. You have led yourself to releasing this fear, but you could see no way other than through pain.

G.:   Yeah, that's true.

MOITA: If there had been another way, you would have found it long ago.

G.:   Yeah. I kept hoping for another way, but it does seem true that this was the only way...
          (beginning to cry)

MOITA: Until you could free yourself from that attachment, you could not give of yourself to
          another... It does not mean that your love is ended.

G.:   No. It feels renewed.

MOITA: And it has changed, matured. You can only live moment to moment while you are here.
          And each moment will contain the seeds of joy if you will unlock the door to them, and they
          may be joys you have not yet conceived of. Your pain will show you your heart, but you
          must give to others what you need yourself: the freedom to change and grow, so each will
          become as much of a light as is possible for them... Your thoughts now affect not just your
          own future but those around you. Acceptance is difficult.

G.:   But necessary.

MOITA: Yes. *(long pause)*

G.:   Thank you.

MOITA: You are looking better.

G.:   I'm feeling better... My heart feels better.

MOITA: Not beating as fast?

G.:   *(laughs)* No. Calmed down. *(pause)*

          (To me, who has been recording this by hand:)

MOITA: You should stop writing.

          (I do, so we can all join hands.)

MOITA: Now I can pour more energy down before I leave.

          (After a period of silence, speaking to G.:)

MOITA: I shall see you again soon.

G.:   Yes, I hope so.

MOITA: Good night.

G./David: Good night.

(A long, silent meditation, as Moita gradually leaves. As Kelly returns, there are tears in her eyes, as there have been several times during the session when Moita's tenderness toward G. was especially strong. Kelly then describes what she alone was seeing.)

Kelly: That's why I cried, right at the end. Moita put her hands around your head, leaned over
          and kissed you on your forehead. And she put a gold cross above David's head in the air. I
          couldn't stand it; it made me cry. There was such warmth.

ৎ   ৎ   ৎ

There are times as this book is compiled when the editor can no longer stand apart. This is one of them, as moments when my own veil has been torn rise out of the past . . . [66N]

I see myself wrenched by friends' criticism into recognizing, amid heaving sobs, that I *am* all that I have tried not to be – till suddenly I realize my perfectionist isolation is over, leaving me to celebrate my rebirth as a child of this Earth . . .

I see my world of meaningful goals shrivelling to cardboard because my beloved will no longer share them – till I befriend my own self, or my Self befriends me, revealing the mystery of all creation within . . .

I see myself becoming a last, tiny dot of identity, crying out to a terrifyingly alien universe – till I disappear into compassion, sharing my vulnerability . . .

I see myself emerging from a therapy session, knowing I shall not be "together" if anyone I should meet – but strangely, humbly proud of that fragility, like a butterfly first opening its glistening wings . . .

Here, at the meeting-place of opposites, lies a marvellous equality of the heart, a wholeness without words. But the way to it is not paved with gold.

H.: I feel like I'm in the spiritual first grade, in that I often lose sight of important things. I'd sure like to graduate from the first grade, but I seem to keep going on. *(pause)*

MOITA: There are many things I could say to you: many things you are already aware of within yourself, why you feel you are not progressing – and yet you *are*. You are in the midst of growth and turmoil. When you pass through your own personal storm and the calm weather has entered into your heart again, you will be able to see the purpose of the storm's passing.

Growth on a spiritual path is not something that can be measured. Each soul develops in its own way, making its own rules as it travels. You have much more knowledge and awareness than you allow yourself to recognize. It is, for now, standing behind you, waiting for you to turn your attention in its direction.

There is never any clear distinction between one phase of your growth and another. One day you shall awaken and realize you are on a different level. Relax and learn joy in all the things that you do. That is the path to self, for if you can learn joy you will learn self.

But joy is complete. It takes in all things, all aspects of yourself and of life. To turn away from one part, you must overemphasize another; and then there is regret, the beginning of the loss of joy. Put your yesterdays behind you and leave your tomorrows to themselves. Live your todays completely, and then you will have no regrets.

In this moment, in each moment that you are fully there, you decide what kind of future you will bring to yourself, and you are deciding what kinds of relationships you will have with others in other lives as well as this one.

H.: I sense the rightness of your words and the ring of truth. I am sometimes at a loss as to how to put the truth into action, or the general into the specific. Maybe those are false worries because they're worries about the future; but yet, I have those doubts.

MOITA: In leaving the past behind, you come into your own. You recognize that all beings have their own view of their past and yours. You will recognize that your own view of the past is a changing thing. There is no truth except how you perceive it. In seeing this, you can know that you need not defend your view of the past. In trying to defend your perspective, you change your reality of the present. You give the past life, substance, energy, importance. It creates a false battleground – people who kill themselves and others through words over dead things, and by so doing also murder the present.

If you know yourself, feel cleansed within yourself, there is no need to prove it to another. Their view is theirs and relates to them. This is fairly practical advice.

H.:　　　　Yes. I appreciate practical advice.

MOITA:　　But the practical application is not as easy as the advice. *(laughter)* From here, it is easier to see these things from a different perspective. When you are in the midst of them, it is not as easy to see what you are doing to yourself, for in the end all that you do you do to yourself, not to another... I have an advantage in being able to see a more complete picture. *(laughter)*

H.:　　　　I'm playing with half a deck.

MOITA:　　Even I must tread this path with care. But for those who do not have this advantage of perspective, other people's paths may seem very confusing, scattered, inappropriate, or even useless, *to you* who cannot see the true purpose behind their experience. *(pause)*

You can make great intuitive leaps. You get messed up in trying to fill in the gaps between your current knowledge and your leap. It need not be straightforward or logical... *(long pause as they gaze at each other)*

H.:　　　　What do you see? What goes on in these periods, from your perspective?

MOITA:　　I watch as different parts of your soul come forth and cry for recognition. I see the many sadnesses that you have gathered to yourself throughout the ages, for these things are in the foreground of your development in this moment. They are seeking release as well as recognition. As long as the depth of these feelings remains hidden, it cannot be released or left behind. That is what I perceive *now*. Since each moment is different, and you are different, what I perceive during quiet times changes.

H.:　　　　I don't even feel that I know these sadnesses well, though I feel something like that. How should I get to these sadnesses that I could release them?

MOITA:　　You have brought them into the foreground of your consciousness partly through your own [past-life] regression – that [incarnation] is one place where you acquired a great deal of sadness – and partly through the experience you have chosen in this life. Each one mirrors to a certain degree that which has happened to you before.

You go through the same lessons, but in a shorter time; and so, learning to let go of the things you have acquired in this life will help you let go of the sadnesses you have brought to yourself throughout time. But you do have sadness within you from this life, and that is the greatest part that needs release. It is your turning from your feelings that causes the dimness that you see in your own sight. It is hard to leave shadows behind, and not all are ready to face their own shadow.

H.:　　　I guess I don't have a clear picture of that: of turning away, you said, from my feelings (?).

MOITA:　　I see you as a being with many levels of thought and feeling. I can go to the deepest level or the one that is closest to the surface. You see things in the surface that are confusing to yourself. From my view, this is what we see: you are not clear within your own thoughts.

H:　　　That's true.

MOITA:　　To seek an answer to your question, I must go deeper in your levels of feelings until I reach a point where you are clear. And so, I see all those things that lie between your clearness and your surface. This is what I am attempting to describe and explain. But you see, you as a conscious entity are still on the surface. It is your job to descend within yourself to seek that clearness. *(pause)*

We would have you remember also that you are only responsible for your own spiritual development. Do not take upon yourself responsibility for another's. Give them the freedom to find themselves. *(smiling)* It can help you release...

(From the conversation afterward:)

Kelly:　　I saw your face change completely, into that life from your hypersentience session. There was a look to the eyes: the first time I saw it, there was a vivid sadness, a strong feeling pulsing out of the face and eyes; the second time, the sadness had matured somehow, gotten to a new plateau of understanding, with more serenity and/or acceptance. I heard something about "You have accepted love into your heart. You are seeing things more clearly now than in any other time you've been in a session. And yet . . . "

H:　　　*(laughing)* I can appreciate the "and yet".

Kelly:　　". . . you recognize it not."

ॐ　　ॐ　　ॐ

I.:　　　I've gone through an intense metamorphosis recently. It's made me think a lot about depths of despair, the depths of emotional feeling, and how going through a thing like that can be a springboard to incredible spiritual growth – that the deeper you've gone, the further you can grow in an immediate sense. I think I've learned a lot about it by having gone through it. I'm wondering how that process looks from where you look. Can you describe it?

MOITA:　　You are doing fairly well yourself.

I.:　　　It seems to me so far that, no matter how far a person progresses, those periods of depth and despair always seem to come. There never seems a point where you don't go through them anymore.

MOITA:　　Not yet. There are points.

I.:　　　There are points?

MOITA: It is not something that *I* experience – have not experienced for a long time.

I.:   Hmm.

MOITA: Here is where you get in touch with the fact of each emotion and feeling to gain understanding of it. And once understanding has been reached, the experience is no longer necessary, for you have that awareness and compassion for yourself and for others who may still be going through those experiences.

I.:   Am I right in thinking that, at this particular stage, getting a clear, deep understanding of the experience of despair could be an important key to finding the core, nothingness, the core of all beings – that once that is experienced, there's no longer anything to fear? That's a very liberating feeling.

MOITA: It is finding that you have the strength that you need to go through the experience and come out the other side and still be whole, still be you. It gives you that . . . certainty that all the emotions, all feelings, can be survived and learned from, can be embraced for their value.

I.:   So that *all* experiences, including the low ones, can be transformed into growth...

MOITA: You continue to have experiences in a life, or over *many* lifetimes, that say the same thing over and over, until you go through it deep enough and strong enough to understand it... All experiences *must* be transformed into growth, sooner or later. When the growth happens, that is when the letting go takes place too.

ભ   ભ   ભ

That we create our own reality is a byword of the New Age. The astounding simplicity of the words – the reason the statement is so often dismissed with disbelief – masks vast complexities that must be worked through personally before their underlying truth is revealed. The difficulties within that first pronoun "we" are sufficient illustration, and go a long way toward accounting for the inner/outer upheavals of our time.

That "we" have indeed been creating our realities largely unconsciously, out of bottled-up emotions and limiting, fear-ridden definitions of life is precisely our problem, and it is these that are being forced to the surface by current "disruptions". The apparent negativity of many changes with which our lives are confronting us today can be traced to this emergence of deep-seated attitudes to consciousness, where they can again be owned as creations for which we have been responsible but which we may now pass beyond.

J.:   How are things where you are?

MOITA: Difficult to describe. *(laughs)* There are many variations. Much depends upon where I look.

J.:   That's the way it seems sometimes here, too. It depends on how I look at things – many different ways.

MOITA: The one you take to your heart will be the one that is real for you. It is the nature of reality that only you can define it for yourself.

J.:   It's hard when your heart is aching.

MOITA: We know. *(long pause, as they gaze into each other's eyes)*

J.:   I'm having a hard time keeping you in focus.

MOITA: Reality is shifting around freely. But, you see, looking into my reality, things are not as sharp in line as they are here for you. Barriers, edges, are not as clearly delineated. Things flow into each much more. Shapes reflect thoughts.

The thoughts you see in your life are sometimes so separate from you [that] they seem to have an identity of their own. It is difficult to become one with them in order to understand where they are coming from. Their angles reflect. That is why, as one becomes more aware of other realities, the patterns of life begin to shift and change. They do not stay still, for you are learning the ability to flow with your own thoughts; understanding them from within instead of seeing them as outside forces over which you have no control and for which you can bear no blame... Letting go of old thought-forms can be distressing, for they become close friends. They are comfortable, for they are known; and it is the unknown that causes fear and uncertainty...

When you can understand the nature of reality – its *true* nature – you will be able to shape your thoughts into those you wish to have around you, for they will reflect your inner nature.

ல்   ல்   ல்

It is a neat trick we perform with these old thought-forms and judgments of ourselves and others, pretending we have no choice about thinking them by having them appear "outside forces" – the objective reality or standard. It is similar to the trick we play getting born into our human egos and forgetting we all come from the same source.

In fact, the origin of our deep-seated barriers can lie not just in experiences from our current life but in other times we have been a personality in a body. These "oldest" of our thought-forms rooted in previous lives can be the most difficult to work with precisely because, not being explainable by this life's circumstances, they appear all the more objective. Failure to understand reincarnation fully *between* lives can add to the confusion, as Moita points out in the following excerpt. The moral is plainly one of detachment and acceptance.

MOITA: Reincarnation can be a useful tool or a dangerous one, depending on how you use it.

K.:   Do you mean knowledge of reincarnation, or reincarnation itself?

MOITA: I mean both. Not all spirits believe in reincarnation, so they are unable to direct it. But even those who do believe and do not understand its purpose can mistakenly direct it...

The one who spends a life in poverty and disease can become the richest man in the world and a fanatic about germs. The one who enjoys torture and battle can become the one who is the greatest crusader against war and torture. But still, in this they have erred, for rather than understanding the lesson they have been shown, they have leaped to the opposite end in an attempt to balance...

As I have always stressed, this life is the most important. Integrating your past lives can help to make this one richer or it can tear this one apart. For, you see, a [past] life is not really past; it is alive... You can...connect with a past self and understand the essence of another part of your soul. Until it is done consciously, with love and acceptance, you cannot go on to another level. The wheel of rebirth goes round and round until you know the whole wheel and can rise above it.

K.: How should we best reconnect with our past lives so that we can gain that understanding?

MOITA: There are many hints in the present that can open doorways to other lives... Strong likes and dislikes are keys. Your relationships with other people, your views on them and yourself, are very often based on past experience. Sometimes you think you can see clearly what you base a judgment on: the person who lies to you, you judge as a liar; and in the future when you meet this person again, though he may have changed, to you he is a liar still, for you have that memory. There you can trace a reason in this life, although it may still have connections in the past. Why did he lie? There may be a clue there too. He may feel he is paying you back for past pain...

You see, many people will become attracted to being together, or repulsed by being together, without clearly understanding why. When man is totally aware of himself and his motives, he will not make mistakes in joining with others for the wrong reasons. You have here many clues to yourself and your past, if you can look at them in the right light. You also have here an opportunity to learn how to let go of your own conceptions and judgments of someone else...

Learning how to let go of your judgments will help you rise above the prejudices of the past you have accumulated. That is the lesson of living in the moment. Each person surrounds himself with false corridors and angles in which to hide from his true feelings, from his true understanding, from himself. It is a never-ending process of breaking down barriers...

Lessons and tests are never easy. If they were easy, they would be useless. When you wish to make great strides in your soul's development, you must place yourself into great difficulties and learn from your reactions more about who you are... I do not believe in mistakes, for to me mistakes are the greatest teacher...

K.: A couple of times I had the feeling that I had caused some bodily pain to [name], and that was related to our difficulties now. Is that the case?...

MOITA: Thoughts are real. How people receive them will decide what effect they have. Here we are responsible for our thoughts, for we understand what they do; we can see them. But where you are, thoughts are still unknown, not understood or taken into account. You learn by seeing reactions to them, what they are and what they can do. This is where man discovers he is a creator, and where he defines his responsibility toward his own creation. But other beings are free to accept or reject the thoughts of another. They cannot find a home if they are unwelcome, or if there is not a resonance within the person that attracts or accepts the thought.

K.:   As an answer to that question, I'm a little perplexed.

MOITA: There are two responsibilities: the thinker and the accepter. It is never as straightforward as we would like. The universe is complex in its reactions and its reasons, but simple in its underlying energy and its overlying purpose. You can get lost in the complexities.

୨ଚ   ୨ଚ   ୨ଚ

Feelings, attitudes and conflicts born of past lives are a factor in the difficulties encountered by a couple – part of a triangle – on the verge of separating. Moita tries to clarify the inner sources of some of their barriers, and goes on to share her vision of love in its true nature, making for a group session we will long remember.

MOITA: I am seeing a life you are living... You are a mandarin, a woman, one who is bound by custom to the home. It is not one of your more pleasant lives.

L.:   Not much joy, you mean?

MOITA: Not from your perspective. It is a culture of bondage during a time when maleness was considered the only proper form of expression.

L.:   I've felt that sometimes.

MOITA: In these past months, this life has paralleled parts of that one, so those feelings would be closer to the surface. Past experiences can tend to fortify current perspectives of reality. It can be dangerous to look through old windows.

L.:   Do you mean dangerous to the present?

MOITA: Being able to see all things in the current moment is something each individual needs to learn. All things are in constant flux and change; nothing remains the same. Experiences can become walls to new perceptions, if you see reality as consisting only of things known, tested and experienced.

L.:   That's true. My perception seems to be changing. Sometimes it feels good and sometimes it frightens me, but it's exciting.

MOITA: As your clearness brightens, more old windows will be brought to light. And as you become aware of those perceptions, you can clear them away. You can take down your structures one piece at a time, until you find yourself in the open and free.

L.:   Mmm. That's a nice thought to think about.

MOITA: Those walls are sometimes harder to unmake . . . *(L. laughs)* . . . than they were to make. Fear comes because you have forgotten the countryside. The walls are safe.

L.:   When I'm out in the woods, it feels like the walls are less there. It feels much better.

MOITA: The energy that is inherent in the Earth is one of change, one of moments. It helps for you to recall experiences on other levels – a time without many walls...

(Then turning to M.:) You lived also in a time where man was considered the only positive, productive force in the world. And in your role you were a man, so you have seen another side. You have been one who subjected others – in the right of your position, and with the backing of your culture – to your will. It is here, in part, you are learning how to let go of your will. *(long pause)*

M.:   And that's what I'm experiencing now?

MOITA: You are in battle with different parts of yourself that are moving in opposite directions. You feel the pull of the culture and the pull of the will. In this life, they do not coincide. They go in different directions.

(For example, the culture says to stay in one's present relationship, and will says to leave it.)

MOITA: To gain what you need, you must let go of both and not know what path you are following – not with your eyes, not with your mind, not with other people's structures or concepts. The path of the moment is a changing path, but one that is changing you to finding yourself. You do not know who or what you are. If you knew, or thought you knew, it would be but one more structure, one more blind alley or false wall...

M.:   I feel the pull of both my will and the culture going in different directions. I like the male force or strength in me. That isn't the same as love, but some of that force feels to me like a positive thing – the strength to follow my own . . . promptings, or . . . to follow my heart.

MOITA: There is a difference between your will and your heart.

M.:   I'm using my will against the culture. Is that . . . ?

MOITA: You have it. That is what you're doing: opposing yourself. The middle way is your heart, the way of love, of sharing, of being able to share in many ways with many people without comparing differences. You must be wholly – meaning completely – where you are. You cannot remain divided without breaking yourself apart...

The main purpose in life is to find your own essence, an essence that can be shared in many forms. Do not limit yourself to one form or the other. Do not destroy your future possibilities by burning your bridges behind you.

M.:   That makes things more confusing for me in some ways.

MOITA: True. But it is a confusion that has been there for a long time, and I am trying to bring it out. The true nature of love – this is what you all are seeking in this and any experience. What form of expression should it take?

Love is many-faceted. It is a jewel of creation, sharing. It has many forms and many faces. It is not limited in any way. If it limits, then it is not love but a shadow and a falsehood, a reflection in the water but not the mountain you are seeking.

You all need to expand your walls to include other forms. There are not better or less in love. Love knows no judge in any way. If you take a jewel and suspend it before a window, and the Sun reflects through this jewel and breaks itself into many colours, one colour is not more desirable or complete than another. They are separate because they have been broken. They are different because they are separate. But they each come from the same jewel. They are all part of the same whole and together make one light, not many.

This is not an easy thing to explain in words, in these structured terms, because your language itself is a barrier to understanding reality and creation. You can see many forms of love around you, know that the love of a parent for a child is different yet no less than the love of a man for a woman. A grandparent sheds a different colour on a [grandchild]. Yet when all are free within themselves, when love is unbound, let loose, they are the same; they come from the same source.

M.:   It is this integration that I'm having trouble with.

MOITA: Do not compare. Each moment is its own beauty. It stands alone on its own merit. It is not meant to be compared. You cannot compare a star to a leaf without taking away something from both. *(pause)*

If love is to make itself manifest in the world, it must first be understood; it must be lived, not talked... Each moment has in it the seeds of your understanding, the seeds of love, spirit; but only if you are *in* that moment to see what it holds.

Being a river flowing over the stones and the falls and the rapids, each one is different yet each one is complete. And the river eventually finds its way to the sea because it does not try to stop the flow of its own moments. *(pause)* You cannot go back from here in time to moments past. In this focus they are very precious, and none should be wasted... Turning yourself against the flow and looking back to the cliff the fall has just descended from will not let yourself climb back up to the top. You can only go forward. Leave the past behind.

M.:   Which past?

MOITA: All pasts. They help you to know the way you have gone, to know your route to the sea. They are there as signposts of your development, and others can sometimes use them to help them find their own way. But they become another obstacle when you turn yourself around to face the direction you have come. Great and monstrous shapes can rise from any past to haunt you. Guilt, despair, loneliness – all of these things can sit on your doorstep, if you give them life. When Christ said, "Get thee behind me, Satan," he was telling the world to put past mistakes behind and not to look upon them ever again.

M.:   I want to ask some questions about what you've said. "Burning bridges behind me" – is that a warning that is what I am about to do or part of my will would do?...

MOITA: *(closes eyes)* When you see...fewer possibilities in your future, you narrow what paths may be open to you. Your reality is what you can conceive. If you conceive that something is impossible for you, you will bring that into reality. It will *become* impossible in your world. Your only limitation is what you can bring to any life situation. Does that help?

M.:   I think so.

MOITA: You are learning to create your own reality.

M.:   Sometimes I think so.

MOITA: It is a lesson many will learn well in future times. All men are creators. The human spirit has a great reservoir of creative energy, but it has been unseen in many years. The universe is open; it has no walls, no structure, no limitations, and no expectations. It is a filled emptiness waiting for mind to bring form to it. Make your forms things of beauty. Fill your emptiness with love and light. You do not want the darkness; I can see that well. *(pause)*

And so, we come and we tell you these things and hope you see a glimmer, a light to follow when things grow dark, a hope to keep in your heart. We come to show you the reality of love in its many forms by being here. *(pause)* Thank you.

M.:   Thank you.

(Later, near the end of the session, Moita takes advantage of a silence to look around the circle.)

MOITA: There have been many great experiences tonight.

L.:   There *have* been.

MOITA: It is an occasion when our worlds touch more closely and a part of my reality enters more clearly.

L.:   It makes my reality more clear also, to join with yours.

MOITA: Soon both realities will become one and no longer separate – no need for bridges...

(Another participant says Moita feels "more here than I can almost ever remember".)

MOITA: Times are changing.

(to M.:) And how are you now?

M.:   Fine.

MOITA: I hope this has been an experience for you to recall in times ahead.

M.:   I think it is that.

MOITA: Unlike your own life experiences that occur in this physical reality, this experience transcends the time-stream, if you can learn to reach it.

M.:   How can I best learn to reach it? For, as you can see, I have trouble sometimes.

MOITA: It is something that has become a part of you, a well in your own heart. Touch love and you shall touch this. You will learn.

M.:   Thank you. I appreciate your light.

MOITA: I must shade it for a time. Good night.

(We hold hands in silence, sharing energy, as Moita departs. This conversation takes place afterward:)

David: M. appeared close to falling into Moita's eyes.

L.:   Yes. It was like being attracted, drawn in. M. was leaning over her.

M.:   We were real close, powerfully connected. What she talked about made a lot of sense – a less simple path than one would hope for.

L.:   I could feel all this energy in your body. It looked like conflict.

M.:   Yep. I was getting a strong feeling of strength of will. Usually my feelings at sessions are quite a bit gentler.

Kelly: Your thoughts were like storm clouds churning around, searching for what to ask. I could see Moita going down inside you, like pulling weeds – bringing things up into the light.

M.:   I feel like I've been thrown back into the stream now.

(L. also says that Moita's face looked transparent, out of focus, and was changing appearance. Kelly says her body was vibrating during the session and still is somewhat. After we talk for quite a while, Kelly stands up and – though her legs are not asleep – she suddenly collapses on the floor. It is as if she has forgotten, she says, how to work her body!)

✎ ✎ ✎

Moita's presence brings a freedom to find our own path ahead, leaving aside the inner pasts – the dead-ended approaches to life – that make for and subsequently tie us to uncreative relationships.

N.:   Why do I stay where there are so many distractions?!... I get to this point where I cease to see what *is* forward and what *is* back.

MOITA: You have reached another crossroads. You must decide for yourself what your values will be, what your goal is. You are torn between commitment to another and commitment to yourself. You still desire to sacrifice your *own* being to another's. And until you are willing to let each man be his *own* guide, and not be a crutch for others to lean on, you will continue to be weighed down by your sense of responsibility. You cannot save the world by being a crutch. You can only destroy yourself and those who lean on you, for then neither one of you can walk. It is sometimes the hardest thing to do: let another fall. That is how a child learns when he first begins to walk. He falls down, and learns how to get up and stand on his own feet. You are *all* children; you are *all* learning how to walk.

N.:   But it doesn't really matter what direction; it's how we walk there.

MOITA: The universe is open. First you must get your feet under you. And then, as you learn to see, you will see different paths, different universes. And whichever one feels right to you, you will be drawn to. Even if you go off in another direction first, it always draws you back. To deny your path does not keep you from it; it merely delays your walking on it.

(Meanwhile Kelly is seeing a roadway with side roads branching off, going around hills, etc., but later rejoining despite initial appearances. Some routes take longer to return than others.)

N.:   Have I ever walked on my path before? Will it be easy to recognize?

MOITA: Each life you have lived has been a step upon the path. You see, the goal is always the same. But your way of getting there is your *own*. That is the path: being yourself. Again, it is not the what.

ℂ ℂ ℂ

Our security can be identified with many outward and inward conditions – a truth we generally only learn when those conditions disappear. This is graphically illustrated in the experience of this close friend who remarks to us, "It's bloody scary to be alone, outside of the routine I've been in all these years, knowing that my [spouse will be] home... Without that, there goes your identity. It's like being put on the Moon. It's like a baby after being born. All my world is back [where I used to live]. I have trouble believing that just me is motivation enough. I'm literally rebuilding my reality. It's terrifying."

But losses of relationships and other forms of security *can* lead us to become intimate with our own inner resources, beyond the walls we have created. Though the way appears to lead even further from others at first, we are larger beings able to give with clearer hearts when next we feel ready to join paths.

MOITA: Very few people know what is happening to another. There is great distance between you, all of you. *(long pause)* It is not an easy thing to bridge the gap. Sometimes the gap must be accepted. Each of you has an individual path to follow. Eventually, gaps will have no meaning anymore. But it still boils down to fear – fear of breaking down barriers from within in order to let others touch you...

O.:   I still have a lot of walls, then?

MOITA: Even *I* have walls. *(pause)* As the inner self expands, and walls fall away, new structures are built; and they too expand, eventually falling away. Someday I shall leave *these* structures behind... But it should not be . . . something to fear. It is a cause for rejoicing: delving deep within and finding self.

O.:   I'm working very hard at it. It's straining on me right now. I have a lot of work to do, and I'm not sure what's the right way to go about it.

MOITA: Don't think of it so much as work. You will find it much easier to flow with. Think of it as an adventure. You are setting a course into the future and putting up signposts along the way. You shall not get lost. And every time you go around a corner, there shall be something new awaiting you – something you may not have even thought of before or seen before or remembered. Make it not a *task* to break down your walls. Let them fall, gently.

O.:   I hope I can. *(pause)*

MOITA: I do not doubt that you shall have success.

ℂ ℂ ℂ

P.:   I was discussing today with someone the necessity of self-love, so the person is able to branch out and love others. What are the most important first steps towards that goal, so that you can stay with it? Sometimes I seem quite able, and other times it seems almost impossible for me to love myself.

MOITA: When you are finding it difficult to love yourself, try and accept that feeling at the moment and see it as a tunnel, knowing that at the end of this tunnel you will come again into the clear sky, into that clear knowingness. And if you feel the need to reconnect with yourself perhaps sooner than your tunnel would let you, you can try and take yourself away from the identity of you by becoming involved in the energy outside. I mean literally outside – in the air, in the Earth.

P.: Divorcing yourself from your ego temporarily, do you mean?

MOITA: Taking a long walk, looking at the trees, watching the clouds, immersing yourself in the Earth, and forgetting yourself for the moment. You may find you are in some way cleansed of that worry. For when you do not love yourself, it is because you are focused in the wrong direction. This helps to unfocus you, so you can regain focus.

Reading helps as well. Anything simple and beautiful that conveys a strong feeling for life will help you touch that life-source. And you can express that energy in a creative form. Try to get it out of yourself and down on paper, so that you can see it, see where it comes from and then accept it. For you must accept yourself even when you do not feel you are loving yourself. Your good moments and your bad are equally as important. And if you try to fight having bad moods, you will have more bad moods.

P.: Yes. That would be your recommendation, then, for breaking up bad thought patterns and starting on a new track. I've just been starting to get wee snatches in my dreams. I wonder if you could interpret one of them in any way that I could understand it a little better – the one where I was picking up buttons in an old part of a city, and dumping them on the seat of a new car that didn't belong to me.

MOITA: I can tell you that these buttons represent your cast-off thoughts that you are now beginning to recollect – things as a child that you have experienced, things that you have desired, things that you have thought of and have put away because you were taught they were things you should not think. So they have been lying around in the corridors of your mind, waiting for you to come back and realize that they have been there. You are beginning to recollect them so that you can look through them and decide which ones you wish to keep and which ones you will put back, or which ones you will give away to someone else.

P.: Why did I wish to show them to these other people?

MOITA: In this experience you used them to represent your parents within yourself – the ideal, the aloofness, the untouchability. Although they seemed friendly, you felt they were hostile, because their friendliness was something that was plastic – something you could see, something that angered you. And you wished to show them these thoughts. You need them to accept thoughts that you have had. You are seeking approval from these inner authorities. Does that help?

P.: Yes. And where did the green field full of blue flowers come from?

MOITA: It is a good image to represent growing that is happening within yourself – your own blooming, the possibility of becoming a field studded with beautiful flowers. *(pause)* But remember that a field, before it grows beautiful, has many things that others may consider unbeautiful put upon it first – the natural fertilizers of the Earth, things that some people would throw away and consider waste, that can be changed and used to help this kind of growth take place... It can come from what you have thought of as waste, and some of those throw-away thoughts that will bloom.

P.:   This field appeared full-grown, in full bloom.

MOITA: I said it is a possibility, one you are working toward – a symbol given to you by yourself...

(From conversation after the session:)

Kelly: It all seemed so clear about your dream.

David: You had told that to Kelly before, right? So Moita was listening in and was working on it in the meantime. She had that all prepared.

Kelly: It seemed like she *knew*, when you asked. I had no inkling of an idea, though, what she was going to say. I mean, even when she started talking, all of a sudden I saw buttons on the sidewalk, and she says, "Aha! The buttons mean . . ." And then poof! This whole thing started coming out. And those are the times that really amaze me, because the answer's happening and I'm scratching my head on the side, wondering, "Golly, that's really interesting – never thought of that!"

P.:   Me neither!

∾   ∾   ∾

(At the beginning of this session, there is a long silence as Moita and Q. gaze toward each other. A little way into the silence, Q.'s sigh shows something is definitely happening. Eventually Q. is ready to speak.)

Q.:   I felt like I almost lose myself. I guess one shouldn't be afraid to lose oneself, or to enter into a different state, kind of.

MOITA: It is not yourself you are losing. It is your perspective of reality that is changing.

Q.:   Yeah. Sometimes it seems there's difficulty, but I suppose that's all part of it.

MOITA: You are learning to touch your own soul, and finding a purpose – in growth.

Q.:   Mmm.

MOITA: There is a great dance that is being performed in your life and with those around you. It has momentum; it has an inner strength. It knows its form. But being only one part of this dance and looking at it from one side, it can be distorted. Your angle is not complete.

Q.:   I can feel that. I have a feeling that it will be more complete. Maybe I'm trying to deceive myself, but it feels that way. Is it complete for each person in the dance? Or . . . how do you mean "complete"?

MOITA: When you see your own part, when it feels whole alone, it is not as necessary to be able to view the wholeness of the entire dance. When your part is clear, you know the dance continues unfolding as it should, and that is the meaning of the dance in the first place – each one becoming whole. The more you touch your soul, the sooner you will find that completeness that lies within it. So fear not.

Q.:   *(smiles, nods)* I feel my fears have fallen away more lately. They don't have the same grip on me. It's a nice feeling. Every now and then I keep grabbing hold. Then it takes a while to shake them again. I don't know if a conscious effort is needed or if they'll just slip away.

MOITA: Your energy travels in cycles as the seasons. As long as you are in cycles, you will rise and fall within yourself. And as the Earth slowly changes its face, you will find your fears slowly lose their intensity. *(pause)*

           These moments in this altered reality are the keys to wakening your own latent ability for perceiving not only your own strength and clearness but others' as well. It is an energy that gradually manifests itself in daily living. It spills over.

Q.:   It's so nice that this energy is here to touch. I've been feeling your energy – it seems, most times at sunset. Maybe it's my own making, but I feel it more then.

MOITA: When the light grows dim in the sky, it sometimes helps to illuminate other lights.

Q.:   That's true.

MOITA: I am not here just in these moments. The more familiar anyone becomes with this energy, the more easily they will be able to touch it at other times. It is not meant for this to become a necessity in order to touch. It is meant for this to help bring about those inner changes that are needed so it will become a living process. This is my purpose...

           (At the end of this rather emotional session involving another, Moita returns to Q.:)

MOITA: How are you taking all of this?

Q.:   It's been feeling like a dance! *(laughs)* I've been feeling the rhythm of it, feeling like I'm floating. What you say has very deep meaning for me too. *(pause)* More and more I sense the great importance of being in touch with my soul. It feels so good when there are some glimpses. It feels really good and strong.

ৡ   ৡ   ৡ

Many of the friends who have appeared in this chapter are present together for this final session, which takes place in early March 1980. With winter soon to end, there is awareness here of cycles and seasons through which our energy travels, leading to a "spring" on many levels. Members of this group are to travel in different directions after this session, reflecting various phases in our search for wholeness, both in and out of relationship. Gatherings will become smaller and less frequent as time goes on, so that the overall pattern of the dance will be much less visible, while each concentrates on getting clearer about his or her own part.

MOITA: *Everyone* here feels different.

R.:   It's been a winter of changes.

MOITA: Each winter will become more and more of a change.

R.:   A lot of the lessons I've been learning have been through painful experience. I'm still too caught up in the emotion of it to grasp the direction I'm moving... The changes, I know, are positive; but sometimes when you're in the middle of the change, it's very hard to see that.

MOITA: That is why man has hope – to get him through the difficult times.

R.:   It's in Edge City where you learn the most, it seems.

MOITA: But it is not there where you apply what you learn. It is a lesson that you take with you to a different place or use in a different way...

We are here for you to draw on in your times of need. And we can be that extra strength that some feel they lack when they are in pain, because of our perspective and our distance...

S.:   I really identify with needing a perspective, a distance, giving one the freedom to . . . be.

MOITA: I can see that...it is important for you to be able to...speak your feelings. Others are not unaware of your thoughts. *You* are less aware of your thoughts than others, in some ways... Distance is not a barrier.

S.:   In some way I feel I've been isolated too long, too used to my *own* thoughts circulating instead of learning how to relate to someone else's thoughts.

MOITA: That is why there is the urge to speak, to share. One man alone cannot do that much. A few people together can do a great deal. But only if they are really together. Otherwise, they will be too busy trying to unbuild everyone else's works.

S.:   That's a lot of the problem I find with talking – to somehow include everybody else.

MOITA: Try not so much to include everyone else as to really touch yourself. They will feel included or excluded whether you include them or not...

T.:   I've been worried about talking to people. The last couple of weeks I've been very open, telling a lot of people a lot of things. I'm beginning to wonder about the wisdom of it. I've been warned by a lot of people not to say this to so-and-so, and not to say that to someone else. Are they fearful unnecessarily, or am I too open?

MOITA: Is there such a thing as being too open?

T.:   That's what I *wonder*. I find so often that being open clears me and often the other person too. But so many people fear I may be giving something away or harming myself for the future. Do you see any threat there?

MOITA: I see more threat to those who are closed.

T.:   Good. I don't like to go around being secretive.

MOITA: Sometimes it is more painful to get things out into the open initially. But in the *end*, everything will come out. Even if you said *nothing*, things would not be *hidden*.

T.:   Even if I feared violence for speaking things, would it still be better to say them? It's almost like provoking an incident.

MOITA: When you work with people, sometimes in order to gain the most desirable result in their growth you must allow them their fear. And if they see you as a threat to their own walls, they will fight you. As long as you remain clear within yourself, and see the purpose behind their actions, it should not make that much difference if you can actually speak with your mouth, so long as you can sing with your heart.

Each situation should be decided upon....its own merits. Trust your intuition, not other people's thoughts...

David: In times like these I seem especially aware of the "heart" within each person. When I hear each person speak, I feel especially in touch with them. In some ways we seem so enclosed in our own lives, changes, dramas, worlds. I sense our hearts groping upward toward that centre where you were saying a group needs to be really together to bring changes. It almost seems like some outward expression of that centre, that unity within the circle, might help make it more real for us. R.'s idea of building a medicine wheel somewhere here in the valley or surrounding mountains comes to mind as at least a symbol of what I'm groping toward.

MOITA: I can see clearer water downstream.

David: I seem to really feel it flowing there.

MOITA: It is good you are not paddling in the other direction! *(laughter)* It is a strong current. *(pause)* The first rush of water in spring is always muddy until the silt settles, assimilating all of the learning of the winter before...

R.: I have the feeling that this spring we're going to be springier than most somehow. I can almost see ice creaking around the circle the way it is on the river now.

MOITA: In leaps and bounds... This will be an important spring for *all* of you. So many changes.

Chapter 7

ERUPTIONS WITHOUT AND WITHIN

As Kelly rises from the group session in Chapter 6 that explored deep feelings emerging from the relationship crisis involving L. and M., she suddenly collapses on the floor! Later that night, Kelly becomes violently ill. She feels better before long. But then, a couple of days later, I come down sick as well. On the fourth night we're able to speak to Moita again. Her first answer reminds us of some inner reasons for the various illnesses, physical symptoms and "accidents" that many involved in consciousness change may be experiencing these days.

David: Having been sick, I'm feeling very fragile, vulnerable, open now. I'm touching the world only very lightly.

MOITA: You are cleansing your body. It changes your vibration rate, and so alters your perception.

David: What made our last session such a good occasion for the two worlds to touch, such a deep and intense experience? And is there a connection between the session and Kelly's getting sick?

MOITA: The more you become attuned to our vibration, the more your bodies will need to adjust themselves. Her body was in need of a cleansing. It had been building for a time. The many emotional experiences she has been going through, through others, has contributed to this need. And my presence, being so much more there than has been usual in the past, was the trigger for releasing a great deal of energy that no longer was needed – a different kind of energy, a lower form.

    There are many factors that influence when our worlds are closer together. The two energy changes that my realm has effected on the Earth in recent times have combined to accelerate the closing of this apparent gap. And it is in this decade that many more will become aware of our presence in and among what you call the living and how we influence their daily existence. Of course, the depth of those hearts who are searching also influences the worlds through a doorway. Their openness helps to determine clarity and depth.

ဆ   ဆ   ဆ

Thus, even through the "eruptions" of Kelly's and my own physical bodies, we are reminded of the larger context for the changes our friends are encountering – the rising vibration rate of our planet and all who dwell within her. Simultaneously, these energy changes are reflected and propelled further by the new intensity with which both Sun and Earth have been erupting during the year of our move to British Columbia. There is a clue here to the future as well.

The world upheavals of 1979-1980, viewed from the perspective of our sessions with Moita and Amar, bear strong parallels to the predicament that will be facing planet Earth and its inhabitants leading up to December 21, 2012, over three decades later. And as the transitional period to a New Age dimensional shift approaches its culmination, the connection between outer and inner changes will increasingly be brought home to us.

In this chapter, then, Moita's words highlight the close relationship – even the mirroring effect – between "eruptions without" and "eruptions within", from solar and planetary levels right down to the individual, during a very changeful year. Some key excerpts from Moita's messages in Chapter 6 also return as touchstones in the latter part of this chapter dealing with Earth upheavals.

One crucial point, already made in the Introduction and Prologue, needs repeating with special emphasis in this chapter, however. Prophecies are readings of the probability lines extending from one point in time forward. These probabilities evolve and change as choices are made and actions taken by beings on all levels. Predictions of dire circumstances are themselves actions taken, which hopefully teach lessons and so help avoid those circumstances becoming actualized.

As of this writing in 2012, Earth's intervening history and current prophecies from many sources suggest the more dire probabilities in this chapter are not coming to pass, for which we can be thankful. They are still included here as they emerged, though – partly to tell our story in context, but also to tell the history of what *might have been*, what at some points was even *likeliest* to have been, so we can appreciate the importance of the choices and gifts of energy that enabled their avoidance.

Solar changes

As all life in our system begins and ends with the Sun, so we should begin with the dramatic heights of solar activity that are recorded during 1980.[67N] We read that the predicted 22-year sunspot peak during January and February becomes a 350-year record by mid-February. The developing magnetic/gravitational forces from an alignment of planets, developing from now till 1982, is suggested as a causative factor in the solar storms, as well as in the year's rising tempo of earthquakes and volcanic eruptions. As it happens, an X-1 type solar flare – to this point, the highest category of radiation – makes the newscasts in July, and early October is said to bring the highest level of sunspot activity since 1609 when recording began.

The disruptive effects of solar storms on such physical phenomena as radio and electrical transmission are well-known, but little recognition is given the more important unsettling effects on the human mind and spirit. Physical science does not understand the internal dynamics of the sunspot cycle, let alone know of a factor from beyond our solar system that may alter that cycle in unprecedented fashion. This is the starting point for one of our most mind-stretching communications to date.

On the afternoon preceding this post-Christmas session, Kelly suddenly feels a difference in energy, as if someone we know is going through an unusual, exciting, almost fearful experience. Her heart is pounding heavily, identifying with this other reality. A while later, she takes a nap and begins to leave her body. She experiences three purifications to prepare for being guided on some journey. But she is interrupted then by young Arista and cannot return to the experience.

Moita session #126 (Kelly and David / December 26, 1979)

(Tonight, just before holding this session, we "happen" to read about sunspots in the newspaper. As Moita comes and opens Kelly's eyes, Kelly suddenly sees a bright, vividly blue star on my upper right chest. Moita cannot convey what Kelly's first experience in the afternoon was about, but does say that it served as a trigger for changing energy and leaving her body.)

David: We were just reading how the sunspot cycle is reaching its peak in recorded history. How do you see that process and the effects it has on the Earth?

(As I ask this, Kelly feels some force begin to drive her out of her body and much energy coming in as if to "take her place". She feels she's going to fall over and is surprised to see she's still sitting upright. She then receives a picture of sunspots being a greater than normal concentration of some of the Beings that comprise the Sun's subtle essence. This explains the huge emissions of energy from these areas. Interference on Earth is due to the frequency of their thought-waves. She will say later that this inward/outward thinking about the Sun is difficult for her to grasp.)

MOITA: The Sun goes through its own periods of awareness that the scientists call cycles of sunspot activity. You are travelling in a direction through space that will bring you closer to a *centre of awareness* in the system. This explains the dramatic increase in the solar activity.

The Sun is reflecting in an outward way this awareness. It is a shift in its energy. It is, in a way, increased mental activity. Just as the brain gives off different waves that correspond to different qualities of thought, so the Sun in its contemplations gives off different kinds of energy. This is a higher-frequency energy, corresponding to the higher frequencies in the human mind. And it serves to wake up consciousness in...the rest of the solar system.

Men seem to be usually more creative during periods of solar activity – near the end of them, once the energy has been absorbed and changed. Man is now learning to utilize the energy as it is happening rather than waiting. He can see the physical effects: the agitation of the planet's orbit and field of energy; and not the Earth's only but all the planets in the solar system are similarly affected. The magnetic field is stretching, reaching, seeking to connect itself with that of the Sun.

David: Some people have received communications to the effect that the sunspot peak we are entering is not going to wane in the same pattern as previous cycles. Could that be due to this area of greater energy that we're heading toward?

MOITA: It will serve to fan the flame, and the greater the awareness of those spiritual beings who live within the influence of the Sun, the stronger and more lengthy the sunspot activity will be.

You see, we have already gone through several energy changes – in part, to prepare the Earth to accept more of this kind of energy. The Earth has many shields and walls that man's awareness has built around it to protect itself. One of these shields has been dramatically decreased over the last number of years: the outer layer of the Earth's atmosphere. For reasons other than pollution, greater (what you call) radiation is entering the Earth through the thinned layer. It has been used as a filter [but] is becoming less of a filter and more of an opening.

(Kelly is reminded of reading about a group monitoring the Earth's ozone layer and discovering unexpectedly that a rocket launched into space created a gap in this protective shield, allowing greater radiation to reach Earth. She is receiving pictures of many rockets being launched, and these as symbolic of man's outward quest for answers. Without knowing it, we are opening up all these spaces for communication between levels – through our desire to touch other worlds, even if the ones we seek are but physical. We are being answered, *because of our very act of searching.)*

(A very long silence follows, in which I experience the most intense visual changes yet in these sessions. As I look steadily toward Moita's eyes, my entire visual field is filled with a golden haze in which figure and ground are continually reversing and the room and her face almost disappear from view. I am feeling very detached and out of this world . . . into another.)

(Kelly will later report that my eyes are quite dilated and unblinking, yet there is no straining, as if my higher self is relaxing them more than I can myself. Kelly is meanwhile seeing a mental image of us both floating above and behind our bodies, Moita and Loria standing, and five or six other beings grouped in a semicircle around us.)

David: I have the feeling my eyes could be closed and I'd still be seeing all this. *(long pause)* And I feel *very* unfocused!

MOITA: You *look* very unfocused!

David: Is this centre of energy you were talking about the same one that is spoken of in the book *Fatima Prophecy*?

MOITA: The energy that the solar system is working its way towards?

David: Mm-hmm.

MOITA: There are not very many of them around.

(This is Moita's typically indirect way of saying yes. Certainly, the intensity of energy both Kelly and I are feeling, to us, lends credence to the startling information being transmitted.)

(As mentioned in Chapter 3, the channelings in Fatima Prophecy *elaborate on the messages received during appearances of the Angel of the Mother of Jesus to children near the famous Portuguese town in 1917. They also refer to energy manifestations in the skies as observed by thousands during the last of the children's visions, including a dimmed "sun's" appearing to spin three times, to send out strange emissions, and then to fall toward Earth. These are said to prefigure a future "cosmic-solar event" that would speed the evolution of man.)*

(As we keep in mind what has been said about probability lines subject to free will, both human and angelic, and the different potential interpretations ranging from literal to metaphorical, here

are excerpts from Fatima Prophecy *relevant to Moita's words:)*

At the present time, the physical solar system heads in space at a great rate toward a mass of cosmic energy and particles which, in the *not-distant* future, will collide with the sun and planets and energize the ionosphere of planets and...the photosphere of the sun – unless it is averted...

Then the cosmic-solar event will begin. The Earth shall be showered with cosmic rays... Then will begin the three days of darkness fulfilling the [Biblical] prophecy...

If man approaches this properly, the evolution brought about by it will be smooth, and many deaths and sufferings will be averted; for the activity of the angelic realms and those who serve them from outside the Earth, would cause the change of conditions that this may be averted, but not unless the consciousness of those beings animate in the solar system and in the Earth, changes, for the Earth *must change in its consciousness...*

Those that survive shall have been changed... A new race of man shall have begun. *The evolution of man shall have been enhanced.*[68]

MOITA: The galaxy moves in cycles as well. Its energy ebbs and flows. There is a season to everything. Man is flowing from a cycle of winter into one of spring. *(pause)*

David: Is there anything more you can say about this *centre of awareness*? This must be a Being, I assume.

MOITA: A number of Beings. You have been told of them before. They were given a name.[69]

David: Well, I was just thinking about Archangels. Is that who you mean?

(Moita's eyes close, and I think Amar is come. Kelly feels "this terrific, golden rush all through my head" and identifies it definitely as Amar's energy. Then it leaves, however, and Moita is back to answer the question.)

MOITA: We have called them "the High Ones". It is the same. The addition of their energy to the Earth will help to bring about a great many of the changes that have been foretold. The added energy of their presence will bring things to a crisis point, so that there can be a breakthrough into a new reality. In order for this change to take place, the reality that exists here now must undergo a transformation. It will not be able to survive otherwise. For those who cannot cope with the changes, new shields will be put in place.

David: Do you mean on another world?

MOITA: In another time-area or reality.[70N]

David: Will this crisis point be right around the year 2000?

MOITA: That is the projected date – near there. The reason why the [Earth's] poles will shift is to adjust to this new energy. It will be a reaction to their arrival. And the magnetic poles will shift as well.

David: Is it possible to say approximately where those [new poles] will be?

MOITA: One shall be in the South Pacific. *(pause)* Quite a change.

David: *(laughing)* Hmm. No more lolling on the beaches.

MOITA: *(laughing)* Unless one is in a bearskin... *(i.e. polar bearskin!)*

(Kelly will say later that during the above conversation she gets a sudden flash of seeing Noah and hearing strange phrases such as "Get thee unto the high mountains." This relates to a potentially dramatic shifting of the poles and resulting change in climates. She can see the point and necessity in preserving as many as possible of existing animal species as well as plant seeds – including those that are not able to grow in our present climate, but which might be able to survive in the new one, and perhaps no longer where they do now.)

(We will look at our atlas and realize how great a shift would be entailed for the South Pacific – if Moita is implying at least a temperate, if not tropical, part of the South Pacific – to become polar. The globe would turn to some degree on its "side" in relation to its current axis. A critical factor, of course, is the gradualness or suddenness of such a change, an issue to which Moita will turn in a future session.)

(As the potential extent of these changes begins to sink in, Kelly experiences thoughts coming to mind like, "Is this real? I mean, here we are and we're being told the future, and is all this stuff really going to happen?" Then a really strong *"YES" answer comes back, and "Wait and see" and something about "This is what is meant by creating your own reality," with parallels to just before Christ's first coming, when all these prophecies were coming through and the momentum was building. As she says later, "And then it actually* happened, *it really* did happen *– it wasn't just a bunch of nuts running around! And this is the same thing.")*

David: It seems I'm looking at you from half-way up the ceiling... *(long silence, as my partial out-of-body experience continues)*

MOITA: At the moment we are floating...

David: I really like each of your and Kelly's many faces. *(long pause)* It's a little hard to believe we're still in bodies, and that when the session is over we're going to . . . be more in them than we are now.

MOITA: You are both floating away. *(long pause)*

David: Like the butterflies on Kelly's ring. *(i.e. a silver coil with two butterflies in turquoise, given as a Christmas present yesterday)*

MOITA: A very apt symbol. You have transformed each other. *(pause)*
          Before you both forget how to return, I should leave.

David: I can feel you withdrawing.

(Things are beginning to feel less spacey, more solid and compact. Kelly feels the energy starting to flow away from her as Moita recedes.)

MOITA: You are becoming very much in tune with my energy. Until another time . . .

David: *(whisper)* Good night.

MOITA: Good night.

(Later Kelly will describe her experiencing during the period above when Moita said we were

floating:)

Kelly: I see a dome of energy around us, and Moita standing behind me pouring energy into the dome or field of energy. Our heart centres become really bright and a beam of light comes out to connect them, heart to heart. I see our third eyes do the same thing, and then the same at our throat chakras, so they are all connected. Next I can see Moita's hands coming on top of our heads, one on each head, and this white flow start where she touches us. Right at the end, before she decides it is time to go, I can feel her hands on our hands, one hand on each set of ours, and this warm pressure and energy flowing into my hands. And I hear her say, "Blessing be unto both of you."

~ ~ ~

Kelly and I have arranged to drive up for an overnight holiday visit with our Kindle Valley friends the following day. After supper we play for them the tape from December 26th and then hold a group session with Moita. C., a short, dark-haired, individualistic woman, has a strong reaction to the tape that brings out some important points, consistent with the *Fatima Prophecy* message about "averting" the worst destruction.

Moita session #127 (Kelly, David, C., Erica, 3 others / December 27, 1979)

C.:   Perhaps I can't accept that things are being done by others to me and sit passively by. What's bothering me is all the talk of all the profound changes in the Earth to happen about 20 years from now, and it *tremendously* seems to me that things should be able to happen in a gentler fashion.

MOITA: I would wish that it will happen in a gentler fashion. Time is running short for that possibility, although it has not yet run out. There are still alternate futures that are open to man.

            You are dealing here on a physical level with the many facets of souls that have manifested in physical form, and their expression in physical form on this physical Earth. You do not see what is happening in a sense behind the scenes. When I say the High Ones are coming and their presence will create a trigger for these changes, it is not that the High Ones have, from some other level, chosen this time to impose change upon man. It is man *himself* who has requested this, this need to change and grow – the soul-self of you and others who have seen the need...

            The Earth needs to change to preserve itself. It too has a right to life. And man is only a part of the life in the universe, and his life is not being extinguished. No life can be extinguished. Once life is created, it goes on forever, and it never dies.

            A birth can be a painful or an easy experience, depending upon the awareness of the child in the womb before it is born. And if those who dwell on the Earth fight change and fear it, they will have a difficult birthing. But they shall be born nonetheless, for they cannot remain in the womb without dying, and they know that the contractions can only last for a certain time before they must make that transition to new life. Those children who are in wombs physically and do not wish to be born – do you believe that their birth is something that is thrust upon them without wanting?...

Erica: Is there anything that will help man preserve the *new* world, to make things not go wrong as it did in this age of the Earth?

MOITA: Do you mean after the transition?

Erica: Yes.

MOITA: To keep the awareness and the ability to communicate with the Earth – this would prevent another such occurrence. But man will be changed in a great many ways. It will not be easy for him to slide into forgetfulness.

ৎ ৎ ৎ

In past history, those who have been aware of communication with the Earth have not found many willing listeners, to say the least of it. Thus, in a subsequent session C. learns perhaps one reason behind her initially negative reaction to the Fatima prophecies.

Moita session #161 (Kelly, David, Jim, Margaret, C., George / November 7, 1980)

C.:   I often feel it does no good when I try to talk about things, because I say a word and a person who hears me puts an entirely different interpretation on it. And the more that one tries to explain, the worse it gets. I think that's very familiar in everybody.

MOITA: Sometimes the exercise is not worth the effort. *(C. laughs; pause)*

C.:   ...What did I do to cause me to be afraid to speak? What happened?

MOITA: You had an experience – what others could call "supernatural" – in another life, and you tried to tell people what happened to you. You were young, and naive or trusting. And the people became afraid because they could not comprehend what you said to them. It came to pass that your tongue was cut out.

C.:   Mmm, Jesus! *(laughs)* Can you tell me where it was?

MOITA: It was in...what is now thought of as Europe... Northern Italy, but it was not called that then. *(Kelly hears "Milan" repeated.)* They were simple people used only to simple things of the earth that they could understand.

C.:   Was it the common people that did this? Was it the clergy, or the local government?

MOITA: The local lord – although the priest had his ear... *(laughter)*

C.:   How long ago?

MOITA: 1200s. Not long.

C.:   *(laughs)* To you, perhaps, not long. Was I a boy or a girl?

MOITA: You were a girl.

C.:   How old was I when it happened?

MOITA:	Sixteen.
C.:	How long did I live after that?
MOITA:	Quite a long time, since you could no longer tell them what you were seeing. *(laughter)*
C.:	*Goodness. (laughs)*
MOITA:	They felt they were being very lenient with you. You could have been burned or stoned.
C.:	What did I see that I told them? *(pause)*
MOITA:	You saw the Sun fall.
C.:	Why did that frighten them so much?
MOITA:	Your conviction, for one; their fear. It is, or was, an instinctive thing.
C.:	What did I see when I saw the Sun fall?
MOITA:	The Earth burn.
C.:	What was it a vision of? What did the vision mean?
MOITA:	You were seeing the time to come. It has not happened yet.
C.:	*Why* did I see it?
MOITA:	Because you will be here when it does. *(pause)*
C.:	Hmm. Wow! *(laughs)* ...Thank you.
MOITA:	You're welcome. Do not let it hurt you.
C.:	I don't think it will. I think I've remembered worse than that and gotten through it quite nicely. *(laughs)* It can help to know . . .
MOITA:	. . . why you have a reluctant tongue?
C.:	Mm-hmm.

(Kelly says after the session she is quite sure what C. saw was related to the cosmic-solar event warned of at Fatima[71N] – though perhaps combined with warfare. Once again, one probability line seen in the 1200s, or the 1970s, need not become reality, at least destructively so. Moita only says she was seeing into "the time to come", not necessarily seeing what will occur physically.)

ও   ও   ও

Where C.'s 13th century vision was probably tinged with that era's emphasis on hellish retribution for human sin, the following dream Kelly receives on April 12, 1980 (our next to last day in the Okanagan Valley after giving our "Swift Wings of Change" workshop) shows the extremely positive potentials amid the dangers that lie ahead.

"Splitting Suns with Void Between" dream
Kelly / April 12, 1980

David and I are walking across a long bridge over a deep canyon with a wide river. There seems some chance that at any moment we'll have to leap off the bridge into the river below to save ourselves. Knowing this, I try to keep an eye out for the deepest spot so we might survive the fall, although at that height I think the chances are slim. I see the scene of us jumping every few feet or so, but we make it across the bridge.

On the other side is a low, grassy hill and some trees – a very beautiful spot. We're watching the Sun set when suddenly the Sun splits in two and separates. Between the two Suns a great black void appears and begins to spread as the Suns move apart. When the Suns stop moving, the void begins to extend toward the zenith, but never passes it. Then deep reds and shocking pinks start to flow out of the void, not quite filling it completely but spilling over past the two Suns, as the Suns sink close to the horizon.

I'm gasping in awe and amazement. David is supposed to photograph this sunset, but is waiting for the best moment. I finally can't stand it anymore. I don't believe the colours, and the contrast against the blackness, can possibly get more vivid and beautiful than they are at the moment. I get the camera out and take the picture, though I'm not sure I have wound it completely and fear a double exposure. Nevertheless, the colours are now fading fast. There is no time for another.

One meaning Kelly gets from this dream is the idea of two New Age centres growing up, one in the Okanagan and one in our own area, which would be strongly linked despite the physical distance. But there seem to be other possibilities as well – and readers may get hints of some we do not consider at this time. One month later, we ask Moita for her perspective.

Moita session #143 (Kelly and David / May 13, 1980)

David: We want to ask about Kelly's dream of the two Suns, and the darkness opening between them, and the many colours issuing from the darkness.

MOITA: On another level, it is also representative of that cosmic-solar event [referred to in *Fatima Prophecy*] and the possibilities for evolution from the experience – the need to be ready and accepting, knowing the right moment. And it represents the splitting of the worlds: both worlds having their own Sun, each Sun being as bright; but they are still separated by a void of understanding, comprehension, acceptance; but many beautiful things can come of that sundering.

And, as Kelly has understood, it also represents two centres, or more, of light on the Earth, and how the gaps can be filled between them with energy, and how that energy will flow out of the gap and spread itself.

ye   ye   ye

My plan for this chapter was to refer at this point to the following story, quoted from the July/August 1980 issue of the *Coming Changes* newsletter:

Hundreds of people out of the estimated 2000 who attended mass at the Grotto of the Three Fountains in Rome on April 12, reported the same extraordinary solar rotation phenomena. The liturgy was being celebrated to commemorate the 33rd anniversary of the appearance of Our Lady of Revelations in the Roman Grotto. Many of the participants testify that the grotto was 'bathed in vari-colored light' during the mass, that the sun began to spin, and that mysterious symbols appeared on the face of the sun. The Church of Rome has not yet taken a stand on the reported miracle.[72]

It is not till this quotation is actually typed for inclusion in our journal *Rays* that I compare the date of these manifestations with the date of Kelly's dream! Thus, the sequence of Fatima-like visions continues through the present, and their energy continues to be shared all around planet Earth.

ৎ   ৎ   ৎ

Earth changes

What is the response of humankind and its Earth to these visitations of higher energies in different forms, ranging from the solar wind of charged particles to Archangelic presences? In order to glimpse the underlying pattern within all the details, it is well to envision the symbolic significance of Earth and the Heavens for humanity. With Moita's help now, see our planet as a mirror of ourselves, with its heart ("core") and aura ("magnetic field") especially receptive to and linked with the cosmos of higher powers.

We have already seen how in a literal/symbolic manner man's outward quest is being answered, albeit in unexpected ways. Now we look to see what is happening on our surface and deeper within.

> *I see you as a being with many levels of thought and feeling. You as a conscious entity are still on the surface. You see things in the surface that are confusing to yourself. To seek an answer to your questions, I must go deeper in your levels of feelings until I reach a point where you are clear. It is your job to descend within yourself to seek that clearness.*
> *– Moita*

Any quaking of the Earth forces us to become aware once again that we live on but the outermost skin of our planet's body, and that deeper within lie dynamics that can drastically transform or put an end to human life – in the same way that personal emotions, if unintegrated with our conscious surface, can suddenly erupt to alter or destroy an individual life. It is more than an analogy, as one major causative factor in Earth changes is human thoughts and emotions. Conversely, the pressures exerted on humanity by the Earth's beginning to shed its old skin will confront us with the need to do likewise.

There are many things for people to discover about themselves, their natures. The Earth is in turmoil and the people are in turmoil with it. If a life was placid and easy and straight, would you look for answers in a deeper place? Strife serves as a means to reach within, to force you to face yourself.

– Moita

In the late fall of 1978, Moita made us aware of two planetary energy changes designed to bring human awareness somewhat closer to her level. Effects were first noticeable on a physical level in weather abnormalities and then as Earth changes strikingly linked to emotional human events. For example, as Pope John Paul II arrived for visits first to the Dominican Republic and then Mexico in January 1979, earthquakes struck those countries in turn, just as a quake shook Iran on the day the Shah went into exile.[73]

Similarly, fall 1979 brings several clear instances of earthquakes tied to a cosmic context that includes human consciousness. That Iran should experience three major earthquakes during the heady days of November 1979 following its seizure of hostages in the U.S. Embassy becomes understandable as a reflection of the turmoil and strife of which Moita speaks above. A huge 8.1 quake off the Columbia coast coincides with a different influence: a conjunction of Mars and Jupiter. Then October 10th brings both the sunspot peak and the worst quake in northern Africa in 275 years, levelling 80% of the Algerian city Al Asnam and killing 20,000 people. And there is yet another quake this fall that has a lower death, but higher moral, toll.

Your mind will seem a prison until you find the key to unlock your heart. In order to connect with your greater self, with your wider understanding of the nature of life, you must pass through your heart first. The heart is that centre which goes into confusion and chaos and comes out as order and balance and meaning.

– Moita

In late November, Italy's worst quake in over 70 years, and the third major one in the last dozen, destroys 81 villages in the country's southern mountains, killing an estimated 3,000 people. Hundreds of tremors continue through the following week – including some at the site of ancient Pompeii, causing (symbolically ominous) cracks leading to closure of the ruins to tourists.

Worst of all, though, is the massive human suffering by thousands of refugees as rain, mud, winds, then snow and hail descend on freezing tent colonies and hampered rescue workers. As if in a nightmare portrayal of the fall of civilization, typhoid and hepatitis break out from the rotting corpses, and newly orphaned children are stolen for sale to the childless. The government is roundly condemned for ill-preparedness. But when it does try to settle refugees in vacant apartment buildings, their owners refuse. Most grisly of all, there are reports of gangs fighting to corner the dwindling supply of coffins in order to gouge the bereaved at the highest bid. One wonders how indicative this is of the state of Italy's – and all mankind's – soul, and thus of drastically needed change.

Moita session #164 (Kelly, David, 2 others / November 30, 1980)

David: We have noticed that major rains have followed several major earthquakes recently. Is this a regular pattern, and what's behind it?

MOITA: It is typical. When the Earth releases tensions through earthquakes, this release significantly alters the electromagnetic field, or the Earth's aura – depending on your view. The Earth considers water a healing substance. It is part of its natural biological mechanisms, its inner clock.

David: I can see the healing quality in the abstract, but in the immediate experience of the people it often only makes things worse.

MOITA: Let me put it this way. We'll use an analogy. At the moment, earthquakes are caused mostly by people's thoughts. To us, [unbalanced] thoughts are dense, hazy, red. It is a festering wound in the skin. As this wound becomes more infected, the body's defences – antibodies and so forth – converge in this one area, like the earthquake would be a pushing out of pus. The people could be considered the germs as far as the Earth's spirit is concerned, and the water the cleansing – the washing away of what caused the infection in the first place. Is that clearer?

David: Yes, I see, from the Earth's point of view. *(pause)* A long ordeal does force people to have time to re-evaluate things more than if there was only a short, sudden disruption.

ഏ   ഏ   ഏ

An extremely clear picture of the interactions between Earth and humanity, particularly as our conscious understanding of Earth changes develops, comes from one of our friends in the Okanagan. A letter written November 4, 1980 describes a feeling, reflected in dreams and shared by several acquaintances, of a pressure building up within oneself – which may, the letter notes, exist within the Earth as well. The pressure builds to a point where one expects and even hopes for an explosion. But nothing happens, and depression follows. The same letter summarizes channelings presented at a recent workshop, identifying Earth changes to be expected in the Okanagan as chain reactions to an initial upheaval in a given location.

Two weeks later, a second letter reports a sudden feeling one evening (again experienced independently by more than one person) that the pressure has been released, followed by the best sleep and mood in a long time. During that night, at about 3:15 a.m., a small Earth tremor occurred, centred at the very location predicted in the workshop channeling.

This experience appears to confirm the faith that those who are sufficiently open and attuned will be able to receive forewarning where and when upheavals will strike. It is also another example of the positive, even liberating side to what many may experience as additional disruptive and destructive events in their lives. Speaking soon after we receive these letters, Moita points out: "They [in the area] all experienced it as a pressure. It is the reaction to it afterwards that is different."

You have drawn a veil between how you feel and its cause, and you are now finding the veil is being torn.

The things that you are feeling fall away are your attachments to those happenings of yesterday. And it is frightening not knowing where your tomorrows are leading you.

– Moita

But cracks or "faults" in the surface stability of Earth and humankind are being felt or uncovered all over the globe during 1980. In North America, tensions grow between various cultural, religious, racial, economic and regional groups as "hard times" pressures increase. Precariousness of personal relationships is mirrored on a national level in Canada by continued talk of "separation" (currently in the western provinces more than Quebec) and heated debate over a new constitution.

On a geological level in North America, faults continue to be discovered within cities and across countryside assumed by most to be quite safe. For example, the New Madrid fault zone underlying five mid-Mississippi Valley states, and responsible for the strongest U.S. earthquake ever recorded (in 1811-1812), is pinpointed – raising fears at the possible destruction if there is a recurrence of the quake that then levelled buildings within 50,000 square miles. Then on July 27th's Full Moon the fault's biggest quake in 25 years strikes Kentucky – and is felt as far away as Ontario.

New evidence swells the list of most earthquake-vulnerable U.S. cities: San Francisco, Los Angeles, San Diego, Hawaii, Anchorage-Fairbanks, Seattle-Tacoma, Salt Lake City-Ogden, St. Louis-Memphis, Charleston, Buffalo, Boston, New York. Canadian cities lying near faults include Vancouver and Victoria on the West Coast and St. Lawrence River centres such as Montreal and Quebec City.

When you pass through your own personal storm and the calm weather has entered into your heart again, you will be able to see the purpose of the storm's passing.

– Moita

1980 is another year of record abnormalities in weather patterns. In North America, an extended heat wave brings extreme drought conditions and over 1,000 fatalities to the south-central United States. Meanwhile, the worst forest fires in decades rage through Ontario and Canada's western provinces. The opposite problems – record-breaking storms, precipitation and cold – prevail in some other parts of the world. In the fall, huge brush fires threaten southern California. And during the sunspot peak of early October, Los Angeles is smothered by the worst smog in its history, closing schools, businesses and airports for 10 days.

As long as the depth of these feelings remains hidden, it cannot be released or left behind. It is hard to leave shadows behind, and not all are ready to face their own shadow.
A clear heart, a true heart, is one with no dark corners or hidden shadows. Shadows do

not disappear when you turn your back on them. They disappear when they themselves are turned into light.

– Moita

Most dramatic of all the Earth changes in 1980, however, are the volcanoes – a total of 30 of which are now active around the world. Rising out of dormancy to awake a complacent North America – a "sleeping giant" to match the Three Mile Island nuclear "accident" *exactly one year earlier* – is Washington state's Mount St. Helens, erupting first on March 28th. Looking back now, we find a dream in Kelly's journal from two weeks before that weaves together several of the meanings for us of that significantly timed eruption:

"Escape Prison before Earthquakes" dream
Kelly / March 14, 1980

I am aware that some earthquakes are going to happen soon, while taking a steep, quick path up a mountain for a fantastic view. Later, David and I are part of a group taken hostage in a women's prison by [my office manager at work], who thinks the prison is a nuclear power plant and seeks to take it over. Having told the other hostages of the coming quakes, we wait for the right moment to escape, and David and I do escape before they begin.

Here, Kelly's office job – which she began in late fall 1979 and from which we *do* soon hope she can escape – represents much about the mental/physical/spiritual confinement of routines and power-seeking, at potentially great cost to one's health (for instance, as with nuclear power). It is against such prisons that quakes are directed, so it is best to escape our own as soon as we are able.

This minor eruption of Mount St. Helens is nevertheless a fascinating phenomenon, and the crowds of sightseers that begin congregating in the area suggest to us that the volcano's attraction works on many levels. We liken the traffic jams to those converging on Devil's Tower, Wyoming, in the movie *Close Encounters of the Third Kind*.

Moita session #138 (Kelly and David / March 31, 1980)

David: Some interesting things are happening on Mount St. Helens. Is it likely this is a sign that other mountains in the same chain will become active before long?

MOITA: There are many volcanoes in that area that have been dormant for a long time.

David: What is causing the blue lightning that we hear is now arcing between the two cones?

MOITA: It has something to do with the lessening ozone layer and the energy that comes from a deeper place into the atmosphere. When the second cone uncovered itself, it set up a polarity between the two. And so, the energy is in some ways recirculating by charging back and forth. It does help . . . to release. *(pause)* It is an attempt at balance.

David: Releasing the energy from deeper, then?

MOITA: And by so releasing it in that manner, helping to cushion the Earth further, in creating new ozone. *(pause)* And it is making energy available to the surface, to be redistributed.

David: A whole lot of people seem to be attracted to this manifestation, almost like people are really after some experience of unusual energy beyond themselves.

MOITA: You could say it is very similar to man's desire to see aliens . . . or his concept of God.

৯   ৯   ৯

It is easy to believe, as many claim, that Mount St. Helens will let out a few more rumbles and hisses and then quiet down again for another century's sleep. But a dream of mine on April 22nd continues to suggest otherwise: the Cascade mountain chain is erupting, and we realize how important it is to be together with our Kindle Valley friends in a large barn with plenty of food.

Then we go camping in the valley on the weekend of May 16-17. As we are thus physically out of touch with the larger world, Kelly experiences the following dream early on Sunday morning.

"Mount St. Helens Explodes" dream
Kelly / May 17, 1980

David and I and another couple are in a Vancouver, B.C. house with a huge window overlooking the water. Looking across the bay, we can see Mount St. Helens – in fact, we also seem to be right at the base of it. The ground starts to shake, and we see the mountain exploding very vividly and realistically. The sky is totally grey. I'm afraid it's much too close for comfort and think we should flee, but then realize there's nowhere to go. Tremors continue for a long time.

I think I see a log floating halfway across the bay, but then realize it's a stick in the water which is now rising up on the other side of our window! I know the volcano has caused a flood and we have to climb higher through a window in the ceiling. Having done so, the water retreats some. But after we go back down, the water rises once more. It seems a logjam is going to crash through the window. I decide we have to leave Vancouver while there's still time. The volcano is just too close.

Much could be made of the symbolism in this dream: that there is a Mount St. Helens close to all of us in a deeper than geographical sense, that the log we see far away may be the mote in our own eye (window), and that we will need to raise our consciousness and *keep* it raised (climb through the ceiling window), if we are not to be carried away in the explosive flood (fear? anger? tears?).

Whether or not we notice this symbolic level, however, it is that very morning we learn from a neighbour who has a radio that the physical Mount St. Helens has indeed just erupted massively – with a force 500 times that of the Hiroshima atomic bomb, blowing off the top 1,300 feet of the mountain, sending ash and steam 12 miles into the sky, and being felt up to 200 miles away. The first reports we hear speak of four people being known to have died near the base of the mountain, and of the waters of Spirit Lake and its outlet rising and falling twice as debris cascades into their once scenic beauty. (And note well this fact: the small city of Vancouver, in southern Washington state, is just downstream from Mount St. Helens.)

The apocalyptic impact of the eruption is brought home to millions through the terror in eyewitness accounts, the eerie photos of gas-masked citizens trudging through towns of the Pacific Northwest lit by street lamps at noon and clogged with grey "snow", and by the sinuous cloud that wends its way across much of the United States and parts of Canada during the week following. That passengers in cars who are in the wrong place at the wrong time can be instantly incinerated, that whole forested mountainsides can be shaved bare and left littered with thousands of smoking matchsticks that were once trees, sends an unmistakable message about the power of the Being whose surface we inhabit. The danger of flooding to populated centres – and a nuclear power plant – downstream, and the gritting up of automobile engines, illustrate the vulnerability of our civilization to the cleansing our host planet now requires.

Volcanic eruptions, of course, occur where quakings of the surface connect with open channels into the heart of the Earth, allowing pent-up vertical pressures to be released. How deeply felt must be the need for such release from within – and for communication between heart and surface inhabitants – when the cost of an eruption in surface life and tranquility is so great.

To see a path clearly does not mean to see one without pain. It means to accept all that taking that path entails, and embracing the sorrow as well as the joy. Sorrow is a doorway to the inner workings of one's spirit. It is a cleansing fire that clears away the unimportant things in its wake, but only if a person can accept it enough and know it for what it is.
– Moita

A week later, on May 25th and 26th, major new eruptions at Mount St. Helens are accompanied by major earthquakes in eastern California. On the 28th, Mt. Margaret, the next volcano nearest Mount St. Helens, will also begin to quake. Meanwhile, fire is making its elemental presence known on the Earth and in the heavens as well, in the form of massive forest fires across Canada and another of the year's great solar flares.

Moita session #144 (Kelly and David / May 27, 1980)

MOITA: The Earth is very busy right now.

David: I know. I wonder how long before many people start getting the idea that this isn't just chance physical happenings – that there is a purpose behind it.

MOITA: There will be many who will never see that. Their whole life is filled with empty chances, and [they] mainly notice "coincidences". There is danger for those who are in the fringes between understanding and not feeling that there is purpose. They still look too much to authority to explain the unexplainable.

David: And yet I gather you're saying that can't really satisfy them. So, what is the danger –

that they'll feel torn?

MOITA: They will accept unacceptable answers – what the authorities say, and therefore lose valuable time in preparing themselves.

David: Speaking of coincidences, the last time Mount St. Helens had a major eruption was in 1857, which is the same year the Los Angeles area had its last very large earthquake. So, are we looking at perhaps the start of major California quakes very soon?

MOITA: It is quite possible that this eruption will serve as a trigger to other areas on the coast. Things that happen deep beneath the Earth do not go in just one direction... It may be that the repercussions of this activity will be felt in the area of Japan before they will be felt on the West Coast. Usually things balance...

You are seeing a physical eruption on the surface, but tensions that are beneath are not as easily measured. There is a place where all these things meet, where each has its effect on each other, even if they are not connected by passages in the physical sense... [You] are learning how much energy the Earth has to release, and how little man is able to do to prevent it, at least on his material plane and with his understanding.

David: It's interesting how it's sort of the counterpart of Three Mile Island a year ago, even as to the shape of the object through which the energy might be released. *(i.e. the power plant's cooling towers resembling two volcanic cones)* It's certainly a lesson – but more easily excused in this case, I suppose.

MOITA: Although both lessons are pointing to the dangers of civilization and technology when they have not been harnessed properly with the right attitude. Man is too secure in his position as ruler of the Earth. And so, his fall will be more devastating, because it is unexpected and considered impossible.

ॐ ॐ ॐ

Subsequent developments turn out to match Moita's words. The interior connections between distant surface points on the Earth are made graphically evident by reports that Miette Hot Springs in the Alberta Rockies is showing a sharp drop in temperature and an infusion of black, murky water each time Mount St. Helens erupts 450 miles away! Additional Cascade volcanic peaks in the U.S. do show renewed activity during June, with small quakes under Mount Hood (near Portland, Oregon) and Mount Baker (close to Vancouver, B.C.) as well as one near Seattle.

Beginning in late June, Japan experiences a series of earthquakes touching off panic-buying in fear a major one is imminent. Three small quakes there on July 22nd coincide with three eruptions of Mount St. Helens the same day, which send ash and steam billowing upward 55,000 feet. August 8th brings another similar eruption, eventually convincing scientists to admit they have no idea what the mountain will do next. Out of the other 29 active volcanoes in the world, Mount Etna in Italy erupts violently on September 2nd, opening up no less than three craters.

When conventional authorities can no longer provide the accustomed secure answers about one's future, one may begin reaching out in other directions. A short news item we hear on October 10th makes us wonder just how great a shock to conventional wisdom may be in store for North Americans because of Mount St. Helens. The radio announces that new tremors have occurred beneath the mountain overnight (coinciding with the record sunspot activity on this date). It also reports that during recent days a "beautiful woman" has been seen more than once by people in the vicinity, who warns of another huge eruption between the 12th and the 14th (of October, presumably). She is reported to have said it will devastate a large area of land. Then . . . she has vanished!

Our minds leap immediately, of course, to other visionary appearances over the past century of a beautiful woman, most often interpreted as the Virgin Mary. But this time the predicted major eruption does not happen. Quakes and minor eruptions of steam and ash do occur throughout the next week, particularly on the 16th to 18th, and we hear no more about the "mysterious woman". But we obviously can't let matters rest there . . .

Moita session #159 (Kelly, David, Jim / October 19, 1980)

David: I must ask about the mysterious appearance . . . *(laughing, as Moita smiles)* . . . of a beautiful woman warning people near Mount St. Helens. What's going on here? Do you know who this is?

MOITA: There is some activity on a lower plane in the area. It is not as high a visitation as may have been indicated at first. You could say it is more the inhabitants putting [together] their thoughts, their apprehensions, their fears, seeking the answer to safety. Once enough people ask the same question, an answer needs to come in some form... They have created a new soul. She is trying to serve her creators... [But] being new on a non-physical level, information is not as accurate as it may be...

Jim: Does this new soul that has been created continue on as an objective form?

MOITA: She *will*. She is also part of the mountain, a conglomeration of energy. There will need to be a split of sorts in her spirit before it will be able to develop independently. Being created near a potential area of destruction connects her very strongly with the element of fire, and earth. I recall that when the group that created me disbanded, there was a period of great confusion and adjustment before I could continue as an individual soul.

Jim: So the group that was involved in creating her very likely will disband, in the sense that likely many people will be moving away (?). *(Or they may simply cease putting their questions together as presently.)*

MOITA: And she is in many ways attached to the volcano, for now.

Jim: It will be fascinating to watch and see what happens.

MOITA: It may also come to pass that this may happen more than once in other places as our worlds draw closer.

Jim: Do you mean there may be lots of new entities or forms created as the world gets more confused?

MOITA: *(laughing)* More confused?!

Jim: As there's more pressure put on people. *(pause)* That makes sense. Because she seems created out of emotion, and emotion makes thought-forms. The rule of ritual is that the stronger the emotion, the clearer and stronger the thought-form usually. So when people are afraid – and lots of people are afraid – it's fertile ground for that kind of thought-form to be created.

MOITA: And our worlds drawing closer together makes them more visible – or rather, makes it more likely they will be seen. They are *always* created. *(i.e. under the circumstances Jim describes)*

Jim: Mm-hmm. *(pause)* So instances like this could start popping up all over the globe.

MOITA: Quite possible. The only problem would be hearing about them.

ക   ക   ക

With this glance ahead, our review of 1980 Sun/Earth changes comes to an end. Undoubtedly reflecting the outworking of the preceding energy changes in late 1978, it certainly *has* been an active period. These 1979/1980 eruptions of various kinds can suggest what is in store for us in the future, in the wake of many energy changes to come.

It is an era of uncertainty for all – not just those living near a volcano, and not just over physical-level possibilities. We on the surface of Earth/ourselves are being confronted now by greater energies from above *and* below. To remember the symbolism is to remember a key to growth through all the upheavals of the turning of an age.

> *My love comes from a clear heart, for I know myself and I have seen my own beauty. It is a place that is reached through difficulty and pain.*
> *It is finding that you have the strength that you need to go through the experience and come out the other side and still be whole, still be you.*
> *– Moita*

Part One began with Kelly and me travelling to the Sunrise Valley and deciding upon a "step in the right direction" for ourselves. Now, as Part One concludes, the valley becomes a focal point for others questioning its rightness – or how *any* of us knows where to be at this turning of an age.

This final session is held after hearing that a person living near Sunrise Farm may be moving due to repeated guidance to him that this whole area is "going under". Our questioner is one who, with Becky, began and still visits Sunrise Farm but currently lives in California. Here concerns about external eruptions lead back to the central, inner questions – what our heart will tell us, if it can.

Moita session #149 (Kelly, David, Anita, Tom / July 6, 1980)
MOITA: Have you one last question?

Tom: Well, in a way I suppose I'm at a crossroads in certain respects of my life. I'm thinking of moving from San Francisco. I'm very aware of imminent catastrophes of various kinds. I'm wondering how the choice of a geographical place to live is arrived at. Is that too vague?

MOITA: You want to know if the valley is safe?

Tom: Well, partly that; indeed yes, yes.

MOITA: For the moment. It is true there is no place on Earth that will not be affected by great changes – either physical or social...

          Believe that where your heart feels best is where you should be when things occur. That will help you to stay grounded throughout the changes, and centred within yourself. If you are meant to survive *(Tom laughs)*, you shall. And if not, then you shall be one who will be born again when the changes are over – which may be an easier path than those who choose to stay.

Tom: *(laughing)* Mm-hmm. I understand that.

MOITA: You will not know for certain which you are until the time comes.

Tom: *(laughs)* I'm sure that's true.

MOITA: You see, death is not something to avoid, from my level. It is to be embraced in its own time, and accepted just as life.

Tom: Well, I see that. It seems also that, although you may not be trying to avoid death, you might feel that you could do more good being alive rather than dead, as far as perhaps helping. Is that an illusion?

MOITA: It is a desire to assist through change – and there are many with that desire... There will be those with that frame of mind who will remain to help through difficulty. You will know when to leave, for you.

          But each must follow his own path in this, for if you are to be any use to help others, you must be able to reach this guidance in yourself first. Many things have been said on where catastrophe will strike and where it will not. But vessels of spirit must be made ready, and tested, so they will not break in time of need. That is why I do not answer your question specifically. It is a question you must answer for yourself.

Intermission

TWO SUCH DIFFERENT SOULS

It is time to explain a bit more about Kelly and me. In my Introduction, I referred to us respectively as "a psychic" and "a mystic". To some, the terms may seem almost interchangeable. But I'm actually using them as opposites – for in our case they are tied to a whole set of complementary tendencies. In this life, they can be traced to the inherent thrust of our personalities as well as experiences that have brought out our basic soul qualities.

On the one hand, it seems unusual that we, quite aware of our differences, come together in as much unity as we feel during these years – in fact, using those differences to cover each other's back, as Moita once put it. On the other hand, there is a point where these differences will propel this story in a new, unexpected direction. Some excerpts from *Mind Leap* and *The World Conspires* will now set out these different qualities of ours, so as to prepare readers for that later development.

On July 12, 1978, two weeks after her first words to us, Moita says this about Kelly and me: "It is very rare that two such different souls decide to spend so many lives together in so many kinds of ways." On August 1st she follows that up with this key sentence...: "Spiritually speaking, you and Kelly stand back to back." Kelly receives the image of two warriors' stances in battle, each protecting the other's blind spot.[74]

A few months later, Moita states that our differences trace back to higher levels, through the different ways that she and my own entity, Loria, came into being. (I first became acquainted with Loria during the two years prior, through channeling experiments with my then-partner Ruth.)

Moita session #56 (Kelly and David / January 9, 1979)

David: Can you tell us...how Kelly and I are so different and yet "stand back to back"?

MOITA: You have been told by Loria that she was created in whole on the level that she now exists in. She was a conscious creation on the part of other entities who were on the same [non-physical] level.[75]

You have also been told that I was created by a group of individuals who took part in the creation consciously but were certainly *not* in existence on that level.[76]

(In other words, the group of individuals that created Moita as their guiding spirit was on the physical plane – though this was in far ancient times when Earth's reality was less dense.)

MOITA: We are your roots... We bring to you different aspects of unity – different views, a different texture or focus. In this way you both represent the greater coming together of the two levels, the meeting of the worlds, even though you yourself have gone through your own wheel and are still on it. The quality of your soul is different because of your roots.

It is important that the two worlds come together as one. Some feel these are contradictory – the differences between Earth and Sun. You have not lost your difference, but you have intermingled your sameness and brought it up.

David: How does that difference get expressed on our level, in our awareness?

MOITA: You are more the dreamer, the creator of high ideals, a weaver of worlds. She is more the sustaining centre, the practical aspect (?), the workings out...Your [own] sustenance comes in a different form – the thing that makes you a healer, a healer of minds.

Do you see the connection?

David: Yes, well, they're all *connected*. They wouldn't work if they weren't.

MOITA: So you see that we have conspired together to bring this about – I on my part, Loria on hers. We have been with you both throughout eternity.

In fact, there is very ancient history behind Moita's comparing us to the differences between Earth and Sun. "There is an early shared incarnation of ours, uncovered by Kelly in September 1978, which will serve ever after as a touchstone in understanding both our difference and our connection, that 'natural bridge' often depicted in my dreams."[77] During her second past-life regression guided by me, Kelly re-experienced the consciousness of that life, as in the Garden of Eden:

I am outside. It is sunny, warm. There is a man on a hill... He is very tall and fair. There is a sense of the Sun in him. He is in some way connected to that energy that pours down upon us. The air itself is alive. It speaks. It has a voice, and we hear it.

He and I are connected. We form a unit and work together. It is a time of great joy. All things happen as they should. There is time enough for everything – a sense of oneness with those things around, a knowing how it works, an understanding of needs and of place...

The Earth is very young and new and filled with the wonder of...its own discoveries. That is why everything speaks – it seems it has so much to say... He speaks to the Sun and I speak to the Ground, and we weave together what we are told and make it whole...

We are the last of a special breed. We have not yet forgotten where we came from. The others have started the long descent into forgetfulness, and parts of the Earth are changing so that the world can no longer speak. There was an attempt to stop this descent, but it proved fruitless and wasteful because none were able to hear what was said. [He] tried to sing to them of the Sun. They did not understand [his] meaning...

Since nothing could be done, we eventually decided to leave and go back to the world we knew and understood, and try to remember it, because we knew a time would come when we also would forget...The rest of our days are filled with wonder and joy. We die the way we lived. We pour ourselves into the world at the same time.[78]

A few months later, Moita would add:

In the life you two lived together alone with the Earth and the Sun, that was a time when [our levels] were much closer. *I* was much closer, and the others here. And you were more open, in touch. We spoke of many things then. We spoke of now...

You saw this as a possible opportunity to accomplish that which you could not in that life: the bringing back to yourself of the awareness of life, and the communicating of that to those around you, so that you would not feel isolated. That life is one of the basic urges that has pushed you in the direction of forming a community: the need to share those feelings and [that] awareness with others, not just for yourself, and not just for those who are aware already, as [were] those...in Musili... And you are not doing this alone. Others are here to help you, have chosen to come here with you for similar reasons, and for their own.[79]

In this present life, then, our opposite poles within wholeness were what attracted Kelly and me. First on the personality level: "Given my introverted, intellectual and mystical bent, her more sensuous, earthy, extroverted personality makes for an interesting contrast."[80] Then spiritually, reflecting our "Earth and Sun" legacy: "When we meet again...and our hands join, particularly in meditation, the energy current is so tangible the very air seems to be vibrating. It is the completion of the circuit of life, the linking and balancing of poles that have been separated too long."[81]

I have also written of those "blind spots" that can arise in each other's absence, or when we fail to weave together our different perspectives:

Yet we are still coming from opposite points of the compass as souls, from poles most clearly identified as Sun and Earth: my inward focusing of the unified pattern or ideal to be manifested, while potentially prone to boredom and sterile alienation "above" life; Kelly's spontaneous flowing with the changing multiplicity of forms, while potentially vulnerable to fear and confusion, becoming immersed in surrounding influences.[82]

Our younger lives before we met, as shared in *Mind Leap*, bore witness to our different strengths and vulnerabilities. Then our coming together proved the maxim about the whole being more than the sum of its parts – especially when beings like Moita are included:

What will result from bringing a born mystic and a born psychic together? The mystic inwardly identifies with spirit as the universal ground of being, seeking balance and oneness through all in life that are its symbols. The psychic, acutely sensitive and responsive to changing surroundings, interacts with the non-physical spiritual realm as real entities. Quite opposite approaches, these.

Then what if, additionally, the mystic and psychic come from opposite life experiences? My own early circumstances afforded many advantages in pursuing a spiritual path. But spirituality is weak if it only reflects a privileged or "ivory tower" existence. The test will come on meeting someone who possesses very different inner powers and who faced cruel obstacles in trying to grow up whole and free. Will people coming from such opposite poles find it impossible to relate, or can they complement, learn from each other, touch and merge?[83]

On ordinary levels, of course, every person represents some merging of these Sun and Earth principles. But the deeper we allow this complementing to go, the wider the way opens to a creative wedding of inner and outer. It makes sense for the opposites to "conspire", does it not? – as a way of...trying to ensure more balance in one's work, drawing on a broader range of experience, communicating to more types of people, operating simultaneously on several levels of meaning?[84]

I wrote these words with our relationship in mind. But it is no accident they also point to some of Moita's own multifaceted qualities and abilities. Yes, "the deeper we allow this complementing to go", there we find Moita. And the effects on others of her communications and sharings – seen in Part One, and as continued now in Part Two – clearly manifest the wisdom in living life thus wholly, freely, creatively.

PART TWO

Chapter 8

BECOMING PARTNERS WITH THE EARTH

If no one interfered in the course of your world, if things went along as it looked they were going with your technological developments and governments, can you see any possibility for man to understand what it means to live a life as a person of the Earth, of the world, and not as a cog in a wheel? The purpose of death is to pave the way for rebirth.
— Moita (September 29, 1979)

Each of our lives shows "the mark of the Beast", the imprint of those forces trying to construct a purely rationalistic, materialistic civilization devoid of Spirit. Thanks to the "interference" of higher levels, though, that nightmarish future line serves mainly as a warning, helping us see which kind of world we wish to create as whole beings. This search begins within ourselves, and each new level of discovery can prove so much more fulfilling than we have come to expect from life that we doubt there can be more. In this great transition, however, no aspect of our lives can be passed over, for none exists in isolation – and the resulting growth in each area reinforces that in all others.

We turn now to more outward, practical changes in our way of life that can move us out beyond the civilization that is dying. That transition can take many forms, suitable to many different environments, so the specifics in this chapter serve as examples only. But one universal can be stated: those who survive the coming changes are likely to be those whose mode of living expresses the fundamental *values* of the next age.

During 1980, Kelly and I are also feeling pressure to bring our inner and outer lives into greater alignment. How can we join with others in being of help, being part of the solution, combining our individual and group work with what Moita once called "something concrete"? This chapter, then, combines sharings toward a spiritual/practical vision of earthly existence with experiences this year that move our own family closer to that goal. The dream that enticed us from the Canadian prairies to the interior of British Columbia now leads us deep into the Kindle Valley. In the same way, life invites everyone to define what is "home" for themselves and find their own unique path to it.

At the time of our "Swift Wings of Change" workshop in the Okanagan Valley of British Columbia, a friend is experiencing one of those intervals between forward leaps. Her question brings a surprising response from Moita that will serve as a keynote.

Moita session #140 (Kelly, David, workshop group / April 9, 1980)
Dorothy: Moita, I seem to have reached a point in the last couple of months where I'm very

happy and very peaceful and very comfortable with where I'm at. But then I have the feeling that there's something else that I should be doing. But I don't really know what that is, or how I can help in this transition.

MOITA: You need to move, first. You need to get more into the Earth. The Earth will be needing more help than even man.

Dorothy: What do you mean "getting more into the Earth"?

MOITA: You are living on a sentient being. The Earth can help you and others understand the best way to prepare for change, or to help avert it. The Earth is seeking partners. Man cannot live on the Earth and apart from it. If you would help in the transition from one age to another, it is time to begin understanding the greatest partner you will have in that transition, learning to live cooperatively with a being whose body you are on – a sharing of joy, one that comes with energy and union. Man's plight...is because he does not understand yet how to cooperate not only with his fellow man but with his Earth. A new way of life will be one that is born of that cooperation.

You'll not get ideas on a New Age without being a pioneer in your thoughts and your actions, without taking steps into the unknown, without opening your heart and extending your hand and walking down the pathway of the future together, creating a newness.

৯ ৯ ৯

Another at the same workshop is in a different phase of New Age commitment than Dorothy – the space of feeling sure what the next step is, and eagerly trying to work towards it . . . but encountering obstacles amounting to a brick wall. Still, Moita's prescription for the period of delay Lena perceives in her life is strikingly similar.

Moita session #140 (Kelly, David, workshop group / April 9, 1980)

Lena: I no longer chafe at the delay, because I know inside that the delay is necessary for growth. I would like to be able to do something to ensure that once we are under way my own spirituality can help further things along...

MOITA: There is an opportunity here for you to delve more into the planetary consciousness, into the Earth, and develop your own relationship with that awareness. For you are not alone. There are many around you – not just from my reality, but of the Earth. Becoming a partner necessitates knowing whom you are working with...

Lena: Is there something that I can do now to get more in touch with my spirituality on an ongoing basis? I have a tendency to flounder once I'm away from surroundings like this, because I'm on my own and I don't have reinforcement on a steady basis other than attempting to look within to find my own strength.

MOITA: Then I shall give you a guide. Find a tree, one that you feel attracted to, comfortable with, and talk to it every day. Do your meditation outside, beneath it, if it is at all possible.

And you shall create for yourself a living partner who has a great awareness of many things. And it will help *you* to increase awareness of the Earth, and to understand that the reassurance you need is in every blade of grass you set your foot upon.

Lena: That's very beautiful.

MOITA: For me life is beautiful, and I wish to share it.

ک   ک   ک

"... knowing whom you are working with." Man's potential partners "in every blade of grass" are Earth's nature spirits as touched upon in Chapter 2. Here the continuation of that same conversation between Moita and Kindle Valley people broaches the unavoidable dilemma: moving to the country to live doesn't only permit sitting under trees; it also can involve cutting them down.

Moita session #125 (Kelly, David, workshop group / December 17, 1979)

Glen: The nature spirits must be distressed with the way man is treating the world these days.

MOITA: Yes, there is much distress.

Glen: So that's probably one of the major reasons we can't communicate with them. They probably don't want to relate to us at all.

MOITA: There is an anger on their part, and frustration as well, for they have tried to communicate but they cannot break through those kinds of walls, where belief in them has been eradicated and the experience of them has grown dim in man's mind.

Glen: Are they negative about communicating with men of any sort at any time? Would their anger neutralize my sincere wish to communicate?

MOITA: They are very much trying to communicate. They have worked through much of their anger, and *are* working through it. Much will depend upon what part of the Earth you are on when you attempt such a communication. But you must understand that before communication is possible there are many things within yourself that need to change. It may take you many years of real effort and desire and belief, of changing within, before you are able to see into their reality and to begin a communication that may go both ways, not just one.

Glen: This seems a trivial thought, but just the fact of getting firewood and cutting trees sometimes really worries me. Although I feel I can't communicate with nature spirits, I'm just wondering if at that point I get even further from communication with them by doing that: by killing trees – put it that way, I guess. It sounds exaggerated; I don't know.

MOITA: By being aware of what you are doing, by showing concern within yourself, an awareness of the consequences, you are coming closer to their kingdom. For it is man who goes through without thought for any consequences or any possibility of other life-forms that creates walls. In the Indian culture there was always that awareness. It did not prevent them from gathering wood when it was needed, nor from killing [for] meat when it was needed. But it did keep them from doing it without reason and without need. There is a difference.

Glen: Are [the nature spirits] pretty much everywhere on the Earth, or are they hiding from some places more than others?

MOITA: It is difficult for them to be in cities, although there are some who do manage in small gardens, depending upon the people. And it is hard for them to use chemicals to help things grow, because [a chemical] is to them an alien substance. It does not react in ways they understand. They cannot manipulate it. They cannot change its energy into energy that will be helpful to the things they are helping to grow. So in those places where there is much pollution, there are very sad nature spirits – or very few.

Glen: Can you foresee them communicating more with men in the future?

MOITA: I can see that as a very real possibility.

Glen: That's good to hear.

MOITA: The Earth is speaking with all of its voices, and it is waiting for man to remember *it...*

Jim: Would it be a good idea to put a lot of conscious effort into contacting and communicating with nature spirits? Is that one way in which we could assist a more peaceful transition to the New Age?

MOITA: There is a reason why you are in the country. It is good to start making that kind of a change in awareness.

Jim: Will they be prime allies in helping to bring about the New Age?

MOITA: They have a great deal to do with all of these rumblings. They are part of the voice of the Earth, and they are reacting to man's influence on the body of the Earth. If you had a tumour on your arm and knew that if you left it there it would kill you, you would want to cut it out if you valued life. It is much the same thing... It is a necessary operation and one that will change the surface of the body, but not the heart.

Jim: Even when the surgery is as extensive as it needs to be?

MOITA: The love the Earth has for all living things is very deep, and it does this cleansing for the benefit of all – not for the hate of some, for the Earth holds no hate for anything that has life. It is part of all life. This is a rejection of death. *(pause)* By acting in this way, it is preserving man when man seems unable to preserve himself. *(pause)* Does that help?

Jim: Mm-hmm. The mythology of the Zapotec Indians of southern Mexico has a whole line of predictions leading up to 1987. Their prediction is that the Pakwachis – which is their name for nature spirits – will leap out from where they've been hiding and leap into the hearts of men. I hope that's what's starting to happen now and that that will signal the end of the ninth hell, as they describe it, and the beginning of a new cycle.

(This is the closest that anyone's questions for Moita come to what will become better-known as the prophecies surrounding the Maya "Long Count" calendar. José Arguelles and others will later refer to 1987 as the year of the Harmonic Convergence, starting a 25-year transitional period leading to 2012.)

MOITA: Is the next cycle a hell or heaven?

Jim: They describe 13 heavens and then the coming of the white man, which started the first of the 9 hells. And then that's the end of their mythology, pretty well. Interesting, isn't it!

MOITA: And so, the next one is open-ended.

Jim: Open-ended. The only prediction is that from thence forward the red man will no longer be dominated, and that the Pakwachis will be in the hearts of men. Sounds nice, but it looks like a lot of trouble between here and there to me.

MOITA: And opening up man's hearts...

Jake: I've been having some of the same doubts that Glen is having about the cutting of trees. There's one place I've been cutting trees for a purpose I've taken upon myself. While I feel love for the place that I've been working in, and for many of the trees that I'm cutting, I wonder what the effect is on the spirit of the place. It's beautiful as it is, but I've taken it upon myself to change it.

MOITA: It is still difficult to make great distinctions in this time of history. If the Earth were only experiencing this one thing, it would not make any impact on the energy of the forest. There is enough energy to replenish a great deal when it is used wisely. But the energy of the land right now, in many places, has been depleted. And it is that kind of lack of care for the Earth that is causing some of the changes that are coming.

You can look at it in a small frame, in the one area, and see that it is not doing any great harm. You are not changing the ecology of the forest. You are not altering its destiny on your own. But if taken on a larger scale, over the whole planet, it can be seen that man has done that and has taken it upon himself.

When things are changed, these doubtings will not be as troublesome. But it is a good sign that more are becoming aware of possible consequences. *(pause)* Even with all of the depletion that has taken place, the nature spirits cannot hate man, for they can see some of the reasons and they know some of the lessons you are all going through.

Jake: I'm not sure what I should learn from what I'm experiencing. Would it be better *not* to continue what I'm doing at this time? It seems all right. But as you say, looking at it as a whole . . .

MOITA: The only thing I can suggest for you to do is to go to that place, and sit down beneath a tree with your back against it, and meditate on these thoughts. See if you can get a clear picture from the forest how *it* feels. This is what they have missed – the chance to help make the choice.

Jake: Thank you.

(Jake will say he is already getting a picture of the particular tree he will sit by. Ten days later, Moita will tell him, "I am glad you have met your tree.")

ৡ৵   ৡ৵   ৡ৵

As spring begins to arrive in these northern woods, Moita again asks Jake about his tree.

Moita session #142 (Kelly, David, Jake, 7 others / April 19, 1980

MOITA: Have you spent much time with your tree?

Jake: I haven't. I was over there today, or yesterday.

MOITA: What did you find? *(long pause)*

Jake: I considered how I've changed it over there and how that felt. And it seems like every time I go over there, I think about lowering the scope of the change. I'm just not sure about what I'm doing there, I guess. And so, what I've been doing is *nothing* – but occasionally walking over there.

           Most changes seem pretty violent, and there's part of me that doesn't like it. And I think there's something else – that feeling of a connection to me in another time, another place – and I wonder what changing it does to the connections. It seems like some of the area has more of a definite form and structure and life-force, and other areas are in a different stage of their life-force where change is easier. Those are about three questions, I suppose, or musings. *(Jake laughs, followed by a long silence)*

MOITA: It is good that you have stopped enough to consider possibilities and feelings. The Earth would *prefer* to change more slowly – not that it is incapable of many fast changes [of its own], but they are more deep. They start from a lower place, fuller place; they are not surface changes.

           In picturing in your mind what you would do, you help to prepare an area for change, warn it in a sense, and give it an opportunity to talk back – an opportunity it doesn't have in most places . . . yet.

Jake: It feels like it's easy for my ambition to run roughshod over whatever subtle and quiet communications come my way.

MOITA: It takes practice to develop an inner ear. *(pause)*

           You are beginning to float! You have touched much of your depth, and your intuitions are stronger than you would let on.

Jake: I wonder if most of my intuitions are wanting to let things alone, and most of my ambition – or whatever it is – is looking at things in terms of changing. I wonder if all that is just a form of egotism on my part that isn't really necessary.

MOITA: It is your decision. *(pause)* Sometimes choices are difficult to make.

Jake: I guess it will take some practice.

MOITA: Practice and dedication – very close sisters – and a letting-go of your own ideas and perceptions.

ശ   ശ   ശ

We return to the session in which Moita suggested Jake's tree meditation. Earlier in the conversation, Moita refers to the Indians' awareness of the consequences of their actions. She says that awareness "did not prevent them from gathering wood...nor from killing [for] meat when it was needed." Margaret now picks up the latter thread.

Moita session #125 (Kelly, David, workshop group / December 17, 1979)

Margaret: We had a discussion around the dinner table tonight about vegetarianism and meat-eating, Moita. What is your view? Is it necessary for modern man to eat meat, or can he fulfill all of his requirements with just vegetables, grains and so forth? Do you find it immoral for modern man to maintain slaughterhouses, for instance, in order to continue his meat-eating habit?

MOITA: I will tell you that the animal kingdom looks upon slaughterhouses much the same as your civilization looks upon the keeping of slaves.

Margaret: What about the small farm areas like we live in here, where each family provides its own meat supply and does its own butchering? What would the animal kingdom think of that? We try to raise our animals as humanely as possible and take good care of them, but most of us are raising animals for meat purposes.

(Long pause. Moita closes Kelly's eyes. Kelly is aware that her own feelings on the subject are making it difficult for her to be a clear channel. Many of us are sensing the parallels in how slave owners might have spoken about their slaves, though Margaret's words are of course true from any "normal" perspective.)

MOITA: There *is* a difference in the feel. *(pause)* With so much of the other going on, it is difficult to separate, at the moment, these differences. If it were that way planet-wide, the animal kingdom might feel differently about it.

Margaret: Which kind of diet is actually beneficial to our bodies in the long run?

MOITA: Much depends on the individual body and the purposes for which they have come, what kind of thing they are here to learn. This is a choice that needs to be made by each in this time. There may come a time in the future where there will be no need to make that kind of a choice, where things in the Earth will be different, [where] there will be not as much of a conflict, when the communications are open between the worlds.

It is these kinds of things that need to be worked out through awareness of yourself first and your own purposes: to have a very distinct idea of who you are and why you are doing what you do, and what you really do or do not need, and which way is the best way to meet *all* of your needs.

Margaret: Do you think what we are doing out here in this area is a good thing – moving away from large cities and striving to take care of ourselves? We generally *only* do that; we don't contribute like city-dwellers do in lots of ways to each other's upkeep. We find ourselves looking after ourselves more and more. Do you think that our lifestyle is selfish, or is it mostly constructive?

MOITA: You are learning more about self-sufficiency, and you are not depending upon...other people's energy to support yourself. [In cities and towns] there is much using of other people's energy. People are contributing parts of themselves to a larger whole or identity they may not be aware of and may not approve of – all of the things that go into manufacturing items, [for example]. There is little satisfaction in putting a nut on a screw on an assembly line. The ability to create, and feel satisfaction from having created something, has been taken away from man in mass production, and other people are becoming dependent upon this kind of almost leach of energy.

So from my viewpoint it is far better to be able to put your energy into what you are doing, for then you will get back from life more than you have put into it. You are interacting *with* life in a more direct way, and you have more opportunity to understand what you are doing. You are taking the responsibility for your own support on the planet on your own shoulders and not portioning off on others.

(Actually, there is a good deal of mutual aid locally here also, but in contrast to mass society it is informal, spontaneous and face-to-face.)

Margaret: Do you think it's possible for the entire world's population to do that? There seems to be so very many people and such very small amounts of land, proportionally speaking, while we're here in the middle of acres and acres. Our political systems are so tyrannical in this way. Can you see a system where all the world's population can support themselves? Do you see this changing in the future?

MOITA: I see a time when there will not be as many people. One of the things that will be a by-product of the Earth changes will be a large decrease in the physical population of the planet back to a point where the planet can support the numbers that are here. And there will be a greater awareness of how to live with the Earth. Man will not have the need to populate in order to control and feel he is dominant. The only reason the Earth has too many people is [that] man feels he can live without the Earth.

Margaret: So large numbers will die, will they? Through what – famine, disease, pollution?

MOITA: All three, and more. But they are not dying, either. *(i.e. as souls)*

Margaret: Oh – no, not in that sense!... But then a lot of young couples have reconsidered about having children for that reason. Do you think they've made a wise decision not to have children because of what seems the coming calamity?

MOITA: If a child needs to be born, he will be. There are so many smaller areas that you can focus in and thereby lose the full impact of the whole picture. All people must make their own choices. And if they feel it is not right to have children in this time, their intuition is probably a good one for them. You are here to learn to follow your inner guidance, and not to worry if your neighbour agrees with what you have received. *(pause)*

Margaret: That can go in a lot of directions, can't it?! *(laughing)*

೭   ೭   ೭

Land, shelter, energy and food are four of the survival needs we have by now touched upon in considering mankind's relations with the Earth. Mention of the potentially calamitous period our world is now entering gives renewed emphasis to another area in which many have already been learning to take greater personal responsibility, rather than rely on mass production and established expertise. Chapter 5 of *The World Conspires* presented Moita's view of the self-created causes for illness and of mankind's potential for healing self and others by natural and spiritual means. Below are some further exchanges on health and healing that relate more specifically to future situations we may face and the attitude changes that may prepare us.

Moita session #170 (Kelly, David, Sue / January 10, 1981)

Sue: Are our physical illnesses always a sign of something we're not accepting or following?

MOITA: Not always. Sometimes they are just things that you think, ways of slowing you down, ways of testing your strength, testing your growth, testing your acceptance.

Sue: Right. So they all must be accepted. Should we accept illness to the degree of using man's earthly crutches?

MOITA: Are you speaking of medications?

Sue: Somewhat, yes.

MOITA: Each is different. I can give no blanket answer to that question. In some cases it helps teach you something about your body and how your mind affects it.

Sue: The disease or the medication?

MOITA: The disease. And there are different forms of medication:... manmade and earthmade. As far as life is concerned, earthmade medications have more wholeness... They give energy to a body, help it to heal itself. Most manmade medications are like thoughts. They disguise the disease, suppress it, distract your attention...from something.

In this culture, it is a great struggle for man to go from one kind of medication to the other. It is a gradual growing process – no easy stopping point and then a starting point on the other side. It is another [case] of flowing, gradual letting go of things that you no longer need, gradually accepting things that have more life to them.

ல   ல   ல

With other people, Moita has stressed more the urgency of change, easy or not – and in this early session, her prescription of one of the earthmade medications could not be more immediate. This session takes place during Kelly's visit to a city several hours from home. The subject of healing comes up because of the congenital skin ailment of the family's newest member, but Moita responds in terms of some graver possibilities for the world.

Moita session #21 (Kelly, Laura, Scott / August 12, 1978)

MOITA: The changes that are coming are one of the reasons why there have been so many healers born right now. Man has become too dependent upon modern medicine to meet his needs. When the changes do come, if the medical institutions are destroyed, there will be no drugs. Even those physicians that survive will be without their tools. So mankind will be forced to look to the natural healers for help. There will be no others available to them.

Laura: Besides psychic healing, is there anything else you would suggest I do to help the baby's face heal more quickly?

MOITA: *(smiling broadly)* As a matter of fact, there *is*. Kelly brought the remedy with her – although she thought she was bringing it for herself.

Laura: And that is . . . ?

MOITA: Red clover. It is a very powerful and useful herb. Kelly will tell you what to do with it.

Laura: Thank you very much!

MOITA: You are most welcome.

ஒ   ஒ   ஒ

Though different individuals will always possess special talents in the healing field, the attitude must change that there are a certain number of "healers" and then the rest of us. We all can learn to heal ourselves and others. This is Moita's point in the next two excerpts, again expressed in a context of dire probabilities. The first is addressed to our friend and housemate Joe, the medical doctor.

Moita session #111 (Kelly, Joe, Alexis / September 15, 1979)

Joe: Is it my soul's desire that I consciously develop my healing energies?

MOITA: You have not become a physician for nothing... We see on this level a potential here of beginning. *(pause)*

       One of the things that will be needed in the coming change of the world [is] healers, for the destruction will topple the institutions of medicine, destroy most of the pharmaceutical companies, disrupt the organization that is now in place. There will be many who are hurt and injured on a physical and on a spiritual level by going through what changes will come. Each of you have come here in order to lend a helping hand to your fellow man through this time, and by so doing you are learning what humility means. You are learning in this life to lose your sense of pride.

ஒ   ஒ   ஒ

Moita session #118 (Kelly, David, Joyce, 3 others / November 10, 1979)

Joyce: I've met now a number of healers who have come to my area. We have the feeling we are all there for a purpose, that when the Earth changes do come we will be there to give help to people. Are we on the right track thinking that way?

MOITA: If there are no medicines, there must be healers of some kind. And if people are not ready to heal themselves yet, there must be channels for that energy. This is a transition period. A time will come when there will be no healers, for there will not be any illness. You will not be out of touch with your other levels and [will] come into the world as whole rather than as a part.

ๆ   ๆ   ๆ

One very down-to-earth way of getting back in touch is this prescription for a friend with foot trouble. It also returns us to our main theme.

Moita session #168 (Kelly, David, Ellen, Connie / December 28, 1980)
MOITA: She must realize that her feet are her foundation. Most people do not consider that they depend on their feet to hold them up... Pain is an indicator of something that is being neglected... They are very much like an abandoned child who desires attention, and the pain is a way of attracting it. They need to be spoiled...

Energy comes through the soles of the feet into the body. It is a grounding mechanism, something that connects you with the Earth. People's soles *(souls?)* have been insulated [from the Earth] for too long... It is a statement with more than one meaning.
Connie: But how may we run barefoot in the snow?...
MOITA: There are other ways of connecting with the Earth energy...than through the feet, providing that the feet are used when conditions permit as much as possible. You reach the Earth through your heart, your feelings. You can help your feet by manipulating them with your hands, giving them what energy you have stored in the rest of your body, if you cannot let them feel the Earth directly.

ๆ   ๆ   ๆ

Pavement is at least as much an "insulation" as shoes – if there are not enough reasons already for living in a more natural environment. How to know, then, where to move, and where to build communities that through mutual aid can achieve enough self-reliance in days to come?

Moita session #140 (Kelly, David, workshop group / April 9, 1980)
Mary: Are there Earth energy points that we should be aware of as possible areas to move to and build community?
MOITA: Most places where there are already people who desire to build community are fairly good places. You can arrive at a fairly accurate description of safe places by looking at the predictions that have been made of possible Earth changes. Mostly, people will be attracted to the areas that are best suited for these purposes, and it is important for them to discover these places on their own, to open up their own awareness and intuition of the Earth and

what may happen. If they cannot do this, if they cannot find places without being told directly, then they will not be able or ready to build a community that will last, so it would do no good to go there.

Mary: But definitely get out of the cities and live a country life?

MOITA: There is certainly more safety where there are fewer numbers of people. The greatest devastation will happen where the highest population is, not just because there are many people there but because of their energy and the amount of it. It will in a sense attract destruction, for it is those places that have affected the Earth the [most], and where there is the least awareness of the Earth and of the Spirit.

Learning to live with the Earth is what is meant by living in the country – or so I *hope*. And it may be different for each. It is becoming part of, instead of living off, the Earth. It will have to come from within. A place that is right will be known.

ဖ   ဖ   ဖ

The story of how a temporary "right place" becomes known to our own family can begin on New Year's Day, 1980. This day is a high point in our first year in British Columbia, for the large hilltop farmhouse we are renting is, for once, filled with a dozen of the Kindle Valley people we have met through our fall workshop. It's a joy to know that this group of new friends want to drive a couple hours from their homes to spend the holiday with us – and that all of us together can create such a warm, relaxed celebration together.

After an afternoon of skating on our "own" lake, a bountiful potluck supper, and a group sauna (*sans* clothes, but complete with snowballs!), we gather in a large circle to invite Moita's presence. Near the end of the session, I speak what is in my heart.

Moita session #128A (Kelly, David, 11 others / January 1, 1980)

David: I feel that Kelly and I are at a point like when we first visited Sunrise Farm, in that we're at a further decision-to-move point – and now, getting quite sure we want to move towards the Kindle Valley. There's a whole lot that we need to start exploring with people about community. And I can't come up with a question about that because it seems such a delicate thing, barely in the sprouting stage. In this wordless situation, can you say anything to help us in that exploring – what attitude to bring to it, what's important to remember?

MOITA: *(laughs)* The only answer at the moment is an answer that you have already been given.

David: Mmm. "Expect the unexpected"? Or another?

MOITA: Another one. "The universe is ready to give you anything you want, providing you will let it."[85N] So relax and put your faith in the world and its wisdom.

ဖ   ဖ   ဖ

We can appreciate the need to be open and patient in the faith that things will work out for the best. But we also tend to believe in the maxim that "God helps those who help themselves." So we squint at government office maps and tramp the snow-covered woods of a couple vacant pieces of land near where our Kindle Valley friends live. By February and March, as we discover numerous financial and legal barriers to our buying or leasing such land – not to mention the practical question whether we, inexperienced and lacking funds, could manage to do much with it – we are forced to recognize something is wrong with the time and/or our approach.

Returning home in mid-April from the Okanagan Valley workshop where Moita talked about moving closer to the Earth – which reignites our own determination – we start exploring again: other pieces of land, the chance to lease land with another friend, and the possibility of a livable dwelling in the Kindle that we could rent for the next year. A few days later at the home of a valley friend, I ask again about our situation.

Moita session #142 (Kelly, David, 8 others / April 19, 1980)

David: Right now we're beginning to work actively toward a way to move to this area. Moving as soon as possible seems the thing to do, as the distance barrier is getting too frustrating. Yet it seems there are so many hurdles to go through before we can actually get settled here.

It would really help at least to know that there's a place out there in the future that we're either being manoeuvred or manoeuvring ourselves toward, instead of just a myriad confusing choices. And then, what do we need to keep before us as the most important attitude and awareness to have in order to get there?

(A silence as Moita looks toward me with a great deal of energy. The answer, said with emphasis, comes as a complete surprise.)

MOITA: *Give in. (pause)*

Try to see others as I see all of you. Bring that into life. It is not in your goal that you shall find peace – it is in the road to it. So do not make the goal the important part, but the moment. Looking too far ahead, you can miss a great deal of joy, and then the ending shall be a disappointment.

David: Mm-hmm. *(pause)* Is it mainly, then, to change our attitude while doing all those things that, rationally and practically speaking, we expect we will have to do to find a place to settle? Or are all those steps not going to be necessary? Sometimes I find it difficult to integrate that intuitive faith with the side of rational, practical action.

MOITA: Regardless of what path you take, you shall not want for physical things. These are always available. *(pause)* It *is* something you must integrate on your own.

David: Well, we'll just have to see how it works out.

৯   ৯   ৯

Having become so wrapped up in the responsibility for finding a future place, it is painful at first to surrender to the moment. But then comes the relief of Moita's indirect assurance that it is all right and not irresponsible or wildly impractical in this case to do so. Further, the hint that our attitude toward others is important lifts me out of my self-absorption, perhaps to glimpse a larger pattern.

It is probably that very weekend that a friend takes me driving up the valley to look once more at possibilities. We go further up the Kindle Valley Road than I ever have had occasion to go before. As the road narrows and begins to leave the more cleared valley floor to wind through tall forest, we spy through scattered birch groves a recently built, two-storey log house. It is owned by an American, I am told, and may possibly be available to rent. We stop and walk up the long, roundabout driveway to the house, perched on the top of a gently sloping hillside leading down to the Kindle River below.

The artfully designed house is so beautiful in its woodsy setting on this warm, sunny day in early spring, it's very hard for me to believe it might be just waiting to fall into our grasp. ("Surely someone else has already laid claim to it, if the owner actually wished to rent it in the first place; and surely he'd want some other kind of people to live there; and surely there would be all sorts of obstacles," etc., etc.) This is how I let the universe give us whatever we want?! And too, I am not without doubts it *is* what we want – so far up the valley, without power, plumbing or phone, a mile and a half from the nearest neighbour, let alone nearly 20 miles from our friends and 30 miles for our children to ride the school bus.

Nevertheless, the log house on the wooded hillside above the river begins to haunt us the next week back at Joe's farmhouse. It is one definite possibility, and the only possibility we yet know about. The following weekend, we are back: to show Kelly the house, and to visit the people we are told the owner has authorized to rent it. Then, we can't believe how easy it seems when they pull out the lease form and say go ahead and fill it out! (Incidentally, these people will become good friends, and one will later attend some of our sessions.) The rent turns out to be only $50 per month, which can be exchanged by doing any needed work on the place.

We begin to suspect some of that "manoeuvring" as we're told that many others have inquired about renting but decided not to because of one condition in the lease: the owner wishes to come up two weeks every fall to use the house while fishing. Inconvenient, yes – but for us, knowing the valley is where we belong, what are two weeks beside the other 50?! So we agree, and are encouraged to think our signed application will be accepted. *[Photo Album #6 and #7]*

In early May, Kelly and I can hardly contain our excitement as we drive up to camp on, hopefully, our future home site. We ask the nature spirits' permission to cut a trail from the house down through the bushes to a meadow by the river, where we begin to work the soil for a garden. We try to return every weekend so the garden will be ready to plant by month end. A circular or oval shape comes intuitively as more appropriate than sharp corners. Our work of raking and digging up the sod goes slowly but steadily, and we're glad the steep hillside between garden and road does not tempt us to use large machinery. Aside from the small rototiller we later borrow, we feel good to be investing our personal energies in a simple, old-fashioned way without extra noise and disturbance.

Sometimes, in the unusually warm spring weather, we cool off by going barefoot and bare-skinned in our secluded meadow, dunking our heads in the river that bears snow-melt from the mountains. Then we lie under the huge cottonwood leaning out over the bank and experience the awakening life around us to the tune of rippling water and singing birds.

Thus we introduce ourselves to our anticipated home. We know exactly what she must mean, and are deeply touched and encouraged, when Moita gives us this sentence on May 13th: "Becoming more involved in the Earth will see you a long way on your road."

Two weeks later, from the farmhouse, we speak again. Moita now hints at more reasons why Kelly and I are to live in a remote cabin in the woods.

Moita session #144 (Kelly and David / May 27, 1980)

David: We feel so strongly drawn to the life we're starting to build up in the valley. I really felt good when you said that living closer to the Earth would take us a long way on our road.

MOITA: I am glad you are going to enjoy the place.

David: Any particular reason we arranged to be living at that place?

MOITA: It is isolated enough, but not too much, to give you the solitude you require. Your life will be not quite as hectic as it would be if you lived closer.

David: Once school starts in the fall, we're going to have long days together, alone – quite unusual for us.

MOITA: It will be a good opportunity to learn the wisdom in silence.

ം   ം   ം

For weeks, though, we have to content ourselves with looking into the almost completely unfurnished house through the windows. It takes some time for the owner to give his hesitant okay to our moving in. Then the keys all seem to disappear! Finally, official authorization is delivered to the one person in the valley who does have a key . . . and in early June we turn the lock and walk in.

The large, open first floor draws us forward to two front picture windows, where we can stand looking over the deck down through woods to the Kindle River below. A third big window to the left brings afternoon sun onto an eating area next to the wood-burning cookstove. The stove and the wood heater behind it share an insulated chimney, rising up through the centre of the house. Opposite the door to the deck, a strong pole ladder angles up to the loft's two bedrooms in the back half of the house, divided from each other but open to the front, each with a gabled side window.

We're enthusiastic about starting with such a fresh and beautiful structure, but we also realize it will take a lot of work to turn it into a home. Our other problem is our truck, which continues to break down during June, requiring a costly repair. Lack of transportation keeps us impatiently back in town, and Kelly at her secretarial job, when we should be planting and then readying the house to move in when school lets out at the end of June.

The great day finally comes, followed by busy weeks of settling in. Early on my agenda is digging a new outhouse with pick and shovel. In exchange for rent, I end up producing a nice two-seater – with styrofoam on top to avoid frozen bums, and a half-door offering a view of the mountains! Then there's my project to insulate and board up the cabin floor from below, hoping to block frigid winds curling up the hill into our living space. Meanwhile Kelly is maintaining the veggie garden, preparing much of our food and running herd on the children.

We soon learn life can be hectic here in the wilderness, not just in town, depending upon the awareness we bring to our days. It takes a conscious change in mental pace sometimes to remember the definite energy in stillness, when one stops to sit on the Earth and feel the life all around. It is certainly pleasant in summer to wander and gaze upon this rolling acreage of birch, cedar, fir, alder and berry bushes – at least, when mosquitoes are about, with the aid of repellent.

Beyond the natural beauty surrounding us, Moita begins to speak of the "healing energy" of this place as well. And during the second session we hold in our new home, she tells us more. (We will return for the full context of this excerpt in Tales of Power #3.)

Moita session #148 (Kelly and David / July 4, 1980)

MOITA: You are in this place for a good reason. There is a good energy here, a whole energy, an energy that is close to the Earth and the Spirit, together. This energy has already started to manifest itself in your life, and you have only been here a short while. *(pause; then softly:)* This used to be a sacred ground, and there is the chance of many visions...

David: This particular piece of land, you mean?

MOITA: Yes.

David: How was it used?

MOITA: It was a place of meditation, a place of visions, of quests...

Over two months later, I'm experiencing one effect of that energy.

Moita session #156 (Kelly and David / September 16, 1980)

David: It seems that as I've been consciously tuning into the land more recently, my dreams have suddenly been coming through much more strongly, after a long period of vague and unremembered dreams. I wonder how far back the knowledge of this place's power goes among the local Indians. Would it be within the memory of anyone living now, or does it go way, way back?

MOITA: *(after a long pause with closed eyes)* I see none who remember. It was more a personal place than a tribal one, belonging to one family and only one living person in each generation. The symbol of the bear appears. *(she smiles)*

David: Would that have been the totem of this family?

MOITA: So it seems. There are always mixtures within each. *(i.e. through clan intermarriage)*
           (Moita's smile is about the she-bear with cub that has made her appearance several times at our compost pile and by the raspberry patches that cover the river meadows. Our closest call is a deep growl from the depths of a thicket right in front of where we're picking berries . . . but not for long!)

೪   ೪   ೪

The Spirit of the Earth begins speaking to both Kelly and me in waking as well as dream, yielding different angles on the same message. One cloudy afternoon in September, sitting on the deck overlooking hillside and river, I become unusually aware of my feelings in the presence of the trees: the ease and comfort in their lack of opinion or judgment, just their acceptance of what *is*. Not taking sides as humans do, how balanced and undivided they are! Then I remember how often I have *not* felt this way in nature's presence – have felt its stillness instead as a cold, ignoring energy, or as an oppressive weight of material fact, or as a beauty and serenity that put me to shame.

Then it dawns that this forest is the landscape of my own mind. It reflects myself back to me in the way I perceive it. Nature can do this precisely because it is so perfectly balanced and open. And when we flow from the centre of all, its beauty is also our own. Contact is never spoiled by too much intimacy, as happens with manmade things when the veneer wears off. The depth of nature goes on and on, an endless mirror of spirit. Like the perfect therapist, it is the secret gift given to all who live close to the Earth: the opportunity to see ourselves reflected in clarity and wholeness.

The experience teaches me more – that these thoughts that flow through me, unbidden but yet as mine, must be the form of channeling, along with dreams, natural to my soul. I have looked for an *outside* source – a higher entity that would come down and speak. Not finding it, I considered myself dense, as I continued to block my true expression. For others, though, it may be natural to experience channeling as from another, and they will become channels when they open to *that*.

Kelly is one who perceives the Spirit speaking as from a higher being, while recognizing we are all part of the same source. Sitting outside near woods in another Kindle Valley spot on the afternoon of October 4th – a key date that will recur in a similar vein – she writes: "I can feel the presence of the Earth's Spirit as a living and viable entity. It speaks to me of becoming a mirror (as I was in Musili), and I see that in order to be a mirror someone or something must reflect itself through me. The voice tells me I should let the Earth be my focus, and then speaks of seeing harmony in disharmony – how, even when things look completely destructive and unnecessary, there's an underlying balance (or overlying harmony) to it all.

"It makes me feel really marvellous, and then I hear someone ask me if I need a sign, as proof of the experience. I say no, I don't think I need one. But then I see a being of bright light standing in the trees and surrounded by shafts of sunlight (though the Sun is not out). I just sit there and absorb it all. The trees become wavy and start to disappear, becoming more like coloured lights than trees. I think that maybe I am seeing what Moita sees, and using my soul's eyes rather than my body's eyes.

"The feeling of oneness and awareness of myself and what I am doing within the harmony/disharmony/harmony balance stays until into the next day. Relationships, including with the children, are a breeze, and everyone seems to pick up on my mellow."

How this suggestion to become a mirror for the Earth finds its fulfillment exactly one year later, through seeking the harmony in disharmony, is a tale for a future chapter.

ᔐ   ᔐ   ᔐ

Spirituality notwithstanding, living on our own in the country brings no escape from material-level challenges. In fact, compared to city living with taken-for-granted services, they can become all the more immediate and pressing. Especially at the beginning, living "cheaply" a distance away from "civilization" also involves some major investments, and many minor ones.

For instance, to avoid the catch-22 of using gas for long drives into town to fill up on gas, we get a pumping gasoline barrel fillable once every few months. But on arriving home, it's a trick to roll that very heavy barrel off our pickup (and not into the woods!), then by stages propping it upright for use. Another useful purchase, but one we *don't* make, would have been a mobile radio tuned to the logging truck frequency to warn us when the next fast-moving monster is about to come round a curve, so we can veer our own vehicle toward the ditch or nearest snowbank!

But above all, there's one major purchase I greatly resist making – due to my ambivalence about tree-cutting as shared with our friends. The challenges of this new life, so far from my earlier academic-musical-religious background, are epitomized by a chainsaw. I know the saw is a necessary tool here, used by all, but it is still very hard to envisage myself wielding one. So, on a camping trip that starts the very day of purchasing my first chainsaw, I ignore cautionary thoughts . . . and allow it to be stolen from our tent! As a result, I'm left without a saw of my own for three months during prime wood-gathering season, until it is returned by the RCMP with winter coming on.

I first see the theft as a "sign" I should have nothing to do with chainsaws. But Moita's comment on the loss surprises me, emphasizing my inner experience of the tool, not what it is in itself.

Moita session #154 (Kelly and David / August 28, 1980)
MOITA: The chainsaw [theft] was a combination of things. You were given warning that it might happen, that it was a possible future line of yours, and in that you did not follow your intuition. And so, your chainsaw has disappeared – a graphic example of what can happen when you lose touch...with your inner self – not only because of what a chainsaw can do to a tree, but because it represents for you an external thing, something you do not feel as connected with, something you are not in touch with, in yourself.
David: Are you saying the warning *(i.e. the fear it might be stolen)* was more about buying one at all rather than, having bought it, leaving it somewhere?
MOITA: There were *both*. It can be a useful tool if it is used with the right awareness and if it is something that you can tune into.

ᔐ   ᔐ   ᔐ

With this to go on, losing the saw does make me aware of my conflicting feelings regarding it: certainly about felling trees, but also the male stereotypes associated with chainsaws, the foreignness to me of my new outdoorsman role, my inexperience and unmechanical mind, etc. The loss also means that I will slowly work my way into the situation – finding alternative wood supplies, going together with Jim on wood-gathering missions, then borrowing a chainsaw for my use. By the time I get ours back, I know a little more, have a clearer sense of the need it fills, and feel it's more of a helpful tool than a foreign object. I then can take pride in rising layers of firewood, from large logs I've sawn and split with a weighted axe, lining the front of our log house. I know the energy stored in those logs, complemented by the "lamplight glow" of kerosene lanterns, will see us through the dark northern winter.

Indoors, our kitchen shelves are lined with a supply of whole foods purchased from the local co-op. Every week, I hand-grind the grain for Kelly's prized bread-making – tricky in a wood cookstove, and uncomfortably hot in summer, but so deliciously full of that sturdy, earthy energy when ready to eat. Another hot job is canning bulk fruit from the Okanagan and our own abundant raspberries, which will add their summery flavour to our homemade yogurt, granola, whole wheat pancakes, and so on, through the winter months. There are also wild mushrooms and other edible and medicine plants to gather, as well as Kelly's bountiful garden to keep up with. And when we join Margaret for an overnight hike up a tall mountain visible from our house, huge huckleberries line the trail.

Surely, in many ways, living here fulfills our hopes in joining with each other and moving to the country. In other ways, though, we will experience the pressures of any nuclear family living in relative isolation on the land. Thus we will come to realize this kind of life is not our final goal, but a way-station on the path that we hope leads to greater community.

Despite the hardships, it is nevertheless satisfying to know where one's heat, light, food and water are coming from, rather than lying at the mercy of an unbalanced, faltering mass society. Even during the winter, when hauling firewood and snow for meltwater, or huddling around the wood heater after getting home to a freezing house, it is a gift to learn the difference between an abstract "standard of living" and true *survival* – which is not in doubt, now that it depends upon what the Earth provides, simple tools, practical knowledge and intuition, and our own human hands. The wood with which I fill the heater on going to bed *will* keep us warm through the night and be there still, as glowing embers, to reignite in the morning. (Those hot coals, shovelled under the engine block, will also help us start our truck on sub-zero mornings.)

Watching the overhead vees of honking geese flying south in fall, or standing silently by the bedroom window on a cold, moonlit night to hear the wolves' truly eerie song from the snowy woods beyond, I feel we have earned the privilege of being here. But then the shimmering, colourful curtains of *aurora borealis* are a grace beyond earning.

Those are some of my thoughts on living with the Earth as a spiritual experience – and all the more practical, in the truest sense, for its spirituality. Indeed, Kelly and I will both experience times when the thoughts in our minds are suddenly replaced by different, more whole and centred thoughts through the simple act of walking outdoors. Yet the effect is far from automatic. We can immunize ourselves to nature's touch by letting inherited structures of thought and reaction gain too strong a hold. Then our purpose in coming here becomes mere abstraction, and we might as well be back in the city.

Moita session #154 (Kelly and David / August 28, 1980)

David: When we came here to the valley, we wanted to create a way of life with a depth of spirit to it. It seems we nevertheless often find ourselves narrowly focused on the surface, physical level. Do you have any comments on the awareness, or lack of it, with which we've been living?

MOITA: You are all falling into a habit of structuring your lives in old forms – things that have been handed down through your experience, from your parents, through your culture, as those that are right to do and be. You are here to try and let go of these structures so that you can find one that is malleable enough to change in need. Being inventive and spontaneous and not worrying about position or talent – in this, you will learn more about yourself and learn how to work together with others, not closing them off from the areas that you consider your own.

Do not let your role trap you until you become nothing but a role. *(pause)* Expand yourself, and remember that this experience is here to help you find that balance between spirit and practical.

ço   ço   ço

One way to reach a depth beneath our roles, and our frustrations about roles, is remembering other times we have lived in the woods and known each other, times when we were very alive to the magic of our surroundings.

One day in winter, we can't believe a very resonant, penetrating sound coming from outside, like a loud "plopping" of objects falling into water. We are amazed then to discover that the sound is coming from a big, black raven perched atop a tall spruce. With my old dream of turning into Raven in mind, I try to imitate the call and attract his attention.[86N]

As days pass, a great variety of unusual sounds come from the ravens who like to fly along the river below us. And more than once a raven will fly over or land on the house at significant times, as when we are just going outside or arriving home. Like the call of the tropical bird – *karuna* – that reminded the inhabitants of Aldous Huxley's novel *Island* to "pay attention",[87] Raven calls me to notice, and feel my way more deeply into, the energy of the moment. (Events in a later chapter will explain Moita's reference below to "timing" and my current "stage in development" – which make Raven's presence all the more significant for me at this point.)

Moita session #172 (Kelly, David, Jake, 2 others / February 3, 1981)

David: In our last session, you said privately to Kelly, "So you have met a raven." I'd like to ask about some of the meanings behind your saying that...

MOITA: All of your lives are connected. Different ones are connected at different points in each life. At the moment you are going through a stage in your development when you are more closely connected to that life in which the Raven was your totem. The raven has been around for a while, but you have not noticed him because circumstances and timing were not exactly perfect. Once you noticed him, he became more than just a bird – for your other self has put energy into him as a symbol, creating a field, an attraction, between you and it.

It is the way that you open up your own [reincarnational] buds – through symbols, learning to connect with them, using them as a means to flow along into the past, to bring energy forward into the future, into your present. This is a lesson in your multidimensionality.

David: We've had hints that my Raven life would be associated with moving here, as when Kelly sought a dream on our connection to Sunrise Farm. Was Kelly also involved in that life?

MOITA: She was in that life, but that totem was not hers. The Raven is a personal totem, for you. *(pause)* Since you are not as prone to receiving images from your other lives during this one, except in dreams, this is a way you have chosen to help you make a conscious connection with other energy. You each have a different way.

David: Do you have any suggestions on connecting more closely with that life's energy through the bird's presence here?

MOITA: Your thoughts on it should be enough, your meditation on it. Do what feels right. It is your experiment. See what happens. Use your imagination.

David: I've had some ideas already.

MOITA: There is probably a reason why – discovering your own guidance. *(long pause as we gaze at each other)*

David: Looking at you with your dark eyes shining makes me think of Carlos Castaneda's shaman teacher Don Juan instructing him how to turn into a crow.[88] *(laughter)*

MOITA: Watch out, I may peck off your nose!

(From the conversation afterward:)

David: That was amazing how much you started looking like a bird there. Like, your shawl was coming down along your shoulder and your back, and started looking like wings or tail of a bird. Your eyes were this bright black, with little star reflections of the light in them . . .

Kelly: I have no desire to turn into a bird.

David: And your nose was starting to look like a beak. *(laughs)*

Kelly: Oh *really*?! *(laughter)*

(In good down-to-earth Kindle Valley style, Jake then points out how ravens love to eat dead frogs on the road. But Raven is an illustrious figure in Pacific Northwest Indian mythology.)

David: After the bird, you turned into the gypsy.

Kelly: I did? Well, at least that's better.

(The "gypsy" is a face identified with Kelly's 15th century life as an herbalist, having a weasel/ermine as her "familiar", a life first described to her by Loria. I, as a village boy, liked to visit the "good witch" in her hut in the woods.[89])

David: It was a very powerful kind of presence, being the bird.

Kelly: You know what? Back when she was talking about totems, all of a sudden I thought of the gypsy life and the ermine.

(We did also spy a weasel last summer on our overnight mountain hike.)

David: Oh! I never thought of that during the session, but the raven naturally connects for me with going as a boy to visit the old gypsy in the woods.

Kelly: Boy, minds work in weird ways, eh? You see the raven, I see the ermine, you see the gypsy, and we both end up in the same life.

৯ ৯ ৯

Some of the changes Kelly and I will undergo in future years of living in the valley will bring us closer to what the gypsy/herbalist and the raven priest represent in us. And of course, behind these figures lie our first incarnations, who immersed in the energy of Earth and Sun in order to remember what a future world would forget.

Moita spoke to us frequently in that "Earth and Sun" life, and conversations with her continue to be a high point and invaluable medium of sharing for us now as valley residents. Starting on one of our moving days in late June and running through Christmas week 1980, we hold a full 20 Moita sessions, usually with friends participating, during our first six months in the Kindle. These sessions we transcribe, edit for *Rays* and send out to subscribers in the valley and beyond – sessions that will eventually fill many pages of these books.

Living in near-wilderness affords many of us a freedom outside the mainstream of present-day society, an opportunity to explore a "marginal" life in Thomas Merton's sense – one of contemplation and voluntary simplicity. But we may also then have to deal with doubts about our value and place vis-a-vis the majority reality, as one of our closest friends expresses below.

Moita session #134 (Kelly, David, Mike / February 24, 1980)

Mike: It's been on my mind that from moment to moment my life is pleasing to me. But sometimes I worry that I don't have a goal, a direction for developing skills that would fulfill needs of people when whatever is going to happen happens – like even professional skills. Maybe I'm lazy, but I don't know what I'm headed to do.

MOITA: You should know yourself well enough in many ways to be able to see to the feelings of your heart, seeing them from a deeper place. It is your clearest pathfinder. But you must do things that will increase that clearness and centredness in your heart. For, although there are many things in the world that need doing, you are only on the Earth for a short time. Most of man's work is not done here; it is done elsewhere. Trying to bring the kind of work you do elsewhere into this world in a more touchable form is what you are here to do.

     Leave off conceptions that have been acquired through many lives of what is worthy and what is not. Let yourself have the freedom to find the unique path that is in you. Worth is not measured by your earthly accomplishments. It is measured by your ability to share yourself with the world. It is not so much a need to change a possible direction you might take, but to change your perception of it – its purpose and the joy you should bring to it as you do whatever you choose to do. Do not judge yourself by the yardsticks you have been given in this world. If you can bring love and joy to even one, you have accomplished more than many men.

Mike: I believe that's true.

♾   ♾   ♾

     The same tension between the majority reality and emerging unknown possibilities can be felt wherever one is. A whirlwind visitor from California (mentioned in Tales of Power #4) asks these questions.

Moita session #155 (Kelly, David, Judi / August 30, 1980)

Judi: Why has there been a shift in my energy recently, a restlessness, some changes in my belief structures that I'm finding alarming? I don't know where these thoughts are coming from: desires to accumulate money (where I've never been a material person before), desires to break out of my regular work pattern (one that's always been satisfying to me)?

MOITA: You are experiencing the unrest of the world. You are feeling the need to prepare yourself for the unknown, for change; the need to be secure, the need to assist, and the need to grow out of old patterns that no longer fit.

Judi: I think a difference this time is that, in the past when I've had this same feeling, it was accompanied by a sight of where I was going. I could see the old pattern fading and I had a sense of a new pattern coming about, where I was heading. In this instance I don't see where I'm going. All I'm seeing is a discarding.

MOITA: Maybe it is time for you not to seek a pattern. A pattern will bind you to its own boundaries... And containing yourself in a pattern, you will limit your view of the world and your own abilities... In order to break the pattern, you must break away a part of yourself. You must break through, fight or destroy your perception of reality... Going forward with no pattern in mind can be a frightening experience, because in a pattern lies safety. Boundaries are set, are known: where you can and cannot go, what you can and cannot do.

     The world is entering a time where it is learning it need not set limits. It can do the unexpected, the impossible, when it recognizes no impossible. What *is* man's need for a pattern? What goal do you need greater than finding yourself? You do not find yourself in a pattern. You are an essence, without form. You are a spirit.

Your body gives you limits, too. Man is learning to leave limits. You are learning to leave yours. Try to leave your fear of what you cannot see behind you. Your greatest teacher and guide is yourself.

ଚ୬   ଚ୬   ଚ୬

Moita session #137 (Kelly, David, workshop group / March 17, 1980)

Carrie: I am feeling really torn. It's between what's happening in the world right now and what I feel I should believe in – I think. I feel that this physical world really doesn't matter in the long run, because everything changes and because what happens here is all for the best no matter what happens. And yet I see so many things happening that I want to get out and change so that other people will feel better. I've always felt that there was something I have to do in this world, and yet I find myself feeling that maybe I should just leave my body and stay out. *(laughs)* It's really bothering me...

MOITA: If you feel you are here to change things, and yet you feel that the physical world is unimportant in many ways, perhaps what you are here to change is how man looks upon his world. The physical world is here because of how man has viewed it, how he views life and his life force. And it is, to me, obvious that he has many fears; and so, he expresses these fears in a physical way.

In order to change the world, one needs to change how one looks *at* the world, for the world starts from thought and then thought is manifested in the physical. So, to change the world, change how you look at it. Look at it as you feel it should be, and see the things in it that are beautiful, harmonious, whole. And keeping that thought before you, and knowing that the physical is just transient, and if there is evil in the world it is a passing thing for most, you can help to change those around you and help to change the world. For if enough people can see the world as a place of beauty, then the world shall *become* a place of beauty. And one must start someplace, and you cannot start with another – you can only start with yourself.

Carrie: *(with a sigh) Yeah.* I think I probably knew that. It's going to take some working on.

MOITA: Many of these concepts are well-known. Living them is something else, and finding that place where they are real, where they do have force and energy. But you have us behind you!

Carrie: I guess I just keep trying, eh?

MOITA: It is not by disliking what you see that you change it, but by finding those things that you like.

Carrie: That I *do* know.

MOITA: It takes a certain kind of focus, and there are always tests of your awareness to see how well you have learned that.

Carrie: Aha, so that's what it is! *(laughing)*

MOITA: Things that you have set up for yourself. For if your awareness comes from a superficial plane, when change *does* happen you will be blown away. It is important for strong individuals to manifest themselves in the Earth right now so that they will stand, and stay, when the time comes. You must be strong within yourself to find that centre. It is like one who pours cement, and then must test it to see if it has the right tenacity to hold together lest it become brittle and break.

Carrie: That helps.

MOITA: *(smiling)* I am glad it helps. *(Carrie laughs)* That is why I am here.

ও   ও   ও

We have now come full circle from our keynote exchange in which Moita tells Dorothy she has to move. For the spirit with which we view our world and the Earth is at least as important as our material relationship to them. And they influence each other in so many, many ways – which is why Moita responds with a rather different emphasis when Dorothy asks this follow-up.

Moita session #140 (Kelly, David, workshop group / April 9, 1980)

Dorothy: Okay, in very practical terms, how can I help? Reading spiritual books sometimes seems very futile to me when there are more practical things that will have to be looked after when this transition does come.

MOITA: The needs of the body will be taken care of if the needs of the spirit are met. Man has the ability to look after himself through this crisis period in practical ways that he is as yet unaware of. The best way to prepare is by becoming more spiritually aware yourself and by connecting with others who are on a similar path, creating a network so that those in need can find help – and not just food for the body, but also food for the soul.

There will be many who will not survive – not because they cannot find something to eat but because they are desperate and afraid, confused and alone, and have lost love and have just realized it. They will find themselves in a world they do not understand or recognize. The help they need will be from those who can show them the *new* beauty and help them find their centre, their grounding, so that they can become whole and then self-sustaining. Man has always put his physical needs before his spiritual ones, and [as a result] this is where he is.

Thus the many levels to being pioneers, which must all interact so that (paraphrasing Moita) we can open our hearts, extend our hands, and walk down the pathway of the future, creating a newness.

ও   ও   ও

Moita session #168 (Kelly, David, Ellen, Connie / December 28, 1980)

Connie: Moita, three years ago I dreamed I was in this old white house with relatives and other people. It started getting very, very windy and I felt to myself, "This is it." The wind got so strong that the house just fell on us, into the Earth. I felt the dirt coming down on me and I went unconscious. Then I woke up and dug myself out. Everyone was all right. I took this person's hand and said, "C'mon, let's go." We came out of the house and saw this whole new world. We went down some stairs into a paradise, where there were people like from a very different civilization. I don't know what that means...

(Meanwhile, Kelly has been seeing what Connie is describing.)

MOITA: It is a good dream!... I knew the ending before you started. It is something I have spoken of many times.

Your house can be interpreted as the structures of yourself, of your society, this civilization of man. And the wind can be the Spirit that is seeking entrance, or it can be the fears of the civilization turning against itself. That the house was destroyed is what is coming to pass here in the near future. This civilization will be toppled by its own fears, but also because some of its members seek something beyond its structures.

Buried in the Earth, the Earth becoming part of you – the Earth is part of this change, for the Earth will be one of the forces that change man externally as well as internally. For when the change is over, man will become a partner with the Earth instead of a user of it. There will be those who are killed, seemingly, when the great change happens. When the Spirit is awakened in the Earth, they can be reborn in the same body and come into the light again.

Connie: That's beautiful.

MOITA: It is looked forward to. Man will remake himself, discover his true nature, and shake off the things that are false...

Connie: Many times I don't feel I belong on this Earth.

MOITA: There are many people that have been born in this age who feel they do not belong. That is because they are here to help bring in the next one. This one does not feel like home because of a vision they were given at birth and before of what the Earth *can* be like – its potential that it does not live up to. If you were happy with the way the Earth was . . . the Earth wouldn't change.

Tales of Power #3

ABUSE OF TRUST AND FRIENDSHIP

Elisabeth Kübler-Ross, the Swiss-born psychiatrist known worldwide for her work with the dying, is in the middle of a controversy involving alleged sexual misconduct and cruelty among leaders and members of her Escondido area retreat fueled by...allegations that during seances there were sexual encounters between individuals and afterlife spirit entities...[90]
– *The San Diego Union* (September 2, 1979)

If not rejected outright, the scandalous news would have shocked the multitude of supporters Elisabeth Kübler-Ross earned through many years of caring, courageous, groundbreaking work on behalf of psychiatric and terminally ill patients and their families. When Kelly and I first heard a report about this – oddly, during our initial stay at Sunrise Farm in the summer of 1979, from a woman visitor who had studied psychodrama at Elisabeth's retreat centre – I was tempted, as well, to disbelieve. How could I *not*, having been so impressed by Elisabeth's warmth, openness and spiritual depth during a treasured meeting in her Chicago home two years earlier?

The day after that memorable visit, Loria told me that "an extended, close relationship will develop between you and Elisabeth this time around, building upon your past associations."[91] At the time, I could not guess that much of my future interaction with Elisabeth would revolve around the *truth* of bizarre reports like the above . . . and the as yet unknown parallels that lay in some of those "past associations".

Not that Elisabeth herself was a party guilty of anything like "sexual misconduct and cruelty", in this life or others. But in 1976 she had been opened to powerful experiences of apparently materializing entities by a self-proclaimed minister, psychodramatist and channeler named Jay Barham. At a time of emotional vulnerability in her hectic life, Elisabeth quickly became dependent on these contacts with and manifestations via Barham – seeing only the best in him, and completely missing the darkness.

So it was that in 1977 Elisabeth founded Shanti Nilaya near Escondido, California, as a holistic health retreat for patients, families and professionals dealing with terminal illness, in partnership with Barham and his psychotherapist wife Marti. The charges against Barham mostly concerned illicit goings-on during his "darkroom" psychodrama seances. He claimed no knowledge of or responsibility for any untoward happenings during these sessions, saying he merely served as a channel for materializing spiritual beings who then interacted for the good of participants as the entities saw fit (despite their being found, once lights were turned on, to look strangely like Barham himself, even a naked Barham!).

The report Kelly and I heard first, though, was simply that spirits were not actually materializing as Barham was claiming and making it appear. Not knowing what to think about this, we sought Moita's perspective at our earliest opportunity. While Elisabeth was sure that her association with the Barhams was simply bringing more tests of her strength in the face of opposition from others, Moita's words suggested quite a different challenge:

It is true that after a contact with an entity, the communication can deteriorate if the person involved in it becomes unclear with her own purposes, or ungrounded in the world; and there are those who can take advantage of someone who is not as grounded as they should be. Deception does happen, not only from a physical point of view but also from a spiritual point of view, when one forgets to question...

It is not that common for an entity to materialize. It takes a great deal of energy, a great deal of purpose, in order to do so. It is feasible that it happened more than once. It is not likely that it happened a great many times; and, in the wake of non-materialization, others whose purposes were not clear to them could make it appear that something was happening that was wished for...

If it is found that a deception is occurring, the reaction that she has to its discovery will make a great impact upon her future. If she chooses to believe that it means nothing was real, she will go into despair, for she has given her life over to the search and the contact with us. If she sees that there is still truth, that we are still there,...then she will be stronger. She will be wary. She will have more discretion.[92N]

After writing to Elisabeth mentioning the rumours we'd heard and the Moita session we'd held, she wrote back to us enclosing the (to us, evidently well-researched) San Diego newspaper article quoted at the top – while dismissing all charges and maintaining her total public and private support for Barham. She did, however, agree to my sending our Moita transcript. This I mailed along with a lengthy letter outlining our concerns – both about the likely truth of the allegations and the way that Barham was trying to avoid any accountability for what was being done by him or through him.

My letter nevertheless expressed ongoing faith in Elisabeth's own work and integrity. The issue was the need for discrimination about someone very close to her who was threatening to destroy all that she was trying to achieve. Elisabeth's responses to us over the next few months continued to be friendly and supportive, but did not express any change of view regarding Jay Barham.

ço   ço   ço

The next year, on returning from giving a workshop in the Okanagan Valley, we receive a letter on April 21, 1980 in which Elisabeth expressed "a strong urge or need to connect with you in person for some reason". She continued hopefully: "Maybe some time during the summer I will be able to do that and we can share...our mutual experiences." Interestingly, we also hear that Joan, a friend from our Okanagan workshop, dreamed on April 19th that Elisabeth was coming to visit.

Then on May 2nd, Judi, Elisabeth's secretary, writes to tell us that Elisabeth will be giving a lecture in late August in south-central B.C. – not too far from the Okanagan, though still very far from us – and that "Elisabeth is very, very interested in connecting with you (as am I!)." Judi's thought, of course, is that we might arrange a meeting down south where Elisabeth will be. But it is the very day Judi is writing (10 days before we receive her letter) that we finally get approval to rent the beautiful log cabin we've found in the Kindle Valley – which we soon realize would be an earthy, peaceful place for us to host a visit from Elisabeth.

As it turns out, on the May 12th that Judi's enthusiastic letter arrives, Joan phones us with more information about Elisabeth's itinerary . . . and the reminder that Roger, another member of our Okanagan workshop, recently offered his small plane to fly some of them – and Elisabeth? – up to pay us a visit sometime.

But that same morning, I have already dreamed about Elisabeth's unexpectedly early visit.

"Elisabeth's Early Visit" dream
David / May 12, 1980

I am typing a Moita transcript. The next thing I know, Elisabeth is here sitting on the floor, leaning against the wall, giving a talk to a gathering of people that includes Kelly and her children. At one point she stands to perform a short piece on a small organ that illustrates raising vibrational levels. She plays the keys and pedals surprisingly well.

Then Elisabeth's short, grey hair grows much longer, and she becomes a woman in her twenties wearing a bright yellow skirt. As some of the group join in conversation, Elisabeth enjoys their spontaneous, informal energy.

All through this, though, I'm wondering how she got here so early, as I know I was to pick her up at the airport. Feeling I must have been asleep when she came, I ask the time and discover she shouldn't have even arrived yet. Then, while going to place an important phone call, Elisabeth jokes how typical it is that the one who's supposed to arrange her stay doesn't know what's going on!

৯ ৯ ৯

We can't wait to inquire of Moita about all these happenings the next evening. While promising nothing, Moita answers with a depth that does nothing to discourage our imaginings.

Moita/Amar session #143 (Kelly and David / May 13, 1980)

David: Something certainly seems in the works with the developments about Elisabeth and connections to our friends in the Okanagan. I don't know what to ask about all that. *(laughs)* We don't want to spoil any surprises, but is there anything helpful for us to know now as whatever this turns out to be approaches?

MOITA: There are no chance meetings in this life. Each one has a potential of fulfilling a great purpose – not just for your own development, but for the development of world-consciousness. It does not mean that each meeting will fulfill its greatest potential. But the more open each individual is to his own higher self and the promptings therefrom, the more benefit on a physical as well as a spiritual plane will be derived from such meetings.

This is a time in man's history of great purpose. This is a moment of destiny for the Earth and its development, and for man and his spirit, for his ability to express his totalness on and with the Earth. You are all going through many tests of your strength and your pureness of purpose. Much depends upon your own awareness, and on letting go of expectations. Each one of these experiences has been carefully choreographed to teach and show you a part of yourself and bring you closer to wholeness. Accepting life with an open hand is your key...

David: We feel it might be important to try to have Elisabeth come up here – not only to see where we are, where we're working, and to meet the people here, but just the energy of this place and this kind of country, away from speaking engagements and like that. Does that sound right to you too?

MOITA: There is a healing energy here that would help her very much. *(pause)* And it would be better for your connections if a meeting took place where you were going to be staying for a while. And the energy would associate itself with the place *and* with you, and the bridge would be easier to build.

David: Yes, I certainly feel all those things too. I'm glad I asked. *(laughs)* It's nice to hear them back from you. *(laughs; pause)*

(Kelly will say later, "There certainly was a lot of energy when she talked about Elisabeth. It got so pointed and focused, it just about blew my head off." As well, at times in the session both Kelly and I have been seeing faces from other lives superimposed on each other. The apparent distance between us has also been changing, reflecting movement out-of-body.)

MOITA: There are other connections that are surfacing at this time.

David: Such as with Kelly's "medicine woman" life?[93N]

(Since returning home from the Okanagan, a waking realization came to Kelly that Roger, who has the small plane, was the chief of the Indian tribe in that life, and that I married the chief's daughter. Roger currently has close contacts with a medicine man in Alberta. And Elisabeth has always felt very close to indigenous peoples, as I could see from all the Indian dolls, paintings, carvings, etc., in her living room the day I first met her.)

David: Maybe that life is not what you had in mind – or only *one*. But I almost asked earlier, does that life include many of these people that we have been meeting in the Okanagan and that may be coming to visit at the end of August? Or did you mean others?

MOITA: Other lives?

David: Other connections.

MOITA: In part, I mean *both*. But the medicine woman life is very important for this life. *(pause)* Remember that wisdom can be learned, but it cannot be shared except with those who have also learned it.

(During the above, Kelly sees images from her "Vision of Glowing Feather" dream in Tales of Power #1, with north representing wisdom and the eagle feather surrounded by white light representing the Great Spirit or Christ-consciousness. She realizes that by showing the feather moving away whenever it was approached, despite her wish to give it to someone else, the dream was demonstrating what Moita has just put into words.)

(After the session, our conversation includes this exchange about possible visitors:)

Kelly: "No meetings in this life are by chance."

David: Sure sounds like it's going to happen!

Kelly: Depending on everybody's openness, right? – how well it happens.

David: How completely its potential purpose is fulfilled.

ço   ço   ço

Two days after this session, I write to Elisabeth and Judi, inviting them both "to visit us and Moita and our friends in the Kindle Valley over the Labour Day weekend". My letter describes the web of events suggesting that things are being manoeuvred to make such a meeting possible. It includes the above transcript where, I say, "Moita reaffirms the importance we feel in inviting you up here, to visit at our new home in the Kindle Valley, despite the additional travel it involves."

At the end of the letter, I say that I am sending them an enlarged "photograph, taken last fall in the early morning near our present farmhouse... It is the photograph that I have begun to imagine on the cover of our book. It speaks of the magical beauty that is now unfolding for us all in this new dawning of the spirit on earth. May it express for you the energy of 'starflower' until we can bring all of our rays together in one place. In the love that creates joyous meetings, [signed]." (Thirty years later, this photograph will indeed appear on the cover of *Mind Leap*.)

While Elisabeth travels, Judi writes back with many thanks, saying that "arrangements for a connection are being given every consideration possible". By mid-June, Judi passes on that "Elisabeth very much wants to come to your new home after her [August 28] lecture . . . and has asked me to accompany her!" But then the obstacle: "We are having a big, big problem with transportation, however. We cannot leave [south-central B.C.] until the morning of Friday, August 29, and must be back in San Diego by Sunday evening, August 31." Given the terrible connections, she asks about chartering a small plane – which, of course, leads us to think of Roger's offer. Judi adds, "I imagine Moita has a smile of amusement at all these endeavors!"

On July 2nd, we receive a letter from Roger, expressing his own "strong need" to visit us and offering to fly Elisabeth, Judi and other friends up to the Kindle Valley in his plane for the Labour Day weekend. I immediately phone Judi at Shanti Nilaya, hoping to confirm their acceptance of this plan so we can begin making the arrangements. But I am then bewildered and most disappointed to hear Judi say that in the meantime, "Elisabeth has received strong guidance that it is very important for us to meet", instead, at one of her speaking engagements in Alberta or southern B.C.!

Ironically, Elisabeth's need to cut back on her now worldwide travel for health reasons is later cited as a concern, but clearly that is not all that is going on. We wonder in what form this contradictory "strong guidance" came and why she is needed back at Shanti Nilaya in the middle of the Labour Day weekend, the third anniversary of Elisabeth's openings as orchestrated by Barham.

For us, not only would we be financially unable to travel south again so soon, but we know that meeting in a hotel room between public events would be far inferior to having quiet time together here, close to the Earth, with friends who have been and will be involved in our work. From our end, this plan still seems possible, but we can't argue with what seems to be Elisabeth's guidance as well as the tight time constraints of her hectic life.

ço   ço   ço

Back in 1977, when Ruth and I first met Elisabeth in her Chicago home, we held a brief session with Loria. Loria warned then of heavy storm clouds gathering around Elisabeth, but said even in the darkest period rays of sunlight would continue to shine. She urged Elisabeth to take time from her work for relaxation and self-care – to give herself some of the love she so abundantly gives others. Now, two days after hearing the news from Judi, we ask Moita's perspective on Elisabeth's decision not to come north. Her answer seems to follow directly from Loria's message years before.

Moita session #148 (Kelly and David / July 4, 1980)

David: I had a strange conversation with Judi in which I learned that Elisabeth told her she'd received strong guidance that it was very important we meet at one of her speaking engagements, instead of her coming north.

MOITA: You would like enlightenment?

David: So we would like to ask why Elisabeth received such guidance, when so many things are pointing to her coming here.

MOITA: The problem is that Elisabeth has not had the time alone to herself which she requires in order to develop a clear enough channel to her own guidance. She keeps herself very busy. She is always involved with other people's energy, and that energy mingles with her own. Unless she makes time for herself to clear her mind of *all* of those around her, she will continue to receive contradictory guidance, even from herself. It is her choice; it is her need. She will have to make the decision.

But if she meets you in a place where she has just given so much of herself away, she will not have the clearness or the calmness to get the most benefit from the meeting. We see she has expectations, and there is a fear that her expectations will not be met. In a possibly hostile environment – at least, hostile to calmness and spirit – expectations that are not met can be explained away to inner satisfaction, so that they do not cause too many tumultuous disruptions in her thoughts.

It is very difficult to let go of expectations when you are coming from so far away – in more ways than one – to meet with someone you have not seen in many years *(meaning me)* and with someone else whom you have not seen in many lifetimes *(meaning Kelly)*. There are many things afoot, more than will ever be illuminated in this life. There are many intricate relationships involved, and personality clashes, conflicts and mergings. You have your own expectations of what such a meeting will bring. It will be better for all if these desires are let go of – if it [is seen as] a special meeting but not one that is of major import to your own development.

You are all travelling along different lines, and there are many possible meetings for *all* of you in this life. You will have to decide *which* meeting place will be the one that will happen in *this* reality; and if meetings do not, there will be others in other lives. Nothing will be lost, but much could be gained with the right frame of mind, the right acceptance.

We would like to see you meet, because there are good possibilities for growth on all parts – which brings us to your next question...

David: Why would her unclearness, or the influence of others on her, lead her to feel it was very important we meet at one of her speaking engagements? Was that related to what you said – it would be easier to explain away expectations that were not met?

MOITA: Yes.

David: Because there wasn't time or . . . ?

MOITA: Because of the place.

David: Mm-hmm. To blame it on circumstances.

MOITA: If she truly wishes to meet you, and Kelly, and me, she *needs* to come to your place where your energy is present, your life is there to be seen, because the things that surround you are part of you. And it is *her* desire to meet, more than it is your desire to renew contact.

(Now the words that were excerpted in Chapter 8 can appear in their full context:)

MOITA: You are in this place for a good reason. There is a good energy here, a whole energy, an energy that is close to the Earth and the Spirit together. This energy has already started to manifest itself in your life, and you have only been here a short while. *(pause; then softly:)* This used to be a sacred ground, and there is the chance of many visions.

David: This particular piece of land, you mean?

MOITA: Yes.

David: How was it used?

MOITA: It was a place of meditation, a place of visions, of quests.

David: Where people would go alone, away from the group?

MOITA: Yes. And with Elisabeth's connection with the Indians, this could be a key place for *her*.

৯৬   ৯৬   ৯৬

———————

Chapter 9

THE HUMAN FAMILY DIVIDED

Just as the Earth is erupting in physical disaster, so is man erupting in anger and fear.
— *Amar (November 26, 1979)*

This civilization will be toppled by its own fears, but also because some of its members seek something beyond its structures.
— *Moita (December 28, 1980)*

You are here to learn to follow your inner guidance, and not to worry if your neighbour agrees with what you have received.
— *Moita (December 17, 1979)*

As the 1980s begin, many people of Judeo-Christian heritage and many following other ancient or new spiritual paths believe the Earth and humanity are entering a period of great troubles. Despite general agreement on basics – potentially massive Earth changes, a possible world war focused on the Middle East, major disruptions of the economic system and modern lifestyles, accompanied by a worldwide spiritual awakening perhaps linked to a "Second Coming" of Christ or other avatar – there is also great disagreement as regarding the *inner meaning* of such events. Underlying the disagreement are different experiences and understandings of the Christ consciousness (however it be named in different traditions) and how that energy plays into human evolution.

There is a cluster of key questions. In the Christian tradition, if the Christ would come again in personal form, would that actual living Presence be recognized better than the last time? Would it be realized that, as before, the Christ consciousness manifests on Earth not just for a "chosen people" but for all? Would we instead try to manufacture a Messiah in our own limited image, betraying the One who comes in ways we do not expect? Would many continue to be taken in by "false prophets", or "black magicians" of any type, who control and turn us against each other, preaching values they do not practise because their real motive is power, greed and their own self-importance?

Moita has described the Christ presence as "the completeness of all of man expressing itself in a single form. It is all of your wisdom and all of your love and all of your acceptance and understanding brought together in one place at one time." The precise opposite attitude is "God is on my side against you, Satan". And as long as the latter prevails, the threat of war remains real. As Moita has also said, "Unless your leaders become more loving and in touch with the spirit within, there is a very good possibility that man will express his fear in this form."

Exploring these subjects now in more depth will make clear the nature and gravity of choices before us. Coming events will bring to the surface much that is hidden and reveal what approach to these "end-times" is consistent with our learnings as souls to this point. The issue is going to be forced, and we each will choose a destiny we believe right for us. Certainly discernment is necessary to make wise choices, and this chapter aims to further our discernment.

Separation of Worlds

Some sources, including Moita, have predicted a substantial lowering of the population of our planet in coming years. This may be through another major war, geological upheavals, manmade disasters, famine and/or plague, the prophesied "Rapture of true [fundamentalist] believers", or simply cutting the rate at which generations are replaced. Is there an inner, spiritual necessity for this possibility? Might it involve the "void of understanding, comprehension, acceptance" of which Moita spoke in Chapter 7, resulting in a "splitting of the worlds"?[94] What will actually occur on a soul level as a death and rebirth of the Earth with its billions of human inhabitants unfolds?

In Chapter 5, Moita explained the reasons behind a "separation of worlds":

Some will not be able to accept newness and change because they have been unable to do so in their own development for a long time. They will be given an opportunity to develop in another place, on another earth, and start the cycle again... This is their "out" they are using,...their escape hatch. They are fearful and afraid and not ready to enter a New Age. It has a great deal to do with their expectations from the *first* coming...

You are all One in one place. But for now things go in different directions..., each to find his way back to home and self. They are making it easier for those who will be left behind, for they are taking their influence away. They are freeing the Earth, in a sense, for they have kept it locked in this particular reality because of their belief and the strength of it and the strength of their fear. By giving themselves this doorway, and leaving *this* Earth behind, going on to that other one that they are expecting, those of you who have chosen to be here through this time and afterward to help remake man's awareness and to heal the Earth will be freer to do so.[95]

To approach this probability in the right spirit, we should recall Moita's saying that both worlds will have "their own Sun, each Sun being as bright", and "many beautiful things can come of that sundering."[96] Thus no one will be cast into outer darkness, unless we believe we *should* be and choose that illusion ourselves. Love surrounds us all, however long we take to recognize it.

What then will be the difference between the two worlds? I believe an answer lies in the quality of relationship between the individual person and the Christ consciousness. With this in mind, we can understand the classic channeling through David Spangler:

I have spoken to you of two worlds. I am the body of one; I am the shepherd of the other. The one is what I am and I am revealed in it. The other knows me only as its shepherd, separate and apart. I do not live within it. I only stand and envelop it... [It] is the separation between those who cleave unto God, their Beloved, in new revelation and new maturity and those who remain in the household of their Father...[97]

Just as we come from the same source, so are we heading toward the same goal – in our own timing, in our own way. But until all can realize and accept this more deeply than words, there will be conflict, on this Earth or another. A final channeling from David Spangler gives much to ponder:

How the worlds will separate is not of your concern. From my standpoint they are already separate and the old does not exist. You cannot be in conflict with the old, for you cannot be in conflict with what does not exist. If you are in conflict with anything through resistance, hatred or fear of it, you are automatically of the old to that degree. This is why I have stated that all who would be of me must build the new consistently and manifest the energies I represent. This is not being blind to the world. It is being open to the real world.[98]

I want to emphasize this openness to those with differing beliefs who wish to join in a mutual search for deeper understanding of what we hold in common and what we do not. Without this understanding of others, my *own* world falls apart, for "others" are in my world as much as "I" am – all part of the universe I am opening myself to experience, or allowing myself to dream, at this moment. As I see it, our common goal is ultimately to become lucid: aware that we are co-creating this "dream" – and that therefore all of its characters and situations are potentialities within me as well as you, seeking to come together finally in wholeness.

As we plunge now into some of those actual situations with which life confronts us – starting very close to home and moving outward – we need to remember that in order for the Christ consciousness to return to a world that can appear dark and empty, we ourselves must become lucid to our dream of it. Only wholeness can perceive wholeness. Surely it is one and the same Light.

      ❧   ❧   ❧

When the buds of the New Age begin to open within us, even if we make no attempt to share our changes publicly, the people around us will notice a difference – and try to account for it, sometimes in surprising ways! And when we do get involved publicly, we should be prepared for even stronger reactions, as our newness is torn from its personal context into that of the non-comprehending group mind. Below, one of our Okanagan friends is experiencing both these levels of response.

Moita session #118 (Kelly, David, Joyce, 3 others / November 10, 1979)
Joyce: Moita, right now all the official channels where I live are refusing New Age activities –

like even astrology classes – access to services and facilities they used to give. It seems they're trying to push underground all of us "weirdos", as we're called. Are these problems going to be overcome?

MOITA: [Your area] is in a way a battlefront. It is an area where the energy of the Earth is closer to the surface. Many people feel this and react to it. Some react in fear, and as the energy changes this will also be intensified. Those who are afraid will become more angry and express their fear in outward forms. They cannot see that they are afraid of revealing themselves *to* themselves and others. So they find labels, external forces, to explain away their fears so they do not have to take responsibility for their own reactions on themselves. This does not entirely answer your question.

Joyce: No.

MOITA: Where there is need, ways are always found. And if it is right, things will come. If you are seeing these battles for *yourself*, it is because you have tuned into them. You have made this a part of your universe. And some of the reactions of others at the moment to you are caused by your rapid opening. And seeing things with your new eye, you feel you are more discerning – and then others sense this discernment aimed in their direction, and so react.

Joyce: *(laughing)* Rather violently at times. *(laughter)* So my neighbour's part of the reaction would be that we are now Jehovah's Witnesses and that I have changed my job.

MOITA: They know *something* has changed. *(laughter)*

෨   ෨   ෨

Such labelling and hostility are no strangers in our own experience, especially as we enter the rural neighbourhood of the Kindle Valley. Our "Psychic Frontiers" workshop in fall 1979 swiftly is judged, with strong emotion, to be the "work of Satan" by one local fundamentalist Christian. In addition, while a guest at one of our workshop sessions in Chapter 3, Ike accuses us of sorcery and trying to hypnotize the participants into our, or Moita's, power. Though Ike's opinions change through actually reading Moita's words, certain local fundamentalist church members – needing no such evidence themselves – remain adamantly, even hysterically, opposed to our activities.

After writing of the "very creditable and professional manner" in which we conducted our fall workshop, the coordinator of the local community college invites us in March 1980 to offer another workshop – this one on dream psychology – for the coming fall. Encouraged, we plan to explore in practice how helpful are the views of Freud, Jung, Fritz Perls (founder of gestalt therapy) and others, as participants share and work on their own dreams – they to be the ultimate judge. After submitting our proposal, we hear nothing until just moving into our Kindle Valley home in late June. Something secretive has happened in the meantime, though, for we then receive a letter concluding our proposal cannot be supported by the college "because it is focused on and aimed at imparting a very specific philosophical-'religious' set of views."

Knowing that our proposal does nothing of the kind, we ask for an explanation. The reply is that our proposal has been "read...in terms of the considerable feedback...received concerning your previous workshops". This decision is among the last acts of the outgoing administrator, whose invitation for us to speak and teach in the valley we appreciated so much the previous year.

Aware that the college never asked the *participants* for a formal evaluation of our first course, and having difficulty imagining many or any of them so misunderstanding our emphasis on individual experience and choice, we are not surprised to learn from the next administrator that fundamentalist church members were a major source of the "feedback"! We *are* surprised, however, at their continuing vehemence – to the point, reportedly, of one pounding on the administrator's desk in a "purple rage". More to avoid further controversy than anything else, the previous decision about this or any workshop of ours is sustained, at least for the current year.

We are at first upset but, despite the loss of income, then accepting – and also rather amused at the ridiculousness of it all. By this time, however, a charge has begun making the rounds that seriously concerns us for its distortion of experiences we hold very close to our hearts. This is the accusation – reported to us over and over from innumerable sources – that "Moita broke up" two of our closest friends' relationship.

Chapter 6 revealed Moita's efforts to help a number of our friends through the painful, confusing period in their personal growth that seems roughly to have coincided with our first year in the valley. That the causes of those separations that did occur existed long before our arrival, and that Moita's message of self-knowledge and openness left its recipients stronger and freer to decide for themselves the right course of action, would be testified to by each of the persons who requested those sessions.

But gossip, of course, does not consult the people involved – with the result that one of the first things many local people hear about our work with Moita is that "Moita broke up . . ." Few hear of the caring, understanding and acceptance Moita (and we ourselves) gave, and helped people to find within themselves, while facing these upheavals in their lives – or, for example, of her talk on love's many colours and the beauty in *not* burning bridges between these varieties of love or between the partners in changing relationships.

The fear of change in these most intimate realms of life and self can obviously be very strong and can control one's total reaction to something new. The teenage girls attending their first session below are basically open to and trusting in their own experiencing – which enables Moita to answer their questions from such a deep level. But they also bring with them an awareness of others' fears – both near and far.

Moita session #153 (Kelly, David, Jim, Lorna, Cindy / August 16, 1980)

Lorna: Why are you here? *(pause)*

MOITA: There are many ways to answer that question. I am here at this moment because others have expressed a desire to speak with me. I am here in my existence because this is the path I have chosen – my work, my purpose: to bring some understanding to your world of the unseen and the unheard part of mankind.

Lorna: You're well-known around this area. I've heard about you for a long time. I have understood from some people that what you're doing here is positive and for good reason, but then some people feel a negative energy and do not feel what you're doing is for the benefit of people around here. You seem to have disrupted quite a few people here in a way which they can't understand, and this life has been disruptive very much for them. Why?

MOITA: Each person that comes to this experience is drawn to it for different reasons. For one thing, disruptions in this life will become more and more frequent, for this is a time of change. The Earth will not be the same. And there will be many who will not be able to embrace change because they are afraid, and they fail to understand because they look no farther than themselves and their own life.

I am not alone in coming here. There are many like me that are trying to communicate with your world, to bring warning of change to come, to let man know he must become whole *now* or he will fail to avert catastrophe, not only for his Earth but for his fellows and for himself. It is true that nothing is ever lost. Even if the world were destroyed, man would still exist as spirit. But it would be a long time before another Earth could be created so that he could continue to learn [the] lessons...needed to become a whole soul instead of part.

Lorna: What is "whole"?

MOITA: It is a process of growth, of accepting all parts of yourself first in one life, and from there being able to accept other parts of your own soul in other lives. As you accept more, you *become* more. You regain experience that you have forgotten. It is difficult to explain in words. Your words lack many shades of meaning, and they lack depth to make the meaning.

People bring their fears. If they are unhappy in their lives and unwilling to look past their life, they will see no good in what I bring...

Lorna: Well, let me explain. Everybody, in themselves, knows that this world isn't "it". But people are afraid of something more because there are a lot of cults, etc., that take people for a ride. So that makes people more closed. They just don't believe anything anymore. So what happens to those people?

MOITA: They must learn the art of discrimination! Just because there are some who are unreal, or who present themselves as something they are not, does not mean that all are untrue. It is up to each individual to discover for themselves what experiences are good for them.[99]

Integrity can be seen in the channelings, in what has been offered. If an entity is attempting to manipulate, there are many ways to determine this – by looking at what is being said, in what way. I have never attempted to control another, to lead people in a certain direction unless it is one of love, one of wholeness and acceptance of themselves.

I do not fear they do not accept *me*. I am not here to be accepted. My reality is real. I am in it; this I know. But I am here to help them to see themselves, and not all will take that kindly, for many people are here to stay away from themselves, to hide from themselves. They are afraid of what they will find. This is not *my* responsibility, but I do take the ones that I *have* seriously. *(pause)*

Lorna: Well, I don't understand a whole lot of things, but I'll think about them more.

MOITA: I am here more to be experienced. That is my . . . gift.

(Moita turns to Cindy, who was feeling nervous at the start.)

Cindy: *(whisper)* Hello. *(clears her throat)*

MOITA: *(softly)* Hello. Are you feeling better?

Cindy: Yeah. I mean, I'm still maybe a little bit afraid – maybe not so much of you, but of a new experience. Do I have reason to be afraid?

MOITA: There is nothing here to fear.

Cindy: *(laughs)* That makes me feel better...

(Later in the session:)

Lorna: Why have you come at this time to warn us of change? Like, why not before? Change has always been occurring. Is it going to be so drastic that we just don't have a clue?

MOITA: This is not the first time a spirit has manifested itself on a physical plane before change. There have been many visions. There have been many experiences and many manifestations and many warnings. It is just that time is so short, there must be more. You would not sit back and watch your world destroyed, would you . . .

Lorna: No.

MOITA: . . . if you knew what would happen and when and how, and could see a way to avoid it?

Lorna: It's already being destroyed.

MOITA: And what are you doing?... Have you thought of anything you can do to help avoid the destruction of your world...?

Lorna: Not take part in the destruction in any way. I'm not going to sign up, for instance. *(laughs)* But, well, just to try to create a positive energy instead of a negative one. I guess that's the main thing.

(Lorna goes on to describe the work that she wants to do with people.)

MOITA: But first you start with you.

Lorna: Mm-hmm.

MOITA: This is what we are here for – to help give people direction, so that they can find new ways to make positive input into the world and stop their useless and disruptive activities. It is something that has been building for many, many years.

Lorna: Why do they bother with such useless activities?

MOITA: They are afraid.

Lorna: Of what?

MOITA: They are afraid of themselves. They are afraid of *this*. They do not want to find out that they are not just themselves but a part of something more. And they do not want to know themselves. They fear their ugliness, and they fear their beauty more.

Lorna: What do you mean "destruction"? Do you mean pollution and stuff like that, or that the world one of these days is just going to blow up or something?

MOITA: The future is still fluid. As yet, there is time to change what can be or what may be. The Earth has been unrecognized as a soul in its own right, as a being you are sharing. It will be your greatest disruptive influence. Pressures within the Earth are building, because man has chosen to ignore and to use.

Man's thoughts affect the world around him. They affect his life and his planet. If he would think negative thoughts, he will create negative action and reaction within himself and his world. Those who will not live for joy will work to destroy the things they feel they cannot have. It hurts them to see another's peace when they have none themselves. It is foolish, but it is true. It is real because man has made it so. He has created this world, and he is trying to uncreate it because he cannot cope with its beauty as a reflection of himself.

Nuclear holocaust is one possibility, one that hopefully will never come to pass. But should it happen, there will be those who are aware enough, who will be able to utilize the energy released and reshape the Earth and make it different. And there will be those who will leave the Earth and never return, for they have . . . stopped up all of their possibilities for this place. They will start anew in another place. The Earth has great power, and it *will* use it because it has no choice. It is either disrupt or die.

Lorna: These people will start at the bottom – the ones who do not come back?

MOITA: I will say that they will no longer be an important influence in *this* world. They will no longer be here to hold this one back... They will leave, or be shut out. When you have two realities that are similar, they can co-exist. But when one changes beyond comprehension of the other, they will not see each other anymore... They will not be destroyed..., start not *all* over, but maybe from where they are now.

Lorna: Has this already happened before? Is that where *we* are? *(laughter)*

MOITA: That is a loaded question! *(laughter)* Eternity is a long time.

Lorna: Mm-hmm. So then this isn't the first one, so we're in the middle of something. Perhaps we here are ones who were shut out of somewhere else.

MOITA: Let us say that I am from an era in the past . . .

Lorna: Uh-huh. And so are we.

MOITA: There are always those who go on and those who stay behind. A soul only develops when it is ready to, and it only listens when it opens its ears. *(pause)*

Lorna: It's weird feeling like a reject! *(laughter)*

Cindy: For some reason – I don't know what it is; I've been listening and trying to figure it out – I've felt really close to you, like I want to be near you all the time. I don't understand why.

MOITA: It is simple. You were created in love, and when love makes itself felt you have the desire to be near it. Love is the energy that feeds you. It feeds your soul. It is nourishment and sustenance. When one rejects it, one is trying not to grow. You seek growth; therefore you seek light, so that you may grow better.

During our last days before moving to the Kindle Valley in late June 1980, I spent a number of hours constructing, burning in, colouring and varnishing a large wooden "Starflower" sign bearing a rainbow-hued version of the design (like a 12-pointed sunflower centre) from our journal's front cover. This I then erect on a rustic sort of easel at the driveway entrance to our new log cabin home, to give people a sense for who we are and to mark the turnoff for visitors.

Over the next few months, though, this sign is repeatedly ambushed – including two shotgun blasts and an attempted burning. The mischief leads us to ponder Moita's words to Joyce: "If you are seeing these battles for *yourself*, it is because you have tuned into them. You have made this a part of your universe."

Do we see the attacks in the context of rumours of "devil worship" circulating around the valley about us? Or do we perceive it as petty vandalism as our friends want to assure us – most likely hunters (widely reputed to shoot at just about *anything*) seeing a chance for target practice? (If so, they missed the bull's eye from only a few feet away!)

Even so, it's a little hard to take, given the energy we put into our symbols and our high hopes in coming to the valley. Kelly responds by posting a note in the valley lodge inviting all those interested in personally learning what we're doing to drop over on Sunday evenings. We leave our sign where it is, and I'm strangely pleased that logging truck drivers start referring to "Starflower" when radioing their location to oncoming rigs.

A few days after the shooting episode, I ask Moita the following.

Moita session #157 (Kelly, David, Warren / September 24, 1980)

David: I want to ask how we can deal with the controversy we're embroiled in in the valley. I wonder about the idea of giving another public talk, trying to clarify what we're doing and what you are really saying, dealing with all the questions and objections people might bring. Do you think such a head-on approach would be useful, or should we just lie low and let things settle?

MOITA: Fear can be a difficult thing to handle. Telling them what I say will not make them feel less fearful. I have not hidden my motives. I have said I am here to bring change, and it is change that is feared. When someone is ready to listen with an open heart, only then will they have the ears to hear what is really being said. If someone comes to you wearing earplugs and sporting a wall, whatever you say will bounce off. You would do almost as much good sitting in the corner talking to yourself, for at least you would *listen*.

Time is a great changer. It brings fast and slow change, but it always brings change. Man cannot remain in one place. He must grow, he must expand – given time... Spend your energy where it is received. But always remain open if someone should ask you a question.

Being involved so closely in the process of communications being channeled from another level takes you into the kind of energy that must be broadcast from within in order to maintain clarity. We see that those who become channels and choose to recruit (in a sense) listeners eventually become useless for that purpose. They are not as centred; they are not magnets anymore. *(smiling)* You will fall into [your critics'] hand, for then they can say you are...seeking followers.

David: Mmm.

MOITA: I have *enough* friends.

ഔ   ഔ   ഔ

Meanwhile, the larger world of which our valley seems such a small, insignificant part is certainly "broadcasting" to us the kind of energy use *it* seems so bent upon these days. Over a year later, we reflect upon these cycles of world unrest.

Moita session #210 (Kelly and David / December 20, 1981)

David: The world situation seems to come in waves. For a while, there won't be much news, and then oftentimes all at once many things crop up together. I wonder how connected world tensions are – why there are certain times it seems "the pot boils over" everywhere.

MOITA: Discontent and unrest and violence breed each other. Just as in many places at the same time discoveries of the same nature are made, so also are discoveries of reactions to situations. It is the domino effect, the avalanche. It only takes one person to recognize that a situation is intolerable to them for it to *become* intolerable to many. It may not be the situation itself that is at fault. It is more often people's reactions *to* a situation..., how they choose to either battle, confront or absorb their lessons.

There *is* a great deal of unrest in the world, a great deal of confusion. Humanity tends to try and keep it under the surface, holding it down, stamping it out, pushing it under. So it only takes one hole for it all to boil back up into the conscious awareness, to be dealt with, to be understood. Unfortunately, it is not usually understood at all. It is pushed back down again, forced back into the subconscious, the unconscious, the collective unconscious, where it festers and broods until it boils to the surface again.

ഔ   ഔ   ഔ

September 1980 does seem to be a time when conflicts are erupting on many levels, as elaborated below. This is first brought home to me by my dream on the 13th.

"Explosion Leaves Flaming Chakras" dream
David / September 13, 1980

I watch an explosion on the horizon that at first makes me think of a volcano, next possibly an oil refinery exploding, and then maybe a grass fire on the prairie. Huge, billowing, dark grey clouds finally engulf my friends and me, sprawled flat on the ground, leaving us flecked with tarred cinders. Curiously, many of us are also left with small flames burning at our throat chakras.

Then on September 23rd, soon after the shooting of our *Rays* sign, I dream definitely of a volcano erupting. The same night, Kelly dreams of a huge column of smoke. In our session the following evening, I raise these dreams and suggest that the first may be precognitive.

Moita session #157 (Kelly, David, Warren / September 24, 1980)

David: In the last few days Iraq has invaded Iran, attacking its oil refineries, threatening to bring about a large-scale Middle East conflict. I feel that these dreams are partly referring to this war, but there may be other levels too. Can you say more, and whether it's likely the war will grow a lot bigger soon?

MOITA: It certainly has the potential to do so. The prairie fire: a quick conflagration that spreads over a wide area. Depending on conditions, it may spread far or burn itself out. It can also be symbolic of your own inner desires being bottled up, not having the attention paid to them that they desire or deserve, and then exploding outward, consuming your attention.

David: I was saying earlier that there's a part of me that wants to see all these dramatic things happen in the news – like even that the war will get bigger and more exciting, because that means *change*. I was wondering how much of that sort of misguided motivation lies behind wars and what's coming to the world.

MOITA: Let us say that...wars start over seemingly small and insignificant things in themselves, but they lead to larger, more significant things. They are out of control. No one knows how to stop the process, once set in motion – as difficult as corking a volcano.

These things could be stopped if there were more honesty between people and acceptance of other people's paths. Allowing freedom to your neighbour ensures freedom to yourself. But man is too afraid of losing what he sees as his, whether he places that on objects or intellectual acrobatics or lifestyles. It is the same, and his fear is the same. And when you fear losing what you...think is yours, anyone who has something that looks different seems a threat because they are on a different wavelength... You do not think they will understand...your point of view.

The whole thing is incomprehensible *(she laughs)*, on one level.

David: I can see at least that as the valley goes, so goes the world.

MOITA: *(laughs)* So do not look for too much excitement here, and the world will go well too.

David: *(laughs)* Yes, we hope gunfire will not proliferate around here.

MOITA: *(laughs)* Symbols everywhere.

ও   ও   ও

Black Magic

Though our moving to the valley in mid-1980 may dampen rather than encourage some of the initial interest there in our work – a typical pattern – coming months will bring a rise in regional contacts that bode well for the future. And there will be developments on a more personal level that also begin to flower in the new year. As will be told in Chapter 11, they relate to those "inner desires" Moita mentions above – for greater openness, communication, sharing, centredness and community – the seeds of which are being sown at the time of my "Flaming Chakras" dream.

As for the international situation, this particular flaring-up between Iran and Iraq *does* seem to want to simmer along for years, becoming just one more element in ongoing world tensions. A few months earlier, Moita used the same volcano symbol quite ingeniously in depicting this general state of the modern world: more and more conflicts and crises leading to . . . what? That session occurred three days after the first eruption of Mount St. Helens.

Moita session #138 (Kelly and David / March 31, 1980)

David: How do you see the phase we're going through now on the planet? There are many signs of approaching crisis: internationally, financially (there are many predictions of an economic collapse in a year or two), and Earth changes starting in a big way in coming years. Are we a little bit ahead of a precipice that's going to cause a lot of people to be shaken up soon?

MOITA: All of those things you mention are manifestations of the Earth and man redistributing itself, its energy, its presence. They are necessary, in that view, since man by himself will not distribute himself evenly or wisely in any of those areas. He has not learned the true meaning of economics, for he sees it as a system or a means to his own glorification, or the elevation of a few being supported by the many. That kind of system has never been self-sustaining. If it were done as it has been conceived of in other times, then the energy of the few would return to the many instead of being hoarded.

David: I'm not sure what you mean by "in other times"...

MOITA: The image of the pyramid with the eye at its head or apex is on one level symbolic of that system of which I speak, where the many support the few but the few are there as a focus for the many rather than [the many] being *used* by those few at the top. It was this kind of an ideal that began your neighbour to the south, an ideal that was short-lived in the reality that was created. There was not a balance, and there is a lack of communication. The flow has been stopped. And so, eventually the pyramid will turn into a volcano, and the power at the top will drain back down to the bottom and be distributed.

This world cannot change in the shape it's in. There are too many of those who are ready to fight for their positions, who are not ready to understand that this is a passing phase and the power they take now will turn on them later. We are trying to re-establish the natural law of the universe – and man does not think there is glory in it.

ళ   ళ   ళ

Speaking of "our neighbour to the South", in fall 1980 the United States enters a different phase from its post-Vietnam, post-Watergate moderation of the late 1970s: replacing Jimmy Carter with Ronald Reagan. At the time, the right-wing, fundamentalist Christian mobilization that helps make Reagan President, with a general as his Secretary of State, looks to us – in conjunction with the Soviet Union's imperial and repressive policies – like one of the gravest threats to peace in recent years. We hold this session the night after the presidential election.

Moita session #160 (Kelly and David / November 5, 1980)

David: It seems pretty obvious what Reagan's election represents: everyone thinking that one man can make all the bad things go away.

MOITA: The parallels with Atlantis are becoming more and more obvious.

David: With respect to the focusing on a leader, do you mean? What parallels do you see?

MOITA: That is one. The other is the emergence of so many so-called religious organizations and orders that are grasping for dominance, seeking slaves; and the trend towards more and more dependence on weapons and the ability to destroy preventing destruction. There are so many factions that are vying for power, and so little wisdom.

(Meanwhile Kelly is getting images of Atlantis in this regard, as she describes afterward: "I see an image of a large continent and a couple of smaller pieces, all divided up into little, fighting sections – with a leader here, a leader there; a temple, a discipline, here and there and so on. The only unity holding the whole thing together is power *– weapons and being able to tap into huge reservoirs of energy. I see Russia and the United States as really symbolic of Atlantis.")*

ళ   ళ   ళ

The early Reagan years will bring paranoia-fueled escalation of the nuclear arms race and global confrontation with the Soviet Union. The fascination with nuclear overkill beyond the point of absurdity, the welcoming of laser weapons and science fiction war games into physical reality, and the transparent projection of one's own evil onto the enemy so that every action serves to justify an oncoming Juggernaut of destruction: these show that not "realism" but man's fantasy life is the actual issue. Nuclear weapons only make obvious the archetypal levels that are increasingly being activated and projected onto the world scene in this battle of blind versus blind.

Trevor Ravenscroft's amazing book, *The Spear of Destiny*, concerns the archetypal weapon, a physical spear that symbolizes the human will utilized for good or ill. The book documents the black occultism in which Adolf Hitler became adept, enabling him to hold such sway over Germany's subconscious. It also tells of the spear that the Roman centurion Longinus used to end the agony of Christ's crucified body so that his bones needed not to be broken – fulfilling one more prophecy.

This ancient and potentially powerful relic, claimed by a succession of "world-historic" European leaders down through the centuries, was seized from Vienna's Hapsburg Museum by Hitler upon his invasion of Austria, and remained in his hands till U.S. forces reached into Germany and General Patton recognized it – thus falling into American hands before the U.S. dropped the first atomic bombs on a human population.

The information for the book was derived from the researches of Rudolf Steiner, arch-enemy to Hitler because of his powers of spiritual perception, and of Steiner's student Walter Stein. Stein deliberately made the acquaintance of Hitler during his period of occult training. Later, during World War II, this familiarity enabled him to advise Winston Churchill on the thinking of the Nazi inner circle. The power of the relic for good or evil – especially in the hands of an adept, according to Steiner – lies in its key role at that culminating moment when the Christ-energy fully entered the Earth-plane, completing its mission of incarnation.[100]

The "spear of destiny" is back in the Hapsburg Museum now. But in view of the prophecies about an Antichrist to come, we might wonder if it will remain there – and if the abuse of psychic powers that played a role in World War II will make a comeback.

Moita session #160 (Kelly and David / November 5, 1980)

David: What can you tell us about the nature of the power associated with the so-called Spear of Destiny?

MOITA: *(slowly)* When a stone such as that . . . connects with a force that is itself from a level far removed from the Earth, it absorbs a certain charge of energy. It is similar to what the alchemist does when he transmutes metals from one density to another. In a small way, each thing you touch retains the memory of you on it or within it. It is the same with the spear, but it retained the memory of Christ in his moment of transmutation. There *was* a great deal of energy involved, and those who have held it since have been attracted to the moment in history, on one level or another, that created it. And so, they have served to strengthen that moment.

(Meanwhile Kelly is seeing the scene at the cross, and an intense white light like lightning hitting the spear as it pierces Christ's side.)

MOITA: Anything can become a talisman, although certain substances can act to retain a charge of energy more readily than others. The Egyptians were very well versed in the technique. The curses they laid upon their tombs are famous, and the process is a similar one for they created an energy presence and placed it within stone with such force that even now some of that energy has survived and its potency is not much less than it was in its origins.

The spear can act much as I do in opening the doorways in a man's mind to other realities, other sources of power and energy. It is not the thing itself that has accomplished or destroyed, but [it is] the instrument that is used.

David: I wonder what possibility there may be of that spear being used again as we approach these end-times of our era. We've also heard predictions [most often by Christian fundamentalists] about a person arising – this is one version of the Antichrist, the literal meaning. Do you see a strong line of probability matching or relating to these interpretations that might lead to Armageddon?

MOITA: So many have come to believe in its possibility that it is becoming more and more probable. And things of power in times of turmoil are rarely overlooked. They act as magnets.

(A long silence follows. Moita's answer carries a very serious feeling. An intense energy is felt pouring into Kelly, and she hears Moita saying, "I don't want to answer this question alone." Kelly immediately wonders if Moita will ask Amar to come – something we wondered about before the session. I, however, get the feeling that Moita does not wish to say more now. I realize that our own values and choices will decide our future, as she says. Therefore I pass on to another question, while Kelly feels the energy gradually thin out again. I only learn after the session that Amar almost came – and am sorry I didn't wait. Amar will finally come to speak on this subject, however – in the concluding session of this chapter.)

ৡ৹   ৡ৹   ৡ৹

The Prologue introduced the issue of power – to use or *not* to use. The nub of the issue of power is the traditional rationalization for its use: to fight for a good cause, to oppose those who are using power for evil. As long as this model of reality prevails, Moita's message that power is not to be used makes little sense, for what she means is not truly seen. This is why we need now to explore the effects of unbalanced thoughts in some depth – and their connection to "black magic".

Of course, most of the sides in conflicts publicly claim to be the "good guys". But in a war of opposites, extremes soon become interchangeable. In both ordinary life and world history, the good for which one thinks or claims one fights readily turns into the evil that one opposes. This becomes all too clear in the following conversation about conspiracies. From this excerpt, one also realizes that "black magic" or "demonology" is the normal course of events in an alienated society, rendering bizarre rituals unnecessary. It also becomes obvious that those who scapegoat open-minded explorers of the spirit for alleged psychic machinations are but projecting their own unconscious will to power, along with their own fear of the consequences.

Moita session #113 (Kelly, David, Becky, Chris, Dawn, Greg, Rick / September 29, 1979)

David: We've been listening today to a tape distributed by an evangelical church concerning a group called the Illuminati that goes back centuries. According to the tape, it's an international conspiracy of psychic adepts, based within certain wealthy families, who are behind everything from rock 'n' roll to the expansion of consciousness movement. It is said to be manipulating many institutions – including liberal religious and political organizations – so as to produce crisis conditions that will enable it to take over the planet.

(The extremist viewpoint expressed on the tape is close to that of Christian fundamentalist

author Hal Lindsey, in regard to the ecumenical movement among liberal churches as a cover for the Antichrist.[101] *But it's fascinating that the Illuminati have been targeted by conspiracy theorists of both the left and right, and of both secular and spiritual backgrounds. Each theory substitutes a different list of evils for which the Illuminati are supposedly responsible.)*

David: Also, today [unidentified "New Age" spokesman] has been quoted as saying that 90% of the world's troubles are related to "black magic" in some sense. I'm sure *his* use of the term is quite different from this tape's allegation about "witchcraft" and so on.

How much do you see public events in the world being controlled, planned – or at least that attempt being made – by people consciously involved in what has been called "witchcraft" or "black magic"? There's all sorts of paranoia involved in imagining what a group like the Illuminati could be, and one's prejudices are obviously actively involved, but there may be some reality to it also.

MOITA: You are living in very paranoid times. *(pause)* I think we may begin this discussion on Illuminati with a talk on demons and their origin...

In a physical body, you do not see very much; you do not see your own thoughts. You are not aware, on a conscious level, of the effects of what you think upon others. But each thought that you think has its effect and its reality, and it can travel from you to another and back again, or go on from there to someplace else.

The thoughts that you have take on the form of the feel behind the thought. Those who are into what you might term "black magic", or unproductive energy, are utilizing the thoughts from their own conscious and other people's consciousness as actual weapons – things that can be thrown at others and that can be used and manipulated for their own purposes.

If you choose to look at it in the light of tradition, any thought that you have that is not coming from a centre of love is in effect a demon – unless you are changed and you go about changing the energy you have released... If there are enough people banded together with the one thought in mind, they can create collectively a single thought-form that expresses their purpose and desire. But no one needs to be affected by those kinds of thought-forms. They are only real if you are open to them.

There are problems in discussing this with terminology, for there is a religion of the Earth *(i.e. Wicca)* that has been called "witchcraft", and there is of course a god Pan who has been termed "Satan" . . . and *is not*. Much depends on what is feared, and it is your fear that is used against you, and your doubt. So long as you do fear and doubt, and do not open yourself up and connect yourself with the higher energy that is within you, do not let it flow forward into the world, there will be people who will be able to change and manipulate you from within. And although on one level you will be aware of it, on this one you may not.

You know that souls reincarnate in groups, as a rule. It is not at all uncommon to have the same kind of situation in one point in history as you do in another – the same kinds of schemes and plans – because they are, most often, the same people, [with] the same energy, that still have not seen what it is they are doing to themselves and continue to believe they are doing unto others.

Many people believe in this world that being able to cause another person to change their life for [their] purposes shows [them] to be [individuals] of great worth. And people who believe this do not think very much of themselves. They are very sad and lonely and have no respect for their own energy. Everyone in the world has helped to create the situation wherein this kind of thing can flourish. They are only externalizations of your own fears and doubts.

Dawn: Why would it be that these same souls keep coming back to the Earth and keep making the same situation that's really a frightful one? How come they don't seem to learn?

MOITA: Because you have not learned, either. You are all tied together. You could say, in some ways, they are the darker side of yourself, the side you have not changed or accepted. You cannot reject anything that is in the world without rejecting a part of you – something you may have been in a past life, or something...you may experience in a future one because you find it repugnant and do not understand it. When everyone can accept others as they are – not by subjugating themselves to another's will, but by being themselves and knowing that they are not unfree – then these expressions will no longer need to come through.

Each one of you has a higher self and each one of you has access to a universal energy. If it is not there, it is because you yourself have cut it off. But this goes for your world, not just for yourself. The condition of...the world's spirit is the unifying of everyone's energy, and everyone plays a part. When you all come up out of your self-imposed darkness and see the world through your new eyes, you will understand that everything is balanced and everything is as it should be, and that your painful lessons were necessary in order to make your world a more beautiful place and a stronger one.

Would you have stayed in the Garden of Eden forever and never have eaten the apple, never known all of these fears and doubts but never understood all of the joys and beauty? You cannot have the one without the other. *(pause)* I am here very well!

Chris: It *feels* like it! *(reacting to the intensity of the energy throughout this entire section)*

ༀ ༀ ༀ

Coming to know our own shadow side – all that is frowned upon by our conscious selves – and finding the way to transform and integrate its potentials is a key step in our growth toward wholeness, or what Jung called the process of individuation. On the other hand, those who passively accept the status quo repress the strength that would enable them to smash the ancient idols and set free their spirit. Hedging their gamble by clinging to old forms of security, they typically find a serpent to blame for their trouble – and preferring to be one-sidedly in the "right", ensure that the "wrong" will always be with them as well.

In this war against human wholeness, myriad horror movies reflect mankind's simultaneous attraction to and fear of power. Having refused the uniquely rewarding challenge to plumb the depths of our own souls, we end up caught in the middle. This next exchange is prompted by Rena's encounter with Leroy, a man of markedly unbalanced energies who is consequently prone to possession by a power-hungry spirit.[102N] Two related excerpts will follow.

Moita session #70 (Kelly, David, Rena, Greg, John, 2 others / February 17, 1979)

Rena: Moita, all these things that I've learned recently from you, Kelly and David, seem to be in conflict with the things I was taught as a child, things related to God and the church. I feel it's a conflict – that I don't know which way to go.

MOITA: All things are one.

Rena: They seem to be opposed to one another

MOITA: The only place things are opposed is *here (i.e. in the physical)*, which I know is not always easy to grasp. But you make oppositions for yourself so you *can* choose. I have no conflicts – not conflicts of opposition, or good or evil, or theory and reality.

Rena: There seem to be good and evil forces, and I have felt some evil forces. I feel like I have no way of knowing how to protect myself.

MOITA: If you stand within the Light, there is no evil that can touch you. Those who are touched by evil allow themselves to be so touched. You create your universe. If there is evil in it, you have put it there. You can *see* it and still not be touched by it, if it exists for others. I do not mean that you should be blind to the evils that others would perform, just more aware of your own part within it, so you can steer your path more consciously...

Greg: Do you mean there is no evil?

MOITA: Here where your life is focused, there is what people call evil. There are dark thoughts that man has made himself, which can seem to act independently of their own will. There are tensions built up from your own thought-forms. All of what you call evil thoughts are to us unproductive thoughts, are negative thoughts, if you will. They go against the grain of creation, against the natural law of the universe. And so, they must be dealt with; they must be absorbed or changed or released. But to us, where we see the pattern, there is no evil. There is balance, and the Earth is striving to awaken its inner harmony in man himself so that balance will be maintained.

Greg: So balance takes the place of good? I sometimes wonder if there are evil thoughts and good thoughts.

MOITA: If you could view thoughts as individual creatures, each by itself; if you could actually see what the thought looks like when it leaves; you would be able to tell from that point of view, from what you saw, whether it was a good or a bad thought.

          If it was a productive or a positive or a balanced thought, it would appear to you to be bright and light and gay and joyful, beautiful – all of those words that you use to describe that side of your nature. On the other hand, if it was unproductive and negative, you would see it as twisted, warped, unbalanced, ugly, diseased, unnatural. And then you would *know...*

You learn from your life by expressing these thoughts and then having them come back to you in situations, in people's attitudes, in the very feel of your life-energy itself, and what you can get out of the Earth and its harmony or what you cannot. And with that learning, you weed out what you would call the good from the bad, or the harmonious from the inharmonious, until you yourself are in balance with your own nature and the rest of the world.

And so, all evil is is your mistakes made manifest, and the accumulated mistakes of your entire race. All that you have all done in the past to set things in the wrong light you must all undo.

John: Is it our ego and our desires that make our thoughts become distorted?

MOITA: To find what makes them *un*distorted is what you're after. It is not necessarily your ego or your desire that makes a thought distorted. It depends on how you express that ego or that desire that decides. One of the things when you meet like this and share your energy and raise your level is to help change some of those thought-forms into ones that are more pleasing.

ৎ ৎ ৎ

Moita session #63 (Kelly and David / January 26, 1979)

(During tonight's session, Kelly feels a kind of fierceness from Moita – that she is showing more of her power than usual. It makes Kelly realize that if she had opened herself up too soon, "Who knows what would have come through?!" Then, as we enter a silent period, we both experience the different spaces Moita's changing energy and expressions can put us through.)

MOITA: You are becoming more aware of how I can change the texture of a moment.

David: I'm getting the feeling of different movements in a symphony or different acts in a play.

MOITA: Or different faces. They are very conscious changes – to show you more dramatically, perhaps, the power of thought and what it can do.

(During a pause, as the intensity builds, Kelly can't help wondering, "Is Moita going to reveal herself all of a sudden as not *the way she has been up till now – as the wrong kind of spirit?")*

MOITA: There are some terrifying aspects to the ability when it is used to control others, which it can very easily be used for. But you see . . . *you* have at least fallen into loving hands. Rena...has encountered the other aspect of this ability. Do you think you would be wise enough to see through it?... It was not always so.

ৎ ৎ ৎ

Moita session #73 (Kelly, David, workshop group / February 27, 1979)

(Moita eavesdrops on our workshop this evening, as Kelly and I respond to questions about

spirits of the dead possessing the living. Then we invite her to speak.)

MOITA: Something needed to be clarified from your conversation earlier about possession. Besides the things that you mentioned..., there is a different level – not of spirits but of thought-forms – that can also act as if independent of their originator.

When you have a thought, it takes on a shape. When you are opening, depending on what kinds of thoughts you are having, you will attract those kinds of thoughts to you. That is why those who are into satanistic trips have demons that they can see, because their thought-forms take on that shape and act towards them as if they were what they were supposed to be. So, you see, your doors are most important – which ones you open.

Pat: So if you don't think of something, it won't come (?).

MOITA: That's right. It has nothing to draw it to you. It is as if you did not exist [for it]. The different universes overlap only where there is a common ground. Those who can become something of the universe they seek will find that universe there. That's also why, if you expect disaster in your life, you will find it, because you will create a universe in which there is a great deal of disaster...

Rita: In other words, you create whatever happens to you. You make that happen...

Pat: So if I don't want possession in my life, all I have to do is not think of it.

MOITA: You have to put your energy into different directions. If your energy is just floating around, there is still a possibility there will be some kind of a hold there, because you all have negative thoughts and that cannot be avoided as yet. But to take the majority of yourself and put it into a positive direction – that's what's needed.

Rita: What, to you, is a positive direction?

MOITA: One that accepts the flow of the universe.

Rita: Hmm, I'll have to think about that one for a while!

MOITA: Well, the universe has its own direction – the *larger* universe, the universe where this one was created from.

Rita: Ah! I see.

MOITA: And so, when you do things that go against the current of the flow, you create blocks for yourself. You see these blocks in your life as difficulties and problems. That is how you are here to learn what is the correct flow.

√ √ √

Before this early session, we listened to a recording of Elisabeth Kübler-Ross speaking, and I commented on the powerful aura conveyed through her voice. After some initial greetings, Moita picked up the topic from an unexpected angle – returning once more to the lessons of the Nazi era. Not incidentally, this session came less than a week before Kelly and I moved to the house on a power point for our last year in Regina.[103] Moita uses the occasion to speak at length on the dangers and subtleties of power, epitomized in powerful speech.

Moita session #35 (Kelly and David / October 25, 1978)

MOITA: Speech is something different and unto itself. It is a very strong power... That was a lesson that Hitler learned well. I'm sure you have seen how someone who knows how to speak can carry a crowd, even if he has no ideas. There were those who could sway another's thoughts and minds with the quality and sounds of their speech... Being able to use speech as a refined form of communication in getting across an idea to someone else in the truest sense is one thing. Using that ability to control someone else's thoughts is another.

Having such a close example in history [of] the power of the spoken word when it is used for personal gain hopefully makes you all more aware of the power that you all have and makes you more wary of using it for yourself. If you could take any individual who has lived through that time, and ask them why they followed and why they did what they were told, you would not get a coherent answer, because they would not know. *(pause)* Any time a power is misused in the past, it must be encountered again in another life and the opportunity is given for it to be misused again. You all have a great deal of influence over others . . . as do I...

(Kelly will say afterwards that, as Moita speaks about speech, she uses her voice in different ways, showing exactly what she is talking about. Kelly also will find that each current block of conversation is very clear in her mind, but that previous blocks immediately become very hazy – making her think, "Did it happen, or didn't it?!" After an ensuing long silence, and other conversation, I ask about the work we are here to do together.)

MOITA: In order to teach others, you must also learn a great deal yourself. And in order to learn, you need to put yourself in different kinds of situations with different people and, from their reaction to you and yours to them, find out more about who you are and how you feel, and gain a better idea of what kind of power you have and how to use it wisely. The closest thing there is to true evil is knowing what you can do with what you are, and then purposely using it to harm others. When harm is done in ignorance, it does not carry as much weight in your soul as it [does] when it is done with knowledge. And before you take that choice, or assume the responsibility for your own path, you must know yourself.

Each time you have reached this point, in other tests you have laid out, you have gained back your power and not taken the responsibility that went with it. And as all power that is controlled, it eventually turns and destroys the user. Of course, you are not the only one in this position. Many of the souls that have chosen to be born at this time must make the same choices and assume the same responsibility. Otherwise, the awareness of the world could not go any further than it has...

David: When you say "reached this point", you mean being aware of having powers?

MOITA: Being able to tap into those forces and control them to a certain extent. This energy is all around you. It is used differently now than it was before, but the energy is still there and can still be tapped. The energy that destroyed Atlantis is the same as it was. It is on a slightly different plane, other levels more subtle, not as easily accessible to the conscious man, but it is still available.

The thing about power is: of itself, it is nothing; it merely exists. And till a conscious being taps it, and uses it, and gives it form, it has no thrust of its own for either good intentions or bad. That is one reason why we stress love, because it is of itself an energy with good intentions, or proper.

You have already learned to tap a great deal of power in this life, but the point I am speaking of is still in your future. But it is when you must make a choice. You desire to take control of your own destiny and walk your own path. But you cannot do it without the knowledge, and the knowledge brings the power, and the power brings the responsibility: to use, or not... It is much more difficult to have the power, and not use it, and *know* it is not something that can be used.

David: The whole concept of "using" implies, I guess, "for one's own ends" in a separative way, as in "using nature", "using human beings".

MOITA: The purpose of life is finding the way back to where you began. But you cannot find your way by nudging at the door or forcing it down. When you force down the door, you find yourself in the wrong room. That is why, when it is not used, the door opens by itself, and you walk through with no resistance.

Ends can be idealistic and full of good intentions. They do not have to be evil or obviously misusing others. When one uses power for *any* ends, it causes destruction, because power was not meant to be used. It has its own rules, its own sense of flow. And when that flow is interrupted, channeled away, taken off and put into other forms, it disrupts and makes changes that usually cannot be foreseen...

Love does give power. But it is also a two-sided coin. If you are not free to be yourself, you are also not free to love – not in the true sense of the word, because that's what love demands. You are all here to learn to be yourself, to find your own beauty, your own sense of oneness, your love. When you find that, then [the power] will not be used. It will flow out. And others will not be able to destroy you, whether they can accept your love or not, because it is a strength – a knowing that life continues.

ം   ം   ം

The exchanges below continue the discussion of power and probabilities from a session first sampled in the Prologue. Here Moita should not be seen as responding to any specific conspiracy theory, but to the questions as asked.

Moita session #77 (Kelly and David / March 9, 1979)
David: During this time, are there groups with access to power of different kinds that might deliberately seek to create a police state on this continent – people with a chance to do it? It

seems to me the establishment has been doing much bumbling along. Am I being naive?

MOITA: Is it bumbling or is it perhaps just starting to get caught at its own doings?

There have been many things that have been done with the view to gain power. The tools are somewhat different now than they were in the past, but the period of history that man has remembered this time has been filled with instances of individuals who have craved power over their fellow beings. Why would this time be any different?

They just feel they are more organized or knowledgeable and have more in control. They can reach more people now than they could ever before, and their wars are more subtle wars. Rather than murdering their subjects and conquering their lands, they win them over with ideas and thoughts, and change them from the inside until they do not know themselves that they have been changed. At least in appearances, they are more aware of their own [hypnotizing].

David: It often seems to me that the people who are involved in doing that are themselves hypnotized like the others.

MOITA: They are probably the most hypnotized of all, because they think they are something they are not, and have not learned that they cannot get away with this kind of energy-changing and not have it affect them personally, or those around them, and the very structure of the world they choose to try and control. They are working on a different level of awareness, and they don't see that the world itself is more aware of them than they would like. But these things do have to be dealt with by many.

David: I know our whole structure of society is oriented around power and control of people's minds in subtle ways – mostly subtle ways. The things I find hard to believe are conspiracies going far outside the structures that are now set up, which would involve a very conscious, deliberate striving to dominate in a way that the persons could hardly fool themselves as to what they were doing. I guess you can always fool yourself, though.

MOITA: They are not fooling themselves as to their own purposes. They are fooling themselves as to how they can or may get away with it. When someone wants to take over the world, it is definitely a very conscious act; and when one wants to conquer another land, that too is a conscious act. That does not change the outcome...

There are those who would try and manipulate others, and they can contact sources that can help them find plausible reasons for doing what it is that they want to do. There are innumerable excuses that individuals can find or manufacture to explain or back up their own thoughts and ideas. That is how their universe is formed. Each one of you look for things that support your own view of the world. And so, this seeking is answered by a different part of themselves. All things serve a purpose.

(At this point Kelly hears this additional thought from Moita: "Aren't you getting from me what you wish to hear, too?" Earlier this afternoon, Moita also was "talking" to Kelly about authority: that we have to be careful of any "Authority" that "knows what it is doing" or says it knows; that there's no true authority except your own inner one. This is one of the ways that you can tell a

fanatical group of any kind, by whether it sets up an Authority. We were reminded then of one supposedly "New Age" organization in particular, and Moita refers to that group in her answer.)

MOITA: The influence that they have over others is something that others must learn to define for themselves. And as long as people are willing to let others do their learning for them, there will be many such groups. You could say [the leaders of this organization] are "slicker" in their approach than many others have been. They are buttering people up and making them feel important and worthwhile. It is good for [people] to feel important and worthwhile, but it must come from within themselves. Otherwise, if their structure was taken from them, they would be worse off than they were before. It is an empty worthwhileness that is being offered – not a very strong foundation to build a new world upon... But the others will have to take care of themselves, since it is each individual's responsibility to cause his own awakening.

∽ ∽ ∽

Shades of War

We have been seeking to understand the elusive balance within or beyond all of man's conflicting thoughts and actions. In early October 1980, Kelly experienced a voice she identified with "the Spirit of the Earth" – a first hint of developments yet a year away. That voice spoke of "seeing the harmony in disharmony – how, even when things look completely destructive and unnecessary, there's an underlying balance (and an overlying harmony) to it all."[104] It is a lesson we will need to remember if war comes – that "alien pestilence", in Moita's words, "that is visited upon the Earth" by man. Kelly's experiences six days later, on the evening of October 10th, the day of greatest sunspot activity yet recorded, ultimately bring a message of hope – while also vividly portraying the "disharmonious" possibilities ahead – for those of us who intend to stay on this Earth through all the labour pain of its rebirth.

Our day begins auspiciously as we hear news about the "mystery woman" of Mount St. Helens. Here is Kelly's description of later that day:

"David, the kids and I stop at [a nearby lake] to eat supper before going to a movie. It is a clear, crisp day, and we enjoy watching the Sun sinking behind the snow-capped mountains across the lake. After eating, I have the urge to wander around the lake and feel the trees and rocks. As I walk through a grove of trees, suddenly I feel a great wave of change in the air. The sense of something disastrous occurring is so strong, I almost lose my balance. The only words that come to mind are [from *Star Wars*], that there has been 'a great shift in the Force'.

"Immediately I wonder if Mount St. Helens has erupted. I walk over to the nearest tree, put my palm against the rough bark, close my eyes and ask, 'Has the volcano erupted?' – instead of asking, as I should have, simply 'What has happened?' Instantly I 'see' a picture of the volcano in my mind – calm, serene and quiet.

"I never do ask the right question, but the experience is very unsettling. I walk over to a large boulder and place my hand on it, closing my eyes again. I am overcome by a sense of stillness and waiting and clarity – no thoughts clutter my mind so long as I am in touch with the rock. I know that I am experiencing its unique consciousness – slow, steady, patient. It helps to ground me. Not long after, we leave for the show."

That is Kelly's afternoon experience. We learn afterward that if Kelly had asked the right question, she might have seen the huge earthquake this day in Al Asnam, Algeria, killing 20,000 of the city's inhabitants. The following description of Kelly's nighttime experience is written while still in the grip of emotion at the most dramatic aurora we have ever seen:

"Tonight, as we are driving back from [town], I look out the truck window and behold a light growing in the east. I tell David that the northern lights are out; and though they are but a wisp of paleness against the black of the clear sky, I sense a power in them and know they are building in strength.

"After we arrive home, get the fire started and the children to bed (reluctantly), I go outside to watch the growing glory of the sky. At first there is a bridge or arc of light that spans the sky from east to west, even [extending] beneath the horizon on both sides. I watch, at first in awe, and then growing fear, as a deep blackness – blacker than the void of space – begins to encroach upon and within this bridge. They are like long, dark, thin, cruel fingers without warmth and understanding, and they separate the strands of light from each other, threatening to break the bridge asunder.

"I think of Canada and the differences that are growing between East and West, and how difficult it will be to bridge the gap, as the forces of fear and misunderstanding band themselves to widen the gulf. But when it looks as though the light will collapse entirely, the bridge rebuilds itself. I see this scene re-enacted several times, and each time it holds a new meaning.

"I see the planet's East/West cultures striving to reach an awareness of their own and the other's road. I see the doubt and fear that thrives when each looks only to its own part; and so, the bridge crumbles to dust. But again it is renewed. I see the desire and hope of the unseen world of light and love stretching out its hands in succour – reaching with all of its love to embrace us, to help us find the way home. Again, many are afraid and see evil and darkness where there is only light and love. But again the bridge rebuilds itself, and this time remains whole.

"I see pale energy drifting from the south – diffuse and dispersed – but as it touches the arc the bridge is strengthened and glows more brightly. I know it is help unlooked-for coming from other, even farther and more distant realms; celestial beings of light who, when added to the whole, each increases its own light a thousandfold.

"David is there beside me to watch the making of the last bridge, and I am glad, for a cold fear of foreboding is coming upon me. When he leaves to tend the fire, I have to leave also, for suddenly the world, the woods, are filled with hatred, malice and ill will.

"Later, the energy from the sky draws me again. We go out together, and I feel heartened and strengthened by his presence. The arc is gone. Curtains of light flicker and wave in the east, and we watch in delight. Then my delight turns to horror as I see a red glow as of blood growing in the East.

It is faint and far away at first, but soon the colour grows in strength and begins to spread itself in ever-widening, darkening bands upward toward the zenith, the centre of all things.

"I turn to see what will happen in the West, and there before my despairing gaze I see the blood rising in wrath to answer the East. It grows swift and terrible, and they meet at the centre in a clash of wills. Above me the battle rages unabated. There are clashing lights exploding all around the centre, and the violence increases until we can hear the sounds of death above us. I think of the children in Garabandal, Spain, who screamed in terror at the visions they were shown by the Virgin in the early 1960s...[105] I see the futility of learning our lessons too late, and of waiting to see if prophecy is true before accepting our responsibility for the future.

"And I suddenly know, with a feeling of terror and awe, that Moita speaks the truth – that the Earth *is* fighting for its very survival, and indeed man will not wake up in enough time to avoid cataclysmic change. Moita's words suddenly have so much more import that I feel dizzy and weak. It is as if I have previously thought the whole thing an absurd game, only to find that now it is no game, but real – and the stakes are higher than I alone can handle. But I know I am not alone.

"I go in the house again, my head spinning and in a daze. We have something to eat and warm ourselves by the fire. But then I know I must go back outside one last time. When I look, the war is over. In its place, in the East but almost at the zenith, is a display of bright lights that make me think of fireworks and celebration. I know it is the promise of light – the dawning of the New Age, the union of worlds in love and harmony, our hope for the future and what the change will bring. My heart is lifted and I feel renewed within. I call David out, and we watch together in wonder. When it is over, we go inside . . . and to bed.

"In the early morning I become quite ill. I vomit for several hours, and am weak for the entire day. Obviously the experience was very intense to affect me so."

While it is Kelly who perceives this level of meaning in the aurora this night, it is the first time either of us has seen that kind of brilliant *red* filling whole areas of the night sky. Her interpretation/ perception of its message for the world, both warning and loving, does not feel out of character to me. Moita clearly does not think Kelly's perceptions out of place either.

Moita session #159 (Kelly, David, Jim / October 19, 1980)

David: Can you tell us the source of the meanings Kelly perceived in the northern lights recently? How would you account for an experience like that?

MOITA: *(smiles)* Is her experience accountable?! *(I laugh)*

The Earth speaks in many languages. The northern lights are, and have always been, a means of communication. To those who know the language, they will reveal many things. They will tell of weather patterns, earthquake patterns on other parts of the globe, Sun patterns – all forms of energy. Those of us who take an interest in communication are also drawn to this particular phenomenon, for it is readily affected by manipulation, thought waves, and it can be made to express many forms. *(pause)* This will not be the first time that someone has seen a great significance in that type of display.

David: You're thinking of one that Lucia of Fatima saw before World War II?

MOITA: That is one that has . . . slipped through. *(humorously suggesting sneakiness on their part, perhaps to lighten the serious subject a little)*

(According to Fatima Prophecy, *the Angel of the Mother of Jesus warned the children in 1917 of five "scourges" to come. The first of these would be another devastating world war – heralded, the eldest, Lucia, was told in 1927, by "an unknown light" in the night sky. The book continues:*

That sign, as prophesied, came on the night of January 25, 1938, when all of Europe and part of North America were lighted by an extraordinarily brilliant display of the *aurora borealis*... Lucia, peering in awe from her convent cell, recognized it as the promised warning of war to come.

*(*Fatima Prophecy *says the remaining "scourges" were the militant rise of communism, persecution/martyrdom of the Church and specifically a pope, and the annihilation of several entire nations presumably due to nuclear war and/or natural cataclysms.*[106]*)*

MOITA: There were a few [prophetic aurora displays] in Egypt and near the end of Atlantis. Egypt once was not as far south as it now is. *(pause)*
           You can say that that energy can help form a link between the worlds. And depending upon the ability and the strength of the channel and the link combined, what is seen will have significance or will be merely astonishing on a physical level. There is *also* that the person's thoughts can actually affect the northern lights display. It is not always easy to tell if the thoughts affect the display or the other way around.

ও   ও   ও

Then it appears to be *my* turn in the prophecy seat. On the Sunday morning a month and a half later – the 39th anniversary of the attack on Pearl Harbor that plunged the United States into World War II – I wake in great agitation from the following dream.

"God's Murder" dream
David / December 7, 1980
I hear a news report that Mount St. Helens has begun to erupt internally, its peak caving inward, and that a nearby volcano is rumbling as well. But next these volcanoes are in the Middle East, as a backdrop to the confrontation of two vast armies.
The fanatical leader of one army mounts a ridge to address the opposite side, his black

figure silhouetted against the red-orange flames of the now fully erupting volcanoes. I hear him begin to speak. But as the rumblings drown out his voice, a TV news announcer takes over, quoting his words. He is threatening the other side with the consequences of resistance, including this: "God's murder will be carried out."

I am astounded to be witnessing such historic news coverage, and overwhelmed by the dramatic rendering of such a demonic figure in what I take to be real life.

My immediate association to "God's murder" is to the Bible story of God demanding Abraham sacrifice his only son Isaac, of which I have just been reading (and to which Moita referred in Chapter 6). But the murder in that story became unnecessary once the lesson of surrender to God's will was accepted. Conversely, the insistence in this dream that the murder *will* be carried out (i.e. no matter what) shows that the fanatic has refused this central lesson – rather, he presumes that God is on *his* side, and that God stands ready to smite them, ensuring the murder of *his* opposition.

Then Kelly adds a second meaning: that those, like the fanatic, who see God willing the murder of their enemies are symbolically or literally the Antichrist, prepared to will once more the murder *of God,* potentially embodied in a returning Christ or Great Teacher.

And Amar will provide a *third* meaning.

<u>Moita/Amar session #165 (Kelly, David, Jim / December 21, 1980)</u>
(Jim joins us for this session on the evening of the winter solstice. When I ask Moita about my dream, a long silence follows. I begin to feel a very concentrated pressure in our linked hands.)
MOITA: We are visiting your dream.

(Long pause, as Moita closes Kelly's eyes and I close mine to delve further into the images. Kelly sees the fire and the black face, feeling all three of us in communion around the dream. Our eyes open at the same time. It takes me a few seconds to put together the clues – the husky voice, the intense energy. Soon I am feeling very at home in a much deeper space, and sense that I am leaving my body – for I feel my arms spread wide, though physically they are at my side.)

(Coinciding with the flow of energy around our circle, Jim begins to see waves of visual changes that astound him as in only one other session. For him, Kelly's face seems at times to turn to stone – but with intelligent, living eyes; sometimes to a bearded male face; more often to an older woman's face; and these are only a fraction of them.)

(Kelly feels her heart pounding very heavily at first, and then little trickles of energy being added over and over to raise her to a clear enough level. She sees the room filled with moving currents of energy. Her sinus congestion disappears, and much energy is concentrated in her neck and shoulders. Her body seems filled to capacity, so that later she can identify with that idea of being made of stone – similar to the heavy, dense feeling in my hands. Kelly hears the words, "It's not dense; it's intense.*")*
AMAR: Hello. *(pause; very strong energy directed at me through the eyes)*
David: So you've finally come.

AMAR: I have considered it before.[107N] Your dream speaks in words like I do – words that have many meanings. *(pause)*

Man will start a war: not from greed, but because he fears his own evolution. He would destroy himself first – the God within. *(pause)*

And there is a Light growing in the Middle East, a Light that has been born. This Presence is making itself felt. Why you all react with fear sometimes is beyond us. There are some who hope he will be killed before the end-times, his mission destroyed.

David: Would he come out of Israel again?

AMAR: He is there now. That area on your Earth is a focus-point for much creative energy. It is for that reason, and no other, his manifestation occurs there. *(pause)*

(Kelly is seeing an umbilical-like cord connecting higher levels to the Earth at the Holy Land, permitting their energy to be directed there more readily.)

David: Does my dream show anything like a scene that may come to be in the future, or is it almost totally on a symbolic level? Could the new Great Teacher possibly be threatened by war in that way? Could the threat become a literal future event?

AMAR: There is no way that Light can be extinguished from that level.

David: I know it won't be carried out.

AMAR: But will the threat be real?

David: Mm-hmm. Will he be the focus of warfare himself?

AMAR: No. He will not come to full recognition until after, when the world will need a Peacemaker.

David: Mm-hmm. That's what I suspected. *(pause)*

Jim: Those who wish to see him dead – are you speaking of people on this plane who seek his death, or on higher levels? *(pause)*

AMAR: No one from a higher level would wish such a thing.

Jim: So those on this level who seek his death – do they know where he is yet?

AMAR: Some of them do suspect, but his identity is being kept fairly secret.

It is appropriate we speak of this on the eve of the return of the light. *(pause; much energy being experienced)*

(to David:) Keep your aims high. *(pause)*

(to Jim:) And your heart clear. *(pause)*

Good night.

Tales of Power #4

TO MEET AN ANCIENT ENEMY

He focuses her attention on a life . . . near Christ.
— Amar (April 18, 1981)

As told in Tales of Power #3, plans for Elisabeth Kübler-Ross to meet Moita, Kelly and me and a few close friends at our home in the Kindle Valley on the Labour Day weekend 1980 become stalled in early July when Elisabeth reports receiving much different guidance than she has before. We have to decline her invitation to meet between her speaking engagements in Alberta or southern British Columbia – not merely for financial reasons but, more importantly, because she, and we, would then not "have the clearness or the calmness to get the most benefit from the meeting" (Moita on July 4th).

Moita then goes on: "If she truly wishes to meet you, and Kelly, and me, she *needs* to come to your place where your energy is present, your life is there to be seen, because the things that surround you are part of you... You are in this place for a good reason. There is a good energy here, a whole energy, an energy that is close to the Earth and the Spirit, together."

However, Elisabeth does invite her secretary Judi along on her late August speaking trip, and urges Judi to realize her own wish to visit us as a way to express the connections among us all. That is the context for Judi's remarkably quick, intuition-guided trip from south-central to remote northern B.C. and back south again, then returning to southern California, all between Friday and Sunday (August 29 and 31, 1980), as told in Chapter 1 of *The World Conspires*, with session excerpts in Chapters 5 and 8 of this book.[108]

One further exchange from Judi's Saturday evening session with Moita needs to be given now. Moita's response serves as a general answer to a frequently asked question about past lives at the time of Christ. But in the context of Judi's question, it is highly relevant to the relationship between Elisabeth and Jay Barham, as we shall see.

Moita session #155 (Kelly, David, Judi / August 30, 1980)

Judi: What is the "Jerusalem connection" that Elisabeth speaks about? I don't feel the importance that she seems to stress, but I'm curious about it.

MOITA: What does she say?

Judi: She says that there is a group of people who live all together in Jerusalem at a point of time [when Jesus was alive].

MOITA: Mmmm.

Judi: Now, my feeling is that this may or may not be true, but I don't understand the relevancy it would have on our work now.

MOITA: There are certain groups of people that do reincarnate together at other points in history at key times, but it does not mean that they will accomplish an end just because they may have been together in another life. The danger in believing in reincarnation comes from seeing your past lives as greater or more important than the one you are leading now. The present moment is neglected in past glories, and many things that can be accomplished are not accomplished because of past structures that you bring forward with you from other lives.

In each life there are opportunities to work for the betterment of your own soul, or [of] others in working on yourself. But each life has its own unique possibilities. The part of your soul that is born in this body is not the same part that was born in another. And though all the parts are connected, no one part is more important or better than the one you have now. *(pause)*

There are many lives in the past that many wish to have been, and it is easy when you are first beginning to learn of past lives to be drawn to the energy that surrounds different personalities in your known history. It is to be taken carefully. In many cases it should be seen symbolically and not literally. And in all cases it should be understood that whether it is literal or not makes no difference. It is the now that is important, not the then. The other possibility that can arise is that you will see past glories and be satisfied with them, and not create pathways of your own or new glories to take with you.

This is my perspective.

We and Judi correspond several times following her August visit, but there is no contact by letter or otherwise with Elisabeth for many months. The next April finds Judi working on her idea that Kelly and I might give one of our own workshops down at Shanti Nilaya. But then we learn of a major interview with Elisabeth Kübler-Ross appearing in the new issue of *Playboy*.[109] We are confounded to see Elisabeth in this interview continuing to back her associate Jay Barham to the hilt as one of the world's greatest healers. After the letter that I wrote to her in late summer 1979, enclosing the transcript of our July 28, 1979 Moita session,[110] we are amazed that almost two years later she seems not to have changed her stance regarding him in the slightest – *except* that we don't know how long ago this interview was actually conducted. These issues feel especially weighty for Kelly and me given the possibility now of being invited down to Shanti Nilaya ourselves.

It is Thursday of Holy Week in the Christian calendar, the day before Good Friday, 1981. It is the night on which Jesus is believed to have been arrested in the Garden of Gethsemane and then tried by the High Priests, before being brought before the Roman governor, Pontius Pilate, in the morning and later crucified. But we have not consciously thought of this connection – and know nothing of another connection, involving simultaneous, startling events in California – as we prepare for tonight's session.

Moita/Amar session #181 (Kelly, David, Nancy / April 16, 1981)

(As we meditate, Kelly knows "something is up" because Moita and whoever else are "doing something to my head – moving things around, straightening things up". Soon she hears this very clear "That should be enough." Right after that, Moita comes. The first part of the session is then devoted to our first-time guest. Finally, Moita turns to me.)

MOITA: You are seething with questions.

David: That's true. *(laughs; pause)* The one that pulls me the strongest is about Elisabeth Kübler-Ross and her relationship with Jay Barham. Can you tell us anything more now about the tie, including reincarnationally, between them: what kind of energy exchange happens between them; why she, almost alone, sees nothing dubious in his actions and character?

(After I say "almost alone", Moita is already closing Kelly's eyes to make a transition. During a long silence, Kelly senses intense energy all down her neck, making it feel very thick. When her eyes reopen, I recognize the characteristic intensity of Amar's gaze, and Kelly notices my eyes reacting to his presence. Kelly feels the energy vibrating through her hand is "so strong" during the following.)

David: I feel like I should say "hello".

AMAR: That you *should. (speaking quite slowly:)* I have been long in the coming . . . waiting . . . for the appropriate . . . moment, as it were, when conditions . . . were more . . . convenient. *(pause)*

            This situation . . . is one which we have an interest in. *(pause)*

David: It seems to be focusing a lot of people's questions about this whole area [of spiritual communication].

AMAR: It is time that many questions need to be asked. *(pause)*

David: What kind of energy is involved in these activities of Jay Barham? *(pause)* Is he . . . sort of two-sided?

AMAR: I cannot see in twos.

David: *(laughs)* Many? *(pause)*

AMAR: He allows himself to be used as a channel by *any*. He has no discretion. We could prevent . . . his use, but we choose . . . not to, for it serves . . . many purposes. *(pause)*

David: Are these entities truly materializing?

AMAR: Some. Not all.

David: Other times it is his body that is . . . moving around (?).

AMAR: Yes. Once it is given up, he has no control. And he is not totally unaware or innocent.

David: What about the tie with Elisabeth? Is it true that when she is present with him, then the energy that comes through is much more positive than is very often the case otherwise?

AMAR: She has a great heart, and more clarity in some ways. She does help to focus his energy. But even then, not all are from as "together" a level as she would believe.

David: Why does she refuse to consider other possibilities? Is there a reincarnational tie that explains a lot, as well as the events in this life that have left her sort of dependent, it looks like, emotionally? *(pause)*

AMAR: He focuses her attention on a life . . . near Christ, . . . because it . . . puts a mist before her eyes. *She* has only good . . . connections . . . with the memory . . . of the Christ . . . and believes anyone else who was there at the time would also only have good connections. And she seeks an experience that is similar; and so, she creates in him a healer, one to replace what she feels she has lost.

David: I'm not sure how you mean "she feels she has lost".

AMAR: Christ as the healer.

David: Are you implying that *he* was there at that time and had a negative kind of connection to that energy then?

AMAR: I am not implying. I am *stating*.

David: Would you say any more on what that was?

AMAR: He was a *Zealot*.

David: The most famous one? *(meaning Judas Iscariot – mainly based on my understanding from reading* I, Judas, *the historical novel by Taylor Caldwell and Jess Stearn – though there have been different views of Judas)*

(At this moment our recording tape runs out! I fumble to change it while Amar waits in suspense-filled silence, interrupted only by the sounds of the cassette not fitting into the slot and the recorder lid refusing to close! Finally I get the tape in place.)

AMAR: No! *(smiling, in loud voice)*

David: But one that had perhaps similar attitudes (?).

AMAR: There is much in his *(Barham's)* background that suggests an affinity for using others. *(pause)*

David: Loria once said that Elisabeth and I would have a long and very close association in this life, based on past connections. There is a possibility that Kelly and I may go down to Shanti Nilaya. Do you have any words on how we might help the potential light in the situation to come to the fore, to teach whatever it's here to teach, and specifically be of help to Elisabeth? *(pause)*

AMAR: Your mere presence would be dangerous enough.

David: To whom? To us?

AMAR: To all. You have yet to meet an ancient enemy. I believe that is your word for it. "Adversary"?

David: *(laughs)* I'm not sure on what level you're talking. *(pause)*

(As the word "adversary" came up in a key past dream of mine involving a dark threatening figure[111], I wonder whether one level would be our inner fears, guilts, etc.)

AMAR: As it stands now, Barham has gained a measure of control over Elisabeth. He will seek to maintain that control. *(pause)* Be *wary*. Be *centred*. *(pause)*

(During this conversation, Kelly hears Moita telling her, "Whatever you do, don't listen *to him." The thought is that he can mesmerize people that way. Note the parallel to Kelly's regression*

to be held two days hence, as given in Tales of Power #2, "Mind Control in Atlantis".)

David: Would it be better for us *not* to be there yet? I mean, are we prepared *(laughs)* any time soon to deal with that, even being in the vicinity?

AMAR: If it is time, things will fall into place. *(pause)* You will learn more as time goes on. *(David laughs)* I am through for now.

David: Thank you for coming...

(Amar closes Kelly's eyes. Moita returns, smiling. I laugh and go on to another question, but a while later return to the subject.)

David: I wish I'd asked Amar more specifically: When he spoke about "an ancient enemy", he seemed to be confirming that we have connections with Elisabeth and Barham as well. Would a hypersentience on that be a worthwhile venture?

MOITA: You *may* be able to handle it. It could help prepare you.

David: I gather he was speaking of both of us as having this connection?

MOITA: The animosity is more open between the channels.

David: Mmm.

MOITA: He *is* the reason she did not come. *(i.e. last summer, when Elisabeth seemed ready to visit us in the Kindle Valley, if possible, but then reported guidance to the contrary)*

David: Through this power he has over her? Would it have been something *consciously* said or done, or on another level?

MOITA: Subtle doubts. *Control* is not that obvious. A casual comment?

David: He does know about us then? We haven't known if he's ever heard about our journal or if she's talked about us or anything.

MOITA: She does not keep *much* from him. She considers him one of her few friends.

David: Could he be affecting us even now – like affecting Kelly's health?

MOITA: He aims his energy in this direction only when he feels threatened. Do not worry overmuch. You have *us*. *(I laugh)* He does *not*. Only what you believe can hurt you *will* hurt you.

David: We'll work on that...

(We have much to share after this session:)

Kelly: I was really surprised at how much information we got.

David: Yes!

Kelly: It seems this is a much larger thing than it looks like on the surface, because otherwise what Amar said doesn't make sense: "We have an interest in this." And *his* level doesn't *take* an interest in little things. I saw energy patterns, world patterns, but I couldn't really interpret them.

He said they don't interfere, because "it serves many purposes." I got a whole bunch of stuff when he said that: to make people question things, to bring things to light, to release energy in California before Earth changes. And it seemed also to have something to do with Biblical prophecies about the Antichrist and false prophets. These kinds of things are channels for that energy, the collective unconscious of man that has been ignored or denied for so many years.

I got that Jay Barham was in Atlantis and he was "on the dark side of the Force". He was an impetus behind Atlantis's sinking, by taking that energy and bringing it in and consciously focusing it, misusing it.

I also got the feeling that [my first husband] Ted *(the sociopath)* was a preparation for Barham, so I would know what power and manipulation were and recognize them when I came across them. I get the feeling that if I meet Barham, he'll remind me a lot of Ted. And Ted was *very* convincing – very honest, big beautiful brown eyes. He was really sincere as he was lying to you through his teeth. And you believed every word he said! It's hard to explain how total that was.

David: Reminds me of the wicked queen in Narnia, who could mesmerize you by talking. *(referring to C.S. Lewis's series of children's books)*

Kelly: And Jim was just telling me about Robespierre in the French Revolution. He mesmerized crowds.

(As most notoriously, of course, did Hitler. I will later recall that Moita's warning about the "power of speech", included here in Chapter 9, was given to us on October 25, 1978, right after we listened to a recording of Kübler-Ross speaking. Elisabeth herself speaks very movingly – her German-accented speech carrying a powerful aura of its own, though an aura of a different kind and used for a different purpose.)

Kelly: Who was *the* Zealot? I don't even *know*! *(i.e. the one Amar said Barham was* not*)*

David: You don't know?!

Kelly: No!

David: Judas!

Kelly: Oh, Judas! He popped through my mind at one point, that's right.

I thought that was really funny with the tape recorder, [when Amar waited to say] "No!" He does have a weird sense of humour. Amar's so different from Moita. Some of those phrases he said, again there was the feeling of them having multiple levels of meaning, and all of them being true. Like the word "she" didn't seem to be always just Elisabeth. There was one it could mean both her and me.

David: What went through you when Amar said, "Your mere presence there would be dangerous enough to all"?

Kelly: Unhealthy.

David: Obviously, dangerous to Barham's control, so . . . he'd want to fight back.

Kelly: And that's how it would be dangerous to us. And it would be dangerous to Elisabeth's sanity to be the centre of the fight – the prize?

David: But he didn't then say it would be a bad thing to go.

Kelly: No, he just said it would be dangerous. But then, they don't seem to worry about danger; they worry about *results. (laughter)* I don't know. I never expected to hear anything

David: Did you get any sense of whether we're going to be ready for this this year?

Kelly: *(shakes head)* They get to things like that and they are just *blank minds*. I can't get a *thing*! They don't let me. If I could get it, we'd know; they'd tell us. They have such control over their thoughts – nothing leaks!

ഗ ഗ ഗ

The next morning, in bed, I suddenly put together Jay Barham's name with the person I think of as the *second* most famous Zealot: Joseph Bar-Abbas, or Barabbas, as it appears in the Bible. I wonder if I should mention this to Kelly, before she has her own chance to receive the identity of that person, as through hypersentience. I mention only that I've had a thought about it, and then Kelly herself pops up with Barabbas! She says this was the name that was going through her thoughts all through that section of the session. She didn't mention it at the time because she felt it could be just her own thoughts. But it seems very significant that apart from Judas once briefly, this was the only name going through her mind repeatedly.

Only then do I realize how Amar might have meant that last night had appropriate energy for him to come and speak about this. This has been the 24 hours during Holy Week commemorating Jesus's arrest, trials and sentencing. The one chance for release of Jesus was Pilate's Passover tradition of freeing one prisoner chosen by the Jews. The gospel of Matthew reports that "the chief priests and elders persuaded the multitude that they should ask [for] Barabbas, and destroy Jesus."[112] That Bar-Abbas thus became "the chosen one" instead of Jesus – just as Barham now has masqueraded or allowed dark forces to take him over, in place of true spiritual presences – certainly fits the Antichrist theme.

Soon I am re-reading *I, Judas*, the novel that has suggested a lot of our understanding about the Zealots. As portrayed in Caldwell's and Stearn's book, Bar-Abbas, the leader of a violent revolutionary party that wanted Jesus only if he would prove a political deliverer, spoke of "manufacturing" a Messiah, if need be for their purposes. The parallels to Jay Barham's manipulative, abusive masquerading today are hard to ignore. As Moita has said with reference to all the controversies at the time of Jesus, which have returned in slightly different forms today: "As the age began, so shall it end."

But it would be wrong to end here. For this ending of an age to bring the birth of something new rather than repetition of the past, what must be different in our approach to meeting our "enemies", up to and including the archetypal "enemy"? In the following excerpts from later this same year, Moita and Amar not only provide more detail about a coming Peacemaker but, more to the point, indicate the new attitude that will emerge through humanity's rising self-awareness, enabling us to become peacemakers all.

Again, readers are reminded that prophecy is subject to the changing probabilities flowing forward from the time period in which it is given. Then, with today's hindsight, readers might consider what personifications of negative energies have been active, say, in the wars and deceptions of intervening decades. (Due to recording difficulties in this session, some wording may not be exact, but the essential meanings are preserved.)

Moita/Amar session #192 (Kelly, David, Wes, Clare, 2 others / August 2, 1981

Wes:	What of the Christ?
MOITA:	He is born...on Earth, as was foretold.[113N]
Wes:	What is his physical age?
MOITA:	In his early twenties.
Wes:	On what continent is he?
MOITA:	He is once again in the country known as the Holy Land. But he is not Jewish, nor a Christian.
Wes:	Does he have a following?
MOITA:	He is in hiding...
Wes:	How many disciples are around him?
MOITA:	The Christ has not come this time to be an example.
Wes:	What is his mission?
MOITA:	To bring man to a recognition of the Christ within.
Wes:	When will he openly declare himself?
MOITA:	After . . . the worst . . . of the devastation . . . is over.
Wes:	You're referring to the Earth changes.
MOITA:	I am.
Wes:	When do they start?
MOITA:	They have *started*.
Wes:	When do they end?
MOITA:	Around the year 2000 – we *hope*, if indeed we find it necessary. *(smiling)*
Wes:	So what are you saying is the reason for the Earth changes?
MOITA:	It is possible to change the picture without going through the upheaval. Man's awareness is the determining factor.
Wes:	And the probability?
MOITA:	Not very high. But it is still possible. After 1985, the chances decrease dramatically for avoiding changes of that nature...
Wes:	Thank you.
MOITA:	You're welcome.
Wes:	Why so solemn?
MOITA:	We have been speaking of solemn things... *(then, turning to me:)* Hello!
David:	Hello. I have some more solemn questions, if possible.

MOITA: Perhaps we could call on an authority!

David: Do you think so?!

MOITA: It is perhaps a good idea. Authorities are usually the best ones to go to when one has solemn questions. Would you care to try?

David: Okay.

(Moita closes Kelly's eyes. In a long silence, energy rises to Amar's level and her eyes reopen.)

David: Greetings. The question I had in mind was a follow-up to Wes's. If the returned Christ is not being brought up within Judaism or Christianity, is he being raised in another religion, such as Islam? Or is he outside of those categories?

AMAR: His childhood has been spent in Islam, although he is now apart.

David: Would he be one of the Palestinian people displaced from Israel, among those who feel themselves persecuted?

AMAR: He is in hiding because he *is* being persecuted.

David: Can you say more on *why* he's being persecuted? Because of things he has done?

AMAR: There are forces at work here which you are not aware of... He disturbs the continuity of what man has begun to see as his purpose...

David: I'm not sure I understand what you mean. How would you see his purpose?

AMAR: Man thinks he is a destroyer... It is a self-fulfilling belief...

Wes: Can I ask, what of the Antichrist?...

AMAR: The collective unconscious of man is...responsible for the creation of the energy that you have called the Antichrist. He is no more than the shadow of man, the unaccepted parts.

Wes: Will it be personified?

AMAR: How can one battle it unless it takes on form?

Wes: When will this be?

AMAR: It will be before the Christ is revealed. The Christ will not be revealed until 2000, or near there – *after* the Earth changes.

Wes: In the meantime the personification of the Antichrist, the shadow aspects of mankind, will be working?

AMAR: It will be soon as an influence. There are many on the Earth at the moment who do not understand the energy they draw upon... [But] the Earth could not attract such energy if man were whole in the first place... He is there because man cannot accept himself. He would not be, if you were all whole. That is why he will be destroyed... He can be cast out by being *loved from within.*

Chapter 10

A DIFFERENT KIND OF EARTH

The good news ("gospel") for our time – in which human development has put the very sustaining of life on Earth at risk – must include rebirth of our threatened planet as well as a transformed consciousness in man. This chapter looks ahead to that "whole Earth" of the future, sustained by a civilization of partnership with, rather than dominion over, nature. But given the current mess we have made of our planetary home, and the resistance in mainstream society to anything approaching radical ecology, is such a positive vision realistic? Getting from here to there can often seem nigh impossible without, say, some very drastic upheavals and cosmic interventions. This is the rather grim outlook that world events seem to force upon us circa 1980.

In fact, many psychic-spiritual sources – from the Fatima visions and Edgar Cayce readings through to these early 1980s – have been predicting cataclysmic Earth changes starting well before the end of the 20th century. We have seen Moita too warning of such events, explaining that Earth cannot long continue in the exhausted, imbalanced state to which it has been reduced. But she also stresses that the timing is not set – and adds (as I have rarely, if ever, seen elsewhere to date) that higher-level entities are purposefully stretching the timeline by adding their energy to the Earth and humanity. If, through this nurturing, human hearts and minds can be awakened from fearful, combative attitudes, and our destructive treatment of the Earth reversed, the necessary changes can be made more gradually and gently than previously anticipated. As Moita has explained before, it is a matter of different probability lines. Therefore she takes a "yet to be decided" perspective on our near future, combined with confidence about our eventual destination.

Tests of Awareness

Amid the latest, stunning psychic predictions of upcoming disaster in the spring of 1981, Moita initiates the topic herself.

Moita session #184 (Kelly, David, Margaret / May 19, 1981)
MOITA: So you have questions on California and whether it will sink into the ocean?
David: *(laughs)* Right. The recent issue of *Coming Changes*[114] reprinted a channeling that predicts in a very definitive manner a chain of events occurring in various California fault systems that will eventuate in major devastation of the state by November of this year. According to the anonymous source, a series of massive earthquakes is to result in much of the state sinking under water. The channeling urges everyone to consult their own guidance for possible corroboration, so I would like to ask you – especially about the predicted

timing. Is it accurate or not? *(pause)*

MOITA: Things have been set in motion. Dominoes are falling, as it were. However, the time is not yet ripe for the events to occur as described. We can . . . stall the devastation some time yet. As is mentioned in the channeling, much depends upon the inner nature of man.

David: The book *We Are the Earthquake Generation* [by Dr. Jeffrey Goodman[115]], which is based on several correlated psychic sources, puts the date for that level of change closer to the end of the decade. Would you see that as fairly likely?

(Goodman's sources actually predict the destruction of California's coastal cities, and the partial flooding of the interior, by the end of 1985, less than four years from now.)

MOITA: At the moment it is up in the air. This is a period of time where future lines are still flexible. They are both possible, although the...latter is somewhat more probable. It would be easier for man to deal with the release of energy that this will cause if it is released more slowly. *(pause)* All the votes are not yet in. All I can say for sure is that we are . . . lengthening the process at the moment. There is still some hope that that level of destruction will not be necessary.

    We shall see what recent events do to stimulate an awareness change in the U.S. It is no accident that thus far Reagan's administration has gone backwards in time. It is a test of the people's awareness. They have been given much evidence in many areas – political, economic, social and environmental. If they cannot piece it together, they will not *get it* together. *(with a laugh)*

Unfortunately, no, the American body politic – falling in love with their Gipper – will *not* "get it together" anytime soon. The clock will be turned back by Reagan's neo-conservative domestic policies as well: elimination of ecological protections ("If you've seen one redwood, you've seen them all"), corporate deregulation and tax cuts for the rich. The consequences of those policies will multiply through future decades, till they produce the environmental, socio-economic-financial and government debt crises of the early 21st century.

୬   ୬   ୬

If the content of prophecy proves wrong (as do, of course, the above channelings about California), the underlying *purpose* may still be served. Tests of people's awareness are growing universally close to home these days, the Kindle Valley included. In recent years, this beautiful area of forest, streams, Indian reserves and small family farms has become a potential target of at least two development schemes initiated from far away.

One, if approved, might eventually turn the heart of the valley into an open pit mine (only temporarily, of course!). The other would clear a broad swath down the length of the valley, spraying it with noxious herbicides (already a serious problem here) to *keep* it clear, so that double transmission lines (with their powerful electromagnetic fields disruptive of animal and human health) can carry power south from one or more dams proposed by BC Hydro for the wild Stikine River canyon and other rivers north of here.

Serious questions have been raised about Hydro's plans by other branches of government and interest groups more powerful than mere Kindle Valley residents. As projected costs rise, actual budgets shrink, and the economy sinks into depression, the utilities empire has had to lower its estimates of future demand for electricity in the province. But that authorities could even *consider* doing these things to our valley and way of life leaves residents feeling very definitely threatened.

That vulnerability, which we share with innumerable peoples, creatures and ecosystems around the globe, is the subject of this next exchange.

Moita session #197 (Kelly, David, Margaret, Jo / August 17, 1981)

(There is a long silence as Moita gazes at Jo, a first-time participant.)

MOITA: It is good to meet you! *(long pause)* You have a great attraction to this area.

Jo: Yes.

MOITA: This *is* a place you have been to before, long ago.

Jo: That's why I felt so at home when I came here.

MOITA: Mm-hmm. In the other time, you have much peace and serenity.

Jo: *(laughs)* But not this time.

MOITA: You can draw on that. Being here in the same place, it helps you to connect with that same kind of energy that you experienced then – with the Earth...

           Many people are being touched by the Earth's fears, and many people have seen or felt its potential for destruction. Each person experiences that touch in a different way. Most times you experience it as a peace, a strength, a feeling of connectedness. And yet, with all of the change that is happening now, you can also experience it as annihilation and destruction. The Earth cries in agony at times. It cannot help itself...

Jo: I want to live in this valley for a *long time*.

MOITA: Yes, it is your *home*. And you are afraid of losing it? *(long pause; Jo sighs, with tears)* If you know where it is that you belong, then you know your own heart.

Jo: I'm afraid the *valley* is not going to be here!

MOITA: With all of the changes that are coming?

Jo: Yes.

MOITA: It is in for some rough times.

Jo: It's going to change it so much.

MOITA: It will be a passing change. *(pause)* At the end, it will change back into something else, something more than what it is. *(pause)*

           When man learns to live *with* instead of *against* his environment, these sorts of threats will not be able to be made. And that is why this time is upon us, and upon *you*. All of these things point the way. They are there as signposts, to show that something is wrong, something essential in the way man sees his world. And no one can hide from it.

That is why man is reaching into all the corners of the Earth. That is why he is scarring his world: so that all of its people will be faced with the difficulties that it represents. What kind of change do they want? Change is coming, yes. But each must decide for himself which way the change will go.

Jo: But a very few could destroy the whole thing.

MOITA: Not if man changed his way of seeing the world. The few control the many because the many allow it, because the many cannot decide for themselves what the many need. They do not know themselves. They hide from their own hearts, in fear, in terror. They see themselves as evil, and they make themselves such because they are afraid to face the truth. They are afraid to see the light that is behind the darkness that they are afraid of.

Jo: But it's still a case of a very few, that are chosen by the many, that are controlling everything. And how can that change?

MOITA: When each person changes within, there will be no need . . .

Jo: *(interrupting)* But they will destroy the Earth before then. We could totally destroy it.

MOITA: The Earth is not idle. If man is going to destroy the Earth, then the Earth will destroy man.

Jo: I'd rather see that happen.

MOITA: It comes to that, that kind of choice. For the Earth can recreate. Man must learn that *he* can create as well. *(pause)* You must follow your own conscience. Do what your own heart tells you you must do to preserve that which you need, that which feels right, that which belongs to you.

࢙ ࢙ ࢙

Jo and Margaret return a week later with Margaret's two young adult children. This time it is Margaret who asks how to awaken man to a different dream than domination – becoming instead stewards and co-creators with the Earth.

Moita session #198 (Kelly, David, Jo, Margaret, 2 others / August 23, 1981)

Margaret: I was looking at photos of the Stikine today, wondering what to do, to do my part to help save that from being flooded by a lot of greedy men and women – wondering whether I could use some form of energy, just from where I am, to help do something about that.

MOITA: If you can get clearly in touch with the Earth spirits of that area, let them know that some humans are behind their wish to remain, they can...help – though they need to have their energy channeled. They are not aware in the same way that man is aware, or unaware, or as man sees himself as being aware. Their spirits are of a different nature altogether. They do not rely very heavily on memory. They understand the natural laws that govern their world and what their purpose is in it. *(pause)* But that focusing can, in turn, bring in other levels.

Margaret: Will the mass effort of the people who want to preserve it focus enough energy to do that – without physical, without political, force?

MOITA: Sometimes, in order to manifest results on the physical plane, steps need to be taken on a physical plane as well as on a non-physical one. There are ways for them to work together, encouraging and increasing each other. You *must* follow your heart. You can see more clearly than many. You certainly see more clearly than those who are about to attempt to control the Earth's energy and force it into their channels. But subtlety is indicated.

Margaret: Yes, I can't see myself leading a brass band anywhere. But there must be something that can be done to change enough people's minds, that can start a chain reaction to change that decision before it can take place.

ல   ல   ல

The next summer, Moita takes another tack in response to a further question from Margaret about the Stikine situation.

Moita session #218 (Kelly, Margaret, Duggan, Rob, 8 others / June 4, 1982)

MOITA: Taking the energy of the Earth and focusing it in certain areas requires people, thoughts. You are the focusers – walking focuses. You take your energy wherever you go. The more people that come together [and] create an energy focused on a single purpose, the more probable that outcome becomes – although the results of the energy can quite often be completely *different* than expected, in order to acquire that desired result. There are often unforeseen steps that must be taken, such as what [transformations] the Earth is going through *now*, in part of humanity's desire to create something more complete, more whole, more *free*. You see, many things have to be undone *before*...

Duggan: What do you mean that things have to be undone?

MOITA: Since you are part of the Earth's aura and the energy that you put out affects the Earth's health, all of the anger and fear and bitterness and hatred that is poured *through* humanity *into* the Earth must be undone or rechanneled. In order to have a *healthy* planet, you need to cooperate with the planet as well as [with] each other. By cooperating with each other and the planet, together, at the same *time*, you will accomplish much more than doing just one *or* the other.

There are many scars that need to be healed. The Earth is capable of healing itself if it is given the opportunity. But at this stage it desires help. It is evolving too. This planet has a soul, has an essence that you are part of, that you share.

How would you feel if you were a planet and you were the home to many beings, creatures; and yet there was one creature on you that continually went around with pins and needles and stabbed you and gouged you and drilled you, and refused to hear you, didn't seem to care that you were in pain, didn't notice that you were alive?

That is why it is very important to redirect that anger, because it affects your planet, not just yourself. And so, you are responsible not just for your own life, but also for the life energy in the sphere in which you live. It comes to a point where either you go completely – are wiped out entirely so that the planet can survive – or you learn to live cooperatively *with* it. A lot of people call it karma. What you have done you are responsible for. Humanity has not taken responsibility for its own actions. It has not become a responsible individual, a responsible creation.

It starts off slow. Only one person can do it at a time, and only each person can do it for themselves. It cannot be forced. You cannot take the masses who are walking around blindly, not seeing who they are or where they are, and *make* them understand.

Duggan: How are things going for healing the Earth?

MOITA: They're looking better than they have for a while.

Duggan: The economy and the general state of things between the Americans and the Russians don't look too good.

MOITA: That all depends on your point of view. Things like that serve to force issues. They make people take a more serious look at themselves – those who are willing to look. Messages come in many disguises. That is what we try to do with apparent negativity: turn it into positive growth by understanding its underlying message.

Rob: Can I bring up the Stikine again? If there is any chance that they *are* going to build this dam, what should I do? Or should I just put it out of my system and put my energy someplace else?

MOITA: There comes a point when battlefronts meet and they become non-productive, because they serve to hide the real issues. Then the battle becomes all-important, not the underlying reasons for it. And then your energy is wasted, because you are throwing yourself against an immovable object.

Rob: So where should I focus my energies?

MOITA: The best place to focus your energy is on yourself – on changing yourself, on your own view of reality.

Rob: Towards that particular issue?

MOITA: Toward *everything*.

Rob: Everything. So I should just let life run its own course?

MOITA: Not necessarily. By becoming more aware of yourself, you should become more aware of those things you feel you *need* to do to *be* yourself. Action is not necessarily bad in a spiritual sense. There are different forms of action... This is the hardest period in development because of the transition: the sense of being bogged down in the old while trying to bring about the new. You will have to work through old systems...

Rob: Like as a whole group of people, all of us together?

MOITA: You have to transform old patterns, but you have to transform them from *within* some way.

Rob: The whole society, you mean.

MOITA: Yes. Things like this happen because people have created the space in which they *can* happen, in which they are proper and expected. The society as a whole is the way it is because of how you have all used your energy. You have created the circumstances . . .

Rob: So what can I do as an individual?

MOITA: [You have] to uncreate them.

Rob: I know. Each one of us has to figure that out.

MOITA: What's the point, if you can't figure it out? This is where you test yourself. This is where you find out what you're made of, what your weaknesses are and where your strengths lie.

Rob: So every negative situation actually strengthens us and makes us see.

MOITA: Depending on how you react to it.

Rob: Ah, what do you mean "react"? How should we react? *(pause)*

MOITA: Being aware that you can choose your reaction is the first step. You can choose to react angrily, violently, aggressively. You can choose to react acceptingly, and try to change that energy into some sort of a constructive input in some way – if not in that place, in another. You can see the reasons why it happened; and if you can understand the underlying roots, start to take steps to change that underlying root.

ৡ   ৡ   ৡ

As these choices are posed to people around the globe, Earth's planetary brothers and sisters apply their own pressure toward restoring balance. But just as planets themselves are multi-leveled beings , Moita stresses that her level, along with ours, can affect the influence of physical factors.

Moita session #191 (Kelly, David, workshop group / July 29, 1981)

Don: In 1982 *(and also near the year 2000)*, according to astronomers, most of the planets will be aligned. How does that affect the Earth here? Is it going to create earthquakes?

MOITA: You are speaking of the "Jupiter effect".[116]

Don: That's right.

MOITA: *(pause; then slowly:)* Gravitational and magnetic alignments take some time to affect physical matter. It is very much like the aura of a person, where the disease first manifests itself in the aura and then the body manifests the disease in the physical.

          We can alter how much the planets will affect the Earth, and by "we" I mean not just those from my level but you as well. The Earth is in need of a healing. If the disease is not removed in the aura of the Earth, then it will manifest itself in the physical. Depending on how much awareness occurs between now and then, the physical manifestations will be sooner or later, or not at all – preferably, in some ways.

          You should watch Earth activity between '82 and '85. It will probably increase. But again, that depends . . . on how many people have learned to channel love into the Earth.

Don: So that depends on people's behaviour.

MOITA: Their state of mind. It is not so much what they do that matters. It is the way they do it, the energy – connecting with their wholer selves, becoming whole.

ဖာ   ဖာ   ဖာ

That a shifting of the Earth's physical (as well as spiritual) axis of orientation may occur, sometime near the turn of the millennium, has been suggested before by Moita as well as many other psychic sources and some independent physical researchers. John White's book *Pole Shift* summarizes numerous proposed causes for this possibility – which, depending how it might occur, would be, as he says, "the ultimate disaster".[117]

Moita session #178 (Kelly and David / March 15, 1981)

David: Now that I've finished reading *Pole Shift*, I'm curious what you would say to be the actual "trigger mechanism", as it's called, to cause the physical Earth to change in that way. Of course, many people in the book are working on it as a purely physical phenomenon. We have some idea of the underlying reasons for it, but where and how would these subtle forces actually affect the physical?

MOITA: *(pause; eyes closed)* We are seeing the different volcanic centres, places where plates meet, as energy lines on the Earth's body – weak points, vulnerable points, places of change and turmoil. When the psychic atmosphere of the Earth is changed by man's encounter with spiritual forces that have been absent, if the reaction is one mostly of fear, the fear will pour down into these areas, jarring loose the crust, the skin, seeking a new balance, a new centre. There is no single trigger mechanism. It all is intertwined.

How the High Ones choose to manifest themselves on a physical plane – or rather, how the [people of] Earth choose to *see* the return – will [decide]. But there is no doubt there will be outside influences – "cosmic" influences, if one desires such a word.

David: You mean the High Ones by that.

MOITA: Yes. The Earth is not travelling through a vacuum.

David: And what you said suggests the crust shifting over the molten core.

MOITA: That is what I saw. This is not exactly my area. So I may not be as accurate an interpreter.

David: Did you ask one of your friends who . . . *(Moita laughs)* . . . does have this as a specialty, or is it a universal source that you seek such pictures from?

MOITA: I asked the air. It is a "universal source". The air here may not be breathable, but it does have its attributes. *(pause)* The electromagnetic field of the Earth is also a factor. It is something that is very subject to change, through thought.

David: The shift of the poles isn't any more likely if man's reaction is mainly fear?

MOITA: It is *more* likely if man's reaction is one of fear. The energy lines of the Earth can be changed without changing the physical structure.

(From our conversation afterward:)

Kelly: The picture of the Earth's crust slipping was very clear. I saw the Earth hanging in space, and I could see the inside and the outside. I saw first the inside spin around, and then the outside slip in the opposite direction, I think – settling into a new balance.

Seeing the tectonic plate theory as *shiatsu* lines was interesting. When she spoke of shifting the energy centres of the Earth without shifting the physical form, I got that that would take a lot of the stress off the plates, making them less vulnerable to slippage. Certainly the mind is going to have a lot to do with what happens. The more people we can convince of that, the better chance we've got of making it the way we want it, creating our own reality.

℘   ℘   ℘

The startling nature of the above material justifies a brief scientific update as of this writing. The probability of a pole shift in *some* sense will be increasingly recognized scientifically in the years between this session and 2012 – ranging from observations of accelerating migration of the magnetic poles, to a likely magnetic pole reversal and to the possibility of a physical (rotational) pole shift.

According to the CBC TV science program *The Nature of Things* with David Suzuki (November 30, 2010), the magnetic north pole was migrating about 10 kilometres annually prior to 1994. This increased to 15 km circa 1994, by 2001 surpassed 50 km and a decade later is in the 55-60 km/year range. The location of the magnetic poles reflects the axis of Earth's turning magnetic core. The magnetic field has been weakening significantly as well, losing 15 percent of its strength in the last 150 years. Progressive weakening of the field is a precursor to at least a magnetic pole reversal, of which there have been many over Earth's geological history. The CBC program did not deal with the additional possibility of a shift in the physical poles marking the planetary axis of rotation, however.

A magnetic pole reversal would greatly affect climates and living things. But the weakening of Earth's protective magnetic field itself allows in increasing amounts of cosmic radiation that can disrupt everything from modern technology to the human mind. Recently, "cracks the size of California" have been recorded in the structure of that field.[118] And according to Lawrence E. Joseph's 2010 book *Aftermath*, NASA's 2008 unmanned THEMIS spacecraft found a pole-to-equator breach in the magnetic field that extended out into space a distance equal to 4 Earth diameters, 10 times further than previously observed. Given the expected solar activity maximum in 2012, such huge breaches of an already weakening field may have major effects.[119]

Finally, Joseph's 2007 book *Apocalypse 2012* quotes geologist William Hutton arguing that the observed migration of the magnetic poles could be due to a "mantle-slip pole shift", whereby the mantle and crust slip over the liquid core. This type of polar shift would eventually change the position of the equator and rotational axis relative to the Earth's surface, which could be cataclysmic if sudden, and in any case would change the centrifugal forces and sea levels influencing different regions and tectonic plates of the Earth, inducing potentially huge seismic and volcanic effects.[120N]

Readers will recognize a "mantle-slip pole shift" as virtually the same image Kelly received from Moita during the last session, though that kind of upheaval remains only one probability of undetermined timing. Current science, of course, does not consider that our openness to higher energies could be stretching a transformational timeline to allow for greater conscious evolution and therefore gentler physical changes.

ॐ   ॐ   ॐ

Change Not Seen in Eons

Our next session is unique in touching upon so many varied, concrete topics, including not only geomagnetic shifts but also climatic change, social and technological evolution, coming mutations in nature and man, and the growth in human awareness in relation to non-physical levels. It would not have happened without the presence of our guests, and particularly Max, a meteorologist with intuitive abilities and strong spiritual interests, who thoroughly enjoys conversing with Moita. As Moita says in May, "This source has become...more informative."[121]

The session focuses first on a question from Max, who assumes here the timeline many sources have been suggesting as most likely: "In the next 20 years or so, how does British Columbia fare as far as Earth changes go?" Moita notes the vulnerability of Vancouver Island, Vancouver and the rest of the B.C. coast to earthquakes and/or tsunamis at a time of Earth changes. On the other hand, unless the scale of upheaval is unexpectedly great, the B.C. interior should be relatively safe – as would, even more so, the Canadian prairies. We pick up the conversation as Moita then raises Max's own specialty, the weather.

Moita session #196 (Kelly, David, Max, Iona, Sharon / August 9, 1981)

MOITA: There will be a great deal of weather changes. They have already begun.

Max: So I've noticed. Very perplexing.

MOITA: Not from here!

Max: No, but it is for my job. My job is a challenge every day I go to work.

MOITA: We put your Earth through an energy change – several of them... – raising the energy level, raising the vibration of the Earth.

Max: This is done from *your* side?

MOITA: Yes. *All* of us from my side were involved in this endeavour – that is a great many – to make it an easier transition for man when his body becomes different.

Max: Will our bodies appear the same, or will we take a different shape?

MOITA: They will appear a little different – slightly taller.

Max: Thinner.

MOITA: Yes.

Max: Finer boned.

MOITA: Longer fingers.

Max: More artistic...

MOITA: There will be more creative energy available. There will be more awareness *of* it. Transportation will change too.

Max: What form will it take?

MOITA: There is a great deal of energy in the Earth's magnetic field, and it can be tapped into without harm. It is much like the aura in a body. It is a high, intense vibration, and there are some right now who are involved in studying the Earth's aura... They are coming close to uncovering its secrets...as they apply on a physical plane...

           And of course, there is the Sun. The Earth will not be running on just one form of energy. There will be many forms.

Max: Does the Earth's magnetic field originate with the Sun?

MOITA: It is affected *by* the Sun.

Max: But it is separate.

MOITA: Yes. It is the Earth's aura. It belongs to the planet, will stay with it. Right now it is weakening, opening itself up to the energy from the Sun – *absorbing* energy, yes. And afterwards it will begin rejuvenating itself.

Max: Like a battery being charged up?

MOITA: Somewhat.

Max: Very interesting. Transportation, then, will depend mainly on vehicles that utilize the magnetic field?

MOITA: Yes.

Max: Fascinating.

MOITA: It is surprising that man has not discovered this before.

Max: I guess we didn't realize the magnetic field contained so much energy.

MOITA: And also you had available forms of energy seemingly in endless supply for running *other* types of vehicles.

Max: *That* was a lie told to us by greedy people.

MOITA: It is *need* that creates new inventions.

Max: Hopefully it will all be put to peaceful purposes.

MOITA: Man can also use this energy for [travelling] in the solar system...[and for] interstellar travel...

Max: The magnetic fields between stars are fairly *weak*, though, aren't they?

MOITA: You can store up magnetic energy in things similar to battery cells when you are near a star, and then use that stored energy to travel between.

Max: Would the storage units be similar to crystals?

MOITA: There are some that are in that shape. Crystals can hold a great deal of energy.

Max: Yes, and they can contain the energy without loss, can they?

MOITA: Oh, they will glow. There is *some* loss.

Max: Okay. What crystals can mankind use – quartz, for one? Must it be melted and formed into larger units?

MOITA: There is a crystal that will be discovered that can be *grown* into the appropriate shape. Crystals can be grown artificially. It is a combination of crystals.

Max: Several elements.

MOITA: Yes. Similar to your discovery of steel – combining.

Max: Very interesting.

MOITA: The blueprint is there.

Max: Is it within us?

MOITA: Yes, it is within the available information of the collective unconscious. Man will not be able to *have* secrets anymore; and so, these things will not be able to be used as weapons. They cannot be held over someone else's head if everyone has them. They are not the *type* of crystal that can be used such as the laser, and there will not be this potential for hoarding and blackmail.

Max: Sounds like a delightful world – no secrets.

MOITA: And the truth shall be revealed to *all*...

Max: Good. So be it. That appeals to me.

MOITA: Yes, government will not be the same.

Max: *(laughs)* I can imagine. There will only be need for very minimal government.

MOITA: People will learn to govern themselves. How can a thief steal if everyone knows he is stealing?

Max: That's right – what's the point? Everybody will have equal access to all things, too. Why steal?

MOITA: Right – except for the thrill, and there is no thrill if you are always caught or prevented.

Max: Sounds ideal. I must think on this. Very good.

MOITA: Wait and see it begin.

Max: I will. I *hope* to, I really do.

MOITA: And then you can come back after it has started and see how it is *progressing*.

Max: I'd like to. There will be fewer people around, though, to get me back.

MOITA: There will be less souls as well.

Max: Because of the separation of worlds.

MOITA: Yes... There will be less souls available for *this* particular Earth, and yet there will be another earth to accommodate the souls that are leaving...

Max: The one you talk about [is] the one that I like.

MOITA: You do not wish to join the others?

Max: No, thank you. Too materialistic.

MOITA: They will probably not mind your not coming.

Max:	Terrific. *(laughing)* I don't think I'll really miss them.
MOITA:	They are working on a quota system. *(laughter)*
Max:	Yes, I have understood. I work with a fundamentalist. He pities me, and I pity him.
MOITA:	Things will be much freer without that type of fear.
Max:	He does seem to operate from fear, and it's sad, truly sad. Thank you, Moita.
MOITA:	You're welcome.
Max:	You're a fantastic lady.
MOITA:	Thank you very much!
Max:	My pleasure...
MOITA:	*(to me)* And how are you?...
David:	We mentioned weather changes. But can any information be given on likely changes in the basic climate of British Columbia after the major Earth changes are over, including a possible polar shift?
MOITA:	It will definitely be warmer here.
David:	Warmer. Less extremes, or like the tropics?
MOITA:	That will depend, but definitely warmer.
David:	Year round?
MOITA:	Winters will not be as severe.

(As we are now in the central interior of British Columbia, Moita's use of "here" would refer to portions of B.C. with a harsher climate than the mild south coast. The cause of "warmer" is also unclear – a pole shift, the not-yet-widely-discussed "global warming" and/or other factors.)

David:	Is it possible to locate the likely positions of both poles if there were a shift?

(In Chapter 7, Moita states that one new pole could be located in the South Pacific.)

MOITA:	A great deal will depend on how long the shift takes – on if it is slow or quick.
David:	That would determine how *far* it shifts?
MOITA:	Yes, and it will be shifting for a long time. *(pause)* It will be a gradual change in your weather – we hope. Should it be instant, it will be very destructive. Besides the crustal displacement, the animals are not adapted to warmer climates very well, nor the trees.
David:	So gradual change would allow time for adjustment.
MOITA:	Yes. You will have very busy Earth spirits. Your Earth will be going through a change of mutations which it has not seen in many eons.
David:	Among the different species, you mean?
MOITA:	Yes.
David:	Both plants and animals?
MOITA:	Yes. There will be new life forms, and old ones will become different.
David:	As to changes in the human body, will there be a difference in the eyes?
MOITA:	That will be . . . personal preference.
David:	Up to individuals, you mean, as they incarnate?
MOITA:	Yes. There will be a great deal of violet eyes, which are not common now.

Max: Will the perception be a broader spectrum?

MOITA: You will see farther into the light spectrum at both ends – and sound also.

Max: Sound, as well?!

MOITA: Of course! You will be coming more in tune with the Earth. Right now you see a very narrow spectrum. You miss out a great deal on what is happening around you.

Max: What about radio waves? Will we be able to see those?

MOITA: You will choose not to – too disruptive to the rest of the environment that you will be looking at. You will be able to use yourself as a tuner at chosen times, so that you can tune *in* or tune *out* what you choose.

Max: Music of the spheres.

MOITA: I know a very good channel! *(laughter)* Listen to the stars. They have a nice song... And the sound of colour is *very* interesting... Each colour has its own sound...

Iona: What kind of time span would you expect this shift to a warmer climate to take?

MOITA: From the time it begins to the time it ends? Probably about 30 years, if things work out my way.

Iona: That soon, eh?

MOITA: That is not very fast when you have all of the Earth fairies aware of what you are doing, and helping – and all the people too. It will be a time of great labour. Thirty years is not from *this* moment. Thirty years is from the end of the Earth changes.

          The weather patterns that are changing now are becoming very obvious, and they are *preparation* for what is to come. And yet it is not really the beginning of the pole shift yet, although it is tilting rather far.

Iona: What time span, then, do you see from now to the beginning of the shift?

MOITA: There is a variable in there. It could begin as early as 1990, or as late as the year 2000... *(or with hindsight, even later – which is a good sign!)*

Iona: What determines the length of time for the pole shift to occur?

MOITA: Man's awareness has a great deal to do with that.

Iona: In other words, if he becomes aware faster, then the shift can occur . . .

MOITA: Slower. And the more aware he becomes, the less the changes will be necessary. The Earth is hitting the mule over the head with a two-by-four. *(laughter)*

(This is Max's imagery from earlier: the need to get the attention of us humans so we can stop making the same mistakes over and over again.)

MOITA: It has given *many* warnings and has not been heard, and time is running short. *We* are helping it survive at the moment, feeding it energy. Another reason why the magnetic field is lessening: it *needs* energy from the Sun in order to continue, and man has depleted its energy supply by overuse, by not giving back, by a lack of awareness of its spirit. The Earth needs love, too, and you are sharing its body.

Iona: What significance does the *aurora borealis* have? There's been tremendous activity in that area in the last few years.

MOITA: That has to do with the magnetic field lessening and the Sun's wind increasing. There is more solar energy at the poles than there has been, and we are playing with it. Messages can come through the aurora that can affect it. The particles are very small and very easily affected by thought – what you call telekinesis.

Iona: In a similar way to what I do with the clouds?

MOITA: And do you change the form of the clouds?

Iona: *(laughs)* Yes.

MOITA: Or do the clouds conform to your thoughts?

Iona: Whichever way.

MOITA: Water vapour is somewhat larger than solar particles – not as easy to manipulate. It is a similar process. And it would not be you directly affecting the clouds, but you communicating with the air fairies. They, in turn, affect the clouds. They are sending you a message. They say, "We hear you." They are waiting to be heard from the other direction.

Iona: All right. I'll start to listen more.

MOITA: They will appreciate it. There are many life forms on the Earth that have not been seen in a long time – those that are of a different vibration level.

Iona: And will they begin to be seen more as the changes occur?

MOITA: When man's body is different as well as his mind, he will be able to perceive their energy, just as he will be able to perceive ours. It will be a *different* kind of Earth than it has been for a while.

ॐ   ॐ   ॐ

Our Universes Will Meet

A differentness exists already, in the new eyes with which more and more of us are looking upon our world, and imagining/helping to create its new face. As we link minds, hearts, hands, we need *not* simply "wait to see it begin".

Moita session #208 (Kelly and David / November 20, 1981)

(This is a "correspondence session" for a couple in the southwest U.S. who have sent questions for Moita and agreed to meditate from a distance with us tonight. I begin by introducing these new friends and where they're coming from. Only a small portion of Moita's initial response is given.)

David: They've written, saying how they feel attuned to our work and in many ways are doing what we're doing – moving into the forest, to the mountains. They feel they've been linked with some other close friends on a spiritual path. And they're very interested in a renewal of ancient pathways – American Indian, Goddess religions. So I wonder about the linking of us with them tonight in our energy, and the coming together of people like us in this time...

MOITA: Yes, a network of light is important. It is a primary goal, in a sense. For now, the world is dotted with small places of awareness of change, of acceptance, of a growing understanding – [which], to be made strong, must be connected. So, those that are connected from other times and other places, and on other levels, have all chosen to come together, all *over* the world, in the midst of chaos and war, to try and start a new beginning before the old dies away, before it is too late to begin anew.

Always it has been this way. Always man has sown the seeds of his rebirth in his destruction. And he has always seen that his seeds were tainted, were wrong somehow, grew crooked – so they must be destroyed again. I cannot say if this time you have all got it right. You are getting it *righter*. Each time around you understand a little more of how the universe works, of what is meant by being awake...

Each planet goes through this process of joining the rest of the universe... And the rest of the universe is awaiting your awakening, waiting to talk, to communicate, to welcome.

୬   ୬   ୬

Moita session #85 (Kelly and David / April 21, 1979)

David: Are the institutions we have now, like universities and such, going to survive into the New Age? *(pause)*

MOITA: It is hard to find the right words. It will be different in different places. For a while you will be a conglomeration of paths. Education and learning will still play important roles. It will be different in nature; the emphasis will change.

Some knowledge will be lost, and some will not. And there will be a clean slate *(smiles)* in some places... And the knowledge that is lost will be more important for having been lost and preventing those who seek it from going on old paths that have been worn long...

The energy that was not available before will be available again... There will be more sharing, more ability to understand the forces around you and know how they can be tapped without being misused.

୬   ୬   ୬

Not a sameness, then, but a way of relating, of participating, our differences. And we will emerge free of the dead weight of the past, free of the structures, patterns, records that have represented an authority greater than the individual spirit. This need not mean ignorance of our past, however, nor a lack of wisdom.

Moita session #129 (Kelly, David, Mike, 3 others / January 19, 1980)

Mike: There are so many mysteries about ancient history still unsolved. Do you see these things coming into our knowledge in the future?

MOITA: As man develops, he will regain the ability to travel backwards in time, and then he will not need written records. Then time in the past will become a living thing, and we will not need historians who record things incorrectly. True history may become *known! (they laugh)*

Not all will have this ability, of course, but many more than do now. It will be a slow-growing thing, a slowly learned talent, not all at once or overnight. But eventually those who are born will be born with the talent instead of having to learn it in a life.

Mike: From mutations?

MOITA: Not just physical mutations, but a change in the awareness of mankind in general will bring about this kind of change, will create the atmosphere for these kinds of births. Man is born into forgetfulness because it is necessary. When it is no longer necessary, he will not be born already without a memory.

ৡ৹ ৡ৹ ৡ৹

Moita session #130 (Kelly, David, workshop group / February 4, 1980)

(Prompted by a question about the ages of souls present:)

MOITA: Creation has not stopped. It continues and will continue for a long time. When the Earth reaches a point where this communication is no longer necessary, when man can once again hear the voice of the Earth and the rest of those who exist in it, those [souls] that are newly created will have just as much wisdom and experience as those who have been here for many years or many lives.

ৡ৹ ৡ৹ ৡ৹

Ours is but the time of transition – barely early spring, much less full summer. So much learning seems to lie between where we are now and where we will be when the way of the universe is obvious to all. So one wonders: Do our higher levels experience the anticipation – both joyful and daunting – that we do, as we take each hesitant step forward?

Moita session #180 (Kelly, David, Fran, 17 others / March 28, 1981)

MOITA: *I* grow too. We all grow together. Your world will change mine, as mine will change yours. We are taking a chance.

Fran: How much of a chance?

MOITA: Think of a universe that [we] have experienced in solitude, and company with those who are the same as [us], in joy and love for what seems to be an eternity. And then add to that a multitude of beings who are searching, who are reaching, who are striving and pulling. Can it stay the same? We are giving up our universe, our reality, *with* you. We are taking a leap into the unknown, into the unknowable.

Fran: Trusting that it will all work out.

MOITA: Knowing it will. But still we must go through it too, even if we are different in our perspectives. Can you imagine your world where one of us can manifest itself as a physical form and speak to you direct? How much will that change your world?

Fran: It would make it much *better*, I would think, if that could happen.

MOITA: It depends upon man's awareness, first. We would come as allies, as friends. We would not come as gods and teachers.

ৎ৹   ৎ৹   ৎ৹

Moita session #197 (Kelly, David, Margaret, Jo / August 17, 1981)

   (This is a later part of the same session with Jo that appeared earlier in the chapter.)

MOITA: I enter your world through this doorway. Only a part of me can come, for there is too much energy in *my* place to focus it all into *this* place. When I say I am more present, I mean I am putting more energy into your reality. And that energy is something that is felt, something that affects others, that changes your reality somewhat, so that it becomes a little of both – a taste of my universe, small as it is, and there is much more behind it.

Jo: Is it a better universe than ours?

MOITA: We are more aware of who we are. Yours is *no worse*. It is different.

Jo: More confusing.

MOITA: Yes, because you have lost touch with this universe. But that is the only reason, and it has been an important part of man's evolution: finding himself alone, and trying to find his way back to home, to self, to wholeness. You have learned *will* this last stage in development, and now will will be joined with being, beingness, oneness. And a new universe will be the result: becoming conscious creators, knowing why things happen, instead of seeing life as being thrust upon you. It will be very different. *(pause)* And we will be a part of it. Our universes will meet. *(pause)* It has been a long time since man allowed love to walk in his world, and that is what he has been missing.

ৎ৹   ৎ৹   ৎ৹

Then there are moments when we realize – *experience* – that nothing at all is missing.

Moita session #191 (Kelly, David, workshop group / July 29, 1981)

   (Nearly 20 people attend this open house in the Okanagan Valley of British Columbia. But the size of the circle does not interfere with this most intimate sharing.)

MOITA: This Earth, your mother, is in need of help. She is looking to her children for succour. She cannot be denied, for she has nourished and given the gift of life. [One of you] speaks of patience with a 16-year-old child. The Earth has learned patience with all of her children. You are adolescents. You are entering adulthood, and it is a time of turmoil, a time of change within, a difficult time for the Earth, who is waiting to accept you as a partner in awareness. She has many beautiful things to offer.

Phyllis: This time of turmoil – is it going to be soon, or may it take a 100 years or longer?

MOITA: Pregnancy is a long time; birth is not as long. The birth process has already begun. The labour pains are obvious. The process will end with either the birth of the child (that has entered into adulthood) or with the death of the mother who is giving birth.

Yes, in your time-sphere it is soon. The next 20 years will tell a strange tale to those who come after. You are living through what will one day become a legend to others. You must decide what kind of a legend you will make.

Phyllis: You mean me as a person, or the Earth as a whole?

MOITA: I mean *both*. No part is too small. All parts must be whole to make a puzzle complete. After the birth, the process of another maturing will take some time. The new awareness will not be instant, although it will seem to be for some of the children who are born later. Those are appearances only. You have all worked towards this end.

(Turning to youthful Tara, sitting to Moita's immediate right:)

MOITA: Hello.

Tara: *(laughs, clears her throat)* Hello.

MOITA: How are you feeling?

Tara: Nervous.

MOITA: Now that I am here you are nervous, where before you were intrigued? Am I that different?

Tara: No. I feel excited.

MOITA: You are looking bright. There are many hard times ahead that will require a great deal of strength to meet the challenges as they come, to experience the pains – not only of your own but of others. But there is joy at the end, to keep you hoping. It is worth it. It is always worth it, even though in the midst of despair you may lose sight of your purpose and its worth. We are *always* there. We never turn away. We are dependable and real.

Tara: You're very beautiful.

(As Tara smiles at Moita, with open, wide eyes, everyone would say the same of her too. She will say that she feels "on Cloud 9".)

MOITA: When you are old enough to learn how to let love become a part of your being, all men know you as beauty, as rightness. Love *is* beautiful, and I am one expression of the energy of love. So are you, and you will grow into it as you remember your own beauty. It is a nice feeling, isn't it.

Tara: It is.

MOITA: It is home. This feeling gave you birth. And all of the journeys in between, leaving home and coming back, become just whispers in the wind – unimportant, once the goal is realized. This feeling you have right now others would call a state of grace. You are open and receptive, totally unblocked. It is funny that the moment, being so real right now, will later become a memory to cling to. When you can remember how to be in this moment, in this reality, in this feeling . . . And it will come again in time.

I know I speak to your heart. I *see* it. That is why I am here: to help you remember.

Tara: *(whisper)* Thank you very much.

MOITA: You're welcome. *(then to Marge, Tara's mother, sitting next to her:)* You too.

Marge: Thank you.

(For Marge is experiencing Moita's presence as directly as her daughter, through the energy flow between them, and Moita knows it. The same is true, if only slightly less so, for all of us.)

MOITA: There is a lot of energy here.

(Moita turns to her left, looking at me, then Clare, then . . . when, in passing, there is a definite "click" between their eyes, and Moita returns to Clare's sudden intensity.)

Clare: *(whisper)* Oh my God!

MOITA: What do you see . . . or feel?

Clare: *(whisper)* I can't describe it.

(While feeling tremendous heat, Clare is seeing glowing white lights in the centres of Moita's eyes – actual circles, not just twinkles. Several days later, Amar will tell her: "You needed a sign... It is by your own openness that you have received it.")

MOITA: You have all made me real! – *allowed* me to become real in this reality. You are *each* doorways. This is but the doorway that speaks. *(pause)* And I can see I am not frightening after all.

Clare: *(whisper)* No. *(pause)* Oh! Can you tell me . . . what I need to know?

MOITA: I am *showing* you what you need to know.

Clare: *(whisper)* But I don't . . . *(the rest inaudible)*

MOITA: It will *be* there.

Clare: *(whisper)* Yes.

MOITA: Life is here to be learned from. Don't worry about making mistakes. That is how I arrived where I am. I would not be in this state if I did not make mistakes first. Learn from your lessons and love yourself for them. We all love you for them too.

We are awaiting the moment when our worlds become one, so that you can see as real all of the things we have meant to man throughout his growing period. You will *change* us. In your growth, we must grow too. So do not be afraid of change. We are returning. Life is there for *all* time, and things pass. Nothing stays the same, except love.

Remember that your heart is the leader of your soul, not your mind. Follow it. It will lead you through pain, but it will lead you to yourself. That is the hardest lesson to learn: how to be yourself.

ॐ   ॐ   ॐ

Chapter 11

INTO THE UNKNOWN, INTO THE LIGHT

In the beginning, there are two . . . later three . . . then four. This is how any organic, stable structure or group is built. We have been reminded that community means first of all people – people, moreover, who have been brought to a point of inner strength and openness that will enable them to work together toward a goal overlighting each and all.

This chapter is a turning point – a new beginning, a deeper level of our search for community. It is another move closer to "home" – but one more direct and intense, because more inward and personal, than the outward moves in previous chapters.

Two conversations dealing with other people's attempts to build community set the stage, and in doing so recall our own hopes to realize a similar vision once before.

Moita session #140 (Kelly, David, workshop group / April 9, 1980)

(In Chapter 8, Moita suggested Lena find a tree to meditate by to nurture her spiritual growth while her community plans were on hold. Here Moita addresses the issue of delay itself.)

MOITA: Nothing happens by accident. When there is a desire to build a community, by those of you who have come into this life to do such a thing, usually the first desire does not bear fruit because there is a tendency to rush into things too quickly, before enough learning of self and others has been done. The foundation for any community must be built upon strong individuals, but individuals who have the kind of strength that is flexible, through spirit. There is a balance that is needed in each person who chooses this path.

There are difficulties that are encountered to ensure that much of what is built stays, instead of dissolving for lack of purpose, lack of strength, lack of dedication. In making the spiritual your life, your path, you will encounter many things that will not sit right with your present personality, for we attempt to shape you into better vessels. You choose to be shaped also, on other levels.

So a delay can be looked upon as a blessing, for in that way what comes of it will be something that is lasting instead of something that passes away and becomes only memory. There are those who have overcome these kinds of obstacles, and as a consequence have destroyed that which they would build, for they have not come to it centred. It is a sign that you are more aware than you would let yourself believe at times...   If the desire is sincere, and the humility is pure, the way will be found to fulfill it.

৵ ৵ ৵

A few months later we receive a similar question from people also seeking to establish a New Age centre. Doubts that their project will work out are cropping up as well – again primarily for people reasons rather than physical ones.

Moita session #148 (Kelly and David / July 4, 1980)

MOITA: It is one lesson among many in how to begin community . . . or how not to. They have already learned a great deal from this experience, and it has changed them. When first we met they were not as consciously aware of the differences in their chosen paths... There are still many changes to go through... All must become more centred within themselves and know their own heart before community can happen and before the New Age can flower.

   (pause) The process of growing towards self can be painful and disconcerting. And in this circumstance each is learning something different; each is learning how to give in a different way. The whole, the three together, are not a balanced whole, because they are not balanced apart. And if each was himself complete, the plans would be complete, working together would be more harmonious, things would "click" as they should.

   So, it is not for me to look upon this and point out their weaknesses. It is for them to look to themselves first and find their own weaknesses and build their own strengths from them. It is something only each can do alone.

David: Is the goal for all three, then, to become centred in themselves and go on to make that balanced whole, or are they more likely to be following those different paths?

MOITA: At this point in time the future possibilities are many. I will not say, so they may remain many.

᭥   ᭥   ᭥

Though there is no escaping the hard work of personal and interpersonal growth, many hope to find a way of "working with the grain", rather than against it, on this difficult project of building something new. How to find the right people, then – even *the intended, destined people* (if there are such!) – with whom to work for the New Age?

That was our question, of course, back in Regina in the late spring of 1979, as we waited for an answer to our request to visit Sunrise Farm. It was in the session held shortly before Becky's invitation arrived that Moita told us she was "paving the way". On that occasion we also discussed a possible further level on which to contact future co-workers.

Moita session #93 (Kelly and David / June 6, 1979)

David: We've just read Peter Caddy's article about the telepathic networking they did with groups all around the world prior to the founding of Findhorn Community.[122] We wonder if there are similar things we can do to link up with people before we meet them, letting them know who we are and what our goals are. *(pause)*

MOITA: There is a good idea there, but you need more people to make it fruitful. You should have at least four including yourselves and have regular sessions. *(pause)*

There is a lot of power in thought. It would be an invisible advertising campaign. Kelly has already seen a telepathic network – more than one – that surrounds the planet. So far you have kept yourselves aloof from that network. You are working on the sidelines until you feel you are more ready to join in. But there are others who are aware of your existence, having no secrets. To one who has the sight, people such as you stand out in the place that is between our worlds.

(In an astral experience several years before, Kelly experienced floating above the Earth, seeing different light energies crossing the planet. Each group was trying to keep theirs secret from others. She found she could tune into each separate network and hear what was being communicated to some extent. She found the Rosicrucian network to be the strongest and most easily tapped by her. Sometime afterwards she perceived a Rosicrucian coming to visit astrally to check her out.)

David: Can you say more about the telepathic network?

MOITA: There are several. There are groups of people who have developed these networks, and they cross the globe. Some of them are secret societies. Many of them keep this kind of activity veiled; it is not spoken of to outsiders. Much happens on your planet that few people know of, and many people would not believe the possibilities. You are still young in your development of these abilities. You are the budding flower rather than the full-grown fruit.

The networks are not isolated to just spiritually oriented groups. There are others... involved in manipulation of different kinds...that also are experimenting with these techniques... There is a power in knowing what another is thinking, and there is a tool in being able to plant thoughts without having the other one aware of your existence. People can be controlled in a sense without their knowledge from very long distances – receiving impulses to do things, not knowing where the impulses come from. We are not the only ones who can influence minds...

If you would be sure of contacting the right network, you must have your minds very clear and your hearts very centred. If you are just looking for information or experience, you could make yourself more known to those who would perhaps not appreciate your goals.

෨   ෨   ෨

We set aside the idea of telepathic networking as we move to British Columbia later that summer and begin to meet new friends in the Kindle Valley. Jim is the most forthcoming the night of our first talk there in his remark about being "New Age catalysts". Three months later, it is also Jim who asks of Moita the key question near the end of our New Year's Day celebration with a dozen valley friends. Earlier in the evening he has given us a Christmas card along the lines of Amar's short but impactful sentence during the workshop: "Make love your reality."

Moita session #128A (Kelly, David, Jim, Margaret, Jake, 8 others / January 1, 1980)

Jim: I've been talking and thinking a lot recently about community and communal energy, people working together. And I've wondered what kind of a love link between people is needed in order to work together effectively in a community. *(pause)*

MOITA: It is important to have a goal that is common to all... This goal [need not] express itself in the same form for each. But you are all here to learn the same lesson. You are all here to learn love – its realness, not its words.

You would have to have people who were willing to take that step into the unknown – have faith in themselves and know that their reality is not . . . what others see them as, but it is as they experience themselves. And you must have people who are able to give all of the others the freedom to make their own choices, and to accept those choices whether they feel to you that they are right or wrong.

If each is headed towards the same goal and able to do these things, there will be experienced a harmony on another level as well as on this one that could well be beyond the expectations of any who are involved in this. But to bring freedom to yourself, and [to create] a place to bring freedom to others, is what life is about. This is your purpose in being here. Purpose is not defined by what kind of a job you can do or how well you can do it. It is defined by how you can give yourself *to* it.

I wish I could answer your question in more depth. It is not an easy question to answer.

Jim: No, it's not.

MOITA: It is a learning experience itself . . .

Jim: Mm-hmm.

MOITA: . . . perhaps a question you will answer on your own.

Jim: Much comes down to trial and error even, it seems.

MOITA: That is how I arrived where *I* am.

(That exchange provokes much interested discussion afterwards:)

Margaret: I think the most interesting thing she said about community was that it doesn't matter with whom or what we build this community, so long as everything and everybody that comes into it has a chance to expand on their own level and do their own kind of growth without interference from the other members. And it isn't so necessary that everybody do the same, or do a job the way somebody else thinks it should be done, but that they do it with the right spirit. And you've got to be ready to hold back with an objection if somebody were to do something that wasn't quite your way of doing it.

Jake: What did Moita say about goals and what should tie it together?

Jim: She said a common goal.

Kelly: But that the manifestation of the goal needn't be the same – the individual interpretation of how to bring that goal into reality.

David: There's got to be a balance between a minimal kind of unity – in spirit and in a way of working together – and leaving the specific forms as free for individuals to find as possible.

There's got to be some agreement, and yet freedom within that. And where that balance lies . . . Well, one of the last things she said was, if you have agreement on that goal and if you meet those conditions, then there will be another level of harmony as well . . .

Jake: Yeah, a bonus opening up.

David: . . . that will produce things that we can hardly expect.

Kelly: Beyond our expectations. Hmm, sounds like Findhorn and their garden.

David: So it seems like one important way for a community to work is to really put an emphasis on being open to other levels working through us – being ready to follow intuition when it may lead in different directions than we would have expected or even agreed with previously. For example, at Findhorn before any group sets to work or to decide anything, they hold an attunement: a silent mingling of their energies, opening to a presence overlighting the group, so that can express itself more clearly within each and all together.

ॐ   ॐ   ॐ

Around this same time, with the turn of the decade, the planet is beginning its plunge away from community and detente, spearheaded by the Soviet Union's invasion of Afghanistan in December. Mutual distrust between the U.S.A. and U.S.S.R. will escalate from this point on, bringing increased fears of war and an ever-darkening shadow of militarism to the world. In the depressing atmosphere of that January, Kelly hits upon the idea of a regular group meditation – regardless of the physical distances separating participants – attempting to break the cycle of more and more fear by sending out positive energy to each other and to the various peoples and leaders on the planet. Thus, with little thought to initiating anything resembling a telepathic network as discussed the previous summer, we begin our "world light meditation".

Whatever small light we may add to the world situation, we soon find these weekly meditations to be potent generators of energy in our own lives. They are also an enjoyable way of linking with some Kindle Valley folks and more far-flung friends, a few of whom independently begin referring to themselves as the "rays" of Starflower. Jim is naturally a participant, being the one we know most committed already to regular meditation. In fact, as the workshop group cast around for something to do in the wake of Amar's message the previous fall, Jim it was who suggested forming meditation circles (as building a medicine wheel was also his idea).

One of these "world light meditations", held the week after Valentine's Day, opens immediately with tremendous energy for Kelly and me. After about ten minutes, Moita pops into Kelly's mind, bringing "fantastic rushes lighting up my whole inside", and tells her she's come to speak. Perhaps guessing that something may be happening, I've been looking over at Kelly several times during my own meditation, and finally notice her eyes are open. . . with a characteristically intent gaze.

Moita session #133 (Kelly and David / February 20, 1980)

David: Are you here to speak?

MOITA: That's why I usually come... You are making an impact with your meditations.

David: Where is it being felt?

MOITA: The most important place...is in those who are participating. *(long pause)* New worlds are built with the heart and the mind before they are built with the hands. You are laying a foundation. *(long pause)* You are opening doors that have, until now, been shut – for you...

David: Is it like we're opening the door to the kind of future we want, or feel would be most beneficial, by envisioning it now, sending our energy toward it and linking our energies together? *(long pause)*

MOITA: *(very slowly)* In creating this bond of energy between different beings, you are also helping to form that bond on other levels. You are freeing energy, allowing it to take form and direct itself, through you and others. Once this energy comes together in a cohesive form, it will release itself into your material plane. *(long pause)*

David: You seem to be blazing with light.

MOITA: Connecting in such a way is similar to opening a dam. The water does not always rush down a channel; it sometimes creates new ones. *(pause)* You are leading a quickened existence. If you are not to be swept away by the flood, you must be firm to a point, *know where you stand.*

David: There are signs of a nucleus developing in this area that might represent a contrasting view to ours – one that might serve a testing or even opposing function. It seems to centre around more traditional values, a more structured approach less open to the free flow of intuition. Now I certainly agree with you on the importance of accepting others' paths. I wonder if you see such opposition as likely; and if so, what we can do to bridge the gap.

(My question arises from the first fundamentalist criticisms of our approach, sparking attempts by some people to seek an accommodation between the two points of view as they see them.)

MOITA: *(very slowly)* Do not expect that this New Age will go unopposed. If you can see that in truth there is no opposition, those who feel they oppose you will have nothing to cling to. Understanding from your deepest heart that all things come from the same source will free you from the need to prove your path is the right one for you. *(pause)* It has been a secret too long.

David: That everything comes from the same source?

MOITA: The true meaning of that. The season is changing. You can expect it to show. And not only the season, but the age is changing too. *(long pause)*

(Then, in her final comments, Moita seems to use my question about differences to make a point in an unexpected direction, though the possible implications are many.)

MOITA: If you are to build, you need more than one plank.

David: You're speaking about people? You could be speaking about *any number* of things.

MOITA: Oh really?! *(mock surprise)*

David: Or *approaches* might be the main point – views.

MOITA: A house is stronger when it has many angles. One cannot put a roof on a wall. And one cannot make a doorway with one pillar.

(From our conversation afterward:)

Kelly:	There was one thing I kept seeing: you and me as two pillars. And after a while I was reminded of Kahlil Gibran, one of his descriptions of couples: the two pillars, separated enough to hold up the roof; if they were too close together, the roof would fall down.

David:	Did you have any sense of why we needed to be told that now?

Kelly:	Maybe it has to do with community, meeting people. Maybe we're becoming distracted by all the different energy from all the other people and forgetting something. She said we needed to be more clear inside ourselves exactly what our goals were, knowing our strength. Every so often I kept hearing we had to be strong as a pillar, but bending as the willow. We needed to be both.

David:	I liked what she said about opposition. I got the picture that our goal for community is not finding one particular road, but the Medicine Wheel idea – the interplay of many different strengths and views; that the openness and freedom are the main thing – and seeing that everything comes from the same source, rather than trying to define what particular path or belief is right for all. But somehow that has to be distinguished from chaos. We have to have a very clear, strong experience of the centre from which all the different spokes come.

She left the impression of things happening, popping up.

Kelly:	"Change coming on swift wings." That's what I kept hearing. I saw us building! – once using sawed planks, another time with logs. And there was something else she didn't say but that I heard: that you and I were "two hearts of the same goal". *(laughs)*

David:	Sounds like a valentine.

Kelly:	I thought it sounded kind of neat. Want to be a heart with me?

ৠ ৠ ৠ

With the arrival of spring, we find our log house in the Kindle Valley, move there in June, and in early September are ready to hold a first housewarming party as valley residents: beautiful sunny weather, a delicious outdoor potluck supper, and sitting and talking around the campfire with a fair number of our acquaintances, including Jim and Margaret.

Our reactions are interesting. After looking forward with anticipation for this day, and enjoying the work of preparation, proud of the place we have created together, I feel strangely let down or passed over – almost as if I didn't really want people to come, removing the solitude of our woodland retreat where we have relied so much on ourselves, living and working as a team (despite the summer's many demands and frustrations). The shift from the aloneness of our partnership to all of these new energies coming in and changing, expanding the atmosphere is a bit too sudden and unexpected for me. On the other hand, Kelly takes advantage of the welcome presence of more people, talking long into the night around the fire after I have gone to bed.

"Two pillars . . . two hearts of the same goal." A difference is revealing itself more strongly now that – having supported each other through the long period of isolation that began in Regina – we have managed to arrive at a place and among people where our visions have a chance to take root and grow. During the next week I dream of the volcano, or explosion, or prairie fire, which Moita later tells us "can also be symbolic of your own inner desires being bottled up, not having the attention paid to them that they desire or deserve, and then exploding outward, consuming your attention" (Chapter 9).

Some of the very common feelings that are going on within but largely unknown to us, as we turn through the fall toward "the season of within" far out in these northern woods, are suggested in this exchange between Moita and an American visiting from the urban East, who hasn't slowed down yet. Though in Canada only on a year's work visa, he quickly recognizes this area is more of a place for him than his native city could ever be.

Moita session #142 (Kelly, David, Herb, Mike, 6 others / April 19, 1980)

Herb: Am I now, in this area, around people that I've known in other lives? Because I feel very at home here, and back East I don't.

MOITA: There are many people that are attracted to this area. This is . . . the second stage of a training ground. *(setting off laughter from all at this apparent bombshell revelation!)*

Mike: What?!

Herb: *(laughing)* What's the first stage and the third stage?

MOITA: The first stage is what brought you here.

Herb: I remember that. And the third?

MOITA: That will be what you *gain*.

Herb: Um, okay, that took care of like five questions. *(laughing, as Moita and others join)* All right. I often feel lost. Like, I've travelled around a lot. But since I moved to this area, I don't feel that way anymore. Would you say this is a good place for me to be? And do I have to leave *(laughing)* when my contract runs out?

MOITA: What you want is a place that you feel you belong, where there are people around you who can understand how you see the world – a kindred spirit. It is not uncommon to feel alone. And it is easier to feel alone when there are many people, for each is so busy being afraid to touch another, they never reach out. The people [you think of in the city] are not very different from those who live here. It is only that they have not realized they're alone – their need for others.

Herb: Does that go against standing alone, like you've spoken of before?

MOITA: Depending upon your wholeness first. Before you can stand together with others, without taking from them what you feel you need to fulfill yourself, you must feel and know that you are a whole being without others to hold you up.

ॐ   ॐ   ॐ

Now that we have come to the Kindle, will we remain figureheads of some abstract cause? Or will we be able to touch and be touched in a personal way, coming home to a wholeness within ourselves and as a group to which we feel we belong?

This fall of 1980, we offer a weekly open workshop at our new home. There are a few better-attended sessions, most prominently our All Hallows' Eve gathering (featured in the Epilogue). But due to our more out-of-the-way location, and perhaps a shift in people's energies, almost no one comes – except for one regular.

Kelly and I regret not being able to renew the experience of last year's workshop group. However, Jim's commitment of interest and energy certainly makes up in our eyes for the missing numbers. Jim already lives as part of a four-member, cooperative land grouping in the valley, including small, custom-made houses of interesting design. But as the one who asked the question last New Year's Day, and who we feel has much to add to a New Age community, we have naturally been thinking of him for a while – despite his seeming reluctance to talk about it – as a potential member of our own.

Moita session #154 (Kelly and David / August 28, 1980)

David: We were speaking today about a few people in the valley who have gone through great changes and heavy experiences in the last year, and how that may be leading them toward community in some form. And I've remembered Kelly's recent dream, in which Amar seemed to talk about inviting people in the hope we might have four "definites" instead of four "maybes". What went into that dream?

MOITA: Before you can build community, you must have the people, and the people must express their dedication to an ideal to work towards. You have many practical things that must be worked through first before a community on a physical level will be possible. The time to start planning and working out your differences is very soon, if anything is to be done in time for those who need such a place, and for you to grow through the experience – being of service to others.

ૐ   ૐ   ૐ

For some time we're not sure what "practical differences to be worked through first" might entail, especially since we find it difficult to arrange concrete discussions about community with interested others. So our sense of waiting continues through the fall, even as we enjoy growing closer to Jim through our weekly evenings together.

As the winter solstice approaches, we plan a gathering and session for which we hope a larger group will be present. By this time it has become almost a joke, though – once again, only Jim shows up! It is this session which Amar attends, giving us some of the material on the Christ and the Antichrist at the end of Chapter 5. Later in the session, my thoughts turn to the three of us present.

Moita session #165 (Kelly, David, Jim / December 21, 1980)

David: It's been a year in which people have been moving apart – both individual couples and in the lack of meetings of last year's group. What is it about the three of us that leads us to feel a commitment or attraction to get together for these gatherings, when others do not?

MOITA: Is it not obvious?

David: Well, I'm sure there are things in your perspective that are not obvious yet to us.

MOITA: Hmm. You three *have* spent lives together. There is a foundation for energy exchanges, working together, exploring new avenues. Things always happen in their proper time. Others must be more centred before they will begin to see the possibilities for growth for themselves and those around them.

David: I know Peter Caddy has spoken of a very important progression from two people to three and then four, leading to a New Age centre or community. I suppose that may be a structure that isn't all that necessary, but . . .

MOITA: It makes for a stronger foundation. Energy builds upon itself. But when uncontrolled influences enter into such a situation prematurely, it can have catastrophic consequences, destroy whatever growth has been accomplished. It also gives an opportunity for you all to explore your own motives and desires before there is pressure.

David: Pressure from *many* people?

MOITA: And expectations from many. You cannot possibly hope to build something new unless you start from the bottom, letting go of your structures as you grow, grasping new ideas, fitting them to you. For this kind of energy, I have said before three is a good number. It forms its own particular vortex. It has enough togetherness and enough solitude built into it.

৵   ৵   ৵

A "transforming third" element – or person – has been prominent in recent changes of couples we know, just as Kelly and I became for each other in relation to previous partners, Phil and Ruth.[123]

On December 30th, almost exactly a year since his question about links between people in community, Jim turns 32 and holds a birthday party to which we are invited. Later this night Jim finds Kelly outside and lets the words come that he has long held back – that he is attracted to her and wants to express that energy which, denied, has been getting in the way of other levels we share. At the same time he stresses to her that he does not wish to do anything that would disrupt her and my relationship – that he will not pursue this if I do not feel okay about it.

Kelly is rather stunned by the whole development, despite having picked up some of these vibrations before with Jim. On top of this, returning home the next morning after not too much sleep, we are shocked to find her ex-husband, Phil, on our doorstep, returning Arista and Donovan earlier than expected from Christmas holidays in Saskatchewan. By the end of that confusing, tiring day, Kelly finds time to tell me of her encounter with Jim during the party. She admits to some doubts, a lot of nervousness . . . and also interest in the possibilities. From her openness in telling it, and Jim's concern for me and us together, I cannot help but feel a part of this breakthrough in communication. The strength of Kelly's and my relationship, the mutual liking and respect among all three of us, and our sharing of the same New Age awarenesses and goals, make all the difference. It is the end of the old and start of a New Year.

In a day or two, Jim comes over so we can all talk it out together. On the basis of this clear beginning, we decide to enter upon an experiment: breaking down the conventional definitions of how we can and cannot relate to each other as individuals. Thus we begin a journey of self-discovery, of personal vulnerability and openness, with no guarantees except a commitment to mutual honesty and trust, so far as we are capable of them. This is not to say that we will always remain this clear within ourselves, or this open to each of the others as time goes on – for one purpose is to bring forward and try to deal with all that hinders us from being so.

The impact of this new chapter in our lives will be not unlike the explosion in my September dream. The flames burning at people's speech centres at the end of that dream, and many of Moita's urgings in recent months – letting go of structures and possessions, working toward mutual honesty, acceptance and freedom – take on fresh significance. Beneath it all, for Kelly and me, is the opportunity to redo in a positive way, and from different positions in the triangle, what Ruth, Kelly and I ultimately failed to do in 1978.

Moita session #169 (Kelly and David / January 4, 1981)

David: It seems to us we have reached another turning point in this life. Could you give us your perspective on changes we are going through now in our relationship and in being drawn together with Jim?

MOITA: You are in the midst of a tremendous learning experience. Such circumstances will serve to help you all gain depth, connect closer with the inner self. I see this much as the process of a seed in beginning its growth, and it pushes the earth aside in order to reach for the sunlight. If you are a good seed, you will grow in the right direction – and the soul knows where the Sun is.

David: It seems I have been working with that image for a few years now.

(Sunseed was the name given to workshops that Ruth and I began in Regina, which evolved into Starflower, a symbol of spiritual community.)

MOITA: Working with an image and living its reality will make it have a different feel. Many souls on this plane are searching for freedom. In order to help them find it, you must learn what it is first. To become a teacher, you must tread the paths and face the perils, so you can show the signposts to those who would follow in your footsteps.

With the birth of memory – the memory of past lives – man will find that his previously held ideals and concepts must change to accommodate what it means to have shared in many ways with many throughout time. But each must learn for himself what is the best route...

David: I remember the liberating feelings that emerged from past relationship crises that felt negative at first. Great discoveries!

MOITA: It is good to watch people grow.

David: It will be good to reach the point of finally knowing that there *is* nothing to fear.

MOITA: And thereby creating a world that has nothing to fear in it. *(pause)* There is so much in both of you that is coming into the light. *(long pause)* I think the time is drawing near.

David: It's been a special time.

MOITA: They are all special for me. Good night.

David: Good night.

✀   ✀   ✀

As our experiment begins, I am naturally hoping that whatever "liberating feelings" are in store will not come at the price of many "negative" ones (for myself in particular!). It is obvious from Kelly's first visit with Jim that an energy quite different from that of our own relationship is starting to release. Even she is amazed and wondering where this will lead, whether she can handle the situation or be engulfed by it. The "unknown" we are entering becomes definitely less abstract and a more uneasy place to be, especially as we realize it will develop a momentum of its own.

For me, the realization strikes that Kelly is creating a separate universe from the one she's shared with me. A baffled apprehension arises, causing me to ponder one of Moita's earlier statements: "When you fear losing...what you think is yours, anyone who has something that looks different seems a threat." Yet, when Jim comes over the next week as planned to renew our threeness, the same mutual respect and appreciation are still there. And if our experiment is turning out to be more intense than expected, at least it is not superficial or haphazard. The depth of connection of which Moita spoke previously is beginning to surface.

Moita session #171 (Kelly, David, Jim / January 17, 1981)

Jim: I had a very intense dream experience a few years ago at the time of my last operation. I was still taking God knows what kind of drugs for the pain. I dreamed of meeting a woman with bright white light shining out of her eyes. When I saw the light, she kind of waved her hand and the two of us were floating off somewhere, out of our bodies. For a time she instructed me about astral travelling. Then, after I failed at returning to my body on my own, she escorted me back and I woke up in the hospital room, remembering clearly every bit of that dream. In some ways that seems to have foreshadowed some of the events of the last year. I wonder if you can tell me about the lady with the light in her eyes. *(pause)*

(Moita looks away from Jim to help Kelly channel the message.)

MOITA: Sometimes the things that we do on other levels are difficult to explain. *(pause)*

When we are in the process of moving people, influencing people to move from one place to another, in order to instill the desire, the motivation, in the right direction, we take our . . . *(laughs)* – there's not a good word for that – . . . "pupils" (?) on excursions when they are sleeping, and sometimes when they are not.

There is a part of the astral body that carries a great deal of the subconscious with it. Under certain circumstances it is very easily separated from the conscious body and is not generally missed. It can be instructed, although it has no conscious memory of the experience when it returns and rejoins with the conscious. However, the subconscious is a powerful influence on the conscious mind. Slowly these experiences, though unremembered, rise up to the surface and begin to move things in the right direction, the desired direction.

We have spent a number of years slowly moving all of you in this direction. Dreams of mountains, encounters with astrals who have no memory, questions that need to be answered, experiences that force a looking deep within, many birthings, some deaths.

You wonder if the lady with the bright eyes is Kelly – *was* Kelly. She is, unknowing to her, a teacher on the astral planes, has been one for many years now, has encountered many people. There were many blocks to *this* one. *(soft laughter; pause)*

Jim: In the dream, it was as if I surprised her. It wasn't as if she was there to meet me or anything like that. She seemed kind of shocked and almost dismayed that I noticed the light shining out of her eyes. *(laughter)*

MOITA: I told you we are tricky. There are many approaches. It is one way to find out if you are conscious enough of what is happening . . .

Jim: Hmm.

MOITA: . . . for it to be of any use. Test.

Jim: In the dream, there was another woman I know who took me to meet her.

MOITA: There are many people on the astral who have met and who know each other well, and yet may never meet [physically]. *(pause)*

Jim: Who would have put the blocks there?

MOITA: To the answer to this question? *(laughs)* She has not as much faith in her ability, since she remembers it not. It is also somewhat unsettling to her concept of reality.

Jim: When I awoke, I did have the strong sense that something was coming, off in the distance. I didn't know where, though. *(pause)* It was a very intense dream...

(Near the end of this three-way session, Jim looks over toward me:)

Jim: Somehow this feels more balanced than before – that somehow your and my entities . . . I feel their presence much more than previous sessions.

MOITA: That is because you have taken a step into the unknown. It is helping to open your own faculties of perception.

Jim: When you step off into the unknown, you've got to be alert.

MOITA: *(laughs) Very.* It definitely is not meant to make you feel safe.

Jim: But it feels more like there's three of us here, more than before when it's been sort of Moita and we are experiencing *her.* From my perception, it feels like we're all here this time. *(pause)*

MOITA:	I think it is time for me to go now, before David falls asleep.
David:	No.
MOITA:	No? Your mind looks somewhat hazy.
David:	I've been feeling Loria close and sort of sinking into that.
MOITA:	Hmmm.
David:	It's probably hazy too. It's a nice haze.
MOITA:	You can enjoy it while I'm gone...

(She closes Kelly's eyes. We have lots to talk about afterwards:)

Kelly:	What was the question from Jim that she was saying I had all the blocks about?
David:	About your astral.
Kelly:	Oh!! How could I forget that?!
David:	Because you don't want to *remember*. *(laughter)*
Kelly:	I can remember I was out there when you started talking about it, and I thought "Uh-oh." I looked at Moita in my head and I said, "Was that *me*?! *No. Couldn't* have been! Oh, come on!" I didn't know what I was talking about – I could only hear my half of the conversation! *(laughing)*
David:	Gee, that suddenly makes me wonder if you appeared in *my* dreams long before I knew you. I mean as a teaching figure – like the woman who taught me how to fly.
Kelly:	Oh, you had one too?
David:	Yep. *(laughter)* Yeah, a really nice lady, and she took me up to her space station.[124]
Kelly:	Oh *no*!!
David:	She taught me that it was thought that directed flying – that it was done with the mind, not the body. It's quite likely it was you, if you've been out there teaching lots of people.
Kelly:	Oh-h-h-h . . . Screech!! Let's stop this! What am I doing teaching people I don't even know and have never met?! *(laughing)*
Jim:	It's funny that I never mentioned that to you guys until I did to Kelly the other day. It's like I'd almost forgotten it. Yet that's exactly the kind of thing we've talked so much about. Why is it that I didn't bring it out before?
David:	Kelly didn't want you to talk about it.
Kelly:	Or maybe there were other things that had to come out first. *(laughter)*
Jim:	*(to me)* I was really feeling something larger where you were sitting.
David:	I certainly felt more of a closeness and a presence in all of us.
Jim:	Your shadow on the wall was fascinating me. When I closed my eyes, I was seeing the shadow as larger than you, and it became identified with higher levels.
David:	Well, I certainly was feeling Loria's presence through the whole session more than usual – a lot of touches all around my head. It was quite nice.

(And Kelly will say later that she was very aware of all three of us together interacting during the session. She felt the tapestry of past lives among all of us. She was aware of Jim and her being souls with a similar energy, and of her and me being souls with complementary energies.)

やや やや やや

"The buds are slowly opening," Moita tells Jim on January 17th, as he sees Kelly's face changing to that of a shared past life. In fact, between the winter solstice and Christmas I have guided both Jim and Kelly in separate hypersentience sessions, using each other as the focus. Jim found her in one of his African lives, and she saw him as an African shaman. He also experienced his part in the life Mike once glimpsed, known to us as Kelly's medicine woman in the Pacific Northwest – a life that she powerfully dreamed about ("Vision of Glowing Feather") while still in Regina, as described in Tales of Power #1, with more coming in #5.

Kelly's regression showed several and hinted of many incarnations shared with Jim – including her life starting as the visionary country girl, as recalled during her very first hypersentience.[125] In another, the "tower and meadow" life in which she was my daughter,[126] Jim was a hermit who occasionally came to visit and play his pipes for her after my death. Finally, Jim's love of popular music in this present life – and his extensive tape collection, from which he selects for Kelly's visits – will lead me to suggest he was the one in Musili who put the music into her magical wall. As Kelly described during her Musili regression, "It is a music that soothes me and thrills me at the same time. It changes my heart."[127]

やや やや やや

Previously held ideals and concepts must change to accommodate what it means to have shared in many ways with many throughout time. But each must learn for himself what is the best route.

There is a great deal in you that is being brought into the light. You are beginning to learn how to illuminate your darker corners, chasing out your shadows.

– Moita (January 4 & 17, 1981)

There are a great many purposes at work in our situation: for each individual, each pair, all three, and beyond. What I can write about these changes inevitably reflects my own perspective and learnings, since from now on I increasingly lose touch with aspects of Kelly's experience. Clearly, though, the differences in us that surfaced at our housewarming party are placed now within a crucible, a vessel for alchemical transmutation. As in any true metamorphosis, the end result will take time to unfold and become conscious for us: the two, and the transforming third.

One thing that will begin to emerge but will take years to really sink in for me is that attraction of one person to a new partner need not be a judgment upon the original one, but a reflection of growth purposes to be served by the new relationship. And growth involves facing both the dark and the light within oneself. Thus Kelly and Jim will discover that intimacy with someone very similar in energy allows them to pull many a shadow into the light – to befriend and transform it at last into joy. Kelly finds that the manifold personal discoveries and experiences she is undergoing require a journal all to themselves – and she struggles valiantly to keep up with them. Jim feels that these new links are a kind of anchor through this painful period in his life, which began a year earlier when his partner of several years and their newborn, beloved daughter began living apart from him.

As men with rather different energies, Jim and I have the greater communication barriers to overcome, despite some striking parallels in our individual histories. Yet, conscious of the tragically destructive patterns men have played out against each other through the centuries and in timeless legend – Arthur, Guinevere and Lancelot come to mind – we strive toward conveying and accepting each other's inner experience: two former war resisters closing in on the roots of war.

For myself, I can at times lapse into apparently negative spaces and selves – jealousy, resentment, closed-mindedness – as I sometimes perceive the spiritual link of our threeness degenerating into two against two, or two against one. Knowing firsthand the difficulty of balancing two realities and relationships, I have to appreciate the sincerity and love with which Kelly responds to my pain and doubts. In turn, I try to be honest about what seem my own rightful needs. Thus I express that it would be only fair for Kelly and Jim to take the children with them on their once-a-week visits together, rather than expect me to be the child-minder, and to this they readily agree.

Unexpectedly, as more dimensions and potentialities of the situation dawn on me, including new opportunities for solitude, I begin to feel exhilarated. One scene crystallizes this for me: walking on bright sunny days upon the frozen, snow-covered river below our cabin, overhung by towering fir trees, as ravens fly and call overhead. This newfound freedom to remember/recreate myself will also give new impetus to sharing my dream-weaving soul with others. As the year progresses, I will deliberately seek opportunities to let my own light shine, rather than relax in the shadow of Moita and Kelly as I have too often in the past – and will marvel at the heartwarming results.

In early spring, another free day offers a lesson in intuition – wrapped in a good story. It begins as I put a blanket, books and lunch in a hiking pack and set out walking along the river. I find an old spruce a little way back from the river cliff and spread my blanket at its needle-covered feet. I meditate, leaning against the tree in the quiet afternoon, and imagine that I'm being so still, I might turn and see the face of an unwitting bear, who wouldn't have known I was there. Then I cast an *I Ching* oracle for my day, which yields hexagram #7 ("Army") changing to #4 ("Youthful Folly").

The first hexagram indicates danger hiding beneath the surface, like water seeping underground or a well-disciplined, powerful army. The commentary on one of the six lines reads: "In face of a superior enemy, with whom it would be hopeless to engage in battle, an orderly retreat is the only correct procedure, because it will save the army from defeat and disintegration." But even as other lines refer to "corpses", I fail to get any definite message, literally or symbolically. The "Army" then changes to "Youthful Folly": "Stopping in perplexity on the brink of a dangerous abyss is a symbol of the folly of youth."[128]

Still wondering what my day's lesson will turn out to be, I take a further walk. When I return, I lie down 50 feet or so from the spruce on a rock overlooking the river. I stay still for at least 20 minutes. Then, feeling hungry, I rise and head toward the lunch left in my pack under the tree . . .

Suddenly, there's a sound and flash of movement near the tree, where I now glimpse a full-sized black bear turning from my pack and – obviously frightened at the sound of an intruder – jumping up to the first large limb, from which it then hangs rather comically by its forepaws. Realizing I'm facing a real, live, earthly danger, I start putting more distance between us. When I look back, the bear has come down and is again snuffling through my lunch. Finally I decide to just leave the area, letting the bear do what it will. Thus, an "orderly retreat" in the face of "a superior enemy" rather than continuing my "youthful folly". Please, no "corpses" today!

When I return after supper in the cabin, I find no trace of my lunch *or* of my aluminum-framed pack! Fortunately, the bear was less interested in my books, which are now mostly just tossed about on the rumpled blanket. But of those, it's the *I Ching* that's damaged – some pages torn or ripped out, the binding broken and the cover chewed. Appropriately, several ripped pages are from hexagram #21 ("Biting Through")!

Therefore the lesson of my day: even you, David, channel true intuitions; so in meditations and oracles, take seriously the messages you're given – always considering literal possibilities! To help remember this, I will never replace my punctured, broken *I Ching*, but keep it as a proud memento – of the bear whom I frightened before frightening me . . . the bear who I suppose must have hiked away with my pack strapped to his back!

ço   ço   ço

Meanwhile, as winter turns to spring and then summer, Kelly's and my couplehood is gradually and meticulously being taken apart, enabling us to see more clearly the difference of our "two pillars" – our respective channelings of spirit – and our independence and individuality. As I will associate my Raven life and dream with the freedom of soaring above past attachments, seeing clearly again in the sunlit air; so Kelly will associate her herbalist "good witch" life with the rich earthiness of her nature. The earlier, perhaps wilder gypsy phase of this life, shared with past incarnations of Jim and Mike, now comes to the fore, helping her release the repressions she has sensed within. Nothing helps my feelings more than seeing the rightness of the pattern – that different does not mean better or worse – and that by clarifying our differences we are enriching our polarity: Sun and Earth, mind and manifestation, aloneness and togetherness, individual and group.

For the present, it is sufficient for me that some of the energy I'd invested in our twoness is returning to me, building my strength so I can let others be, while enjoying what is irrevocably my own. Simultaneously, Kelly and I grope towards a new form of relationship – something always changing as more elements come to consciousness. Through the various negative sides of this experience, the sense of positive yet remains – almost *because* of the negative, and in living tension *with* the negative, for the two together are so effective in pointing the way ahead.

This is an ongoing change – like a prairie fire – that, just as Moita predicted, occupies much of

Kelly's and my attention throughout 1981, and continues past another New Year's. Thus do we encounter – in our own way, and once again – many of the conflicts and choices which friends of ours have been asking Moita about in recent years.

Moita session #178 (Kelly and David / March 15, 1981)

(This is one day after my 34th birthday, preceded on the 13th by a largely symbolic but quite meaningful hypersentience experience guided by Kelly.)

David: Do you have any comments on the way Kelly has become more conscious of her astral experiences lately? Very often in these, and also in dreams, she's contending with a lot of intrigues, spies, enemies, etc., often in the context of flight and space travel. What's the nature of the forces she's dealing with?

MOITA: Well . . . *(we laugh)* . . . A lot of it has to do with her own inner battles with authority. She is usually the spy battling undercover, behind the scenes.

David: Against her own inner authorities?

MOITA: Yes. Attempting to take more control away from them. There are many things here that need to be dealt with, and there are many levels of mind involved. The out-of-body experiences are her discovery of one of the levels where these dreams originate, becoming more conscious of the dream process, and in that sense becoming more in control *of* it. And there are fears. You always have more fears to work through.

All growth goes in cycles. You make great strides forward and then, thinking you have arrived, end up sliding back down the hill some ways, until you realize you are sliding and turn around and start to climb one more time. Mostly you are going more uphill than down. But, as the seasons, it is to be expected. You learn, and then must assimilate. Then you are ready to learn more and build upon what you already know. *(pause)* This is just a natural progression, just as inevitable as spring...

David: The last few months, I've repeatedly lost touch with my wholeness and experienced a lot of doubts. And I've realized how over the years I've gone through cycles, and cycles within cycles, of knowing who I am, where I'm coming from, and then almost choosing to let go of that awareness in order to plunge into some experience that will threaten it or be new, anyway. Sometimes that goes farther than intended, so I really *do* get lost, but then eventually recover my perspective again. Do I choose to lose touch with my centre in order to feel . . . in order to learn things?

MOITA: There is a fine line between centredness and isolation. You seek a balance between allowing yourself the freedom to experience and keeping your centre at the same time. If you *are* centred too much into self, you will lose touch with the world around you and with those who are in the world *with* you. When you are truly centred, it is not difficult to reach out and enfold another, for then you are not afraid of losing your self. It is just a different focus, and when you turn around you are still there and are richer for having had an experience.

David: Mm-*hmm*. *(pause)* Yes, being truly centred doesn't mean isolation, doesn't *have* to mean being alone.

MOITA: And it does not mean being afraid of losing something.

David: And I can lose my centre whether I'm being alone or with other people. *(pause)* I guess what I was sensing was that I seem to go through periods when I feel I need to stretch myself. And so I agree to certain changes, consciously or not, which mean I deal with a lot of emotions that pull me from my centre.

MOITA: It is a cleansing process. Just as the body needs to become less dense, so does the heart and the mind. It *is* a stretching, learning to accept change in yourself as well as others.

David: And what surprises me is that, in working through things to reach some new stage, I tend to forget awarenesses that I've had years ago. Then I come back to them and have to ask, "How did I lose touch with *you*?!"

          I also want to ask about the blazingly bright angel in my hypersentience, who brought the message of the Light coming back into the world through the heart of man. There was so much energy to it. What can you tell me about that presence?

MOITA: *(long pause; then slowly:)* It is very much an archetype, a representation of your need to fulfill your pledge and to remind yourself of your own connections with other levels from within. *(pause)* Much of it is . . . your own soul-creation. *(pause)* It fulfilled a need in you for contact. In many ways you feel unworthy and left behind. Part of you does not see your contribution, does not understand your talents, does not accept your own uniqueness.

David: *(after a long pause)* I know those are all true. When you say my "soul-creation", you mean a lot of it is a symbol created by my soul to express that contact? *(Moita nods)* Can you say any more about my "pledge"?

MOITA: *(laughs and coughs; long pause)* Some of it you know already. In fact, most of it you know in different parts of yourself, for you would not have been led here; you would not have put yourself through so many difficult situations; you would not have kept it up, retained your faith in the universe, in beauty. You are trying to learn more of what the world is, of what you want to make the world; and in that search for a true reality, many things that are merely appearances will fall away. *(pause)*

          The two of you have come into this life in order to learn the balance between the Sun and the Earth. It is not something you will be able to discover alone. Learning how to share and accept differences as well as similarities will prepare you for a new world. You want to be here when it begins. *This has been its beginning. (pause)*

          The more you learn to set aside your doubts and your fears, the easier life, change, growth, will become. It is all in how you look on it – and you are the one who chooses.

ও   ও   ও

Though Jim, Kelly and I are breaking new ground in our own lives – not only in *what* but in *how* we are doing it – we acknowledge our part in a "conspiracy" (a "breathing together") pursuing similar directions all over the planet in these times. Witness this woman, writing in a Quaker newsletter, quoted by Marilyn Ferguson in *The Aquarian Conspiracy*:

> We will recognize that each person needs to nourish and be nourished by many persons, and we will not seek to restrict them through fear. We will know that we can only keep that which we set free... We recognize ourselves as members of the family of human beings. It is right, even necessary, to make [ourselves] available to one another in new loving, caring, and fulfilling ways – without the spectres of old guilts at loving widely.[129]

Always in conjunction with the personal dimensions of our change, we wonder what our discoveries imply for community. Comm-unity: how to make a whole with others; *and*, how to be whole in oneself, with or without others. Perhaps, in abstraction, neither comes first. But for each of us the polarities will forever be moving into and out of balance – always a next step to take deeper into what can seem a coincidence of opposites. This tension gives us *life*, as no static structure or stereotyped ideal ever can. And the parallels to Regina in 1978 strike me with the force of *déjà vu*.

There were Ruth and I, locked into an image as prospective founding couple of a community-to-be, the authoritative source and model with their respectability to uphold, the initiators who should have reached a level of maturity and spirituality which excludes further challenges, already knowing the basic outlines of what is to follow. These everyone else can either like and join (whereupon the initiators must prove their ability to "make it happen"), or dislike and reject (as one more "cult of personality"). Such is the idolatry which even Peter and Eileen Caddy and Findhorn Community members have had in recent years to shatter – in order for them all to breathe more freely and pursue wholeness in their own ways.[130]

Otherwise, the hopes of many for a personal New Age would seem to depend upon the spokespersons, authorities, gurus – and how *they* define *their* lives; whereas, in truth, that hope and that self-definition are responsibilities that only each can bear for him or her self alone. If Kelly and I can at times be catalysts (and Jim too, obviously!), it is only because we are continually and often unknowingly "arranging" these tests: whether we can remain open to sharing our deepest selves rather than walling them off; whether we can recognize the spirit's workings even when that clashes with our own or others' expectations about the path ahead. "Leaders", it turns out, too often end up being ruled by their "followers".

We do not escape some of these latter pressures during 1981, as in some ways our actions do not match others' images of what channels for the New Age should be. And sometimes we are perceived and criticized for trying to be models or leaders in ways we don't at all intend or wish to be. There are opportunities here for learning from *both* sides of these episodes, if we can remember – despite our different starting points – that we are seeking to grasp the same dimly lit maze, all groping for the same clues that, when put together, can set the whole alight.

This year we lose a friend who was close both to us and to Moita – partly on account of these changes in our relationship, which are perceived as contrary to Christian morality. Doubtless Terry is not an isolated case.

Moita session #187 (Kelly, David, 3 others / June 29, 1981)

David: How is Terry feeling about us? We haven't heard since his letter in which he . . . was feeling pretty distant.

MOITA: Threatened. He was feeling threatened. *(pause)* It is a common reaction whenever your concepts of reality are challenged, whenever your expectations are not met. To be open to the truth as it is instead of as you wish it to be: that is wholeness.

He is here to learn how to change not what he believes for himself, but in accepting how others believe for themselves as valid for them. There are many tests you each go through. This is a time of testing – more so than other times – since the vessels that will be here in [time of] need will be more important than they have been at other times. Their clarity or their unclarity will greatly affect the outcome.

Souls are being pushed, forced to face parts of themselves that they have buried and hidden. Your unique situation goes against preconceived notions of morality and truth. He is beginning to see this, beginning to feel more at ease with himself, but he still cannot let go – let go of structures, let go of the past, let go of his own reasons for being here, his own need to sacrifice himself. Part of him fears that he will be disintegrated, lost, dissolved, absorbed – a loss of individuality. *(pause)*

It is a crisis point. *(pause)* The question is: Can he accept love, or will he continue to fear it? You have accepted and been transformed into wholeness. And yet, you have not lost your individuality or your uniqueness. You have gained – both of you, all three of you.

David: It's definitely worth it.

MOITA: Life becomes a celebration.

ও ও ও

Given the circumstances of our coming together in this life, Kelly and I want to ensure we are not deceiving ourselves but truly learning the lessons of love *and* freedom – in relationships and elsewhere – seen from each of the possible perspectives. There are complementary lessons here, and another person's current learnings may not resemble ours in the slightest. But we do have reason to care about each other's openings. So I want to say: let us celebrate the breaking open of all the idols, wherever they occur, by those whose destiny it is to break them, that the spirit of truth and wholeness be renewed and flow more strongly from our hearts.

Can we live without our idols? Can imperfect people of many different outlooks join together in harmony without a charismatic leader who inspires, and entertains, and enslaves according to his own pattern? It strikes me now that true community can come about only in that absence, which *is* an emptiness – an openness to who we are as a creative mystery-self in the ever-present now.

If Kelly and I have any gift to give those who may invite us into the community of their presence in coming years, I hope it will be in helping to dispel such illusions. A community truly belongs to no one; it lives only in individuals, both alone and together, leaving behind the congealed past to explore their *next* reality, a new integration of living forces. In this there can be no preconceived or untouchable structure. The "sacredness" of such a "place" will lie in the respect it grants each person to choose a way of life, a spectrum of relationships and a manifestation of Self that suits her or his turn on the spiral journey.

The alchemical opus is the work of individuation – which means, as Teilhard de Chardin once wrote, "to establish, in and by means of each one of us, an absolutely original center in which the universe reflects itself in a unique and inimitable way."[131] The complementary emphasis is just as valid: that an original and unique centre becomes possible for us only as we discover that the whole of the universe is indeed open to our touch everywhere, both without and within.

That is the direction of our essential learnings this year: such a heightened awareness of our different, separate selves – and yet also, such new levels of merging! And the same is true *within* each, as the different personalities we have been, the different energies we have tapped in other places and times, grow more alive and vivid, seeking integration and expression in this present life's focus as well. Thus it is that we come upon new spirit names by fall – names better able to channel these energies: Siofra Bradigan ("spirited elf") to eclipse Kelly, eventually for all purposes; and Ravenstar, or Raven Sky, to stand behind the David of daily life.

Too often, the goals of spirituality and community have been co-opted by authorities – outer as well as inner. They have become, at times, ideals that hang above our heads, judging whether our inner beings measure up. Yet these and all their derivatives are precisely the structures we need to let go, if we would truly start to build from the bottom, creating our own ways of touching Earth and Spirit and each other.

We must find where it is that we stand, as whole beings alone and together. Is it a structure to which we retreat, or is it a finer and finer line – perhaps only a ray of light – that we travel, deeper into the centre of life? How can we be both strong as a pillar and bending as a willow? The foundation for any community is strong individuals – which to me is coming to mean individuals able to accept freedom – one's own and each other's, the mystery of creation as an act of love. Is that a foundation for a new world?

Our evolution may proceed at times, outwardly speaking, from one extreme to its opposite – from all-out conflict to miraculous union. Thus, in the midst of otherwise happy times during the summer of 1981, the tension in Kelly's and my relationship, triggered by her other universe with Jim, reaches a breaking point. I become very concerned that all we have worked for, and our partnership itself, are being left by the wayside. Neither of us wants this to happen, but our struggling to preserve them comes out distrustfully as an attack upon each other and as a moving apart.

In late July, we are scheduled to begin a series of Moita sessions and readings in the Okanagan Valley. Temporarily, our conflict is submerged as our work begins: a large open-house talk and session (excerpted in these chapters), followed by several days of appointments. Nevertheless, "fate" arranges a free evening out of a booked-up schedule and frustrates our every attempt to spend it at the movies (we never find the theatre!). We are left by ourselves to talk, speaking out of our conflicting worlds . . . strangers who no longer have any common ground, or so it seems . . . until the non-words of the heart break through the gathering gloom.

Suddenly we find ourselves face to face, literally only inches apart, searching each other's eyes, and finding to our surprise that we are recognizing and being recognized as if for the first time. Touching and embracing, love penetrates to those inner levels of fear and self-doubt that only our conflict could have uncovered. Our sharing is deep because of our estrangement. How well does darkness reveal the light! Our trusting – our "natural bridge" – is restored . . .

A week later, near the end of a group session in another city, Moita turns to me with one of her cryptic questions.

Moita session #195 (Kelly, David, workshop group / August 7, 1981)

MOITA: And what have you thought so far of all of our plans?

David: "Plans"?

MOITA: You have looked through them.

(We laugh, as I am still confused.)

MOITA: I told you that this would be an interesting journey and that things were planned for you *in* it. And *now* I am asking how you have experienced this interesting journey that we have helped you to arrange.

David: Um, in a lot of ways I feel we've sort of hit our stride now, and I can imagine things just flourishing from here on.

MOITA: Energy has a tendency to build on itself. *(pause)* It is good that you are learning how to touch another's mind. It is a step in the right direction.

David: Do you see that happening especially in my hypersentience work with people?

MOITA: Hypersentience work is benefiting *from* it. Have you deciphered the riddle yet?

David: "Touching another's mind" – on another level?

MOITA: Not necessarily. You had an encounter not long ago, in the Okanagan, where you and Kelly met . . .

David: Yes.

MOITA: . . . *truly* met. This is the experience I am referring to.

David: And you see that as a meeting like we haven't had before?

MOITA: Not in this life.

David: Hmm.

MOITA: That was a very special meeting. That was the creation of a reality. And from it you can draw a great deal of strength.

David: Yes, we can do that. I can see that.

MOITA: You will know that you never really left. And the more you recreate it, the more real it will become – just like this. *(i.e. just as these sessions build upon themselves)*

You are learning *how* to create your own reality – as a *fact*, instead of a concept. And it becomes more and more your own creation as time goes on.

David: I'm sure glad that's there.

MOITA: This helped bring that about. You have *all* changed a great deal with being exposed to this energy.

ဢ   ဢ   ဢ

As life moves on, the end of August finds me again expressing my feelings about what seems to be getting lost in Kelly's and my relating, and Kelly voices to me more of her experience as well. Then we and Jim have a very clear, loving talk and agree together on other practical arrangements that I have requested. It is good for me to work these things out on the home front as I prepare to teach a psychology class through the local community college. Still, my body lags behind, strained by all the changes.

Moita session #199 (Kelly, David, Jim, Margaret / September 4, 1981)

David: What can you tell me about why my shoulders and neck have been so extraordinarily stiff the last couple of weeks?

MOITA: Your body is having difficulty adjusting itself to a higher level of energy. *(pause)*

David: Specifically coming through the energy centres in that area?

MOITA: The connection that you two have made together is activating your centres. All of them are involved. There is a block that has begun to dissolve in your throat centre. It has been pent up for a long time, and as it is released it causes this discomfort. It is a good sign that it is being released, that it has opened. It is your speech centre, your ability to communicate your thoughts to others, to feel *free* to communicate your thoughts, to express yourself, to have in some way control over your environment, learning to create your own reality.

It is very similar to what happened to Kelly when you two first met and her sciatic [nerve] went out – only yours is in a different place.

David: Yes, a lot of that fits. And I'm aware of the influence of that change spreading out into other areas of life.

MOITA: Your coming teaching position is at the appropriate moment for you to have an outlet to release some of this newfound awareness and energy.

David: Yes, I've been wishing for something like that in the last year, and here it is.

ဢ   ဢ   ဢ

The late summer and early fall do bring a rising spiral of experiences of union on closer, inner levels between Kelly and me, and Kelly and Jim, and also – on rare but memorable occasions, and in a different way – among all three of us. These are indeed the creation of a reality that builds upon itself, outside of physical time. (And the energy that is building is soon to reveal itself in unexpected form.) So it makes no difference if we end by recounting an experience that occurred back in early June – for it is one in essence with every such experience in whatever time: an unfolding of all that community can mean.

From Kelly's journal for June 7, 1981:

David, Jim and I are sitting around the kitchen table after having a delightful dinner alone together. We are all feeling quite mellow and connected, and I suddenly have the urge to link hands and meditate.

We sit there for a while as the energy starts to rise. I become aware suddenly of a number of strong presences in the room with us, and "see" a bright white light flowing out of them onto us, bathing each of us in radiance. The love is vivid, strong and real – so is the understanding, compassion and acceptance.

[David: Three inner images of my own during this meditation are of a flower, a baby, and a cup pouring forth sparkling water.]

Then I open my eyes and look out the window that is directly in front of me, and gasp, because there, hovering in the bushes, I see Moita – a beautiful, blue-white light surrounding her. And for a brief moment I see the world through her eyes. Each leaf is covered with brilliant specks of dancing light – vibrating – and it is <u>so alive</u> and so bittersweet and piercing and haunting all at once; tears roll down my face, and although I am the only one who sees, both David and Jim share in my joy and in the love and wholeness we each feel flowing around and through us in this moment.

Chapter 12

CREATING A NEW REALITY

Only the ones who are unafraid of change, or at least willing to face the fear of change,
will be capable of such a commitment.
– Moita (March 15, 1981)

Jim is not the only Kindle Valley friend with whom a particularly close tie develops over the course of 1980-1981. There is one other . . . through whose personal changes our hope of community will become quite a bit more concrete than before. In March of 1981, though, we are still groping toward this next important connection.

Moita session #178 (Kelly and David / March 15, 1981)
David: It was way back last August that you said we should soon be talking practically with people about community, if we were going to be ready in time. Since then we have come much closer to the personal side of community with Jim, but there seemed to be more levels to your words. Are we now reaching a time when we should ask if people are committed to a physical building of community – or would that be pushing it?
MOITA: It is probably too soon yet to phrase questions as directly as [that]. However, there is nothing wrong with the idea of discussing community in general: what people's concepts of community are or might be; what kind of experiences they have had already; what they have learned; what growth has taken place within themselves; how they see their path. It is difficult to get commitments as yet. But there *are* those who are committed, even when they are not aware of it. Only the ones who are unafraid of change, or at least willing to face the fear of change, will be capable of such a commitment.

୨େ   ୨େ   ୨େ

The openings among Kelly, Jim and me take the place of any specific plans for work together, though our respective strengths might easily be seen contributing to the same centre for living and growth in a New Age direction. Over the next two months, with Moita's words in mind, we do propose the idea of a retreat to discuss experiences and visions of community, possibly to be held out at Sunrise Farm. Unfortunately perhaps, that idea never gets off the ground. Something totally unexpected comes our way, however, on May 12th, from a good friend whose commitment has not been realized by us till now – perhaps not even by her.

Margaret came to the Kindle Valley earlier than some we know, homesteading a farm with her husband and two young children through many hard-working years since the late 1960s. Starting from a conservative religious background, and a determination to make their foothold in the bush a success, Margaret's outer and inner realities eventually collided head-on as her marriage deteriorated. This is how she describes it to us one evening in May:

"All I could see was that there was destruction of some kind going on. All the things I had been building, so many years of work to build something constructive – at least, that's what I *believed* I was doing. And when you see the imminent collapse of the thing you've worked for for that many years, you just literally don't have a thing left for strength. I had abandoned my poetry completely, abandoned all my domestic thing. I'd been such a baker and cooker, and out there feverishly stacking up piles of firewood, and almost feeling guilty if I took any time off. All of a sudden I just let all of that drop. I didn't care about it anymore."

Personal liberation demanded some deep-going change, but for a long time the direction of that change was unclear. Only one new interest sustained her: she had found Jane Roberts's Seth books.

"At night I'd hit the Seth books and fall asleep with them for months and months and months. And I was beginning to sound like a record, trying to find any poor sucker who would lend me his ear and have it poured full of Seth! *(laughing)* But that was my only worthwhile reality. I stopped thinking about the future, and started to cut myself away from the idea that I was going to live there and have anything to do with the farm. I had to start this whole divorce procedure in my head before any of it really happened, so that I could *bear* it, when I knew inevitably that down the road, not very far away, it was coming.

"You guys arrived in the valley here just maybe a month after I left the farm for the first time. I remember hearing about you. I'd been waiting for some opportunity to just get on the train and go see Seth. That's all I had in my head. I had to get there! God, it was a long way away *(to New York State)*, you know, but I *(laughing)* was going to make it one way or another, because I was going nearly crazy, and reading the Seth books was literally my only touchstone with any kind of *hope*."

If Margaret's memory is correct, we were leaving Regina for B.C. at the very time she took her first physical step toward a different life and self. In the winter of 1979-1980 we met Margaret, an intense, determined but also imaginative, artistic woman in her later 30s who had by then returned to the farm. We found her anxious to discuss Seth with us and to begin what became quite a series of Moita sessions. That same winter she casually (or so it seemed to us, at least) mentioned that there was vacant land on her farm on which we might build and live, but we gave this little thought since her husband was not in on the invitation.

Our friendship with Margaret expanded for other reasons than psychic communication. We shared her deep interest in nature and in ways of enjoying its gifts of food and beauty. We also appreciated her refreshing openness – as shown, for instance, in all our conversations that lightened an otherwise painful experience for Kelly, as her hip went out while the three of us were on an overnight hike up a nearby mountain that August.

Another experience of pain, this time Margaret's, drew us closer as well. Once, she and Jim decided to stay the night in our log home after sharing a Moita session. Margaret ended up on a temporary bed downstairs not far from the wood heater. A few hours after we'd all gone to sleep, repeated shrieks shattered the stillness. Margaret must be having a nightmare, I instantly decided, though I would have thought she'd woken herself up by now! It turned out this was an *awake* nightmare – an excruciating pain in one of Margaret's ears, with the added horror that something seemed to be chewing into her brain! Probing with a Q-tip quickly proved the wrong tactic, agitating whatever was in there, prompting more screams.

Three remaining adults, and we couldn't think what to do about an apparent creature inside our friend's head . . . other than get Margaret into our truck for the long drive to the health station in town. So I drove, with Jim in the middle to comfort and restrain Margaret as needed, preventing any delirious flailing from sending us off the road.

Thankfully, the nurse at the station did know what to do first – pour oil into Margaret's ear to drown the intruder so it no longer moved. Then the on-call doctor arrived and with light and proper instruments extracted a now-dead tiger beetle. This striped beetle – to my memory, at least a half-inch long – must have come into the house on the firewood stacked near our heater, and found a warm, moist cave to crawl into. Before we headed home, the doctor offered Margaret the beetle corpse as a souvenir – which she accepted, resolving to write a poem about it someday.

ॐ ॐ ॐ

Now it is May 1981 – a year in which a U.S. astrologer has informed Margaret a "miracle" will happen for her. Margaret has been living in town for months, part of the time with an Indian male artist. She has let go of many past attachments and begun to create a new life. It is becoming clear she cannot go back to live as she once did on the farm. Yet she loves the land, her children and friends, her poetry, drawing, print-making, batiking and other crafts. She decides that with the divorce she will return to occupy her part of the family land, living in a house built for herself. And as a start toward creating community, she invites us to move and build there as well!

Thus in one stroke Margaret cuts through our thick fog of doubt and uncertainty how we will ever find and afford our own land for the centre that we feel is meant to be. The many ways this arrangement might meet the needs of all concerned leave us breathless – but we hesitate to even believe it yet. We think the higher-level manoeuvrings that obviously have been arranging this should perhaps be left alone for a while more to solidify their creation, without our blundering in and upsetting what seems such a delicate possibility. Nevertheless, Margaret's old determination is coming back in full force behind her new project. And Kelly dreams of travelling into the future through a series of six concentric crystal balls: finding a clear image of our community growing up right there where Margaret is envisioning it.

A week after Margaret's offer is extended, we gather with the intention of discussing the many physical-level possibilities that have suddenly begun buzzing about our heads. Moita's response takes in some of the more dire probabilities ahead for this part of the world, but as usual reminds us of the yet bigger picture spiritually.

Moita session #184 (Kelly, David, Margaret / May 19, 1981)

Margaret: Knowing that things are going to change in the Earth and for many people's lives soon, we've been asking ourselves what we could do now that's practical and concrete to prepare, to be of help. We want to use the time available in a useful way rather than wandering aimlessly in directions that might just be a waste. It seems that, if there is a great upheaval to take place, someone has to be thinking of how to survive it and of what will come after. I'm wondering if you have ideas on this.

MOITA: There are many levels to preparation. First, the physical preparation is the easiest and the least time-consuming in many ways *because* of the fact that they are concrete, touchable, and...you can see probably what needs to be done. Obviously food is an important factor. We cannot guarantee that *anyone* will have stored away enough. But . . . there will be ways opened up to make whatever food supplies there are around at the time stretchable.

(We think this might mean reducing intake by drawing on higher energy sources – and Kelly gets the image of Christ's feeding the 5,000. Materialization would be another interpretation.)

MOITA: You see, it is not just preparing for a disaster. It is also preparing for the changing of the world. We will be closer to you. There will be more cooperation between our levels, and everything you see around you was created by thought.

Margaret: So whatever may be needed on the physical plane could be created by thought to fill the needs that were there (?).

MOITA: Once people calm down enough to tune in. But the other preparations, the *inner* preparations, are the most important, since it will be your inner strength that will sustain your life-force through cataclysmic changes – and help you to adjust to a new environment, a different reality, once those changes have passed by.

Margaret: Might that be one of the reasons I'm going through such change now – to prepare *me*, for instance?

MOITA: Many people are going through many changes *(laughs)* at the moment, for that very reason: to prepare your soul, your life, your personality, your ego, for change. The changes you are going through and have gone through are very small by comparison to what is coming.

Margaret: I'm sure.

MOITA: They are a first step. In this life you have gained much practical experience for physical, everyday things. It is time for you to put much of that behind you now and devote yourself to the inner world. Those talents, that knowledge, will not be lost by being turned away from for a while. When the need arises, *if* the need arises, ish tal . . . *(laughs at her mix-up)* . . . – the energy! – it shall be there for you to draw on. (Mmm! I must concentrate better on this one [speech] centre.) You understand?

Margaret: Yes.

MOITA: Fulfill your soul – it is of prime importance. Even if you do not survive, you will have benefited a great deal from the effort. And then you can return, if you so wish! There is, however, a high probability of your survival *(laughter)* – even if you do not want it *(laughs)* at times.

Margaret: Yes. There have been a lot of times when other people wished they hadn't survived things. What I'm putting a lot of my energy into now is to develop my artistic talents. Would they be of importance or help to those in that kind of a state of upheaval?

MOITA: Will *you* be of help if you are unwhole?

Margaret: I see.

MOITA: What we *need* here are whole beings. We must help to create oneness between people – centredness, balance within. In order to stand on a mountain that is erupting, you must learn the art of levitation! I mean this not in a *literal* sense.

Margaret: Several weeks ago, I had an experience which made me feel very whole for just a few moments – a very high, euphoric feeling which I still haven't forgotten. I'd like to know why I was lucky enough *(laughs)* to have that happen to me, and if I have any more in store.

MOITA: Only if you *want* them.

Margaret: Oh yes, I do.

(From here on, as Moita speaks intently, the energy focused on Margaret and among us all grows very strong – as described afterward.)

MOITA: When a soul reaches a certain stage of development,...when [you] are ready to give in or give up the search, as it were, it is at that moment the doors between the worlds are opened, and *our* energy can flow into your world, your reality. You connected with your greater part, and you also briefly touched the soul of the Earth. We are your strength, when we are opened to. Some people call that grace, that moment.

Margaret: Mmm, that was really a state of grace. I wonder if it was precipitated by the talk I had with the woman on the ferry, that woman that I came to feel so close to in just a few moments. It started just after I talked with her.

MOITA: Yes. *(pause)* You have crossed a threshold into another reality – one where past, present and future are no longer quite as distinct as they have been for you. You have known that woman before, in another life. This was the very first time for you that your soul actually crossed through the barrier of reality around you and touched another you in another life. It was part of that opening of doors. You see, then there was not just you. There was you, and then there was you in another life – which makes you more than you know yourself to be...

(A section is omitted on negative patterns from the past – in this life and in other lives.)

MOITA: There is a door in front of you, and you are ready to take the plunge. You are preparing yourself to walk through the door. You are casting off old values and trying to open yourself up to new ones. And it is a painful process at first. As old skin tears away, the new skin underneath is still tender, vulnerable. *(pause)*

But then, the seed – when its shell bursts apart – experiences a similar pain. Although it is also mingled with the joy of release, finally being able to put your demons behind you, your *own* demons; gaining clarity and learning to live in the moment, *truly* leaving the past behind – not to forget it entirely, but not to let it rule your present as it has so often before.

Margaret: That's a *lot*.

MOITA: I *know*. But there is a great deal of joy coming your way.

Margaret: I'm glad to hear that.

MOITA: I am here to show you that it is possible to leave the past behind. It *does* work and I *know* the process, for I have been through it. It is one of the few things that I *can* do – prove that it works – by being here, by being a light and shining as much as I can, so that even in your confusion, even in your fear and doubt, you can still see a glimmer of hope at the end of a long, dark tunnel of struggle with yourself, with others. The price is worth it, for the gift is the gift of life...

(Near the end of the session, Moita gives us this:)

MOITA: I do have a piece of news. I am sure you have noticed that this source has become more open, more informative.

David: Yes. *(recent sessions bearing this out)*

MOITA: A new cycle is beginning, and it has a great deal to do with preparation. It is a time of action, of doing; a time you have been prepared *for* by our earlier channelings, and by the tests that you each have gone through and the growth that you have allowed yourself to experience. *(pause)* There is still opposition ahead, but not as *much*, or of a different nature than has been. Things are coming together.

David: We have noticed! *(i.e. the links with Jim and with correspondents elsewhere, reconciling letters exchanged with Ruth leading to the visit of her and the boys a month from now[132], and of course, Margaret's offer)*

MOITA: *(coyly)* Be prepared for more surprises! We always keep at least one or two tucked away to keep your life more interesting. I am sure you appreciate our efforts.

David: *(laughing)* You're right!

(From the conversation afterward:)

Kelly: *(laughs)* Oh Margaret!

Margaret: Dear me, how can I stand it?! *(laughter)*

Kelly: That was *great*, it really was. The energy exchange between you two was just terrific. I was basking in this love and warmth. There was the image of a hand reaching out and drawing you upward somehow. I saw her kiss you on the forehead and put her arms around you. And I got a feeling for that "miracle" that that astrologer in the States said was coming up for you this year. Miracles come in many guises, you know! It could be she's talking about an inner miracle. I am just *buzzing*. I feel like I'm on Cloud 9 or something.

David: I had a real feeling for what she was saying about a doorway before you, and you're ready to move through it.

Kelly: It's really neat to be on a threshold. When we're on this side of the door, there may still be fears and doubts about what's going to happen when you cross over. It's an unknown world over there – an unknowable, unpredictable world.

David: What Moita has called "a fairy tale existence".

Kelly: Right, that was what it was like for me one moment during the session – living a fairy tale, seeing things coming together. The energy was like being on the space shuttle or something. And I got this feeling of unreality in the midst of it, like I was watching a play or a movie that someone else was directing, all of a sudden seeing where each of us fits in and each of us is playing our parts perfectly. It was just gorgeous!

(Later, turning to Moita's talk of "a time for action, for doing":)

Kelly: It seems to be people action.

Margaret: Yeah, you've got to have people with really good intentions and willing to give a little and take a little.

Kelly: And work through themselves.

Margaret: Yeah, and work's going to mean something different than material things, as in a lot of communes. Of course, there will be gardens and such, but that's not going to be the end-all and be-all, is it.

Kelly: No. There's got to be something more, or there's no point in building it. That seems obvious.

Margaret: Sort of a mend-a-soul clinic.

Kelly: Right, that's it! *(laughing)* Everyone's there to try to mend his own soul, and help the other guy try to mend his.

Margaret: A real community of people.

ℳ   ℳ   ℳ

A few days later Margaret hits us with another surprise – showing that she understands "a time for action" in other ways too. Her unassailable logic runs something like this: "You've been thinking you may have to move out of this log house you're renting before winter anyway. Why not move into the cabin near my land that I fixed up and stayed in a while last winter? You'd save rent, we'd be closer to each other, and you'd be handy to start building your house on my land the next spring!"

Again, we see manoeuvring at work, offering not only a solution to our immediate practical needs (the chilliness of our house last winter, landlord problems, skyrocketing costs for gas for our long drive into town and for others to come visit us – though we will certainly also regret leaving the beauty of our first valley home). We also see in the cabin idea an opportunity to establish a foothold in physical reality for the new direction Margaret has recently given our dreams. Whatever the difficulties of moving our family of four by fall into a tiny, old log cabin in another fairly isolated location, on Crown land, up a winding, hilly road – though still much closer to town and friends – the energy of it does feel like another "step in the right direction". *[Photo Album #8 and #9]*

Then one week later a bunch of conflictful interactions with valley people crowded into virtually a 24-hour period seem to send this message: don't be led astray by overconfidence now; release your expectations of others and concentrate your energies where they are desired, where a sense of common goals is now strongest. Still, as Moita makes clear, despite the differently perceived hurts of the various personalities involved, we are all in the same boat.

Moita session #185 (Kelly, David, Jim, Margaret / May 30, 1981)

David: A flurry of negative emotions came our way from several friends one day this week, and Margaret too experienced the same sort of things around that time. Is there some group-mind reaction here, or some cycle playing itself out?

MOITA: Any time there is a change in level, there is a battle that must be fought within those who are changing. The Earth's cycles are accelerating. These disruptions on a physical plane will come more frequently as the time grows closer. They are cleansing; they are necessary. They cause searchings within, questions, growth.

There is *always* more than one truth, and each has a part of the truth for themselves. You are seeing more the different truths that others have...of what the world is experiencing. Together you *can* create a balance. There will be turnings-away and leavings-behind when the worlds depart from each other's embrace. Each must choose for himself which world he will go with. You are seeing fear and doubt and learning acceptance.

David: I gather this change is the one you referred to at the end of our last session, leading to a more open channel. How does it relate to the energy changes in the fall of 1978?

MOITA: Those changes that we worked are now being felt. I said it would be some time before the results of those energy changes would be manifest on a physical plane, and that the first such patterns to be disrupted would be weather patterns. We have worked through the weather patterns and have come home to roost in the souls of men, who are now also becoming disrupted and their patterns are changing. They are seeking a new balance. But for a while there will be an imbalance, an apparent imbalance, that always happens when anything shifts from one stage to another. Transition is always wavy, as it were.

David: And one effect, I gather, is we're now more aware of, and maybe actually have, greater power or responsibility to create our reality in ways that we weren't able before?

(Kelly seems to have gotten this message in an out-of-body experience during the last week.)

MOITA: You are seeing not just other people's fears but your own; otherwise, they would not come close enough to your heart to feel. You have doubts as well to work through before you can leave behind the old and embrace the new. All of you together are helping to manifest these things for each other – giving choices, different perspectives, opportunities to see how things work. In that sense you are more responsible for the reality you have created and for choosing how to look upon it: as a lesson of love, or as one of pain.

(Then more softly, and with greater feeling:)

MOITA: There comes a time when any who would teach a spiritual path must be able to look upon [others] with an open heart and accept their fear with understanding and be patient. *(pause)* I have waited through many lives for this one where you become more aware of my presence, where you become a partner instead of a child. And so as you grow into adulthood, and leave behind many things that once were a part of you because you no longer need them, you will become more aware of those things you have left behind and see them in others, where before you did not notice they existed.

David: There's a lot for us to ponder there.

MOITA: And it is only the beginning.

∾ ∾ ∾

During the summer Margaret tells us she needs a new name to confirm her crossing a threshold into new self-awareness. (However, to avoid confusion, we will continue to show her as Margaret here.) During one of the last sessions held in our first valley home, she asks Moita's reaction to this more natural, poetic, lively name. Moita's response applies to any such name change – such as the one that Kelly also, stimulated by Margaret, will soon embark upon.

Moita session #197 (Kelly, David, Margaret, Jo / August 17, 1981)

Margaret: Do you think my choice of a new name is a suitable one?...

MOITA: Names can be very tricky things. Their sounds have certain vibrations. If you name yourself something different, you will *become* something different. For then you will be able to cast aside those traits in you that you associate with the name you bear now and explore what you would like to be – what lies beyond what you know as yourself, as this name. If a name vibrates within you, if it feels comfortable or exciting, then it is probably a good name for a time. As you change, as you grow in awareness, your name can change *with* you. It can help to redefine your reality – who you are, or who you are becoming.

   My name was chosen *for* me for this communication because of a past association...[133N] I have borne many names throughout the history of man, and I will bear many more. And yet, they are all me in essence. *(pause)* You too have had many names already...

Margaret: Do you know where I picked this name from? One is the name of a tree, and the other is the name of an element in nature.

MOITA: Earth names are good names. They help you to resonate with Earth things, and Earth things are not as limited in their scope as manmade things have become. The name you choose, the parts of nature you are drawing from, will become a part of *you*. Their attributes will become yours. That is how the Indians chose their names. They looked into the world, and they saw what things they had an affinity for, what things in nature expressed a certain part of their personality, of their soul makeup.

∾ ∾ ∾

One other session from the summer – actually the first held in the cabin to which we are to move in September – presents a portrait of Margaret, our dear friend and anticipated co-worker, on her many levels. These levels cover the spectrum of changes many are reaching toward, in our own ways, to make the New Age a uniquely personal experience.

Moita session #190 (Kelly, David, Margaret / July 23, 1981)

Margaret: I've done a lot of thinking about the attempt to build a community, and my hopefully helping *(laughs)* rather than hindering. A number of questions are on my mind. I have done considerable worrying about the physical construction of the buildings that we'll want to inhabit and use. Do you know of a shape or form that would be more beneficial for our use than, say, rectangular? Do you perhaps think a pyramid design would be helpful?

MOITA: I believe that one conception of the centre is a pyramid [or] cone. Those types of structures help to focus energy that would be used to encourage inner growth. Tipi shapes will make very good meditation centres.

Margaret: Hmmm!

MOITA: The idea of setting up small buildings or tipis in fairly isolated places where those who feel the need to be alone can go for meditation, for communion with nature, with themselves – that is something that should be thought about and used.

In such an experiment as you are going to undertake, there will be a need for innovation, for reaching into your own creativity, your intuition – allowing the inner to flow into the outer – so that the structures you build will become an extension of your inner self instead of merely a place to put a body.

Margaret: Mm-*hmm*.

MOITA: Letting go of some ideas of what a home should look like will help a great deal, being creative with shapes and form, looking to nature for ideas.

Margaret: Yes. I feel that I personally would like to live in a home where I could look *up*. I spent too many years, I think, in boxes with little windows to look from, and corners that got dark and stayed that way. I conceive of living within rounded, tall shapes – even having trees growing out through my roof, that kind of thing; *(laughs)* indoor gardens, much glass, and bringing the outdoors in, living with it as much as possible in our rather severe climate...

All right, I had for me what I feel is a happy incident this week, making progress with my artistic endeavours *(laughs)*. I was very, very, happy with this opening. Do you see this progressing from there?

MOITA: As long as you are following your heart, things will fall into place – as I have said. You will create those opportunities and experiences around you when you are on your right path. When you are doing what brings you joy, joy will come back *to* you. Energy is always returned, and usually it is returned in more abundance than it is given.

It is the way of the world, when one learns to create one's own reality. This is what you are doing. You have been opened to the concept of creating your own reality many years ago when you first began to read the Seth material. Seeing it now as an actuality, learning how it really does work from your own personal viewpoint, your own personal life, will help you to understand what it is we are talking about...

Margaret: Would you happen to know where I've mislaid my poetry? It's driving me a little crazy. *(laughs)* I'm pretty sure it's close by, but I've looked and I can't find it. Is it here in the cabin?

MOITA: It is quite possible! *(Margaret laughs)* You must learn to let go of worry. You create loss from your worry. When you put so much energy into worrying about things, other things begin to happen to give you something more concrete to worry *about*.

Margaret: I *see*.

MOITA: That is your greatest lesson in this life: learning not to worry so much about the future, about your next step, about possible endings or possible beginnings. You will learn a great deal of that with this experiment you are beginning to undertake.

Margaret: Ho-ho-ho!... *(laughs)*

MOITA: You have learned a great deal *already* in your circumstances over the past year: your not having a steady place to live in and such, and not having a steady income, and so forth. These are things you have created to help spur you in the direction of not worrying, so that you can put that energy you have wasted in worry into more constructive areas.

Margaret: Yes... I hope that I'll be able to reach out and take my freedom in my own hands soon. I can feel a real need to be able to decide exactly what I'm going to do every single day all by myself, willingly and freely. I think that only then will I be able to be really creative – when I have a grasp on my days, and I don't feel the compulsion or need to give part of them to anyone else, because then real giving can start.

MOITA: Giving from the heart.

Margaret: Yes, instead of a sense of obligation.

MOITA: Yes... You are passing through a stage right now, and when you get on the other side of this particular stage in your development you will change your view somewhat. It will be less important to be entirely free to be whatever you want to be in the moment, because you will have gained a *true* freedom and be able to be free no matter where you are or what you are doing or what sort of demands are placed upon you. You will be able to see yourself through it all. You will not be afraid of losing who you are.

Margaret: That will be a really nice place to be.

MOITA: It will be a while yet. But that is what you are going through now, heading in that direction. And many of these questions that you are coming up with are all pointing *in* that direction. But the experiences must come first, and it is through your experiences that you will define the reality that you want, so that you will be able to create it.

Even though it is not wise to have specific expectations about what you want to have in a life, it is important for you to define the type of reality that you will make your own. And in that type of reality that you have created for yourself, things will flow *towards* you. Some people will create a reality in which there is much destruction and guilt and such; and so, they will propel themselves into situations where they do things they feel guilty about, or [where] they are used and so can feel self-righteous about the destruction in their life. And they *create* these walls and barriers.

You must decide whether you want a reality where your barriers are gone, which leaves you vulnerable and open to other people, but also at the same time gives you the opportunity to discover the strength in vulnerability. You have to go through the initial shock first before coming out on the other side, to discover the strength that is hidden in everyone – the *true* strength, the strength that will carry you through *all* of your lifetimes and the in-between states, the one that will propel you into a whole soul, into union with your higher self without fear of losing individual freedom or individuality.

Margaret: That must be one of my big fears, then – losing my individuality (?).

MOITA: It is a very *basic* fear. It is something that everyone must work through at one time or another. The more you understand your own fears, the more gracious you will become, the more you will understand other people's fears.

Margaret: And I will have nothing to lose by giving.

MOITA: Right. And you also will have nothing to gain by judging. It will teach acceptance and understanding, such as I have gained.

Margaret: You are very *here* now.

MOITA: Yes, I am. *You* are very here too!... *(Margaret laughs)*

Margaret: I was going to ask more about my personal preferences for colours. I love bright colours...

MOITA: The love of bright colours is very much an inner interpretation of the love of nature.

Margaret: Mmm.

MOITA: For in nature there are many brilliant colours mixed together in fascinating combinations. And a lot of people are reluctant, or reticent, about combining brightness in articles of painting or clothing or art of any kind.

Margaret: Its intensity frightens them.

MOITA: Yes.

Margaret: It's a little like being alone: you don't know what to do with something so intense.

MOITA: And you have very intense feelings.

Margaret: Yes.

MOITA: You are an intense person. And so, it is natural for you to want to express yourself in intense forms. Through your art and poetry, you try to express that inner part of yourself. The things that attract you are usually an expression of a part of your inner nature, a clue to who you really are...

Margaret: I feel I'd be very happy in an area with lots and lots of sunshine and white sand and rocks. I won't be finding it here, I don't suppose. I guess that's why I like to be down by the river. It does on warm days remind me a little of where I'd like to be.

(On August 23rd, Moita will tell Margaret that she once spent a life as "a willow by the river in

the sun", or that she merged awareness with this willow's life — which will bring instant recognition. And soon a few of us will be told of our lives in ancient Greece . . .)

Margaret: I mean, I don't want to *leave* here. All my heart strings are wrapped right around this place. And there's so much beauty here, I can't imagine there being more somewhere else anyway. To go looking for greener pastures seems futile...

MOITA: True. *(Margaret laughs)* If you cannot find enough beauty to blind you in this spot, you will not find it anywhere else either.

Margaret: I'm sure of that. So we've picked a good place to try our experiment.

MOITA: You have all been led here. You are all here at the same time.

Margaret: Yes, isn't it something!

MOITA: Isn't it amazing!

Margaret: *(laughing)* Well, I'm going to do my best – I hope not try too hard or worry too much.

MOITA: And you will have *me*.

Margaret: *(laughs)* I sure hope you don't leave us!

MOITA: I am not planning on doing so *yet*!

Margaret: Not till we're able to stand on our own feet anyway.

MOITA: At least. But I must leave you *now* . . .

Margaret: Yes.

MOITA: . . . at least temporarily.

Margaret: Thank you for all your help.

MOITA: You are getting much better at asking questions. *(Margaret laughs)* I shall see you again soon.

ဆ   ဆ   ဆ

Do "miracles" ever really happen, and in the predicted time? How can we contemplate what a miracle would mean in one's life – if it truly *is* one, outside the boundaries of our previously known or knowable reality? This fall will bring an answer.

One session yet intervenes. Jim and Margaret join us for an evening of time-travelling through a life we once shared (as told in Tales of Power #5). It is a life as Indians, a life that required dealing with the abuse of psychic powers. Later Margaret wonders to Moita whether her own incarnation was involved in that abuse. Her question leads to the repeat of a frightening perceptual change that she once experienced during a Moita session a year ago. That the frightening experience should recur now reflects an inner block that is almost ready to give way.

Moita session #199 (Kelly, David, Jim, Margaret / September 4, 1981)

(The energy of that other lifetime as Indians, added to this one, has been intense through the session, as Moita turns to Margaret:)

MOITA: How are you doing through all of this?

Margaret: It's pretty heavy. I feel more expanded.

MOITA: Don't worry, you won't lose touch with this reality. Tenuous as it *is*, it is also obstinate...

Margaret: Was I then involved in misusing power that I might have gotten through my position?

MOITA: *(pause)* No. *(pause)*

Margaret: Your face is very mask-like, ominous-looking.

MOITA: You have many fears of using power wrongly. You need to let go of them. What you fear will become a reality – if you fear it enough.

Margaret: What connections would *I* want to make with that life in order to help this one?

MOITA: A sense of acceptance, knowing you belong, connectedness to Earth, to symbolism... You have always had a strong attraction to the Indian culture, the Indian way of things... Theirs is a way that speaks to the heart instead of the mind – an example that shows that the way of the heart can work, and *has* worked; and though the mind that [has developed in this culture now] will change the heart, the heart is still there. You need to believe in the power of the heart to do good, to make change, to learn love.

(Margaret suddenly gasps, then closes her eyes, sighing.)

MOITA: That is what you are *all* here to do, and [to] love yourself first. *(pause)* Many beautiful things in your world have been destroyed because man thinks of himself as an evil being. Man does not love himself – how *can* he love his world? *(pause)*

Margaret: That seems so very *obvious. (pause)*

MOITA: He seeks it all the time. And he seeks in the wrong places, so he cannot find what he looks for. *(pause)* When you all see yourself as beautiful and worthy, your world will be a beautiful place. *(pause)*

Margaret: So we have no enemy, and we have no problems other than those we manufacture in our own hearts... *(pause)*

MOITA: If you *know* your heart, then you can follow it. It is learning to know your heart first that is the most difficult step.

Margaret: Because it means facing the unknown.

MOITA: And accepting your own shadows, as well as your light...

(From the conversation afterward:)

Kelly: Why did you *gasp* like that?

Margaret: Oh God.

Kelly: I thought maybe some sort of a monster had walked into the room!

Margaret: Sitting right there. Your face tightened right up. You had a horrible little gaping hole for a mouth with one tooth hanging around it. Oh, you were just horrible. It changed right into it. I closed my eyes. I didn't want to *watch* anymore.

David: Was that one of many things you were seeing on her face?

Margaret: Well, yeah, it was changing all back and forth. Lots of Native masks, and then this horrible creature, with pale, pale skin. You had one watery, pulled-shut, horrible eye a lot of the time, and one eye that was open and glaring like an old woman with one eye that's gone bonkers.

Jim: That's similar to what *I* was seeing. I saw you get *very* old, old to the point of almost horrible old, but still not horrible. Then it would flash and I would see a young Indian face. It seemed to become a very *long* face as it got older – almost twice as long as now.

Kelly: I was feeling very *tall* there a couple of times, like my energy was extended up. That feeling might affect what you see.

∾   ∾   ∾

As if to underscore that something is up for her this morning slightly over a month later, Margaret falls on her ankle, spraining it badly, just before hobbling up the hill to meet us for this session, joined by a very open woman who has travelled all the way from the Okanagan.

Moita session #204 (Kelly, David, Margaret, Clare / October 16, 1981)

MOITA: How are you doing?

Margaret: Much better, thank you. I sure screamed a lot. I tried to scream the pain away... Am I punishing myself again?

MOITA: You were trying to get yourself back into this reality. *(meaning physical, conventional reality)*

Margaret: Having too much fun in the other one, was I?

MOITA: No.

Margaret: I don't understand.

MOITA: I know. I can see it. Do not put yourself down so much. *(as in guilt for enjoyment)*

Margaret: I've been trying out lots of different methods for [psychic] communication, and trying to change my way of looking at things.

MOITA: *(suddenly very determined)* Then change how you see *me*. Go through your last barrier. See me not as fearful, as you have in the past. Do not be afraid to love. Until you can cross over and see me as beauty instead of as pain and fear, you will continue to do these things to yourself.

(Moita reaches out, placing her forefinger on Margaret's third eye, then lets her finger travel down Margaret's nose and face to come to rest on her heart centre.)

MOITA: Close your eyes. *(in a whisper:)* And open your heart and mind. *Feel* us, let us become one, let us out. Accept. *(whispers again:)* Accept love. Accept beauty, and joy.

(Margaret starts to breathe heavily, in rhythmic gasps, and to cry.)

MOITA: It's all right. You can do it. You know we are *here*. We are about you. Relax. Let it be. *(Margaret continuing to cry)* Relax . . . Good. *(pause)*
     See? There's nothing to be afraid of. Potent, yes . . . Power, yes . . . Fear, no. Just flow. There is no such thing as evil. There is no evil *anywhere* in the universe, except in the mind

of man. So let your heart *rule* you instead of your mind.

Yes. *(whispers:)* You *do* see. *(Margaret nodding, still crying)* Welcome.

Margaret: *(crying) Thank* you.

MOITA: Now your name will *mean* something. Now you can be [new name], and you can let your soul-self out.

Margaret: *(with much feeling)* I don't want those doors to close again.

MOITA: A door that is shattered in such a way is hard to close. *(they laugh)* You may turn your back on the *door*, but you cannot close it again. You can focus yourself in different realities, in different directions, but you will always be able to turn around again, and the door will still be open.

Margaret: I feel really good.

MOITA: You are much brighter than when you came in! Unexpected, eh?

Margaret: *(laughs)* Yes.

MOITA: We have been building up to this for a long time. Step by step, one step at a time, until you were ready for that.

Margaret: It was very beautiful. I'm going to try to write something about it.

MOITA: Fine. It is no less beautiful the next time.

(Margaret laughs. Moita turns to me:)

MOITA: Do you know now what is meant by "The channel is ready"?

(Coming chapters tell the history and fuller meaning of this phrase – which will also explain what is different about "Moita" in this session, most explicitly from this point on.)

David: I have a feeling I'll keep learning more.

MOITA: Most assuredly... *(to Margaret:)* Now you know you are not alone.

Margaret: It's been a monster for me.

MOITA: It is man's greatest fear. But you are *not* alone.

Margaret: I feel like I could do anything.

MOITA: In this moment, in this place, you probably could. This is the in-between place, the place where magic works, where magic is alive. *(pause)*

Margaret: Your face doesn't go bad now.

MOITA: No. You have broken through that one and come out the other side. This is the miracle that you were told of that would be given to you this year, and you have worked for it.

Margaret: *(laughs)* Haven't I.

MOITA: You've also worked against it. *(Margaret laughs)* Yet, in the end, your true nature wins. It always wins in the end.

Margaret: And it's my only real search, for that true nature. Going to keep on looking. I'll never be comfortable if I'm not looking.

MOITA: All things grow, all things evolve. It is only the shell that decays and is left behind. The essence remains – changed, and yet also the same. Do you *like* waking up?

Margaret: Yes. I slept for a long time. I want to be awake every minute.

MOITA: That will be a little difficult . . . *yet*. And yet, you will never again be truly asleep, not as asleep as you were. The moment will fade when you enter "reality" again.

Margaret: I understand about that.

MOITA: But the memory is strong, When you enter *this* reality again, it will be back – alive and well and whole – and gradually you will be able to have more of this there. You want to heal hurts of the world?

Margaret: Some of them.

MOITA: You have made a good beginning by letting yourself be healed.

Margaret: It's very good.

MOITA: When man is healed, [the Earth] will be made whole again. Then there will be no more battles, for there will be no more fear, and man will know he is *not alone*. And so, you will help...by accepting yourself.

Margaret: My acceptance of others will follow.

MOITA: Acceptance of self is first. You will recognize more of yourself in others and, through you, will understand where they are coming from and why they do what they do. You will learn compassion instead of pity. You will gain understanding instead of living in confusion. The world will become bright and clear instead of dark and foreboding, and you will see the meaning of death and its necessity – the births that follow it...

(The conversation afterward reveals more of what actually took place this day:)

Margaret: As soon as I closed my eyes there was this fire or burning sensation which started in my chest, and it just filled my whole body up. All of a sudden I felt terribly vulnerable, and not sad really, just completely overcome by the experience. I felt all trembling and I broke down. Actually, I reached a point where I was hysterical almost. And she said, "It's all right." And so I thought, "Well, okay, it's all right." I calmed down a little bit.

I didn't understand what it was at all, except that it was something really strong, and I was supposed to give way to it and accept it. So I did. And things started to look really nice, and she was just coaxing me along there, telling me, "Now you're feeling it, aren't you," and I said yes. And then she started talking about the door having opened.

It was like a meltdown on my insides. That's the best I can describe it – a great relief. I *felt* like I'd crossed something, like I'd left something behind me, not even fully understanding what that thing *was*. It was probably *many* things: a lot of fear, leftover guilt and self-accusation.

I've just felt really nice since. I feel differently about [a personal situation] just about overnight. It was just a real adrenalin shock which I needed. This time last week I was getting the blues really bad, but I didn't even know *why*. Now that I look back on it, I can see how I was just feeding myself all these leftovers over and over again, reswallowing a lot of the pain that I'd been going through, giving myself one last lethal dosage of it before I was ready to finally not think about it again. She just put the cap on it.

Kelly: So you're not going to see Moita as a demon anymore.

Margaret: I don't think I ever saw her as a demon, but she had power that was threatening. You didn't want to step into it too far, in case you got swallowed up. And that's one of the things that people had been trying to tell me. Several people had been trying to impress me with the idea that maybe I was giving over my mind. I never really wanted to believe that, but they must have had more of an effect on me than I thought. It must have been a basic fear, that I *was* giving up a part of my mind, and I didn't want to. I'd struggled too hard to get my mind back once already, and I didn't want to give my mind to someone else again. Even though I liked what she was giving me, I didn't want to hand over the whole piece of cake to her because my trust was still . . . Well, you know, maybe something could happen to me. Maybe something terrible could happen even from *this*. So I kept that little bit of reserve. It's like having 25 to 30 pounds of cement taken off my shoulders that I've been carrying around all this time. It was really nice.

Kelly: It looked really beautiful from this end. It seemed too that afterwards your perceptions were much more vivid, more clear; that you were picking up on changes much more readily than you have before. You were *noticing* more. You were more conscious of what was going on and the processes involved in your end of things too.

Margaret: It was really quite an experience, and it'll probably be a long while getting the repercussions from that in different ways.

Kelly: I could see how they've been building all of us up for that. Remember when we were talking about the step-by-step kind of thing, and all of a sudden Moita announces that you're ready. This is it! The time has come!

Margaret: It really just gonged me. That was my miracle that was supposed to be raining down on me (?). I was expecting a new Mercedes *(laughs)* or somebody to hand me a nice new body to start over with. But I wasn't expecting anything like *that* at all.

As far as I could see, it was going to be more or less the same kind of thing between her and me and whatever else was out there for quite some time to come, until I was ready. I felt I had a lot more proving up to do. I didn't know I was ready for anything. I would never have said, okay, I'm ready now. I thought to myself, okay, maybe five years down the road.

Kelly: She's been talking about that for a while, that the threshold was there and you had to decide when you were ready to cross it. So it was another part of you that decided it was time to cross the threshold.[134N]

ॐ   ॐ   ॐ

_____

Tales of Power #5

THE MEDICINE WOMAN

It is a struggle that you can end . . . by understanding the enemy within—for there is no true enemy and never was. It has all been a sham.

This is a ritual death, not a real one, that the Earth is going to go through. Death has many parts, and this life is itself an initiation . . . for things to come. Many things are dying and being left behind so that the new can be born. And you have all chosen, of your own free will, to be here and to go through it.

— Moita (September 4, 1981)

On August 30, 1981, Kelly and I receive a long-awaited letter from Elisabeth Kübler-Ross, which she dictated back on June 30th:

> Since I have talked with you by letter the last time, many things have happened. I had an almost-fatal spider bite on my face. I recuperated from that. Four weeks later, on the day before Good Friday, part of my house burned down with many of its beautiful contents. And later on yet, on Father's Day, my two partners, especially Jay, had to be dismissed from Shanti Nilaya... The details of this are much too cumbersome and difficult to describe... I just wanted you to know what big windstorms...we have had here at Shanti Nilaya and that you know we are in very, very good spirits, that we are also feeling a sense of new beginnings and incredible growth and peace...
>
> I would be most happy if Moita would give me a message in terms of her opinion about all the new growth, the new changes, the new spring cleaning, as I call it, here at Shanti Nilaya, and give me some message as to the opinion of the unobstructed world about the choices we have taken.

Thus we learn that in April, even as we were discussing Elisabeth's pro-Barham magazine interview and holding the Holy Thursday session with Moita and Amar about her connection with Jay Barham (Tales of Power #4), Elisabeth was in the midst of dramatic lessons about his perfidy—such as her suspicious house fire on the 16th, the very day of our session. Kelly's hypersentience on Barham in Atlantis came two days later.

In spring 1981, Elisabeth's growing, well-founded distrust of Barham had been provoking him, or whatever possessed him, to strike back. Thus a series of life-threatening events – or "attacks" is likely more accurate – finally convinced Elisabeth she must break all ties. As she would later write in her autobiography (even avoiding to write his full name), "The series of freakish incidents threatening my life – the spider bites, the [automobile] brake failure and the fire – was too close for comfort. I believed my life was in danger... I felt I had to get away from B. and his evil energy."[135]

In response to Elisabeth's request for a message from Moita about her changes and choices, we plan the following session. We decide to invite Jim to add to our energy, and as Margaret (non-accidentally) appears at the moment we are inviting him, we naturally invite her as well. This is appropriate given the events surrounding the four of us in our moves toward community this year. And as seemed true in Kelly's and Carla's regression (Tales of Power #1), we will learn that our joining in this session is actually affecting, and being affected by, ourselves in another reality.

Moita session #199 (Kelly, David, Jim, Margaret / September 4, 1981)

(We four sit holding hands in a circle, with a candle burning at the centre. We close our eyes in meditation and Moita makes her presence known. During some early conversation, Jim feels her energy as "very clear and very solid". Meanwhile Kelly is seeing us sitting around a campfire, with Moita also present. Kelly will say later: "I see her with long, voluminous robes and a tall crown sort of like a pope's headdress. It's like she came as a vision to me in [the life she is going to tell us about]. I start to hear words about what the connection is and that it is important. She also tells me, 'I have appeared to you in all of your lives in one form or another.'")

(Then Kelly feels the energy click, *"like somebody cranked it up about 10 notches." To her, we look "about 10 miles away, all floating up on the air together", with a spinning feeling.)*

MOITA: How was *that* for a change?

Jim: I feel like a vessel.

MOITA: You are floating!

(Long pause as they look at each other. Then Moita introduces the life we are to visit with one of her leading statements, and more to come.)

MOITA: All of you have sat before a campfire before. *(pause)*

Jim: In this same time and place? Another time and place?

MOITA: In another time and place, together. *(long pause)* There is a parallel doorway to what you call the past open at the moment, and it is affecting this life and you are affecting it. This energy here is important to something else that is happening in the same moment in another time.

Jim: So our selves at that other time can make use of some of the energy we are producing here?

MOITA: Indeed, without it there would be a failing. *(pause)*

Jim: Can we still affect choice and probabilities, then?

MOITA: Time is always fluid, including the past. The only thing that makes the past the past is your memory of it. Changing your memory of the past changes the past's effect on *you*. It changes the past itself. What you choose to focus on will become a reality in your present. So choose well what you will remember. *(pause)*

Jim: This is a four-part remembrance. We have to harmonize those four parts of our . . . *(long pause)*

MOITA: This relates to your questions about Elisabeth and Barham. *(turning to Margaret)* And this also relates to your questions about what life, or lives, you and Kelly have shared. These are all interrelated issues from this plane. And it is the medicine woman life.

(The medicine woman life is what we now call the life Kelly remembered in her joint hypersentience with Carla. While that life lies in Kelly's future evolution as a soul, it's unclear when it occurs in the development of the rest of us. Historically, the time is around 900 A.D.)

Margaret: Kelly's medicine woman life?

MOITA: Yes, so it has been termed... *(Margaret laughs)* And Elisabeth is in it, and so is Barham.

David: Hmmm!

Margaret: And all four of *us*.

MOITA: And all four of you.

Margaret: We were Indian tribesmen together (?).

MOITA: Members of the same tribe.

(From pieces received at different times in different ways, we know Kelly is the medicine woman of a tribe of Indians that ranged from what is now the northern Washington/Idaho region into the northern interior of British Columbia, although generally staying to the south in B.C. In Kelly's hypersentience on this life [Tales of Power #1] and in a regression I guided Jim through in December of last year, there are elements of black magic or contact with "dark" spirits. Kelly has the role of spiritual protector of the tribe who must counter these forces with strength, clarity and understanding. From a position of weakness, the tribe has to grow and learn in order to avoid destruction by the power that their lack of balance would give to these other forces.)

David: Can you tell us the story?

MOITA: Barham was cast in the role of antagonist in that life as well. It is a role he has chosen in many lives. He is still working through . . . the pitfalls of power. *(long pause, her eyes remaining closed)* There are still some parts here that cannot be told... *(pause)* He was what you thought of as the enemy, the evil force that was making the tribe move to a new place... *(pause)*

(slowly) But it is a struggle that you can *end* . . . by understanding the enemy within – for there is no *true* enemy, and never was. It has all been a sham. *(long pause)* Recognizing that in this time – letting go of the battle, ceasing to struggle against self – will help to make a new beginning . . . now, as well as then. He needs to be released so he can free himself.

(to Jim:) Your experience in that life – out of body, bondage, trapped, an evil – you visited the inside of your own mind, faced your own fears, were confronted. You died a ritual death, not an actual one.

(According to Jim's understanding of his hypersentience session, he and others were sent by

Kelly, as medicine woman, to physically attack the man who was psychically attacking us, causing fires to consume our land. Simultaneously, Kelly would attempt to stop him from a non-physical level. However, Jim's mission apparently ended with his being imprisoned by beings of the dark side, and seemingly dying in the process. But now Moita clarifies this was not a physical death he underwent but potentially a transformative dying and being reborn.)

Jim: Was it a kind of initiation that I was forced through or that I chose?

MOITA: You were not forced.

Jim: You said before that that hypersentience experience was somewhat garbled and mixed with some other things. But the part of being bound, then, was connected to that life.

MOITA: As with many things that come from that life, it was an experience on an inner plane rather than an actual physical level.

Jim: It didn't seem to relate to the rest of the hypersentience in a physical way. I couldn't understand that. But the memory of that part ended without any resolution.

MOITA: That has to do with the flow of time, or its folds and convolutions. There are certain things that you cannot remember in a past until you have gone through something that releases that connection in a present... *(pause)*

On the inner planes all times are connected. Times of similar energy are all available and open – to investigation, to memory. And as your understanding of the processes involved increases, then your ability to discriminate between the different kinds of experiences will also develop. You will gain more *from* them . . . *and* from [these sessions], for this is an experience that is connected on *all* of the planes at once.

Jim: So, by connecting this moment with occurrences in that life, if we handle it right, we can improve our situation in both.

MOITA: And of course, our input has something to do with it as well, since I am also present in *all* of the lives.

Jim: And so are all of our higher selves.

MOITA: Yes. On my level, they are in the process of becoming one. There are many such groups in the world that are involved in the same process of growth, of evolution. *(long pause)*

(to David, referring to Kübler-Ross and Barham:) You can tell Elisabeth that she is wise to let things go. It is not her responsibility to hold up another. And she is, in some ways, or has been, holding back his own progress by being associated with him so closely. You *each* need to learn to walk alone before you know *how* to support each other in the right way, a way that does not cripple.

She is learning how to let go of crusades. This is the lesson for this part of her life, and I think she is beginning to see that now. *(pause)*

David: Have you told us all that you can at this time about those incidents in the medicine woman life, or the roles that each of us might have played?

MOITA: *(very long pause; eyes closed)* We can pass on that Margaret was Kelly's sister in that life, and became one of the chief's wives. *(to me:)* And you are her son.

David: Hmmm. *(pause)*

MOITA: *(smiling)* Elisabeth will not be happy to hear that she is a man *(I laugh)*, and she is Barham's son. *(pause)*

(Elisabeth has written – could Barham be the source of this? – that a soul incarnates as the same sex throughout all *of its lifetimes. Thus Moita is teasing that she "will not be happy to hear that she is a man".)*

MOITA: *(to Jim:)* You are not blood-related to anyone I can see – not that you do not have blood relations. *(laughter)* You came to the tribe as an infant from a battle, from another tribe.

Jim: It strikes me now that I *didn't* die young, as I thought I probably did during the hypersentience. Or at least, I've been seeing Kelly's face as a very elderly Indian woman, more elderly than she was in the hypersentience – which indicates to me that somehow I survived past that point.

MOITA: Those moments are always . . . changeable. In each life, where you are at a crisis point, there lies the potential of changing the future in that life. When you first went into the hypersentience, you were tuning into the possibility that you did not survive your test – *(smiling)* partly, because you were going through one in *this* life, and you weren't sure if you would survive *that* one. *(David laughs)*

Jim: Ah! And maybe both are yet to be finally decided. *(laughter)*

(Jim's hypersentience session, guided by David, took place in December 1980, about a week before he first spoke of his growing feelings for Kelly. Moita refers to Jim's test involving those feelings – not knowing whether and how to act on them, with what result.)

MOITA: The universe is in flux. *(laughter)* It is only your conceptions of reality that keep it *here*. *(pause)*

Jim: And of course, death in initiation is in many ways a true death.

MOITA: Yes. Death has many parts, and this life is itself an initiation . . . for things to come. And many things are dying and being left behind so that the new can be born... This is a ritual death, not a real one, that the Earth is going to go through. And you have all chosen, of your own free will, to be here and to go through it...

David: Can you tell me anything about my role in the events with Barham?

MOITA: You were close friends with Elisabeth at the time, and Elisabeth was in conflict. She saw, and sees, you as a supporting figure. *(pause)* You believed in her and her integrity, and that in the end she would overcome her obstacles. *(pause)* That is all for the moment.

David: One last thing. I'd like confirmation, if possible, of the role we seemed to get for Barham in the life at the time of Christ. *(i.e. as Bar-Abbas, the Zealot)* Did we pick that up accurately? *(laughs)*

MOITA: It is accurate.

David: What, then, was Elisabeth at that time – or is that something to wait?

MOITA: That should wait. She already has her own perceptions of what she was. It would not do to give her too much new information all at once.

It has been good.

David: It has.

MOITA: *(to Jim:)* I have enjoyed your energy. *(to Margaret:)* And yours.

Margaret: I hope I was a help.

MOITA: You were very wide-eyed. Your energy was flowing in many directions. There was plenty there for me to tap.

Margaret: *(laughs)* That's good.

MOITA: I will see you later. Good night.

(Moita closes Kelly's eyes and her energy departs. We continue holding hands during a long silence. From the ensuing conversation:)

Kelly: It's one of those things it's hard to let go of, isn't it. *(laughs)*

Jim: I really liked the stuff about the initiatory death. When Moita said the Earth is going through a ritual death and not a real one – wow, is *that* a heavy comment! *(laughs)* She said that softly between other things, like it wasn't the central thing she was saying, but it was like dropping a *bomb* really lightly or something.

Margaret: So if Jim died a ritual death and got rid of old fears and old conceptions of how things were, instead of dying a physical death, then the Earth would be shucking off old concepts of how it is and how it's supposed to be, and bringing in a new era for itself, through a great deal of change and turmoil that would lead up to this ritual death. That could be the significance of the pole shift.

Jim: About Barham, I got the impression that if the power trip or fear or role he's gotten himself entrapped in is overcome, he could be a great instrument for good.

Kelly: It seemed Moita was talking about him when she spoke of the chance for a new beginning: when all of his ancient enemies let go of him as being an enemy, and maybe he has a chance to find out who he is and what he wants aside from being an adversary or a battleground.

℘   ℘   ℘

Since we hold this session because Elisabeth asked Moita's opinion on this year's choices and changes, I soon mail her the session transcript as well as all of the reincarnational information we have received about Barham, herself and us. Then we wait, growing more disappointed with the passing of each month. Receiving no reply, we will never know how this material strikes or affects her. Only the next April, after I write to inquire, do we hear from Elisabeth, who tells us: "As soon as I got your very confidential sharing I wrote you a long letter with my reaction to it."

Unless Barham managed somehow to interfere one last time, perhaps there is some good reason that Elisabeth's letter never arrived. Perhaps it was necessary – regardless of how Elisabeth reacted – so we could let go of expectations and potential dependency and continue, rather, on our own paths. As Moita said when a meeting was still a live possibility: "You have your own expectations of what such a meeting will bring. It will be better for all if these desires are let go of – if it [is seen as] a special meeting but not one that is of major import to your own development. You are all travelling along different lines, and there are many possible meetings for *all* of you in this life."

Through the quality of her own spirit, we can say that Elisabeth eventually overcame her tragic involvement with Jay Barham in this life. As a result, according to her autobiography, she learned "the ultimate lesson about trust and how to discern and discriminate".[136] Obviously, this came with costs: loss of personal belongings and mementoes in Elisabeth's burnt-down house, endangerment to her health and even life as Barham's attacks grew more flagrant, and loss of reputation both personally and, for a while, to the whole field of spiritual communication due to the publicity that Elisabeth's endorsement gave Barham's abuses. But challenging the glamour of supposedly "spiritual" spectacles was also positive and necessary – which explains, I believe, Amar's saying to us back in April 1981: "This situation . . . is one which we have an interest in. It is time that many questions need to be asked."

Before long, Elisabeth will leave Shanti Nilaya as her worldwide work continues, including trying to found another healing centre in Headwaters, Virginia, this time focused on children with AIDS. Through her remaining years, she likely practises better the self-care that Loria and Moita consistently urged upon her: giving herself more time for quiet and relaxation, helping to ensure a clearer channel for her own wisdom and guidance.

In those terms, then, it is good to be able to end this saga by quoting from the letter Elisabeth dictates on July 12, 1982 [abridged, with some transcription corrections], while still at Shanti Nilaya. If an initiatory ritual death awaits ourselves and our Earth, this letter leaves us with images of the new life that opens after our lessons are learned.

I think what I have learned more than anything in the past 10 years working on the path and getting closer to the harmony between the physical, spiritual, emotional and intellectual quadrants is that all things happen when the time is right. And that there are really no mistakes – not even my 4 years work with the Barhams was a mistake – as I had to learn firsthand how psychic energy can be misused the way they did, and can be used as a marvelous God-given gift in healing, which I have been very successful with in times of emergencies only, when I do not have time to think about it.

Whether we meet in person or not is also terribly irrelevant, though my physical-being self would like to connect with you and spend at least an afternoon or evening, quietly sharing and talking about things that cannot be put into a letter easily.

I do have a beautiful private life in that I have a gorgeous mountain cabin, above the Indian reservation here: a dream house, with a sun porch where the sun rises and sets every day, with bluebirds and hummingbirds, salamanders and bunnies, rattlesnakes and all sorts of wildlife.

So between my children, my friends, my gardening, my making hundreds of preserves and my enjoyment of the wildlife and sunshine, there is enough recharging of the batteries to go on the road again, to tolerate airports and motel rooms, instant cups of coffee and all the trivia that go with being a world traveler. I will be able to keep this very special, holy place for me, where there is nothing but silence, interrupted occasionally by the sounds of the crickets or the birds.

Chapter 13

THE GODDESS AND THE AWAKENING DREAM

This Earth, your Mother, is in need of help. She is looking to her children for succour. She cannot be denied, for she has nourished and given the gift of life. The Earth has learned patience with all of her children. You are adolescents entering adulthood, and it is a time of turmoil, a time of change within, a difficult time for the Earth, who is waiting to accept you as a partner in awareness. She has many beautiful things to offer.
– Moita (July 29, 1981)

One of the last pieces to the puzzle that has been coming together since the start of the year finally emerges in what seems a completely unrelated way before summer ends.

By August of 1981, our truck is on its last wheels – clearly unreliable for the coming winter. The best place to get a better, yet affordable one is Vancouver, hundreds of miles away. So one morning I head off south, via thumb and then bus. Staying in a Vancouver hostel, I search the classifieds and locate another mid-60s pickup that has been the pride and joy of a carpenter who needs to give it up. Then, before leaving the city, I stop into famous Banyen Books, since New Age material is not easily come by up north.

There I discover Starhawk's 1979 groundbreaker, *The Spiral Dance: A Rebirth of the Ancient Religion of the Great Goddess.* Though I'm not yet very familiar and am not entirely comfortable with Wicca, I recognize this is precisely where Kelly's energy and interests have been leading her all year. I know that bringing home this book will both delight her and reinforce this direction for our future – destination unknown. So that is what I do, and both will turn out to be true – though Kelly's evolution toward the energy of the Goddess was already well under way, furthered by the opening with Jim since January. Truly, we can say our journey toward the Goddess began with Moita's own coming, but accelerated through our life in the mountains of the B.C. interior.

ዮ   ዮ   ዮ

In September 1981, our family of four moves with some difficulty to a one-room, wood-heated cabin, again without power or plumbing, within a tall evergreen forest along the western ridge of the Kindle Valley, up the hill from Margaret's land. Driving the winding mountainside road will provide us some thrills and chills in winter especially, haunted by steep drop-offs while contending with ice, snow or mudslides. (Once, when a snowplow doesn't arrive for days after a particularly heavy snowfall, we load the family into the truck and head downhill – only to get stuck and need rescuing, by local Indians with snowmobiles.)

Visitors coming in our grassy driveway first see a stovepipe rising high above a low, L-shaped log cabin lit by lamplight within. Though I will later add an entry area with new wood and large vertical windows, the original door ushers visitors immediately through a "kitchen" (sink, shelves, counter with camp stove, and nearby wood heater) to a dining table where we can sit together looking out double windows onto a tiny meadow surrounded by tall fir trees. Past the table is our "corner office": a small desk with typewriter for transcribing, preparing *Rays* and writing letters. Then in the short part of the "L" to the right, our double bed lies atop the family clothes dressers. A narrow aisle between the dressers and another window leads to the children's bunk beds against the back wall. In summer, mosquito netting hangs from the rafters, surrounding the beds.

It will be a challenge for us to live here, obviously – as it was years ago, even more so, for Margaret, her husband and their two babies. But despite the summer's upheavals (both breakdown and breakthrough) in our relationship, and warnings from friends that we are likely to get depressed if not actually go crazy in such tight, dark quarters, this move has brought us close to the land that we hope may become the site for a community, and to the people who may create it with us.

And there will be abundant bright sides to living here so deeply into nature. Only steps away from our cabin, a path winds down into a small rainforest ravine through which a creek flows. A fallen fir tree provides a walking bridge spanning the high creek banks. And standing slightly back but surrounding this part of the creek is a grove of giant cedars, including the one that Kelly names Grandmother (pictured with me on the back cover), contributing their elder serenity to this babbling, mossy, ferny "faery glen". Ravens calling overhead and an array of imaginative totem poles in the nearby Indian village add to the mythic environment.

This mystical atmosphere enlivens several of my dreams during early September. In one, Kelly and I explore a passage beneath a friend's house and discover many elaborately detailed, old-fashioned rooms of an underground mansion or museum that turns out to belong to Margaret – an image for new dimensions of consciousness, or further past lives, waiting to be discovered here.

Then two intriguing dreams come on September 13th.

"Glowing UFO Passes Through Us" dream
David / September 13, 1981

Walking through hills, Kelly and I come upon a once-seen landscape I've been hoping to find again – with Celtic harp music in the air and a rainbow above. "This might be it," I say. Next, a flying saucer of glowing, pastel colours appears and disappears in the sky. It comes right down toward us and, amazingly, passes right through us! I realize this is an encounter with higher levels, not a physical craft, as I wake and meditate in the rising energy.

"Pan as Green, Wrinkled Old Indian" dream
David / September 13, 1981

I notice several men coming out of the woods near our cabin: an old Indian and some younger white men. The younger men, apparently from the government land office, hassle me about not owning or paying taxes on this place. When I go to tell Kelly, she appears alongside the old Indian, who is of a different mind from the others. He says that another old Indian used to own this land and that we should go ahead and stay here, leaving him to deal with the government people. Now seeing his green, wrinkled face, I realize that actually he is Pan, or the legendary Green Man, with his own views and ways of protecting the Earth.

જી   જી   જી

A week later, it is the night of the autumn equinox. Kelly and I sit together on our bed, holding hands with a candle between us, the silence of our meditation interrupted only by the occasional sounds of cats, sleeping children, or an owl in the deep, surrounding woods.

Moita session #201 (Kelly and David / September 20, 1981)

David: Welcome to our new home.

MOITA: You are finding the energy here somewhat different?

David: Yes. Feeling more immersed in the Earth, perhaps feeling the presence of Pan both in a dream and the other day down in the big cedar grove, the "faery glen" by the creek. Do you have any words for us on the particular quality of energy here, or on what we may learn through being here? *(pause)*

MOITA: It is another step, a step closer to your goal, to seeing the Earth with new eyes. It is a deeper place. And though your time here will be short, it will be rich. *(very long pause)*

David: Do you have anything to say on our changes, or the evolution of your level and ours?

MOITA: The essence of the pattern is beginning to unfold. You are beginning to see your part of the pattern and the pattern as a whole. You move yourself about from one part of the pattern to another and become immersed in the single threads, the single lives that you lead in different places and different times. As your conscious awareness of pasts, futures, rises to the surface, your ability to see the whole pattern will also evolve. You will gain that detachment that comes with distance, and yet not lose that ability to immerse.

Consciousness runs on cycles, just as all things in the Earth and between the heavens runs on cycles. You come up to us and touch us; then you turn away and become focused once more in this reality. But each time you rise above your ordinary awareness, the descent is less; and so, we are closer, because the gap is not as wide between our worlds...

It is good to be able to focus your energy in a single direction. That is the art of concentration. You will be learning control of the different states of your consciousness, and learning acceptance of those states that you are usually not aware of or have not encountered. But all states are states of mind, and so, are neither good nor bad, nor sane nor insane. They just *are*. In order to do that properly, you must leave fear behind – at least, learn to accept fear as a part of yourself and not let it rule your actions.

It was in late August that Kelly began to hear in her head the phrase, "The channel is almost ready." In September, the "almost" is dropped. Then, on several occasions of mergence between Kelly and Jim, and Kelly and me – times of intense vulnerability and openness – Kelly begins to channel an energy-presence identifying itself as the Earth Goddess or Earth Mother, the soul or spirit of the planet as a whole. Happening spontaneously, none of these experiences is recorded.

However, Kelly begins to receive "previews" of a session when the Goddess will come by plan and perform some kind of ritual with Jim and me. Kelly lets the two of us know something is in the works. And once all appears ready, Jim arrives at our cabin one evening in early October. As we begin, none of us knows quite the extent and depth of this unique experience on which we are embarking. It will prove an initiation: for all of us into the Earth Mother's realm, and for each of us into a deeper, three-way community.

This unprecedented session (in more ways than one!) begins as Moita's familiar presence focuses itself down into our physical reality, enters Kelly's awareness and opens her eyes. We gaze at each other for a while, sharing the energy that is already quite strong.

Moita/Earth Goddess session #202 (Kelly, David, Jim / October 4, 1981)

David: I feel like I want to go really deep into my dream-self tonight.

MOITA: Actually, what you are doing is waking up. *(pause)* It serves to think of this as a dream for a while. It makes it easier to accept, until you reach a certain level where you realize what you thought was a dream was your awareness, your self – and what you thought was real was the dream.

David: I think I've always thought dreams were more real.

MOITA: They have even more substance when you have them when you are awake. Words seem to lose their distinction. All words seem to mean the same thing.

(These last two sentences have become familiar: Moita's way of moving us beyond logical thought into a deeper state of consciousness.)

David: And one word can mean almost anything, too.

MOITA: Or *all* things... *(long pause)*

David: What about those strange faces I was seeing at the end of the last session[137], that were all sort of ugly or old, depending on your point of view? We talked about one of the aspects of the Goddess – the Crone.

MOITA: The Crone is the Goddess's most fearful aspect, the least understood. Death has ever been man's greatest fear. And is not ugliness and age associated with death?

David: Both the dying and the destroying aspects of that, together.

MOITA: And yet when one looks on the other side, there is wisdom and serenity, acceptance.

David: They didn't bother me. I was just seeing them with interest... *(laughs)*

MOITA: And what kind of a dream would you create?

David: *(laughs)* I feel it should be partly one that surprises me. I don't feel like I should . . . *(we laugh)* . . . plan it out.

MOITA: Oh, surprises. I see.

David: Best to leave things open-ended somewhat.

MOITA: You like to create things "on the run", as it were. *(pause)* How is your heart?

David: It's quivering – pulsing fairly quickly, not pounding.

MOITA: *(turning to Jim:)* And yours? Is your heart centre also activated?

Jim: More so in the last few seconds. *(laughter)*

MOITA: Being in the direct line of the energy has something to do with it, I suppose.

Jim: As I had my eyes closed earlier, I felt far out of my body. I still feel like my arms are incredibly long and I'm sort of floating in back of my body, looking at this. *(pause)* My heart's still troubled and clouded by my separation pains from my daughter, and I keep going through cycles where that's easier to deal with and then harder.

MOITA: Man has ever been one to ride the roller coaster of his emotions... *(long pause)* We plan on activating *all* of your centres tonight.

David: So *you* have plans.

MOITA: Yes, we have plans. We shall see which plans bear fruit and which do not. *(pause)*

David: Is there any way we can help that activation?

MOITA: You're very good at picking up cues, aren't you!

(We laugh, but I'm not quite thinking of the "cue" Moita intends.)

David: Shall we do the meditation we tried at our last workshop? *(i.e. focusing on each chakra in turn, from bottom to top)*

MOITA: Actually, we have another tool which will be useful for this particular situation. It is time for us to take a journey together – although Kelly has her misgivings, I must hasten to add. *(smiling)* She has seen some glimpses of this journey we have planned. But in order to break down the barriers that stand in the way, it is necessary.

The time has come. You will be meeting someone else. I am but here to pave the way this evening, to raise the energy to the proper level first.

David: We've made a good start.

MOITA: Ah, and we shall go farther. *(pause)* It is a leap into the unknown. *(pause)* And you will not be able to speak to me for a while this evening. We shall speak of your experience, whatever it may be, later.

David: Do you mean you won't be back at the end?

MOITA: I may, I may not. The energy may be too intense – for me, for this kind of exch . . . exchange. *(laughs)* I am being blocked. The time has come. *(sighs)* You know who to expect?

David: Mm-hmm.

MOITA: Before I go, I have one more thing to say to you: I *am* one aspect of this energy, and I yield to another. Perhaps you would never expect to hear me say this, but it is time for you to get stoned.

(Very true, as this will be the first time we have ever gotten stoned during a session – by physical means! – and virtually the only time Kelly and I have been under any influence of a psychedelic since we met three and a half years ago.)

David:	How do you mean?
MOITA:	Your pipe.
David:	Smoking? It's funny, I had that thought before Jim ever came.
MOITA:	As I say, you are good at picking up cues.
David:	All three of us, then, or . . . ?
MOITA:	I would suggest it. This journey needs an extra push.
David:	All right. We'll do that now?...
MOITA:	Yes, it is over there on the counter.
David:	Shall we use Jim's special smoke? *(homegrown and cured)*
MOITA:	You might as well. It is next to it.
Jim:	I have more with me, if it's required.
MOITA:	I think not. Not much will be required.
Jim:	And the level has been rising ever since you said it was time.
MOITA:	You are experiencing it? And your centres, are they activated?
Jim:	Yes, increasingly so.

(I can't get the package open. Jim takes it, opens it and starts to fill the pipe.)

MOITA:	You are all nervous...
Jim:	I don't know what to expect, where this journey is supposed to be heading. I'll find out soon enough.
MOITA:	We will *all* find out soon enough. We will monitor this from our level as well as we can. *(Jim laughs)*

(The match is lit and there is a long silence as we begin to smoke, taking two to three tokes each. When the pipe comes around to Kelly/Moita:)

MOITA:	This is funny. *(followed by more silence with our eyes closed, and then . . .)*
GODDESS:	*(whispered with intensity:)* Yes.

(She opens Kelly's eyes, then looks toward me. There is a long silence, my face quite close to hers. She then speaks with dramatic emphasis:)

GODDESS:	Greetings!
David:	*(responding in kind to her strangely dramatic energy:)* Hello!
GODDESS:	I thank you for this opportunity. It has been a long wait. *(pause; laughs)* Intense?
David:	Yes, you are.
GODDESS:	I have much to learn about how to control my presence. I know man's soul intimately, and yet there are some things . . . that will always remain . . . a mystery. *(pause)*
David:	We can know things . . . and yet they are mysteries.
GODDESS:	*(sighs)* The more we know of the thing, the less we understand, the more there is to

discover, uncover, unveil, strip away, reveal. The more I know of you, the less I know, for there is always more. And yet I know more than you about many things, from a different side of things, a different experience of life.

I am always touched, even by those who cannot see me, those who do not hear. And sometimes I am . . . I am touched in anger, in pain, in fear. Not often am I touched with love and understanding. *(pause)*

Of all my children, of all of the creatures that live upon my body, man is the only one who has ever treated me with pain and fear. My soul is being destroyed. I am being raped, dishonoured, tortured, and yet few hear my screams. I am told that I am going to go through a death. I can well believe a death is in the offing. I have fought off death for a long time. Still, I give where I can, where I can enter men's hearts. There I find a doorway.

Each month, as the Moon, three days does [man] see me in darkness. And so, he thinks I have died and gone away, only to return again. But I have only turned my face away to face the Sun, for the Sun is the centre of life.

In this other death that is heading towards me, the Sun itself will turn its back on me. And my children will cry out in the darkness, for they will know that life has been taken away – the life-giver.

David: They don't feel themselves part of you.

GODDESS: No, they are like the child who is fighting his parent. I gave them birth, I sustained them, and they scorn me. *(shocked tone)* They see me as wrathful, as angry, as judging. And yet, I am not thus. They only see in me what they see in themselves. But they have tried to stamp me out. They have tried to control me, through torture bend me to their will, mould me to their likeness. And I have not been able to give in in this slaughter. I have grown angry, as they see me.

But that is only a passing thing. I have been here for all time. *(pause)* I see you feel my pain.

(turning to Jim:) And you, you see it too. In your child, in your separation, you are made to experience a little of what my existence has been like. I am only given fleeting glimpses of my children's potential. Pain is a clearer. It is the fire that purges the soul. So I must accept my pain, as you must accept yours.

(She now moves and stands, as Moita has never previously done.)

GODDESS: I am good to those who know me. I visit upon those few all that I am, all the joy and the unbounded love that is mine to give. *(pause; sighs)* Do you know me now?

Jim: Trying to make a beginning. There's so much to know. And much of the potential still sleeps.

GODDESS: I can pour more of myself in this place than I have ever been able to before.

Jim: I'm open.

GODDESS: I have prepared this body and mind so that I could be received. I am not bound to immobility. I am a creator . . . a doer.

(to me:) You too have things within you that are not spoken, potential that lies sleeping. You have barriers – words and sights.

(whispers) Open. I have drawn you from yourself before. *(reaching to touch me here?)* I have taken you with me. *(pause)* You are safe. *(pause)* Perfect love and perfect trust: that is what it means to experience me. *(pause)* Rise up, turn around, meet yourself – he who guides you from behind. Fly between the stars – the Raven that flies in the void of space, between the points of light in the sky, the jewels that shine down on all of man! But remember that the Raven is part of the Earth. Remember your beginnings. Even if you have been named son of Sun, you are also son of me.

(turning to Jim:) And you – searcher, seeker, always looking, never finding, never seeing what lies before you waiting: see now. For you, it is not behind. You need not turn around. For you it is before you, and always has been. It was never hidden. The chalice, the cup, the light and the love, were ever there for you to grasp, for you to drink from. *(pause)* Be centred. *(long pause; touches him here?)* Let it rise to the surface. *(pause)*

Jim: *(whisper)* What does it look like?

GODDESS: It looks bittersweet. *(pause)* Many things are falling off of you, falling off to the side. They are just dead skin. You need them no longer; and yet, after, you will pick them up off the floor and put them on again.

There is no moment but *the* moment. There is no time. All that has happened in the past, all of Earth's history, man has created in his dream. And the end of time will come when man wakes up and realizes he has been dreaming.

(to me:) Do you understand?

David: Some. *(laughs)*

GODDESS: You have been *asleep*! It is time to wake up! And yet you will still be here with the other dreamers. And so, you must learn to flow in their dream and help them wake, so the dream may end, so I may die . . . so we may all be reborn together.

I am also afraid of this death. A part of me . . . wonders if I will come out the other side. So I am here in the dream *too*, trying to change it, trying to wake enough of you up so that when the time comes I will not stand alone. I need food, sustenance, support. All of the things I have given, for all these ages, I need in return. That is why I *gave* them, because I know the joy of *receiving*.

This is not the only place I can manifest. It is a good clear manifestation, though, and it is well that things have come to a head as soon as they have. There is much to learn. The dream accelerates. You must learn it in order to be ready.

Jim: For the death and rebirth?

GODDESS: And for what comes before it. Not *all* those I connect with will make it to the end. And much will depend upon their ability to absorb energy.

Jim: And adapt, change.

GODDESS: Yes. To *mutate*. I gave special attention to your plants this year *(laughter)*, planning for this moment. My fairies and elves were most particular about what kind of energy they drew up through the roots, about the Sun's warmth.

Jim: It *is* the best yet, this year.

GODDESS: It is an herb I placed on this planet . . . not to tempt man with, but for man to use at the proper time, in the proper way. But like so many of my gifts, its use has gone astray, and the understanding of it and its use has also gone astray. With it, I can build a doorway; you can build a doorway. And the doorway can be to self-recognition and union – or self-destruction, depending on the focus of the user.

Jim: Can it be a doorway into this place, this communion with you?

GODDESS: Is it not? Are you not here, communing with me? It helps you to wake up.

Jim: When I was on the [fire lookout] tower, you showed me your rainbows, and the thunderstorms and sunsets.

GODDESS: Yes. And I have given up my northern lights. I have danced in the heavens. And I am the dance, the dance of life.

(And when Kelly did her creative dance at night around the bonfire for the local women's festival, the northern lights danced with her – according to our friend C.)

Jim: May we reap what potential we have left with that dance.

GODDESS: *(laughs)* Do you think there is more – more potential?

Jim: In us, and in you. *(pause)*

GODDESS: Which of my many faces are you seeing now?

Jim: A dark one.

GODDESS: One of fear.

Jim: Oh, I don't fear it. Just dark and different.

GODDESS: One of power?

Jim: Yes.

GODDESS: I have the power of the earthquake, the hurricane, the volcano. I have a great deal of power. I have the power . . . *(pause, as she comes closer to Jim or touches him)* Now you can feel my aura, my energy in yours, can you not?

Jim: *(whisper)* Yes.

GODDESS: Now *I* have the power again. *(pause, looking at her hands)* Hands . . . are but an instrument to focus attention. *(long pause, punctuated by sighs)*

It is time to call in my brothers and sisters. *(pause)* I do have *them* on my side. *(i.e. the entities of the other planets)*

(pause) Now you see that you can trust me, for I hold you in the palm of my hand and you are still safe.

(to Jim:) I see you are trying to let in the God. *(i.e. the Horned God as experienced in the Wiccan tradition) (long pause)*

(to me:) And what do you think of this dream we are creating? Are there enough surprises for you? *(I laugh)* Is this more than you expected?

David: Yes.

GODDESS: And how do you feel?

David: It strikes me suddenly very much like one evening last summer, in particular.

(I refer to the night when Kelly and I had felt in conflict with each other but then came together in openness and, according to Moita, "touched another's mind" and "truly met".[138])

GODDESS: And yet it is more than that.

David: Yes. That's one time which shows . . . I was getting the image before of how each of us has our stems going down into you, inside. It comes out our eyes sometimes.

GODDESS: You have me for the evening!

(She stands, picks up the crystal ball and holds it in her hand.)

GODDESS: *(sighs)* A beautiful thing, is it not? A solid tear. *(Kelly's recent dream image)* Solid water. Stone. Shape of the Earth. Mirror reflecting, crystal absorbing. Whole, one piece. All of its surface touches and connects with all of its other surfaces. You must be careful what you see in a crystal. Oftentimes things of pain come through. But though they were gifts to man – my tears – they were painful as well... *(pause)*

And do you think this is a dream? Or are we beyond that?

Jim: I don't know how to define what a dream is anymore. *(pause)*

(She gets the pipe, and then the grass.)

GODDESS: I see you have a match, and I have a pipe!

(We smoke once more.)

GODDESS: Ritual: a good energy focus. *(sighs)* And the elements: air, fire, water and earth. *(pause)* Surround the house with a beacon of light, *(whisper)* a band of light. So we can build our power . . . into a force, a force that can help heal me . . . by healing man. *(pause)*

(to me:) Know that you came from the Sun. That is where spirits that do not start off as bodies are born. A piece of the Sun breaks off and is given sentience, individuality, purpose. And you seek to find your way back to the Sun. When you came here first was the "Earth and Sun" life.[139] That was your first incarnation, and your best in many ways. For there you knew who you were, what you were, where you came from. And in this life you will learn again how to *sing* to the Sun. For you will know his song. *(whisper)* You will be his channel!

(pointing to Kelly:) And this, this part, began as Earth, as me, in my incarnation, the one I chose to learn about man, to try to speak my agony.

(to Jim:) And you began here, as one of the incarnations of the God.

And so we three are learning again where we came from and who we are. *(arms spreading to include all, whispering, smiling)* Awaken! Remember! Remember who you are! We are joy and beauty – different reflections, yet part of the same place.

(to me:) For were you not born here too, on Earth? So you are not only the son of the Sun, but the son of the Earth as well. And the only way back to the Sun is through my heart, my core, my fire. So you have become part of me too. And you are trying to descend to my

depths, so you may burst out, and know your Self!

(whisper) All these things are true in one place. Do you understand why there are archetypes? Do you see their purpose? It is man's only way to learn to free himself, by remembering these places he can go and become one with.

(whisper) So awaken, you both. See each other for the different kind of beauty that you are. The God is but a reflection of the Goddess. First was the Goddess and all was her. Then she looked into a mirror and saw herself and fell in love with the image. And so, the image became separate, became apart, so she could delve into it, explore it, and try to *understand* the beauty that was her, since she had never seen it before, because she was all. *(pause)*

How many places we are going! How many places have we been?! *(pause)* This is a *real* place. It has more substance to it than other places you have gone. This is *home.* Welcome! *(pause)*

David: Is the only difference from others that we are more awake? Doesn't everyone have the same relation to the archetypes?

GODDESS: *(laughs)* There are many that have that same relation to the archetypes, since these three archetypes are infinitely repeated. And there are other threes that are discovering each other and their archetypal significance.

And I as the Goddess am in many places. People are beginning to remember me. And as they remember, I become more real. And as I become more real, I enter into the dream and make others aware of my presence. *(pause)* But not all will experience it *this* way. Each way is different. *(pause)* The first time I spoke to you, you knew who I was.

David: This life . . . or the Sun life?

GODDESS: In this life. *(presumably meaning in recent weeks)* It is not always easy to pinpoint these things exactly *(we laugh)*, time being what it is. And yet all lives are the same life, just seen in a different way.

(She sighs twice, looking up at the ceiling, where hang posters of Sulamith Wulfing's paintings – "The Star" and "Silence".)

GODDESS: Yes. Sulamith, she is one who hears me. She is one who sees me walking near, guiding the star. And she sees me in the Sun. And she sees my beauty and my transparency . . . my hidden power . . . and my mystery. And so we come again to mystery.

(to Jim:) What are you thinking?

Jim: I'm thinking that Kelly's still here through this, but she's gone off to the side.

GODDESS: *(laughs, whispers)* Oh yes! We would not exclude her from this experience, even though she is such a small part now. But through Kelly we have uncovered Siofra, and Moita, and me, and Amar . . . And what do you find in these things?

Jim: I don't know if the word is "comfortable". *(pause)* Your presence is comfortable.

GODDESS: Familiar?

Jim: There's that too.

GODDESS: *(sighs; pause)* We'll get into another grinning contest. Faces certainly can flow into many different positions as you think your thoughts onto them!

Jim: Hmmm. *(he laughs)*

(Long pause. She goes to hunt in the box where our tapes are kept, and returns.)

GODDESS: I have uncovered the object of my search, on the first try. *(laughter)*

(She holds Buffy Saint Marie's Illuminations *tape.)*

Jim: I'm afraid if I move or talk, we'll all wake up.

GODDESS: No, no, you *are* awake. You cannot wake up much more than you are right now. You will not fall back asleep. *(laughter)* I will not *let* you, not for *now*. I'll keep you up here . . . where you need to be.

(She hands the tape to me to place in the recorder. She stands and prepares to build a cone of power with the energy of all three of us. The music begins to play and Buffy chants, passionately and entrancingly, Leonard Cohen's words in "God is Alive, Magic is Afoot".)

(As the other-worldly chant rises gradually in volume, the Goddess stands before us, her arms outstretched at first toward our feet. We then feel the energy change as her arms slowly rise, and by the climax of the song reach above her head, whereupon the Goddess releases the cone of power.)

GODDESS: Yes! *(exclaimed, provoking murmurs from Jim and me)* That was well done!

Jim: Maybe Buffy was one with you when she put that to music. And Leonard Cohen was one with you when he wrote the words.

GODDESS: Perhaps he is just another who is awake.

Jim: In momentary flashes, anyway. *(laughter)*

GODDESS: He was definitely awake when he wrote that.

Jim: The only thing is it's in the midst of a novel, and nothing else in the novel is anything like it. [140] *(laughs)*

GODDESS: *(laughs)* May I say that your life leading up to this moment does not at all look as if it is connected?

Jim: *(laughs)* Okay.

GODDESS: Appearances may be deceiving. The ways to learn how to wake up are many, and often do not make any sense unless you are inside of them. *(pause)*

(The energy between them shifts, as Jim feels the Horned God come close to channeling through him. Kelly wonders for a moment if she'll lose the Goddess because of it.)

Jim: If I bring him through, would I sprout horns?

GODDESS: No. *(Jim laughs)* Would you be *afraid* of sprouting horns? *(laughter)* You have not sprouted horns thus far!

Jim: *(laughs)* As long as it wasn't permanent, it might be all right.

David: You could wear a hat over them.

Jim: *(laughs)* Wear a toque for the whole year.

GODDESS: Almost as bad as being Mr. Spock with his ears. He surely must have been an elf at one time. He looks good in ears.

Jim: Are the elves beginning to come back?

GODDESS: They have never been gone. Man's dream has left them behind, but they have always been there on the outside of the dream.

Jim: But there has been a withdrawal of some kind.

GODDESS: Confusion – as I am sometimes confused by man's behaviour. They do not understand him, even less than I.

Jim: But with the big changes afoot now, are they making any . . . ?

GODDESS: Anxious. They are anxious. Some are excited at the possibilities, even though they do not understand the implications!

Jim: Do they feel that they are to play a role in the coming changes?

GODDESS: They will be the ones affected first. They do not feel they have much say in the matter. It is *my* choice. They are but an extension of me. And so, they know this – but I decide when and where and how, and *if*. I can be persuaded – persuaded to not need that kind of manifestation, that kind of death. But there must be enough of you to persuade me. I must have enough in order to know the rest will follow.

Jim: Then we must become good at persuasion.

GODDESS: You are most attentive, and we appreciate that. You have very good energy, and you let it flow. And it is sustenance to us, food. And so, we give back as much or more in exchange, to show our gratitude and our acceptance of your gift of self. And it continues to accelerate, because it bounces off each other, each one showing just as much appreciation and giving back more.

            But you are only one, and *(turning to me)* you also are only one. And there are many, many different parts scattered all over the Earth that do not help, do not know *how* to give, do not know to let go of fear *enough* to give. Fear is *always* present. It is a partner to man. It helps him know what direction he is going. It keeps him from going too fast, but in the end does not keep him from going.

Jim: Fear can accumulate around a time of crisis and become a burden.

GODDESS: To an already overtaxed Earth, there is much fear added from man.

Jim: It's about to increase in these next coming times, it appears. But maybe you will force more to transcend it.

GODDESS: Perhaps. Perhaps then the fear will be gone, for those who fear the most.

Jim: Well, there will be more transcending it. But will it be enough more?, is the question.

GODDESS: So we begin a little early, trying to stack the deck.

Jim: None too soon, I think. *(laughs)* It's a difficult deck to stack. It takes some skill to know how to do that.

GODDESS: I have had a great deal of time to plan, and few distractions – before man came. *(pause)*

            Good. You gave in. You went through another barrier, and relaxed enough to let fears slide away. *(pause)*

Jim: You showed me that dark face again.

GODDESS: Hmm! *(pause)*

    (I've had my eyes closed, but open them as I feel the energy of the Goddess turning toward me.)

GODDESS: I'm getting so present that you feel my eyes as I look at you.

David: Mm-hmm. And your arms before. *(i.e. during the cone of power)*

GODDESS: Did you enjoy my dance? We released a great deal of energy and sent it somewhere else, where it will do the most good.

David: Many other places . . . or on another level?

GODDESS: It is always best to send that kind of energy to one place. For in the sending it to many you break it up into the components with which you built it up. So it becomes again part of the dream instead of something that can break into the dream.

David: So you sent it to one place?

GODDESS: The place where it will do the most good – *the* place, *one*. *(pause)* Thoughts?

    (laughter, as Jim may suggest a joking possibility)

    That's how we become *awake* again, more awake, *(whisper)* is to give away these extra thoughts that we no longer need. So once more we are in the present moment, and all those moments have passed away. *(pause)*

    It is a little different than some other journeys you have undertaken.

David: Quite. *(pause)*

    (She touches one of my centres, or passes her hand over some. I feel the energy shift and clear.)

David: Thank you.

GODDESS: You're welcome. *(pause)* You are enjoying yourself?

David: Mm-hmm.

GODDESS: And what kind of faces do you see?

David: Hard to describe. There were some Indian ones, like masks some were, it seemed. All beautiful and mysterious.

GODDESS: I have not always chosen the form of beauty.

David: Yeah, I just slipped into the other. *(laughs)*

GODDESS: I need to experience all aspects of life – the decay as well as the growth.

    Shining light glows upon my brow. The energy centre is open so much, it shines forth like a star.

    You two should also see each other, not only me. We are all three equal here at this moment. *(pause, as Jim and I turn to gaze at each other)* Are you suspicious? *(laughter)* Does it feel uncomfortable?

David: For a second. *(pause)* Just different.

GODDESS: What kind of differences do you see?... *(pause, as she touches my speech centre)* Open. Open. Words are necessary vehicles for drawing energy out, and releasing it.

David: *(still facing Jim)* Two men is different. Less familiar. Less a feeling of . . . Like we are more on the same level at this moment, whereas with you there is a feeling of something encompassing all. It could be more like a mirror, *or* it could be . . . the other half. *(pause)* The same love – a different form.

Jim: It doesn't flow as easily somehow – the pattern of it. But it's just another direction of the pattern only, which isn't really significant. *(pause)*

GODDESS: *(as I face her again)* And does this pattern now look somewhat altered?

David: It's another alteration to come *back. (laughter, then long pause)*

GODDESS: The energy bounces from one eye to the other, and it's passed around the circle.

Jim: The God is just as connected to the fate of the Earth as the Goddess is.

GODDESS: Since the God and the Goddess are one, it is so. *(pause)* One of the God's forms is Pan. And you will *not* grow horns. *(Jim laughs)* And his are really *very*, quite dainty. *(pause)*

Jim: He doesn't have all of your sensitivity. Kelly's still there.

GODDESS: *(whisper)* Yes. *(long pause)* He has sensitivity. And you remember her from me.

Jim: And what do you remember from her?

GODDESS: I remember being able to *(whisper)* be touched. *(pause)*

(to Jim as the God:) We needed to separate so that I would understand man when he came to this place, when he came to this point. I would not have become as alive, as vibrant, as searching, if I had been content to stay with myself and be whole. If I had not birthed desire to connect, I would not have searched. And then the Earth would have died, for I would not be able to speak. You have helped give me a great gift. You have helped me learn how to speak, how to share my energy, in new forms. And you have helped me to see beyond man's dark side to the beauty behind the darkness, to the stars that are revealed when the light fades. Do you see?

Jim: And I have learned as well.

GODDESS: There must be learning on *all* sides in any exchange of energy, when it is a gift, freely giving and freely accepting. *(pause, turning to me:)* And you have helped me also learn to speak. *(long pause)*

David: I have difficulty myself.

GODDESS: What kind of difficulty?

David: Finding words at the moment.

GODDESS: There are many languages. You see? I'm not an untouchable Goddess. I am alive. Nor am I distant, observing and watching and judging. I participate. This is where you learn to co-create. *(pause)*

David: People very often are scared even of *us* when we try to let some of this through.

GODDESS: And yet there is nothing fearful in it. They are afraid of finding out it has all been a dream, and then deciding it has been a dream not worth having.

David: Like the dwarves in the stable. *(i.e. in C.S. Lewis's final Narnia book[141N])*

GODDESS: Yes. And the farther you delve into yourself, the more you will find. That is why I can spend an eternity looking, because there is always more to uncover... *(pause)*

GODDESS: *(to Jim:)* I am an initiation, and your initiator. It is time for *you* to find a new name.

Jim: *(pause)* A clear one hasn't risen yet.

GODDESS: I can see it rising. In order to complete your initiation, you must have a new name.

Jim: It seems only right as being a first step, a new level, new experience.

(She rises and stands behind Jim, placing her hands on top of his head. After a while she reaches down Jim's spine, then returns toward his head, drawing up the energy.)

GODDESS: *(long pause)* Let the energy heal.

(Jim then utters the name that he hears.)

GODDESS: ...For now, we will know you as [name], and your name is safe with us. *(pause)*

(She sits down and turns first to me, as Jim and I face each other.)

Ravenstar, I give you [Jim's new name]. Meet, so you will know each other when next you meet.

(turning to Jim:) And [Jim's new name], know Ravenstar. For he is a companion along the way, and has been waiting for your arrival. And you will keep each other safe, safe from harm, and you will be a haven unto each other in times of storm.

We can now count him as one of our number. Perfect love and perfect trust. The next step is to pass the kiss around the circle and end your initiation – in a clockwise direction. And so, I accept you. *(kissing Jim)* Now pass the kiss.

Jim: Ravenstar. *(He kisses me.)*

David: [Jim's new name.] *(I turn and kiss Kelly.)* Siofra.

GODDESS: And so it comes back home. The circle is unbroken. Welcome to you both. I will leave now, in a way; or rather, should I say, I will recede now into the background of this dream, until the time comes for me to wake it up again. And as you named your sister Siofra, it is she who will return. *(pause)*

(Her eyes close, and Kelly soon opens them.)

David: Feel any different?

Kelly: Not *much*, I must admit. I feel a difference in the way I talk, and the energy of my words is missing, but it's still pretty high. This has been even better than the previews! There were a lot of gaps. What *rushes* I'm getting! Whoo-ee! Oh! . . .

David: I was struck for a while by how much of a personality she had. And then I realized I was comparing her to Amar – a movement upward in that sense, more distance. But then I realized she's the *opposite* of distance.

Kelly: She seems to be a tapestry of different facets, a really rich tapestry – *whatever* she is in reality, whatever *that* is. *(laughs)* Are we ready to believe that we've dreamed this entire Earth's history? *(laughs)* And maybe we can change the dream? . . . If I even remember what happened when I wake up, I'll be lucky *(laughs)* – I mean, when I go to sleep! *(laughs)*

Once I cross over a certain threshold, the energy flows freely back and forth and I don't have any say in it, but I don't have any say *against* it, as it were. *(laughs)* Does that make sense? I just sort of flow *with* it. What else can you *do*?!

(to Jim:) How are *you*?

Jim: Well, I really felt a lot of rushes. A few times there, *boy*, your face just changed to this really empty blackness. It was somewhat a face, but it didn't have features except for eyes. It was solid, like wood or something. It was *power*. When she touched my hand and chest, there was really a strong vibration.

Kelly: I could just *feel* the rushes you were getting – and you too.

David: Her hands really had an effect, especially when she went down my chest and then went up. It made everything really warm and tingly. She seemed to drain out something that time – there seemed a little excess in my solar plexus as she started – or just balance it.

Kelly: Gee, that was an awfully potent cone of power.

David: Pretty amazing.

Kelly: Did you watch the hands, or did you just experience with your eyes closed?

David: Both. I would mostly have my eyes closed, but I opened them a few times very briefly to check where her arms were.

Jim: I had my eyes closed through that.

Kelly: You felt the cone of power *leave*. Don't ask me where she sent it. She sent it up into the Earth's atmosphere with the message coded into it that this energy will go to the most needed place on Earth. And after it disappeared over the horizon, I lost sight of it, so I don't know where it landed... I wonder what's going to be on the news tomorrow! *(laughs)*

(No particular news the next day, but the following morning we learn that President Sadat of Egypt is assassinated! (gulp) Seriously, though, we'd like to think that, if our energy is sent to the Middle East – hardly unlikely – it adds strength to those keeping alive Sadat's vision of peace.)

Kelly: The beacon of light she put around this house must have lit up the whole countryside. Of course, she needed all that power in order to come, in order to stay. She didn't make just a circle. She made a band from the ground all the way up to the roof of the house, surrounding it on all sides.

Jim: *(sighs)* I feel drained, like I just did 10 Tarot readings or something.

Kelly: Oh yeah, right! We have to open the circle. The last thing she told me when she left was, "Don't forget to open the circle."

(Turning now counter-clockwise, Kelly opens the magic circle:)

Kelly: The circle is open but unbroken. May the peace of the Goddess go in our hearts. Merry meet and merry part. And merry meet again. Blessed be.

(Kelly then urges us to "earth the power" – visualize all the excess energy draining back into the Earth from whence it came:)

Kelly: Let the light go down into the core of the Earth, and give it to her heart. Then we will feel normal physical weariness, not a nasty magical weariness.

(Then we feast on toast and nectarines, since "Magic is hungry work!"[142N] A little later:)

Kelly: I wasn't too sure I was going to be able to let this thing happen. I had a lot of doubts and misgivings, wondering how much I would be programming myself. Then I realized that when you get into those moments, you have to suspend disbelief in whatever is happening. If you're crazy, you're crazy, and that's all right. You can let the Goddess talk, and you can let her be real. And the more you can suspend disbelief, the more real she becomes. And the less you have to worry about whether it's real or not, the more you find out it's true, whether you want to believe it or not!! *(laughter)*

I must say that sometimes the Goddess really pierces my heart: when I go outside and I see the leaves and see the moss and see the stars, and I see all these things that she's put here for us, and I see all these things man has done to all the things she put here – taking her gifts and gouging them out, stomping on them and tearing them down and messing them up, and slapping her in the face constantly. I wonder how she's put up with it for this long. And she says she's being raped constantly, and all she wants is lovers. That's all she needs.

She's like the Garden of Eden personified. She'll give us absolutely anything we'll ever want if all we'll do is love her, and love her for herself and all the things she likes to give us.

ॐ   ॐ   ॐ

There is a history of personal and interpersonal challenges and transformations among the three of us joining in this session without which this manifestation of the Goddess would have been impossible. From the point of view of her coming, and the archetypal roles she ascribed to us this night, the necessity and significance of those changes become much clearer than they often were during the past year. Still, we were guided at most of our turning points by faith in a light such as shone so brightly this night.

The printed page cannot convey the vibrancy of a personality, nor the passionate personal power with which the Goddess encountered Jim and me. Hers is not an abstract spirituality but a fully embodied, sensual, emotional presence, which never seems to lose its centred wisdom for all her participation in the multi-faceted forces of her domain. A shock of recognition accompanied her tale of abuse by mankind, for the victim now suddenly acquired a painfully human identity. The consequences were suddenly a matter of life and death as real to us as any individual's – except that the Earth Mother's fate at once determines the fate of *all* individuals and beings of our world. Her wording suggests that our interaction with the Earth is an erotic act – with all the potential for perversion *or* transcendence such intimacy allows.

Her personal words to me – about my spirit name Ravenstar, from my first archetypal/ reincarnational dream 13 years ago, and about the origin, quality and potential of my soul as linked to the Spirit of the Sun – carried the conviction of knowing me from the inside: striking home intuitively with great force; yet knowing me better than I do myself, because at a far deeper level than I can say that I know.

The effect of her walking about the room and manipulating our energies with a wave of her hand was unprecedented in these sessions, showing that an entirely new, sometimes daunting dimension of realness has been added. Question-and-answer exchanges, punctuated by occasional interior experiments, have been left behind – for, whatever was coming through Kelly was now *actively* present before and *with* us, *alive* in our house!

Her awakening of us to our true identities was indeed a homecoming – and so, too, her opening of Jim and me to each other. While we have been friends, strongly respecting and enjoying each other, our meeting with that degree of vulnerability, open at all the levels of self evoked by Ravenstar and [Jim's new name], held the delicate tension of a bud's hushed explosion in spring. The ceremonial poetry that the Goddess lent to our "meeting" – which could easily appear mere platitude, apart from the energy of this final experience – drew me out beyond my lingering doubts for my own worthiness to be a friend and brother, bearing my new name, to glimpse the waking dream we might all create together if we'd affirm our inner being as wholly as she does.

I remember feeling like a shy young maiden waiting for Jim to kiss my lips. A simple act, but a very new and forceful one – not merely because not normally practised in our society, but because of the depth of meaning we all gave it. *This* is ritual magic: making something outwardly simple glow with energy from within, recreating the world in translucent beauty. Tonight, in perfect love and perfect trust, we took the leap of self-recognition as three someones deeper and wholer than we had let ourselves remember. It is a gift to know the tender strength of such perfection – a gift that wants and needs to be shared.

ॐ   ॐ   ॐ

Less than two weeks later is the session in which Margaret undergoes her own personal breakthrough, as told in Chapter 12.[143] So it should be understood that the power catalyzing Margaret's "miraculous" opening that day (October 16th) is linked to the development bringing the Goddess a fortnight earlier. However, Chapter 12 did not acknowledge the Goddess's emergence, soon after Margaret's "miracle" in that October 16th session. This omission is corrected below, with some dialogue repeated and now correctly attributed. (Actually, there are so many facets to this key session that further portions will appear in Chapter 14 and the Epilogue as well.)

Also participating in this morning's session is Clare. Compelled to visit us after participating in our summer workshop in the Okanagan (including the session that ended Chapter 10), she has driven a long way to get here – in perfect timing. In the following excerpts, Clare's third eye has already been exceedingly active as Moita begins what is becoming a familiar incantation.

Moita/Goddess/Amar session #204 (Kelly, David, Margaret, Clare / October 16, 1981)

MOITA: It is good to get into a place where words have lost . . . their meaning, or where meanings no longer fit words.

Clare: There is only a feeling for it, and each time it's only stronger.

MOITA: Each time builds upon the last. This is a reality outside of time and space. It does not depend upon man's conceptions of reality. This is *my* world – part of it...

(A very long silence, as the Earth Goddess becomes present.)

GODDESS: *(to me)* Are you less daunted now?

David: Not really daunted, no. *(pause)* Will it ever be clear again when it's Moita and when it's the Goddess? *(pause)*

GODDESS: It has *been* Moita. *(pause)* There are many sides to me . . . and I have no boundaries. Let your own energy rise, until you have no boundaries either.

              (turning to Margaret) You, too, have joined us. *(pause)* The more empty you let yourself become, the more filled you will be. And there is no loss; there is only gain.

(During a long silence, Margaret and Clare gaze at each other.)

GODDESS: What see you now?

Clare: *(whisper)* Oh my God. Like a connection. I don't know how to describe it. Something coming from all your eyes, between each of you, both of you.

GODDESS: *All* of us.

Clare: She *(Margaret)* is much more beautiful now than when she came in the door.

Margaret: I feel very warm.

GODDESS: Well met, and you have seen each other. Now you know you are not alone...

              When man is healed, I will be made whole again. Then there will be no more battles, for there will be no more fear, and man will know he is *not alone*. And so, you help me by accepting yourself.

Margaret: My acceptance of others will follow.

GODDESS: Acceptance of self is first. You will recognize more of yourself in others, and through you will understand where they are coming from and why they do what they do. You will learn compassion instead of pity. You will gain understanding instead of living in confusion. The world will become bright and clear instead of dark and foreboding, and you will see the meaning of death and its necessity – the births that follow it. And you will help prepare me, through your understanding, for my *own*, so I may be reborn *with* man instead of beyond him. For I, too, am afraid of being alone.

Margaret: It's a good purpose, a reason to be alive.

GODDESS: Man is the only being on this planet that can *choose* me. All the others are mine already. They know me, they love me, yet they have not *chosen* me of their *own* free will – I merely *am*. And I need to be chosen so that a pathway is formed *between* man and me – one that can [be travelled] in two directions.

Margaret: I hear so many things in your words.

GODDESS: You see? The Earth, too, has a soul.

Margaret: You are the Earth Mother.

GODDESS: Yes. And all forms are my form, and yet this is the only form with speech. My other voices have gone unheard, for the most part. But perhaps this voice will touch the hearts of men.

Margaret:	And you need speakers to speak for you?
GODDESS:	Speakers who will let me speak.
David:	What way of life at a centre here would also speak for you?
GODDESS:	A life that involves my other forms. A life that allows me to ... give ... of my energy, to participate in creativity, to shower you with my gifts and sustain you with my presence. The more things that touch my Earth, the more channels are open to touch back.

The seeds have been planted within you, and they will germinate in this place. Yes, this is a place of power. This is a place where my body is more aware of your presence. This is a place where you can make an impact, where you can spread this energy, let it grow. I can use it to help. I can shape it. I can put it where it needs to go. I can change the structure of the planet, eventually. And I will, with man's help.

Here, at least, you are more in touch with what I *have been*, instead of what I have *become* in many places. I cannot touch those in the city. Their bodies are separated from me by substances which I cannot affect, which are not a *part* of me. They are alien to me. In time, perhaps, I could learn how, but they have grown too quickly. They have come too fast. I have not been given time to adapt, and that has happened because man lost touch with *me*, and did not listen when I tried to tell him he was going too quickly, that he was racing ahead of his life-force and leaving it behind. And so, that is why you are all alone – or seem to be...

Clare:	Being a city girl, you must not be too pleased with me.
GODDESS:	I had to get you away from the city in order to reach you.
Clare:	I came joyfully. I much prefer it here.
GODDESS:	You will notice my lack much more now than you have before.
Clare:	It was very strong before. There are not enough places to go and see you, not anymore.
GODDESS:	And even my sky is changed, and so is the Sun.
Clare:	Do you feel my hurt when I look around me?
GODDESS:	Your pain is my pain. You feel what I feel...

(Soon after this, Amar also comes, as will be told in Chapter 14. Then, from the after-session conversation:)

Margaret:	I could really feel the pain that was in the Earth Mother's messages. The *pain* was just pouring out of her eyes – what she was going through and her vulnerability. For her to admit that she was afraid of being alone was really eye-opening for me. I didn't expect her to admit basic vulnerability like that, that what we did would affect her so profoundly. I always thought about the Earth as feeling ... no matter what man did, it might suffer a lot but it was capable of pulling itself up and over. And it would do *without* us eventually and wouldn't need us. It could go on with all the other beings that were on it.
Kelly:	That was neat about her needing us to *choose*, that we were the only being capable of conscious choice, that it was so important to be chosen like that.
David:	That kind of choice – the consciousness and freedom of it – seems to be really

important if we are to become co-creators.

Kelly: And she doesn't want worshippers – she wants *partners*. It seems that our [traditional] concept of God has been that He wants to be on top of things and in control, where the Goddess wants us to be a *part* of her and *share* all she has with us, so we can come up to where *she* is and she doesn't have to be alone.

Margaret: That's a complete contradiction to the old God.

David: Of course, way, way back, at least in one cycle of consciousness, we were part of the Earth Mother, but not aware of it ourselves. So this is, in a way, a culmination.

Kelly: We were like all the other beings on the planet, like the deer and the whale and such, where we just naturally flowed with things, and weren't aware of ourselves as being different or separate. That's probably the reason why we went through will in the first place, so we could get self-identity. Then we could go back to that being one with the Earth Mother, and still be self.

Margaret: I think a lot of people are struggling their whole lives against a feeling that they're not important; that if they died, nobody would miss them. That's the thing that impressed me most about the Earth Mother. Plus, it was a revelation that she . . . I never talked to the Earth in my whole *life*, you know – not *that* way, eyeball to eyeball!

Kelly: No kidding! How do you think I feel having her talk through me, cell to cell?!

Margaret: Oh, I couldn't even imagine. But it was relevant to me. In my own way I'd been talking to trees and the sky and stuff for years, and we never passed any words, but feelings were very intimate. That was the one thing in my life that I did *trust*. It made me feel good when nothing else could.

Chapter 14

RELEASING THE MAGICAL CHILD

The more you look within, as you have begun, the more clear you will become. It is that clarity that is important to you. Let yourself express the inner. Search your depths and do not be afraid to let them out. There is no one answer, for you are each your own answer.
– Moita (July 29, 1981)

Sometimes the right question from a first-time attender allows Moita to weave together many aspects of a whole answer, framing her message to us in fuller perspective. Below, Moita seems to have this book's title in mind as she sums up key themes and introduces this final chapter.

Moita session #212 (Kelly, David, Kate, Donna / February 27, 1982)

Kate: How do we stop the world from being violated here, all the wrong things that are being done on and to the Earth?

MOITA: *(softly)* First, you become aware of yourself, and then you help others to become aware of themselves. It is your world, and you must decide what to do with it.

This is the test, you see? You have created the world. You have created the civilization. Now you must decide what you will do with your creation. You must become conscious creators and make conscious choices. And to do that, you must wake up from this dream of life, be aware within the dream; and then you can move it in the direction of your choices. What has been created can be uncreated. The Earth can be healed . . . through your own energy coupled with others, joined together, becoming conscious and awake, recognizing your own divinity, your own beauty.

Thresholds are always hard. You can almost see through the door to what is possible beyond it. It is *time* for this planet to join the rest of its universe and recognize itself. You are only one life-form in this, but you are the life-form that has free will. We would have willing partners, not unconscious ones. That is why you must all wake up.

In some ways I represent not only the past that has been lost but also the future that can be claimed. I span *all* of the times, from past to future, for I exist outside of time. I can [come into] this world, but I am not a part of it. It is my choice to be here, to share the possibility of other dimensions, of other ways of seeing energy. I bring more questions than I do answers, because I am from such a different sphere. My answers cannot be yours. I am here to help you find your own answers, to help you become your own being, to create your own universe.

I could tell you how I might change the world, but then you might try to do it *my* way.

Every planet, every soul, has its own uniqueness to it. I would not make the universe a reflection of myself. And so, my answers are not easy answers. They require commitment from those who are seeking, a commitment to being honest and truthful, and looking at themselves even if they are afraid of what they look like – to *know* themselves, so they can make their own answers.

You are growing up. *(pause)* This is the adolescence of your world – rebellion . . . trying to find your own way . . . The fact that we *can* be reached is an answer in itself.

Kate: Why won't you have the world a reflection of yourself?

MOITA: For I, by myself, am not whole. I am a part of the universe. If I made the universe a reflection of myself, it would not be able to sustain my view. It would collapse. It would not *change*. The universe thrives on diversity, on differentness, on uniqueness. Imagine: no two snowflakes are the same! No two leaves are alike! No two people are identical! Nothing repeats itself except differentness. If I made the world sameness, it would not be alive!...

It must be a collective choice, not an individual choice, in the *end*. But each individual must also make a choice *alone, first*. One who is awake has a greater capacity for bringing about change than one who is asleep – merely because they are aware of the process. They know they are dreaming...

A great many difficulties on this planet would be solved if differentness was not looked upon as wrong, or evil, or contradictory. Each one of you is busy trying to prove that your view of the universe is right. Each one of you is attempting to create a world in your own image, to make it a reflection of yourself, instead of embracing the differences.

Not every person needs to embrace personally all differences, but when differences are accepted they no longer become so important. Many people are violent mainly because they are not accepted as they are. The violence is not necessarily an expression of *what* they are but *how* they feel about not being accepted.

We see your secrets. We hear your hidden thoughts. We view your entire life, and all of your lives. We see your mistakes. We see your guilt. We watch you punish yourself for things you think you have done wrong. We accept all these things. But you do not accept them in yourself or in each other!

Every one of you do things, say things, feel things, want things, are afraid of things, desire things, wish to reach out and touch things – and each one of you is afraid to do that for fear that another one of you will think it wrong, or condemn you, or shut you out, or not accept you, or tell you that you are bad, you are unworthy, or treat you as less than they treat others.

You are all doing the same thing to each other. You have not recognized your commonality in your differences. The differences are more on the surface than they are in the depths. There are differences in how the universe is perceived, or in how it is related *to*, but not very many differences in how each being feels towards a universe. A universe is something that [each being] plays itself off from; [it] creates a stage, a place in which to be real... *I* know I am real. You must know you are real too. Are you?

ço   ço   ço

That is why the God and the Goddess created the Sun-Child: so they would not get lost in their own reflection.

– Moita (October 30, 1981)

This final chapter is about each of us becoming more real, by giving birth through the heart to a new, more unique expression of Self while honouring each other as the different individualities we are. This is the spirit of the Medicine Wheel, expressed in Moita's own nature as a group entity, that has guided Kelly and me since the beginning. It envisions a participatory universe in which unity and diversity, individual and group, co-exist harmoniously in and by virtue of each other. The turning of that wheel within our daily lives provides the endless challenge of perceiving the spirit with which each of us would invest our changing, often seemingly contradictory, forms. Through the change of perspectives it makes possible, the Medicine Wheel seems an essential image and tool for community: the healing of ourselves, our relationships, our civilization, our Earth.[144]

When we travel from one thing to another merely, we are but a rolling stone moving along the perimeter of the wheel. If, however, each aspect of life we touch – like the four functions of thinking, feeling, sensing and intuiting, the masculine and feminine, looking inward and looking outward, and other polarities – can be recognized and made our own, integrated in an enduring manner, we then follow a spiral path toward the centre of our personal mandala. In the end, as with the circular labyrinth traced on the floor of Chartres Cathedral, though coming close many times, we cannot actually attain the centre until we have encountered every nook and cranny of the maze.

Within the Medicine Wheel of Kelly's and my relationship, our differences in interests and energies on a personality level continue to show more strongly through the fall of 1981. But we allow space for those differences through arrangements for "loving more than one", and by a deepening experience of each other on an archetypal level.

Spontaneous rituals of sensuous, telepathic merging and transcendence develop, as Kelly comes to embody the Goddess energy and I too begin to experience myself as the Horned God making love to the Earth – her seas and hills and caves alive with the emotions of a mythical being. At a later stage, I begin entering imaginatively into the consciousness of the spiritual Sun, or Universal Mind, projecting itself outward into material form, caressing with hands and lips and soul all the alien diversity of the universe now recognized as my own long-forgotten innermost nature. Neither memory nor words can truly reproduce such a multi-levelled, yet tangible, experience. That Kelly and I can both give ourselves up freely to our corresponding archetypal roles reflects both upon the strong connection between us and our very different qualities of soul.

At fall's end, the winter solstice provides a good occasion to reflect on these things.

Moita session #210 (Kelly and David / December 20, 1981)

MOITA: All things are connected. It is in seeing whole patterns instead of seeing pieces of patterns that you find wholeness. You learn how to become one with your particular role, your part, your facet. You learn how to change faces – from the centre of the wheel, looking out, turning around in all directions. You also grow eyes in the back of your head *(smiles)*, for you see not with your physical senses but with your mind, with your soul.

(to me:) You have had some good experiences lately: touching the Sun, becoming a part of the creative force.

ಀ   ಀ   ಀ

Truly becoming one's own particular facet of the jewel is equivalent to becoming one's own channel. Paradoxically, but in line with all Moita has said in the past, it is through recognizing and accepting my sharp differences from Kelly that I move nearer to being that channel. While my few attempts at channeling in Kelly's sense have never gone very far, a step is taken in early October 1981 toward a form more my own. The visit of Clare, our friend from the Okanagan whose energy is closer to mine, proves the catalyst. By seeking to draw *me* out and being receptive to *my* leadings, Clare begins to play the role I have long assumed relative to Kelly.

Here channeling is something I feel I myself am doing; yet not an ordinary I, but an I that flows with the wind moving through the trees of our forest, letting fly the brightly coloured leaves of autumn. And the unique joy of Clare's visit is that all three of us become channels in our individual ways – a presentiment of what it will be to live in community in the New Age. Clare is present with Margaret and us for the major session on October 16th, but Moita also comes spontaneously for this session the day before.

Moita session #203 (Kelly, David, Clare / October 15, 1981)

MOITA: *(to me:)* You are learning what it means to be a channel.
David: Yes.
MOITA: It is good. *(very long pause, as we gaze at each other)*
David: How might my form of channeling be different from Kelly's?
MOITA: It will be different in form, but not in substance. You will have more . . . You will *need* more conscious control over your channeling. You will not be an open door all of the time, or most of the time. But you are learning how to open your *own* door, and how to create the type of communication that will suit you best..., connecting with your larger self, your higher self, your roots. *(her voice growing gradually softer)*

You have done much more time-travelling than you have been aware of, and yet you are becoming more aware of your travels than you have in the past. You know that this moment is the only real moment, and that all of your future moments are built upon it. You *can* be a lucid dreamer. *(pause)*

You see, the ban has been lifted.

(Moita refers to our not holding hands in a circle, as we have in virtually all previous sessions, since she came spontaneously this time without our planning. But Moita is also suggesting that this physical means of sharing energy is no longer necessary for us.)

MOITA: We are One. Our merger is accomplished. It is a fact. And as you learn, with yourself, more will come through this door. I am your mirror. You *use* me to help you see how far you have gone. *(pause)*

I am *all* of you. I am one of you. I am each. I am none. I am real, because I *affect*. You are real, because I *see* you and I *know* you. Self-recognition. As long as there is another being in the universe who sees you as separate, you exist as separate, as real... *(pause)*

I come where I am needed, and when. You all know my pattern. I am a steady friend. Because I can spread myself...throughout time, I can be with you in *all* of your roles, in all of the pain, for each of your questions. I am there...

(later, to Clare:) When you come out of this reality, your other self – your other *selves* – will have many doubts about what you have perceived here, but there is a part of you that knows that this is true and real. This is no put-up job. *(soft laughter)* You have the proof you need. If you will accept it, then more proof will be forthcoming. But you must take one step at a time.

Thoughts flow from one thing to another. They do not seem connected, if you try to pick them apart. And yet, as we flow through this conversation, communication, you can see it is all interwoven, for you are experiencing it as one tapestry instead of as many little tapestries. Even though my words must come singly, you are hearing them all at once. *(pause)*

The task is the meeting of two worlds. It is like learning how to talk to a dolphin, who has a completely different experience of reality than you, and yet is no less intelligent and no less real. It is like talking to an alien species. So many of those stories stem from this inability to communicate things exactly as they are meant...*in* the reality they stem from.

(to me:) The description of you as a part of the Sun relates to this. Learning how to communicate your own uniqueness to someone else whose background, in all aspects of spiritual existence, is alien to yours, you are both *(i.e. Kelly and I)* seeking to comprehend the vast differences – and the sameness – behind your realities and how they function. How to step inside another person's skin and see the world through their eyes: it is the only way to truly understand another's concepts of reality. But it is not a giving up of self. Self is lost only temporarily, and it is found on the other side of merge.

You are no less important than any piece in this play that you have created, helped to create. Each piece must play its part. Each must become perfect in its own sense. And there is no better; there is only different. *(pause)*

There is no praise in being a channel.

David:	That would be only a distraction. There is joy in the moment.

MOITA:	I am the part that understands you, and you are releasing the part that understands *me*. *(pause)* The in-between moments are merely little trips, non-essential and basically unimportant, because here they are left behind, and they fade into insignificance, as they should. *(pause)* You have grown a great deal, and we are pleased with you, still.

David:	*(laughs)* I was remembering the last time you said you were pleased with me. *(i.e. in the summer of 1978 in Regina, in the midst of our tests with Ruth and the group there)*[145]

MOITA:	Yes. Another time of difficult choices that must be made alone, in order to be made right.

જ   જ   જ

Now we move ahead one day, dipping once more into the remarkable October 16, 1981 session. This morning, not "only" do Moita and the Goddess speak, but also Amar – as if to emphasize the range of qualities and levels of energy that are becoming available to humanity in this transitional period. We pick up the conversation after the Goddess's main response to my question, "What way of life at a centre here would speak for you?", as given in the last chapter.

Moita/Goddess/Amar session #204 (Kelly, David, Margaret, Clare / October 16, 1981)

GODDESS:	You are learning to be a creator. This is your own creation. You can manifest it or not, as you choose, or as you learn. *(pause)* Your Sun-self is rising.

	(Long silence, as she touches my heart centre and my heart starts pounding amid rising energy.)

David:	I can see the roses, and the purples, and the golds . . . and rays shooting up.

GODDESS:	Now you know where the names came from. *(i.e. our "Sunseed" workshops and "Rays from Starflower")* The seed of the Sun is within you. *(pause)* And so, you began naming yourself...

	We have another . . .

	(Amar's energy is rising as Kelly's eyes close. After Amar reopens them, he comments to Clare about meeting her before, the exact words lost as I change the tape.)

Clare:	Have I met you here, or back home?

AMAR:	Not here . . . yet.

Clare:	Amar is the only other one I met before.

AMAR:	Yes.

Clare:	But Amar did not smile before.

AMAR:	Amar did not come after the Earth Mother. *(an example of Amar's wry humour!)*

Clare:	You are clearly different now... – even than a minute ago! Why is there a different spot to see with each personality?

AMAR:	You could say that each cell has a memory locked within it.

Clare:	I see. Yes.

AMAR: It is the third eye. It is the eye you are seeing with. You do not see these things with your physical eyes.

Clare: Sure feels like it.

AMAR: That is how your mind interprets it.

(There's a pause as Amar turns to Margaret:)

Margaret: Am I looking at Amar now?

AMAR: I hope so...

(This being Margaret's first experience of Amar, she has some trouble identifying Amar's particular energy. Kelly, meanwhile, feels like a wheel of different personalities that turns, clicking into different grooves as Margaret's thoughts turn, determining who is there or how much the entity can be present – whether Amar needs to speak through another kind of focus linked to Margaret's thoughts or not. Amar is intentionally showing us how each participant is the "tuner" of Kelly's channeling. When Margaret clicks into Amar's own energy, the experience is wholly different.)

(Then Kelly feels as if she's floating, detached from her body. I also am feeling the intensity of Amar's eyes, and the reality of the room changing, the air becoming thick and wavy.)

AMAR: It is a matter of focus.

Margaret: Mm-hmm. And I'm struggling with it.

AMAR: Each time you go through a different thought, you bring forth something else... It is in this manner that you find out where your mind *is*! – by seeing what changes are wrought in the channel. Where you are focused will determine what comes through. You are all part of this . . . process...

(A period of adjustment as they look into each other's eyes)

AMAR: There. Now you are hitting the right ones. *(pause)* You see how the presence fades and then comes in stronger? We are always here. It is your focus that changes.

Margaret: You seem male. Are you male?

AMAR: I am perceived as masculine. I am neither one nor the other. But the amount of focus it takes in order to be present is a masculine type of energy.

Margaret: Seems quite . . .

AMAR: Yes. It needs to be. I am from a much farther place.

Margaret: Ah! You are a teacher also?

AMAR: Yes.

Margaret: What is it you would like to teach me at the present moment?

AMAR: You are already learning it! You have been perceiving much better. You could say this entire experience has been a test. Each one of you has undergone a different kind of test through it. *(pause)* Can you see the beauty in severity, or in what you perceive as severe?

Margaret: Mm-hmm... You would be more severe, then, perhaps more *decisive* in what you felt had to be done?

AMAR: I have very distinct ideas. I am much more aware of the pattern. The further from the pattern you go, the more clear the pattern becomes.

Margaret: Yes. I've learned a little of that.

AMAR: There are fewer of us on this level. We have merged with each other in order to get here. In order to gain the distance from the pattern, we have absorbed the pattern itself...

(turning to me:) Are you perceiving *more* of this pattern, the way the interwoven parts are connected?

David: I guess. *(pause)* What can you teach me about singing to the Sun?

(I'm connecting the Goddess's mention today of my "Sun-self" to her statement two weeks earlier that I would "learn again how to sing to the Sun" – a reference to our "Earth and Sun" incarnation, where we tried to reawaken awareness of the unity of life.)

AMAR: Listen. The song has begun.

(Suddenly a chorus of birds begins to sing outside our window. A squirrel chatters and comes right up to the glass to look in before scurrying away. A cloud moves away from the Sun, and the light becomes bright and clear, almost dazzling after the semi-darkness.)

AMAR: You see? *(pause)*

David: I'm hearing it inside. *(not facing the window, I have barely noticed the above)*

AMAR: And you are hearing it without.

(As if on cue, the squirrel chatters once more.)

AMAR: The Earth is the voice of the singer. The singer is the song. *(long pause)*

Yes, I am part of the Sun, too. *(pause)* That is why I chose the name "Amar" for this communication. One name for the Sun has been Rama, or Ra.

You are all gods and goddesses. You are just in their sleeping state.

David: I've dreamed of waking up gods and goddesses before.

(And again, we hear the birds are singing . . .)

෴   ෴   ෴

The image of sleeping gods and goddesses leads off on several related pathways. One is my "First Direction" dream of spring 1976, which prefigured the challenges and achievements of my time with Ruth,[146] including starting Sunseed and the Loria communications, leading in turn to Kelly and Moita. During the "chase scene" climax to that dream, I leaped and flew over a body of water, reaching down to touch first my pursuers and then major Tarot card figures. On being touched, these figures transformed into Greek gods and goddesses, now awakened or brought back to life. Another pathway is the life shared by the four of us here, as Moita will describe to conclude this remarkable October 16th session, a life centred around a temple to Aphrodite in ancient Greece. Kelly was also a channel at that time, while Margaret was my teacher, as I was Clare's, in this Greek islands life on which we can all wax nostalgically.

Consistent with that shared incarnation, my deepest associations to Greek religion are to the ancient dream healing temples of Asclepius and other Mystery schools of spiritual initiation. The Earth Goddess on October 4th told Jim that she was his initiation and that now he was "one of us".

Similarly, after her breakthrough on October 16th, the Goddess told Margaret that now she had "joined us". After these first comings of the Earth Mother, I begin to wonder then to myself, "But who says *I've* been initiated?!" Perhaps it is my own thought that brings it, but the desired experience is soon furnished me, again set to all appearances in ancient Greece.

On November 28th and 29th, two dreams refer to a U.S. president as having died or as having his health examined – in symbolic terms, reflecting concern for the well-being of the "executive", my conscious self or ego. Here is the final dream in the series, in which doctors and teachers help me to cross my own threshold, acknowledging the wholeness on which the little self depends.

"Gates of Divine Buddahood" dream
David / November 30, 1981

The U.S. president is in a coma and undergoing brain surgery amidst controversy over the succession of power. I see his soul as a second body apart from the physical one the doctors are working on. Finally the physical body moves, signifying return of the soul and completion of a successful operation. A male figure then appears, reading from the New Testament about dying and death.

Next the robed figure of a female teacher appears, walking along a path to a couple of stone stairs into which have been carved the words "Gates of Divine Buddahood". It is perhaps the earlier male figure who follows her, and I in turn follow him. Before climbing the steps, I ask permission of the teacher. She replies, "Yes, there are large and small here as well." I understand her to mean the Whole and the Individual as cosmic principles – and that the other man and I are representatives, respectively, of these.

The stairs lead to a stone courtyard backed by a high stone wall, bearing the engraving of a plant, such as wheat grass, expressing the same organic relation of part to whole. The teacher speaks of a stellar constellation linked to my own energy and of related Greek and English words, including the root of "educate" (literally, to "draw forth").

Finally, she asks if I have come of my own free will. I realize how important is my having chosen this, and reply yes. I am then pulled by an invisible force toward a doorway in the stone wall. Reaching the entrance, I stoop slightly under the low arch. Just inside the entry, I see a metal grating at the base of the opposite wall, which I immediately identify as a hearth. I know this hearth means the heart – the centre of all things – and that it is here as a real/symbolic presence at the climax of my initiation.

I know that the hearth embodies the heart-centredness each person must attain in order to cross the threshold into this new reality. I do so in all humility as a strong energy rises, focused at my own heart centre. Having become lucid to the dream as I was being ushered toward the doorway, I now awake, wondering at the significance of this crossing.

§ § §

On October 16th, of course, Margaret experienced an initiation of the heart as well. And in the same last days of November, Kelly receives quite a dramatic dream about Margaret in the same vein. Kelly's dream will be told at the end of the session below, in which the Goddess once more appears. It is attended by C. – whose empathy with the Earth has led her also into Wicca – and a Margaret conscious of the changes set in motion by her last session. Her opening description matches well what Kelly and I have long said.

Moita/Goddess session #209 (Kelly, David, Margaret, C. / December 1, 1981)

Margaret: I felt you coming very distinctly this time.

MOITA: What did I feel like?

Margaret: A sort of humming electric current starting, vibrating in my head. It makes the rest of the house melt away, and it's not quite as real when you're here.

MOITA: It's much more like a prop.

Margaret: Yes.

MOITA: Seeing through your own disguises.

Margaret: I increasingly am not worrying about what I am, and increasingly aware that I'm all things, and that I really don't have to stay in one mould. It's kind of a relief not having to put one cloak on and leave it on all the time.

MOITA: Good. That is how you all learn how to be a channel.

Margaret: *(soft laugh)* That's not going to happen to *me*, is it? *(laughs again, loudly)*

MOITA: There are different kinds of channeling. Everyone has a different kind of channeling that is suited to them. The form that it takes is unimportant. It is its substance – the ability to flow, to become one with all things – that is of the essence. Some speak; others touch, show, share in different ways. You can be a channel in many moments, and a different kind of channel in *each* moment. When a friend comes to you in trouble and you find a comforting or intuitive thing to say, you are being a channel for your self, for your own intuition.

Margaret: My greater self comes through these times (?).

MOITA: Yes. You tap into all that you are, all that you are capable of being...

(Omitted here is their discussion of an instance showing Margaret's greater openness to clairvoyant information. In the next section, she mentions the recurrence of an image previously dreamed – but the connection made this time quite surprises us!)

Margaret: I had a glimpse of myself as a very old lady this morning.

MOITA: Again?

Margaret: Yes! *(laughs)* Rather ugly, yet still with a sense of humour, rather tough.

MOITA: *(turning to me, with a smile:)* David, you have met the old hag.

David: *(in amused surprise)* Really?! The one at Kyrionis?

MOITA: Yes.

David: That's *very* interesting.

Margaret: *(laughs)* Kyrionis: the place with the fire meeting.

MOITA: The earthquake, and then the meeting and the fire.

(As Margaret recalls from reading Kelly's regression transcript,[147] our reincarnational ancestors encountered an old hag outside the long-ago city of Kyrionis in Asia Minor, before they began migrations west and east to found new civilizations at Musili and in the Himalayan region. The members of this large group were sitting around a campfire in the hills outside quake-ridden Kyrionis, on the night before dividing to begin their long journeys. There was much arguing and indecision, exacerbated by lack of food. A passing hag asked to join the circle, but was told to go away. Kelly had the impulse to run after her with some food, but gave in to group pressure.)

David: Was she never able to join up with us then?

MOITA: Not in that life. But that was the life that started you on this path – the meeting of ways in that place – since you were not rejected by everyone. It awakened a spark of curiosity.

Margaret: I was a bit of an old tyrant, wasn't I, in some ways?

MOITA: Not an entirely pleasant personality, true. They were difficult times.

Margaret: Yes. *(pause)* I've had glimpses for the last two weeks into other lives. Some of them have been very surprising and very clear. And I'm not quite sure why I'm seeing them, but I feel quite certain about where they've come from. Is this to eliminate fear?

MOITA: It is to help you start integrating your selves, so that you *can* be all things and understand what it means to have *been* all things – to know that you have worn many cloaks. And knowing that you have worn many cloaks takes away the necessity for wearing only one at a time.

Margaret: Yes. And if one need not identify with one cloak, then you have nothing to lose.

MOITA: As they say, but fear itself. *(Margaret laughs)* Man clutches at fear and tries to keep it with him. He thinks it will keep him safe.

Margaret: Hmm, that's strange.

MOITA: *Isn't* it. Safe from *himself*, and all of his other cloaks. You are experiencing the effects of what we did to you.

Margaret: Yes. I know that. I'm just constantly amazed at it, and that it's not frightening. It's just sort of exciting in a quiet kind of way. I'm not even really frightened about what it might do to me in the future. *(pause)*

MOITA: And what is the future but what you make it?

Margaret: Yes. *(laughs softly; pause)* Glad I'm having a lot of fun.

MOITA: Then you shall learn *a lot*. *(Margaret laughs)* Certainly you will learn much more than the one who hides in the house and is afraid to encounter life in all of its different facets.

           Each experience that you have, be it positive or negative in your eyes, serves a very useful function – especially now, for it touches a chord within you that helps to waken these other lives that you are leading and helps teach you how to integrate those lives with this one. *You* are now learning that reincarnation is not just a philosophy or a concept, but a reality that exists in the eternal now. In *all* of your moments you are in all of these places, right in this moment. They are not dead, and they are not past. And they *affect* you, and in turn you affect them.

Margaret: Yes. It's going to feel good to change my past, for better.

MOITA: You can also change *this* life's past for better too. It too is not dead. You can help give yourself the understanding you need in order to get through the things you have gone through.

Margaret: I can see it working. I can see people looking at me differently, and looking at what I've done differently, all the time. There are people who want to cling to old concepts of what I was, but even *they* are changing in spite of themselves.

MOITA: That is because your awareness is stronger than their unconscious attempts at keeping the status quo, at being safe.

Margaret: "Strong is beautiful." That's one of my latest little finds.

MOITA: Yes. It does not have to be destructive or frightening. *(pause)* The Earth Mother is strong and beautiful too.

Margaret: I think of her strength in falling water. *(long pause)*

    (Kelly's eyes close . . . and then reopen. Margaret only gradually realizes the change.)

GODDESS: *(sighs)* Rising into another reality. *(pause)* I too can change cloaks. That is what *all* of those things are, you know – learning how to change cloaks, how to let each one be itself completely, without the interference of other selves, in order to experience it in its purest form, in order to remember it correctly.

Margaret: There is a correct way to remember it, then?

GODDESS: A complete way.

Margaret: Hmm. Who are you now?

GODDESS: *(laughs)* Whoever I *wish* to be. I am in the midst of change. I am travelling.

Margaret: Hmm. Moita and a higher level.

GODDESS: Or a different level. There is no higher, lower. There is merely different. Sometimes more intense, perhaps. Each universe has its own rules, and in each reality the rules of energy govern what can happen within that reality. Our combined concepts of the structure of the universe, of the nature of life – those are the things that we build upon. When we change our concept of reality, we change reality itself. For it is not something that stays still. It is *always* in motion, always evolving. *(pause)*

    I am the Earth. *(to Margaret, opposite her:)* You are in the position of the Sun at the moment – the element of fire, emotions, feelings. *(turning to C., on her left:)* You are the unconscious, the Moon, all those things that lie underneath the mind of man and wait to come out and spill into the world and shed its reflection on all of its mountains and oceans, thoughts. *(to me, on her right:)* You are the clarity, the thoughts, the air, the clear thinker, the sword, the east.

    As the Earth, I contain all change and am yet unchanged by the other elements. That is how the Earth can be all and still be itself. *(pause)*

I am here enough. *(an understatement)*

Margaret: Yes.

C.:   I hope I wasn't squishing your hand. *(with a laugh, having forgotten herself in the energy of this first-time meeting with the Goddess)*

GODDESS: No. *(pause as they look at each other)* You see my energy field.

C.:   A little. *(long silence as they continue to gaze)*

(The Earth Mother's message to C. relates back to our November 5, 1979 session in which Moita confirmed C.'s feeling she had once existed as an animal – specifically, an otter, who gained the desire to be human through being freed from a trap.[148] The Goddess's comments need to be understood as well in the context of other exchanges with Moita in which C. has stressed that the conditions of most people's lives through history, as well as some predicted, possible disasters in the transition to a New Age, seem unnecessarily harsh and contrary to human freedom.[149])

(Now speaking softly, intimately to C., with great tenderness:)

GODDESS: You are the one who experiences my pain more than my joy. You find beauty in my pain, though, I can see. My heart beats for you. *(pause)*

But do not grieve for me yet. As long as there are those who can hear my voice, who can feel my words as I speak to you through your life and touch you with my being, I will still be. A way will be found – maybe not the best, but there will be a way found to free *all* of my children, so that we can meet and learn of the other and accept our natures as right and beautiful.

You are afraid to see because of your association with pain in the past. We have been one, you and I. We will be one again, but in a different way, a *new* way. You're lost because you've changed form. You haven't lost me. I'm still there. But your body, your humanity, has made you feel apart from the Earth as no other form could have, because you are no longer consciously aware at all times. *(pause)*

You've chosen this path to help bridge the gap between the Earth and humanity. You are one who was sent forth to try to understand what it was to be human, and why we lost contact with man. You are learning. *(pause)* All these different parts coming together, making a whole, an understanding, a newness, leaving old structures behind – it is a death and a rebirth we will *all* go through together. We will all die and leave our old selves behind. I will understand man, and he will understand me. *(pause)*

It looks as if I have made this nose run.

(This is the usual reaction of Kelly's body when deep feelings are flowing. I too have felt tears during what seems a culmination of our contacts with C.)

David: I feel like you were in my dream, initiating me this week.

GODDESS: You could say that that was a part of me, yes – and Kelly's dream *(as given after this session)* about the heart of the Earth and you *(Margaret)* lying upon it.

David: How do you see what happened in that dream of mine?

GODDESS: I see it as you coming home, coming back to the centre of things. The heart is the centre from which all things flow, all things radiate – or at least, should. There is a great deal of heat at my centre...

It is time to change. *(long pause as the Goddess energy withdraws)*

MOITA: We are very much like your dream, you know – where you represented the individual and [the other man] the unconscious, the wholeness... Where she is the whole, I am the specific – even though I am much less specific than *you*.

David: And all part of one plant.

MOITA: All part of one tree, yes. Root, tree and branch... It is a very ancient symbol, the tree of life...

(turning to C.) How do you feel?

C.:   Fascinated... Now you're Moita again, and were you acting as a medium for the Earth? Like that was kind of the way I perceived it to be. Is that your perception of it?

MOITA: That could be partly true, yes.

C.:   Your appearance certainly went through changes. *(laughs)* Not spectacular, hallucinating changes, but you looked quite different. *(pause, looking)* Mm-hmm! *(laughs)*

MOITA: I feel like my energy is not quite as overwhelming. It is more contained, perhaps.

C.:   I don't know how I'd describe the impression.

MOITA: There certainly did seem to be a recognition happening between the two of you. It was good to see.

C.:   Yeah. *(pause)* You certainly look different at different times.

MOITA: All of my different cloaks.

C.:   Uh-huh! *(laughs)*

MOITA: I have worn many faces. They come in handy.

(In the conversation afterward, we all agree "how beautiful it was with C. and the Goddess" – how much feeling was present, how much energy was released from the heart. In addition:)

Kelly: So we meet the old hag, huh? Hi. *(Margaret laughs)*

David: It seems such a nice circle – what is happening in this life, starting from there.

Kelly: Yeah, that's *right*! Because now *she*'s the one with the land! *(laughing)* It's like the opposite this time.

(Finally, Kelly's dream about Margaret, from a few nights before, as told after the session:)

Kelly: You were creating this really amazing film that started off with an avalanche. After that – I'm sure it's related to your poem about the glacier – you made this tortuous path through mountainous regions. It was getting steeper and harder to climb. Then, as you finally clawed your way up this last ridge, you could hear this booming sound going through the Earth under you. As you got to the crest, you saw that the heart of the Earth was in the ground, and you were hearing the beating of this heart. You crawled over on top of it, and you laid all over it and let it beat through you. I thought it was the most fantastic film I'd ever seen, and I figured you should get at least an Oscar for it. *(laughter)*

I really identified with you in the dream. It was like we were one, but it was also just you – it was both. A lot of it relates to your poetry and your own understanding about the Earth Goddess – looking out at sunsets, northern lights, glaciers crashing down, all the ways the Earth speaks to us.

ও   ও   ও

Initiation, transformation, death and rebirth . . . the refining fire, the hearth, the heart . . . Does not the beating of the Earth's heart in Kelly's dream recall our fetal experience within the womb pervaded by the beating of our mother's heart? And yet, symbolically, how many of us can hear that beating through the insulating, isolating walls of the cocoon mankind has wrapped round itself?

On November 20th, ten days before the above session, Moita said:

> We see man covered in his own membrane, just before his birth, surrounded, feeling he is suffocating, unable to break through such a thin veil. Such little force is needed. And all the dramatics he creates to teach himself to break through are essentially unnecessary. He seeks to fool himself. He is his own enemy. The only thing that keeps him from being where he wants to be is the fear of being there – the unknowable.

The time for metamorphosis is upon us. The obsolete membranes of mind and behaviour can be cast aside. A leap in the dark leads to the light. The nightmare fades, and the Sun-child emerges to greet the new day.

This final session excerpt begins within the maze from which may emerge the seeker, when ready. Here it is obvious that the "magical child" free to enjoy a magical world has little to do with physical years, and everything to do with the human spirit – our own and all humanity's.

Moita session #211 (Kelly, David, Margaret, Jim / February 18, 1982)

Margaret: I've sure been meeting an awful lot of different people lately.

MOITA: Are you seeing the worth in each one?

Margaret: Yes, I think so.

MOITA: When you let yourself see the worth in another, you help them to see it in themselves. You help others to see their own beauty and their potential for action, for change, for growth.

Margaret: Yes, I like doing that. I've been practising on *kids. (laughs)* They're not kids, but they're in kids' bodies. *(referring to her work in a local youth drop-in centre)*

    I just wonder if there's some kind of plan in my being put with these people who seem to be bent on self-destruction sometimes. And yet you can see them wanting something besides that. They don't want to destroy themselves, but they don't know how *not* to.

MOITA: When you are in the midst of a pit of darkness, a single light makes a very large impression – sometimes a single word.

Margaret: Yes.

MOITA: It will stay in the awareness of the individual and lead them in new directions.

Margaret: I hope so. I'm trying to give as many of those words as I can. These children – why are they going through that, those kinds of lives?

MOITA: Because of their parents' parents' parents who started the cycle. You see, if you can start an upward trend, how much better your children's children's children will be able to enjoy the Earth and life.

Margaret: I'm amazed at how brave they can be in bad situations. When you can see it knocking them, see them struggling with it, it's hard to watch without wanting to help.

MOITA: You are doing something worthwhile by becoming more active, by participating in giving your energy.

Margaret: I hope so.

MOITA: Just do not let it tear you apart.

Margaret: Yeah, I could see where a person could be burned out awful quick. You have to be able to remove yourself each night and start fresh all over, forget what happened the day before. *(laughs)* Otherwise, anger would build up, the feeling that you weren't accomplishing.

MOITA: Mm-hmm. That's why it is important that each day begins as a new day. That is why you are learning to live in the now, so that the past doesn't hold its pattern on you...

There are so *many* patterns that need to be broken and seen through. If those patterns fit you, then that is all right; that is what they are there for. But when a pattern is propagated purely for its own sake – when it loses its purpose, its usefulness, it is not cast aside at the right time – then it becomes a master, and you become a slave to the pattern.

Margaret: Yes. You can't see new patterns.

MOITA: Right. Because the old one obscures your vision... This is one of the purposes for UFO sightings: breaking patterns. The concept that man is alone in the universe is a very large pattern. *(pause)* We've been living beside you for a long time. *(pause, gazing into each other's eyes)* You see? Once you pass the first threshold, the next one is much easier.

Margaret: I'm wondering if there's going to be another one.

MOITA: You usually find out *after* you walk through the door.

Margaret: *(laughs)* I can feel something coming. I just don't know what.

MOITA: You're letting yourself bloom.

Margaret: I saw images of myself healing, too. *(pause)* Perhaps I'll do that more with words than with touch.

MOITA: Perhaps words and touch are just different forms of the same thing.

Margaret: Mmm. *(pause)* Well, I feel ready for whatever it is when it's ready to come.

(There is no time like the present. Kelly's and Margaret's conversation after the session shows what occurs during the long silence as they continue gazing . . .)

Kelly: At first the shadows on your face turned it into this very mask-like, almost cartoon-like character. You didn't look like you were a person. When that happened, I realized it seemed a reflection of when you saw Moita's face so funny and strange. So I thought, "Ah-hah, there must be a fear here *I* have to go through too!"

The energy just kept getting higher and higher, the farther I let myself look at you and see that really weird, weird face and get it very, very clear, like I could reach out and touch it. And then all of a sudden it changed into a child! Your face was much slimmer, your hair was blonde, your eyes were more wide-eyed. I was seeing [your daughter] on your face!

Margaret: I went and regressed. I went from 12 years old, and then I went back getting younger and younger, and being in different places and doing different things until I was a little baby, like in the pictures my mother gave me. Then I just sort of melted into Moita as mother. Her face changed a little bit. Like the eyes – I thought maybe they were going to pop right out of the head for a while, they were so intense. They were just little *beads* of energy, just throbbing. Her eyes just looked like they were made of agate or something, but *vibrating* agate. Then she seemed to have finished.

(Moita breaks the silence of these experiences. Margaret's words below unwittingly recall some of the last words of the astronaut in Kubrick's 2001: A Space Odyssey, *as he begins to enter the monolith, from which he will return as the Divine Child.)*

MOITA: How are you taking this?

Margaret: It's *strong*!

MOITA: *Isn't* it! Are you seeing things? *(Margaret nods)* What do you see?

Margaret: A big universe, empty.

MOITA: Alone?

Margaret: No, not alone.

MOITA: Filled?

Margaret: Filled. Filled with *everything*.

MOITA: The farther in you go, the larger you become. *(pause)* You're awakening the child. *(Margaret laughs, while scenes flood through Kelly's mind)* All those beautiful moments that you had in your childhood . . . *(more softly now:)* . . . all those wonderful walks in the woods . . . *(half-whisper)* . . . the ocean, the sand, the rocks.

Margaret: I did have a *beautiful* childhood.

MOITA: *(softly)* Reconnect with it. Let it awaken. Let your joyousness flow out. The intimate wonder of a single leaf . . . *(pause)*

Each one of you has a part to play. Each one of you is just as important as each other. There is no better. There is only different. You each have a talent, a perspective, to bring to the whole. And without one part, the whole is different; it is not the same...

Margaret: I just wrote down a small sentence last week that is going to be a poem, I think, about how my childhood years have lost me – or I've lost them. And through children, I've been collecting little parts of what I was.

MOITA: *(softly)* Come . . . over here . . . *(Margaret moves into Moita's arms and they hug, while she whispers:)* . . . and let the child out. *(Margaret breathing deeply and close to tears for a while, till they part)*

Margaret: Is that why my mother gave me my baby pictures? *(on a recent visit)*

MOITA: Is there any coincidence? *(Margaret laughs; pause)* I must move on for a while. *(turning to Jim:)* How are *you*?

Jim: Amazed.

MOITA: Amazed at what?

Jim: *(emotional, in a husky voice)* At what I've become in the last few minutes.

MOITA: How do you perceive your change?...

Jim: Each time I try to put it into words, I lose some more of it.

MOITA: You need not explain it to me. I understand without words...

Jim: I am who I was. I'm about six years old – without the things I learned after that, and without the things I *haven't* learned after that... It's a place where my daughter has been taking me. But this experience with Margaret has magnified it and really brought me there strongly. My older mind had specific questions I was going to ask, but I'm not that anymore.

MOITA: That is why the child is magical. He does not try and define the universe into smaller parts. He sees them all as a whole. What sense is there in defining a part? – for in defining it you take it away from the wholeness and you change it.

Jim: It seems that . . . I've lost so incredibly much more than I've gained since then.

MOITA: But now that you are reconnecting with it, it is no longer *lost*. The experience of the awakening child is like holding two concepts of reality in your mind simultaneously, and not losing either one – coming from below and above. *(pause)*

Jim: It feels at least like holding two lifetimes (?). *(pause)*

MOITA: You have had many experiences with shifting realities. Once you rediscover a reality you have been out of, you can always shift back into it.

Jim: I hope so.

MOITA: Do not hope. *Know.* This is a key. Take it. *(touching Jim's third eye here?)* Memory, open. Let things go. Let the door open wide. Through the child is the larger Self, the pattern-seer, the part of you that understands and can express in different ways that understanding. *(pause)* If you lose worry, you will not forget the key. Worry is an insecure thought-form. The more you worry about losing something, the harder it is to find it again... *(pause)* *(to me:)* How are you feeling?

David: I've been connecting . . . When you and Margaret were talking, I was back in my childhood, and then through Jim I was with my son Michael quite a bit. So *(laughs)* the same patterns hold true for all of us.

MOITA: And you are all awakening together.

David: *(looking at the others)* I'm very aware how beautiful each one of us is. *(laughing warmly)*

MOITA: Yes. It is good for each of you to see the beauty in the others. *(pause)*

I am leaving... Good night. *(this exchanged with each of us individually)*

(Then, from the conversation afterward:)

Margaret: I lived in lovely places. I never lived in an ugly place, never. I lived on a beach when I was tiny. I lived in a forest, like you say. I had an orchard of my own. I had a swamp of my own I could raft on, where I caught minnows. I was always up to my knees in the water or eating wormy apples in the orchard. *(laughs)* I had an old barn I could explore that I could go to anytime, with cherry trees nearby. Me and my sister had an old tractor we were demolishing. *(laughs)* Then from 12 we moved back to the beach.

Thank God I had a nice childhood till I was about 14, I'd say. I was still a pretty free spirit till I was 14. But by the time I was 15, I was fairly miserable. *(laughs)* I was a wretch from that period until I got married.

Kelly: Listening to you, I was realizing that every single one of us had a *completely* different kind of childhood. But through being able to get back into the childhood scenes, and the younger self or child within, we can touch yours and bring out all the neat things in ours too. Like, I know all of the bad stuff from mine; it's right up on top. But to get down into the nice stuff takes a little bit more. Like remembering going through the woods behind where we lived, the huge trees and monstrous rocks, the neat cliff faces we used to climb with all kinds of handholds in them.

When Moita was talking about the small light in the darkness, it one more time tuned me back into the time when my father told me that I had "magic hands". *(referring to her healing gift)*

Margaret: The only nice thing he ever said to you.

Kelly: Yeah, and I never forgot it! It was like some strange thing out of the middle of nowhere...

Margaret: The exchange of energy with Moita was really powerful. It seemed like she wanted me to see that it was just *huge* out there and just full, and it's worlds and worlds and worlds to know. I get this feeling of really powerful things going on that I'm expected to try to understand a little bit and catch up with, as it were. It's like she's sort of saying, "Okay, work a little harder now. You can do it, so get busy and try."

ço   ço   ço

We end with a channeling from the Goddess, which comes as Kelly writes a letter to a woman she shared a tent and impromptu Moita session with at last year's Women's Festival in the valley. It is given just as it was first written, except "sons" is added to "daughters" in the fifth paragraph.

Earth Mother written channeling #216 (Kelly / April 11, 1982)

GODDESS: I am not here to shatter worlds, and prove foundations to be unsafe, but to point out that the foundation has been neglected, lost touch with, uncared for – in need of attention and repair. But how can you fix a crack if you refuse to look at it? Once recognized, it is not hard to <u>mend</u>, and then you are each stronger, more certain of your part in the Universe.

I have spoken to you in the still quiet of midnight, stealing into your dreams, whispering in your heart, opening doorways to the inner realms of mind and magic and . . . love.

And I said you were the seed for the new man . . . so sow well what seeds you can understand how to give, and remember that no seed grows on barren soil, but a strong wind may blow it away one day, to land on the fertile ground of humanity's collective mind.

You are a <u>part</u> of the collective unconscious – so the attitudes and attributes you express are available to <u>all</u> humanity, should it choose this path. You are pioneers into a new realm of expression – children, if you will – and you are bound to make mistakes as you learn this new language – twist concepts as a child mispronounces words – and the adults watch and listen, amazed at how a simple phrase which is so innately understood because of the body of experience that goes behind it is changed and altered through the innocent naïveté of the child's mind, and limited experience.

You see, I have not been neglecting you, daughters and sons, but my words and presence in and among your lives has gone, for the most part, unnoticed. I have had to wait until your ears developed, so you could hear me. And wait for your eyes to open so you could see me. And wait for your spirits to awaken so you could touch me – and feel my touch.

So now we are aware of each other. You <u>can</u> hear, and see, and touch – and are also learning to <u>feel</u>.

I am there, whenever you let down your focus, whenever your mind is still and quiet – my voice is soft and gentle like the sighing wind – or strong and angry as the hurricane or tornado. I have many voices – and now not only can I speak through the animals and weather of earth, but through you, and Siofra, and many, many others – with a single, multi-levelled voice – and I will Sing once again the Ancient Harmonies, and return to the stars, as is my right as the planet which revolves in grace and beauty and love around the Sun, the centre, of my universe, my solar system – and together my brothers and sisters will sing an even greater song, and the stars will hear our voice!

A vision of what <u>can</u> be. Love is a hard road to follow at first – but the rewards are many, and the joys limitless, boundless, timeless. Be at peace – each of you – and know that I <u>am</u> <u>aware</u> – and will be here, all ways.

Epilogue

THE NAMING TREE, AND THE END OF TIME

The world and time are a unit, and it all moves together. Those things which happen before and after affect what is happening now. And so, by connecting yourself to your past and drawing on that energy you had in that different world that existed before, and by pulling that energy along with you, it is that energy of differentness that has a great deal to do with the changing of the universe now...

It is not becoming the way it was, *or* is, *because all that goes between impresses itself on the energy. And so, you create something new and different. You bring the two concepts together as one.*

— Moita (September 15, 1978)

During our session on October 19, 1980, excerpted in Chapter 4, Moita mentions that, long ago, what is now British Columbia "served as a colony for the continent" of Mu, or Lemuria, and that "The Eskimo culture is a remnant of the Mu culture." There follows a silent period in which Moita and I gaze on each other.

Then I say, "The thought just came through: wondering if the reason I saw you, especially in the first year of these communications, as maybe Eskimo might be tied to . . ." I am suggesting I may be seeing the face of her incarnation in Mu. Moita laughs, either appreciating my insight or amazed it has taken me so long (!). I continue, "Even a dream I had – before I even knew Kelly – in which a voice told me, "You can't do it alone, but maybe with the Eskimo . . ." Moita laughs again, followed by a long silence as I continue to look on her face. "I think she's trying to come back." And Moita smiles as we gaze in more silence.

ର   ର   ର

In time, others, too, will glimpse this visage. From the same Okanagan Valley workshop session that ended Chapter 10, these are some earlier and later segments that help account for its extremely high energy. We have been very moved by Brian's letters to us after his encounter with Moita's words in *Rays*. Now Kelly and I meet him for the first time (at least, in this life): an older man in body and soul undoubtedly, but young in spirit.

Moita session #191 (Kelly, David, workshop group / July 29, 1981)
MOITA: Hello!
Brian: Hello.

MOITA: I have seen *you* before!

Brian: Would you like to tell me about it?

MOITA: I met you once in an orchard, where there were blooms on the tree.

Brian: Many moons ago.

MOITA: Yes.

(Long pause as the energy exchange grows extremely intense. For me the whole room is shimmering, hazing over, figure/ground reversing, all disappearing into sheer light.)

MOITA: There is good energy passing between us.

Brian: Beautiful. Thank you.

MOITA: It is by your own sacrificing, your own openness, that you are able to receive this gift.

Brian: That's encouraging. Why me?

MOITA: Yes. Nourishment, love, encouragement. You are pointing yourself in the right direction.

Brian: I hope so.

MOITA: All who seek are eventually answered. It is when you stop looking for the answers that you discover they have come.

Brian: I've heard that so many times. It seems to take a long time to learn the lesson.

MOITA: And yet now you have a glimmer of what it means.

Brian: Yes.

MOITA: The universe is within you. All you have to do is let it out. It is not a matter of searching *for* it and *finding* it. It is a rediscovery of what you have always known...

(Returning to Brian later in the session:)

MOITA: And do you really remember me?

Brian: No, I can't say I do really at all – not consciously, anyway.

MOITA: You were a very small child at the time – no more than six.

Brian: I could imagine that, but it's all lost in so many other recollections. That would be the time if I ever did. *(pause)*

MOITA: But even if you do not remember the incident, you recognize the energy.

Brian: It's really *something*. *(pause)*

MOITA: Have you noticed how the room has become thicker?

Brian: Yes.

MOITA: The air seems to have gained substance...

Brian: It's gotten much warmer too.

MOITA: That is a common complaint. *(laughing)* There are definitely many things in the air tonight, and you are all rising up to meet them, to see them . . . as real.

Brian: Something has happened to you. *(pause)* It's almost Oriental at times.

MOITA: My body, when I was in Mu, *could* be seen as somewhat Oriental. *(pause)* Each of you will see on me a different face. *(pause)* I have worn many forms.

Brian: I have read most of your transcripts. I think you *have*.

MOITA: Is it different – reading, meeting?

Brian: I have no doubt at all – much difference.

MOITA: And now, when you go back and read again . . .

Brian: It'll probably look different too. There'll be more to be got out of the reading than there was the last time, as a result of *this*.

MOITA: Yes.

Brian: Thank you.

MOITA: That is why I would wish to be able to touch all who read my words, such as they are, so that they understand the words are merely a vehicle.

Brian: It's very important at this time that more and more people understand.

MOITA: Yes. More important now than it has ever been before. That is why we have come.

Brian: There need to be many more of us to spread the word.

MOITA: You will each touch others, and they in turn will touch more. Many great things have begun with one – one who truly believes.

Brian: Right.

MOITA: That one is important. If you do not believe that you can make a difference, you will *not*. Remember that those who cannot see yet have just as much love in them as [those who can]. If not in this life, in another, they will realize their dream...

(Meanwhile, another participant has been feeling the strong possibility Moita is about to be seen in materialized form – from his perspective, more of an American Indian face.)

Carl: What kind of encouragement do you need to come on further?

MOITA: You want more than you have received already?

Carl: There are possibilities of more there, because I can see it in the background.

MOITA: Oh, there is *always* more in the background. But the time is not always ripe for them.

Carl: Well, that's right. I agree with you.

MOITA: The time has been ripe for many things tonight. We are not quite ready for the next step.

Carl: Would you take the next step – I think you know what I'm thinking about – if it did . . . If the situation was ripe, would you be interested in going the next step?

MOITA: *(laughs)* There are definite possibilities in the future. There is still some cleansing to do in the channel, and there is a situation to set up, at the proper time – not just for the people who need to be present in order for such a thing to occur, but also from our level to make sure that the worlds are close enough to permit it. It requires great energy.

           I *know* you can almost see me already.

Carl: That's right!

MOITA: There are some who can see without that particular step, and then it is not needed as much. *(long pause)* You see?

Carl: Pretty *near*!

ॐ   ॐ   ॐ

"She's trying to come back," I said, as the Eskimo/Oriental visage emerged out of Kelly's face. She has been coming for years now . . . The lady of Mu, the feminine side of man, who gave birth to human consciousness. She is coming through many of us.

> *We are to weave the strands into a circle. A young woman turns and says she would like to be my partner in this game of identity. My name is irrelevant. She begins embracing me with surprising intimacy as we sit together on the floor. Utterly entranced, I return her passionate kisses. She whispers in my ear, "We are one person . . . one person." We walk toward and through a grove of trees in the dark . . .*
> *– from David's "Game of Identity" dream (December 14, 1972)[150]*

> *I am standing in a grove – a singing grove – of trees, with many women sitting on the ground in a circle around it. There is a sense of newness and wonder in my song. It is a time before there are words, but the sounds themselves are an explanation of how the world works. It is the beginning of language, of naming. A great outpouring of love and life is very evident throughout.*
> *– Kelly's memory of Mu (surfacing in spring 1978)[151]*

All Hallows' Eve was traditionally a festival celebrated at the dark of the moon nearest the midpoint of the autumn equinox and winter solstice. In 1980, this new moon falls on November 7th. We have arranged a gathering including four close friends: Jim, Margaret, C. and George. We form a balanced circle on this night when "the door between the worlds" is already more open than usual. Near the end of a long session, however, our energy has been winding down as we talk of surface things . . . when a quite different level of question comes to me. Moita's unexpected answer takes us back to her description (Chapter 4) of the changes in consciousness that brought an end to Mu civilization – and on back to the Clear Light (Chapter 2) that is the origin of all.

Moita session #161 (Kelly, David, Jim, Margaret, C., George / November 7, 1980)

MOITA: *(turning to me:)* Have you any questions for me?

David: I do have one question: the name that we have for you. You've said it is Kelly's own for you. And we know that sounds have meaning and power. I am wondering if anything *can* be put into words as to where that name came from, if it has some sort of history or meaning that could be put into words.

MOITA: You ask a great deal.

(Long pause as Moita looks down. The energy of her presence and shared within the circle changes completely.)

MOITA: It has more than one meaning.

(Still looking down, Moita now closes Kelly's eyes. Then speaking quite slowly, with

unnameable feeling:)

MOITA: It has as many meanings as *I* do. *(pause)*

It comes from my last life – the name I gave myself underneath the Naming Tree. In that moment, I saw myself as a centre from which all names were born. *(pause; opening her eyes)* And so, I am "The Namer", "The Bringer".

Is it not fitting that I who gave birth to the word would return to help it find its death . . . and renewal?

(Another pause. Then she looks up and toward me.)

MOITA: It is not lightly I tell you these things.

(Long pause as we gaze toward each other. Then Moita turns to Margaret.)

MOITA: That is how a path is born: in a single moment of choice. So I have followed it here, to help others find their way out of the maze I helped to create. *(pause)*

(Jim's next comment relates to Moita's earlier explanation of the end of Mu: "When language was born, memory came after. When things could be named, they achieved identity. And when we recognized their identity, we could remember them when we named them."[152])

Jim: But surely memory has been a positive tool as well as a problem.

MOITA: I know all sides of it. *(pause)* It has needed to be grown through in order to be understood. But still, my path was decided then: to see it through to its ending. It has brought understanding, and it has brought veils.

Jim: Is the time near for it to pass?

MOITA: Let us say, its nature will be changed as man learns to understand it. For he yet does not know its power. It remains undirected. *(pause)* Before he can work through it, he must remember *all*.

Jim: The whole of the Akashic Record?! *(i.e. all history, including our past lives)*

MOITA: Why would the Universe remember if it did not intend to give it back?

Jim: It sounds like it would be a tremendous task, to see it all.

MOITA: Each man will see his part – *all* of his parts. And then all man together will see it as a whole. It will be a great step in his evolution – like the step I took, only different. You cannot possibly comprehend what the new man will truly be, until you become him. Those who had no memory could not possibly put themselves in the place of those who did. The difference excludes understanding. *(pause)*

Jim: So, much of what the new man will be will be bound up in remembering – remembering everything. Many presents tonight.

MOITA: The door is just opening...

Margaret: How did you help create the maze that we're in? Are you a creator?

MOITA: You are each creators.

Margaret: Yes, but small-time. *(laughter)*

MOITA: I created language. There could be no memory without language, without names.

Margaret: That's why you say you are The Namer... All language?

MOITA: All language. It sprang from the same source. In the beginning, all language was one.

Margaret: *(pause)* And they all got garbled and made different. Due to what?

MOITA: Due to will, because will birthed desire, and man desired to be different and keep secrets.

Margaret: Hmmm.

MOITA: But the language I created holds no secrets.

Margaret: Isn't the language that you like to use more than anything else [one] without words? Or have we just not heard this original language? Is it comparable to any language in use now anywhere in the world?

(Kelly sees Moita looking at China, then Japan, then the South Pacific.)

MOITA: The closest the Earth has is Polynesian.

Margaret: Hmmm.

MOITA: But it is very far removed.

Margaret: It's not Sumari, is it? *(i.e. in the Seth material, the language given by the Speakers)*

MOITA: I know of what you speak now. That too is but a memory, though it is closer.

I see you have woken up! *(noting her great interest)*

Margaret: *(laughs)* I just start to see bigger implications in your words, of what you are. You're a creator of language. You can create a body for yourself if you have to. What else can you create?

MOITA: In a way, I created Kelly, her being a part of myself.

Margaret: So you formed Kelly's body from your mind or makeup?

MOITA: Her soul's essence was once a part of mine.

Margaret: And it's growing on its own now.

MOITA: Yes.

Margaret: Do you often have little offshoots starting up?

MOITA: I am fortunate in that I do not have many, for they must be tended . . .

Margaret: Yes.

MOITA: . . . like all growing things. *(pause)*

But perhaps it needs to be made clear what creation *is*, for it is the channeling of love that creates... All who create are used as channels, even when they aren't aware of it. The channel helps to give it form and direction, but the energy itself is of the Universe – the fabric that holds it together.

Margaret: So no creative person can claim creation as their own.

MOITA: They can claim the form it takes, and they are responsible for being a clear or unclear channel for that energy.

Margaret: Mm-hmm. But they're not using their own energy, their own force? They're being given it.

MOITA: You are all the same energy. It is difficult to explain. All things were created from the same source, and all things still come from that source. You are each separate, but you are all together. You are all in essence the same; you are, in direction, different.

Margaret: And we hold ourselves accountable for how we used the energy in the end.

MOITA: And how you use your direction, or what direction you take. *(pause)*

(Moita looks toward C.)

C.:   I was wondering about something I perceived a little while ago, how it relates to what you would call language. It seemed like I perceived, above the language we use, a language of abstract images. And above that one, I don't know if you could call it a language but perhaps a language which consists of patterns which are the link between . . . which are the thought itself, the pattern of links or connections between all the images and ideas that go together to form the thought. What would *that* be? Where does that come from? How does it all tie in with the language we've got now?

MOITA: It is a gradual sinking down into appearances rather than actualities. The first language explained the essence and the place of each living thing, and its connections to all other living things. It was a *whole* language. It left nothing apart. It has gradually been dissected so that things stand alone. That is why each word stands for a different thing, instead of standing for a wholeness of a thought.

C.:   So are we developing into beings who think in an utterly different fashion and communicate in an utterly different fashion from . . . ? It seems like the edge of something that was happening when I received this. It's hard to explain in a way, of course. *(laughs)*

MOITA: I know. But that is why nothing can be hidden with that language. For when the nature of a thing is known, so are motives, if there are any.

C.:   What is it in us that separates us from this language? Obviously, the fact that we're used to speaking English. But is there anything beyond that that keeps us from this language?

MOITA: *(softly)* Your distance from us.

C.:   Is the language we speak, in itself, the distance?

MOITA: It is one manifestation of it. *(pause)* But you must learn to use the tools you are given to communicate with others, if they cannot hear *our* language.

C.:   Is it possible for people to communicate with each other, speaking English?

MOITA: There is a part of them that understands the meaning behind the words, even if this part appears not to...

C.:   How *better*, then, can we attempt to communicate?

MOITA: *Touch. (pause)* By not being afraid to open up the other organs of language that you have. Distance between minds, as reflected in distance between bodies, is one symptom of fear – in the inability to communicate what is there, not being understood.

Language is a *whole thing*. It includes not just your words, but your eyes and your heart and your hands, the feelings that you radiate through the air.

(Here Moita answers C.'s question about her fear of speaking, by relating the reincarnational episode told in Chapter 7 – what was done to her for revealing a vision of apparent end-times. Finally, Moita turns back to me:)

MOITA: Well, you asked a leading question. *(laughter)* It is time for me to go. Good night.

(From the conversation afterward:)

Kelly: *(to me:)* You and your questions.

Jim: That was a real breakthrough.

Kelly: Well, she sure did pour a lot of herself into me when you asked about her name. I thought I was going to pass out!

C.:   Her presence changed entirely. It was as different from her usual presence as from your present personality.

Margaret: She didn't seem to like doing that much.

David: I wasn't sure she wanted to.

Kelly: There certainly was a lot of pain associated with it, or sorrow; remorse, maybe. I think it's more a tremendous sorrow that it had to be done. Like, someone had to do it. Language definitely had to be created. We had to go through all this stuff.

David: This is the first time in this context that she has said "I". Always before it was "we". I pictured a group of people there in Mu. Tonight, it sounded like she was the channel at the centre of that group when that first came through.

Kelly: She *did* emphasize "I". I noticed. I was rather uncomfortable with that. *(laughs)* Now, Polynesian was about the *last* thing I expected her to say. *(laughs)*

(It's not really surprising, though, since Mu was in the South Pacific. And I have read anthropologist Dorothy Lee's book Freedom and Culture *with its articles on worldview and language, including those of the Trobriand Islanders and Tikopians in the South Pacific. These cultures have no words for development over time. Instead, they have many words for different states of what we would call the same thing – all in the present. They do not concentrate as we do on the passage of time. Instead of general categories of things and qualities that can be combined together, there are longer and much more specific descriptions.[153])*

(Owen Barfield, in Saving the Appearances, *says that the further back we go toward the origin of language we find the "holophrase", a "long, rambling conglomeration of sound and meaning", where meaning is not divisible into inner or outer. "The self, so far as there yet is one," writes Barfield, "is still aware that it and the phenomena derive from the same supersensible source."[154])*

Jim: Sitting under the Naming Tree. That sounds like a fascinating . . .

Kelly: I had that experience. I actually was there. Before Moita started talking through me, that was one of the first super-strong experiences I had. I was lying in bed, going to sleep, and all of a sudden I saw myself standing under this huge tree, and all around me were these women in a big circle, and I was singing these words. As each word was spoken, I knew the description and the understanding it gave of what it spoke about, how it described the entire evolution and place and connection.

           Now I know where all those legends come from of the power of words.

C.:   Right, right!

Kelly: And in this case it was true! Because, if you had the true name of something, you had complete knowledge of it.[155N] There was such joy in the words. They're impossible to describe. It was really vivid. It was like music.

࠯ ࠯ ࠯

Clare, who visits us in October 1981, was also present there in the Okanagan on the night in July when Moita's Mu incarnation was seen by Brian and Carl and others. The glowing white disks of light she saw in Moita's eyes were quite sufficient for her that summer evening. But "the gift of seeing" that Moita tells her she has been given reveals more during the autumn morning session in our Kindle Valley cabin that has already been quoted extensively. To start with, Clare now feels the white lights are beckoning her.

Moita/Goddess/Amar session #204 (Kelly, David, Margaret, Clare / October 16, 1981)

Clare: If I could ever get down that white path, I would see you.
MOITA: As I *am*.
Clare: Ah, I would love to walk on that path. Do you put it there for me?
MOITA: The light? *(Clare nods)* Yes.
Clare: How do I get near?
MOITA: Into the light, or onto the path?
Clare: Down the path, because that's what it means.
MOITA: Yes, this is a *true* doorway. *(long pause, as they gaze)*
Clare: *(very slowly)* I can hardly see Kelly's body and face.
MOITA: You are discovering that material matter is not as *solid* as you once believed.
Clare: And your voice seems to come from everywhere in the cabin, instead of where it usually comes from.
MOITA: That is because you are at the centre.
Clare: Does that mean at this moment that I am centred?
MOITA: Yes.
Clare: Now I know . . .
MOITA: Now you know.
Clare: That is what I asked.
MOITA: And as you can see, it is something that must be experienced to be understood.
Clare: I feel like I am burning.
MOITA: No – *shining*. Just let it out. Do not try to contain it or give it substance or form. Let it find its own form.
Clare: I see black hair around a face that I can't see!
MOITA: Relax. The face will come.
Clare: Brown skin.
MOITA: Not Indian.

Clare:	No.
MOITA:	Not Oriental.
Clare:	No! Very pretty!
MOITA:	This is my first and last form on a physical Earth.
Clare:	Where is she from?
MOITA:	It is from Mu, from the Naming, from the birth of language.
Clare:	Can I touch it?
MOITA:	I am not distant.
Clare:	There's a brown mark here. *(indicating Moita's forehead)*
MOITA:	Yes. It is from the band I once wore. It is a brand.
Clare:	*(very softly)* You are melting. You are going.
MOITA:	There are others. *(long pause)*
Clare:	Your face is thinner.
MOITA:	And narrow.
Clare:	*Yes, very* narrow.
MOITA:	And I am tall, very tall.
Clare:	And you are more severe in this . . . reality . . . than you were in the other one. Things are more serious to you.
MOITA:	Yes. There is more purpose, more will. In Mu there was no will. This was a time when will was born, after the Naming. This is my form as the Speaker. This is a body I created out of the universal substance. *(pause)* It was in this form that we came to try to teach men how to control the power that was theirs, to give them understanding of it.

ço   ço   ço

"Remember – Shine – do not Burn! You have been told before that you have a great capacity for Love within you – Remember . . . "

An echo from Moita's first written channeling through Kelly. Or *is* it an echo? Moita has said that for her these communications are continuous . . . and timeless.

So it is appropriate to end with another written message, this one given in the same fall of 1981. "As the age began, so shall it end." But I do not know any longer which era I am talking about.

A great inward quiet has pervaded me all morning as I have woven the materials of this final section. A slowness . . . a fullness . . . reverberating through me, which has all the time in the world – or none at all, for time has ceased to matter. To matter, time has ceased.

The cycle of these four years is ending. In its beginning, time seemed so compressed, accelerating . . . Now, from a different point of view, it slows . . . expanding outward to include more and more . . . of a single pattern, endless reflections and renewals. More than a four-year cycle is coming to a close. The end of one phase is the beginning of the next.

Moita written channeling #200 (Kelly / September 16, 1981)

(This experiment at automatic writing begins with a string of ink – a scribbly line that becomes words, but the words are not separated at first. As Moita takes greater control, they become spaced, but with capitals and underlinings as given – emphatic translations of the energy accompanying Moita's thoughts.

(Obliques are added at the beginning here to separate the strung-together words for comprehension. Kelly's eyes are closed till the asterisk, then open.)

MOITA: hear/my/prayer/love/love

yes/my/name/is/unimportant/why/i/am/here/is/very/important – YOU ARE NEEDED to help/perform a great/work – This you feel* on an unconscious, albeit very strong, level. Why are you here? What are you waiting for? GO FORTH NOW not later. Your life is before you – grab it with both hands – EMBRACE LOVE & your Eternal Soul shall once more know PEACE, not the illusion, but the reality that is every being's inherent right.

Am I a part of you? Yes – you know in your heart of hearts that I speak through you so well because of how closely we are connected. Your thoughts, your hopes & your desires are my own – I love you & am part of you – We, together, are complete – yet still there is more for you/us to learn, to express & to communicate.

I am the Namer, the Bringer, not only of words, of names, of power, of Will, but also of Self-recognition, of an acceptance of Beauty – of an ability to actively & uniquely express that Beauty and individual Oneness.

Why are you seeking the answers to such questions? What is it that you are after? You, like all Beings, are after love & acceptance. Our mutual discovery of Universal Truths – of REVELATION – of defining of our own understanding of our Universe – has brought us to a point of merger much sooner than we had anticipated. The Time is now – and TIME is short for your Earth.

How many times must the World destroy itself before it sees the folly of power – the fear of death. All men seek immortality – they seek to hide from death itself – DEATH, the Great Change Bringer – the Transition from one state or idea to another – Yes – it is all the same Source – All the hints, the hidden meanings in books, in conversation with friends & acquaintances – It's all OUT THERE because you are still too afraid to see these things WITHIN yourself.

Communications such as this can become sporadic and meandering when the Channel's mind is not as clear as it should be. I focus the pattern of my thoughts on your mind – at a low, sub-atomic level – & as it rises through to your brain-cells, its original imprint can be distorted or changed by your own unclarities & lack of concentration as well as by your own concepts of the Universe & how it functions.

You are doing very well at the moment.

However, we must get back to the original question which you asked. Do you remember it now? Who are you? What are you called? Why are you here?

And why <u>am</u> I <u>here</u>! Do you know yet? Do you know who <u>I</u> am? What names I have been called? What parts I have played throughout the history of your world? Do you know <u>which</u> Earth <u>you</u> are on yet? The last one – the last one that will ever BE – because, as I said before, TIME has run out. In the New Age – & <u>I</u> would not then be calling this beauteous goddess you abide on <u>EARTH</u> – TIME will have ceased to be. It is flowing <u>out</u> of things. You have had time as a concept for the past 50,000 years. You have played a game with it, trying to understand what it is. But each cycle has its death & in death a new beginning. Time's cycle is at an end.

How will man handle the knowledge that a concept of linear time has, in effect, <u>prevented</u> him from answering the question that plagues man <u>most</u>? Its very conception <u>precludes</u> an understanding of "The Way Things Are" since they "are" only what you make of them.

Someday – before the End of Time – you will see me once again, & this time you shall know me in all my Glorious Light & Shining <u>Presence</u>. Nothing shall be withheld, least of all my Love & Acceptance.

But keep <u>going</u>, no matter what the blocks that present themselves. FOLLOW YOUR HEART – & it will lead you to your heart's desire. Remember my words – NOTHING IS UNATTAINABLE!! Soon you shall not only hear, but <u>understand</u>.

Good night – May the blessings of Love & Light be yours through the pain of life & trial – We are always with you – even in your darkest <u>hour</u>!!!

M

Afterword

THE MOMENT OF CHANGE

So we begin a little early, trying to stack the deck.
– Goddess (Earth Mother)

How early is "a little early"? The year 1981 has already brought many deep changes for Kelly and me when Moita makes an announcement a little way into November. While couched in such good energy, on such a bright, glistening early winter's day, we get no inkling of its meaning, or many meanings – or its timing. We might easily imagine Moita is speaking of a mysterious "moment of change" coming to ourselves personally, perhaps within the next year (?). *Not* so easily that she really means coming to us and the entire planet – so many as *30 more years into our future* . . .

Moita session #206 (Kelly, David, 3 others / November 3, 1981)

David: I'm feeling that today is turning more and more magical: the sun and the snow and blue sky outside; and links between people that always seem surprising when they suddenly reach the surface.

MOITA: Yes, we've watched the stars sitting on the leaves outside. *(pause)*
              You are coming closer and closer to the moment of change. Change is becoming more obvious.

David: "The moment of change." *Many* moments or *the* moment? *(laughs)*

MOITA: There is *one* moment, in essence!

David: In *all* of them? Or one that's coming?

MOITA: One that's coming. A pivot moment (?). Things on *this* side of that moment have a certain flavour, and things on the other side of that moment will be completely different! And yet the other side *leaks through*, as you grow closer and closer to the moment.
              Of course, it is also true that what you see as magic has always been here. It is you that have changed your perception of reality, and so have allowed that kind of energy to enter into your life.

ඔ   ඔ   ඔ

[TO BE CONTINUED . . .]

PHOTO ALBUM:

"STEPS IN THE RIGHT DIRECTION"

(1) In the funky living room of Sunrise Farm: David perhaps writing down a dream?
(2) Morning outside a log cabin at Sunrise Farm: Christopher chopping firewood.
(3) Workday at Sunrise Farm: Becky herds goats above house and Chris carries pail below.
(4) Taking in morning sun and mountain view: Kelly and Arista on Sunrise Farm deck
(5) From Dr. Townsend's farmhouse: Barn and hill in winter – imagine a brilliant dawn!
(6) Our first Kindle Valley log home, with birch trees, from snow-covered driveway.
(7) Other side of log cabin, with deck looking down wooded hillside to Kindle River.
(8) Our second, more primitive Kindle Valley log home, with smoke from tall stovepipe.
(9) From above Margaret's land: View of Kindle River Valley on clear day in winter.

Descriptions are on pp. 41 (#1 to #4), 91 (#5), 217 (#6 and #7) and 326 (#8 and #9).

Appendix A

POWER, PROBABILITIES AND PROPHECY*

Power

Man has split the love energy of creation into the power of controller vs. controlled. Throughout this book, Moita has analyzed the nature of power and pointed the way toward wholeness.

Many lessons have been given showing how power can destroy if it is not used properly... If you would come into your heritage and know yourself, you must also know how *not* to use power.

The thing about power is: of itself, it...merely exists. And till a conscious being taps it, and uses it, and gives it form, it has no thrust of its own for either good intentions or bad. That is one reason why we stress love, because it is of itself an energy with...proper [intentions]. (pp. 21; 258)

When one uses power for *any* ends, it causes destruction, because power was not meant to be used. It has its own rules, its own sense of flow. And when that flow is interrupted, channeled...into other forms, it disrupts and makes changes that usually cannot be foreseen... You are all here to learn to be yourself, to find your own beauty, your own sense of oneness, your love. When you find that, then [the power] will not be used. It will flow out. (p. 258)

After the birth of memory and things were defined, the birth of will was not far behind... In the age of Atlantis, will ruled man. He did not learn control or the understanding of power, of what its use could do or undo... So there were seeds from the beginnings – seeds that craved dominion over others, and greed. Such small beginnings, and such devastating results. The first small descent, and man plummets!... Atlantis was very much like this culture is now in an outward form. (p. 116)

You know that souls reincarnate in groups... It is not at all uncommon to have the same kind of situation in one point in history as you do in another – the same kinds of schemes and plans – because they are, most often, the same people, [with] the same energy, that still have not seen what it is they are doing to themselves and continue to believe they are doing unto others. (pp. 252-253)

The period of history that man has remembered this time has been filled with instances of individuals who have craved power over their fellow beings. Why would this time be any different? They just feel they are more organized or knowledgeable and have more in control. They can reach more people now than they could ever before, and their wars are more subtle wars. Rather than murdering their subjects and conquering their lands, they win them over with ideas and thoughts, and change them from the inside until they do not know themselves...

---

* Page numbers after paragraphs are to assist readers in reviewing the original context of these excerpts.

They...have not learned that they cannot get away with this kind of energy-changing and not have it affect them personally, or those around them, and the very structure of the world they choose to try and control. They...don't see that the world itself is more aware of them than they would like... They are not fooling themselves as to their own purposes. They are fooling themselves as to how they can or may get away with it.

This world cannot change in the shape it's in. There are too many of those who are ready to fight for their positions, who are not ready to understand that this is a passing phase and the power they take now will turn on them later. We are trying to re-establish the natural law of the universe – and man does not think there is glory in it. (pp. 248; 259)

Many people believe in this world that being able to cause another person to change their life for [their] purposes shows [them] to be [individuals] of great worth. And people who believe this do not think very much of themselves. They are very sad and lonely and have no respect for their own energy. Everyone in the world has helped to create the situation wherein this kind of thing can flourish. They are only externalizations of your own fears and doubts...

In some ways, they are the darker side of yourself, the side you have not changed or accepted. You cannot reject anything that is in the world without rejecting a part of you...When everyone can accept others as they are – not by subjugating themselves to another's will, but by being themselves and knowing that they are not unfree – then these expressions will no longer need to come through.

Each one of you has a higher self and each one of you has access to a universal energy. If it is not there, it is because you yourself have cut it off. But this goes for your world, not just for yourself. The condition of...the world's spirit is the unifying of everyone's energy, and everyone plays a part. When you all come up out of your self-imposed darkness and see the world through your new eyes, you will understand that everything is balanced..., and that your painful lessons were necessary in order to make your world a more beautiful place and a stronger one. (p. 252)

Love...flows freely and does not bind itself to anything, for everything it touches is also love. The love has always been here, and it always will. The only thing that has changed is man's awareness. Man has cut himself off from that...in order to learn . . . *not* to. (p. 25)

You desire to take control of your own destiny and walk your own path. But you cannot do it without the knowledge, and the knowledge brings the power, and the power brings the responsibility: to use, or not... It is much more difficult to have the power, and not use it, and *know* it is not something that can be used.

The purpose of life is finding the way back to where you began. But you cannot find your way by nudging at the door or forcing it down. When you force down the door, you find yourself in the wrong room. That is why, when [power] is not used, the door opens by itself... (p. 258)

 formula formula formula

Probabilities

World events from 1980 to 2012 and current prophecies suggest the more dire probabilities as many sources earlier perceived them are now unlikely. Those in this book are included in order to tell the history of "what might have been", so we can appreciate the choices and gifts of energy that enabled their avoidance. Through it all, Moita, Amar and the Goddess have been clear that the transition to a New Age depends on human transformation, supported by non-physical beings that have been guiding us as well as holding off destruction as long as possible to increase our chances.

On another level, you all experience each possible future line of your development and your world's development... You are all aware of the lesson that you are learning from that other set of possibilities or circumstances... Those who see other levels also act as a warning to show where the possibilities may lie, and how they can be prevented from happening. (p. 22)

This time period is a nexus, a whirlpool, a crossroads. There are paths before you that lead into the future – some of them not pleasant, some of them extremely promising. That is why we are here: to help you choose the road that leads not to destruction but that leads to life, and to this change of man and his awareness, to the reuniting of [our] worlds... (p. 141)

Since you are part of the Earth's aura and the energy that you put out affects the Earth's health, all of the anger and fear and bitterness and hatred that is poured *through* humanity *into* the Earth must be undone or rechanneled... You are responsible not just for your own life, but also for the life energy in the sphere in which you live. It comes to a point where either you go completely – are wiped out entirely so that the planet can survive – or you learn to live cooperatively *with* it...

The Earth is in need of a healing... If the disease is not removed in the aura of the Earth, then it will manifest itself in the physical. Depending on how much awareness occurs between now and then, the physical manifestations will be sooner or later, or not at all... All I can say for sure is that we are lengthening the process at the moment...

This is a period of time where future lines are still flexible... There is still some hope that that level of destruction will not be necessary... But again, that depends on how many people have learned to channel love into the Earth... It is not so much what they do that matters. It is the way they do it, the energy – connecting with their wholer selves, becoming whole. (pp. 276; 279-282)

[The energy changes] which we initiated have brought our worlds closer together. In a sense, we are more like rubbing each other than having a space apart. This energy, we knew, would affect people in many ways: frighten many people; some would definitely lose their grounding. But it was their choice not to be ready enough when it happened, a lesson for some to take to another time to understand what steps are needed in order to be ready.

But the happenings that the world has planned for Earth are closer than many would think – not just the physical ones, but the political and social and economic changes as well. It would not do for us to wait too long, because then things would have started...their downward movement... So we begin a little early, trying to stack the deck. (pp. 86; 358)

Just as the Earth is erupting in physical disaster, so is man erupting in anger and fear... War is like an alien pestilence that is visited upon the Earth and all of its spheres of influence... Unless your leaders become more loving and in touch with the spirit within, there is a very good possibility that man will express his fear in this form...: not from greed, but because he fears his own evolution. He would destroy himself first – the God within. (pp. 104; 140; 265)

As man begins to evolve, and begins to pass through these fears that he has built up over so many centuries, those fears will begin to form to make their last stand, to fight for...their existence, for they cannot live without man and his belief... That energy, that conglomeration of fears from all of man, will make itself known, and many will call it the Antichrist, for it is in many senses anti-life... [But] the Earth could not attract such energy if man were whole in the first place. That is why [the Antichrist] will be destroyed. He can be cast out by being *loved from within*. (pp. 142; 274)

Some will not be able to accept newness and change because they have been unable to do so in their own development for a long time... They are fearful and afraid and not ready to enter a New Age... They are choosing not to stay and try to work through [man's problems on Earth]...They will be given an opportunity to develop in another place, on another earth, and start the cycle again...

You are all One in one place. But for now things go in different directions..., each to find his way back to home and self. They are making it easier for those who will be left behind, for they are taking their influence away. They are freeing the Earth... By giving themselves this doorway, and leaving *this* Earth behind,...those of you who have chosen to be here through this time and afterward to help remake man's awareness and to heal the Earth will be freer to do so. (pp. 140-141)

Do not think that you are in this alone... We are there to add our energy, our compassion and our understanding to all of the pain and all of the fear you will have to go through in order to see the end of this darkness... And we are not at all ashamed to ally ourselves with you, for we see your beauty and we see your light, and we are here to help you let it shine...

You cannot change another so that their energy is better..., because then you are neglecting the prime responsibility for changing yourself and giving others the freedom to do their own learning. This is how the world will change, in one time or another. This is how each can help to alleviate all those possible futures, so that perhaps the easier one can be chosen, the one with the least amount of pain. If you all love life and enjoy it, life will be good to you. (pp. 92; 143)

৯ ৯ ৯

Prophecy

Perhaps the world has lived in darkness too long. It is a time of awakening, of returning; a time of many lessons... Perhaps you can look on this as the true coming of spring in man's development. He has spent the winter sleeping. Now it is time for him to wake up. (p. 24)

You are travelling in a direction through space that will bring you closer to a centre of awareness in the system... We have called [these Beings] "the High Ones"... The addition of their energy to the Earth will help to bring about a great many of the changes that have been foretold. The added energy of their presence will bring things to a crisis point, so that there can be a breakthrough into a new reality. In order for this change to take place, the reality that exists here now must undergo a transformation. It will not be able to survive otherwise... When I say the High Ones are coming..., it is not that the High Ones have, from some other level, chosen this time to impose change upon man. It is man *himself* who has requested...this need to change and grow. (pp. 180-184)

When change comes, it has swift wings; it waits for no man. And if you would be ready, you will prepare yourself. It is no easy task that we undertake, to turn about the destiny of the world when it is running headlong into disaster. If it was something we could accomplish alone, it would have been done eons ago... The key is within... I cannot turn the lock... If you know this is what you are here for, you have already opened the door. Now it is up to you to make your opening not just an idea but a reality... Will you make a world of light or one of darkness? You are at a crossroads, and time is short. Make love your reality – and then we can all be together, and One. (pp. 103-104)

There are many people that have been born in this age who feel they do not belong. That is because they are here to help bring in the next one. This one does not feel like home because of a vision they were given at birth and before of what the Earth *can* be like – its potential that it does not live up to. If you were happy with the way the Earth was, the Earth wouldn't change... (p. 229)

How would you feel if you were a planet and you were the home to many beings, creatures; and yet there was one creature on you that continually went around with pins and needles and stabbed you and gouged you and drilled you, and refused to hear you, didn't seem to care that you were in pain, didn't notice that you were alive?...

They speak of this as a New Age because the Earth is being reborn..., and it is going through a death first before it can be reborn... The changes the Earth is going through are its cleansing of itself, so that it will be ready to receive man as a partner... There are many scars that need to be healed. The Earth is capable of healing itself if it is given the opportunity. But at this stage it desires help. It is evolving too. This planet has a soul, has an essence that you are part of...

And so...it is important for each individual to take it upon himself to see the world change for better. To do that, he must see himself change towards wholeness. And that is the message we are here to bring: that you can change the world, and you can do it by starting from yourself. And if enough of you do it, indeed things will have changed and the face of the world will be different...

When man is healed, [the Earth] will be made whole again. Then there will be no more battles, for there will be no more fear, and man will know he is *not alone*... Each planet goes through this process of joining the rest of the universe... And the rest of the universe is awaiting your awakening, waiting to talk, to communicate, to welcome. (pp. 139; 142; 279; 290; 336)

We are awaiting the moment when our worlds become one, so that you can see as real all of the things we have meant to man throughout his growing period. You will *change* us. In your growth, we must grow too. So do not be afraid of change. We are returning.

Think of a universe that [we] have experienced in solitude, and company with those who are the same as [us], in joy and love for what seems to be an eternity. And then add to that a multitude of beings who are searching,...who are striving and pulling. Can it stay the same? We are giving up our universe, our reality, *with* you. We are taking a leap into the unknown, into the unknowable...

Can you imagine your world where one of us can manifest itself as a physical form and speak to you direct? How much will that change your world? It depends upon man's awareness, first. We would come as allies, as friends. We would not come as gods and teachers. (pp. 291-294)

There is a Light growing in the Middle East, a Light that has been born... He will not come to full recognition until after, when the world will need a Peacemaker... The Christ has not come this time to be an example, [but] to bring man to a recognition of the Christ within...

When the Christ-consciousness manifests itself on Earth, it is, in a sense, the completeness of all of man expressing itself in a single form. It is all of your wisdom and all of your love and all of your acceptance and understanding brought together in one place at one time. And this kind of physical manifestation only occurs at key points in man's evolution – places where he has opened a door into himself. Man chooses when this will occur. (pp. 138; 265; 273)

We [bring] a practical way to use love,...to find out what love really is, and to let it flow out into the world again where it has been so sorely missed and has been misunderstood in its entirety...

There will be many who...are desperate and afraid, confused and alone, and have lost love and have just realized it. They will find themselves in a world they do not understand or recognize. The help they need will be from those who can show them the *new* beauty and help them find their centre, their grounding, so that they can become whole and then self-sustaining. (pp. 36; 228)

[Man has felt cut off because] it was necessary...to develop a sense of selfhood... But the time is coming to reunite the other parts that have been left behind and to become more in touch with the world and the things in it... You have learned *will* this last stage in development, and now will will be joined with being, beingness, oneness. And a new universe will be the result: becoming conscious creators, knowing why things happen, instead of seeing life as being thrust upon you...

The energy that was not available before will be available again... There will be more sharing, more ability to understand the forces around you and know how they can be tapped without being misused... There are many life forms on the Earth that have not been seen in a long time – those that are of a different vibration level. When man's body is different as well as his mind, he will be able to perceive their energy, just as he will be able to perceive ours... Your Earth will be going through a change of mutations which it has not seen in many eons... There will be new life forms, and old ones will become different... It will be a *different* kind of Earth than it has been for a while. (pp. 43; 287-292)

How will man handle the knowledge that a concept of linear time has, in effect, prevented him from answering the question that plagues man most? Its very conception precludes an understanding of "The Way Things Are" since they "are" only what you make of them.

In the New Age..., Time will have ceased to be. It is flowing out of things. You have had Time as a concept for the past 50,000 years. You have played a game with it, trying to understand what it is. But each cycle has its death and in death a new beginning. Time's cycle is at an end...

All that has happened in the past, all of Earth's history, man has created in his dream. And the end of time will come when man wakes up and realizes he has been dreaming... You have been *asleep*! It is time to wake up! And yet you will still be here with the other dreamers. And so, you must learn to flow in their dream and help them wake, so the dream may end...so we may all be reborn together. (pp. 353; 399)

You are living through what will one day become a legend to others... The New Age is yours to experience in its beginnings, but not in its flower – not in this life. But the flower must be nourished, and the seed must be sown... After the birth, the process of another maturing will take some time. The new awareness will not be instant, although it will seem to be for some of the children who are born later. Those are appearances only. You have all worked towards this end...

As man develops, he will regain the ability to travel backwards in time... Then time in the past will become a living thing... True history may become known!... Not just physical mutations, but a change in the awareness of mankind in general will bring about this kind of change... Each man will see his part – *all* of his parts. And then all man together will see it as a whole. It will be a great step in his evolution...

When the Earth reaches a point where this communication is no longer necessary, when man can once again hear the voice of the Earth and the rest of those who exist in it, those [souls] that are newly created will have just as much wisdom and experience as those who have been here for many years or many lives... You cannot possibly comprehend what the new man will truly be, until you become him. (pp. 36; 290-293; 392) [156N]

Appendix B

INDEX OF COMMUNICATIONS*

* Page numbers locate all session excerpts. Separate references to one session are identified by letters after a repeated date ("1976-08-06a").

Date	Source	Key phrases	Pages
1979-03-09b	Moita	Inwardness expressed in outward form	23
1979-03-09c	Moita	Get the main characters of a life together	77, 83
1979-03-09d	Moita	Their wars are more subtle wars	258-260
1979-03-24	Moita	You are weaving a network of light	24-25
1979-03-29a	Moita	You must know how not to use power	19-21
1979-03-29b	Moita	Our worlds will come closer together	52
1979-04-05	Moita	Many patterns are put off as coincidence	23
1979-04-14	Moita	Smallest stone can start an avalanche	28-29
1979-04-21	Moita	There will be a clean slate in some places	290
1979-04-29a	Moita	A spiritual interpretation of "big bang"	51
1979-04-29b	Moita	Stars are outward manifestations of beings	52-53
1979-06-06a	Moita	I am here to pave the way	33
1979-06-06b	Moita	Telepathic networks cross the globe	296-297
1979-06-11a	Moita	When beings go between realities	71-72
1979-06-11b	Moita	Bermuda Triangle is a time-flux area	117-119
1979-06-14a	Moita	You are reuniting with many old friends	33
1979-06-14b	Moita	You would be closer to our realm	37-38
1979-06-24a	Moita	To help found a new world	7
1979-06-24b	Moita	A guide, a door and a mirror	9
1979-06-24c	Moita	Co-creators to help found a new world	34-37
1979-06-24d	Moita	Pyramid is instrument to gather energy	122
1979-06-24e	Moita	Control-oriented man controls nothing	123-124
1979-06-24f	Moita	Offer something concrete to others	204
1979-07-03a	Moita	Much can be done from this level	38-39
1979-07-03b	Moita	Mother/father in Mu, Atlantis and Egypt	124-125
1979-07-16	Moita	Not a wise child who destroys his mother	42-47
1979-07-28a	Moita	Getting down to exploring doubt and fear	47-48
1979-07-28b	Moita	Deception happens, physical and spiritual	231
1979-08-08a	Moita	Whales are very delicate, gentle creatures	68-69
1979-08-08b	Moita	Each state has its own consciousness	85
1979-08-11	Moita	It would not do for us to wait too long	86
1979-09-15	Moita	Healers needed in coming changes	213
1979-09-26	Moita	Devastation still could all be avoided	88-90
1979-09-29a	Moita	Animals have a visible, living blueprint	67-68
1979-09-29b	Moita	World will change by changing yourself	92-93
1979-09-29c	Moita	Creative One (God) cannot be described	127-128
1979-09-29d	Moita	Everything planned in Great Teacher life	131
1979-09-29e	Moita	If no one interfered in course of world	204
1979-09-29f	Moita	You are living in very paranoid times	251-253
1979-10-12	Moita	Let go of fears, let yourself flow outwards	95-96
1979-10-15a	Moita	You could see a flying saucer or angel	73
1979-10-15b	Moita	An optimum future line converges here	93-95
1979-10-15c	Moita	Creation happens all around you	128

Date	Source	Key phrases	Pages
1979-10-15d	Moita	When Christ-consciousness manifests	138, 237
1979-10-27	Moita	You will feel what must be done	96
1979-11-05a	Moita	Animals can gain a desire to be human	69
1979-11-05b	Moita	My energy serves as doorway for many	96-100
1979-11-10a	Moita	If people not ready to heal themselves . . .	213-214
1979-11-10b	Moita	They are afraid of revealing themselves	239-240
1979-11-10c	Moita	If seeing these battles for yourself . . .	245
1979-11-18	Moita	War is like an alien pestilence	140, 237, 260
1979-11-26a	Moita	It is time for hiding to cease	102-106
1979-11-26b	Amar	You are at a crossroads, time is short	102-106
1979-11-26c	Amar	Not easy to turn about destiny of world	107
1979-11-26d	Moita	Those who have seen Christ once . . .	133
1979-11-26e	Amar	Make opening not just idea but reality	152
1979-11-26f	Amar	Man is erupting in anger and fear	237
1979-11-26g	Amar	Make love your reality	297
1979-12-16a	Moita	If reincarnation were left in Bible . . .	132
1979-12-16b	Moita	For now, things go in different directions	139-140
1979-12-16c	Moita	This is their "out". They are freeing Earth.	238
1979-12-17a	Moita	Many different types of nature spirits	62-63
1979-12-17b	Moita	Earth speaking with all of its voices	206-208
1979-12-17c	Moita	Interacting with life in a direct way	210-211
1979-12-17d	Moita	Learn to follow your own guidance	237
1979-12-26a	Moita	Expect unexpected, must walk fine line	131-132
1979-12-26b	Moita	We have called them "the High Ones"	180-184
1979-12-27a	Moita	Earth needs to change to preserve itself	184-185
1979-12-27b	Moita	I am glad you have met your tree	208
1980-xx-xx	Moita	A: Your mind will seem a prison	153
1980-xx-xx	Moita	B: Be guided by your higher awareness	153-154
1980-xx-xx	Moita	D/E: Your heart is leader of your soul	154-157
1980-xx-xx	Moita	F: Shadows disappear as turned to light	158
1980-xx-xx	Moita	G: Clear heart through difficulty, pain	158-160
1980-xx-xx	Moita	H: If know yourself, no need to prove	161-163
1980-xx-xx	Moita	I: Experience and come out other side	163-164
1980-xx-xx	Moita	J: Only you can define reality for you	164-165
1980-xx-xx	Moita	K: To me, mistakes are greatest teacher	165-167
1980-xx-xx	Moita	L/M: Love is unlimited, faceted jewel	167-171
1980-xx-xx	Moita	N: Cannot save world by being a crutch	171
1980-xx-xx	Moita	O: Let your walls fall gently	172
1980-xx-xx	Moita	P: Finding difficulty in loving yourself	172-174
1980-xx-xx	Moita	Q: A great dance performed in your life	174-175
1980-xx-xx	Moita	R/S/T: We are here to draw on in need	176-177
1980-xx-xx	Moita	DL: The more you attune to our vibration	178
1980-01-01a	Moita	Relax and put your faith in the world	215

Date	Source	Key phrases	Pages
1980-01-01b	Moita	Important to have goal common to all	298-299
1980-01-19	Moita	True history may become known!	290-291
1980-02-04a	Moita	Life is on all planets, physical or not	70-71
1980-02-04b	Moita	When language born, memory came after	110-111
1980-02-04c	Moita	Jesus came as living, unfiltered Presence	126-127
1980-02-04d	Moita	You're not alone, you have many allies	141-143
1980-02-04e	Moita	Creation will continue for a long time	291
1980-02-04f	Moita	Memory came after language	392
1980-02-20	Moita	A house is stronger with many angles	299-301
1980-02-24	Moita	Do not judge self by world's yardsticks	225-226
1980-02-25a	Moita	On another line, the world was destroyed	21
1980-02-25b	Moita	Each animal species has its own oversoul	67
1980-03-02a	Moita	Bright, colourful union at Full Moon	59
1980-03-02b	Moita	Currents of energy running through Earth	61-62
1980-03-02c	Moita	Ark of Covenant was for communication	129
1980-03-17a	Moita	You are climbing a great mountain	129-130
1980-03-17b	Moita	Many levels to Christ-consciousness	134-135
1980-03-17c	Moita	Look at world as beautiful, harmonious	227-228
1980-03-31a	Moita	The volcano is an attempt at balance	192-193
1980-03-31b	Moita	Power they take now will turn on them	248
1980-04-07a	Moita	Spirits near Earth became physical	69-70, 72
1980-04-07b	Moita	Great Pyramid leaves our future open	122
1980-04-09a	Moita	Opportunity to develop on another Earth	141
1980-04-09b	Moita	The Earth is seeking partners	204-205
1980-04-09c	Moita	Reassurance in every blade of grass	205-206
1980-04-09d	Moita	Becoming part of, not living off, Earth	214-215
1980-04-09e	Moita	Help others find their centre, grounding	228
1980-04-09f	Moita	Some will not accept newness and change	238
1980-04-09g	Moita	When there's desire to build a community	295
1980-04-19a	Moita	Earth prefers to change more slowly	209
1980-04-19b	Moita	Not in your goal shall you find peace	216
1980-04-19c	Moita	It is not uncommon to feel alone	302
1980-05-13a	Moita	Cosmic-solar event, splitting of worlds	187
1980-05-13b	Moita	Becoming more involved in the Earth	218
1980-05-13c	Moita	No chance meetings in this life	232-234
1980-05-13d	Moita	Void of understanding and acceptance	238
1980-05-27a	Moita	Gnostics and orthodox made battlefield	136
1980-05-27b	Moita	As the age began, so shall it end	138, 272, 397
1980-05-27c	Moita	Man is too secure as ruler of the Earth	194-195
1980-05-27d	Moita	Glad you are going to enjoy the place	218
1980-07-04a	Moita	This used to be a sacred ground	219
1980-07-04b	Moita	We would like you to meet, for growth	235-236
1980-07-04c	Moita	She needs to come to your place	266

Date	Source	Key phrases	Pages
1980-07-04d	Moita	They are not balanced, together or apart	296
1980-07-04e	Moita	Many possible meetings in this life	343-344
1980-07-06	Moita	You should be where your heart feels best	197-198
1980-07-17	Moita	Sun is the eye of spirit, the life-giver	53-54
1980-08-11	Moita	Earth also has a greater spirit	60
1980-08-16a	Moita	When I was last here on Earth . . .	110
1980-08-16b	Moita	The Grail means union with the soul	137-138
1980-08-16c	Moita	Man must be whole now, or catastrophe	241-244
1980-08-28a	Moita	We could still use the Crystal Skull	117
1980-08-28b	Moita	Chainsaw useful tool with right awareness	221
1980-08-28c	Moita	You are here to let go of structures	223
1980-08-28d	Moita	People must express dedication to ideal	303
1980-08-30a	Moita	Man's body was not as dense as now	128-129
1980-08-30b	Moita	Time for you not to seek a pattern	226-227
1980-08-30c	Moita	It's easy to be drawn to people in history	266-267
1980-09-16a	Moita	Memory was the death of Mu	111-113
1980-09-16b	Moita	The first descent, and man plummets!	116
1980-09-16c	Moita	Atlantean records as legend and prophecy	120-121
1980-09-16d	Moita	It was more a personal than tribal place	219
1980-09-24a	Moita	I have not hidden my motives	245-246
1980-09-24b	Moita	Wars could be stopped with honesty	247
1980-09-24c	Moita	Inner desires bottled up, then exploding	302
1980-09-24d	Moita	When you fear losing what is yours	306
1980-10-19a	Moita	Eskimo culture is a remnant of Mu	114, 388
1980-10-19b	Moita	The inhabitants have created a new soul	196-197
1980-10-19c	Moita	Northern lights are means to communicate	262-263
1980-11-05a	Moita	It connects to your Raven dream	41-42
1980-11-05b	Moita	Parallels with Atlantis more obvious	249
1980-11-05c	Moita	The spear retained the memory of Christ	250-251
1980-11-07a	Moita	At New Moon, hidden things illuminated	58
1980-11-07b	Moita	You were seeing the time to come	185-186
1980-11-07c	Moita	I who gave birth to the word	391-396
1980-11-24	Moita	They all experienced it as a pressure	190
1980-11-30a	Moita	The Universe began to diversify	50-51
1980-11-30b	Moita	This is not the first universe	51-52
1980-11-30c	Moita	Saturn's rings are like northern lights	54-55
1980-11-30d	Moita	Spirit is cause; matter is effect	67
1980-11-30e	Moita	Many civilizations have been lost in time	113
1980-11-30f	Moita	Earthquakes caused by people's thoughts	190
1980-12-21a	Moita	Astronomical data passed from Atlantis	53
1980-12-21b	Amar	Man will start war, fearing own evolution	264-265
1980-12-21c	Moita	For this energy, three is a good number	304
1980-12-28a	Moita	People's soles insulated too long	214

Date	Source	Key phrases	Pages
1980-12-28b	Moita	Man will become a partner with Earth	229
1980-12-28c	Moita	Civilization will be toppled by its fears	237
1981-01-04a	Moita	So much in you is coming into the light	305-306
1981-01-04b	Moita	Sharing in many ways throughout time	309
1981-01-10	Moita	Earthmade medications have wholeness	212
1981-01-17	Moita	We've moved all of you in this direction	306-309
1981-01-17a	Moita	Astrology given as symbol to reconnect	138
1981-01-17b	Moita	So you have met a raven	224
1981-01-17c	Moita	The buds are slowly opening	309
1981-01-17d	Moita	Learn to illuminate your darker corners	309
1981-02-03	Moita	This is a lesson in multidimensionality	224-225
1981-03-15a	Moita	Earth does not travel through a vacuum	282-283
1981-03-15b	Moita	This has been beginning of a new world	312
1981-03-15c	Moita	Willing to face the fear of change	320
1981-03-20	Moita	Earth is being bombarded with energy	55-56
1981-03-28a	Moita	Other planets have chosen form like yours	74
1981-03-28b	Moita	Religion is attempt to regain lost unity	123
1981-03-28c	Moita	We're giving up our reality, taking chance	291-292
1981-04-16a	Moita	He is the reason she did not come	268-272
1981-04-16b	Amar	You have yet to meet an ancient enemy	268-272
1981-04-16c	Amar	We have an interest in this situation	344
1981-04-18	Amar	He focuses her on a life near Christ	266
1981-05-19a	Moita	We can stall devastation some time yet	275-276
1981-05-19b	Moita	This source has become more informative	284
1981-05-19c	Moita	Preparing for the changing of the world	323-326
1981-05-30a	Moita	Seeing a tree from all times, perspectives	61
1981-05-30b	Moita	There is always more than one truth	327-328
1981-06-29	Moita	Souls being pushed to face hidden parts	315
1981-07-06	Moita	One of Pan's favourite places	64
1981-07-19	Moita	Pan is a manifestation of the Earth Spirit	64
1981-07-23	Moita	Creating one's reality, how it really works	329-332
1981-07-29a	Moita	Other-planet beings concerned for Earth	73-74
1981-07-29b	Moita	We can alter how planets affect Earth	281-282
1981-07-29c	Moita	Our worlds will become one	292-294
1981-07-29d	Moita	Earth, your Mother, is in need of help	346
1981-07-29e	Moita	You are each your own answer	368
1981-07-29f	Moita	My body in Mu could be seen as Oriental	388-390
1981-08-02a	Moita	To bring recognition of the Christ within	273-274
1981-08-02b	Amar	The Antichrist is man's unaccepted parts	273-274
1981-08-02c	Amar	By your openness, you received a sign	294
1981-08-07	Moita	You and Kelly, a very special meeting	317-318
1981-08-09	Moita	It will be a different kind of Earth	284-289
1981-08-17a	Moita	If man is going to destroy the Earth . . .	277-278

Date	Source	Key phrases	Pages
1981-08-17b	Moita	New universe results, conscious creators	292
1981-08-17c	Moita	Names can be very tricky things	328
1981-08-23	Moita	Take physical and non-physical steps	278-279
1981-09-04a	Moita	Becoming free to express yourself	318
1981-09-04b	Moita	No true enemy – it has all been a sham	338
1981-09-04c	Moita	Accepting your own light and shadows	332-334
1981-09-04d	Moita	Medicine woman life relates to Barham	339-343
1981-09-16	Moita	In New Age, Time will have ceased	398-399
1981-09-20	Moita	Seeing your part of the pattern	348
1981-10-04a	Goddess	End of time when man wakes up	7
1981-10-04b	Goddess	Begin a little early, stacking the deck	8, 358, 400
1981-10-04c	Moita	You will be meeting someone else	349-363
1981-10-04d	Goddess	I'm not an untouchable Goddess	349-363
1981-10-04e	Goddess	Learning to Sing to the Sun	375
1981-10-15	Moita	Ban lifted. Our merger is accomplished.	371-373
1981-10-16a	Moita	Change how you see me, your last barrier	334-337
1981-10-16b	Goddess	This is the miracle you were told of	334-337
1981-10-16c	Moita	A place where words have lost meaning	364-367
1981-10-16d	Goddess	I will be made whole when man is healed	364-367
1981-10-16e	Goddess	Your Sun-Self is rising	373-375
1981-10-16f	Amar	You are sleeping gods and goddesses	373-375
1981-10-16g	Moita	This is my form as the Speaker	396-397
1981-10-30	Goddess	Why Goddess and God created Sun-child	370
1981-11-03	Moita	Coming closer to the moment of change	400
1981-11-20a	Moita	A network of light for a new beginning	289-290
1981-11-20b	Moita	Man in membrane, just before birth	382
1981-12-01a	Goddess	Man sees evolution from the other end	65-66
1981-12-01b	Moita	You and I have worn many cloaks	377-382
1981-12-01c	Goddess	Will find way to free all my children	377-382
1981-12-20a	Moita	Humanity tries to keep unrest unconscious	246
1981-12-20b	Moita	Seeing whole patterns instead of pieces	371
1982-02-18	Moita	Through the child is the larger Self	382-386
1982-02-27	Moita	You must wake up from the dream of life	368-370
1982-04-11	Goddess	I will Sing again the Ancient Harmonies	387
1982-06-04	Moita	How would you feel if you were a planet	279-281

Appendix C

INDEX OF DREAMS

Date	Dream Title	Dreamer	Pages
1981-10-(early?)	Crystal Ball as Solid Tear	Kelly	355
1981-11-28	She Climbs Peak, Lies on Earth's Heart	Kelly	381-382
1981-11-28 & 29	[2 dreams: U.S. president's death/health]	David	376
1981-11-30	Gates of Divine Buddhahood	David	376, 380-381

INDEX OF REGRESSIONS

Date	Regression summary	Subject	Pages
1978-09-15	Re: Kelly & David as Earth and Sun	Kelly	200
1979-01-19	Re: Kyrionis and journey to Musili	Kelly	85, 378
1979-03-02	Medicine woman / Indian maiden	Kelly/Carla	77-83
1979-07-14	Re: Atlantis destroyed, migration, return	Kelly	41
1980-12-21 to 23?	Re: Kelly in Africa; medicine woman	Jim	309
1980-12-24	Re: Jim as African shaman, and others	Kelly	309
1981-03-13	Re: Priest with visions of angel	David	313
1981-04-18	Atlantean priestess fights mind control	Kelly	144-151

Series Preface: MIND LEAP 1960S/2012

Today the gauntlet of crises facing life on Earth is undeniable: from extreme poverty-hunger-disease to financial system upheaval, from religious-ethnic-political fanaticism to massive weapons proliferation, from pervasive ecological destruction to escalating climate change and natural and/or manmade disasters. The Hopi's discerning understatement clearly applies:*koyanniquatsi*, "life out of balance". Indeed, without a fundamental, planet-wide change of course, scientists have warned that within the next decade, perhaps even by 2012, we may pass one or more "tipping points". Thereafter, spiralling events could spell the decline of nature and civilization.

However, simultaneously, many voices around the world have been portraying this same period of years, leading to 2012 and beyond, as a time of rare transformative potential.[157] The collapse of existing structures brings the opportunity to reinvent society on a surer, more resilient foundation. But more than the obvious socio-economic and environmental challenges are involved here. The voices of transformation urge we now prepare for the descent of spiritual energies, and synchronous rising of human energies, that will open up our blinkered view of what is real. For life again to flourish on this planet, humanity's consensual, working reality must expand to include higher dimensions of being.

This opening to higher levels can begin as simply as tomorrow morning's dream. But it has vast implications. It is essential in restoring the perspective we lack: on *who we are*, where we have come from and where we are going, individually and collectively; on our *sustaining relationships* with non-physical energies able to generate inspiration and insight toward solving our many practical and existential dilemmas; and on the as yet *unknowing power* of human thoughts and emotions to reflect outward, co-creating our world. In other words, there can be no lasting solutions to external problems without overcoming our spiritual estrangement and achieving wholeness from within. By reconnecting with our source, we will rediscover what is truly essential in life and how to manifest it, helping to heal ourselves and our Earth.

Not the first new world to be born in the death throes of another, say seers of far ancient days. I include the Maya – by whose Long Count calendar the fifth World Age begins at the December solstice 2012 – and those you will meet in the *Mind Leap* series. While perceptions of what lies ahead vary, it is certain that humanity's future consciousness will diverge from the one creating these crises, and will represent a new evolutionary stage. Therefore a journey of transformation beckons us all – which means opening our minds and hearts and entering the unknown. That will always be the starting point in this series.

Of course, within our collective memory there was another period of widespread change, of leaps in consciousness and alterations of lives, though generally lasting only a few brief years. Yet they were a harbinger, those late 1960s and 1970s – and a preparation. Various groups and personalities spring to mind as representatives of that era, be they cultural heroes who pioneered and clarified the new awareness or self-aggrandizers who exploited and profited from its facsimile. But out of the public spotlight, certain others delved deeply, exploring new territories of experience with minimal distraction.

Today humanity needs to rediscover and share all that we can learn about transformation and the challenges now staring us in the face. To do so, we must move beyond our safe positions, whether of uncomprehending ridicule or understanding silence. Accordingly, you hold in your hands one of the first very public sharings from a couple of those relatively quiet explorers, two of us forever changed by encounters with energies of whom I have spoken.

The names that humanity has given these energies are much less important than how we can connect with them. And now, establishing more conscious relationships with higher levels has become an evolutionary necessity – as inevitable a quest as searching for physical life on other planets, and much more urgent. But far from alien, this connection is the most intimate thing in the world, for it flows from listening to our dreams, feelings and intuitions, perhaps eventually blossoming into more direct forms of communication. It is the fulfilment of our growth, our reaching toward joy.

Such communication has been spreading more widely than many suspect, expressed and understood in whatever ways individuals find most natural. Directly or indirectly, it has helped energize and enlighten movements toward peace, human rights, community and reharmonizing ourselves with nature. On the other hand, those who wish to preserve the old limits on consciousness, who try to resist the rising energy environment we are entering, may face mounting pressures they are not able to explain.

True, mass culture has made sport of forms of communication called "channeling". And yes, the trivialization and abuses of supposed "spiritual" contact are obvious. But part of the mainstream attitude toward channeling – as also toward the wondrous communications called "crop circles" – is a nervous, adolescent reaction to something important. This is an actual mystery that reaches much deeper than its media image. Perhaps more are now ready to look carefully at the reality behind the caricature and examine the workings of this bridge between worlds.

We must be clear: good communication with the non-physical or "subtle" worlds is a cooperative endeavour between levels of being, both ends of which need to be clear and whole. That is why information should not be believed merely because it *appears* to come from a higher source, and why anyone wishing to evaluate a body of non-ordinary communications should seek an *inside view* of how it emerged and evolved. One should be on guard against dishonesty and manipulation: those putting on a front of all-knowingness and "spiritual" perfection for influence or financial gain.

One should also look into how the communications addressed the psychic and very human problems of those involved. The true value of a guiding philosophy shows in how it is conveyed and applied, both day to day and in life's emergencies – like the intensity attending the birth and early evolution of our own contact. That is why we have chosen to share these life-changing experiences, and we invite readers to glean from them what is universal and/or useful to yourself.

Through the *Mind Leap* series, we introduce Moita, a friend and teacher speaking through Kelly (Siofra Bradigan). We convey the manner of Moita's coming: the learnings and choices that opened us to her reality so that eventually we could share her and her own higher levels with hundreds of session participants. Then, we invite you into our sessions, providing verbatim the most revealing conversations with these energy presences – their wisdom and even "cosmic humour" – as well as spontaneous reactions by those who participated.

Future offerings will continue our own journey and share many more communications of an experiential and prophetic nature. The fact is, much that has been happening to our Earth, and is now being suggested may emerge circa 2012 and beyond, was mentioned or hinted at decades ago – and explained to us in the context of human and planetary consciousness evolving toward a new stage of co-creation. Though no definite target date was given, the similarity between the transition as then projected and what is developing and being spoken of now is impossible to ignore. Because of this, however difficult the period ahead, I feel assured that love and growth will be at the root of extraordinary changes to come. Special-effects movies aside, this is not a prophecy of ultimate catastrophe, but of transformation and renewal.

No one yet knows the degree of awareness and commitment humanity will bring to this transition. But today the harbingers of co-creative wholeness are everywhere: as gossamer as sudden intuitions, meditative visions and lucid dreams; as down-to-earth as farmers' fields graced with amazingly complex, inspiringly beautiful "crop circles" (like the one on our title page); and as bravely outgoing as those prophetic pioneers who would lift present-day civilization from its cynicism and destructiveness toward "One Earth", a green and just "peaceable kingdom".

Without human beings, obviously, no new vision can be incarnated. A high source whom you will meet in this series once put it very bluntly: *"If it was something we could accomplish alone, it would have been done eons ago."* We face tests continually, small and large. Choosing well eases the whole world's struggle toward rebirth.

David W. Letts
January 2011

Mind Leap Series

A CHANNELING FOR DECEMBER 20, 2012

What will December 21, 2012 mean for us and our Earth? How may we expect our reality to change, and how should we prepare for it? Critical questions, these – since the awareness we bring to this event will be crucial to the outcome. But most important of all – and most absent from the public debate – is recognition that *non-physical, higher levels of nature and human nature on this planet*, with whom we are inherently connected and able to learn to communicate, lie behind such transformative events.

Amid major societal/economic/environmental disruption, with a growing sense that our world is conspiring toward a pivot point of change, consider just two current and now converging factors: (1) nearly universal awareness of the 2012 December solstice as a so-called end-of-the-world date in an ancient Mayan calendar; and (2) the much lesser known but stunning evolution of "signs in the fields", or "crop circles", in the course of the 1990s and 2000s – including the huge formation that appeared at Avebury Manor, Wiltshire, England, on July 15, 2008, depicting the exact astronomical positions of our entire solar system as of that same December 21, 2012 date.

Of course, many wonder whether any date should be singled out as definitive – even if it is the turning point from one World Age to the next in the Long Count calendar of the Maya. Should those who look to a New Age be focusing rather on a transitional period of decades or even centuries that includes many significant junctures? Compounding the uncertainty, even from those convinced the 2012 December solstice will bring *the* pivotal change, we've heard widely varying suggestions, reflecting disparate world-views, of what may transpire – ranging up to the extremes of "apocalyptic" earth upheavals, UFO landings of "space brothers", universal "instant enlightenment" and/or "the end of time" (which itself can mean quite different things).

I do assume the 2012 December solstice will mark a significant point in our evolution – in part, due to all the attention from human consciousness – but also fall within a decades-long transition that has been underway since at least the 1960s and will continue beyond 2012. There may or may not be obvious *outward* changes on or near the 2012 world-shift date – certainly the probability of large-scale Earth changes has retreated since 1980 as energies have risen from within and beyond our planet, according to current sources. But to me, the nature of the *inward* event is not in doubt. Despite likely differences in magnitude, I believe the best key we have to the essence of 12/21/12 lies in previous *progressive energy changes toward a meeting of worlds*, as Moita has described.

I'm convinced the communications in this series apply throughout the ongoing transition, being as relevant for the present and future as when they were first given. But if we are now to consider their specific implications for 2012, everyone must be free to reach their own conclusions. As Moita has said: "In the end analysis, you are the only one who can decide what you perceive of all this, and what applies to you directly." On this basis, I offer interwoven channelings from Moita that we can together imagine being delivered, to our expectant ears, on the Winter Solstice Eve of 2012.

The Channeling*

Something is happening tomorrow, to everyone on the planet. It requires my *complete presence*. There have not been many things in a long while that have required all of me. There is a great deal of energy bent in this direction.

I see the planet covered with the tides of change. There are times in the Earth's history when a single word, spoken at the right time and place, can change the face of the world. This is one of those times. The Earth has had many faces. The one that you have on it now will not last much longer. As each of you are in this age striving to find out who you are as an individual expression of being, so is your Earth finding out who it is. It, too, has a soul.

These communications have been happening throughout history. We have spoken through many people – ancient prophets and modern ones. You all have gone through a period of development where you have drifted away from your source. You have gone into forgetfulness, and you think the world is asleep and does not remember. Now you are beginning to come back up out of that forgetfulness, to remember where you came from and who you are, and to know what you can do. In a change like that, the world will wake up.

Our worlds co-exist in the same space but are separated by vibrations of energy. Your eyes are so accustomed to seeing physical matter. You are narrowly focused on one thing – this life, this reality. We are another form of this existence, the same as you, but our energy is a much less dense energy. Your world is in the process of raising its energy level, and we are reaching down to touch it, so that our worlds will come closer together. It is closing a gap. It is *all* of us who exist in this universe being able to touch each other and work together towards creating a more whole humanity.

For us, this change is a great responsibility. Our whole sphere of influence will be drawing close. It will mean a great shift in your energy towards our level – and being that kind of change, will cause unrest and growth, some unwanted. It need not be as chaotic as it might. We are trying to soften it as much as possible, to be here as closely as possible and add our energy to these changes and to each of you. We have to gauge these things as delicately as we can, so the most good is done with the least ill. There is a chance that some of the physical changes could be avoided if many people can change their level of consciousness in enough time.

---

* The text blends Moita channelings through Siofra Bradigan during 1978-1980, as included in the *Mind Leap* series. I have merely abridged and rearranged the transcripts, making slight stylistic changes for continuity of presentation.

Let me explain the connection to you in this way. Each time you have a thought, you have created a thought-form with its own particular energy. If many people are sending out negative thoughts, many negative thought-forms build up. They mass together and form great pressures that eventually affect your physical reality when there are too many of them. And there are too many of them now.

As in an earthquake or a volcano, when pressure builds until the Earth must shift in order to relieve that pressure, so also with thought-forms. When they build to such an intensity, something must change in order to release that pressure. Some of these changes will be from those who are punishing themselves. If you could all learn that one lesson – that self-punishment is not the way to learn – there would be much fewer physical rumblings. And if you have enough people together putting out strong positive thought-forms, they would negate the negative forms and the built-up pressure would be released in a different way. The more who rise above, the fewer who will be left behind and fewer physical manifestations will occur.

It will be you who makes the difference, whether it is a destructive or a constructive change. Each individual has as much responsibility for this as each other. It must start from one. And hopefully it will make you all realize how important you really are to the world that you have created – and how much power you have over it, to change it for good or ill.

One of the things we bring, our gift, is the inability to hide – from each other, and from yourself. It is not a gift many will take kindly. In a body, you feel you can hide your thoughts and failings from others. But our energy coming closer will destroy that apparent ability. There is much unrest over this. What do you think would happen if everyone could read everyone else's thoughts? It would be rather difficult to run a government if everyone *knew* when you were lying. There are no such things as secrets.

We also bring a message of remembering. You have gone through a long period of not being able to remember who you are or where you come from. It is as if, when you are born, a spirit places a bud inside your head. Inside this bud is the memory of *you*, of all those things you cannot remember while you are alive. One of the changes that will happen is that these buds will begin to open for the many – not just for the few, as it has been in the past.

People will remember in different degrees, depending on where they are in their development. Some will just remember this life, and all of the things they have conveniently tried to forget. Others will remember many lives, and see how they all flow together to make one. Many times that have been forgotten need to be remembered and the energy to be renewed. Those who remember their pasts while they still live in a body will not have to forget, the next time they are born.

The whole point of being here is to bring to the world your awareness, to become a whole being instead of one who is one part in the day and another at night. When you sleep, you leave your body. You go into other worlds, other realities. You meet teachers, you go to classes, learn lessons, some of which you bring back in dreams, some in intuitions and hunches. The problem is the separation of the two forms of consciousness. It is a very artificial separation, and the one thing you are striving for is to bring these two worlds back together, so the one can work with the other.

You were separated from our level of feeling and intuition in order to create in you the sense of the ego, a rational mind, the intellect. And now that that has been accomplished, you are hopefully seeing many sides of what it can do. It is time to bring that quality together with the spirit, so that you will have more purpose, more understanding of the creative forces of which you are a part.

If you can go through this change with the right attunement, you will gain an extra source of energy. As in all things, it takes a great deal of awareness to do that. You who are trying to build a New Age, have you thought of the kind of New Age you are trying to build, what you will do with that energy you will have access to? That is why so many of us are here. We would not see the world destroyed another time.

Warnings about power have been given to many people over the centuries in every age. And there are many more people here now, when the change in the world comes, who will have access to that power. It is very important to realize that whatever you do with it – however you choose to use it – you do it *to yourselves*. You must become very aware of what you are doing and what kind of energy you are putting into it. If you let yourself delve into your lower centres, they too will be amplified.

I am explaining this to you so you will have a clearer understanding of what you are doing. There will be feats that can be accomplished in this new universe that others would not have believed possible. It is important that you realize you must build this reality slowly and carefully, so it will have a strong foundation.

Much consciousness needs to be developed in everyday life. Each moment must be made a meditation, an awareness on another level of your purpose and why you are here, what you are doing and what you wish to work on. There is no such thing as unimportant, and the effects of doing things the wrong way will be felt immediately. It is not an easy spot you are put in, but how can you continue unless you are? It sounds like a hard road, but once it has been taken, it is hard no longer. It has many rewards.

What is needed in this time is not starry-eyed prophets who have no firm basis in the Earth, but those who are balanced in both worlds, who can take the wisdom that we can offer and the experience of our sharing, and bring it into the world in a real and physical way to help shape it and change it. That is what the New Age is all about: trying to discover who you are, being yourself without losing your integrity and without destroying things around you; being an individual expression and a unique interpreter of all of your experience, but working with a sense of cooperation and love.

We have watched for a great many years, and now there is a drawing together of worlds, a time when the two worlds may touch and not be destroyed by each other, when they may integrate and understand. The coming together of our worlds will not change just yours, but mine. It will affect us as much as you. There is a great difference between watching over a soul and its development when it is not aware of you, and participating with a conscious soul in its own development. Life will never be the same again.

As our levels become more in tune, there will be *many* manifestations, for those who have eyes to see them. The texture of the world is changing, and all those who are already partially tuned into us will feel the effects at a highly accelerated pace. Time has been compressed for a reason. Your bodies are changing. Your other senses that have lain dormant are beginning to wake up. We are preparing you for the inevitable shock of seeing us as we really *are*.

It is the world discovering itself. And those who do not wish to discover who they are do not look forward to the changing of the world, because when the world changes to what it *is* and people recognize it, it will be unavoidable – for *all*.

We are entering a New Age of humanity. Instead of man creating only on his own, as an individual self set apart from the rest of the universe, this time he is involved in a co-creation – and *we* are the co-creators. Those who are here have arrived to help found a new world.

Do not look on us as higher beings who know all the answers, for then you limit yourself and you limit us as well. You put us into a role that is difficult to break. It is that I am more aware of what I know, not that I know more. We have much to share. We have much love to give to the world and to its people. And we are building that bridge so that the energy that has created the universe can shine out from the Earth and its inhabitants.

We shall see what tomorrow brings on the road to awareness. And we will shine our love on you all. Good night.

ABOUT THE AUTHOR

David W. Letts was born in 1947 in New York City. He grew up in a Lutheran minister's family with his older sister and brother. David entered college to study music, but in the shadow of the Vietnam War switched to history and sociology. He filled his extracurricular hours with peace education/activism and, after being rejected for conscientious objector status, became a war resister by publicly returning his draft card to the government in 1968.

David later graduated Phi Beta Kappa from the University of Oregon, majoring in psychology and minoring in philosophy. He earned his M.A. at the University of Saskatchewan (Regina), Canada, with a holistic critique of the typical textbook introducing psychology to university students.

As a Ph.D. student, David's research on lucid dreams led to "midwifing" two women's openings to psychic-spiritual communication. He was a regular participant and transcriber for over 300 of these individual and group sessions, shared with hundreds of participants from 1976 to 1985. He also edited the journal *Rays* devoted to selected transcripts and related experience.

David has applied his holistic outlook in his writings and in teaching a variety of university psychology courses. He has led or co-led dream workshops, among other groups, and guided past-life regressions, across western Canada.

Since the mid-1980s, David has also worked as an editor in two Canadian provincial governments, including several years for a New Democratic Party caucus and premier. David notes this proves that exploring non-ordinary realities need not impair one's social, rational (even pedantic) side. "Editing government legal publications is as far from the intuitive psyche as one human mind would ever want to stretch. Yet it has balanced me in useful ways."

A new, fulfilling phase of life began in 1986 when David met his soon-to-be wife Margi. Between 1987 and 2011, they lived in Victoria, British Columbia, which enabled them to explore Vancouver Island and the rest of B.C. and the West Coast. With retirement from full-time government work, David and Margi returned to Regina, renewing former contacts. David has given presentations at Saskatchewan's annual Paranormal Symposium: on "The Reality of Crop Circles" in September 2011, and on "Channeling and 2012" in the year this book is published.

Readers are encouraged to email the author at dwletts@gmail.com with feedback on this book and/or interest in arranging talks, seminars, workshops, etc.

ABOUT THE CO-AUTHORS

Siofra Bradigan (a.k.a. Kelly) has consulted on aspects of the *Mind Leap* series but prefers to continue her healing work (which no longer involves extensive Moita sessions) without this kind of public profile at this time. Meanwhile Moita undoubtedly continues her own joyful work – under any of her many names, or none.

ACKNOWLEDGMENTS

I wish to thank the hundreds of participants in our Moita sessions for sharing their energy and curiosity, their experiences and heartfelt concerns. They contributed greatly to the variety and deep relevance of this material.

I am grateful to my wife Margi for choosing to be my companion through these past 26 changeful years and for continuing to sustain me, during this writing, in all the ways that she does. Margi also took the back cover photo of me hugging Grandmother Cedar in 1991. (The front cover photo is mine from East Sooke Park on the southwesternmost tip of Vancouver Island.)

I acknowledge the sources listed below regarding significant excerpts included:

Illustration reproduced from "2009 – Crop Circle Communication" (web article), courtesy of Bert Janssen [www.CropcirclesandMore.com].

The Mysteries of Clear Light: A Timeless Legacy, by Thespian Michaels and Esmi Fernau. 1st Trilogy. (IN: Trafford, 2006).

Fatima Prophecy: Days of Darkness, Promise of Light by Ray Stanford (TX: Association for the Understanding of Man, 1974).

Coming Changes newsletter (July/August 1980), edited by Rich Green.

"Allegations of Sexual Misconduct, Cruelty at Ranch Stir Controversy" by Henry Fuentes, San Diego Union (Sept. 2, 1979).

Revelation: The Birth of a New Age by David Spangler. 2nd ed. (CA: Rainbow Bridge, 1976).

The Aquarian Conspiracy: Personal and Social Transformation in the 1980s by Marilyn Ferguson (CA: Tarcher, 1980).

BIBLIOGRAPHY

Andrews, Synthia and Colin. 2008. The Complete Idiot's Guide to 2012. NY: Penguin.

Ardagh, Arjuna; Argüelles, José; and 24 other contributors. 2007. The Mystery of 2012: Predictions, Prophecies & Possibilities. CO: Sounds True.

Association for the Understanding of Man. 1974. Fatima Prophecy: Days of Darkness, Promise of Light. TX: A.U.M.

Barfield, Owen. 1988. Saving the Appearances: A Study in Idolatry. 2nd ed. CT: Wesleyan University.

Bethune, Brian. 2007. "The End of Days". Maclean's Magazine (Feb. 26, 2007).

Carter, Mary Ellen. 1968. Edgar Cayce on Prophecy. NY: Warner.

Castaneda, Carlos. 1974. The Teachings of Don Juan: A Yaqui Way of Knowledge. NY: Pocket.

Cohen, Leonard. 1966. Beautiful Losers. ON (Canada): McClelland & Stewart.

Edinger, Edward F. 1973. Ego and Archetype. MD: Penguin.

Ferguson, Marilyn. 1980. The Aquarian Conspiracy. CA: Tarcher.

Findhorn Community. 1975. <u>The Findhorn Garden</u>. NY: Harper & Row.

_____. 1980. <u>Faces of Findhorn: Images of a Planetary Family</u>. NY: Harper & Row.

Findhorn Foundation. 1978. "Interview with Peter Caddy". <u>Onearth 5</u> (Spring 1978).

Flem-Ath, Rand and Rose. 1995. <u>When the Sky Fell</u>. ON (Canada): Stoddart.

Garvin, Richard. 1973. <u>The Crystal Skull</u>. NY: Doubleday.

Goodman, Jeffrey. 1979. <u>We Are the Earthquake Generation</u>. NY: Berkeley.

Gribbin, John, and Plagemann, Stephen H. 1977. <u>The Jupiter Effect</u>. NY: HarperCollins.

Hawken, Paul. 1975. <u>The Magic of Findhorn</u>. NY: Harper & Row.

Holy Bible, The. Authorized or King James Version. [no date] PA: Winston.

Huxley, Aldous. 1962. <u>Island</u>. NY: Harper & Row.

Jenkins, John Major. 2002. <u>Galactic Alignment</u>. VT: Bear & Co.

Joseph, Lawrence E. 2007. <u>Apocalypse 2012</u>. NY: Random House.

_____. 2010. <u>Aftermath</u>. NY: Random House.

Kübler-Ross, Elisabeth. 1981. "Interview". <u>Playboy</u> (May 1981).

_____. 1997. <u>The Wheel of Life: A Memoir of Living and Dying</u>. NY: Simon & Schuster.

Lee, Dorothy. 1959. <u>Freedom and Culture</u>. NJ: Prentice-Hall.

LeGuin, Ursula. 1971. <u>The Wizard of Earthsea</u>. UK: Puffin.

Lewis, C.S. 1980. <u>The Last Battle</u>. UK: Collins.

Lindsey, Hal. 1977. <u>The Late Great Planet Earth</u>. MI: Zondervan.

MacDonald, Bruce. 2010. <u>The Thomas Book</u>. NY: Strategic Book Group.

Michaels, Thespian, and Fernau, Esmi. 2006. <u>The Mysteries of Clear Light: A Timeless Legacy</u>. 1st Trilogy. IN: Trafford.

Moore, Marcia. 1976. <u>Hypersentience</u>. NY: Crown.

Pagels, Elaine. 1979. <u>The Gnostic Gospels</u>. NY: Random House.

Pinchbeck, Daniel. 2007. <u>2012: The Return of Quetzalcoatl</u>. NY: Tarcher/Penguin.

Ravenscroft, Trevor. 1973. <u>The Spear of Destiny</u>. NY: Putnam's.

Roberts, Jane. 1972. <u>Seth Speaks</u>. N.J.: Prentice-Hall.

_____. 1973. <u>The Education of Oversoul 7</u>. N.J.: Prentice-Hall.

Spangler, David. 2011. <u>Apprenticed to Spirit: The Education of a Soul</u>. NY: Penguin.

_____. 1976. <u>Revelation: The Birth of a New Age</u>. CA: Rainbow Bridge.

Starhawk (Simos, Miriam). 1979. <u>The Spiral Dance</u>. CA: Harper & Row.

Stearn, Jess. 1968. <u>Edgar Cayce – the Sleeping Prophet</u>. NY: Bantam.

Steiner, Rudolf. 1972. <u>An Outline of Occult Science</u>. NY: Anthroposophic.

Storm, Hyemeyohsts. 1972. <u>Seven Arrows</u>. NY: Harper & Row.

Stray, Geoff. 2005. <u>Beyond 2012 – Catastrophe or Ecstasy: A Complete Guide to End-of-Time Predictions</u>. UK: Vital Signs.

Teilhard de Chardin, Pierre. 1961. <u>The Phenomenon of Man</u>. NY: Harper.

Thomas, Andy. 2011. <u>The Truth Agenda</u>. UK: Vital Signs.

White, John. 1980. <u>Pole Shift</u>. NY: Doubleday.

Wilcock, David. 2011. <u>The Source Field Investigations</u>. NY: Dutton.

Wilhelm, Richard (tr.). 1967. <u>The I Ching, or Book of Changes</u>. 3rd ed. NJ: Princeton University.

ENDNOTES

1   See Bert Janssen's website www.CropCirclesandMore.com for much fascinating analysis.

2   An ellipsis representing the omission of text from a quotation appears as three closely spaced dots (...). On the other hand, three dots spaced apart (. . .) indicate a pause, interruption or unspoken conclusion. Exceptions: in centred, italicized quotations and on pp. 406-412 and 426-429, omitted or reordered text is *not* indicated by ellipses, in order for the quotes to flow without interruption.

Channeling sessions are given in excerpt form, usually without indicating what preceded or followed. The text of a section excerpted, however, is shown precisely, with any internal gaps indicated by ellipses and any text substituted or added for clarity, grammar, etc., put in square brackets. The words of session participants, however, are occasionally abridged without notice.

Italicized phrases or sentences within round brackets during session transcripts provide experiential descriptions, connections to related material or other information about the subject being discussed.

3   While the present book can well be read on its own, previous volumes in the Mind Leap series add the context of earlier events surrounding Moita and Amar, Kelly and me: *Mind Leap: Intimate Changes and Communication Between Worlds* (2010, updated readers edition) and *The World Conspires: Weaving Our Energies to Renew the Earth* (2011).

4   Only in hindsight will it be recognized that 1980 marked the start (2016 being the end) of the 36-year period of alignment between our Sun's rise on the December solstice with the equator of the Milky Way, being thus the start of the transition from one precessional era to the next (i.e. from Age of Pisces to Aquarian Age). This alignment has been subjecting Earth to more powerful energies generated from the galactic centre, and John Major Jenkins has concluded it is the astronomical target of the Mayan calendar "end-date" of December 21, 2012. Might this galactic alignment help explain the 1980/2012 parallels? See Jenkins (2002), pp. 249-256.

5   See Findhorn Community (1975; 1980) and Hawken (1975).

6   See Ch. 3, pp. 84-85.

7   Kelly's account of her earlier life can be found in *Mind Leap*, Ch. 8.

8   See the transcript of Moita's first words in *Mind Leap*, Ch. 10, p. 219.

9   This "rarest exception" is described in *The World Conspires*, Ch. 9, pp. 207-208.

10 *Both Sides Now*, #101-102, pp. 18-19. While Kelly and I were living remotely in British Columbia in the early 1980s and, as always, sharing our sessions and workshops at minimal or no charge, we lacked the means to publish our journal *Rays* properly. Having connected with us from Texas in the usual synchronistic fashion, Elihu Edelson offered printing, distribution and even calligraphy services to enable *Rays* to continue publishing, and in considerably more professional fashion than previously.

Thirty years later, Elihu's own long-time journal continues to inform and enlighten on a quarterly basis. *Both Sides Now* can be reached at http://bothsidesnow.freeservers.com or by mail at Both Sides Now, 10547 State Hwy 110N, Tyler, Texas, U.S.A. 75704-3731.

11 See Federation of Light channeling for June 14, 2012 at www.blossomgoodchild.com.

12 Adapted from "The Three Clarities" in *Mind Leap* (2010). I have revised terms after David Spangler's suggestion in *Subtle Worlds*. "Inner" communications refers to messages via our inner senses.

13 For an extensive, contemporary look at evidence for alleged conspiracies, see Thomas (2011).

14 See two early books by the Associations of the Light Morning community (1974; 1983). Their website is www.lightmorning.org.

15 The story of my partnership with Ruth may be found in *Mind Leap*. Early in Ruth's channeling, Loria explained that she was the entity for both Ruth and me, her current earthly expressions.

16 See *Mind Leap*, Ch. 1, stepping-stone #4, pp. 38-39, plus pp. 328-330..

17 The image of a bobbing cork of changing identity is Moita's, from our first year.

18 Michaels and Fernau (2006), p. 6.

19 *Ibid*, p. 6.

20 See *Mind Leap*, Epilogue, p. 319.

21 See *The World Conspires*, Ch. 6, pp. 146-147.

22 See Findhorn Community (1975), pp. 101-125.

23 See further discussion of this topic from these August 8 and November 5, 1979 sessions in *Mind Leap*, Ch. 14, pp. 295-296.

24 Findhorn Foundation's "Links with Space" (1970), as channeled through David Spangler, stated that: "The proper means of travel between systems...is through projection of the soul itself" – i.e. not by physically colonizing but by a soul's actually incarnating on the other world. This would especially be the practice in Earth's case since "the life-forms and civilizations on the planets in your immediate celestial neighbourhood are etheric [non-physical] in their manifestation." (p. 14).

25 See *The World Conspires*, Ch. 6, pp. 129-130.

26 Findhorn Foundation (1970), pp. 14-15, stated that extraterrestrials that were making contact with Earth did not exist physically but rather on the etheric plane. Consistent with this, the channelings described a plan during the 1960s to evacuate the more evolved humans from Earth, *if* the planet faced imminent nuclear destruction, as entailing great effort and risk – since beings and craft would have to be densified from the etheric into physical form to accomplish it. Obviously, the plan proved unnecessary. In that regard, and in line with Moita's saying Earth was destroyed in October 1962 on another line of probability, these 1970 channelings confirmed that "man came extremely close to the point of disaster several times over the past decade."

27 UFO abduction and other contact experiences, as extensively reported from the later 1980s on, may be understood in this light: essentially non-physical beings who can interact with humans in physical dimensions by raising and lowering vibrational rates, controlling the physical and mental states of contactees, and materializing forms and various types of physical evidence.

28 For Moita's links to the Virgin Mary, see *Mind Leap*, Ch. 8, p. 161; also *The World Conspires*, Ch. 16, pp. 17 and 312-327.

29 See Moore (1976).

30 Compare my own experience as a subject in *The World Conspires*, Ch. 4, pp. 90-91.

[31]   Freely abridged from *The World Conspires*, pp. 270-271 and 284. Also see next note.

[32]   See *The World Conspires*, Ch. 14, pp. 280-286. Further related regressions continue to p. 293.

[33]   See *The World Conspires*, Ch. 15, pp. 308-311.

[34]   See *The World Conspires*, Ch. 12.

[35]   See *The World Conspires*, Ch. 1, p. 25.

[36]   See session transcript in *The World Conspires*, Ch. 15, pp. 298-302.

[37]   See *Mind Leap*, Epilogue, for this material appearing in our journal *Rays*.

[38]   See *The World Conspires*, Ch. 5 and 6, pp. 113-116 and 146-147.

[39]   See *The World Conspires*, Ch. 7, p. 160.

[40]   See *The World Conspires*, Ch. 7, p. 160.

[41]   See *The World Conspires*, Ch. 11, pp. 240-241, including Amar's interpretation of the dream as relating to the arrival of "the High Ones".

[42]   Roberts (1972), pp. 286-299 and 348-351.

[43]   *Ibid*, pp. 75-102; Roberts (1973), pp. 247-259.

[44]   Barfield (1965).

[45]   Flem-Ath (1995) with a consensus of other sources.

[46]   Garvin (1973).

[47]   Stearn (1968), pp. 226, 230, 235-237; Carter (1968), p. 55.

[48]   Quoted from *Mind Leap*, Ch. 8, p. 167.

[49]   See www.edgarcayce.org/_AncientMysteriesTemp/hallofrecordsupd.html.

[50]   See Steiner (1972), pp. 108-114 and 385-388.

[51]   *The Holy Bible (King James Version)*, p. 975.

[52]   Association for the Understanding of Man (1974), pp. 59-60 ff. *Fatima Prophecy* actually lists several heavens, not just one.

[53]   See *The World Conspires*, Ch. 8, pp. 194-195.

[54]   See Roberts (1972), pp. 415, 435-437. There is a fascinating parallel to Seth's version of the crucifixion story in Bruce MacDonald's *The Thomas Book* (2010).

[55]   See Roberts (1972), pp. 240-246.

[56]   Carter (1968), p. 135.

[57]   Pagels (1979).

[58]   Spangler (1976), as quoted in Ch. 9, p. 239, of the present book.

[59]   *The Holy Bible (King James Version)*, Matthew 22:37 to 39, p. 784.

[60]   Edgar Cayce predicted invention of the laser 25 years before it happened. The process is similar to the Atlanteans' use of their "firestone" (ruby) to focus energy for purposes of power generation but also as a weapon. See Stearn (1968), pp. 235-237.

[61]   Unwittingly, I titled the *Mind Leap* chapter in which Kelly's current life story is told, "From Shadows, a Bright Lady", referring to both Kelly and Moita. As I was one of these "rogues" Kelly mentions, is my using "Bright Lady" a remnant of the life she is recalling?

62 See *Mind Leap*, Ch. 8, pp. 166-167.

63 See *The World Conspires*, Ch. 3 (p. 66), Ch. 4 (pp. 87-89), Ch. 7 (pp. 160-161) & Ch. 12 (pp. 255-256), where different pseudonyms were used. Also see Ch. 9 of this book, pp. 233-234.

64 See *The World Conspires*, Ch. 15, pp. 304-305.

65 Gerald and Eileen (she to be mentioned shortly) are a couple who were within our group in Regina – for example, see the August 11, 1979 session excerpted in Ch. 3, p. 86, of this book. Roy was another close friend in the group there, as described in *Mind Leap*.

66 See *Mind Leap*, Ch. 1 & 2, where all these "stepping-stones" to greater awareness, are described.

67 The changes to our physical environment described in this chapter were taken (at the time it was first drafted in the early 1980s) almost entirely from an extremely useful newsletter of scientific and other news then circulated by Rich Green, entitled *Coming Changes*. Unfortunately, I can no longer access the original issues to provide specific references.

68 Association for the Understanding of Man (1974), pp. 108-113. Bracket and italics in original.

69 See *The World Conspires*, Ch. 11 and 12, pp. 241, 246-247 & 255.

70 The splitting or separation of worlds is first referred to in Ch. 5, pp. 139-141, of this book. See also the heading "Separation of Worlds" in Ch. 9.

71 Re: cosmic-solar event, see quote from *Fatima Prophecy*, p. 182 above, and the attached endnote.

72 Rich Green, Coming Changes (July/August 1980).

73 See *The World Conspires*, Ch. 12, especially pp. 263-264.

74 See *The World Conspires*, Ch. 16, p. 318.

75 Regarding Loria's creation and an entity involved, see *The World Conspires*, Ch. 17, pp. 332-333.

76 Regarding Moita's creation and Kelly's origin through her, see *Mind Leap*, Epilogue, pp. 311-312, and *The World Conspires*, Ch. 13, pp. 276-279, and Ch. 17, 332-333.

77 See *The World Conspires*, Ch. 16, p. 318.

78 *The World Conspires*, Ch. 16, p. 319.

79 *The World Conspires*, Ch. 16, pp. 321-322.

80 *Mind Leap*, Ch. 9, p. 183.

81 *The World Conspires*, Ch. 17, p. 337.

82 *The World Conspires*, Ch. 17, p. 335.

83 *Mind Leap*, Ch. 8, pp. 152-153.

84 *The World Conspires*, Ch. 17, p. 337.

85 Nearly verbatim from Nov. 11, 1978 session, when we were living in Regina, not knowing where we were headed, as quoted in Ch. 1, p. 27; also see *The World Conspires*, Epilogue, p. 349.

86 The first link between our B.C. life and my "Raven" dream was noted in Ch. 1, pp. 41-42, as Moita (in a Nov. 5, 1980 session) connected that dream with another of mine about Chris of Sunrise Farm.

87 Huxley (1962).

88 Castaneda (1974), pp. 162-169.

89 See *Mind Leap*, Chapter 10, p. 197.

90 Fuentes, Henry. "Allegations of Sexual Misconduct, Cruelty at Ranch Stir Controversy". *The San*

Diego Union (Sept. 2, 1979).

[91] See *Mind Leap*, Ch. 6, pp. 118-120 (quoting April 21, 1977 Loria session).

[92] See *The World Conspires*, Ch. 7, pp. 161-172, for the full session transcript, my letter as described in the next paragraph, and some aftermath that is supplemented here in Tales of Power #4 and #5.

[93] See the joint hypersentience about this life in Tales of Power #1, to which more will be added.

[94] See Ch. 7, p. 187.

[95] See Ch. 5, pp. 139-141.

[96] See Ch. 7, p. 187.

[97] Spangler (1976), pp. 73-74 and 80.

[98] *Ibid.*, p. 93.

[99] See *The World Conspires*, Ch. 7 ("The Art of Discretion").

[100] Ravenscroft (1973).

[101] Lindsey (1977).

[102] A month after her first three closely spaced Moita sessions – and after deciding on her own not to see Leroy again – Rena is struggling to integrate these experiences. See *The World Conspires*, Ch. 4 (pp. 87-89), Ch. 7 (pp. 160-161) and Ch. 12 (pp. 255-256), where the pseudonyms Darryl and Jill were used instead of Leroy and Rena.

[103] See *The World Conspires*, Ch. 9, p. 211, for the part of this conversation dealing with channeling.

[104] See Ch. 8, p. 220.

[105] See reference to Marian apparitions at Garabandal in *The World Conspires*, Ch. 16, pp. 312-314.

[106] Association for the Understanding of Man (1974), p. 24. Also see *The World Conspires*, Ch. 16, pp. 312-314.

[107] Undoubtedly referring to our Nov. 5, 1980 session earlier in this chapter, when he almost responded to the subject of prophecies about Armageddon. Regarding Amar's next statement that "Man will start a war...because he fears his own evolution": In addition to ethnic warfare in Eastern Europe and Africa, a sequence of wars linked to the Middle East featuring a great deal of absolutist rhetoric will indeed come during 1980-2012. Besides the Iraq vs. Iran war that started in September 1980, there is Gulf War I following Iraq's invasion of Kuwait, the 9/11 attack on the World Trade Centre and other terrorist attacks attributed to al Qaida, the ensuing Western allies' war in Afghanistan, and then Gulf War II, being the U.S.-led war in Iraq. As of 2012, high tension remains in the Middle East between Israel and the Palestinians and over Iran's alleged nuclear ambitions.

[108] See *The World Conspires*, Ch. 1, pp. 34-36; and Ch. 5 (pp. 128-129) and 8 (226-227) of this book.

[109] Interview in May 1980 issue of *Playboy*, available for purchase in April.

[110] See *The World Conspires*, Ch. 1, pp. 162-164.

[111] See "First Direction that Comes to Mind" dream in *Mind Leap*, Ch. 3, pp. 68-69 and 322-323.

[112] *The Holy Bible (King James Version)*, Matthew 27: 20.

[113] It is interesting that in Roberts (1972), pp. 389, 395 and 397, Seth also predicted return of the Christ. Seth deliberately gave virtually no information about the life (e.g., no time or place of birth) but did say the mission would be completed before 2075: "He will undermine religious organizations – not

unite them. His message will be that of the individual in relation to All That Is. He will clearly state methods by which each individual can attain a state of intimate contact with his own entity; the entity to some extent being man's meditator with All That Is."

[114] Rich Green, *Coming Changes* newsletter. Specific references are no longer available to me.

[115] Goodman (1979).

[116] Gribbin and Plagemann (1977).

[117] White (1980).

[118] Brian Bethune, "The End of Days", Maclean's Magazine (Feb. 26, 2007), referring to Joseph (2007).

[119] Joseph (2010), pp. 38-42.

[120] Joseph (2007), p. 53. Joseph also quotes Edgar Cayce's Reading 3976-15 from January 19, 1934. After predicting large-scale land mass changes, eruptions, etc., in the later 20th century, the "sleeping prophet" predicted a physical pole shift would follow: "there will be shifting then of the poles – so that where there has been those of a frigid or the semitropical will become the more tropical, and moss and fern will grow."

[121] May 19, 1981 session.

[122] Findhorn Foundation (1978).

[123] See *Mind Leap*, Ch. 9 to 14; also *Mind Leap*, Ch. 1, Stepping-Stone #5, pp. 40-43.

[124] See *The World Conspires*, Ch. 5, p. 122, for my 1972 dream "Flight to Space Station".

[125] See *Mind Leap*, Ch. 10, pp. 217-218.

[126] See *Mind Leap*, Ch. 14, pp. 296-301.

[127] See *The World Conspires*, Ch. 14, pp. 287-293.

[128] Wilhelm (1950), pp. 20-24 and 31-35.

[129] Ferguson (1980), p. 397.

[130] Spangler (2011).

[131] Teilhard de Chardin (1961) quoted in Edinger (1973), p. 105.

[132] See *The World Conspires*, Ch. 17, pp. 340-341.

[133] This comment relates to the question I ask Moita in the Epilogue.

[134] Regarding transformative "threshold" experiences, see *Mind Leap*, "The Transitus and the Medicine Wheel", pp. 12-20.

[135] Kübler-Ross (1997), pp. 230-235.

[136] *Ibid.*, p. 240

[137] Referring to later in the Sept. 20, 1981 session excerpted above.

[138] See Ch. 11, pp. 317-318.

[139] See the Intermission, pp. 199-202.

[140] Cohen (1966).

[141] Ref. to C.S. Lewis's final Narnia book, *The Last Battle* (1980). The dwarves experience as a mangy stable the same space that others perceive as a beautiful, heavenly meadow.

[142] The Wiccan phrasings employed at session end are drawn from Starhawk (1979).

[143] See Ch. 12, pp. 334-337.

144   See quotes from Storm (1972) in *Mind Leap*, "The Transitus and the Medicine Wheel", pp. 18-19.

145   See the July 11, 1978 session in *Mind Leap*, Ch. 11, p. 241.

146   See *Mind Leap*, Ch. 3, pp. 68-69 and 322-327.

147   See *The World Conspires*, Ch. 14, pp. 280-286.

148   See Ch. 2, p. 69, and Ch. 7, pp. 184-185.

149   See *The World Conspires*, Ch. 3, pp. 58-61.

150   See David's full dream in *The World Conspires*, Ch. 6, p. 150.

151   See *Mind Leap*, Ch. 9, p. 182.

152   See the entire discussion in Ch. 4, p. 111.

153   Lee (1959).

154   Barfield (1988), pp. 121 and 123.

155   Compare this with the magical environment of Ursula LeGuin's *The Wizard of Earthsea* (1971).

156   Also see the earlier compilation of prophetic excerpts from the Mind Leap series on pp. 425-429.

157   *The Mystery of 2012: Predictions, Prophecies & Possibilities* (Ardagh, Argüelles, et al. 2007); *Galactic Alignment: The Transformation of Consciousness According to Mayan, Egyptian, and Vedic Traditions* (Jenkins 2002); *2012: The Return of Quetzalcoatl* (Pinchbeck 2007); *The Complete Idiot's Guide to 2012* (Andrews and Andrews 2008); *Beyond 2012 – Catastrophe or Ecstasy: A Complete Guide to End-of-Time Predictions* (Stray 2005); and others.